DATE DUE

DEMCO 38-296

CONTEMPORARY MUSICIANS

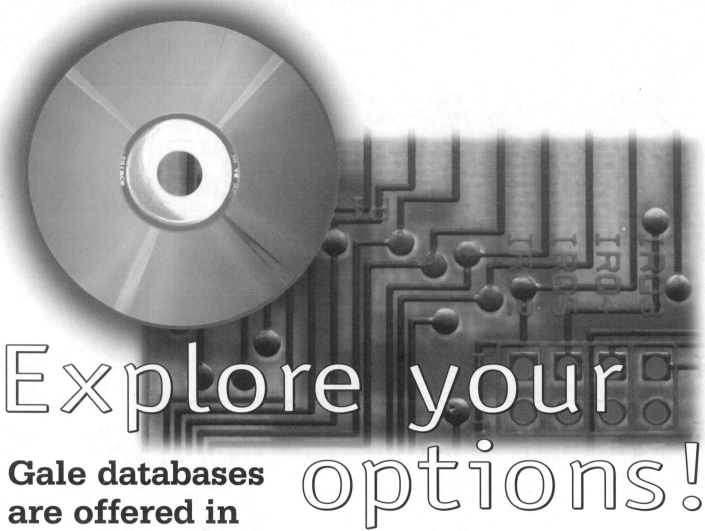

Explore your options!

Gale databases are offered in a variety of formats

ISSN 1044-2197

CONTEMPORARY MUSICIANS

PROFILES OF THE PEOPLE IN MUSIC

STACY A McCONNELL, Editor

VOLUME 19
Includes Cumulative Indexes

GALE

DETROIT · NEW YORK · TORONTO · LONDON

STAFF

Stacy A. McConnell, *Editor*

Maria Munoz, *Associate Editor*

Suzanne Bourgoin, Rich Bowen, Carol Brennan, John Cohassey, Ed Decker, Robert Dupuis, Nicole Elyse, Brian Escamilla, Shaun Frentner, Simon Glickman, Daniel Hodges, Robert R. Jacobson, Mary Kalfatovic, Christine Morrison, Kevin O'Sullivan, Sean Pollock, Joanna Rubiner, Pamela Shelton, Sonya Shelton, Geri J. Speace, B. Kim Taylor, David Wilkins, Link Yaco, *Contributing Editors*

Neil E. Walker, *Managing Editor*

Marlene S. Hurst, *Permissions Manager*
Maria Franklin, *Permissions Specialist*
Andrea Grady, *Permissions Assistant*

Mary Beth Trimper, *Production Director*
Deborah Milliken, *Production Assistant*
Cynthia Baldwin, *Product Design Manager*
Barbara J. Yarrow, *Graphic Services Supervisor*
Randy Bassett, *Image Database Supervisor*
Pamela A. Hayes, *Photography Coordinator*
Willie Mathis, *Camera Operator*

Cover illustration by John Kleber

This book is printed on acid-free paper that meets the minimum requirements of American National Standard for Information Sciences— Permanence Paper for Printed Library Materials, ANSI Z39.48-1984.

This book is printed on recycled paper that meets Environmental Protection Agency Standards.

ISBN 0-7876-1064-X
ISSN 1044-2197

10 9 8 7 6 5 4 3 2 1

Contents

Introduction   ix

Cumulative Subject Index   257

Cumulative Musicians Index   281

Marc Anthony 1
   Simmering salsa singer and screen star

Albert Ayler 5
   Unorthodox "free jazz" sax groundbreaker

Bad Livers 8
   Down-home bluegrass popular with punkers

The Beautiful South 11
   Catchy yet cynical pop band

Better Than Ezra 14
   Alternative pop/rock radio hitmakers

Eubie Blake 18
   Original ragtime piano player/composer

Victor Borge 22
   Slapstick spoofer and ivory tickler

Brandy 26
   Pop-soul crooner and teen queen

The Breeders 29
   Rambunctious, blowout alternative rock

The Cardigans 32
   Syrupy yet serious Swedish popsters

Terri Clark 34
   Award-winning country success story

Albert Collins 36
   "The Iceman;" red-hot blues guitarist

Coolio 39
   Down-to-earth West Coast rapper

Carl Craig 41
   Detroit techno turntable wizard

Billy Dean 44
   Rugged, romantic country crooner

Bryan Duncan 47
   Soulful Christian gospel mainstay

Ian Eskelin 49
   Busy Christian technopop artist

Cesaria Evora 52
   "Barefoot diva" of mournful morna music

Fred Frith 55
   Avant-garde father of noise guitar

Front 242 58
   Eurohip industrial-dance club faves

Gary Glitter 61
   Glam cult phenom known for jock anthem

F. Gary Gray 64
   Respected R&B/rap video director

Erskine Hawkins 67
   Swing trumpeter; penned Tuxedo Junction

David Helfgott 70
   Troubled classical pianist from Shine

Walter Horton 74
   Blues harmonica genious and mentor

Helen Humes 77
   Lusty, tender, funny jazz/blues singer

Engelbert Humperdinck 80
   Gentlemanly heartthrob lounge perfomer

Jesus Lizard 83
   Stage-diving indie rock thrashers

Antonio Carlos Jobim 86
Bossa Nova master and mainstay

Eric Johnson 89
Master guitarist of the "post-Jimi Hendrix" era

Thad Jones 92
Outstanding postwar jazz trumpeter

Joy Division 97
Gloom-and-doom postpunk goth rock

R. Kelly 100
Producer/performer of sexy but spiritual R&B

Chaka Khan 103
Smooth and funky vocal stylist

Dave Koz 106
Critically acclaimed jazz sax player

Barbara Lamb 110
Old-time country/bluegrass fiddler

Lisa Loeb 112
Breathy, bookish folk/pop songstress

Frank Loesser 115
Broadway bigwig; created Guys and Dolls

Luscious Jackson 119
Contagious, danceable meld of melodies

Mahavishnu Orchestra 122
Trailblazing jazz fusion group

Liza Minnelli 125
Versatile, high-energy showbiz institution

Alanis Morissette 130
Raw alternative-rock vocal sensation

Nas 133
Witty, gruff, poetic rapper

Peter Nero 135
Genre-spanning pianist, composer, arranger

Northern Lights 140
Bluegrass/swing/folk eclectic ensemble

Offspring 144
Southern Cali ska/punk/pop

Joan Osborne 147
Bluesy alternative/pop singer

Pigface 150
All-star industrial/alternative lineup

Awadagin Pratt 153
Avant-garde classical pianist

Lou Rawls 156
Soulful R&B master

Leon Redbone 159
Enigmatic folk/blues guitarist

Reverend Horton Heat 163
Fiery Texas punk-metal-rockabilly

LeAnn Rimes........................166
Powerful young country singer

Ryuichi Sakamoto 169
Prolific composer with technological edge

Adam Sandler 173
Wacky comedian with songs up his sleeve

Carlos Santana 176
Influential jazz/rock guitarist

Screaming Trees 180
Original grunge rockers

DJ Shadow 183
Groundbreaking trip-hop techno artist

Shaggy.............................186
Raucous and funky reggae

Horace Silver 188
"Hard-bopping" jazz giant

Social Distortion 191
Old-school tattooed gravelly punkabilly

Spearhead 194
Quirky, catchy blend of soul, reggae, R&B

Spencer Davis Group 197
Upbeat British pop rockers

Steeleye Span......................201
Traditional and longstanding folk group

Sting..............................204
Ex-Police man with buzzing solo career

Sublime 209
Lively alternative/ska band

Talk Talk 211
  1980s Britpop drum-machine pop group

Leon Theremin 214
  Electronic music machine inventor/innovator

Traffic 217
  Psychedelic-influenced 1970s rock act

Uriah Heep................................... 222
  Harmonic but heavy 1970s fantasy rock

Ventures 225
  Vanguard surf-guitarists ....

Gene Vincent 229
  Once dubbed "America's favorite Folk singer"

Weather Report 233
  Founding fathers of jazz fusion

Slim Whitman 238
  An original folk/pop musician

Gerald Wilson 241
  Unique jazz arranger

Mac Wiseman 244
  "Voice with a Heart" bluegrass musician

Jimmy Witherspoon 248
  Gospel-tinged jazz/blues belter

Wu-Tang Clan 251
  Gritty, urban hardcore rap

Introduction

Fills the Information Gap on Today's Musicians

Contemporary Musicians profiles the colorful personalities in the music industry who create or influence the music we hear today. Prior to *Contemporary Musicians,* no quality reference series provided comprehensive information on such a wide range of artists despite keen and ongoing public interest. To find biographical and critical coverage, an information seeker had little choice but to wade through the offerings of the popular press, scan television "infotainment" programs, and search for the occasional published biography or exposé. *Contemporary Musicians* is designed to serve that information seeker, providing in one ongoing source in-depth coverage of the important names on the modern music scene in a format that is both informative and entertaining. Students, researchers, and casual browsers alike can use *Contemporary Musicians* to meet their needs for personal information about music figures; find a selected discography of a musician's recordings; and uncover an insightful essay offering biographical and critical information.

Provides Broad Coverage

Single-volume biographical sources on musicians are limited in scope, often focusing on a handful of performers from a specific musical genre or era. In contrast, *Contemporary Musicians* offers researchers and music devotees a comprehensive, informative, and entertaining alternative. *Contemporary Musicians* is published twice yearly, with each volume providing information on more than 80 musical artists and record-industry luminaries from all the genres that form the broad spectrum of contemporary music—pop, rock, jazz, blues, country, New Age, folk, rhythm and blues, gospel, bluegrass, rap, and reggae, to name a few—as well as selected classical artists who have achieved "crossover" success with the general public. *Contemporary Musicians* will also occasionally include profiles of influential nonperforming members of the music community, including producers, promoters, and record company executives. Additionally, beginning with *Contemporary Musicians 11,* each volume features new profiles of a selection of previous *Contemporary Musicians* listees who remain of interest to today's readers and who have been active enough to require completely revised entries.

Includes Popular Features

In *Contemporary Musicians* you'll find popular features that users value:

- **Easy-to-locate data sections:** Vital personal statistics, chronological career summaries, listings of major awards, and mailing addresses, when available, are prominently displayed in a clearly marked box on the second page of each entry.

- **Biographical/critical essays:** Colorful and informative essays trace each subject's personal and professional life, offer representative examples of critical response to the artist's work, and provide entertaining personal sidelights.

- **Selected discographies:** Each entry provides a comprehensive listing of the artist's major recorded works.

- **Photographs:** Most entries include portraits of the subject profiled.

- **Sources for additional information:** This invaluable feature directs the user to selected books, magazines, and newspapers where more information can be obtained.

Helpful Indexes Make It Easy to Find the Information You Need

Each volume of *Contemporary Musicians* features a cumulative Musicians Index, listing names of individual performers and musical groups, and a cumulative Subject Index, which provides the user with a breakdown by primary musical instruments played and by musical genre.

Available in Electronic Formats

Diskette/Magnetic Tape. *Contemporary Musicians* is available for licensing on magnetic tape or diskette in a fielded format. Either the complete database or a custom selection of entries may be ordered. The database is available for internal data processing and nonpublishing purposes only. For more information, call (800) 877-GALE.

Online. *Contemporary Musicians* is available online through Mead Data Central's NEXIS Service in the NEXIS, PEOPLE and SPORTS Libraries in the GALBIO file.

We Welcome Your Suggestions

The editors welcome your comments and suggestions for enhancing and improving *Contemporary Musicians.* If you would like to suggest subjects for inclusion, please submit these names to the editors. Mail comments or suggestions to:

The Editor
Contemporary Musicians
Gale Research
835 Penobscot Bldg.
Detroit, MI 48226-4094
Phone: (800) 347-4253
Fax: (313) 961-6599

Marc Anthony

Singer

Marc Anthony is a vocalist whose contemporary version of salsa has been embraced internationally by Latino audiences *and* criticized as controversial by old school music critics. Not even thirty years old, Anthony has reached more lofty goals than many accomplish in the course of their entire careers. " I was born to be a singer, it has never been a question for me," he told *The Globe.* In addition to his many recording credits, Anthony has appeared in several films.

Marc Anthony attributes much of his own unique style to a diverse musical upbringing. He was born in 1969, Antonio Marco Muniz, to Puerto Rican guitarist Felipe Muniz and his wife. Raised in the tough neighborhood of East Harlem, New York Anthony was exposed to two competing musical worlds; the street sounds heard on the sidewalks of his neighborhood and the authentic Puerto Rican jibaro music generating from his father's Friday Night Jam Sessions. Jibaro music is the prominent music of Puerto Rico defined by the "le lo lai" of the vocalist. As he elaborated in the February 1996 issue of *GTTV,* "I would walk down third avenue and out of one window I could hear Ruben Blades' music, while Gloria Gaynor came blasting out another and Doobie Brothers sounds from the window of a passing car's stereo. But to be honest with you, I never liked salsa because it didn't cater to the younger generation. And I couldn't relate to it. I thought it was uncool." Like many rebellious youngsters Anthony did not appreciate his parents' tastes until much later in his life. However, at a very young age Anthony was taught music and composition by his father probably influencing his decision to pursue a career in music. While his childhood home was suffused with the background soundtrack of Ruben Blades, Hector Lavoe, and Willie Colon, Anthony credits his most relevant musical influences growing up as Air Supply and Puerto Rican superstar Jose Feliciano.

"M-I-C-K-E-Y" launches vocalist's career

At age 12, Marc and his sister were discovered by commercial producer David Harris, in the midst of belting out the Mickey Mouse theme. They were used almost exclusively by Harris for quite some time, providing background vocals for his productions and commercials. Ever since that fortunate break, Anthony's career has been on the upswing.

While still in school, Anthony began writing songs. One of his compositions "Boy I've Been Told" caught the ear of his good friend and singer Sa-Fire. Anthony ended up recording background vocals for the dance siren's entire album, as well as writing "You Said You Love Me" and "I Better be the Only One." The single "Boy I've Been Told" went on to became a top-40 hit. During his teens, Anthony also worked with groups such as the Latin Rascals as well as Menudo.

With his interests moving toward club hip-hop and dance music, Anthony was fortunate enough to team up with DJ and producer Little Louie Vega who is described by Rebecca Mann of the *Latin Times Magazine* as "the nicest most talented star maker in New York." Though Vega and Anthony had been acquainted though the New York Club scene for years, it wasn't until a low-budget movie *East Side Story* that their professional paths finally crossed. Vega had written the score for the film in which Anthony sang and had the main role. Louie impressed and delighted by Anthony's abilities, asked if he would consider forming a partnership. Anthony agreed and the result was his first album *When the Night is Over* (Atlantic Records) produced by Vega and including appearances by India and the legendary Tito Puente. A showy single from the record, "Ride on the Rhythm" reached number one on the Billboard dance chart.

Star-Slated Salsa Sensation

Ambitious and driven, Marc Anthony created a series of far-fetched goals for himself. Before the age of 35, he wanted to sing at Madison Square Garden, perform at Carnegie Hall, and to have a number one record. With the fiery success of the dance smash "Ride on the Rhythm," Anthony managed to achieve one his coveted goals before even reaching legal drinking age. At this point in his career he was a champion of the urban dance music

For the Record . . .

Born Marco Antonio Muniz, September 16, 1969 in New York, NY; son of Felipe Muniz, Puerto Rican jibaro guitarist; single; one child: Arianna

Marc Anthony was discovered at age 12 by commercial producer David Harris; as a teenager, he wrote songs and performed with Sa-fire, The Latin Rascals, and Menudo; at age 19, opened for Danny Rivera at Carnegie Hall; opened for Tito Puente's 100th Album celebration at Madison Square Garden November 22, 1991. Released his debut album *When the Night is Over* (Atlantic Records) in 1991. Single "Ride on the Rhythm" reached number one on *Billboard* magazine's dance singles chart; appeared in the MGM film *Hackers*, 1995.

Awards: *Billboard* Award, Best New Artist of the Year, 1994; Todo a su Tiempo,Tu Musica Award Best Tropical Album of the Year, Quadruple Platinum; *Otra Nota-* Double Platinum, 1994 Lo Nuestro Award, Ace Award, Diplo Award in Puerto Rico.

Addresses: *Office*—Marc Anthony Productions, 1385 York Avenue, Suite 6F, New York, NY 10021; phone: (212) 396-0963

known as "freestyle" which basically is an ethnic combination of hip-hop and disco. Even though he was inherently proud of his heritage, the musician was not yet associated with the salsa music for which he became celebrated. At age 19, Anthony achieved the second of his desired goals when he participated at a Carnegie Hall concert with vocalist Danny Rivera. The third and most notable of success was accomplished on November 22, 1991 when he opened the tribute to jazz legend Tito Puente at Madison Square Garden on the occasion of his 100th album.

Searching for a New Goal

Upon achieving his aspirations, Anthony, still incredibly young and feeling invincible, began searching for a new path. The next road for the musician was paved by his friend and manager David Maldonado and Ralph Mercado(the president of Soho Latino/RMM records). The pair offered him and other artists such as India, who shared a similar musical background, the opportunity to cross over, to record a salsa record for the Soho Latino label. Anthony considered the record offer, thought it an

interesting opportunity, and agreed. The successful vocalist was also interested in the opportunity to work with RMM main producer Sergio George. George and Anthony both were fans of each other's work. At the time, Anthony was being mentally revisited by the sounds of his parents' homeland and finally he was inspired by the music he had rejected as a child. He was elated when the legendary Tito Puente jumped on-stage with him at a Ne York Palladium performance, and through personal contacts he was happy to be able to land a gig as a "water boy" for legendary Ruben Blades. In this very glamourless position Anthony would run to obediently greet Blades with water should the star's thirst present a need. In an ironic twist of fate through the course of his career, his relationship with Blades has developed from idol-worship, to being a colleague, and finally culminating in a friendship.

The highly praised first salsa album by Marc Anthony was entitled *Otra Nota.* The record, sung entirely in Spanish, contains compelling versions of songs by musicians Jan Gabriel and Ian Chester. One original song on the album that received much attention, "El Ultimo Beso," was written by none other than Anthony's father. In a 1996 concert series at the Luis A. Ferre Performing Arts center in San Juan Marc, Anthony had the honor of performing this song with his dad. He told *The San Juan Star* in July 1996, "It's special anytime you can give something back. For me it's a very special concert, for him it's a great big moment in his life. I know what it means to him and it means so much to me to be able to make his dream come true". The album was a breakthrough success from the start. In January 1993, just 5 months after its release, *Otra Nota* went gold. The album eventually claimed double platinum status.

Otra Nota was a sales success and managed to gather a host of good reviews. In *Billboard* magazine *Otra Nota* was described as "a smashing salsa premiere and showcasing his (Anthony's) emotive bari-setto searing over George's customary fine arrangements." The album was met with a lot of controversy regarding its authenticity as real salsa, generally from people at odds with the younger generation's interpretation.

Rejected Old School Dress Code

"My critics say my take on salsa is heresy, but I say I just do salsa the way I would sing it." Anthony claims that while he was initially attracted to the music, he couldn't relate to the old school open shirts, gold chains and ultra flashy style. Rejecting the social requirement of dressing flashy to perform salsa, Anthony instead often dons a pair of jeans, T-shirt and a baseball cap on stage. "When I recorded my first album I didn't know anything about technique. People sent me cassettes of traditionalists and said, 'Here learn this, you're doing it all wrong.' I said, 'No way. Let me contribute something new.' I just closed my eyes and did it the way I heard it from my experience and thank G-d I did it the way I heard because now looking back I can say I have a style of music that is mine"

Translating His Songs

In June of 1995, Anthony released the super smash *Todo a su Tiempo*. The album gained platinum status literally overnight in an twenty-four hour sweep. The title translated into English means all "in due time." Anthony found it an appropriate name due to the album's two year, very detailed and demanding process of completion. "The record has that title," Anthony explained to the *El Daily News,* "because I think artists cannot do things in a hurry" Since its release, the recording has gone quadruple platinum and has brought not only international acclaim but has also substantiated Marc Anthony as a force to be reckoned with within the music industry. The album was arranged and co-produced by Anthony and contains compositions by Omar Alsano, Rudy Perez, Victor Victor and Manny de Gado. In addition to its success, *Todo a su Tiempo* managed to place Anthony side by side with idols Ruben Blades, Willie Colon, and Celia Cruz as a 1996 Grammy nominee in the tropical album of the year category.

Marc Anthony's career has demanded many live appearances. In 1995 the Salsa sensation hit the concert trail with vigor, spending an exhausting 50 out of 52 weeks on the road. His relationship with his fans and his pride in his heritage are of great importance to him personally and appear significantly in his music as well. On stage Anthony is described by Elizabeth Roman of *GTTV* as "shining like no other, as he displays an aggressive energetic passion that almost always brings the audiences to their feet." During his performances, he always pays a tribute to the Puerto Rican Flag. He brings out the flag not In the essence of the performance but to express pride in his heritage. Anthony often sells out concerts, playing multiple nights at a single venue, and was described by Christina Veran of *Newsday* as having a similar stage strut to the provocative Rolling Stone singer Mick Jagger.

Hollywood Hopeful

Marc Anthony's prolific charms, besides developing a

gigantic fan base, have attracted additional attention by Hollywood big-wigs. He has starred in three major motion pictures to date. In the film *Hackers,* released in 1995 by MGM Entertainment, he portrays a young secret service agent. In *The Substitute,* Anthony is a gang leader who controls a high school and in *The Big Night* he appeared opposite legendary actress and model Isabella Rossellini. Though Anthony enjoys the challenges of acting, he reportedly has no intentions of giving up his musical endeavors. As he explained to *the San Juan Star,* "The day movie making satisfies me as much as music is the day I will be able to decide between the two."

Making Time for Things That Count

Anthony's career still maintains an accelerated pace. With prospective movie deals and musical opportunities, the singer has had many demands placed on his time. In 1997, Anthony sought to change that burden to accommodate what he described in *Latina* magazine as "the current love of his life," his infant daughter Arianna. Anthony insists his next album will follow the same lengthy recording process as *Todo a su Tiempo*, with a possible two-year wait. In the meantime, after turning down many opportunities, he chose to accept a role in the much-anticipated Broadway play Capetown so he could stay close to Arianna in New York City. In the play, expected to open in summer 1997 on Broadway, Anthony will star along with his longtime hero and colleague Ruben Blades. Both men play the convicted-murderer-turned-lauded-writer, Salvador Algron. The music is composed by Paul Simon.

Anthony is fortunate and humble. He explained his gratitude to *GTTV:* "The truth is I'm doing what I was born to do. God gave me this gift and the tools to do this and even if it's just to instill Puerto Rican pride in others, I am doing what I was born to do. What keeps me going is knowing my daughter will have all the options I never had"

Selected discography

Todo A Su Tiempo, Soho Latino/RMM Records, 1995.
Otra Nota, Soho Latino/RMM Records, 1992.
When the Night is Over, Atlantic Records, 1991.

Sources

Periodicals

CashBox, July 1 1995, p.16.
Billboard, February 13, 1993, p.92.

El Daily News, June 8, 1995, p.23, June 22, 1995.
Guia de Television & Entretenimiento, February 1996, p.18.
Latin Beat, August 1995,p.33.
Latina Magazine, Premiere issue, summer 1996, P.12.
Newsday, July 20. 1995.
The Daily News, Viva Suppliment, March 1997 p.18.

The Globe, date unknown, Page D17.
The San Juan Star, July 18, 1996, P.41.
Urban, The Latino Magazine, Summer Issue.

—*Nicole Elyse*

Albert Ayler

Jazz saxophonist and composer

Photo by Ken Settle. Reproduced by permission.

Although his professional career lasted only about a decade, Albert Ayler was one of the most influential saxophonists and composers on the cutting edge of jazz in the 1960s. Ayler's unwillingness to play by the accepted rules of harmony and rhythm created the special emotional spark that propelled his music. At the same time, it guaranteed that he would never be heard by the great majority of conservative-eared listeners, to whom Ayler's brand of free jazz was nothing more than irritating clatter. In the years since his death, a generation of jazz innovators has recognized the brilliance of Ayler's work, and has carried the freedom principle that he helped pioneer to ever greater heights of sonic ecstasy. In 1983, 13 years after his mysterious death, Ayler became the 57th member elected into *DownBeat* magazine's Hall of Fame.

The iconoclastic Ayler was born on July 13, 1936 in Cleveland, Ohio. At the age of seven, he began taking alto sax lessons from his father, Edward, who played both saxophone and violin. At ten, he began to study with Benny Miller, a former Charlie Parker and Dizzy Gillespie sideman, at Cleveland's Academy of Music. Ayler developed professional-caliber skills very quickly, and he was performing regularly in rhythm-and-blues bands at Cleveland clubs while still in his teens. At the age of 16 he toured with bluesman Little Walter (Jacobs). Ayler was known around Cleveland as "Little Bird" (a reference to Parker). Other early influences on his playing included sax greats Lester Young and Sidney Bechet.

Ayler served in the Army from 1959 through 1961, and while there he switched from alto to tenor sax. Stationed in France, he was able to come into contact with some of the great expatriate musicians based in Paris, such as Dexter Gordon and Don Byas. After his discharge, he decided to stay in Europe, where the climate for his increasingly experimental musical ideas was more hospitable. In 1962 Ayler moved to Sweden, where he made his first recordings. The following year, he went to Copenhagen, Denmark to record the album *My Name is Albert Ayler*, which has become something of an underground classic. During his stay in Scandinavia, Ayler made the acquaintance of pianist Cecil Taylor, who became a frequent collaborator over the next few years.

Ayler returned to the U.S. later that year, settling in New York. In 1964 he formed a quartet with trumpeter Don Cherry, bassist Gary Peacock, and drummer Sunny Murray. With this group, Ayler began to create the body of work that established him as a giant of modern jazz. His compositions combined elements of New Orleans-style group improvisation with melodies from black spirituals and other folk music forms, all infused with an avant-garde no-holds-barred sensibility, in which no sound that you can figure out how to make is off limits. Of course, Ayler's own playing was not confined to random blurts. His upper register featured a soulful, shimmering vibrato, while his low range retained traces of the gruff r&b honking of his youth. As with most visionary artists, critics in New York had trouble deciding whether Ayler was a genius or a fraud. His seamless shifts between a huge, wavering, sentimental vibrato and piercing bleats tended to confound even seasoned listeners.

Inspired Generation of Free Jazzers

In 1965 Ayler formed a new group that included his brother Don on trumpet, Charles Tyler on saxophone, Lewis Worrell on bass, and again Murray on drums. This group recorded "Bells," one of Ayler's most influential albums, live at a concert in New York's Town Hall. Over the next few years, Ayler's supporting cast included at various times bassist Alan Silva, drummers Milford Graves and Beaver Harris, and many others on such unlikely instruments as harpsichord and cello. During the mid-1960s Ayler recorded many of his most important works, including "Ghosts" and "Spirits" mostly on the Impulse! label, which was putting out much of the era's best avant-garde jazz. Although Ayler's music still failed to capture a wide audience, his saxophone peers and a host of younger players began to take notice. John Coltrane, Pharoah Sanders, and Archie Shepp were among the well-known reedmen whose styles were noticeable influenced by Ayler, particularly his floating sense of rhythm.

Towards the end of the 1960s, Ayler began to veer away from total abstraction in order to focus more on his musical roots. It is not entirely clear whether this new direction was a heartfelt shift on Ayler's part, or a response to suggestions from Impulse! that he try to sell more albums. Either way, Ayler's r&b recordings of the late 1960s did not sell particularly well, and succeeded in alienating some of his hardcore free-jazz fans. The release of *New Grass*, which was more or less a rock and roll album, was especially annoying to Ayler's more noise-oriented listeners.

Haunted by "Apocalyptic Visions"

Meanwhile, as he sought to simplify his music—to make it music "for the people"—Ayler's own internal life was becoming increasingly more complex. He spoke, according to his *New York Times* obituary, of having "violent, apocalyptic visions: flying disks shooting colors, and the devil's mark branded on foreheads." Shortly after his return from a 1970 European tour, Ayler was reported missing, and his body was found a few weeks later floating in New York's East River. Ayler's death was declared a suicide, although the circumstances remain somewhat murky.

In the years since his death, Ayler, who was barely able to eke out a living playing music, has become widely recognized as one of the preeminent figures in the development of free jazz. The list of important saxophonists and composers who cite him as a major influence is huge, and includes such luminaries as Henry Threadgill, Roscoe Mitchell, and Joseph Jarman. Music as strange and haunting as the kind conceived and played by Albert Ayler during his peak years may never catch on with the mainstream American CD-buying public; but if it ever does, Ayler will certainly be regarded as one of the genres most important progenitors.

Selected discography

My Name is Albert Ayler, Fantasy, 1963.
Vibrations, Arista Freedom, 1964.
Witches and Devils, Arista Freedom, 1964.
Spiritual Unity, ESP, 1964.
Bells, ESP, 1965.
Spirits Rejoice, ESP, 1965.
Albert Ayler in Greenwich Village, Impulse, 1966.
Love Cry, Impulse, 1967.
New Grass, Impulse, 1968.
Music is the Healing Force of the Universe, Impulse, 1969.

Sources

Books

Lyons, Leonard, and Don Perlo, *Jazz Portraits: The Lives and Music of the Jazz Masters,* Morrow, 1989.

Periodicals

DownBeat, August 1983; July 1994.
New York Times, December 4, 1970; September 23, 1996.

—*Robert R. Jacobson*

Bad Livers

Bluegrass band

Hailing from Austin, Texas, the Bad Livers are on a mission--to bring the tradition of bluegrass to the general public. "We feel that we are providing a service," Mark Rubin, bassist and tuba player, said just before a March 1997 show at a Detroit pool hall. And they are. The crowd at that show sported cowboy hats, pierced eyebrows, ripped leather, and retro suits. Not your typical bluegrass crowd, but then the Bad Livers are not your typical bluegrass band. Drawing on an eclectic range of influences, from bluegrass legends Flatt & Scruggs to jazz greats Thelonious Monk and Charlie Parker to punk artists the Misfits and Iggy Pop, they have crafted their own form of bluegrass—"Bad Livers music," as the band calls it. The diversity of their audience is due in part to their early penchant for covering punk rock classics.

Music critics quickly labeled them "bluegrass-thrash." Though this moniker resulted in wider exposure for the band, it also threatened to exile them to the land of kitsch. The Bad Livers would have none of it. "We remembered what John Hartford once said. 'Don't get famous doing something you hate'" said Rubin. So they stopped the covers and focused on the music. Their audience, initially drawn by the novelty, stayed, drawn to the top-notch musicianship, the lightening-fast playing, and the old-time bluegrass soul pulsating through each song.

The Bad Livers' story begins in 1990. Danny Barnes, banjo madman and long-time Austin music scene sta-

ple, enlisted Rubin and fiddler/accordionist Ralph White to form the Danny Barnes Trio. Barnes, a native Texan who began banjo picking at the age of ten, brought the band a reverence for bluegrass. Rubin, a former roadie for The Flaming Lips, brought a punk sensibility honed by listening to college radio in Norman, Oklahoma. White, a tree-cutter by trade, brought a no-nonsense love of traditional music and a burning desire to play. Together the three of them set out to make some good music.

They soon landed a regular gig at a local bar. Saddled with the task of performing four one-hour sets a night, the band, having been together less than a year and with little original music, turned to covers. They applied their bluegrass twist to everyone from Miles Davis to Johnny Cash to Motorhead. During this time they coalesced as a group—getting tighter, playing stronger—and somewhere in the midst of it all the Bad Livers were born.

Banjos and Tubas and Punks, Oh My!

Word began to spread about this little bluegrass trio that did outrageous covers of punk classics. They became the band to see in Austin—not a small feat considering that there is quality original music coming out of every corner bar in town. Paul Leary of the Butthole Surfers, another Austin export, was hooked. In June of 1991, he produced the bands first recording—a 7-inch cover of "Lust for Life," Iggy Pop's classic punk anthem—in his living room. Soon after, the Bad Livers toured with the Butthole Surfers, playing for young alternative fans across the nation. Critics, at a loss to describe the band, labeled them "bluegrass-thrash" or "punk-bluegrass." At first the band let this reputation ride. Barnes told *New Country Magazine* in a 1994 interview, "People who aren't familiar with the kind of music we can play, bluegrass, don't hear it. But if you play something they already know and whap it, then you've got their attention. That's what we did with the crazy covers. It's kind of a sad comment on the music-listening public, but it worked."

It worked well enough to get the attention of record label executives. Leery of being signed as a novelty act, they carefully reviewed each offer and eventually signed with Quarterstick, a division of Touch and Go Records, a Chicago-based indie-rock label. "They were the only label willing to give us absolute freedom to do our own thing," said Rubin. This collaboration, while giving the band artistic freedom and helping to expose bluegrass to a wider audience, would also reinforce the punk connection in the eyes of the public.

In September of 1992, their first album, *Delusions of Banjer,* was released. Produced by Leary, the album received widespread acclaim, both with the indie-fans

For the Record . . .

Members include **Danny Barnes** (born December 21, 1961, Temple, TX), bango, guitar, and vocals; **Bob Grant** (born March 11, 1966, Astoria-Queens, NY), mandolin, banjo and guitar; **Mark Rubin** (born August 18, 1966, Stillwater, OK), upright bass and tuba; **Ralph White** (left group 1996), fiddle and accordion.

Group formed in Austin, Texas, c. 1990; released 7 inch *Lust for Life* cover on Cargo Records, 1991; signed with Touch and Go's Quarterstick label and released *Delusions of Banjer*, 1992. Quarterstick re-issued *Dust on the Bible* on cassette, 1994. Released *Horses in the Mines*, 1994. Signed to Sugar Hill Records and released *Hogs on the Highway*, 1997.

Addresses: *Agent*—Davis McLarty, P.O. Box 3156, Austin, TX, 78764. *Record company*—Sugar Hill Records, P.O. Box 55300, Durham, NC 27717-5300. *Website*—http://www.hyperweb.com/badlivers/ and http://www.southern.com/southern/band/BADLV/biog.html. *E-mail*—mdrubin@bga.com.

and, to a lesser extent, the bluegrass purists. The album consisted almost entirely of Barnes' original compositions. Songs like "Git Them Pretty Girls" and "I Know You're Married" pass as bluegrass music pure and simple, but the cover of Leary's "The Adventures of Pee Pee the Sailor" reminds you that this is Bad Livers bluegrass, after all.

Quarterstick's commitment to the band was reiterated in 1994, when the label re-released *Dust on the Bible*, a tape the band had self-produced in 1991. Originally intended as a Christmas gift for family and friends, the tape, recorded in Barnes' living room, consisted of classic bluegrass spirituals. Songs like "Workin' on a Building (for my Lord)" and "Crying Holy Unto the Lord" resonate with a down-home pureness that recalls Sunday afternoon church picnics. "It doesn't get more non-commercial than gospel music," Rubin told *CMJ's* Dawn Sutter in 1994. Like *Delusions of Banjer*, the tape was praised by music critics, but garnered little financial gain. Still, the label kept their faith in the band and soon financed a second album.

With the goal of producing an old-timey feel on the album, the band built a wooden shed to serve as the studio. There, they recorded the mostly original tunes on an eight-track analog recorder. The result was 1994's *Horse in the Mines.* Background noise, idle chatter between songs, and Barnes' barking dog, Judy, pepper the album throughout, evoking a sense of authenticity— music the way it was before technology got a hold of it. As Rubin told Sutter, "The idea was to make a more organic record." The sixteen tracks feature traditional bluegrass instruments like the banjo, upright bass, fiddle, and mandolin, but, consistent with Bad Livers penchant for the unexpected, the tuba also figures prominently, most nicely on the Dixie-land tinged "Turpentine Willie." Other highlights include the fiddle-driven "Old Folk's Shuffle," a lament on the realities of aging and the plaintive title track inspired by Emil Zola's novel about a depressed French mining community. The one cover song, "Blue Ridge Express," is a traditional bluegrass tune that Barnes first learned to play as a child.

Punk Reputation Blocks Their Way

The band and the critics were pleased with the album. Bluegrass aficionados, previously turned off by the band's punk antics, embraced them. They received invitations to perform at bluegrass festivals, including the prestigious Telluride Bluegrass Festival. However, because the album was on the Quarterstick label, it found it's way on to the editorial desks of thrash and metal reviewers who also raved about the band, prompting bookings at alternative venues. Wherever they performed, they quickly won over the audience with their furious playing and good-time attitude. Album sales, however, were dismal. "We knew something had to change," said Rubin just before the Detroit show, "and it wasn't the music." Despite Quarterstick's belief in the band, the label was not able to generate interest in the type of audience that would appreciate it. "It's good to open the music to a new audience, but the crowd would request 'Lust for Life' and then request it again, and we knew they weren't hearing it. They didn't understand." Despite their musical inroads, they were unable to shake their quirky cover band reputation. Both the band and the label, realizing this, initiated an amicable break. Summing up the experience, Rubin said, "It was good thing and a bad thing. We got exposure, but if we died in a car wreck tomorrow, we'd be remembered as the band that did the wacky bluegrass covers."

Following *Horses in the Mine*, the band toured heavily, racking up thousands of miles on their van's odometer. They traveled alone—no roadies, no manager, no merchandisers—just three dedicated musicians with a truckload of banjoes, fiddles, and guitars. (And of course Rubin's trusty tuba.) When not on the road, they worked on other musical projects. Rubin also plays bass for conjunto accordionist Santiago Jimenez, Jr. Barnes produced an album for Texas mandolin player Steve James. And both players have been known to keep nimble by doing polka gigs. "It gives me a wider palette," Rubin told *Rolling Stone* in 1994. During this time, the trio began to work on the material that would form their next album.

Followin' the True Bluegrass Road

In 1996, the group signed with Sugar Hill Records, a label known for it's bluegrass and country acts, and in 1997 released *Hogs on the Highway.* The album is straight-ahead bluegrass with the usual Bad Livers intensity. This time, however, there are no funky covers to draw attention away from the quality of the music. Chris Riemen-schneider, in a 1997 article in the *Austin American-Statesman* described the album and the band like this: "A deeper change has taken place ... one where novelty has been left behind for maturity, modernization for traditionalism ... they're the same good ol' boys, just with a more respectable twist."

Hogs on the Highway is composed of songs drawn from the band's touring experiences. The knee-slapping title track refers to the time their van was stuck behind a truckload of pigs. During the Detroit show, Barnes related the incident to the audience. "One pig in the back of the truck fixed his eye on me, and I knew, he knows where he's goin' and I know where I'm goin'." "Shufflin' to Memphis" was based on their first out-of-town gig. "We were this little band from Austin and they [the promoters] completely ripped us off," recounted Barnes. "It was music-biz 101." Other highlights of the album include "Counting the Crossties," described by Riemenschneider as what "might well be the best Bad Livers composition ever, with richly wry lyrics complemented by Barnes' warm-as-a-campfire, nasally drawl."

Just prior to signing with Sugar Hill, Ralph White, tired of touring, decided to leave the band. Bob Grant, a mandolin and banjo player from New York City quickly took his place. It was an amicable split and White has remained close to the band. Both he and Grant appear on *Hogs on the Highway.* The new label and the band's continuing commitment to bluegrass should help the Bad Livers' finally break free of their punk past. "We are confident what we do is valid," Rubin ventured. "We will find an audience because of the music. True music fans will seek us out."

Selected discography

Lust for Life, 7 inch, Cargo Records, 1991.
Delusions of Banjer (includes "Git Them Pretty Girls," "I Know You're Married," and "The Adventures of Pee Pee the Sailor"), Quarterstick, 1992.
Dust on the Bible (includes "Workin' on a Building (for my Lord)" and "Crying Holy Unto the Lord"), Quarterstick, 1994, reissue.
Horses in the Mines (includes "Turpentine Willie," "Old Folk's Shuffle," and "Blue Ridge Express"), Quarterstick Records, 1994.
Hogs on the Highway (includes "Shufflin' to Memphis" and "Counting the Crossties"), Sugar Hill Records, 1997.

Sources

Periodicals

Austin American-Statesman, January 1997.
Black and White Magazine, June 12, 1995.
CMJ, June 13, 1994.
Rolling Stone, February 1995.
New Country Magazine, June 1994.

Additional information was obtained from a March 1997 interview with Mark Rubin and materials from the Bad Livers sites on the World Wide Web (http://www.hyperweb.com/badlivers/).

—*Candace LaBalle*

Beautiful South

Pop band

A band as well known for their gin-soaked cynicism as their catchy and lush pop melodies, the Beautiful South have had enormous impact in their native England, while success in America has been limited to cult status. Music critics on both shores and beyond, however, have praised the South and in particular, lyricist and singer Paul Heaton, for his cockeyed views on love, the music business, and whatever else comes up, as well as his and songwriting partner Dave Rotheray's innate ability to invent hummable tunes with irresistible pop hooks. Named for the not-so-beautiful debilitated neighborhoods of South London, their name, like their songs, is an exercise in irony. As *Spin*'s Jonathon Bernstein observed, their music consists of "intricately constructed melodies serving as safe houses for bilious attacks on men and women—and that dumb, doomed dance they do together."

Formed from the remnants of the breakup by the Housemartins, another cynical band, albeit with a more political bent, singer/songwriter Heaton, along with Housemartin drummer Dave Hemingway started the Beautiful South in 1989 in their hometown of Hull, a gray, working-class city in the north of England. With guitarist/songwriter Rotheray, bassist Sean Welch, drummer David Stead, and vocalist Brianna Corrigan, the South presented a more expansive musical playing field than what was offered in the Housemartins. With Hemingway, now a singer not a drummer, Corrigan, and Heaton, the band was able to move seamlessly through the vocal characterizations of three quite different lead vocalists. "Their voices," Parke

Puterbaugh observed in *Stereo Review*, "one a croon of limited range [Heaton], the other more of a sing-speak [Hemingway]—are joined by Corrigan's girlish mouse-squeak and backed by a crack three-piece band of guitar, bass, and drums."

Songs for Whoever

The Beautiful South stormed out of the gate with their debut single, "Song For Whoever," a magnificently sardonic view of syrupy love songs which feature women's names as a protaganistic prop. Released in May of 1989, the song went to number two on the charts in the UK and marked a stellar introduction to the new band. The next single, "You Keep It All In," also a hit, featured all three vocalists bemoaning the stodgy, reserved tendencies of the British. Both songs appeared on their debut album, *Welcome to the Beautiful South,* released in October of 1989. "Make a list of qualities that define great pop music," *People* magazine's Michael Small suggested in his review, "and you've got a pretty fair description of the Beautiful South." The album did exceptionally well in England but received a cooler response in America, despite praise from the likes of Small and his colleagues. "They aren't yet a classic pop band," *Spin*'s Tony Fletcher asserted, "but *Welcome to the Beautiful South* remains exactly that—a warm introduction to an enticing new proposition. Here's to the sequel."

The sequel turned out to be 1990's *Choke,* an album that cemented their reputation as biting ironists. *Stereo Review*'s Puterbaugh describes the album as a "mix of lyrical quirks and music-hall and cabaret-influenced pop.... [which] stops just shy of being cute and charming, however, and gives the songs here a devilishly droll edge." For their part, just before the album's release in an interview with *Melody Maker*, Heaton and Rotheray expressed some regret to being thought of as mere cynics. "It's just the way I write. Unfortunately," Heaton offered. "I'd like to be able to write just straight in some ways.... I think there's a bit of immaturity in the way I write actually." Hemingway confessed he didn't like that people saw the band as cynical. "I don't think we are," he said. "It's just that the bubble of unreality is there and there are not many people bursting it. So we took it upon ourselves to burst a few bubbles."

Alcoholism, Nudity, Etc.

It was 1992's *0898 Beautiful South* that had the most bubbles bursting. With *0898* being the English equivalent of America's 1-900 sex lines, the album opened with "Old Red Eyes Is Back, a lush and airy tale of alcoholism.

For the Record . . .

Members include **Paul Heaton**, vocals and song writer; **Dave Rotheray**, guitar and songwriter; **Dave Hemingway**, vocals; **Brianna Corrigan** (left band 1992), vocals; **Sean Welch**, bass; **David Stead**, drums; **Jacqueline Abbott**, (joined band 1993), vocals.

Formed 1989 in Hull, England. Heaton and Hemingway had previously been in the band, the Housemartins, which disbanded 1989; released first album, *Welcome to the Beautiful South*, 1990; album received good reviews and the band toured America, 1990; released *0898 Beautiful South* which contained the controversial song "36D," 1992; Corrigan left band, 1992; compilation, *Carry on Up the Charts-The Best of the Beautiful South*, became third fastest selling album ever in the UK, 1994.

Addresses: *Record company*—Polygram Records, 825 Eighth Ave., New York, NY 10019.

Labeled a "pop album with fangs" by *Stereo Review*'s Puterbaugh, he also declared "Old Red Eyes Is Back" as his nominee for song of the year, and commented on the song being "compassionate while noting the waste of a life. It is this kind of juxtaposition of serious themes and sunny music that makes the Beautiful South stand out from the pack, and *0898 Beautiful South* contains a dozen songs that can equally be hummed, pondered, and puzzled over." Heaton, in an interview with Stuart Maconie of England's *Q* magazine, discussed "Old Red Eyes," asserting that it wasn't a morality tale. "It's looking at the more humorous and sad side of being drunk.... It sold respectably but the radio didn't really play it. I don't suppose they like songs about alcohol abuse."

Another song from *0898*, "36D," caused even more furor. Written about England's Page 3 girls, women who appear topless on the third page of some London tabloids, Heaton and Rotheray's intention was to attack the industry that supports it, not the women themselves, but mixed messages in the song reflected otherwise. "We all agree that we should have targeted the media as sexist instead of blaming the girls for taking off their tops," Hemingway admitted to Eric Puls of the *Chicago Sun-Times*. "It was a case of rushing headlong into the recording of the song." Vocalist Corrigan refused to sing on the song and when she left the band after the album's release, rumors intimated that it was the sexist lyrics of "36D" that prompted her exit. Corrigan said that may

have been an impetus, but not the reason. "I left really because it was the right time for me to go," she told Gary Crossing of England's *The Big Issue*. "My reservation about some of the lyrics became like a trigger to spur me on." Creative growth played a role as well, Corrigan admitted. "I'd always written songs for myself, but I knew there wasn't going to be an opportunity for that in the band. As a woman in this business you're always in a much stronger position if you perform your own stuff."

Following the exodus of Corrigan, the band took some time off and returned with *Miaow*, a 1994 album featuring new vocalist Jacqueline Abbott, whom the band discovered singing at a party. While only available as an import in America, the album didn't fare well in England despite critical praise. After hearing the album Peter Paphides of *Melody Maker* declared "Heaton (not the smug, flat-capped curmudgeon we'd have you believe) oozes more humanity from his tiniest cuticle than any of the lemon-faced irony-challenged Americans we blindly laud." The small reception didn't seem to bother Heaton, however, confessing to *Melody Maker*'s Sylvia Patterson, "Sales figures certainly aren't important to me, that's a dangerous way to think.... People know what I look like , they still like me and that's more important.... I'm genuinely happy I've enough money to go into a bar, buy another gin and tonic and people have enough time to give me a smile—that seems like a fair enough agreement."

Carryin' on Up the Charts

Heaton and company wouldn't have to worry about record sales much longer. In November of 1994 *Carry on Up the Charts-The Best of the Beautiful South* was released and became the third fastest selling UK album of all time. At the same time, Heaton was questioning how much further he could go with the band. "I was feeling a bit unconvinced about me own future in music," he told Patterson. "Because I just feel a bit old for it.... I was just thinking how I'm not sure, as a singer-songwriter in a band, how long you can go in the pop industry. There are four songwriters I can think of, and they're all better than me, who started off in bands and went solo: Paul Weller, Neil Young, Elvis Costello, and Van Morrison. If I was gonna be like that I'd have to be a lot stronger in terms of personality and security than I am now. Right now, I can't even imagine going to New York by meself. I'm just Paul Heaton, I'm not able to do it. I haven't got the confidence."

Towards the end of 1996 the band released *Blue is the Colour*, another album available only as an import in America. Jennifer Nine of *Melody Maker* described it as, "charming, subversively luscious business as usual." So it seems Heaton will carry on with the Beautiful South admitting to Patterson in 1995 that he's, "starting to write really good lyrics now. I'm starting to get proud." Not that he'd ever describe himself as a good songwriter, however. "Because I'm not," he told Patterson. "Because I'm not Otis Redding and I never will be." But Heaton does confess that the Beautiful South, aside from exploring the undiscovered hooks and melodies of pop, is furthering the mission begun by The Clash, The Jam, and the Sex Pistols. "It's all a question of putting people on the right train," he told Patterson, "telling them to watch out, there's things in people and society to be angry about."

Selected discography

Welcome to the Beautiful South, Elektra, 1989.
Choke, Elektra, 1989.
0898 Beautiful South, Elektra, 1992.
Miaow, Go! Discs, 1994.
Carry on Up the Charts: The Best of the Beautiful South, Mercury, 1995.
Blue is the Colour, Go! Discs, 1996.

Sources

Periodicals

Big Issue (England), May 27, 1996, p. 29.
Chicago Sun-Times, June 26, 1992.
Melody Maker (England), September 29, 1990, p.8; November 10, 1990, p. 47; April 2, 1994, p. 34;December 2, 1995, p. 20; November 9, 1996, p. 51.
New Musical Express (England), November 11, 1995.
New York Times, October 24, 1994, p. C14.
People, May 7, 1990, p. 31.
Q (England), March 1995, p. 42.
Spin, May 1990, p. 75; July 1992, p. 18.
Stereo Review, April 1991, p. 86; September 1992, p. 79.

Additional information for this profile was obtained from the Beautiful South page from Polygram Records, www.polygram.com.

—Brian Escamilla

Better Than Ezra

Rock band

Photo by Frank Ockenfels/Elektra Entertainment. Reproduced by permission.

After the so-called "revolution" of alternative or modern rock music in the early 1990s, the airwaves were flooded with new acts that slipped out of sight almost as quickly as they stepped into the limelight. Similar to the phenomena of punk rock and new wave in the late 1970s and early 1980s, the atmosphere of popular music in the 1990s has been one of frenzied record company executives and talent scouts ravenously signing myriads of new artists in hopes of finding the newest sensation. The result has been an often dizzying assault of one-hit wonders and mediocre records amidst truly talented gems. In such a confused setting, the New Orleans-based trio Better Than Ezra has toiled to prove they are not an overnight sensation or prefabricated trophy band of the record industry, but an outfit dedicated to quality songwriting, whether under the label "alternative" or otherwise. "We've been working in overheated vans for years, and I think we're realistic about the chances of success in this business," drummer Tom Drummond told the *Los Angeles Times*, "Playing night in night out is the only way to become a tight band. We want longevity ... We want to be in it for the long haul." With two favorably received major label albums under their belt, *Deluxe* and *Friction, Baby*, in addition to the independently released *Surprise*, Better Than Ezra has demonstrated the knack for well-crafted, if not truly innovative, rock.

True to the tradition of many independent rock bands, Better Than Ezra traces its origins to high school amateurism and garage rehearsals. In 1980, at age 13, future Better Than Ezra singer and guitarist Kevin Griffin found his first, although modest, success with his rock band Aces Up. After winning a local talent competition, Griffin and his band were awarded a chance to press their own record, "Seek, Find, Destroy." The record's flipside, a cover version of Kiss's "Cold Gin," demonstrated a love of 1970's classic rock, which Griffin carried over into Better Than Ezra's music. Despite a promising start, however, Aces Up quickly disbanded, leaving Griffin to tinker with his guitar alone for over half of the decade before forming a new outfit.

While in college at Louisiana State University in Baton Rouge, Griffin began weaving the first true threads of Better Than Ezra. After meeting drummer Cary Bonnecaze, Griffin decided it was time to form another group. However, differences with the bass guitar player recruited by Griffin and Bonnecaze halted the project for a year. In 1988, Griffin and Bonnecaze again decided to launch a rock trio, this time advertising for an able bass player in the local paper. The first applicant, Tom Drummond, then 17, was adopted immediately. The band harvested its initial lineup, and needed a catchy name. From an apparently random passage in Ernest

Hemingway's book *A Moveable Feast,* "anything was better than Ezra learning to play the bassoon," the threesome snatched their new name, ready to make their stage debut.

Self-Made Success

Throughout 1988, Better Than Ezra began making a name for itself. With benign trickery, Griffin booked his new band's debut performance at a Baton Rouge nightclub where he worked, slippinga bogus band name into an open slot in the venue's show schedule. Luckily, Better Than Ezra was received well enough by the audience so that Griffin was not fired. After a modicum of local live success, the band hastily assembled a five song cassette and a press kit to precede them before they trekked to Boston, where they managed to play every possible club. In the meantime, the trio began writing and revising the songs that would comprise their first full-length album.

For the next several years, Better Than Ezra stuck to a routine of extensive touring around Louisiana, playing bars, fraternity houses, or parties. In the process, the band was able to shape enough material in a live format to round out an album. In the spring of 1990, just as Griffin was receiving his degree from Louisiana State University, Better Than Ezra released *Surprise,* which the band recorded itself and distributed to record stores across several Southern states. While *Surprise* did not exactly take the world by storm, its first pressing of six thousand copies was quickly digested by a local market whose appetite was apparently whetted by Better Than Ezra's saturation of energetic live performances. The band was rapidly pulling itself up by its own bootstraps.

On the brink of larger success, however, Better Than Ezra collapsed once again. In the fall of 1990, the band was struck by the death of close friend Joel Rundell, who had briefly played rhythm guitar with the group. Rundell's death marked a moment of reflection for Better Than Ezra's members, who questioned the directions in which their lives and careers were going. "You're twenty, you're out touring in a band, partying, and suddenly you've lost a close friend," Griffin remembered in a press release. "I think we were intelligent enough to see that there was a plateau there, the possibility of stagnation. Bar band purgatory was just around the corner." Attracted by a more conservative career path, both Drummond and Bonnecaze enrolled in programs at Louisiana State University, while Griffin headed to Santa Fe, New Mexico. Once again, Better Than Ezra had stalled out.

Slowly, but surely, the band regained its level of commitment. Griffin, who had moved again, this time to Colorado, received numerous letters from fans of Better Than Ezra—later to be called "Ezralites"—who tried to coax the band to reform. By the end of 1990, Griffin followed the fans' directives and was able to reunite the band's other reluctant members for a performance in their hometown of New Orleans. Still uncertain whether or not rock music was merely an adolescent pipe dream, Better Than Ezra opted to play occasional gigs when time allowed instead of being the touring machine they once were. Despite these doubts, the band was motivated enough to write fresh material, in tentative hopes of recording a second album. Haphazardly, the band recorded demos of their most recent creations, and forwarded the tape to a Los Angeles-based fan magazine. To their surprise, the trio was contacted by several interested record companies, and upon this reinforcement became a full time band once again.

It took several years before Better Than Ezra managed to congeal its energies into something as concrete as an album. Using ragged recording techniques in a friend's home studio, the band began recording demos in the spring of 1992. As Griffin recalled in a press release, "we had to mic the guitar amps from our [19]'82 Dodge van parked two stories below. I guess the sound qualities of shag carpeting were such that we got great guitar tones." After a full year of tinkering and re-recording, Better Than Ezra finally released its second album, *Deluxe,* on the group's ownSwell Records label, complete with cover artwork by the band's members.

Building on the style already established on *Surprise*, *Deluxe* was created as a solid rock album somewhere between 1970s classic rock and the earlier, folksier work of R.E.M. Covering diverse ground, yet never straying too far from a center of heavy guitar-driven melodies, the album's songs are more concerned with emotional conveyance than narrative or precise lyrical images. As Drummond told the *Los Angeles Times*, Griffin, the group's primary writer, "likes to leave every song open to each listener's personal interpretation. That's why we don't include lyric sheets with the CD. Just one word can totally change someone else's meaning of what a song is about."

Critically, Better Than Ezra was in a kind of netherlands. On one hand, the band's fairly traditional rock approach discounted them in the eyes of American independent, or "indy", evaluators, who valued experimentation and irreverence as hallmarks of quality. On the other, the band was technically still independent and only just attaining visibility outside the realm of industry talent scouts and "Ezralites." Nevertheless, the band gained momentum through increasing word-of-mouth buzz and touring exposure, and were approached with more and more contract offers. In late 1994, the threesome performed at the influential CMJ convention in New York City, a showcase for breaking talent. With *Deluxe* nearing the sizable 50,000 in sales, with no help from a major label and little advertising, it was almost inevitable that Better Than Ezra would soon invade a truly mass market.

Major Label Success

At the end of 1995, the band signed a contract with Elektra Records, which decided to re-release *Deluxe*, this time with a lavish advertising campaign. After the single release of the song "Good," drawn from *Deluxe*, sales of the album topped half a million copies. A hastily shot video was produced for the track, and within months, Better Than Ezra had become modest celebrities. Ironically, the group was jeered by some critics and music fans who claimed that Better Than Ezra was little more than an overnight success pasted together by record companies eager to cash in on the success of alternative rock. "People who didn't know our history thought we were just another pop hit band. Nothing could be further from the truth," Griffin defended in a press release. "In one article we were called an 'MTV confection' and in another we were lumped in with another bunch of bands who'd `never spent one day on the road in an unheated van.'" Subsequently, Better Than Ezra has been assaulted with similar criticism, despite the fact that much of the band's success has been the result of their own hard work.

At the peak of its popularity, Better Than Ezra fell back into one of its integral old patterns —extensive touring. This time, the band included Europe on its slate of American gigs, now that major label exposure allowed the band to reach an international fan-base. Although the *Deluxe* tour had its share of disappointments for the band, the overall experience was positive. On the road, new songs were crafted and tested out on audiences to collect for a new album. "We definitely like to try things out on the crowds...," Drummond told Steven Batten in a *Scene* magazine interview. "It gives us a good indication of if it's good live or if people are into it." After the tour was completed, drummer Bonnecaze decided to part ways with the band. Although Bonnecaze remained friends with the group, his resignation created a void for the rising Better Than Ezra.

Luckily, the drum slot was quickly filled by Travis McNabb, also a New Orleans denizen, whose band The Beggars had just been deserted by their record label. McNabb, who was familiar with Better Than Ezra's music, quickly meshed with the band. "We couldn't have asked for it to be any better. He came in and nailed the new songs," Drummond told the *Scene*. "He's a powerful drummer, but he offers a little more on the finesse side. And he's a really nice guy. Everyone's a lot happier now." Unimpeded, the new trio invaded the studio in early 1996 to begin recording a new album.

Friction, Baby, released in August of 1996, became Better Than Ezra's first record made under a major label banner. With a large budget, a high-tech studio, and veteran producer Don Gehman overseeing the project, the band was able to make its most polished album to date. Accordingly, this only gave leverage to critics who claimed Better Than Ezra was not an "alternative" act but a major label puppet. Yet the band had never committed itself to such labeling and felt quite at home within the indulgence of rock. In Griffin's words, "[w]e wanted to record a big overblown, self gratuitous album and I think we did. But we got more ... a lot more." As with their earlier releases, *Friction, Baby* offered a share of straightforward rock numbers. In *Los Angeles Times* critic John Roos' words, "[t]he first few songs are hard hitting rockers that kick up a pile of dust but offer little that hasn't been heard before." However, as the album unfolds, songs like "Still Life With Cooley," "King of New Orleans," and "At Ch. DeGaulle, Etc.," reveal that the trio was trying to branch out, adding new instrumentations such as horns and strings.

Better Than Ezra saw *Friction, Baby* as its strongest, rawest work yet, and the album received a generally warm critical reception. Yet while the record's sales were solid and the band's older fans held fast, the album lacked a runaway hit single to carry it, as with *Deluxe*'s

"Good." In addition, the diverse nature of the album may have turned away fair-weather listeners seeking only the catchiness that made "Good" so popular. Nevertheless, it still could not be said that Better Than Ezra was a one-hit-wonder, and the band has continued to tour and write with the same attitude it has maintained from the start. "We've tried to learn and improve with each album, and I think we understand now—with input and guidance—the importance of how a song should feel," Drummond told the *Los Angeles Times.* With pathos as their guide, Better Than Ezra proved that a band's music does not have to change with commercial success.

Selected discography

Surprise, 1990.

Deluxe, Swell, 1993; re-released on Elektra, 1995.
Friction, Baby, Elektra, 1996.

Sources

Periodicals

Los Angeles Times, March 27, 1995; October 11, 1996.

Online

http://clevescene.com/961107/mus_1107.htm

Additional information was provided by publicity materials from Elektra Records.

Eubie Blake

Pianist

African-American ragtime pianist and composer of over 300 songs and musical pieces, Eubie Blake enjoyed a career which took him from the early years of African American stage theater to television and concert appearances in the 1970s. In his classic work *Early Jazz: It's Roots and Modern Development*, Gunther Schuller commented that Blake "was probably the leading exponent of the ragtime piano style that developed somewhat independently of the Midwestern branch all along the Eastern seaboard as far south as Charleston, with headquarters in Baltimore." Blake's piano pieces revealed a strong folk ragtime strain that prevented him from being associated historically with some of the lesser commercial work associated with the publishing industry of New York City's Tin Pan Alley. Apart from a talented keyboardist, Blake conducted, composed, and arranged music that helped cultivate and broaden the role of African American stage theater.

James Hubert "Eubie" Blake was born in Baltimore, Maryland, on February 7, 1883. Former slaves, his parents John Sumner Blake and Emily Johnston, in-

AP/Wide World Photos. Reproduced by permission.

Born James Hubert Blake, February 7, 1883, in Baltimore, MD; died February 12, 1983, New York, NY; son of James Sumner Blake and Emily Johnston; married Avis Lee, July 1910-1939; Marion Gant Tyler 1945-1983;

Began career as ragtime pianist in 1898; composed first piano rag, 1899; performed in Dr. Frazier's Medicine Show in 1901 and toured with the stage show *Old Kentucky* in 1902; performed as a pianist at the Gold-field Hotel, Baltimore, 1907-1915; met Noble Sissle in 1915 and began musical association; toured with Sissle as the Dixie Duo, 1915-1920; appeared as a member of Jim Reese Europe's orchestra, 1916-1919; composed music for stage musicals *Shuffle Along* (1921), *Chocolate Dandies* (1924-1925); recorded and toured with own orchestra in the 1930s; toured with U.S.O. during World War II ; appeared at 1969 Newport Jazz Festival; recorded and performed on television programs in the 1970s.

Awards: Honorary degrees from Brooklyn College of the City University of New York (1973); Dartmouth College (1974); Rutgers University (1974); The New England Conservatory of Music (1974); University of Maryland (1979); received Presidential Medal of Freedom 1981.

stilled the values of hard work. A literate man who had been taught to read by his former master's daughter, Blake's father "never stopped preaching to his son about the evils of race hatred," wrote Al Rose in *Eubie Blake.* "Even though he'd been a slave, he insisted there were good and bad white people just as their were good and bad Negroes."

Blake learned his first rudiments on a Estey organ purchased by his mother. Not long after he received instruction from his next door neighbor, Margaret Marshall, a young organist at a Methodist church. Around age six Blake studied piano with Llewelyn Wilson, sang in church, and later played cornet in a local bi-racial band.

Without the knowledge of his parents, Blake worked Aggie Shelton's bordello at age fifteen, entertaining customers with light classics and popular rags such as "Hello, Ma Ragtime Gal" and "After the Ball." With little interest in school, Blake sought to become a full time musician, and at age sixteen performed professionally

in a Baltimore nightclub. In 1899 he composed his first piano rag later titled the "Charleston Rag." The piano roll of "Charleston Rag" (1917), observed Mark Tucker in *Ellington the Early Years,* "features a walking bass in broken octaves, flashy appregiated breaks, chromatic seventh chords, and certain rhythmic tricks."

In 1901 Blake danced and played melodian with Dr. Frazier's Medicine Show. In the following year, he joined the touring company *In Old Kentucky,* which took him briefly to New York City. From New York, Blake returned to Baltimore and landed a job as a relief pianist for Big Head Wilbur at Alfred Greenfield's saloon, an establishment built by light weight boxing champion Joe Gans. After two years at Greenfield's, Blake found steady work at Annie Gilly's sporting house. In *This is Ragtime,* Blake related how he "ragged" popular songs and classics from Wagner to Viennese waltzes. Able to transpose numbers in any key, and possessing a finger span of twelve notes, Blake earned a reputation as one of the finest ragtime pianists of the eastern school.

"Professor" Blake

In 1911, Blake wrote his piano rags, "The Chevy Chase" and "Fizz Water." During the next few years, Blake was kept busy through seasonal work in Baltimore and Atlantic City where he performed at such places as Ben Allen's Boathouse and the Bucket of Blood. The great stride pianist, James P. Johnson heard Blake in Atlantic City during the summer of 1914. "[Blake] was playing at The Belmont," recalled Johnson in *Jazz Panorama,* "Eubie was a marvelous song player. He also had a couple of rags. One, 'Troublesome Ivories,' was very good." In 1915 Blake met Noble Sissle while performing with Joe Porter's Serenaders at Baltimore's Riverview Park. Within a few days, Blake and Sissle wrote the number "It's All Your Fault" which became an immediate hit for singer Sophie Tucker. Their number "Have a Good Time Everybody" subsequently found its way into Tucker's repertoire.

With the Great James Reese Europe

In 1916 after Sissle joined James Reese Europe's Society Orchestra, he urged the famed bandleader to hire Blake. Accepting the offer, Blake came north to join the Harlem-based orchestra. "As performers, both Sissle and Blake fit the Europe model of the black professional entertainer perfectly," wrote Reid Badger in *A Life in Ragtime.* "Blake had both experience performing and writing for whites, and they both understood how to please them without demeaning their own personal or professional dignity." Blake soon received promotion from solo pianist to assistant orchestra leader. "Jim Europe was the biggest influence in my musical career," stated Blake in *Eubie Blake: Keys of Memory*. "He was at a point in time at which all roots and forces of Negro music merged and gained its wildest expression."

Shuffle Along

When Sissle arrived back in New York after serving in France with the 369th Infantry Division, he and Blake toured on the Keith circuit as the Dixie Duo. In 1920 they met the comedy team of Flournoy E. Miller and Aubrey Lyles in Philadelphia. Along with Miller and Lyles, Blake and Sissle created the 1921 musical stage production, *Shuffle Along*. Based upon Miller's and Lyles' proposed Broadway-style show, "The Mayor of Jimtown," *Shuffle Along* emerged as the first all-black post-World War I stage production. Responsible for the music and lyrics, Blake and Sissle provided several classic numbers including "I'm Just Wild About Harry," "Bandana Days," and "Love Will Find a Way." Originally planned for a black audience, the show ran two weeks at the Howard Theatre in Washington D.C. and at the Dunbar Theatre in Philadelphia, before opening at New York City's 63rd Street Music Hall on May 23, 1921. After 504 performances, *Shuffle Along* closed with a reported gross of eight million dollars. In the work *The Cotton Club*, Jim Haskins noted that *Shuffle Along* succeeded because "in earlier shows, ragtime had been hidden under the heavy overlay of operetta. By the time the show opened in New York, Blake had already won fame as a composer, and ragtime was present in pure form in *Shuffle Along*."

The success of *Shuffle Along* ushered in a new era for Blake— one that, as he stated in *DownBeat*, had taken him "from barrelhouse pianist to writing a Broadway musical." In 1924 he wrote the score for *The Chocolate Dandies*. Traveling to Europe in 1926, Blake and Sissle dropped the name the Dixie Duo for the stage title "American Ambassadors of Syncopation." They played in England and Paris. Back in America the duo broke up in 1927. In October of the same year, Blake organized a new act with Broadway Jones for the Keith circuit.

Changing Times in Stage Theater

After launching the show *Shuffle Along Jr.* in 1928, Blake earned $250 a week with the 1930 production of Lew Leslie's Blackbirds, billed as "Glorifying the American Negro." The experience with the show brought Blake together with famed lyricist Andy Razaf. In describing Razaf's skills, Blake told Al Rose in *Eubie Blake*, that his song writing partner "never had to change anything. His meter was perfect, and he could write the words nearly as fast as I could whistle the tune. God, he was smart!" Their collaborative efforts included the number "You're Lucky to Me." In *Eubie Blake* Al Rose explained that the number "introduced new and modern concepts about intervals that challenged other musicians and won enough adherents to become permanently incorporated into common musical idiom." Years later, the number was performed as an instrumental by Benny Goodman and the Casa Loma Orchestra.

Due to the affects of the Depression, the Blackbirds production closed after two-month run. Blake then wrote music for Jack Scholl's "Loving You the Way I Do" which became the Broadway hit of the year. In 1933 Blake, Miller, and Sissle attempted to take a rendition of *Shuffle Along* on the road. Though a fine production, the show was forced to close. During the 1930s Blake recorded with his own orchestra and wrote shows under the funding of the Works Progress Administration (WPA).

Elder Statesman of Ragtime

During World War II, Blake served as musical director with several U.S.O (United Service Organization) tours. In the late 1940s Blake went into retirement and studied the Schillinger System of Music at the University of New York. The ragtime "Scott Joplin" revival of the 1950s brought renewed interest in Blake's music. Rudi Blesh's and Harriet Janis's book *They All Played Ragtime* (1950) and Gilbert Chase's *America's Music* (1955) helped find a new audience for one the last of the original ragtime pianists and composers.

In 1968 music impresario John Hammond organized a session for Blake which brought forth the 1969 two-album recording *The Eighty-Six Years of Eubie Blake*. That same year, he played a successful concert at the Newport Jazz Festival. In 1971 Blake launched his own record company, Eubie Blake Music Inc. During the heightened "Scott Joplin boom" of the 1970s, he appeared on the cover of *Time* and *Newsweek*, and was a guest on television shows hosted by Johnny Carson, Mike Douglas, and Merv Griffin. At the pianist's ninetieth birthday party at New York's Hampshire House, jazz writer Dan Morganstern observed, in a 1973 issue of *DownBeat*, that Blake was "in better shape, mentally and physically, than many a man 20 years younger." When Leonard Feather referred to Blake, during a Down Beat interview, as "ninety years young" his spright subject immediately answered "No, I'm 90 years old and proud of it."

During the 1970s Blake was awarded honorary degrees from such distinguished institutions as Dartmouth College, Rutgers University, and the New England Conservatory. In 1976 he provided the introduction for Terry Waldo's book, *This is Ragtime.* In 1981 he received the Presidential Medal of Freedom at a White House ceremony. Suffering from pneumonia, Blake was unable to attend several celebrations held in his honor of his 100th birthday. He died in New York on February 12, 1983. About five years before his death, Blake told his biographer Al Rose, in *Eubie Blake,* "When you leave the theater, it feels like you're leavin' the real world and the fake world is out here in the street where nobody knows anybody else." Though Blake belonged to a close knit creative fraternity, his music touched the lives of several generations of listeners who resided outside the world of the musical theater.

Selected discography

Albums

The Wizard of Ragtime Vol. I, 20th Century Fox, 1958.
The Marches I Played on the Ragtime Piano, RCA, 1959.
The Eighty-Six Years of Eubie Blake, CBS, 1969.
Rags to Classics, Eubie Blake Music, 1971.
Eubie Blake and His Friends, Eubie Blake Music, 1971.
Jazz Piano Masters, Chairoscuro.
Live Concert, Eubie Blake Music, 1973.
Tricky Fingers, Quicksilver.
Memories of You, Biograph, 1990.

Compositions

"Charleston Rag," written 1889 and originally titled "Sounds of Africa," Ampico piano roll 1917.
"Fizz Water," 1911.
"Brittwood Rag," 1911.
"The Chevy Chase," 1911, piano roll 1917.
"Troublesome Ivories," 1911.
"Novelty Rag," 1910.
"Blue Thoughts," 1933.
"Blue Classic," 1939.
"Blue Rag in Twelve Keys," 1969.

"Memories of You," piano roll, QRS, 1973.
"I'm Just Wild About Harry, piano roll, QRS, 1973.

Stage Music

Shuffle Along, 1921.
The Chocolate Dandies, 1924.
Elsie, 1924.
Charlot's Revue Of 1924, (contributed compositions).
Blackbirds of 1930, 1930.
Hot Rhythm, 1930, (contributed compositions).
Shuffle Along Jr., 1933.
Swing It, 1937.
Tan Manhattan, (contributed compositions), 1941.

Blake was also the subject of a documentary: *Reminiscing with Sissle and Blake,* 1974.

Sources

Books

Carter, Lawrence T, *Eubie Blake, Keys Of Memory,* Balamp, 1979.
Haskins, Jim. *The Cotton Club,* Hippocene Books, 1977.
Jazz Panorama: From the Birth of Dixieland to the Latest 'Third Stream' Innovations: The sounds of Jazz & the Men Who Made Them, edited by Martin Williams, Collier Books, 1958.
Ragtime, Its History, Composers, and Music, edited by John Edward Hasse, Schirmer Books, 1985.
Rose, Al, *Eubie Blake,* Schirmer Books, 1979.
Schuller, Gunther, *Early Jazz: It's Roots and Musical Development,* Oxford University Press, 1968.
Tucker, Mark, *Ellington: The Early Years,* University of Illinois Press, 1991.
Waldo, Terry with a foreword by Eubie Blake, *This is Ragtime,* Da Capo, 1976.

Periodicals

DownBeat, March 29, 1973; May 24, 1973.

Victor Borge

Musical Comedian

AP/Wide World Photos. Reproduced by permission.

The scene is as timeless as its performer. A classical pianist in an immaculate tuxedo walks across the stage of a hushed concert hall. Reaching his waiting piano, he sits down with quiet majesty and falls over backward with a loud crash. The audience titters. The pianist gets to his feet, apparently unruffled, rights the bench, and drops the piano lid on his hand, knocking over his microphone stand in the process. The audience laughs. Shaken but undaunted, the pianist nervously adjusts the sheet music in front of him which unaccountably flies up in the air to land all over the stage. The audience howls. In sheer desperation, he launches into a Beethoven sonata, pounding the keys faster and faster, losing control of the tempo, and suddenly stops abruptly in mid-piece, turns to the audience and exhales smoke. The audience is convulsed with laughter.

For many classical musicians, such a nightmarish scenario might tempt them quit the stage permanently, but for Danish musician and comedian Victor Borge, it has been the foundation for a career. For over half a century, Borge has entertained audiences worldwide with a mix of slapstick pratfalls, absurd monologues in heavily accented English, and over-the-top performances of classical standards, almost, but not quite, disguising his complete mastery of the "serious" classical music idiom. Sly satirizing the starch-collared mannerisms of classical performances, Borge aims to make classical music accessible by emphasizing its humorous aspects without detracting from its beauty. Ironically, in doing so he has become one of the most widely recognized classical musicians in the world today.

Born Borg Rosenbaum in Copenhagen, Denmark, in 1909, Victor Borge was the youngest son of Bernard Rosenbaum, a viola player in the Royal Danish Philharmonic Orchestra, and the former Frederikke Lichtinger, a gifted pianist. As might be expected for a family of musicians, Borge was immersed in music almost from birth. He began reading music at age four and by age eight, had performed his first piano recital. The young Borge often accompanied his father to his job at the opera house and became fascinated with conducting, so much so that he would borrow symphony scores from the library and memorize them. By age ten, his musical gifts were widely evident and he received a scholarship to study at the Royal Danish Music Conservatory with the leading Danish pianist of the era, Victor Schioler.

In tandem with his musical ability, Borge also developed an acute comic sensibility. Often asked to perform at private parties from an early age, Borge would play practical jokes on his audience by spontaneously improvising musical pieces with absurd titles such as "Beethoven's Sonata no. 112" and then listen gleefully as

Born Borg Rosenbaum, January 3, 1909, in Copenhagen, Denmark; son of Bernard Rosenbaum (a professional musician) and Frederikke (Lichtinger) Rosenbaum; married Elsie Shilton, 1932 (divorced 1951); married Sarabel Scraper in 1953; children: (first marriage) Roland, Janet, (second marriage) Sanna, Victor Bernhardt, Frederikke ; Education: Ostre Borgerdyd Skole (Copenhagen); Royal Danish Music Conservatory (Copenhagen); Vienna Music Conservatory (Austria); studied in Berlin with Frederic Lamond and Egon Petri.

Comedian, Pianist, Conductor. Began performing in 1923. Has appeared with the New York Philharmonic, the Cleveland Orchestra, the Philadelphia Orchestra, the San Francisco Orchestra, the Chicago Orchestra, the London Philharmonic, and the Royal Danish Philharmonic (Copenhagen). Appeared Bing Crosby's *Kraft Music Hall* in 1942-43; *Victor Borge Show* for NBC in 1946; on Broadway in one-man show, *Comedy in Music*, from 1953-1956.

Awards: Knight First Class, Order of Saint Olav (Norway); Royal Order Daneborg (Denmark); Order of Vasa (Sweden); Brotherhood Award; Wadsworth International Award; Georg Jensen Silver Award; Shubert Foundation Award.

Addresses: *Home*—Greenwich, CT. *Management*—Gurtman and Murtha Associates, 450 Seventh Avenue, Suite 603, New York, NY 10123.

audience members commented that the piece was one of their favorites. At school, he became known for his pranks and abilities as a burlesque artist, inventing skits that mocked the rigid standards of public conduct that were the norm for the early twentieth century Denmark.

The Beginnings of a Comedic Calling

In his first major public appearance at age fourteen, Borge was called upon to perform the piano solo for Rachmaninoff's Second Piano Concerto with the Copenhagen Philharmonic Orchestra. Looking over the audience, as he recalled in a *Saturday Evening Post* Article, he saw that "half of them were falling asleep, and the other half sat gravely, like witnesses at an execution. It suddenly dawned on me that the whole thing was extremely funny." He surreptitiously winked at the audience; in reaction to their titters orchestra began to play faster. The disconcerted conductor lost his place in the score, so Borge stopped playing, walked over to the podium, and pointed out where he should be. The audience response was howls of laughter and the seed for Borge's future as a comedian was planted.

For the moment, however, he continued his training to be a "serious" classical musician. At sixteen, Borge left Denmark on a scholarship to study at the Vienna Music Conservatory. From there, he went on to Berlin and apprenticed with Frederic Lamond and Egon Petri, two of the most prominent piano teachers of the time. Lamond did not particularly encourage the young pianist, but Petri did, seeing some raw talent in his student. As Borge recalled in a New York Times article, Petri "gave me a quality of finesse I never had.... I was on my way to becoming a first class concert pianist."

In 1932, he returned to Denmark to pursue a full-time career in music, but as chance would have it, he was destined for other things. Although Borge's piano playing was critically praised, he suffered from dehabilitating attacks of stage fright. To counter-act this potentially career-threatening problem, he started engaging the audience in informal comedy routines and bantering between pieces. Borge's quick wit and keen sense of the absurd was highly appealing to his listeners and this aspect of his performances came to overshadow his playing. By the late 1930s, he had become one of the most successful nightclub acts in Denmark, as well as appearing in six films, commanding the highest salary of any Danish entertainer.

Forced to Flee

Events taking place on the world stage, however, would cast a pall on Borge's rising career. While in Berlin, he had witnessed the emergence of the Nazi party. Hitler's seizure of power in 1933, marked by aggressive rhetoric toward Germany's neighbors and strident anti-Semitic propaganda, was very disturbing to Borge, both as a Dane and as a member of Denmark's small Jewish minority. He began to include pointed satirical references to Hitler and Germany in his act, sparking threats from Danish Nazi sympathizers. When Germany forced Denmark to sign a non-aggression pact, Borge sarcastically commented, "How nice. Now the Germans can sleep in peace, secure from the threat of Danish aggression." In April, 1940, the German army occupied Denmark. Borge's name figured prominently on a list of Danish intellectuals and artists to be arrested, but fortunately when Gestapo agents appeared at his house in Copenhagen, he was on tour in Sweden.

Borge had narrowly escaped imprisonment or worse, but the future in war-torn Europe looked bleak. As his wife, Elsie, was an American citizen, she was able to book passage for the two on the last ship leaving from Northern Scandinavia for the then neutral United States. However, to accompany his wife Borge needed an exit visa, an item difficult to come by with the immense refugee problem the war had created. In a stroke of good luck, the American consul in Stockholm happened to be a fan of his, so Borge was able to obtain the papers he needed and catch the boat just as the gangplank was being pulled up. After a nerve-wracking voyage that included passing through mine fields and severe over-crowding on board ship, Borge disembarked on American soil in August, 1940.

A Danish Comedian Reinvents Himself

In the new and unfamiliar world in which he found himself, Borge was a virtual unknown, so like any number of immigrants before him, he re-invented himself. Adopting the Americanized name Victor Borge—prior to this, he had been known by his birth name, Borg Rosenbaum—he applied himself to reading comic strips and watching gangster films so as to grasp the idiosyncracies of American speech and translate his Danish comedy routine into English. The complexities of the new language, which Borge nonetheless managed to pick up quickly, became a staple of his stage act and remain so to this day. His deliberate mispronunciations of words, coupled with "phonetic punctuation," a system of non-verbal sounds to indicate commas, periods, and other elements of punctuation would prove to be enormously popular.

Borge's first performance on the American stage however, a small part in a 1941 Ed Sullivan Broadway revue, was anything but encouraging. Rattled by last minute changes in his laboriously perfected act, Borge forgot his lines and was promptly fired. He was undiscouraged, performing in Florida to good reviews and then making his way to California where appearances on band leader Rudy Vallee's radio show exposed him to a national audience for the first time. Americans found the specta-cle of an apparently serious classical musician stopping in mid-piece to engage in irreverent asides in a deep Scandinavian accent hilarious and talent scouts for Bing Crosby's show, *Kraft Music Hall*, lost no time in signing Borge. He would go on to perform fifty-four times on Crosby's show and become one of the most popular and highest paid nightclub performers of the early 1940s, on a par with Red Skelton, Henny Youngman, and George Burns.

By 1945, Borge was a substitute host on a weekly radio show for NBC and shortly afterwards, the network signed him to a show of his own, the *Victor Borge Show*. Although such a meteoric rise for someone who just a few years before had been a refugee from the Nazis was astounding, Borge was still not satisfied. Convinced that the constrictions of performing within the format of a radio show or nightclub act stifled his creativity, he tended from the late 1940s on to appear exclusively before live audiences in concert halls and auditoriums, a forum in which he was free to set his own material and time limits. Left to his own devices, he flourished, developing many of the routines that would be his trademark for the next half century.

Apart from the delightfully low-brow satire of high culture that was the basis for his act, perhaps the strongest element of Borge's appeal was the spontaneity with which he carried things off, particularly as he became more comfortable in his adopted language. As he explained in a *Piano Quarterly* interview, "On stage I'm like a bat throwing out my radar. I listen to those sounds and they tell me the direction I should fly." Audience members arriving late, his dog accidentally following him on to the stage, a bug landing on his nose as he played, all provided a focal point from which to improvise absurdly witty monologues. Musically he was just as creative, starting a serious piece by Beethoven, playing a few bars, and then switching into "Happy Birthday." Although Borge did have some standard numbers, he was largely able to give the impression that he was making his routine up as he went along, a feature which kept his clowning fresh in the eyes of his audience.

Sets a World Record

On October 2, 1953, Borge opened as a one-man show on Broadway under the title *Comedy in Music*. It was a risky move and the show was expected to close after only a few performances. Afflicted with severe opening night jitters, Borge was convinced that the show was a flop; it was not until he received glowing press reviews the next morning that he realized he might have some-thing. *Comedy in Music* proceeded to run almost three years with some 849 performances, ranking to this day in the Guinness Book of Records as the longest running one-man show in theatrical history. At the end of the show's Broadway run, Borge took it back on the road and toured worldwide for the next four decades.

Perhaps because of his reputation as a comedian, it is not always recognized that Borge is a great musician in his own right. His childhood fascination with conducting led him to begin appearing from the mid-1970s on as a guest conductor with a number of prominent orchestras including the Philadelphia Orchestra, the Cleveland

Orchestra, the New York Philharmonic, and the London Philharmonic. But it is his piano playing, on those occasions when he does not stop halfway through a piece to crack jokes, that transmits his deep feel and understanding for music. Borge, a throwback to the golden era of piano of the late nineteenth and early twentieth centuries, retains a graceful touch and lyricism to his playing, which a *New York Times* music critic described as "warm, rich, highly nuanced ... [reflecting] a school of piano playing that is almost extinct."

In a testament to the longevity and appeal of his gifts, Borge continued to appear into the late 1990s. One of the last great comedians from the era of vaudeville and burlesque, his quirky sense of humor seems to appeal to audiences as much as ever, even after fifty years of performing essentially the same act. A 1990 video of a Borge performance entitled *The Best of Victor Borge* sold over 2,600,000 copies, and a 1993 PBS special, *Victor Borge: Then & Now,*" has been widely featured on fundraising specials. Borge continues to keep up a schedule that would tire out someone half his age. When asked by a *New York Times* interviewer about this, he responded, "Why not...? I know life. I have had a full measure of experience. Shouldn't I take advantage of it? The fruit is on the tree. Should I let it rot?"

Selected discography

An Evening with Victor Borge, Columbia, 1948.
The Blue Serenade, Columbia, 1948.
Comedy in Music: Vol. II, Columbia, 1954.
Comedy in Music: Vol. I, Columbia, 1954.
Victor Borge Plays and Conducts Concert Favorites, Columbia, 1959.
The Adventures of Piccolo, Saxie and Company, Columbia, 1959.
Great Memories from Old Time Radio, Columbia Musical Treasuries, 1960.
Borgering on Genius, MGM, 1962.
Victor Borge at His Best, PRT Records, 1972.
Borge at His Best, PRT Records, 1972.
Thirteen Pianos Live in Concert, Telefunken, 1975.
The Two Sides of Victor Borge, Borge Productions, 1987.
Live at the London Palladium, Marble Arch, 1991.
Live, Sony, 1992.

Sources

Periodicals

Chicago Tribune, July 28, 1996.
Musical America, January 1989.
New York Times, December 21, 1984; December 5, 1989.
Piano Quarterly, Vol. no. 130, 1985.
Saturday Evening Post, February 16, 1957.
Symphony Magazine, June/July 1981.

Additional information for this profile was provided by Gurtman and Murtha Associates, New York, NY.

—Daniel Hodges

Brandy

Singer, actress

AP/Wide World. Reproduced by permission.

Brandy Norwood, television's talented African American teen idol, boasts a successful singing and acting resume that many an entertainment veteran could envy. With a flash of her broad, contagious smile, and a toss of her signature mane of glossy braids, the award-winning singer turned her focus to acting and captured a television audience as star of the UPN sitcom *Moesha*, causing *Entertainment Weekly* to note, "She's one of the few pop-music stars who can act even better than she can sing."

Brandy's parents, Willie and Sonia Norwood, recognized stand-out talent in both their children—Brandy's younger brother Willie, Jr., called Ray-J, is also a singer—and launched a non-stop business plan aimed at early careers in the entertainment industry. They moved the family from Mississippi to Los Angeles when Brandy was four Ray-J was two, and started their vocal training in a church youth choir. "My brother and I were always in the front as featured singers because our dad was the choir director," Brandy explained to *Rolling Stone*. "Then I started being directress of younger choirs, and, well, I was just really hot in the church."

Church was Brandy's first stage. Willie handles the kids' musical grooming, while Sonia serves as business manager/chaperon. Brandy calls her "Momager," and Sonia takes the job to heart. Mom must okay clothing, costume, diet, social, and career choices. "She says, 'I'm going to be as big as Whitney [Houston],'" Sonia told *TV Guide.* "It's our job to go out there and help get her there."

At age 11, Brandy won second place in a talent contest and was singing at local events; at 12, she earned a spot singing backup for an R&B group named Immature. In 1993, when she was 14, Brandy signed her first recording contract with Atlantic. Several months later she landed a role on the ABC sitcom *Thea* as 12-year-old Daneesha, daughter of the title character. The show didn't last long, which suited Brandy fine. "I'm always smiling and happy," she told *People*, "Other people on the set weren't. I was miserable. I couldn't wait for it to go off the air."

Brandy used the extra time to polish and launch her debut R&B album, simply titled *Brandy.* The recording was a wild success, rocketing to the top of musical charts with triple platinum sales, producing best-selling singles "Baby" and "I Wanna Be Down," and two videos featured prominently on MTV. Jeremy Helliger in *People* remarked, "Brandy's well-groomed blend of gently lilting hip hop and pop-soul has a more timeless appeal. With the poise and sassy confidence of a diva twice her age, Brandy mixes her love songs with tributes to her little

Born Brandy Norwood, February 11, 1979, in McComb, MS; daughter of Willie (a choir director), and Sonia (Brandy's manager) Norwood; one brother, Willie, Jr. Education: Enrolled at Pepperdine University, Malibu, California campus.

Co-starred on ABC sitcom *Thea,* 1993; recorded album triple platinum debut album entitled *Brandy,* 1994; embarked on 13-city solo tour and spent two months opening for Boyz II Men; star of United Paramount Network's (UPN) sitcom *Moesha,* 1995—; contributed songs to *Waiting to Exhale* and *Batman Forever* soundtracks.

Awards: Grammy Award; American Music Award, favorite new artist, 1996.

Addresses: *Home*—Los Angeles, CA. *Record company*—Atlantic Records, 75 Rockefeller Plaza, New York, NY 10019.

brother ("Best Friend"), God ("Give Me You"), the perfect man ("Baby") and older crooners like Aretha and Whitney ("I Dedicate"). While this isn't groundbreaking stuff, Brandy has the pipes to become more than the latest teenage next-big-thing."

The Versatile Brandy

Brandy embarked on her first 13-city tour of U.S. high schools and a two-month stint as opening act for Boyz II Men's national tour. Her credits include songs on two major motion picture soundtracks, "Sittin' up in My Room" from *Waiting to Exhale,* and "Where Are You Now?" from *Batman Forever.* Winning a Grammy award and being named "Favorite New Artist" at the 1996 American Music Awards legitimized her musical talent on a national level.

Brandy followed up with another high-profile career move. Nabbing the star role in the United Paramount Network (UPN) hit sitcom *Moesha* has elevated her status to prime time. The highly-rated comedy series focuses on the everyday life of the Mitchells, a middle class black family living in south-central Los Angeles. Brandy plays Moesha Mitchell, the bright, 16-year-old daughter who copes with the normal pressures and complications of teen life with the help of best friends and well-meaning family members. She has a mischie-

vous little brother, hard-working car salesman father, and a new stepmother who teaches at her high school.

When Brandy initially read the script for the show, she was struck by the similarities between the lead character and herself. "Brandy kind of matched Moesha," the actress explained to *TV Guide.* "Her attitude is the same. She's interested in boys, but something else comes first—her schoolwork, her family. She hangs out with her friends. She's very nice." Clarifying her position about the show in *Jet,* Brandy said of her character, "She's responsible and listens to her dad. Her friends are wild, but she isn't. Most of the black shows on TV now are so unreal. There's no moral. There is a moral on *Moesha.*"

Moesha, deemed "one of TV's most winning sitcoms—and a fresh alternative to its tire competitors" by *Entertainment Weekly,* is hailed by critics for the normalcy of the Mitchell family's life. Story lines deal with happy and sad moments, sibling rivalry, teen temptations, and parent pressures. For instance, the 1996-97 season introduced a street-smart rapper to the set as Brandy's love interest. Brandy, afraid of her father's reaction to her dating someone so different from his expectations for her, struggles with the issue of telling her father the truth. These types of issues are proving to be important to *Moesha's* fan base. Show co-creator Ralph Farquhar commented in *Jet,* "Teenagers are aspiring to be adults. It's interesting to see teenagers finding out who they are and how they interact with parents." But Farquhar is pleased that the show is not just a hit with teens. "I get a lot of calls from parents saying `Thank you. Finally a show I can sit down and watch with my children,'" Farquhar told *Jet.* "We like to say stuff, but we're not preachy about it."

Brandy leads a large and talented cast. For the time being, she relies on instinct, help from an acting coach, and advice from fellow performers for her new role. Her life is crowded with television rehearsals and tapings, school—Sonia insists on three-hour tutoring sessions daily—and continued work time spent in the recording studio. The schedule leaves little time for dating or down time with peers. She still tries to fit in phone calls and trips to the mall with friends—although now she takes a body guard along.

Brandy is not finished spreading her wings. Brandy's first love is still music, and she considers herself more a singer than actress. In fact, she sings the *Moesha's* theme song, though Moesha, the character, does not sing on the program. Future plans include a second album for which she hopes to help write songs and contribute to production. A four-day television work week leaves little time for school, but Brandy earned a high school diploma with independent studies and tutoring. She continues her studies at Pepperdine University,

Malibu campus, and hopes to earn a degree with an emphasis on entertainment law.

Fame and fortune has not made Brandy sidestep family influence or forget her religious roots. She still counts on her parents for reality checks and her faith for stability. "I think it's because of God that I am where I am today," she told *Jet*. "And I thinks he's the cause of all of us being here. I don't ever want to forget about him."

Selected discography

Brandy, Atlantic, 1994.
Batman Forever (soundtrack), Atlantic, 1995.
Waiting to Exhale (soundtrack), Arista, 1995.

Sources

Periodicals

Entertainment Weekly, November 8, 1996, p. 56.
Jet, February 26, 1996, pp. 59-61; November 25, 1996, pp. 56-59.
Newsweek, March 25, 1996, p. 69.
New York Times, April 2, 1995, (Section 2) p. 43.
People, October 24, 1994, p. 20; November 21, 1994, p. 99; July 31, 1995, p. 23; May 6, 1996, p. 140.
Rolling Stone, April 6, 1995, p. 32.
Seventeen, April 1995, pp. 158-161.
TV Guide, April 6, 1996, pp. 30-32.
USA Today, July 26, 1996, p. 2D.

—*Sharon Rose*

The Breeders

Rock band

Ohio's Breeders, *Guitar Player* proclaimed, "create one of the most wonderfully unpredictable sounds in rock." The band was born from the ashes of two seminal alternative rock bands, The Pixies and Throwing Muses. After various personnel changes, the band had a mainstream hit with "Cannonball," a rambunctious blast of the group's off-kilter rock sensibility, in 1993. Yet the group soon seemed to split off in different directions, with singer-guitarist sisters Kim and Kelley Deal pursuing different projects and the latter hampered by drug problems. Yet the band continued to occupy an important place in the hearts of alternative rock fans, as indicated by the excitement surrounding rumors of a new album and tour planned for 1997.

The identical twin Deals grew up in Huber Heights, a suburban community near Dayton. Their father was a physicist who worked at nearby Wright Patterson Air Force Base, and they grew up adoring hard rock by the likes of Led Zeppelin and AC/DC. Even so, they would one day form an acoustic duo and perform country songs at truckstops. The strong bond between the

Photo by Ken Settle. Reproduced by permission.

Wiggs was drafted into the group, as much for her attitude as her chops. "I just thought she was cool," Kim told Michael Azerrad of *Rolling Stone*. "She looked like [TV horror-movie hostess] Vampira." With drummer Britt Walford, skinsman for the band Slint, operating under the pseudonym Shannon Doughton, the Breeders ventured into the studio to record an album with esteemed producer Steve Albini. The result was 1990's *Pod*, which Azerrad called "starkly beautiful" and *Alternative Press* eventually included in its "Top 99 of '85-'95."

After being fired from the Pixies in 1992, Kim focused her energy on the Breeders. She brought Kelley into the band despite the latter's lack of musical experience. "I couldn't make chords," Kelley recalled in *Guitar Player*. The Breeders released another record, the EP *Safari*, before undergoing more personnel changes. Donnelly left to form her own band, Belly, and Walford—who had moved on to a salacious new pseudonym, Mike Hunt—was replaced by Jim MacPherson. "I grew up with three sisters," the new drummer pointed out in *Request*, "so joining this band wasn't that big an adjustment for me."

Last Splash Had Impact

The Breeders made their first definitive statement with the 1993 album *Last Splash*. Co-produced by Kim and engineer Mark Freegard, the album most clearly defined the band's oddball sensibility. Reviewer Ned Rust of *Rolling Stone* praised the record's "fresh and vital sounds," which "are not those of painstaking musical craftspeople but the raw progeny of an unabashed, unconventional creativity." Melding noisy but joyful guitar rock, pop melodies, surf music, country and a variety of other styles, *Last Splash* caught the alternative audience's imagination. This was helped in large part by the video for the first single, the irrepressible and strange rocker "Cannonball," which was directed by Sonic Youth's Kim Gordon and Spike Jonze; the latter would eventually become one of the hottest names in rock video.

The success of the album led to an appearance on the heralded alternative rock festival Lollapalooza and a European tour with the band Luscious Jackson, among other adventures. Wiggs and Luscious Jackson drummer Kate Schellenbach eventually became romantically involved. Kim, meanwhile, began a seemingly permanent engagement to *Spin* writer and musician Jim Greer, who played bass for a while in the Ohio band Guided By Voices, for whom Deal did some producing. The Breeders also covered some GBV songs on an EP release.

sisters was established at an early age; when asked by *Entertainment Weekly* about "the best birthday present [she] ever received," Kim replied, "Kelley." The two failed to live up to the alternative-rock stereotype of tortured adolescence, as well. "Yeah, we were popular girls," Kelley quipped in *Spin*. "We got good grades and played sports. You got a problem with that?" Kim attended seven colleges, including Ohio State University, but never graduated from any of them. During the late 1980s, she hooked up with the alternative rock band the Pixies, playing bass and singing backups; over the course of several albums, however, the band recorded only a couple of her songs.

Formed As Side Project

In 1989, she formed the Breeders with Tanya Donnelly—herself a second banana in the similarly influential Throwing Muses—as a side project. Bassist Josephine

Drugs, Amps and Other Tributaries

Kelley Deal, meanwhile, got hooked on heroin; in 1995, she was arrested for accepting a parcel that contained the drug. "She has no life right now," Kim lamented in a *Spin* interview, "she has heroin." Kelley's difficulties—following on the heels of several other high-profile addictions and overdoses in the rock world—got substantial media attention, but Kim emphasized the personal cost. "You don't know what it feels like," she asserted, "it's so horrible to have to watch your twin sister, your best friend in the whole world, lose her self-worth, lose her self-esteem, lose all sense of who she is, lose everything. It's the worst f—ing feeling in the world." During the unfolding of this crisis the Breeders were, of necessity, put on hold.

Kim released an album, *Pacer*, in 1995 under the name the Amps; her touring lineup for the group included MacPherson, guitarist Nathan Farley and bassist Luis Lerma. "When I first wanted to do the album, it was going to be a solo album," she told John Chandler of the *Rocket.* "I was going to play all the instruments. I recorded six songs in my basement on a four-track [tape machine]. That's a new thing. I'd never started a record that way before. I'd learned to play the drums recently and really had fun with it." She added that her sister had taken to calling her "The Artist Formerly Known as Kim," in a joking reference to the moniker-shifting pop star Prince.

Wiggs, newly ensconced in New York, formed her own side project, the Josephine Wiggs Experience, and released an album on Grand Royal, Luscious Jackson's label. Kelley eventually entered a rehab program in Minnesota, played in an ad hoc ensemble that featured metal bad boy Sebastian Bach, and released an album on her own in 1996 as the Kelley Deal 6000. The record, *Go to the Sugar Altar,* earned some fine reviews; *Entertainment Weekly* deemed it "an uneven effort, but in the best sense: Kelley takes chances musically and lyrically, and comes up with something raw, off-kilter, and unexpected. Nothing saccharine about it."

What did leave an unpleasant flavor in fans' mouths, however, was the uncertain future of the Breeders. Where they only on hiatus, or had they broken up without a formal declaration? Rumors of a new EP and album and a pair of concerts were reported at the end of 1996 by *Addicted to Noise,* but the lineup for the two Northern California shows in question led *ATN* reporter Gil Kaufman to wonder, "is it the Breeders if Kelley's not there?

Sure, we guess. But is it the Breeders if Josephine Wiggs isn't there either? Um, maybe. But is it the Breeders if, it's, uh, the Amps?" Kim's pronouncements on the subject were vague, at best. Asked by *Tweak* if there would ever be another Breeders album, she replied, "If none of us are in jail we're going to do one soon, yeah." Whatever the eventual outcome, the Breeders had already made a huge splash in the crowded pool of alternative rock.

Selected discography

Pod, 4AD/Rough Trade, 1990.
Safari (EP), 4AD/Elektra, 1992.
Last Splash (includes "Cannonball"), 4AD/Elektra, 1993.
"Iris (Live)," *No Alternative*, Arista, 1993.
"Head to Toe" b/w "Shocker in Gloomtown" and "The Freed Pig," 4AD/Elektra, 1994.

As The Amps

Pacer, 4AD/Elektra, 1995.

As Kelley Deal 6000

Go to the Sugar Altar, Justice Records, 1996.

As Josephine Wiggs Experience

Bon Bon Lifestyle, Grand Royal, 1996.

Sources

Periodicals

Addicted to Noise, December 23, 1996.
Entertainment Weekly, October 1, 1993; July 12, 1996.
Guitar Player, November 1993.
Request, October 1993.
Rocket, April 24, 1996; July 10, 1996.
Rolling Stone, October 14, 1993; October 28, 1993; January 26, 1995; June 1, 1995.
Spin, September 1993, December 1993, March 1994, July 1995.
Tweak, 1996.

Additional information was provided by the Elektra Records web page on the Breeders.

—*Simon Glickman*

The Cardigans

Rock band

The Cardigans's sound—which *Rolling Stone*'s Nilou Panahpour called "loopy '60s lounge pop sweetened with wistful female vocals"—helped them to break through to mass international success in the mid-1990s. "We make happy music, but it's not silly," insisted Nina Persson, lead singer of the Swedish band the Cardigans, in *Option.* "It does have some real emotion in it. We're always happy-sad—that's the Cardigans state of mind. "Yet the band resisted the "retro" pigeonhole as much as possible, and indeed, their songs often explored dark lyrical themes; the Cardigans even managed to salute their metal roots on disc, covering songs by hard-rock titans Black Sabbath. "Easy listening is just one part of our music," Persson proclaimed in the *San Francisco Bay Guardian.* People always want to labelize you. It's a hard job to describe music, and I guess that's the only way some critics can do it." The critics, however, mostly fell for the band, just like audiences from Japan to Britain to the U.S.

The band coalesced in late 1992 in the town of Jönköping. Guitar Peter Svensson, bassist Magnus Svenigsson, guitarist-keyboardist Lars-Olof Johansson and drummer Bengt Lagerburg formed the instrumental lineup. "I knew Magnus from high school, and the band needed a girl," Persson told *People* with typical modesty. "They didn't have anyone else so I agreed, even though I was basically a novice as a singer. I never expected for us to achieve any success at all." Svensson and Svenigsson had been in heavy metal bands together, but Persson speculated in *Option* that even in their headbanging days they were better suited for pop. "Even when they were playing angry music, I don't think they were very angry," she mused. "We were all instantly comfortable making Cardigans music."

"You Can't Sound Modern"

The fivesome cohabited in a house big enough for their eclectic interests, and were soon collaborating on the material that would wind up on their Swedish debut, *Emmerdale.* The album was recorded by producer Doc-Tore Johansson (no relation to the band's keyboardist), who helped mold the Cardigans' sound in his studio in the town of Malmö. "We didn't consider ourselves very '60s until we started recording at Tambourine Studios with Tore," Svenigsson told *Rolling Stone.* "He brought this view of music to us because he felt we had good songs, but we had to add something to be complete. So he started to teach us about '60s music, and we adopted his theories." The bassist—who writes a portion of the band's compositions—elaborated on the Tambourine experience in *TV Guide:* "The studio is equipped from the '60s and '70s, so basically if you record there you can't sound modern."

The album fared well not only on the band's home turf but in England—where all manner of nostalgic pop was storming the charts—and Japan, where fans no doubt appreciated the Cardigans' frothy melodies and unaffected cuteness in equal measure. Similar enthusiasm greeted their sophomore album, *Life,* which was a platinum seller in Japan.

Impressed with Playful Pop

The band's penetration in the U.S. was largely underground, but they sound found themselves with numerous yank fans thanks to college radio airplay of the American version of *Life,* which combined material from the first two Swedish releases and appeared on the respected independent label Minty Fresh in 1996. The band's playful pop recalled everything from the newly resurrected "lounge" and "exotica" recordings of the 60s to the sophisticated pop of Burt Bacharach. Svenigsson, however, insisted he was the only Bacharach fan in the group. The Cardigans also put their delicate spin on a Black Sabbath song, "Sabbath Bloody Sabbath." Declared *BAM* magazine, "The band's generous borrowings from the palette of 1960s pop are the perfect vehicles for fluffy romanticism." Reviewer Michael Ansaldo concluded by calling the album "a grand slam for

For the Record . . .

Members include **Bengt Lagerburg**, drums; **Lars-Olof Johansson**, guitar and keyboards; **Nina Persson**, vocals; **Magnus Svenigsson**, bass and **Peter Svensson**, guitar.

Band formed 1992, Jönköping, Sweden; signed with Stockholm Records and released debut album *Emmerdale*, 1994; American debut, *Life* (comprised of tracks from first two Swedish releases), released on Minty Fresh label, 1996; signed with Mercury Records and released *First Band on the Moon*, 1996; song "Lovefool" featured on soundtrack of film *Romeo and Juliet*, 1996.

Addresses: *Record company*—Mercury Records, 825 Eighth Ave., New York, NY 10019. *Fan mail*—The Cardigans, c/o Trampolene Records, Box 20504, S-161 02 Bromma, Sweden. *Website*—http://lindstedt.mech.kth.se/~moch/cardigans/cardi.html.

a band batting cleanup behind that unholy trinity of Scandinavian bands: ABBA, Roxette, and Ace of Base."

This sort of comparison—even when it accompanied such praise—rankled the Cardigans greatly. While they admitted to an admiration for 70s Swede pop superstars ABBA, whom Svenigsson called "great, great songwriters" and "a brilliant pop band" in *TV Guide,* being lumped in with their younger hitmaking compatriots was clearly irksome. "Ace of Base," he sneered in the same interview, "have done nothing."

Blasted Off, Thanks to Shakespeare

The promise shown by *Life* led to a deal with the American label Mercury, which released the Cardigans' next effort, *First Band on the Moon,* in 1996. This time the band toughened up its sound a bit, and explored some darker lyrical territory. "*Life*'s lyrics were very shallow— stories about nothing, really," Svenigsson insisted in *Rolling Stone.* "I think at least 10 out of 11 songs on the new album are about really deep, serious shit." *Addicted to Noise* reviewer Gil Kaufman proclaimed that with *First Band,* the Cardigans "provide a blast of fresh, spearminted air to the moribund alternative nation."

In addition to melodic rockers like "Been It" and "Losers" and another Black Sabbath cover, "Iron Man, "*First Band* features "Lovefool," a song of romantic masochism placed in a sunny, upbeat musical setting. The song ended up on the soundtrack for director Baz Luhrmann's hit film version of Shakespeare's *Romeo and Juliet.* Luhrmann "asked us if he could use a Cardigans song," recollected Persson in *People.* "We gave him a slow ballad, but Baz asked for something 'jollier.' I like almost all of our other songs better than 'Lovefool.'" Even so, the song became a huge hit in the U.S., moving from alternative rock radio stations to Top 40. The Cardigans were rock stars in America. As a result, they found themselves confronting a lot of myths—not only about Swedish pop, but about them personally. "A lot of people thought we were very glamorous, fashionable people, but we aren't," Svenigsson explained in *Rolling Stone.* Perhaps most important for Persson was dispelling the idea that the Cardigans were purveyors of joke-pop or camp. "We're not being ironical," she asserted in *Addicted to Noise.* "We're taking this thing seriously and some people want to call it kitsch, but I think it's rude to our music. I feel very strongly about it. Tell [Americans] to go out and buy the album," she advised the publication. "And ... tell them not to laugh!"

Selected discography

Emmerdale, Stockholm Records, 1994.
Life, Stockholm Records, 1995.
Life (U.S. version; includes "Sabbath Bloody Sabbath"), Minty Fresh, 1996.
First Band on the Moon (includes "Been It," "Losers," "Iron Man" and "Lovefool"), Mercury, 1996.

Sources

Periodicals

Addicted to Noise, June 18, 1996; August 24, 1996.
BAM, June 14, 1996.
Musician, May 1996.
Option, September 1996.
People, February 3, 1997.
Rolling Stone, September 19, 1996.
San Francisco Bay Guardian, June 12, 1996.
TV Guide, January 31, 1997.

—Simon Glickman

Terri Clark

Country singer

Photo by Matthew Barnes. Courtesy of Mercury Nashville. Reproduced by permission.

Terri Clark became something of a country music sensation in 1995 with the release of her debut platinum album, entitled *Terri Clark.* The first single, "Better Things to Do" was a number-one hit on the country charts. In the summer of 1996, she was voted Star of Tomorrow by the TNN (The Nashville Network)/ Music City News Awards, a fan-voted honor. She was also nominated by the Country Music Association for its prestigious Horizon Award. *Billboard* magazine recognized her achievement by awarding her Top New Female Country Artists of 1995. In her native Canada, the awards were even higher with the Canadian Country Music Association awarding her Album of the Year, Song of the Year and the Vista Rising Star Award for 1996.

Clark was born in Montreal, Quebec on August 5, 1968 to Les Samson and Linda Clark. As a child, the family moved from Montreal to the heartland of Canada, the prairie province of Alberta. She was educated in the public schools of Medicine, Alberta and was exposed from a very early age to country music. Her grandparents had been country music performers and both her parents were musical. Clark herself began playing guitar at the age of nine. Throughout her childhood she was thrilled by country music and became a huge fan of The Judds, Reba McEntire and other big country stars. All her life, she wanted to be a country music performer, she told Victoria Forrest of *American Country* magazine. "When I was growing up, that is all I talked about. I slept, ate and breathed country music. I always loved the sounds from Nashville and couldn't have imagined doing anything else with my life." Succumbing to her daughter's drive, in 1987, her mother brought her to Nashville, country music's Mecca, where the 18-year old hoped to make a career. The chances of it making it in Nashville, of course, were extremely slim.

Still, Clark and her mother had faith that Terri had what it would take to make it. Incredibly, soon after their arrival, Terri got a job performing at Tootsie's Orchid Lounge after taking the stage one day while the regular performer was on break. She told the story for her record company's promotional department: "I was fresh from the prairie. We went into Tootsie's and there was a guy playing for tips. I boldly went up and asked him if I could go on during his break; and I started singing. I did these impersonations of John Conlee and John Anderson and George Jones and people started filtering in from the street. By the time I got ready to leave, the place was full. They hired me."

After securing a job and a place to live, Clark was left on her own by her mother who had to return to Alberta. She took part-time jobs and continued singing and writing music. She worked for a while in a boot store and waited

For the Record . . .

Born August 5, 1968, in Quebec, Ontario, Canada; daughter of Les Sauson and Linda Clark.

Addresses: *Record company*—Mercury Records, 66 Music Square West; Nashville, TN 37203.

tables at all sorts of restaurants, including a Chinese restaurant where one of her jobs was to rub down the steamed rice to keep it from getting too sticky. In addition to singing at Tootsie's, she sang at Gilley's and at the Wax Museum. While critics and fans often consider that she was something of an overnight sensation— since her very first single was a hit— the truth is she worked long and hard at her craft and put in her time knocking on doors trying to get noticed. She spent eight years living on the edge of the Nashville country music scene before catching the attention of Luke Lewis, president of Mercury Records, which signed her in 1994.

Getting Discovered in Nashville

Clark described the ordeal of trying to get "discovered" for an interview in *Country Song Roundup* in 1996. She said that all her running around for all those years in Nashville gave her a good sense of what is and what isn't a hit. She also said that she often wondered if she shouldn't just abandon her dreams and try to put together a life for herself beyond country music. "I wondered if I was ever going to have a normal life. 'Am I just going to keep chasing after my dream, or am I going to settle down, buy a house and raise a family like a normal person?'" Her perseverance, however, won out and she was granted a performance before Lewis. Having been given the opportunity to perform before the president of one the largest labels in the country, Clark selected a few of her favorite compositions, performing "Was There a Girl on Your Boys' Night Out?" and "The Inside Story" among others.

Terri Clark the album was completed in 1995 and contains 12 cuts, all but one of which were written by Clark, in collaboration. These include: "If I Were You" (first number-one hit), "Catch-22," "Is Fort Worth Worth It?" "When Boy Meets Girl," (second number one) Tyin' A Heart to a Tumbleweed," "When We Had it Bad," "Better Things to Do,"(third number one) "Suddenly Single," "Flowers After the Fact," "The Inside Story," "Was There a Girl on Your Boys' Night Out?" and "Something You Should've Said." Almost immediately after its release, the praise started piling up. In 1996, she went on the road, opening up for country music superstar George Strait and drawing quite a bit of attention herself.

In the fall of 1996, Clark released her second album, which has received largely positive reviews. The album contains eleven songs, eight of which Clark wrote or co-wrote. These include: "Emotional Girl," "Poor, Poor, Pitiful Me," "Just the Same," "Something in the Water," "Neon Flame," "Any Woman," "Twang Thang," "You do or You Don't," "Keeper of the Flame," "Not What I Wanted to Hear," and "Hold your Horses." Dating back to her pre-record deal years, the Warren Zevon classic "Poor, Poor, Pitiful Me" has been something of a standard for Clark, and, as such, it was the first single from her sophomore effort. It piqued at number five on the *Billboard* charts. Overall, Terri Clark has shown Nashville and country fans that she intends to stick around.

Selected discography

Terri Clark, Polygram Records, 1995.
Just the Same, Mercury Records, 1996.

Sources

Periodicals

American Country, 1996.
Country Song Roundup, 1997.

---*Jim Henry*

Albert Collins

AP/Wide World. Reproduced by permission..

Although he went largely unrecognized by the general public during most of his career, the Texas-born musician Albert Collins eventually was acknowledged as one of the most talented and distinctive blues guitarists of his era. He established his fame by creating a unique sound with his Fender Telecaster guitar that was based on unusual tunings and scorching solos. His nickname "Iceman" was bestowed on him because his guitar sounds were piercing and could scorch the ears, just as icicles were sharp and could burn.

Peter Watrous wrote in the *New York Times* that "Mr. Collins made his reputation by combining savage, unpredictable improvisations with an immediately identifiable tone, cold and pure." "In the Iceman's powerful hands," said Jas Obrecht in *Guitar Player,* "that battered Tele could sass and scold like Shakespeare's fire, jab harder than Joe Louis, squawk like a scared chicken, or raise a graveyard howl."

Musicians ranging from Jimi Hendrix to Canned Heat to Robert Cray have cited Collins as having a major influence on their styles. He was especially known for his frenzied live performances during which he would often stroll into the audience and dance with the fans, his playing arena extended by a 100-foot extension cord attached to his electric guitar. Often he would start talking a blue streak, regaling his fans with hilarious and lewd remarks.

While his crowd-pleasing improvisations made him an extremely popular performer over the years, his recordings sold erratically until late in his career. His ultimate fame was also delayed by the long-time domination of Chicago blues over the Texas-based version. While the Chicago blues of performers such as Muddy Waters and Howlin' Wolf emphasized group jam sessions, the Texas variety was more of a showcase for individual talent where guitarists tried to outplay each other. Few could compete with Collins in these "bouts," but his talent didn't bring him widespread fame until he was brought to the attention of rock fans in the late 1960s.

Relatives Were Noted Blues Guitarists

After moving to the Houston ghetto as a child, Collins first became interested in music while listening to the pianist in his church. He took piano lessons at school, then learned about playing guitar from his cousins, blues guitarists Willow Young and Lightnin' Hopkins. His cousins turned out to be major influences on Collins's trademark style. He emulated Young's style of playing without a pick, and learned to tune the guitar in a minor key from Hopkins. By using his fingers rather than a pick,

For the Record . . .

Born May 3, 1932, in Leona, TX; died November 24, 1993, of lung cancer, in Las Vegas, NV; married in 1968, wife's name Gwendolyn.

Blues guitarist, singer, and songwriter. Born to a share-cropping family; moved to the black ghetto of Houston, TX, as a child; learned to play piano as a youth and grew up listening to big-band music of Jimmie Lunceford, Count Basie, Louis Jordan, and Tommy Dorsey; learned to play guitar from cousins Willow Young and Lightnin' Hopkins; began playing blues at local clubs with Clarence "Gatemouth" Brown, 1947; played with his own group, the Rhythm Rockers while working days on a ranch and driving a truck, 1949-51; played with Piney Brown's band, early 1950s; became session player, 1953; recorded and performed with Little Richard, Big Mama Thornton, and others, 1950s; recorded first single, "The Freeze," 1958; recorded million-selling single, "Frosty," 1962; released first major album, *Truckin with Albert Collins,* for Blue Thumb, 1965; signed with Imperial label, 1968; sang for the first time on an album *(Love Can Be Found Anywhere (Even in a Guitar),* 1968; toured extensively throughout California, late 1960s; performed at Newport Jazz Festival and Fillmore West, 1969; stopped performing and began working for a building contractor in Los Angeles, 1971; signed with Alligator record label, and formed the Icebreakers, 1977; performed at Montreux Jazz Festival, 1975; performed with George Thorogood at Live Aid Concert, 1985; was chief attraction at American Guitar Heroes concert at Carnegie Hall, New York City, 1985; performed on Musicruise Dayliner circling Manhattan on opening night of JVC Jazz Festival, 1987; appeared in film, Adventures in Babysitting; was subject of television documentary on PBS, *Ain't Nothin' But the Blues,* 1980s.

Awards: W.C. Handy Award, best blues album *(Don't Blow Your Cool),* 1983; Grammy Award, best blues album *(Showdown,* with Robert Cray and Johnny Copeland), 1986; W.C. Handy Award, best blues artist of the year, 1989.

his playing developed a more percussive sound.

Collins claimed in *Guitar Player* that he made his first guitar out of a cigar box, using hay-baling wire for strings. Through his teen years he wanted to be an organist, but his interest in that instrument waned after his organ was stolen. While Collins said that his greatest influence was Detroit's John Lee Hooker, he spent much of his youth listening to the big band music of artists such as Jimmie Lunceford, Count Basie, and Tommy Dorsey. At one time he considered becoming a jazz guitarist, and his playing often shifted between blues and the horn-driven sound of a jazz big band.

After Collins switched form acoustic to electric guitar, he began listening to T-Bone Walker, Clarence "Gatemouth" Brown, and B.B. King to refine his talent. Brown was a key influence due to his horn-driven sound that Collins found especially exciting. Collins emulated Brown by starting to play with a capo and a Fender guitar, an instrument that would become inextricably linked to him. Since he couldn't afford to buy the guitar at that time, he started by having a Fender Telecaster neck put on another guitar.

By age 15 Collins was playing at local blues club with Brown. Then he formed his own group, the Rhythm Rockers, in 1949, with which he performed at honky tonks in Houston's all-black Third Ward on weekends while working during the week as a ranch hand and truck driver. Next on his career path was three years of touring with singer Piney Brown's band.

In the early 1950s, Collins's talent earned him positions as session players with performers such as Big Mama Thornton. He later replaced future guitar great Jimi Hendrix in Little Richard's band. By this time Collins had established himself as a great eclectic who could produce unusual sounds with his guitar playing. As David Gates wrote in *Newsweek,* Collins "tore at the string with his bare hands instead of the ostensibly speedier pick, used unorthodox minor tunings instead of the more versatile standard ones and unashamedly clamped on a capo (a bar across the fingerboard, which raises the pitch of the strings), making the already stinging Telecaster sound even more bright and piercing."

Recordings Established "Ice Man" Persona

Collins cashed in on the popularity of instrumentals ushered in by performers such Booker T., Duane Eddy, and Link Wray in the late 1950s. His first recording, an instrumental called "The Freeze," featured extended notes played in a high register. Collins told *Guitar Player* that the record sold about 150,000 copies in a mere three weeks.

Collins lost a chance to play with soul music star James Brown in the late 1950s because he couldn't read music. Meanwhile, he still didn't feel that he could make his living entirely from guitar playing, and he worked as truck drivers and as a mixer of paint for automobiles. Then he hit the blues big time with his recording of "Frosty," released in 1962, that sold over a million copies and became a popular blues standard. This song confirmed his reputation as a player of "cold blues," and his producer urged him to continue this theme in his song and album titles. He even named his backup band The Icebreakers.

With just his fingers and his capo that he would move up and down the neck of his guitar, Collins produced a wide range of effects ranging from the sound of car horns to footsteps in the snow. He released a series of singles for small record labels such as Kangaroo, Great Scott, Hall, Fox, Imperial, and Tumbleweed that had moderate success at the regional level. He continued playing through the 1960s, but recording very sporadically and was unable to tour because of his day job.

According to Peter Watrous in the *New York Times,* Collins' first significant album was *Truckin with Albert Collins* in 1965. The album featured what would become famous blues recording of his previously released "Frosty," "Sno-Cone," and other songs. Following the release of his compilation album, The Cool Sound of Albert Collins, he quit his paint job and moved to Kansas City in 1966. While there he met his future wife, Gwendolyn, who would become an important motivator for him as well the composer of some of his best-known songs. Among her compositions for Collins were "There's Gotta Be a Change" and "Mastercharge."

Gained New Popularity with Rock Fans

Blues music gained in popularity in the late 1960s due to various rock performers such as Jimi Hendrix and Canned Heat stressing the importance of blues as inspiration for their work. A major boost to Collins' career came as the result of interest in him by Bob Hite. Hite recommended Collins to the Imperial, which was affiliated with Canned Heat's label, Liberty/USA. His understated singing style showed up on a recording for the first time on *Love Can Be Found Anywhere Even in a Guitar,* the first of three albums that he recorded for Imperial. Later he recorded albums for Blue Thumb, then Bill Szymczyk's Tumbleweed label in Chicago in 1972.

Appearances at the Newport Jazz Festival and at Fillmore West in 1969 gained Collins more exposure and acceptance with young rock audiences. He also appeared at the Montreux Jazz Festival in 1975. While jamming in the 1970s in Seattle, he met and played with Robert Cray. More than a decade later, he teamed up with Cray and Johnny Copeland on a Grammy Award-winning blues album, Showdown. As late as 1971, when

he was 39 years old, Collins found it necessary to work in construction because he couldn't make a sufficient living from his music.

More comfortable playing for small audiences than mass gatherings, Collins nevertheless agreed to perform in the 1985 Live Aid Concert which was aired to an estimated 1.8 billion viewers. Right into his fifties, he maintained his flamboyant stage presence. Eventually, Collins was well established as the leading blues celebrity second to guitarist B.B. King.

Selected discography

Albums

Truckin' with Albert Collins, Blue Thumb, 1965.
Love Can B Found Anywhere (Even in a Guitar), Imperial, 1968.
Trash Talkin, Imperial, 1969.
There's Gotta B a Change, Tumbleweed, 1971.
Ice Pickin', Alligator, 1978.
Frostbite, Alligator, 1980.
Live in Japan, Sonet, 1984.
Showdown, 1985.
Molten Ice, 1992.

Sources

Books

Kozinn, Alan, Peter Welding, Dan Forte, and Gene Santoro, *The Guitar, the History, the Music, the Music, the Players,* Quill, 1984, pp. 84-85.
Larkin, Colin, editor, *Guinness Encyclopedia of Popular Music,* volume 1, Guinness Publishing, 1992, p. 531.

Periodicals

Audio, June 1988, p. 148.
DownBeat, February 1992, p. 48; February 1994, p. 14; May 1994, p. 56.
Guitar Player, May 1988, p. 87; July 1993, p. 30; April 1994, pp. 69, 70, 72, 75-77.
High Fidelity, May 1987, p. 79.
London Times, November 26, 1993, p. 23.
Los Angeles Times, November 25, 1993, p. A22.
Newsweek, December 6, 1993, p. 84.
New York Times, November 25, 1993, p. D19; November 26, 1993, p. B23.

—*Ed Decker*

Coolio

Rap artist

Unlike other rappers out there just saying what they see, Coolio offers solutions. "Just because you're from the west coast, and you talk about some real s---, you get labeled a 'Gangsta Rapper,'" Coolio complained in *Rap Sheet*. "I'm not a political rapper. I don't rap about love all the time and s--- like that. I rap about all of it. I'm a well-rounded person and I might say anything." It is important to Coolio that he makes that clear, because there are messages he *does* want to send, and they are positive. Although his "Gangsta's Paradise" was the best selling single of 1995, Coolio is just telling it like it is.

Artis Ivey, Jr., never pictured himself as the rapper Coolio when he was a kid. If anything, he dreamed of going to Harvard University. He was one of the four smartest kids in his elementary school, and although he was small and had asthma, he learned to take care of himself despite the violence of inner city life. His father had left the family when Coolio was two, and his mother moved them to Compton, California, when he was eight. The library was just a block away, and Coolio read every book he could.

Lessons Learned at an Early Age

Coolio's life started getting sidetracked when he was promoted from fifth to seventh grade. The older kids bullied him. At about the same time, Coolio's mother and stepfather broke up. At first her paycheck kept the family going, but when she lost her job she started drinking. Suddenly the boy did not have that family foundation under him anymore. That is when he started running with the neighborhood gangs, creating a sort of crazy man role for himself.

Either a case of mistaken identity, or taking the rap for a friend, landed Coolio in jail for ten months when he was accused of trying to cash a money order stolen in an armed robbery. He turned 18 while incarcerated. Coolio learned his lesson, never wanting to go to jail again, and tried to get out of that scene. But by 1985 he was addicted to crack cocaine. When he finally saw his life spiraling out of control, Coolio looked for help.

Coolio went up north to San Jose, California, and moved in with his father. He got a job with the California Department of Forestry fighting fires in the mountains. Between will power and faith in God he came back out of those mountains 18 months later clean and sober. Coolio had already turned to rap for solace in the early 1980s and even had a single out that got some local airplay. With the death of his mother of a brain hemorrhage in 1987, Coolio immersed himself fully in the burgeoning rap scene.

As a kid, Coolio's mom had always called him Boo. He even had it tattooed on his arm in eighth grade. Although Boo or Artis is still what the family calls him, the street name Coolio came about in a more amusing fashion. Sitting around one day in Compton in his 20s playing guitar, one of Coolio's friends came up and said, "Who do you think you are, Coolio Iglesias?," referring to Latin crooner Julio Iglesias. The name stuck.

From the Streets to the Charts

Over time, Coolio recorded music with his friend Spoon under the name NuSkool. Then he joined WC and the MAAD Circle, whose album, *Ain't a Damn Thing Changed*, came out on the Priority label in 1991 and sold about 150,000 copies. Coolio still did not have it made though. He had to experience the ignominy of being recognized by fans while in line for his welfare check. But in 1993, Coolio's manager sent a four song demo tape to Tommy Boy Records in New York. They liked what Coolio had to offer, but at first only signed him to do a single. But when they heard what he had done in the studio, Tommy Boy signed him on for a full album.

The result was 1994's *It Takes a Thief,* and that record put Coolio on the map. The album went platinum with the help of the inviting, dreamlike crossover hit single "Fantastic Voyage." He proudly calls himself a thief—his own management company is called Crowbar. Their motto is "We're getting in, one way or another"—he acknowledges using samples of others' work in his own music. As Mike Rubin put it in *Spin,* "Coolio has mined a vein of multi-platinum ore by combining his slightly wooden vocal delivery with vintage, test-driven grooves."

In 1995 Coolio wrote "Gangsta's Paradise" for the soundtrack of the film *Dangerous Minds.* The song sold millions, paving the way for the album of the same name. If people thought his first hit record was a fluke, *Gangsta's Paradise* proved them wrong. In *Spin* Barry Walters wrote, "[Coolio] has the power to appeal to folks alienated by '90s hip hop insularity because his lyrics are about things that concern everybody—Aids, family love, respect, daily life, revolution."

Coolio has got a conscience and a definite drive to help make the world a better place through his lyrics. He is the father of six children and knows he is responsible for molding them into good people. Coolio feels it is high time for other folks in this world to start setting a good example.

Selected discography

(With WC and the MAAD Circle) *Ain't a Damn Thing Changed,* Priority Records, 1991.
It Takes a Thief (includes "Fantastic Voyage"), Tommy Boy Records, 1994.
Gangsta's Paradise (includes "Gangsta's Paradise"), Tommy Boy Records, 1995.

Sources

Entertainment Weekly, November 10, 1995; Year End Special, 1995.
People, January 29, 1996.
Rap Sheet, December 1995.
Rolling Stone, December 14, 1995.
Source, February 1996.
Spin, January 1996; March 1996.
USA Weekend, August 16, 1996.

Additional information for this profile was provided by Tommy Boy Records press materials, 1995.

—Joanna Rubiner

Carl Craig

Techno artist

Techno music sustains a particularly unique Detroit music legacy. Like its predecessor, the Motown sound, techno was born underground in makeshift studios and basements in some of the grittier parts of the city. Both musical genres came as a result of a dedicated few who channeled their personal visions into aural innovation. And techno, like early Sixties R&B, draws upon a rich array of African-American musical traditions. However, the artists that Detroit techno produced, Carl Craig among them, remain far more famous abroad than in their own city, and their heady, almost intellectualized sound has failed to find any mass, MTV-viewing audience.

As with that of his turntable peers, Craig's music rests somewhere between dance-club beats and avant-garde composition, and the one-time teen techno prodigy was the first among a new younger wave of DJs/recording artists to sign with a major label. In an interview with *Urb* magazine's Tim Barr, New York producer Joey Beltram called Craig "a true innovator. He has his own sound and his own identity. You hear other people's records and you can tell they've been listening to his stuff. There just isn't anybody else like him."

Craig, who records under the aliases Paperclip People, 69, Psyche, and BFC, as well as his own name, is several years younger than most of Detroit's more celebrated techno artists. Born in the early 1970s, Craig grew up on Detroit's west side and attended the Cooley High immor-

talized in the Seventies movie of the same name. In his formative years, he was as much enamored of white alternative music—including groups like Bauhaus and the Smiths—as he was the current and past Motown sounds and Prince. He also loved the cool metallic sounds of German avant-garde act Kraftwerk, which he discovered at the age of twelve. When Craig was a few years older, he began accompanying his cousin, a lighting technician, to jobs at dance clubs. One such venue was a Detroit discotheque called Cheeks, a legendary draw in the early- to mid-Eighties; there Craig witnessed the power of the star DJ, observing Cheeks' mixmaster, Jeff Mills, play European disco tracks intermixed with the first rap records of the decade.

Homemade Tape

Craig also became a participant in the burgeoning techno scene, which took off in the mid-Eighties helmed by a trio of young Detroiters—Derrick May, Kevin Saunderson, and Juan Atkins. At private loft parties and techno nights at large city clubs, hundreds danced themselves into "group bliss" with the help of the thumping, hypnotic tracks mixed by these three, and by the others who followed. Inspired, Craig borrowed recording equipment and began experimenting in his bedroom. He made a tape—without any beats since he didn't yet have a drum machine—and then took it to the home of Derrick May after simply finding out where he lived. Craig was just seventeen, and May was on his way out the door to catch a plane to Europe, but gave him a minute. He told Craig to work on it some more, which he did, and Craig brought it back.

May then took Craig into the recording studio to record a track called "Neurotic Behaviour," and another song entitled "Elements" (recorded under the tag Psyche) was included on the Virgin Records compilation *Detroit Techno II*. By this time, techno's Detroit epicenter was the Music Institute, a downtown Detroit club that turned away throngs every weekend. In the spring of 1989 Craig, still a teenager, went to London with May's Rhythim Is Rhythim DJ group. "It was like a big thing for me to be in London," Craig told *Mixmag*'s Tony Marcus, "in a club, this was like a dream, I think it's kind of where I caught the bug." He liked the city so much he stayed another six months, and would make it his intermittent home for several more years. Craig still remained tied to Detroit, however, and continued his collaboration with May. His mentor's Transmat and Fragile labels released Craig's another two singles, "Crackdown" (also recorded under the moniker Psyche) and "Galaxy" (recorded as BFC), both in late 1989.

For the Record . . .

Born c. 1970, in Detroit, MI.

Joined Derrick May's Rhythim Is Rhythim DJ group, 1989; co-founded RetroActive label, 1990 (label dissolved); worked in a copy shop for a time; founded Planet E Communications (record label), 1991; signed with Blanco Y Negro (a United Kingdom subsidiary of Warner Brothers); released *Landcruising*, 1995; released *More Songs about Food and Revolutionary Art* on Planet E, 1996.

Addresses: *Home*—Detroit, MI. *Record company*—Planet E Communications, 139 Cadillac Square, Suite 601, Detroit, MI 48226.

Founded Two Labels

The following year, Craig co-founded a Detroit-based record label called RetroActive. He worked in a copy shop to make ends meet, though he was already gaining a reputation as the "boy genius" of the scene. In a rudimentary studio in his parents' basement, Craig created and engineered the RetroActive sound. "That was a good time," Carl recalled of the era in the *Urb* interview. "Nobody had expectations that I conform in a certain way.... At heart, I was just making music for myself." In time, conflicts within the tight-knit techno community severed Craig's ties with his RetroActive partner and even with May—though the two later reconciled, and Craig still refers to him as a profound influence.

In 1991, Craig founded his own label, Planet E Communications, whose first release was the EP "Four Jazz Funk Classics." The record's title is homage to a similarly-named album from Throbbing Gristle, an avant-garde industrial act fronted by former Psychic TV instigator Genesis P. Orridge—yet another of Craig's startling musical inspirations. Another Craig record, "Oscillator," released around the same time under the moniker Paperclip People, also broke new ground. The Paperclip People alias would serve as home for Craig's more traditional dance-club tracks.

Instigator of Jungle

What many critics consider Craig's most profound record came in 1992 under the alias Innerzone Orchestra. "Bug in a Bassbin" has been credited with fertilizing the ground from which the jungle music movement germinated. (The record achieved such fame that upon its re-release a few years later, a DJ/techno magazine called *Jockeyslut* devoted an entire feature article to the song in homage; it included interviews with some of the most famous names in the business who had remixed versions of it.) "Bug in a Bassbin" and Craig's other work eventually attracted the attention of Warner Brothers, and he signed onto its United Kingdom subsidiary Blanco Y Negro. His first full-length record, *Landcruising,* took a long time to come to fruition before its 1995 debut, he told Barr in *Urb,* because he held out for a budget that would allow him to record it the way he felt it should be done.

Designed as a smooth, interlocking whole—not simply a collection of disjointed singles—*Landcruising* "relocated techno in a shinier, glossier future," wrote Barr. During this period of his life, Craig was crisscrossing the globe for DJ gigs, from Europe to Tokyo. "'Landcruising' catches a sense of motion and flight," wrote *Mixmag*'s Marcus, "city lights all over the world seen glittering from a thousand different aeroplane windows." *Landcruising,* however, didn't fly with critics. Others, Craig included, also believe that the label bears some of the blame for poor sales, since they gave generously for its recording then failed to promote it enough to recoup their investment.

Back to Cadillac

By early 1997 Craig had retired from DJing, exhausted at playing countless clubs from Tokyo to Amsterdam, and somewhat disillusioned with the greed of the scene-machine. He also felt that he needed to make Detroit a more permanent home base and start recording in earnest. "It's definitely more rewarding being here," Craig confessed to *Raygun*'s Dan Sicko after he moved back and forsook the DJ gigs, "even just contemplating making music—rather than to go somewhere, sit in a hotel for eight hours and try to get pumped up for something you don't know whether or not it's going to be good." Becoming more settled also allowed him to look to new horizons for inspiration. One definite influence has been former Sun Ra drummer Francisco Mora, who introduced Craig to even more outré experimental jazz percussion as well as Afro-Cuban rhythms.

Such influences found their way to Craig's second full-length LP, *More Songs about Food and Revolutionary*

Art, released in 1996 on Craig's Planet E label. Named in homage to a lauded Talking Heads album, the record, asserted Barr in *Urb*, "is a *tour de force*, the classic example of what happens when sweat, genius and circuit-boards collide with beats, rhythms and melodies that sound like they come from a future time." The science-fiction novels Craig loved as a kid, Mora's exotic meters, the futureworld of all-night techno parties held three floors underground to elude Tokyo's vice police, the changing Detroit landscape—all found their way into the grooves of *More Songs*. "Many tracks have a cinematic effect, as if Craig were composing for a movie of his own mind," wrote Barry Walters in *Spin*.

Critically Acclaimed

Craig's second effort also included a collaboration with May, "Frustration." The influential music-industry magazine *CMJ* predicted *More Songs* to go down as the techno released of the year. Kuri Kondrak, writing for *Resonance*, also heaped praise upon it. "*More Songs* combines styles from Craig's past and present in a way that breaks the mold of the traditional Detroit context while still maintaining a link with the original manifesto," Kondrak declared. Craig liked the record, too. "It's my ultimate album," he *Urb*'s Barr. "Everything that I love, everything that I can listen to a hundred million times, is on there." Around the same time, Planet E also issued *The Secret Tapes of Dr. Eich*, a collection of his Paperclip People work, including the much-lauded "Oscillator." Reviewing it for *Alternative Press*, Dave Segal praised its melding of "globular funkiness and cyborgian synth squeals."

Craig takes the visiting European journalists who come to interview him on personalized tours of the Motor City. His favorite stops include such unusual Detroit landmarks as Tyree Guyton's found-art streetscape known as the Heidelberg Project, and the Eastern Market loft buildings where techno was born. Crag's Planet E offices are located in downtown Detroit not far from the legendary but now defunct Music Institute. Another favorite spot is Belle Isle, the large island in the middle of the Detroit River that serves as the city's park. Teenagers still congregate on here on hot nights with their cars and elaborate mobile sound systems booming from the trunks, but when Craig crosses the bridge into the park late at night, he is reminded of the paradox of techno's great fame abroad, and its failure to catch on in Detroit and America as Motown did. The city, seen from this slight distance, symbolizes that to him for the moment. "People are going to recognise what is happening in this city," Craig predicted in *Mixmag*. "We are the future and we are right here and we are not getting recognised and

very time I come to this island that's kind of what I feel. It's like this power that comes, it's something that hits me in my heart."

Selected discography

As Carl Craig

Landcruising, Blanco Y Negro, 1995.
More Songs about Food and Revolutionary Art, Planet E, 1997.

As BFC

"Please Stand By," RetroActive, 1990.

As Psyche

"Neurotic Behaviour" (reissue), Art, 1993.

As 69

Four Jazz Funk Classics (EP), 1991.

As Paperclip People

"The Climax," RetroActive, 1990.
"Oscillator," RetroActive, 1991.
"Throw," Open, 1994.
The Secret Tapes of Dr. Eich, Planet E, 1997.

As Innerzone Orchestra

"Bug in a Bassbin," RetroActive/MoWax, 1992.

Sources

Periodicals

Alternative Press, April 1997.
CMJ, March 1997; April 1997.
Details, April 1997.
DJ, April 1997.
The Face, March 1997.
Jockeyslut, August/September 1996.
Mixmag, March/April 1997.
Muzik, March 1997, p. 38, p. 103.
Raygun, March 1997.
Resonance, March 1997, p. 20.
Spin, May 1997.
Sweater, May 1997.
Urb, Spring 1997, p. 50.
Vox, May 1997.

—*Carol Brennan*

Billy Dean

Singer, guitarist, songwriter

Photo by Beverly Parker. AP/Wide World Photos. Reproduced by permission.

Tall and ruggedly handsome, Florida native Billy Dean falls squarely into the romantic balladeer category within country music. A string of contemporary, country-flavored singles have charted Dean as a solid performer, and his most successful song, 1991's "Somewhere in My Broken Heart," have garnered him a Grammy nomination as well as a nomination for the coveted Country Music Association's Horizon Award. In the years since, Dean has built on this success as both a songwriter and vocalist.

William Harold Dean was born April 2, 1962, in Quincy, Florida. He inherited both his name and his musical talent from his father who, in addition to being an auto mechanic, led his own local band, the Country Rock. Dean learned to play the guitar while still in elementary school and made his first appearance on stage in his father's band when he was only eight years old. Telling his guitar-playing son that pickers were "a dime a dozen," Billy's father encouraged his son to develop his natural talent as a vocalist instead. "They used to stick a guitar in my hand that wouldn't have the volume turned up, and that ticked me off ...," Dean recalled to Parry Gettelman of the *Orlando Sentinel.* "I got old enough to play finally, and they found out I was a pretty good player after a while and let me turn it up a little louder."

Dreams of a Career in Music

By the time he was fifteen, Dean was performing gigs along Florida's Gulf Coast, where he developed a regional following. Dean Sr. continued to support his son's desire to become a musician. "Son, it won't surprise me if you make it, but it will surprise me if you don't," he once told Billy Jr. Unfortunately, the elder Dean would not have the chance to witness his son's national success—he passed away in 1983, when Billy was twenty-one.

The 6'4" Dean let go of his musical dreams for a short while when he attended college in Mississippi on a basketball scholarship. But after a year his attention wandered off the court and back toward music. Dean left school and toured with his own band, entering the 1982 Wrangler Star Search competition when he was nineteen. Despite the competition, Dean became a national finalist, placing tenth. Looking out from the Grand Ole Opry Stage during the finalist performances was inspiring for the young performer. And the encouragement he received from members of the panel of country music professionals assembled there as judges inspired Dean to move to Nashville to live out his dream.

For the Record . . .

Born William Harold Dean, April 2, 1962, in Quincy, FL; son of William and Odean Dean; married Cathy Massey, 1990; children: William Eli, Hannah Catherine. Education: Attended .

Began performing professionally c. 1980; songwriter and backup singer, Nashville, TN, beginning 1983; signed with EMI (music publisher), c. 1988; signed with Liberty/SBK Records, 1989; recorded debut, *Young Man,* 1990; has appeared in commercials and on television series, including *Lois & Clark.*

Awards: Best New Male Vocalist and Song of the Year awards, both Academy of Country Music, both 1992; Grammy award nomination, best male performance—country, 1992, for "Somewhere in My Broken Heart"; TNN Songwriter award, 1993, for "Billy the Kid"; Rising Star award, Country Music Television Awards, 1993; Grammy Award (with others), best country gospel album, 1996, for *Amazing Grace;* several BMI certificates and awards.

Addresses: *Record company*—Capitol Nashville, 3322 West End Ave., Nashville, TN 37203.

Once he'd made the move to Music City USA, Dean began networking and soon found work as a vocalist, both as a commercial jingle-singer and as a backup singer for other artists. At the same time, he fell in with a new crowd of music professionals—songwriters. "I didn't really consider myself a writer, but it seems like the first people I met were writers," Dean told Vernell Hackett in *America Songwriter.* "... and most of the musicians who were gigging at night were writing during the day. That was a pattern the people I met were in, so I fell into that pattern too." He began to develop his own songwriting skills, maturing his talent and gaining the professionalism that would ultimately give him the break that he needed. Artists like the Oakridge Boys, Ronnie Milsap, Les Taylor of the band Exile, and Shelley West recorded his compositions, and efforts at co-writing were also successful—Earl Thomas Conley recorded "Brotherly Love," which Dean helped to write. His contract to write for publisher EMI would be his first step to a recording contract.

Music City Connections Lead to Recording Contract

After several years in Nashville, Dean's track record as a songwriter was established. Then new traditionalist Randy Travis took a look at "Somewhere in My Broken Heart," a song Dean had co-written with Richard Leigh, and liked what he saw. In 1989, while Travis was still considering the song for a single on his *No Holding Back* album, Dean signed a contract with Capitol Nashville/SBK and recorded the song himself. It would appear on his 1990 debut, *Young Man.* Two of the album's singles—"Somewhere in My Broken Heart" and "Only Here for a Little While"—went to the top of the country and adult contemporary charts, boosting the album to gold. Dean's musical career was in gear and rolling.

The following year would find Dean walking away with best new male vocalist honors at the 1992 Academy of Country Music Awards presentation, the first of many awards the singer-songwriter would win during his career. Meanwhile, his second album, simply titled *Billy Dean,* was equally popular with fans. "You Don't Count the Cost" and "Only the Wind" soon sailed into the top five, while "Billy the Kid" made a rapid climb to the number one spot after the album's 1991 release. *Billy Dean* eventually went platinum.

Extends Talent as Songwriter

Dean co-wrote five songs on his second album—songs that showed him to be a keen observer of life and love. His gift for storytelling rings true in ballads like "Billy the Kid," which is both touchingly nostalgic and deeply introspective, and "If There Hadn't Been You," an ode to love. Billy believes that today's country audience is looking for a more sophisticated slant to lyrics, although he believes country songs are not usually hailed for their depth. His own songs tend to be what he terms "a little vague, like pop music in the '70s, when songs could be interpreted in several different ways. In country, for the most part, you have to spell it out." While Dean's own taste in songs runs to those that have lyrical depth and a sophisticated structure, he will be the first to admit that the songs he records have to fit the country radio format. Although Dean began his career as a vocals, after six albums, songwriting would become his main creative outlet. "I will always be a songwriter first and foremost," he told Hackett in 1996—"my passion is inventing the music, and that's what I love the most."

Dean's songwriting efforts were rewards by more than just his fans when "Somewhere in My Broken Heart" won the Academy of Country Music award for best song in 1992—the same year that Dean himself walked away with best new male vocalist honors.

Hard Work Fuels Journey on Path to Success

The years following the release of *Billy Dean* have found the musician on the road with such country superstars as the Judds, Alan Jackson, Clint Black, and Merle Haggard. Along the way, he has also picked up a family—Dean married former sales executive Cathy Massey Dean in 1990 and became a father when young William Eli Dean appeared on the scene in mid-1993. A daughter, Hannah, was born to the Deans in 1995.

Meanwhile, he put in a full schedule in the recording studio. Dean's third album, *Fire in the Dark,* also contained several original compositions, including the title track, which he co-authored with collaborator Tim Nichols. The 1993 release also featured several tunes that were, well, slightly out of character. "I've had a lot of ballads out because those are the kinds [of songs] I love to write," Dean told Bob Paxman in *Country Song Roundup.* "But I always wondered how people would perceive another side of me, and I also wanted to start writing more about grow-up situations." Together with Tim Nichols, Dean wrote his first cheating song, the title cut, which was embraced by radio and country fans alike.

Men'll Be Boys, which Dean recorded in 1994, didn't exactly wow the critics. While the album contained several ballads—Dean's specialty—including one—"I Can't Find the Words to Say Goodbye"—co-written with David Gates, former lead singer of the 1970s pop group Bread, the album had limited successes on the charts. As Dean would later tell *Billboard,* "The music wasn't right.... And quite honestly, I was feeling burned out." Dean's active touring schedule had taken a toll as well, keeping him from songwriting and draining his creative energies.

Rethinks Priorities

The pressures of staying on top in the music business were taking their toll on Dean's family as well, and after the release of *Men'll Be Boys,* the singer-songwriter took a break from his music to spend time with his young son and wife Cathy, then pregnant with the couple's second child. "It seemed like the time to let the dust settle," Dean explained to Susanna Scott in *Country Song Roundup.* "We had a baby,... the record label was changing from Liberty to Capitol Nashville, and I'd been having voice problems. As a result of the time off, I've fallen in love with writing and performing again. I couldn't have experienced this renewed enthusiasm if I hadn't taken time to step back."

During his year off, Dean did some acoustic gigs that began to renew his passion for songwriting and for performing. He came back strong in 1996, with a new album and a new burst energy. *It's What I Do* showcases a more mature talent, not only in terms of musical experience but in terms of life experience as well. "I didn't really plan to target [the 30-something] audience, but so many people are going through the same things I go through," Dean told Deborah Evans Price in *Billboard.* "I really put my heart on my sleeve with this album. I'm singing from a different place now.... I noticed a change from where I was drawing my inspiration from, and it was coming from much deeper within me." Dean co-wrote several cuts on the album, including the retro "Play Something We Can Dance To," and incorporated several ballads from other top Nashville songwriters. The title cut, the Tom Shapiro-Chuck Jones penned "It's What I Do," is especially reflective of Dean's new outlook: it's the story of a man totally focused on his career to the exclusion of everything else in his life, until he learns to look beyond business for life's true meaning. And singer Linda Davis joins Dean on another single, the poignant "Leavin' Line." Dean accompanied his return to recording with a return to touring, accompanying country superstar Reba McEntire on tour in the spring of 1996.

Because of the highs and lows that are part of a music career, Dean is looking ahead to broadening his creative horizons to include acting. He signed with Creative Artist Agency in the early 1990s and has appeared in commercials and on *The Tonight Show* and *Good Morning America,* as a host on several television awards shows, and, more recently, on such national television series as *Lois & Clark.* In addition to his own albums, Dean has also recorded material on the compilation albums *Common Thread: The Songs of the Eagles* (1994) and the Grammy Award-winning *Amazing Grace* (1996); on the soundtrack album *8 Seconds* (1994); and with Dolly Parton, on her 1993 recording *Slow Dancin' with the Moon.*

Selected discography

Albums

Young Man, Liberty, 1990.
Billy Dean, Liberty, 1991.
Fire in the Dark, Liberty, 1992.
Greatest Hits, Liberty, 1994.
Men'll Be Boys, Liberty, 1994.
It's What I Do, Capitol Nashville, 1996.

Bryan Duncan

Christian singer

For 25 years, Bryan Duncan has spread the Christian gospel in his songs, concerts, and 17 albums — released both as a solo artist and a member of Sweet Comfort Band. Duncan's music is a mainstay on contemporary Christian radio and has earned him a long list of awards from the industry. He was nominated as male vocalist of the year in the 1994 and 1995 Dove Awards, for example, and named *Christian Research Report*, male vocalist of the year in 1993.

Baby-boomer Duncan was born in Ogden, Utah, on March 16, 1953. While in college in 1973, he was a founding member of the trio Sweet Comfort, which featured drummer Rick Thomson, bassist Kevin Thomson, and Duncan on keyboards and vocals. The group quickly developed a regional following in Southern California and, in the course of a dozen years together, climbed to the top of the Christian music charts. One writer called Duncan's music "infectious, groove-oriented, blue-eyed soul delivered with passion, emotion and precision."

In 1996, guitarist Randy Thomas joined Sweet Comfort and the band recorded its first song, Golden Ages, for the Marantha Music label collection *Marantha V*. The following year, Marantha released the group's self-titled debut, which received airplay on Christian radio and on mainstream stations in Southern California. After that first album, *Sweet Comfort* signed with Light Records and released five albums between 1979 and 1983. Three songs from 1979's *Breakin' the Ice* reached Christian radio's Top 20. Two years later, *Campus Life, Billboard* and *CCM* all named Sweet Comfort's album *Hearts of Fire* one of 1981's Top 10 Christian recordings. With the release of *Perfect Timing* in October 1983, it was time for Duncan to go it alone, however. Sweet Comfort announced that it would break up and, in early 1984, said goodbye during a three-month farewell tour.

Duncan launched his solo career by signing with Ray Ware Artist Management in June 1984. The following year, he toured Australia and Light Records released his solo debut album *Have Yourself Committed*. The title song as well as "Child's Love" reached the Christian music charts. In the last half of the 1980s, Duncan toured regularly, released videos, and recorded the albums *Holy' Rollin'*, *Whistlin' in the Dark*, which spawned four singles, and *Strong Medicine*—which received solid airplay and ranked 16th in sales among 1989's Christian albums.

Duncan then moved to the Myrrh record label and released *The Anonymous Confessions of a Lunatic Friend* in 1990. The album delivered five singles which topped the Christian music charts. In 1992, Duncan achieved similar success with the record *Mercy*—which *Christian Research Report* (CRR) named Album of the Year. On the strength of *Mercy*, Duncan was voted *CRR*'s male vocalist of the year for 1994 and nominated for the same honor by the Gospel Music Association. His follow-up album, *Slow Revival*, spawned four more No. 1 hits on the Christian music charts. In 1995, Myrrh released *Unidos En El*, a Spanish language recording of Duncan compositions, and *Christmas is Jesus*—on which Duncan performs with a choir and full orchestra. The record also kicked off a Christmas tradition of popular tours on which the singer performs with local choirs and orchestras.

In 1997, Duncan released the upbeat *Blue Skies*, which he described as the third part of a trilogy that included the records *Mercy* and *Slow Revival*. The trilogy and recounts Duncan's journey from the recognition of his need for God, through his efforts to deal with that need, and finally to his arrival at spiritual peace. "*Blue Skies* is saying, 'Hey, there's a clearing in the sky,'" Duncan told interviewer Bob Lupine. "I mean, it doesn't always stay stormy. And sometimes you can't help help but have good things happen to you, even of you're not trying. It's just a matter of recognizing them when they're there.... One of my favorite songs on the record is 'After This Day is Gone.' I like singing it, because in the chorus it goes, 'I believe after this day is gone, long after all the damage is done, there's still a place in your heart for me.' That song is me reaffirming that God loves me, because it's so easy for me to talk myself out of believing that."

For the Record . . .

Born March 16, 1953, in Ogden, UT; married, wife's name Jodi; children: Brandon, Devin.

Awards: Named Christian Research Report's male vocalist of the year in 1993; twice nominated as male vocalist of the year in Christian music industry's Dove Awards.

Addresses: Home—Riverside, CA. Agent—Ray Ware Management, 1102 West Main St., Franklin, TN, 37064.

Writer Douglas McKelvey called *Blue Skies* "a portrait of a man who has stumbled upon a reservoir of peace, faith and joy even in the midst of his perseverance.... Running the gamut from plaintive, heartfelt ballads to soulful mid-tempo numbers to upbeat tunes reminiscent of James Brown in his heyday, the songs ... reveal a consummate vocalist and performer." A review in *CCM Update* described *Blue Skies* as one of Duncan's best records in years and said it "moves beyond the blue-eyed soul that's become his trademark ... to dig deeper into R&B and jazz influences—think equal parts Smokey Robinson and Sting." Reviewer John M. De Marco, writing in *Christian Retailing*, said the album "is more organic, less slick, and features fewer effects" than past Duncan releases, while "showcasing his straight-ahead natural voice. The album's lyrical content is intimate."

Selected discography

Have Yourself Committed, Light Records, 1985.
Holy Rollin,' Light Records, 1986.
Whistlin' in the Dark, Modern Art Records, 1987.
Strong Medicine, Modern Art Records, 1989, Modern Art Records.
Anonymous Confessions of a Lunatic Friend, Myrrh, 1990.
Mercy, Myrrh, 1992.
Slow Revival, Myrrh, 1994.
Unidos En El, Myrrh, 1995.
Christmas is Jesus, Myrrh, 1995.
Quiet Prayers: My Utmost for his Highest, Myrrh, 1996.
Blue Skies, Myrrh, 1997.

With Sweet Comfort Band

Sweet Comfort, Maranatha Music, 1977.
Breakin' the Ice, Light Records, 1979.
Hold On Tight, Light Records, 1980.
Hearts of Fire, Light Records, 1981.
Cuttin' Edge, Light Records, 1982.
Perfect Timing, Light Records, 1983.

Sources

Periodicals

Christian Retailing, Nov. 11, 1996.
CCM Update, Nov. 25, 1996.

Online

http://place2b.org/cmp/duncan/
http://www.myrrh.com/

Additional material used in this profile came from interviews with Bryan Duncan conducted by Bob Lepine and Douglas McKelvey and published on the Internet.

--Dave Wilkins

Ian Eskelin

Christian singer

Ian Eskelin, the 26-year-old pop star, snowboarding enthusiast and novice skydiver, has been making a name for himself within the Christian youth music scene since 1992, as both the solo artist, iAN, and as frontman for the newly formed quartet, All Star United. While attending high school in Charlotte, North Carolina, Eskelin played keyboard for the local band Business & Industry, which opened for dance acts like C&C Music Factory and Information Society. Eskelin's involvement with the Christian music scene is pervasive. He has worked as both a producer and a performer, touring as keyboardist with Code of Ethics and Seven Red Seven. He has played with the bands Zero and Fell Venus and formed ICE Ministries. Ian Eskelin does not sit still. His newest incarnation is as frontman for Reunion recording artists All Star United.

Born in Springfield , Missouri on October 17, 1970, Eskelin grew up in Charlotte North Carolina. His family was always active in the Christian community. As a youth, Eskelin held his self-proclaimed 'worst job' as "chicken gutting boy" for a Caribbean restaurant. He

Ian Eskelin (center) with All-Star United.   Courtesy of Reunion Records. Reproduced by permission

For the Record . . .

Born October 17, 1970, in Springfield MO. Education: Wheaton College, B.A. Communications

Has played with various bands, including Business & Industry, Code of Ethics, Seven Red Seven Brand New Language and All Star United.
Formed International Concert Evangelism, also known as ICE Ministries, in 1995.

Addresses: *Record company*—Reunion Records, 1540 Broadway Times Square, New York, NY 10036.

enjoyed watching *Real People* and *Gilligan's Island*, and listened to 1980's glam rock. After graduating from high school, he attended Wheaton College in Illinois, coming away with a degree in communications. At Wheaton, Eskelin decide to play music with a message. From then on he wrote with God in mind. Eskelin took a four month hiatus from his studies to travel around the world. He played with Code of Ethics while pursuing his masters in communications. All the while, Eskelin was working on his own sound. "It was in that time that I just went where God led me—and it blew my mind!," he recalled. "I finally felt called to something."

Meaning through Music

Before Eskelin began spreading his brand of Christian techno-pop he played in the mainstream techno-dance band Brand New Language. Of his early experiences in the dance club scene, Ian has said "Those experiences impacted me a lot. I learned that people are people, and that they are almost always searching for meaning." That search for meaning is something Eskelin soon began to address in his lyrics. In 1994 Eskelin released *Supersonic Dream Day.* "Those songs are meant as an encouraging call to get up and put faith into action," he has said. "They're fun songs about the body of Christ getting motivated and inspired." Eskelin has spread his message to a steadily growing audience through performances at dance clubs, churches, roller rinks, coffeehouses, and schools. He strives to bring a deeper understanding of what living as a young Christian in the 1990's is all about to a wider demographic than those reached by the more traditional hymn and gospel forms. His label, Reunion, is one of the top three in Christian music.

In 1995, Sparrow, Reunion, and Word united to create WOW, a multi-artist compilation series. The series features popular as well as newer contemporary Christian artists from each of the labels. Sparrow president Bill Hearn has said of the series, "We're going after the general market as well as the Christian marketplace. We're really trying to show people that Christian music is very quality oriented. It's slick. It's great and it really appeals to the masses."

Success with Christian Message

Eskelin has already shown a grasp of popular alternative music sensibilities, delivering two top-five Christian Radio hits. He has also released a three song video package featuring a liveperformance by Eskelin, an interview with the artist, and a little bit of skydiving. Eskelin has found a receptive audience among 12-18 year old Caucasian Christians. "I really think of my concerts as high energy praise and worship," he has said. "I try to break down the barriers between myself and the audience - to make sure that everyone is participating." That participation sometimes includes stage diving, dancing and singing along. Concert-goer John Turpin wrote in his October 1995 internet review of iAN's show with The Echoing Green, "Not only did I pick up a new enthusiasm for my faith, but also some good stage-diving advice from Joey [Joey Belville, frontman for The Echoing Green]." This kind of physical accessibility and personally revealing lyrics makes these acts all the more popular. "Having fun is great," said Eskelin, "but having fun under the curtain of Jesus Christ is so much more fun." Talking about his 1994 Reunion Records release, *Supersonic Dream Day,* Eskelin summarized, "These songs are words that I've felt God saying to me ... to hear the voice of God say, 'Come to Me, I know you well, I know what you need', or 'Ian, this is what it takes to be free—staying close to Me when everything around you is crazy', those very foundational things that are actually true, and they are a great comfort when I'm feeling frayed around the edges."

Eskelin and All-Star United

Eskelin's new band, All-Star United, sell their CD's, t-shirts and other promotional wares themselves at a display after each show, talking and joking with the audience. Also on Reunion Records, All Star United is comprised largely of those musicians backing up iAN as a solo act. The current lineup consists of keyboardist Patrick McCallum, 20; bassist Gary Miller, 25, who, following the completion of their self-titled debut, replaced original member Rob Wayner; 26 year-old Christian Crowe on drums, Dave Clo on guitar, and Eskelin as lead singer. Their self-titled debut was released

February 1997 three months into their tour with Third Day and Seven Day Jesus and their sound is described as British rock which, according to Lucas Hendrickson of *Contemporary Christian Music Magazine,* is akin to Oasis, Green Day, and the Monkees. All Star United cites diverse influences The Beatles, The Kinks, Blur, Stereolab, and Ben Folds Five among others. "This record stretched me to write from a very personal point of view," Ian said.

"I really had to find ways to be vulnerable with what I've learned about grace, freedom in Christ, and how God opened my eyes to so many new things," Ian said, discussing his latest effort. "Over the past few years I've realized that in many ways, I've been living in some kind of Christian bubble, where everything was polite, but fairly surface-y. God has broken that bubble and shown me just how big a world this is..."

In September, 1995, Ian formed International Concert Evangelism, also known as ICE Ministries. The organization is dedicated to introducing Christian music acts on an international scale. The mission of ICE Ministries, as outlined by Eskelin, is to unite the Christian community through concert events in those places where they are oppressed and/or at a disadvantage because of politics or discrimination. "ICE Ministries is set up for me to be a servant, a resource for local churches to use to get peoples' attention." After a concert is held, organizations like Youth With A Mission and Reaching Unreached Nations, along with regional church groups, pursue establishing a supportive Christian connection with the attendees.

In 1996, Eskelin and Brian Whitman, guitarist for All Star United, played for U.S. soldiers, Bosnian civilians and defense department civilians on a 12 day, 28 show tour through Hungary,and Bosnia-Herzegovina. The tour was sponsored by the Armed Forces Professional Entertainment Office and took the duo to 20 bases by Humvee convoy or Blackhawk helicopter. Eskelin and Whitman participated in live performances, worship services and prayer breakfasts and were told to travel lightly in case of attack. Of the Experience, Ian has said, "This trip was really an amazing experience. It made me realize how big the world is and how many opportunities there are for bands like All Star United to have an effect on people around the world."

Selected discography

Supersonic Dream Day, Reunion, 1994.
(With All Star United) *All Star United,* Reunion, 1997.

Sources

Periodicals

Contemporary Christian Music Magazine, 1997.

Additional info gathered from publicity materials provided by Reunion Records.

—*Kevin O'Sullivan*

Cesaria Evora

R & B singer

Commonly called "the barefoot diva" because she often performs on stage in bare feet, Cesaria Evora of the Cape Verde islands is the world's reigning interpreter of a mournful genre of blues music known as morna. Morna is based on the Portuguese fado and features bluesy vocals set against a background of acoustic guitars, fiddles, accordion, and *cavaquinho,* which is a small, four-string guitar. "For years, the master of the morna has been Cesaria Evora, a Cape Verdean with a rich alto voice who has been accurately described as a cross between Edith Piaf and Billie Holiday," wrote Geoffrey Himes in the *Washington Post.* Evora's repertoire over the years has featured the compositions of top Cape Verdean songwriters such as Nando Da Cruz, Amandio Cabral, and Manuel De Novas.

Largely unknown until she was propelled into international acclaim at the age of 45, Evora has attracted legions of fans with sentimental, intimate songs that are delivered "with a pitch-perfect, full-toned resonance," according to Himes. "My songs basically express feelings about relationships, love relationships, and they sing about the lack of rain in the country," Evora said in *Pulse!.* Singing in a Creole variation of Portuguese known as Criuolo, Evora has won over legions of fans who do not understand a word of her soulful ballads. "Well, now I've been to different countries and the way people respond to me tells me that they really like the music, even though they don't understand the language," Evora told the *San Francisco Bay Guardian.*

Many of Evora's songs are filled with a sense of longing and homesickness that strikes a chord in her homeland, since over half of all Cape Verdeans have emigrated out of the country. "Life in the islands is not easy, because there are very few resources, and you could say that my life and life in the islands are related," she told *Pulse!.* "But in reality, the people are very happy. They enjoy life." Evora's songs offer advice to young people, pay homage to the elderly, lament the loss of a lover, and address other nostalgic themes. Her shoeless performance mode has been said to be her way of symbolizing the plight of poor women and children in her native land, although some accounts indicate that her nickname stems from a visit to Paris when she refused to wear shoes. "I got that name because the first record I recorded in France was called 'Barefoot Diva,'" claimed Evora herself in the *New York Times.*

Cesaria Evora was born in the port town of Mindello on the Cape Verde island of Sao Vicente, and lived for many years under Portuguese colonial rule until the country gained its independence in 1975. Life was a struggle for her as a child after her father, a violinist, died at a young age and left her mother to take care of seven children. Most of her siblings emigrated to other countries, but Evora stayed in Cape Verde and has always felt strong ties to her homeland.

Surrounded by music as a child, Evora started singing at an early age. "I started singing in the neighborhood where I lived, just with my friends ... It was just to amuse ourselves," she told *Rhythm Music.* She began performing in various bars in Mindello, and took up morna at age 16 after a romantic involvement with a guitarist. After a recording she made on national radio made the rounds, she began to be invited to sing in bars throughout the ten islands that make up the Cape Verde chain. According to Nonesuch Records, "With a voice conveying power, vulnerability and an emotional affinity for this style, Evora quickly found a niche for herself in Mindello's musical life and through committed performances gained a distinguished reputation as the 'Queen of Morna.'" Evora's frequent accompanist at the time was the well-known clarinetist Luis Morais. "In Cape Verde ... I used to sing for tourists and for the ships when they would come there'" she said in the *San Francisco Bay Guardian.* "That's why I always thought that maybe if I made it, people from different countries would love my music."

By age 20, Evora had achieved a measure of fame at her local radio station. A few tapes of her performances at the station made their way to Holland and Portugal in the 1960s and were recorded into albums. Despite this exposure, Evora never left Cape Verde for many years, and she stopped singing altogether in the 1970s. "There was no real progress," she acknowledged in *Pulse!.* "I

For the Record . . .

Born 1941 in Mindelo, Cape Verde; married and divorced three times; two children.

Began singing in bars in Cape Verde, 1950s; was discovered in Europe when tapes of her radio performances were sent to Holland and Portugal, 1960s; recorded two songs for a Cape Verdean woman's music anthology, 1985; recorded first album, *La Diva aux Pieds Nus*, in Paris, France, 1988; achieved major success with *Miss Perfumado*, 1992; went on world tour, early 1990s; had first major U.S. tour, 1995; performed in Montreal Jazz Festival, 1995.

Addresses: *Home*—Sao Vicente, Cape Verde; *Record company*—Nonesuch Records, 75 Rockefeller Plaza, New York, NY 10019.

wasn't making any money out of it, so I just stopped."

Found Fame in France

Evora came out of retirement in 1985, when she went to Portugal and recorded two songs for a women's music anthology at the request of a Cape Verdean women's organization. Her big break came in the 1980s when she met José da Silva, a Frenchman originally from Cape Verde who became entranced with her singing. Da Silva convinced Evora to go to Paris with him to record some of her music for his Lusafrica label. "Because I couldn't find anyone to help me out in Cape Verde, I had to start recording in France in 1988," she told the *New York Times*. That year she recorded *La Diva aux Pieds Nus*, then followed with *Distino di Belita* in 1990, and *Mar Azul* in 1991. Her 1992 album, *Miss Perfumado*, made her a major star in France and Portugal, and sold over 200,000 copies in France alone. This recording featured two of her most popular songs, "Sodade" and "Angola." "The record shimmers throughout as strings and accordions mingle deliciously around Cesaria's sublimely relaxed voice," noted Banning Eyre in *Rhythm Music*. Evora's reputation across the world soared after this release as she went on tour in Europe, Canada, Africa, and Brazil. At the age of 51, she had suddenly become a major star.

When Evora began her first major U.S. tour in the fall of 1995, she was greeted by sell-out performances across the country. She received thunderous standing ovations at the Montreal Jazz Festival that year. "I know this is my

opportunity," she noted in *Pulse!* in discussing the tour. "They're going to feel my message through my presence and my music." Her 1995 release, *Cesaria Evora*, on Nonesuch Records was cited by *New York Times* music critic Neil Strauss as one of the ten best albums of the year. In the *San Francisco Bay Guardian*, Josh Kun called the album "remarkable." The record went double gold in France and reached number seven on the album charts in Portugal according to *Billboard Magazine*, claimed Nonesuch Records publicity materials.

Simplicity has been a hallmark of the Evora style, as was emphasized by Jon Pareles in his *New York Times* review of a 1995 performance at the Bottom Line in New York City: "She [Evora] stated melodies almost unadorned, lingering with vibrato at the end of a phrase and sometimes languidly sliding down to a note." Pareles added, "In her tranquil contralto, there were painful memories and unsatisfied longings, a sense of pensive reassurance and of inconsolable loss." Evora also found a very appreciative audience at a performance at Birchmere in Washington, D.C. that year. *Washington Post* reviewer Mike Joyce said, "Evora projected an unusual combination of vocal power and emotional vulnerability." "At times Evora not only sang of heartache, she seemed to personify it, each gesture reflecting the weight of her experience and pain," Joyce also noted.

Personal Setbacks Influenced Music

Much of the emotion of Evora's singing draws on her own experience. Known as a heavy drinker and smoker, she has endured three painful divorces and the blindness of her mother, in addition to her father's untimely death. She vowed never to live with a man again after her third divorce, according to Neil Strauss in the *New York Times*. "I am married to my mother [with whom she still lives], my children [a 35-year-old son and a 27-year-old daughter], and their two children," Evora said in *Rhythm Music*.

Most of Evora's albums have one or more morna songs written by her uncle, the well-known morna composer Francisco Xavier da Cruz. For a number of years her main performance venue has been The Piano Bar of Mindello on Sao Vicente where she lives. She has performed in numerous world music festivals, and as the opening act for top stars such as Natalie Merchant. Evora is dedicated to her Cape Verdean roots and has not been lured by the trappings of stardom or affected by the globe trotting and international fame of her later years. "I wasn't astonished by Europe and I was never that impressed by the speed and grandeur of modern America," she said in *World Music*. "I only regret my success has taken so long to achieve."

Selected discography

La Diva aux Pieds Nus, Lusafrica, 1988.
Distino di Belita, Lusafrica, 1990.
Mar Azul, Lusafrica, 1991.
Miss Perfumado, Lusafrica, 1992.
Cesaria Evora, Nonesuch, 1995.

Sources

Books

Broughton, Simon, Mark Ellingham, David Muddyman, Richard Trillo, *World Music: TheRough Guides,* The Rough Guides, 1994, pp. 278–79.
Sweeney, Philip, *The Virgin Directory of World Music,* Henry Holt, 1991, p. 30.

Periodicals

Christian Science Monitor, September 29, 1995, p. 12.
New York Times, September 21, 1995; September 23, 1995, p. C13; January 4, 1996.
Pulse!, October 1995, p. 42.
Rhythm Music, September 1995.
Village Voice, October 3, 1995, p. 67.
Washington Post, September 22, 1995, p. D11.
Washington Post Weekend, September 15, 1995, pp. 15–16.

Further information for this profile was obtained from Nonesuch Records publicity materials and the website for the *San Francisco Bay Guardian* on the Internet.

—*Ed Decker*

Fred Frith

Guitarist, composer

In Frith's musical world, anything that makes a noise that he likes is fair game. "The history of my playing is a gradual demolition of the guitar over a period of about 15 years." The 1986 *Guitar Player* magazine article that included this quote also called Fred Frith the "Orville Wright of deconstructive guitaring." And not without good reason. Over the course of his career, Frith has banged, pelted, and scraped his electric guitars with a variety of objects and substances that has included rice and barley, scrub brushes, and electronic bows of his own invention.

Frith was born on February 17, 1949, in Heathfield, East Sussex, England. He began taking violin lessons at the age of five. Since his father was an accomplished pianist, Frith had access to pianos from an early age as well. In the early 1960s, he switched to guitar. His first band, the Chaperones, was a pop band that covered Ventures songs and others of that ilk. In about 1964, American blues became all the rage among young British musicians, and Frith was carried off by the same blues wave that formed the musical ideas of such rockers as the Rolling Stones and Eric Clapton. He also began listening to important guitarists from other idioms, such as jazzer Django Reinhardt. Frith absorbed it all, and soon became proficient in a number of guitar styles. When he moved to Cambridge to go to college, he started playing guitar at folk clubs. He also performed with blues bands, composed music for experimental theater, and even dabbled in flamenco guitar.

Absorbed Cage's Views on Noise

By the mid-1960s, Frith was listening to every type of music he could get his hands on, and each kind contributed in some small way to the development of his unique sound. A major influence during this time was the philosophy of avant-garde composer John Cage, who wrote of a blurring in the boundary line between music and noise. Frith also became enamored of several branches of Eastern music, and those styles also percolated into his own work. A breakthrough moment came when he disassembled a telephone mouthpiece, and used the little microphone inside of it to amplify the sounds from the "wrong" side of his hand on the guitar fingerboard. Frith has been experimenting with the gadgetry of sound ever since.

In 1968, while still at Cambridge, Frith teamed up with saxophonist and classmate Tim Hodgekinson to form Henry Cow, an avant-garde rock band formed to explore ideas that were radical both musically and politically. Henry Cow was a fiercely independent entity, refusing to rely on record companies in any way that might force the group to compromise its musical approach. Gradually, a batch of bands with similar views on the music industry and politics in general formed a collective called Rock in Opposition, with Henry Cow at its core. Henry Cow lasted for ten years, during which time the group recorded six albums (starting with *Leg End* in 1973), performed hundreds of concerts, and influenced a generation of cutting edge rockers in Europe.

Launched *Guitar Solos* Series

Around the time that Henry Cow released its second album, 1974's *Unrest*, Frith made the first of his solo improvisational records. Titled simply *Guitar Solos,* the album featured a number of technical innovations that have been much copied since then. One of the trademark techniques featured on the album is the "hammering on" method using both hands on the fingerboard side of the guitar, a move that has become a staple of guitar rockers in the Eddie Van Halen mold. Frith recorded two more albums in the *Guitar Solos* series during the 1970s, and pieces from those recordings were rereleased on CD in 1991. These recordings featured collaborations with other free-form experts, including Derek Bailey, Eugene Chadbourne, and Hans Reichel.

As Henry Cow began to fall apart in the late 1970s, Frith launched a splinter project with vocalist Dagmar Krause and percussionist Chris Cutler called the Art Bears. Unlike Henry Cow, the Art Bears were not a live perform-

For the Record . . .

Born Fred Frith, February 17, 1949, in Heathfield, East Sussex, England. Education: Attended Cambridge University.

Formed first band, The Chaperones, c. 1963; played guitar in a variety of styles at pubs and coffeehouses throughout England, 1963-1968; recorded and toured with Henry Cow, 1968-1978; released first solo album, *Guitar Solos*, 1974; recorded with the Art Bears, 1979-1981; recorded landmark solo album, *Gravity*, 1979; formed the band Massacre, 1980; recorded and performed with Skeleton Crew, 1984-86; guest appearances with dozens of artists, both live and on recordings, c. 1973–.

Addresses: *Record company—* RecRec Genossenschaft, Switzerland; East Side Digital, 530 North 3rd St., Mineapolis, MN 55401.

eventually stopped calling them guitars. In 1988 he released another solo album, *The Technology of Tears*. He also began to compose more music for film, theater, and dance, as well as pieces to be played by other musicians. A 1991 documentary, *Step Across the Border,* chronicled Frith's career beginning with Massacre, and Frith also released a soundtrack CD of the same title. In the early 1990s, Frith moved to California, although he maintained a strong New York connection through his frequent collaborations with the equally prolific John Zorn. He was a regular performer with Zorn's band Naked City. Keep the Dog is another band with which Frith was active.

At some point in the 1990s Frith moved his permanent base back to Europe, where experimental music has always been received in a friendlier manner. In 1996 he released *Allies—Music for Dance, vol. 2* on Switzerland's RecRec label. Although he remains as innovative as ever in his approach to sound, Frith has outgrown his former reputation as a noise rocker who bashes his guitar with objects; he is now generally regarded as a more or less serious avant-garde composer. In the case of Fred Frith, however, such labels are meaningless. It's only the noise that counts.

Selected discography

Solo albums

Guitar Solos, Caroline, 1974.
Guitar Solos 2, Caroline, 1976.
Guitar Solos 3, Red, 1979
Gravity, Ralph, 1980.
Speechless, Ralph, 1981.
Live in Japan, Recommended, 1982.
Cheap at Half the Price, Ralph, 1983.
The Technology of Tears, SST, 1988.
Top of His Head, Crammed, 1990.
Step Across the Border, ESD, 1991.
Allies—Music for Dance, RecRec, 1996.

With Henry Cow

Leg End, Virgin, 1973.
Unrest, Virgin, 1974.
In Praise of Learning, Virgin, 1975.
Western Culture, Interzone, 1980.

With Art Bears

Hopes and Fears, Random Radar, 1978.
Winter Songs, Ralph, 1979.
The World as It is Today, Recommended, 1981.

ing entity. The Art Bears' three LPs reflected a politically-charged, if rather dim, world view. As the 1970s drew to a close, Frith moved to New York, where he quickly recorded what many consider to be his masterpiece, the solo album *Gravity*, in 1979. In sharp contrast to his work with the Art Bears, the mood of *Gravity* is utterly uplifting. Its material is lifted from the dance music of many different cultures from around the world.

Frith joined forces with Bill Laswell (co-founder of the band Material) and drummer Fred Maher in 1980 to form a group called Massacre, a raucously loud and energetic band tailor-made for the surging New York downtown club scene. Massacre lasted only a couple of years, after which Frith put together another loud trio, Skeleton Crew, with Tom Cora and Zeena Parkins. Meanwhile, Frith was collaborating and guesting with every cutting-edge musician in sight, including appearances on recordings by Brian Eno, the Violent Femmes, the Residents, John Zorn, and too many others to list. He also followed up *Gravity* with the solo efforts *Speechless* (1981) and *Cheap at Half the Price* (1983).

Moved Back to Europe

As the 1980s continued, Frith's prepared guitars, which are played lying on a table (the guitar, not the player), began to resemble guitars less and less, until he

With Massacre

Killing Time, Celluloid, 1981.

With Skeleton Crew

Learn to Walk, Rift, 1984.
The Country of Blinds, Rift, 1986.

Sources

Books

Gagne, Cole, *Sonic Transports: New Frontiers in our Music,* de Falco, 1990.

Periodicals

DownBeat, January 1983.
Guitar Player, August 1986; December 1992.
Musician, March 1983.

Additional material was obtained from the RecRec label website, http://www.music.ch/recrec/artist/fred2.html#bio.

—*Robert R. Jacobson*

Front 242

Industrial ensemble

Front 242 might find a place in the history of alternative music as one of several simultaneous co-founders of a European industrial music scene that was later watered down and made palatable to angst-ridden teens everywhere via acts like Trent Reznor's Nine Inch Nails. Arising out of the same leftist stew and love of sampling that produced acts like Germany's KMFDM and Italy's Pankow, the Belgium-based Front 242 achieved fame with several singles that reached American club audiences during the mid-1980s; they received a major-label break in 1990 when they signed with Epic. Yet after releasing three records, Front 242 seem to have vanished after participating in the badly conceived and best forgotten 1993 Lollapalooza tour. Nevertheless, Front 242's music primed listeners for the assault of the more accessible—and out to shock—artistry of Ministry and Marilyn Manson.

Front 242 coalesced around 1981 in the Belgian capital of Brussels after erstwhile design students Daniel Bressanutti and Patrick Codenys, joined by Jean-Luc De Meyer, formed "Massif Central" (also the name of a plateau in southern France) out of their shared passion for synthesizers and anti-establishment sentiments. Bressanutti would later drop his last name and become known as simply Daniel B; he and Codenys programmed and played the complex instruments while De Meyer served as vocalist. A year later, in 1983, they were joined by drummer Richard Jonckheere, who would similarly drop his last name to use the moniker Richard 23; he served as an extra vocalist and drummer. The group would eventually rename themselves as well; "Front 242" came from a variety of sources—the famous Resolution 242, for instance, was the legislative act that created the state of Israel; "242" was also the name of a certain kind of motor in Fiat automobiles. The "front" part reflected the band's political orientation, being a trans-European term understood in several languages as a type of organized, popular uprising.

Rise of Industrial Music

At this point in time, various European acts were taking advantage of affordable synthesizer technology that had recently appeared on the market, and Front 242 was part of this wave. Like other young musicians, they were politically-minded, well-versed in history, artistic movements, and the classical pantheon, and worried about the rampant consumerism and media addiction that seemed to be exerting pressure upon Western civilization. "242 are political. But rather than present a concept through lyrics alone, the whole band is a concept, a microcosm of the multinational corporations and survivalist factions their songs suggest," wrote Melody Maker's Simon Price. Yet while Front 242 often mocked the police state by posing ominously in sunglasses and even brandishing pistols in still publicity photos at times, such imagery was easily misunderstood and they were soon labeled a "fascist" band. "Well, Europe has a background of Fascism, it's still in their minds, and they think we are too close to it," Bressanutti theorized to Melody Maker's David Stubbs.

Technology Changes Everything

Early Front 242 songs were recorded with basic four-track technology. The band released their first single, "Principles," in 1981, followed the next year by "U-Men"; both were on the New Dance label, which would also release the band's first full-length LP, Geography, in 1982. Bressanutti drew heavily from sampling various sounds taken from everyday life as well as the artifice of media. "We are always busy recording samples," he told Steven Newburry in Melody Maker. "We have so many TV channels here on the continent that it is quite easy to get interesting samples." He even carried a portable cassette recorder out in public with him. In time, a full cassette of samples would be passed around to Codenys and De Meyer, who would add their own synthesizer-generated sounds to it. The end result was either spoken-word bits or lyrics combined with abrasive, fast-paced rhythms; in the case of vocals, De Meyer or

Richard 23 virtually barked or growled over the sonic assault. The mood emitted was described at various times as cold, robotic, hollow, machine-like, and impersonal. Their songs were also less than listener-friendly. De Meyer once told a *Melody Maker* writer that "just because our songs have no intro, no middle break, no chorus doesn't mean that they are unstructured."

The Front Catches on

Front 242 gained ground in Europe as industrial music caught on, eventually morphing into what would be tagged "electronic body music," or danceable metal. They toured with Ministry in 1984, in the Chicago-based ensemble's pre-industrial, alternapop days. They eventually became affiliated with the Chicago label that would make Ministry famous, Wax Trax, and released several singles and records over the rest of the decade. These included the 1985 EP *No Comment, Official Version,* and *Back Catalogue,* both released in 1987. *Official Version* even rose to Number 2 in the Belgian charts, right behind U2's *The Joshua Tree,* but it had taken time for Front 242 to win the support of the Belgian music scene. It also took time to catch on elsewhere, but it helped that the band loved animosity from audiences. "In Italy it was

completely exciting because they were totally against us, throwing coins at us, and we had to convince them," De Meyer told Stubbs. Bressanutti rarely appeared onstage with the band, instead running the sampler tracks and complex machinery from behind the scenes. Smoke, screens, and video imagery completed a visual assault designed to complement the sonic one.

Le Corbusier's Atom

Writing for *Melody Maker* in 1988, Stubbs tried to encapsulate Front 242's artistry. Their music, he explained, is engaged in "the politics of effects, capturing the dangerous and alluring crackle of the media environment either directly...or indirectly, by the nature of their massive, electrocuted, grid-iron sound." One single from this era, "Welcome to Paradise," was a massive hit in American clubs, mocking the rise and scandalous fall of televangelism by sampling a bit from a minister summoning his electronic flock with the words, "Hey poor! You don't have to be poor any more...Jesus is here!" Other singles, such as "Headhunter," also became huge dance-floor hits. Stubbs tried to describe another creation, the song "Masterhit"—"its presence is arbitrary, devastating, solemn, and perilously distracting," he asserted, much in the same way as Le Corbusier's giant vision of an atom, a large public sculpture in Brussels.

"Masterhit" was included on *Front by Front,* the group's final release on the Wax Trax label. "Funk Gadaffi," inspired by media images of feared Libyan leader Moammar Gadaffi during the 1980s, was another of the 1988 release's tracks. During this era, the band was also fond of posing in very dark glasses and sometimes weapons for publicity stills. Codenys tried to explain this to Stubbs: "It seems that images of militarism, commando outfits are simply the strongest of images, the most shocking," adding that television is the most potent of all images. In another interview for *Melody Maker,* with the paper's Simon Reynolds, Bressanutti explained that "terrorism is very close to publicity in its techniques, it's just a little less subtle. In publicity, you don't shock people. You don't cut a throat in TV and then say, 'Buy a Band Aid.'"

Major-Label Debut

Despite these somewhat ominous opinions, Front 242 attracted the attention of Epic Records and signed with them. Prior to their first release, the band toured all nine Epic offices and briefed the design and marketing staff regarding how best to sell their music. "I think America is just ready for electronic music," Codenys told Reynolds. "And Epic might have guessed that through watching the rise of Depeche Mode." Reynolds surmised that Front 242 might catch on with young American Europhiles. Bressanutti concurred, noting "in a sense, Front 242 are the real thing for these people, in that we have a cultural heritage, and that makes us more authentically grounded than some band from Utah trying to mimic the Eurobeat sound."

Front 242's major-label debut came with 1991's *Tyranny for You*. The "tyranny" replaced the "terrorism" of their earlier creative efforts, Bressanutti told Reynolds, referring to the tyranny of media images that exerts control over people's opinions and spending habits. By this time both De Meyer and Richard 23 were singing onstage, though the latter kept less to the actual lyrics and instead repeated or elaborated on the former's words, or provoked responses out of the audience. In between two releases on Epic in 1993—*06:21:03:11 UP EVIL*, released in the early summer, and that autumn's *05:22:09:12 OFF*—Front 242 went on the road as part of the 1993 Lollapalooza tour. They were the only industrial act of the national tour that year.

Less Guns, Perhaps Butter

As the Nineties waned, Bressanutti and Codenys had become ensconced in their Flemish countryside headquarters, a state-of-the-art recording studio with motion-detector shutters to thwart curiosity-seekers. The two had also formed the Brussels-based company Art & Strategy, a record label and design firm. Simon Price of *Melody Maker* visited the country retreat prior to the Lollapalooza dates, and asked the band about its new image. De Meyer explained the about-face as a new way to go incognito: "When we take our glasses off, no one recognises us! I always hated all that rock 'n' roll star system. We have abandoned those ideas of commando-terrorism, dark glasses, and so on. We have a more open attitude and a more open image because ... this is the Nineties!"

Selected discography

Geography, New Dance, 1982.
No Comment (EP), Wax Trax, 1985.
Official Version, Wax Trax, 1987.
Back Catalogue, Wax Trax, 1987.
Front by Front, Wax Trax, 1988.
Tyranny for You, Epic, 1991.
06:21:03:11 UP EVIL, Epic, 1993.
05:22:09:12 OFF, Epic, 1993.

Sources

Books

The New Encyclopedia of Rock & Roll, edited by Patricia Romanowski and Holly George-Warren, Fireside/Rolling Stone Press, 1995.

Periodicals

Billboard, June 5, 1993, p. 71.
Melody Maker, September 3, 1988, p. 25; December 9, 1989, p. 45; January 19, 1991; May 29, 1993, p. 12; September 4, 1993, p. 49.

—*Carol Brennan*

Gary Glitter

Rock artist

AP/World Photos. Reproduced by permission

Though best known for a rousing rock anthem that has become a trademark sound at American sporting events, Gary Glitter was far from a one-hit wonder. His recording career began in the early days of rock and roll, and morphed through a hippie phase, glam rock, bad Seventies rock, finally, Eighties revivalism. But it may be for the wildly successful "Rock and Roll (Part II)," released in 1972, by which Glitter will be remembered. "Instantly nostalgic, but like nothing else on earth, `Rock and Roll` cut though everything that was around that English summer, through the T. Rex sparkle and David Bowie sashay, through Slade's patent stomp and Sweet's candied pop," wrote Dave Thompson in *Goldmine*, "and though it didn't quite make #1, it hung around the chart so long there's not another song on earth that recaptures the moment like [this] one."

"Gary Glitter" was one of several aliases Paul Gadd used during his long recording career. Born in 1944—or, by some accounts, 1940—Gadd grew up in Croydon, a South London suburb, and as a young teen became enamored with the music of early rock pioneers like Elvis Presley and Ray Charles. His first performances came at a local club's open-mike night, and though still a teen was easily hired for singing engagements in nightclubs. Some were swanky, but others were reputed gangster haunts. In 1958 Gadd formed his first band, Paul Russell and the Rebels; the Russell was his stepfather's name. With them he cut his first record, "Alone in the Night"; it was not a hit, but by this point he was earning enough money on the nightclub circuit to move out into his own apartment; he was just fifteen.

Raven to Glitter

Gadd changed his name to Paul Raven around 1960 and started touring England; the gigs, though sometimes a flop, helped get him signed with EMI subsidiary Parlophone the following year. He recorded a few singles, was halfheartedly promoted as "Britain's first R&B singer," then dropped. Gadd then worked as a session musician and even did commercial work to get by. His fortunes changed around 1965 when he came to the attention of Mike Leander, a noted production genius of the era along the lines of Andrew Loog Oldham (who worked with the Rolling Stones) and George Martin (sometimes called "the fifth Beatle"). Leander hired Gadd for the Mike Leander Show Band, another abysmal failure. But out of the ashes of this nine-piece band emerged Boston International, Gadd's next back-up act. With them Gadd (as Paul Raven) toured Europe during late Sixties, achieving some minor success.

For the Record . . .

Born Paul Gadd, May 8, 1944 (some sources say 1940), in Banbury, Oxfordshire, England. Divorced; one son.

Glitter began his career as Paul Russell the late 1950s; performed and recorded singles as Paul Russell and the Rebels, Paul Raven, Rubber Bucket, and Gary Glitter.

Addresses: *Record company*—Rhino Records, 10635 Santa Monica Blvd., Los Angeles, CA 90025.

Hippie Chanting

In 1968 MCA named Leander head of its United Kingdom division, and he immediately signed Gadd. Another change of name marked the occasion: Gadd now became Paul Monday. He released a few more singles, which went nowhere, then with Leander hitched onto the hippie craze and renamed Gadd once more, to the implausible Rubber Bucket. This moniker's closest brush with fame came with the 1969 single "We're All Living in One Place." There was a large group of hippie squatters camping out in a building next to MCA's offices, and a sit-in protest occurred when police tried to evict them. Leander sent Gadd down to the scene with recordinggear. "By the end of the day, he had a tape of a 3,000 strong choir of voices, with Paul's way up in the mix, shouting along to an arrangement of `Amazing Grace,'" wrote Thompson in *Goldmine.* The single, Thompson noted, "remains one of the most bizarre, but strangely captivating 45s of the era." Sadly, it received almost no airplay, and sales were equally nonexistent.

Gadd covered George Harrison's "Here Comes the Sun" in a falsetto voice as Paul Monday—another flop—before the glitter-rock scene broke. Hippies, sit-ins, peace and love, folk songs and beads gave way to androgyny, outrageous makeup (especially on men), dance rock, silver lamé outfits and dangerously high platform shoes. Marc Bolan, with his band T. Rex, and David Bowie were among the most successful of this era, though Slade, Sweet, the New York Dolls, and eventually punk rock itself would emerge from glitter rock's wake.

Adapting once more to suit the times, Gadd almost became Horace Hydrogen before settling on the slightly more earnest Gary Glitter. He and Leander reworked an old demo into what would become "Rock and Roll (Parts I and II)." A long studio session that was perhaps more of a party resulted in fifteen minutes of tape that was cut down into two songs. "Part I" was just the words "rock and roll," repeated, while the more successful "Part II" was even more brief—a simple "hey" and no more. Both were built around stomping rhythm and blistering fuzzy guitars reminiscent of kazoos.

The song was released in the spring of 1972, and took a few weeks to get off the ground before word-of-mouth made it a hot record. It finally launched Gadd's career in earnest, but years of living on the fringes of rock and roll had taken their toll. "Visually, he was disastrous," wrote Thompson. "A slightly middle-aged, slightly overweight, slightly daunting creation, a cross between the failed nightclub rock `n' roller he had once been, and the space aged mutant he now wanted to be, Gary Glitter was born out of one more afternoon in the studio with Mike Leander." The success of "Rock and Roll (Part II)" made Glitter rich. He began spending wildly on outrageous stage gear, including lamé jumpsuits and a reported fifty pairs of platform shoes—a look the press often took aim at. Some even claimed Glitter's chest hair was a wig.

First Attempt at Burying Himself

Undaunted by barbs and with quite healthy record sales backing him up, Glitter recorded several other singles with Leander that also did well. These included "I Didn't Know I Loved You (Till I Saw You Rock and Roll)," released later in 1972, and the following year's "Do You Wanna Touch Me (Oh Yeah)." Meanwhile, the British music press discovered that Bowie and the other glam-rockers once recorded syrupy pop tunes that were either never released—or, as in Glitter's case, went largely unnoticed—and began introducing fans to these gems. To avoid this situation, at the height his fame Glitter engineered a publicitystunt in which a ship was chartered and all the old Paul Russell, Paul Raven, Paul Monday, and Rubber Bucket vinyl was dumped in a coffin and tossed overboard. Yet in an outcome symbolic of Glitter's success itself, the coffin refused to sink and instead floated away down the Thames River.

In March of 1973 Glitter played his first concert in London. It would be one of the first rock shows ever at the venerable Palladium. That summer he finally had a # 1 hit in the British charts with "I'm the Leader of the Gang (I Am)," followed by another #1, "I Love You Love Me Love." He also toured the U.S., and though "Rock and Roll" had reached #7 in United States, Glitter's tour received little attention Stateside. The record was, however, making inroads with a new generation. Rocker Joey Ramone of the Ramones told *Goldmine*'s Thompson that he bought the record as a teenager and got chased out of the Queens record shop for it. Furthering his newfound fame, Glitter even made a movie during this period. It was designed to be a documentary, but evolved into a feature film entitled *Remember Me This Way*, "in which an ever-so ludicrous plot allowed our hero to indulge in his wildest rock star fantasies," wrote Thompson in *Goldmine*. "The Kung Fu sequence alone is worth the price of admission."

Nearly Succeeded Second Time

Glitter released a live album of the same name from that tour. He also had another # 1 song in June 1974 with "Always Yours," and released three more singles in 1975 before announcing his retirement. He put on a farewell concert in early 1976 that was televised in Great Britain, and it would be a swansong of sorts—though he later admitted it was, once again, planned as a publicity stunt. His profligate spending had begun to catch up with him, and Inland Revenue--the British version of the Internal Revenue Service—began questioning his finances, and Glitter has admitted to spending excessively not just on sparkly suits and platform shoes, but on drugs and alcohol as well. Televised farewell concert or not, Glitter had never stopped recording, but found much less success with his efforts. The year 1980 was perhaps his lowest point, marked by bankruptcy and a suicide attempt.

The good reception of his 1981 autobiography, *The Leader,* (it was a U.K. bestseller) helped turn things around. Gadd decided that resting on his past laurels was indeed acceptable, and revived his career in an annual oldies tour known as the Gangshow, with Gary glitter as the headliner. From the early Eighties onward it toured smaller venues during the Christmas weeks, but by 1996 it was selling out Wembley Arena.

An Enduring, Respected Pop Star

Glitter made minor appearances on the scene during the Eighties apart from the Gangshows. He appeared on a English television show called *How to Be Cool* alongside Roger Daltrey of The Who, and had a hit with 1984's "Dance Me Up." In 1987 Glitter even re-recorded four new versions of his most famous hit with renowned producer Trevor Horn, but it was the Seventies-era revivalism in the Nineties that renewed interest in Glitter. The Justified Ancients of Murecorded a version of "Rock and Roll" under the name Doctoring the Tardis in which the brief lyrics were changed to "Dr. Who," In homage to the cult British sci-fi television series of the same

name. Glitter was cast as the Godfather in a tour of The Who's Quadrophenia, and performed at the World Cup concert in 1994 in Chicago. "He stole the show," according to Thompson.

Glitter continues to record, most recently a 1996 cover of the classic-rock dirge "House of the Rising Sun." His Rhino LP *Rock and Roll* has become a standard at sports stadiums throughout North America—"Rock and Roll," much like Queen's "We are the Champions," is a crowd favorite and seems to incite a near frenzy. It is likely to survive another two decades. Even Trevor Horn's versions, according to Thompson, were nothing new—"though they add little to the majesty of the original recording, even technology could not destroy the sublime purity of that hammerhead beat."

Selected discography

Singles

"Rock and Roll (Parts I and II)," Bell, 1972.
"I Didn't Know You Loved Me/Hard on Me," Bell, 1972.
"Do You Wanna Touch Me/I Would If I Could, Bell, 1973.
"Hello Hello I'm Back Again/IOU," Bell, 1973
""Leader of the Gang/Just Fancy That," Bell, 1973.
"I Love You Love Me Love/Hands Up It's a Stick Up," Bell, 1973.
"Remember Me This Way/It's Not a Lot," Bell, 1974.
"Always Yours/I'm Right," Bell, 1974.
"Love Like You and Me/I'll Carry Your Picture Everywhere," Bell, 1975.
"Papa Oom Mow Mow/She Cat," Bell, 1975.
"It Takes All Night (Parts I and II)," Arista, 1977.
"Superhero/Sleeping Beauty," GTO, 1979.
"When I'm On I'm On/Wild Horses," Eagle,1981.
"Be My Baby/Is This What Dreams Are Made Of," Bell, 1982.
"Dance Me Up/Too Young to Dance," Arista, 1984.
"Love Comes/Boys Will Be Boys," Arista, 1985.
"Rock and Roll (Parts III and IV)," Priority, 1987.
"Rock and Roll (Parts III, V, and VI)," Priority, 1987.
"House of the Rising Sun/Rock and Roll (Part II)," Attitude, 1996.

LPs

Glitter, Bell, 1972.
Frontiers of Style, Trax, 1988.
Rock and Roll, Rhino, 1991.

Sources

Goldmine, July 4, 1997, pp. 20-30.
New Statesman & Society, December 16, 1988, p. 44.
People, June 17, 1996, p. 122.

—*Carol Brennan*

F. Gary Gray

Film, video producer

Gray has the been the object of a fair amount of attention himself, having earned more awards than perhaps any other video director for his work with smash acts like TLC, Coolio, and Ice Cube, as well as his feature film work. "I'm single-minded," F. Gary Gray told *Source* magazine. "When I'm working on a project all my attention is there." After breaking into music clips and making his way to the top of the video world, he directed a funky, low-budget comedy that earned ten times what it cost to make; his next venture, an action drama, saw him enter the Hollywood mainstream. Yet he refused to allow his newfound celebrity to change his focus. "These people will put you on a pedestal," he said of filmdom's star-makers, "and then knock your ass down."

F. Gary Gray was born in New York City, but did most of his growing up in South-Central Los Angeles. The lure of the street there was particularly strong, however, and during his teens he was sent to live in Highland Park, Illinois with his father. "I went to a predominantly white, rich high school," he recollected in *Source,* adding that the resources at this midwestern institution "were much better than anything I had ever seen. I knew I had to take advantage of this situation."

"Taking advantage" in this case meant exploring video, learning how to direct and edit programming for the school's cable-access TV station. He demonstrated considerable ambition in his chosen field, and upon graduating, he came back to Los Angeles. There he pursued college studies in film and television. "From a young age, I knew I was going to be a filmmaker," he insisted in *Source.* He landed camera-operator jobs for various television programs, including *Screen Scene* for the Black Entertainment Network (BET) and *Pump It Up* for Fox. At the Fox network, more importantly, he met rappers W.C. and the Maad Circle—which featured a then-unknown MC named Coolio—and talked them into letting him direct their video. "The first thing I did," he recalled, "was use my director's fee to shoot the video in 35 millimeter, like actual films are shot." The larger frame size—most videos are shot in the smaller 16 millimeter format—fit Gray's swelling ambitions.

Video Triumphs Led to Film

Fortunately, Gray had talent to match those ambitions, and word of his directorial skill spread to other acts. Soon, he found himself directing clips for Mary J. Blige, Coolio, TLC, Ice Cube and Dr. Dre, among others. The video for Ice Cube's "It Was a Good Day" was listed among *Rolling Stone*'s "Top 100 Videos of All Time." Gray garnered multiple trophies at the 1995 MTV Video Music Awards, including four awards for the TLC clip "Waterfalls"—including Video of the Year—and the Best Rap Video honor for Dr. Dre's "Keep Their Heads Ringin'." By 1996, Gray's video-related honors would include 16 awards and 23 nominations.

Due to the success of Ice Cube's "It Was a Good Day," Gray earned his first opportunity to direct a feature film. Co-written by Cube, *Friday* is a broad comedy inspired by the pot-fueled antics of 1970s comedians like Cheech and Chong. The novice filmmaker was given a paltry $3 million budget to make it. "I've been doing videos for about four years now, and I've been wanting to direct a feature since I was about 17," Gray told *High Times* magazine. "I knew that I had to deliver something that was high-quality. There was a lot of pressure, because with making motional pictures, when you're a first-time filmmaker, if the dailies don't look good the first week, if the performances aren't good the first week, the director gets fired."

"Double-Edged Sword"

Any concerns Gray may have had regarding his abilities were unfounded. His instincts allowed him to plan the shoot and still leave room for improvisation. Co-stars John Witherspoon and Chris Tucker, Gray told *High Times,* "are so funny on the fly and right off the cuff that I didn't want to miss any of that, so I said, 'Stick to the

For the Record . . .

Born c. 1969, New York, NY. Education: Attended Los Angeles City College and Golden State College.

Video and film director, c. 1990s— . Worked as camera operator for BET and Fox television networks; directed music videos for W.C. and the Maad Circle, Coolio, TLC, Ice Cube, Dr. Dre and others, c. 1992-96; directed feature films *Friday* (1995) and *Set It Off* (1996).

Awards: Best Rap Video and Best New Artist Rap Video for Coolio's "Fantastic Voyage," 1995 Billboard Music Video Awards; four awards, including Video of the Year for TLC's "Waterfalls" and Best Rap Video for Dr. Dre's "Keep Their Heads Ringin'," 1995 MTV Music Vdeo Awards; numerous other video awards.

Addresses: *Home*—Los Angeles, CA. *Publicist*—Bragman Nyman Cafarelli, 9171 Wilshire Blvd., Penthouse Suite, Beverly Hills, CA 90210-5530.

script for the first two takes, and on the third take, do it how you want to do it.' When I got to editing, I used most of the third takes because they were so funny, especially Chris' facial expressions." Cube, meanwhile, "has a lot of discipline," Gray reported. "It helps me as a director for him to have that much discipline and be the star of the movie," he added, "because if everybody wanted to run wild, then it would just be a big babysitting session and you lose a lot of time. Cube doesn't play that whole 'I'm a star' trip."

Friday may not have been a favorite with critics—*Times* reviewer Peter Rainer was in the majority when he declared the film a "scattershot jokefest"—but its lean budget helped it go into the black quickly, and it eventually earned 10 times what it cost to make, and turned out to be one of the most profitable releases of 1995. "These movies are a double edged sword," Gray reflected in the *Los Angeles Times*. "Though any other comedy would have three times the budget and twice as long to shoot, I appreciated New Line [Pictures] giving me a shot. How often does anyone write a check like that to an unproven 23-year-old?" Gray pointed out that after making such a splash directing rap and R&B videos, "I was besieged by hip-hop offers." After *Friday*, he explained in *Vibe*, "I didn't want to be pegged as an in-the-hood-type director. It's just too easy to get that title." He informed *USA Today* that he "was offered every regurgitated action comedy idea that Hollywood has done."

Instead, Gray took on a far more ambitious project: an urban heist thriller with four female protagonists. Though the hit film *Waiting to Exhale* had demonstrated the box-office potential of black women, the edgy *Set It Off* brought in action elements designed to woo male viewers. And, added Gray in *Vibe*, "these women are just exhaling all over the place." Co-starring rapper and television star Queen Latifah and budding star Jada Pinkett, *Set It Off* tells the story of a group of down-at-heels women who turn to armed robbery. Gray's conception for the film was, he asserted in *Newsday*, "dramatic smart action." He had already used many of the elements of action filmmaking—such as helicopters—in his videos, and wanted to reach beyond the usual trappings of the genre. "I didn't want to use the action gratuitously because then it has no weight," he claimed. The sequences just become set pieces for action. It's not worth it." He had been looking, he said, for material with "something for the emotions."

Patience Pays Off

In *Set It Off*, Gray found the right combination of elements. "It takes a lot for me to get passionate about something," he told Thulani Davis of *Newsday*. The film, he ventured in *Detour*, "has always been in me. But it was definitely a leap. I would shoot for 14 hours, then I would watch dailies for two, then I would rewrite and work on the script for three hours. If I got five hours of sleep it was like heaven: usually it was two or three." Perhaps the biggest challenge of the film, Gray mused to Davis, was its female focus. "It's a male-dominated industry," he averred. "Stories are told from a male point of view. I wanted to create a women's perspective." He sat down with the cast members and talked about a range of issues; but he also took them to a firing range to make sure they looked natural using guns onscreen. "I would also create special rehearsals," the filmmaker told *Detour*. "normally, you go straight for the script, but when you have characters who have a history with each other, you have to create that feeling, and it has to be as genuine as possible. So for the first week, I would take the actors out for meals and movies to create a camaraderie that comes second-nature." The results, he added, were "fantastic."

Critics didn't entirely agree, however. Kenneth Turan of the *Los Angeles Times* admired the production's style but complained of "genre contrivances that are the obstacles to [the film's] being taken seriously." The director received both praise and blame in Turan's review. "Though he is obviously talented," the critic wrote, "Gray is also 26 years old, and *Set It Off* is characterized by the youthful director tendency to be overambitious, to try to squeeze every possible movie moment into one finite film." *USA Today*'s Susan Wloszc-zyna, meanwhile—while admitting the film was "more fun to watch than it has any right to be"—nonetheless dubbed it "overlong, overdone and overwrought." Gray, she continued, "knows how to ignite high-octane action, but the dramatic passages drag like a rusted tailpipe."

Opportunity and Creativity

Although he hasn't dwelt on it much in interviews, Gray's celebrity derives in part from his success in the mainstream as a black filmmaker. Yet he never claimed to have encountered adversity because of race. "The strong battles, the battles that are historical for blacks in Hollywood, I haven't experienced any of that," he pointed out in *Newsday.* "I've had the opportunity to make a film that I think is good." And in *USA Today,* Gray warned against pigeonholing audiences. "I know a lot of people who enjoy rap music who aren't black," he pointed out. "You can't just say it's black music. To segregate films the way Hollywood likes to segregate films, ultimately everyone loses." Gray's assessment of the present-day situation in Hollywood was mixed. "I can honestly say it's changing," he said. "I can see my colleagues getting opportunities they didn't have even five years ago. In the same breath, it still needs more of a major change. I think ultimately black filmmakers need more options and more support—everything from getting the best material to getting the best financial support to make it right."

Gray shared a bit of his creative method with *Detour.* Budget constraints, he allowed, forced him to "prioritize" shots in order of importance. With that part of the process completed, "I'll sit back with a cigar and some classical music, and read the scene, start to envision it, and write it down shot for shot," he explained. "Sometimes you can't come up with a shot to save your life, and sometimes shots come so fast that you start misspelling words because you're writing so fast." He added that his visual sense compels him to "put the camera where the story is, so I dissect a scene and think about it in the context of the whole movie and decide how I'm going to cover it." He discussed his strategy for overcoming a lack of creative flow in *Vibe,* "Sometimes I get slowed down by writer's block or visual block where I can't find the shot," he admitted. "But I don't worry. Creativity is a mansion. If you're empty in one room, all you have to do is go out into the hallway and enter another room that's full."

After the release of *Set It Off,* Gray's career itself began to resemble such a mansion. The *Los Angeles Times* deemed him a "face to watch in 1997," and he discussed his options with the paper. "I'm not afraid of a big studio film; I trust my instincts," he insisted. "But for me it's not really about box office. It's about looking back on your work and not having to apologize for it. I'm trying to keep my blinders on and continue to perfect what I do, because I'm very young and I have a lot to learn." At the same time, Gray recognized that he brought something unique to the table. "I think the movie audience is starving right now for new material and fresh ideas," he noted. In *Detour,* he described directing as "a love it or leave it job," and confessed to feeling doubts at times. "Sometimes you think, Am I out of my mind for doing this?" he reflected. "But then you sit back—I just got back from the Boston Film Festival, and we had a standing ovation for [*Set It Off*]—you take really deep breath and you say, 'It was all worth it.'"

Sources

Detour, November 1996, p. 70.
High Times, June 1995.
Los Angeles Times, April 26, 1995, p. F2; April 23, 1996, p. F1; November 6, 1996, p. F1; January 5, 1997, (Calendar) pp. 6-7.
Newsday, November 3, 1996, p. C14.
Source, January 1996, p. 27.
USA Today, August 21, 1996, p. 7D; November 6, 1996, p. 8D.
Vibe, September 1996.

Additional information was provided by publicity materials from Bragman Nyman Cafarelli, 1996.

—*Simon Glickman*

Erskine Hawkins

Jazz trumpeter, composer

At the peak of his popularity during the golden age of swing, Erskine Hawkins's trumpet mastery earned him the nickname "The Twentieth Century Gabriel." The group of musicians that made up his orchestra produced some of the big band era's finest and most influential music. Ironically, it took another artist, Glen Miller, to make a true smash hit out of Hawkins's most famous composition, "Tuxedo Junction." Nevertheless, while swing was king, Erskine Hawkins and His Orchestra was among the handful of big bands that defined the sound of the era, and its popularity approached that of bands led by giants like Duke Ellington and Count Basie.

Born and raised in Birmingham, Alabama, Hawkins was surrounded by music during his youth. His father was killed in France in World War I. Along with his three brothers and one sister, Hawkins was exposed to music early by his mother, a schoolteacher. Initially a drummer, Erskine learned to play several other instruments as well, including baritone saxophone and trombone, before turning his focus to trumpet at age 16.

Several members of Hawkins's first serious professional ensemble had been childhood friends. After high school, Hawkins enrolled at State Teachers' College in Montgomery, a hotbed of jazz performance and study. Hawkins got into the school on an athletic scholarship. Within a few weeks, however, it was clear to all that music was his true calling. A number of his musical pals from the neighborhood were also students at the college. After a brief stint with the 'Bama State Revelers, the college's second tier jazz ensemble, Hawkins quickly became the star of the school's top jazz band, the 'Bama State Collegians. At State Teachers' College, Hawkins quickly developed a sizable following. His most important asset as a trumpet player was his tremendous range. Solos by Hawkins invariably featured squeals higher than could commonly be coaxed from that instrument.

Moved to New York

Along with classmates and bandmates Haywood Henry (clarinet and saxophone); Avery Parish (piano); Bob Range (trombone); the Bascomb brothers, Wilbur "Dud" (trumpet) and Paul (saxophone); and others, the Collegians became immensely popular throughout the region. The band would play out several nights a week, bringing their textbooks along to study between sets. Its leader at the time was J. B. Sims, a singer in the Cab Calloway mold. In 1934, the Collegians made their first trip to New York City, where they played the Harlem Opera House, the Apollo Theater, the Ubangi Room, and other bustling jazz venues of the time. The group's reception in New York was so good that school soon became more or less an afterthought. The balancing act between career and scholarship became untenable, and all of the band's members gave up on academics.

Like countless trumpet players of the time, Hawkins was profoundly influenced by Louis Armstrong. From Armstrong, Hawkins learned how to dazzle an audience with flourishes in the upper register, frequently ending songs with bursts of high notes. It was this showmanship, not to mention his ability to emulate Armstrong's solos, that made Hawkins the natural choice to take over as leader when Shims left the band in 1936. The band made its first recording that year, under the name "Erskine Hawkins and His 'Bama State Collegians." Their first recordings, mostly cheap and scratchy, did not sell particularly well. Record sales to white listeners were practically nonexistent.

Hawkins et. al. began reaching a wider audience around 1938. That year, Hawkins hooked up with Moe Gale, a well-connected booking agent and majority-owner of the Savoy ballroom. Gale negotiated a recording contract with RCA Victor, and the band began releasing records on the company's Bluebird label. The band became a regular attraction at the Savoy, and Hawkins became the de facto house bandleader. Gale also booked national tours for the group, which was now known as "Erskine Hawkins and His Orchestra," since the "'Bama State Collegians" moniker had to be returned to the college's next generation of jazzers.

For the Record . . .

Born Erskine Ramsey Hawkins, July 26, 1914, in Birmingham, Alabama; died November 12, 1993, in Willingboro, New Jersey; son of Edward and Cary (a teacher) Hawkins; married Florence Browning, 1935 (marriage ended); second wife's name, Gloria Dumas. Education: Attended Alabama State Teachers' College.

Led and performed with local bands in Birmingham, Alabama as a teenager; 'Bama State Collegians, Alabama State Teachers's college, 1930-34, became leader in 1936; toured as Erskine Hawkins and His Orchestra, 1938-c. 1957; performed regularly at Savoy ballroom, 1936-c. 1954; RCA Victor recording artist, 1938-50; recorded "Tuxedo Junction," 1939; led band at Concord Hotel, Kiamesha Lake, NY, 1967-89; numerous festival appearances, including 1979 Nice Jazz Festival.

Awards: Honorary Doctorate in Music, Alabama State Teachers' College, 1947; Lifetime Work Award for Performing Achievement, Alabama Music Hall of Fame, 1989.

Recorded "Tuxedo Junction"

"Tuxedo Junction," the song for which Hawkins is most frequently remembered, was ironically recorded as last-minute filler at the end of a 1939 recording session. The tune, named for an area in Birmingham, became the unofficial theme song of both the Hawkins Orchestra in its various forms and the Savoy itself. The song was co-written by Hawkins and bandmates Bill Johnson and Julian Dash. It is also interesting to note that the song's most memorable trumpet solo was not played by Hawkins, but by Dud Bascomb. It was actually quite common for Bascomb to take the more sophisticated, jazzier solos, while Hawkins's delivered his customary on-slaught of high-not pyrotechnics. Hawkins's playing style did not always endear him to the critics. He was frequently taken to task for "showboating," a criticism that was occasionally leveled at Louis Armstrong as well. While his playing style wa certainly designed to grab attention, Hawkins was not a spotlight hog. A large part of the band's success stemmed from the virtuosity of all its soloists, and each was given ample opportunity to show off his chops.

Hawkins's next big hit, "After Hours," was recorded the following year. Composed by pianist Avery Parrish, the tune was also largely created on the spot in the recording studio. Several more successful songs were released over the next few years, and the band graduated from the Bluebird label to Victor, the label of RCA's bigger jazz names. 1941's "Someone's Rockin' My Dreamboat" in 1941 and "Tippin' In," recorded in 1945 were among the more successful songs released by Hawkins and company during its peak years of popularity. During the second half of the 1940s, the Hawkins band was a fixture in New York City, performing frequently at the Savoy and the Apollo. Annual tours to the Midwest and the South were also sprinkled into the group's schedule book, as were occasional trips to California. Hawkins's recordings were also received enthusiastically in Europe.

Downsized His Band

Hawkins's popularity gradually waned through the first half of the 1950s. By the middle of the decade, the Savoy had gone out of business, symbolic of the overall decline of the big band music. As bebop, played by smaller combos, became the predominant form of jazz, the venues became smaller, and Hawkins decided to strip his orchestra down to an eight-piece ensemble, mostly out of financial necessity. He shuffled through record labels, signing with Decca in 1954. The band continued to shrink, consisting of six members when it recorded an LP for Decca in 1961. Eventually Hawkins was leading a quartet, sometimes adding a female singer to the lineup.

In 1967, Hawkins signed on for a week-long engagement at the Concord Hotel, a resort in upstate New York's Catskill Mountains. The Concord proved to be an ideal setting for Hawkins's old fashioned swing. Assuming the role of venerable jazz master, he ended up playing there regularly throughout the 1970s and most of the 1980s. Throughout this period, Hawkins worked primarily with a small band behind him, although occasional jazz festivals and cruise ship gigs would find him again fronting a full big band like those of his glory years.

No real consensus exists among jazz historians as to what position Hawkins holds in the annals of the genre. Critic Barry Ulanov wrote the Hawkins band off as the "most slavish imitator" of the Lunceford Band, a swing group popular with black audiences. He contended that the Hawkins band "leave[s] an impression of crude strength and undeveloped talent...." French writer Hugues Panassié, on the other hand, listed Hawkins as the leader of one of the best dance bands around from the late 1930s to the early 1950s. Perhaps the existence of such divergent opinions is the best evidence of an artist's importance.

Selected discography

Complete Erskine Hawkins, 1938-39, RCA Black & White.
Jubilee, RCA, 1943.
One Night Stand, RCA, 1946.

Sources

Periodicals

Jazz Journal, July 1972, p. 12; August 1972, p. 14.

Los Angeles Times, November 14, 1993, p. A32.
Mississippi Rag, May 1990, p. 7.
New York Times, November 13, 1993, p. 31.
Times (London), November 29, 1993, p. 21.

—*Robert R. Jacobson*

David Helfgott

Pianist

Helfgott became known to international audiences as the troubled Australian pianist depicted in Australian director Scott Hicks' 1996 film *Shine*. A child prodigy, Helfgott eventually suffered a mental breakdown after his overbearing father forbade him to accept an invitation from Isaac Stern to study music in the United States. After more than a decade in and out of mental institutions, during which he underwent electroshock therapy and was forbidden to play the piano due to his delicate health, Helfgott gradually recovered, first playing piano in a wine bar in his native Perth, then returning to concert halls in Australia with the help of his wife, Gillian. Following the success of the much-acclaimed *Shine*, Helfgott released a highly popular CD recording of his rendition of Rachmaninoff's Concerto No. 3, and in 1997 embarked on a worldwide concert tour to sold-out audiences.

David Helfgott was born in 1947 in Perth, Australia, two hours northwest of Sydney. The second of five children born to Elias Peter and Rachel (Granek) Helfgott, he was a delicate child who early on exhibited signs of agitation. Many commentators of the film *Shine* argue that the seeds of the son's later illness were first evident in the father. Elias, who was generally known by his middle name, Peter, was the son of a Hassidic rabbi born in 1903 in the Jewish settlement of Kamyk, near Czestochowa, Poland. Raised in a region then under Jewish occupation, Peter grew to despise his father and his religion, even going so far as to try to cut off his beard. In *Love You to Bits and Pieces*, Gillian Helfgott's memoir of Helfgott's life, Helfgott recounts wistfully: "He chased his father around the table with scissors, because my father wasn't scared of his father, you see. He stood up for himself in the world." The elder Helfgott ran away from home when he was 14 and eventually learned that both of his parents had died in the Holocaust. In 1944 he married the then 24-year-old Rachel Granek, a Jewish girl from Czestochowa whom he had met while working with her father Mordecai and brother Morry.

Perhaps it was the loss of his family and the associated guilt he felt for his treatment of that family that led the elder Helfgott to alternately cherish and abuse his son as his love gradually gave way to a deeper envy throughout his life. The early 1950s were financially dark times for the Helfgott family. In 1953, the year David started grade school, he began to develop frequent bladder control problems that may, even at the age of five years, have been related to stress in the family home.

Peter Helfgott, a failed violinist for whom music was a great passion, prompted his son to develop his talent from an early age. David's childhood years were often

Born in 1947, in Perth, Australia; son of Elias Peter and Rachel (maiden name, Granek) Helfgott; married his first wife, Clara, 1971 (divorced, 1974); married Gillian (an astrologer), August 26, 1984; late 1980s, became naturalized citizen of Tasmania. Education: studied at Royal College of Music in London, c. 1962.

First performance at a country festival, 1955; was offered an invitation from Professor Isaac Stern to study music in the United States, c. 1961; eventually left to study at the Royal College of Music in London, c. 1962; last major exhibition before his breakdown, 1964; returned to playing in wine bars, then concert halls in Australia, 1980s; released CDS *Shine: The Soundtrack, David Helfgott Plays Rachmaninoff Concerto No. 3 in D,* and *David Helfgott Plays Mussorgsky and Rachmaninoff,* 1996; released *David Helfgott Plays Liszt* and undertook world concert tour, 1997.

Awards: Marmaduke Barton Prize, Hopkinson Silver Medal, 1969.

Addresses: *Record company*—RCA Records, 1540 Broadway, New York, NY 10036.

spent learning the difficult works of Russian composer and pianist Sergei Vasilievich Rachmaninoff (1873-1943) and Hungarian composer and pianist Franz Liszt (1811-1886), as well as preparing for or performing in piano competitions. Starting at the age of nine with a performance at a country festival, Helfgott received his first major approbation from his father when he failed to win. The elder Helfgott expected his son to win and was personally wounded when he failed. Wilmoth commented of Scott's treatment of this period of Helfgott's life in *Shine:* "Living vicariously through his brilliant son, Peter Helfgott became his son's tutor, mentor and, as the filmgraphically and controversially shows, tormentor."

Pressure on the Teenage Prodigy

In 1958, the Helfgotts financial situation improved and the family was able to settle into a comfortable house in Highgate, Australia. By the late 1950s the hardships of the elder Helfgott's began to affect his health and nerves, and he began to experience frequent heart attacks. As a teenage prodigy during this period, Helfgott studied under a local teacher, Frank Arndt, and

continued to compete in increasingly prominent piano competitions. The same year, at the age of 14, Helfgott was offered and invitation from Professor Isaac Stern to study music in the United States. Perhaps because he saw it as threatening his own and the family's stability, or because it meant his son would leave the family home, Peter Helfgott forbade David from going. Acting against his father's wishes, the younger Helfgott eventually left to study at the Royal College of Music in London. Peter Helfgott disowned his son, exacerbating his son's emotional problems and precipitating what would eventually become full-fledged breakdowns that David later described as "fog" and a state of "being damaged."

Helfgott's talent was gradually refined by his experience in London, and he took part in numerous exhibitions and competitions that in 1969 led to him being awarded the Marmaduke Barton Prize and Hopkinson Silver Medal from Queen Elizabeth at the Royal College of Music. Around this time, David's tortured attempts to master Rachmaninoff's Concerto No. 3, in combination with his still unresolved feelings regarding his break with his father, contributed to a major breakdown. Although Helfgott's mental condition was diagnosed as schizoaffective disorder by his psychiatrist following the breakdown, Helfgott's overall condition has eluded clear diagnosis; as of 1997, he was unable to perform on consecutive days, and he expresses himself in a rapid-fire, often unintelligible fashion that often gives the impression that his speech can't keep up with his thoughts. Yet Kyle Pruett noted in the *New York Times:* "As a psychiatrist, I try to fit him into the analytic flow charts and diagnose him into comprehensibility. But he doesn't fit anywhere.... The blunted emotions of schizoaffective illness are completely belied by the relentless passion, the vitality, even the humor of his piano playing."

In 1971, Helfgott was discharged from his first stay at Charles Gairdner Hospital in Perth. In July, he married his first wife, Clara, immediately feeling it was a mistake. A mature divorcee with four children, Clara had asked him to marry her and was suspected by family members to be after Helfgott's money (benefactors had set up a trust in his name); soon after, she sold David's piano. Helfgott remarked in *Love You to Bits and Pieces.* "It was a marriage made in hell and consecrated by and presided over by the devil."

Helfgott divorced Clara in 1974. On December 29, 1975, Helfgott's father died. Contrary to Hicks' treatment of this event in *Shine,* in which Helfgott finds emotional release and comes to a peace of sorts with his past, Peter's death had little visible effect on Helfgott, who was readmitted to a mental hospital in March of 1976. Helfgott spent time in and out of hospitals during the 1970s but eventually began playing piano again at a wine bar in Perth, where he gradually attracted a substantial following. In 1983, Helfgott met Gillian, an astrologer fifteen years his senior, when the two were introduced by Chris Reynolds, the owner of Riccardo's restaurant in Perth who had hired Helfgott to play there.

On August 26, 1984, Helfgott married Gillian, adopting her daughter Sue and son Scott from Gillian's prior marriage. Although still on medication, Helfgott gradually returned to the piano circuit. In the late 1980s, he became a naturalized citizen of the Australian state of Tasmania.

The Debut of *Shine*

Scott Hicks, an Australian documentary film maker living in Adelaide, made Helfgott's acquaintance in 1986 after reading an article about Helfgott and going to see him play an informal concert. Hicks told Bernard Weinraub in the *New York Times:* "I had never seen anything quite like this extraordinary personality playing this extraordinary music." Ten years later, *Shine* debuted in Australia and was first shown to American audiences at the Sundance Film Festival in January 1996.

Shortly afterward, the film was released by Fine Line Cinema and opened in theaters worldwide and became an immediate popular and critical success for its inspirational treatment of Helfgott's battle against mental illness and for Australian actor Geoffrey Rush's sympathetic portrayal of Helfgott. As of March 1997, the film was playing at 1,050 theaters, had taken in $27.6 million, and was nominated for seven Academy Awards, including best picture, best actor, and best director. Rush won a Golden Globe for best actor. Helfgott reportedly liked the film better than *Ben Hur,* according to his wife, "and when it was finished, David clapped and asked them to put it on again."

Hicks' portrayal of Peter Helfgott in *Shine* has attracted some controversy, particularly for the scene in which Helfgott rebels against him and he beats his son into submission. Although Hicks told Fox Butterfield of the *New York Times* that "everything in the film" was based on factual research, he acknowledged that Helfgott's older sister, Margaret, who now lives in Israel, objected to his portrait of her father. Despite Margaret's comment to Scott that "Dad was a Saint" and never hit David, Helfgott is quoted by Beverley Eley in her biography *The Book of David* as verifying at least one incident in which "Daddy gave me a backhander" while in the bath "and I wrestled with him around the house."Helfgott told Wilmoth: "I had plenty of bad times with the dad. And

many good times too. Most of the time was fine." Asked whether he blamed his father for his breakdown, Helfgott commented: "I was told never to apportion blame ... but when I was in London I always blamed father and Margaret for my condition. I thought it was their fault."

The soundtrack to *Shine,* which made use of recordings of Helfgott's work, was released in 1996 and became Number 2 on Billboard's Classical Crossover Chart. Helfgott's recording of Rachmaninoff's Third Piano Concerto, released by RCA Victor, became the No. 1-selling classical CD despite a wave of negative reviews (Anthony Tommasini in the *New York Times* called Helfgott's playing "pallid, erratic, and incoherent"). Hicks responded to critical views of Helfgott's CD as clumsy and inexpressive, asserting to Butterfield: "We've put Rachmaninoff to the top of the charts. I don't think he is rolling in his grave. The man lived and died in Beverly Hills."

Helfgott Returns to the Concert Circuit

In 1997 Helfgott began a world concert tour that included Germany, Denmark, and six sell-out concerts in New Zealand. He began his American 18-performance, 10-city concert tour at Symphony Hall in Boston March 4, again to sold-out audiences. Most critics agreed with the assessment of Butterfield, who felt that audiences seemed "more attracted by the movie and Mr. Helfgott's inspirational life story than by his music, which has been panned by critics." Some argued that the concerts were less a celebration of Helfgott's return to mental health than a freak show that threatened Helfgott's's fragile health. Tommasini commented that Helfgott was "seemingly touchingly connected to his listeners," yet described his sound as "weak and thin" and "blankly unemotional." Despite the negative reception, the tour represented "the culmination of a lifelong dream," as reported by Gillian via Butterfield. Gillian countered against prevailing criticism: "I think there are probably people who are coming to see a man who has fought his way through the wilderness. But if they come for that reason, I think they leave deeply touched."

Helfgott reportedly remained in good spirits throughout his tour, which for him represented the realization of a lifelong dream. Sitting next to his wife Gillian in an interview with Wilmoth, he commented: "It's been pretty good [the publicity]. I feel very privileged, because I reckon you're the luckiest man in the world, David, because you've got a film made out of you and a biography and an autobiography. That's good isn't it darling? And I'm very grateful and thankful until the end of eternity. You've got to enjoy the here and the now."

Selected discography

Albums

Shine: The Soundtrack, Phillips, 1996.

David Helfgott Plays Rachmaninoff Concerto No. 3 in D, RCA/ Victor, 1996.

David Helfgott Plays Mussorgsky and Rachmaninoff, ARP, 1996.

David Helfgott Plays Liszt, Rhapsody/ARP, 1997.

Sources

Books

Eley, Beverly, *The Book of David,* HarperCollins, 1997.

Helfgott, Gillian, with Alissa Tanskaya, *Love You to Bits and Pieces: Life with David Helfgott,* Penguin Books (Australia), 1996.

Periodicals

Adelaide Advertiser, May 28, 1986.

New York, December 2, 1996.

New York Times, November 17, 1996; November 20, 1996 (late ed.); January 21, 1997; March 5, 1997; March 6, 1997.

Newsweek, November 25, 1996.

Rolling Stone, December 12, 1996.

Time, November 25, 1996.

Online

http://www.helgott.aust.com/
http://www.usatoday.com/life/enter/movies/lef526.htm
http://atlas.onthe.net.au/~robb/davetext.html

—Sean Pollock

Walter Horton

Harmonica player

Photo by Steve Kagan. AP/Wide World Photos. Reproduced by permission.

Big Walter Horton was a virtuoso blues harmonica player who, ironically, never achieved the fame of the renowned harpists he taught and inspired—including James Cotton, Little Walter Jacobs, and Rice Miller. Horton is remembered as a gentle man who never quite escaped poverty and poor health he was born into. Bruce Iglauer, who produced the 1972 record *Big Walter Horton with Carey Bell*, called him one of "only four great creative geniuses of modern blues harmonica," ranking him alongside Jacob, Miller, and John Lee 'Sonny Boy' Williamson. Those three harp players were "recognized, honored and extensively recorded with their own bands," Iglauer wrote, but Horton remained relatively obscure at his death in 1981. "Perhaps ... this shy, withdrawn man (was) never aggressive enough to hustle a contract with a major record label. Or perhaps ... his harmonica is so subtle, so delicate, that it requires hard, concentrated listening to appreciate."

Horton crafted "a unique, fluid style that fused blues feeling with an uplifting jazzlike tone," wrote Chris Smith. "The beauty that he created through his music was in striking contrast to the troubled life he lived. Walter Horton was a shy, sensitive man who had to deal with poverty and illness most of his life. Often uncommunicative in conversation, he 'spoke' through his instrument, creating a world of lyric beauty, wit and energy." Writer Charles Shaar Murray offered a similar assessment in *The Blues on CD,* "Despite the greater fame and popularity of Little Walter, James Cotton, Junior Wells, and Paul Butterfield, many connoisseurs regard Horton as the finest of all the great post-war harp men."

Horton was born in Horn Lake, Mississippi, on April 6, 1918. He was given his first harmonica at age five and soon was playing it on the street. "The decision to opt for a career in music was essentially made for him, because he lacked both the physical strength for menial work and the education for anything else," Murray wrote. In his early teens, Horton moved to Arkansas and then to Memphis, where he played with the Memphis Lug Band and performed in Handy Park alongside Johnny Shines, Floyd Jones, Furry Lewis, and Eddie Taylor. "I met Walter, really, in 1930," Shines once said, "and he would be sitting on the porch, blowing in tin cans, you know, and he'd get sounds out of those things."

In the 1940s, Horton met and taught harp players Little Walter and James Cotton, worked in Memphis as a cook and an iceman, and traveled briefly to Chicago—where many Memphis bluesmen were settling—and played on Maxwell Street for tips. He also became a critical part of the post-World War II blues scene in Memphis. In 1951, the legendary Sam Phillips recorded Horton at his Sun studios, both as a sideman and occasionally as a

For the Record . . .

Born April 6, 1918, in Horn Lake, MS; died: Dec. 8, 1981, in Chicago, IL..

Played harmonica with various artists throughout the decades, including Muddy Waters, Eddie Taylor, and Fleetwood Mac. Had a cameo appearance in the 1980 movie, *The Blues Brothers*.

featured artist. Those recordings later were collected by Ace Records on *Mouth Harp Maestro*. An early Horton instrumental song called "Easy" is still considered a masterpiece of amplified harmonica playing.

In 1953, Big Walter moved to Chicago for good and replaced Junior Wells in Muddy Waters' band. Over the years, he worked in clubs, recording studios and on the road as both as a solo artist and a sideman for Waters, Otis Rush, Willie Dixon, Johnny Shines, Johnny Young, Jimmy Rogers, Jimmy Reed, Tampa Red, and Big Mama Thornton. Horton's erratic, mushmouth singing style garnered him the nicknames "Mumbles" and "Shakey"—which he did not like. His harmonica virtuosity, however, kept him in demand.

Horton's Music Appeals to the Masses

During the 1960s, Horton's career prospered as white audiences discovered the blues. He toured the United States and Europe, performed with Willie Dixon's Chicago Blues All-Stars, and recorded his first album as a bandleader. The record, *The Soul of the Blues Harmonica*, was issued by Argo Records in England in 1964 and later re-released by Chess—but it was largely unsuccessful. In the late 1960s, Horton performed with blues-influenced rock 'n rollers Johnny Winter and Fleetwood Mac.

The 1970s began with promise for Horton, but ended with deteriorating health and professional stature. He recorded his second album as lead artist in 1972, along with his protégé, harpist Carey Bell, with whom he toured and played South Side Chicago bars. That album and another, *Can't Keep Lovin' You*, have been called the best recordings from Horton's later years. He also rejoined Muddy Waters on the blues legend's 1978 album *I'm Ready*. "His reunion with Muddy Waters was one of the very few bright spots of the '70s, as far as the increasing-

ly alcoholically-challenged Horton was concerned," Murray wrote. Late in his life, Horton was back playing for tips and drinks on Maxwell Street—as he had when he arrived in Chicago four decades before. In a street scene from the 1980 movie *The Blues Brothers*, in fact, he is seen doing exactly that, playing his harp behind John Lee Hooker on the song *Boom Boom*.

"(Horton's) harmonica playing, both on his own records and in his uncompromisingly lyrical solos on just about everyone else's, is breathtaking," Peter Guralnick wrote in *The Listener's Guide to the Blues*. "In a sense, he embodies the classic definition of a musician's musician, an artist universally recognized by his peers who has had an enormous impact on musicians who are much better known." Along with Little Walter Jacob, Guralnick wrote, Big Walter Horton raised "blues harmonica playing to new heights and created a new role and a new standard for this once lowly instrument." Horton died in Chicago on Dec. 8, 1981.

Selected discography

Mouth Harp Maestro, Ace Records, 1951.
Sun Records Harmonica Classics collection, Rounder.
Harmonica Genius, from recording sessions for Blind Pig records, Black Magic.
Fine Cuts, Blind Pig.
Can't Keep Lovin' You, Blind Pig.
The Soul of the Blues Harmonica, Chess.
Johnny Shines with Big Walter Horton, Testament.
Harmonica Blues Kings, also featuring Alfred Harris, Pearl records.
An Offer You Can't Refuse (one side of the album is by Paul Butterfield), Red Lightnin' records.
Big Walter Horton with Carey Bell, 1972, Alligator Records.
Big Walter "Shakey" Horton: Live at The El Mocambo, Red Lightnin', 1973.
I'm Ready, with Muddy Waters, BGO, 1978.
Little Boy Blue, 1980 live recordings, JSP.

Sources

Books

Guralnick, Peter, *The Listener's Guide to the Blues*, Facts on File, Inc., 1982.
Murray, Charles Shaar, *Blues on CD: The Essential Guide*, Kyle Cathie Limited.
Scott, Frank, *The Down Home Guide to the Blues*, a capella books, 1991.

Online

http://www.island.net/~blues/big_walt.html
http://www.alligator.com/artists/35/AL4702.html

Additional information found in the liner notes from the album
Big Walter Horton with Carey Bell, 1972, by Bruce Iglauer,
copyright Alligator Records.

Helen Humes

Jazz singer

AP/Wide World Photos. Reproduced by permission.

Blues shouter, pop singer, ballad interpreter—in a career touching five decades, Helen Humes defied categorization. From her earliest recording as a tender teenager through stints with such jazz institutions as the Count Basie band, the Red Norvo Trio and Jazz at the Philharmonic, Humes displayed a virtuosity and consistency rare in any endeavor. She brought to her art a clear, sunny voice, impeccable time and a no-nonsense approach to lyrics and melody. Though often reasonably compared to legends such as Billie Holiday, Mildred Bailey, Ella Fitzgerald and Bessie Smith, Humes modestly rejected labels and preferred to think of herself as "just a singer."

This singer often told of beginning her musical life as soon as she was able to reach the keyboard of the piano in her Louisville home. Her attorney father and teacher mother provided generous encouragement as Helen worked her way through aborted tries at the trumpet and clarinet, before settling upon the piano for serious study. Humes was equally generous in praising her major teacher, Miss Bessie Allen, under whose tutelage many fortunate Louisville youngsters got
their start, including such jazz stalwarts as trombonist Dickie Wells and trumpeter/leader Jonah Jones.

With this group and others, frequently led by Miss Allen, Humes performed in a variety of settings in and around Louisville, including those at community center and church affairs, as well as dances and county fairs, often both singing and playing piano. During this period, she recorded in St. Louis at age 14; it is thought that guitarist J. C. Johnson was at this session. In his
American Singers: 27 Portraits in Song, Whitney Balliett describes Humes's early singing: "It was a kind of singing that we can barely imagine learning now. It preceded the microphone and demanded a strong voice, Ciceronian diction, and an outsize presence. The singer was alone onstage. It was also a kind of singing that relied on embellishment and improvisation, on an adroit use of dynamics, and on rhythmic inventiveness. The singer jazzed his songs."

In 1935 Humes migrated to Buffalo, NY, where she worked with tenorman Al Sears's band. This trip began as a vacation visit with Louisville friends, but ended in a two year stint in which Humes actually began her professional singing career, leaving behind her bank secretarial job in Louisville. In addition to the Spider Web Club and Vendome Hotel work with Sears, she did radio work in Schenectady, Albany and Troy, then returned home. She later re joined Sears in
Cincinnati in 1937 at the Cotton Club. It was here that Count Basie first heard Humes and offered her a singing job with his band. As Humes tells the story, Basie offered

the same $35 per week she was already earning, plus road travel with a band that had not yet made its mark nationally. Eventually, she and Sears did end up in Harlem's Renaissance Ballroom, on a night when jazz's super scout and promoter, John Hammond, was in the audience. Largely through his encouragement, Humes finally did join Basie's band, replacing Billie Holiday, but only after recording with the fledgling band of trumpeter Harry James in December, 1937, and January, 1938.

By now, the Basie band was deservedly being recognized as the swing powerhouse remembered by all. Its lineup was stocked with jazz legends, including premier blues shouter Jimmy Rushing. Assigned mostly ballad vocals, Humes nevertheless acquired a reputation as a blues singer. After about three years of recording and traveling with Basie, she worked as a single in several New York clubs, including the Famous Door, the Three Deuces and the Cafe Society Downtown, and recorded in 1942 with the Pete Brown band. Beginning in 1944, Humes appeared in Norman Granz's Jazz at the Philharmonic tour, her first of many. During this period she also toured with pianist Connie Berry, finally settling in California for an extended residence, punctuated by various far-ranging tours.

Humes Has a Hit

In 1945 Humes recorded her signature hit record with Bill Doggett, "Ee-Baba-Leba," a precursor to the rock and roll era that was to follow, and an albatross to her career for many years. Commercially she was expected to duplicate that popular performance; artistically she sought out songs that displayed her versatility and enlisted the sympathetic accompaniment of music masters such as vibraphonist/leader Red Norvo, with whom she played numerous clubs and successfully toured Australia. While on the west coast, she also took part in film shorts; recorded film sound tracks; appeared on television; acted and sang in stage productions; and participated in a wide range of concert and club appearances with various groups. Included in this era was a 1962 tour of England and Europe.

Though all this activity might seem to constitute a busy career, Humes experienced many down times. Her 1959 appearance at the Newport Jazz Festival sparked a revival of sorts, punctuated by three hallmark recordings with Contemporary beginning in that year and the subsequent 1962 trip to Europe. Dates at Shelley's Manne Hole in Los Angeles, Honolulu clubs and Chicago's Playboy Club provided filler, but not a full career, and Humes returned to Louisville in 1967. At this time she took care of her ailing mother, and later her father, until their deaths. For nearly two years she worked in a munitions factory and at other jobs; she claims she never sang a note until 1973—"never even hummed."

At this point, jazz writer/promoter Stanley Dance convinced Humes to participate in the 1973 Newport tribute concert to Count Basie, causing her career once again to take off. Whisked off to France, she recorded two albums for Black & Blue and sang at European festivals, including the 1974 Montreux Festival, preserved on the British Black Lion label. Interspersed with these festival appearances were extended stays at New York's Cookery, somewhat regular events beginning on New Year's Eve of 1974 which drew rave reviews and enthusiastic crowds. A tour and recording with old friend pianist Connie Berry provided one extended, relaxed stint.

Throughout the remainder of the 1970s club dates and concerts in this country and abroad were punctuated by a variety of appearances on radio and television, as well as by notable recording dates. Among the latter are 1975's *Talk of the Town* for John Hammond on Columbia, which featured pianist Ellis Larkins and guitarist George Benson, and 1980's valedictory recording for Muse, "Helen," featuring trumpeter Joe Wilder, bassist George Duvivier and old Basie compatriot, tenor man Buddy

Tate. The latter, recorded only about a year before Humes's death, shows her in top form—lusty, teasing, tender, humorous, musical—serving the songs and having fun with jazz and her fellow players.

Rhythm, Time, and Humes

Because she replaced Billie Holiday with Basie, comparisons are inevitable. The most persuasive likeness is the singers' horn-like quality. Each possessed an innate ability to phrase and swing like a good trumpeter or saxophonist. Both stuck close to the melody, utilizing inflection and a great sense of rhythm and time, rather than wild improvisation, for variation and emphasis. Humes could toy with time, sometimes holding back, then catching up, but always in a seemingly unhurried manner. Humes employed dynamics much more than Holiday and could, indeed, shout or whisper as the mood of the song was served. Ella Fitzgerald and Mildred Bailey might also be compared with Humes, if only because of the general quality of their voices. Each produced a light, sunny sound, almost girlish. Humes's voice deepened and darkened very little as she grew older, but she retained the ability to project that Bailey never demonstrated and that Fitzgerald showed only in a limited way. Of her style, Humes told Balliett: "I've always been myself. I didn't model myself on anyone when I started out. Somebody'd tell me to listen to So-and-So's record, but I'd only listen, if I listened at all, after I had learned the tune myself."

Helen Humes leaves a legacy of joyous music-making, grounded in the blues, informed with musicality and intelligence, unrestricted by type or era. Some critics have heard these qualities passed on to newer singers such as Della Reese, Aretha Franklin and even Janice Joplin. As critic Nat Hentoff has written: "And so it is that even present day hipsters ... have suddenly discovered wondrous roots, farther back in time, on coming into a place like the Cookery and hearing Helen Humes. Hearing her summon[s] up the mighty spirit of those cabarets and dance halls where the good times rolled before there was rock and where the human voice was a force of nature."

Selected discography

Helen Humes and the Muse All Stars; Muse LP, 1979.

Helen Humes: Helen; Muse LP, 1980.
Helen Humes: Let the Good Times Roll; Classic Jazz LP, 1973.
Helen Humes: Songs I Like to Sing; OJC CD, Contemporary LP, 1960.
Helen Humes: 'Tain't Nobody's Biz-ness If I Do; OJC CD, Contemporary LP, 1959.
Helen Humes: The Talk of the Town; Columbia LP, 1975.

Sources

Books

Balliett, Whitney, *American Singers: 27 Portraits in Song*, Oxford University
Press, 1988.
Chilton, John, *Who's Who of Jazz*, Time-Life, 1978.
Erlewine, Michael, et al, Eds., *All Music Guide to Jazz*, Miller Freeman Books,
1996.
Feather, Leonard, *The New Edition of the Encyclopedia of Jazz*, Bonanza Books,
1965.
Harris, Sheldon, *Blues Who's Who: A Biographical Dictionary of Blues Singers*,
Da Capo, 1979.
Lyons, Len and Perlo, Don, *Jazz Portraits: The Lives and Music of the Jazz
Masters*, William Morrow, 1989.
Rust, Brian, *Jazz Records 1897-1942*, 5th Revised and Enlarged Edition,
Storyville Publications, 1982.

Periodicals

New York Times, September 14, 1981.

Liner Notes

Black Lion BLP 30167, *On the Sunny Side of the Street*, notes by Alun Morgan, 1974.
CJ 120 LP, *Let the Good Times Roll*, notes by Nat Hentoff, 1973.
Contemporary LP 7571, *Helen Humes: 'Tain't Nobody's Biz-ness If I Do*, notes by Nat Hentoff, 1960.
Columbia PC33488 LP, *The Talk of the Town*, notes by Michael Brooks, 1975.

—Robert Dupuis

Engelbert Humperdinck

Adult vocalist

Maintaining a multiple decade career as a singer is not an easy task. Remaining a sex symbol for that duration is even harder, yet that is precisely the achievement of England's balladeer Engelbert Humperdinck. Knighted "The King of Romance" by fans and the popular music press, Humperdinck has sold an average of five million records a year since the mid-1960s and has established himself as one of the world's premiere live performers in a number of sold out tours. However, it has not been Humperdinck's bronze-skinned good looks alone that have caused the attraction but a truly remarkable voice capable of spanning three-and-a-half octaves. Tempering talent and devotion with a humble, genteel persona, Humperdinck has become a veritable institution of the entertainment industry.

The early years of Humperdinck's life are unremarkable and sometimes have been embellished by zealous publicity agents. Born Arnold George Dorsey in Leicester, England on May 1, 1936, Humperdinck grew up with ten brothers and sisters in a working-class family. His dabblings in music began at age 11, when he took up playing the saxophone. Although amateur attempts at singing soon followed, Humperdinck did not commit himself to music until after he had served two years in the British armed forces, stationed in Germany during the mid-1950s. Upon his return to England, Humperdinck soon found himself singing publicly for the first time. His first break came in 1958, when he was tapped by a talent agent who had seen Humperdinck perform in a local talent contest. Impressed by the vocal precision of a singer lacking formal training, the agent managed to cut a deal with Decca Records. A year later, Humperdinck released his first single, "Crazy Bells," under the name Gerry Dorsey.

However, a record deal does not ensure success, and the sporadic Gerry Dorsey records made for Decca would only be a footnote in Humperdinck's career. The singer continued along the British club circuit with only moderate recognition until he was adopted by manager Gordon Mills. Mills, who later helped Welsh singer Tom Jones achieve fame, became Humperdinck's mentor, creating the suave image that the singer retained throughout his career. Rather than marketing his protégé as a teen pin-up, Mills opted to focus upon Humperdinck's "gentlemanly" personality. It was then that Humperdinck dropped the name Gerry Dorsey to step into the name of a 19th century German opera composer. With a new image of charm and an association with high culture, Humperdinck was soon to take off.

In 1967, in a turn of events seemingly taken from a musical or film melodrama, Humperdinck was contacted to be a last minute replacement on the popular variety show *Saturday Night at the London Palladium* when its scheduled star, Dickie Valentine, fell ill. Humperdinck performed "Release Me," a single that had just been released on Parrot Records, and the result was almost instant stardom for the singer. The song quickly hit the number one slot on the British music charts, and this success reflected on the U.S. music charts as well. At its peak, the "Release Me" single sold an unprecedented 85,000 copies daily, but moreover, the slow, powerful ballad became Humperdinck's signature tune, and a staple among adult vocals fans.

Almost immediately, Humperdinck began to amass legions of devoted fans, most of them female. On these grounds, coupled with the fact that most of Humperdinck's recordings are love songs, some critics immediately dismissed the singer as a mere "crooner." While Humperdinck cannot be said to have made significant musical innovations, the freshness, energy, and range of Humperdinck's delivery set him apart from other show business Romeos. As Humperdinck told the *Hollywood Reporter*'s Rick Sherwood, "if you are not a crooner it's something you don't want to be called. No crooner has the range I have—I can hit notes a bank couldn't cash. What I am is a contemporary singer, a stylized performer."

A Nightclub Legend

Throughout the rest of the 1960s and into the 1970s, Humperdinck continued to produce million-selling al-

bums of love songs on the Parrot label, and developed increasingly more extravagant stage shows, sometimes over one hundred per year. While the mood of Top 40 radio quickly changed, Humperdinck's music, more akin to Broadway show tunes than post-Beatles rock, did not. Subsequently, Humperdinck's live performances became more crucial in reaching his fans, and the singer responded by producing lavish, energetic extravaganzas that set the standards for Las Vegas-style glamour. "I don't like to give people what they have already seen," Humperdinck was quoted as saying in a 1992 tourbook. "I take the job description of 'entertainer' very seriously! I try to bring a sparkle that people don't expect and I get the biggest kick from hearing someone say 'I had no idea you could do that!'"

By the late 1960s, Engelbert Humperdinck fan clubs had begun to sprout, first in England, later around the globe. By the next decade, the fan mania had grown to giant proportions, reportedly the largest such club in the world, with chapters including "Our World is Engelbert," "Engelbert...We Believe in You," and "Love is All for Enge." While an occasional fan ventured into the realm of obsession—several fanatics claimed to have been pregnant with the singer's offspring—Humperdinck's following of a reported eight million members guaranteed record sales with limited radio air play. "They are very loyal to me and very militant as far as my reputation is concerned," Humperdinck said of his devotees to Sherwood. "I call them the spark plugs of my success."

Critical Recognition

The release of the album *After the Lovin'* in 1976 was a relative watermark in Humperdinck's career. For one thing, it was the first record Humperdinck made for the Epic label, after almost a decade with Parrot. In addition, the album received a nomination for a Grammy Award, the first major nod Humperdinck had received from critical corners. Perhaps part of the reason behind Humperdinck's critical neglect stemmed from his lack of involvement with the recording of albums, whereas he had so much control over live presentation. Until the late 1980s, Humperdinck had little say in which songs were selected for each album, a fact that might have supported claims that he was little more than a pawn of his label's executives. Over the years, this arrangement slowly changed, giving Humperdinck full creative freedom. Humperdinck's albums began to cover more musical terrain than ballads alone.

By the 1980s, Humperdinck was fast approaching his fifth decade of life, yet he was still producing albums regularly, performing sometimes more than 200 concerts in a year, and he was still a source of attraction for his female fans. Despite all this, Humperdinck had managed to maintain a solid family life with his wife, Patricia. Perhaps a mixture of business and pleasure had contributed to this success: Humperdinck's four children are involved in their father's career in some way. A truly jet-set family, the Humperdinck/Dorsey clan shuttled between homes in England and Beverly Hills, California, where Humperdinck had purchased the Pink Palace, a lush mansion once owned by film star Jayne Mansfield.

A Quarter Century

Humperdinck had reached the point in his career where he had transcended stardom to become a legend. In 1989, he was awarded a star on the Hollywood walk of fame, as well as a Golden Globe Award for Entertainer of the Year. He had met the queen of England and several American presidents. Still, he retained his element of humanism, and began major involvement in charity foundations. In addition to involvement with The Leukemia Research Fund, the American Red Cross, and the American Lung Association, Humperdinck contributed to several AIDS relief organizations. For one of these, Reach Out, Humperdinck even penned and performed an anthem for the organization's mission, called "Reach Out." As longtime friend Clifford Elson said of Humperdinck, "[h]e's a gentleman in a business that's not full of many gentlemen."

In 1992, the singer launched a gala world tour to commemorate 25 years of performing as Engelbert Humperdinck. The tour showcased a career's worth of middle-of-the-road favorites, as well as songs from a special anniversary album recorded with the Royal Philharmonic Orchestra on Polydor Records. Like most of Humperdinck's tours, the anniversary was almost completely sold out. By the time his 1996 record *After*

Dark hit the stores, Humperdinck had sold 130 million records, including 23 platinum and 64 gold releases, and he showed no signs of decreasing his output. "The last twenty-five years have been an adventure, a story without a script," Humperdinck told fans in his anniversary tourbook. "I never knew what was coming next but it's been a wonderful journey. I hope the chapters of my life to follow allow me to continue to keep giving back all the love and respect that I have been given."

Selected discography

Release Me, Parrot, 1967.
We Made it Happen, Parrot, 1970.
King of Hearts, Parrot, 1974.
His Greatest Hits, Parrot, 1975.
After the Lovin', Epic, 1976.
Last of the Romantics, Epic, 1978.
Love is the Reason, Critique, 1991.
Engelbert Humperdinck: The 25th Anniversary Album, Polydor, 1992.

Sources

Periodicals

Hollywood Reporter, December 1991, pp.1-4, 10.

Additional information gathered from publicity materials, including a press release from Baker, Winoker, Ryder, July 11, 1996 and *The 25th Anniversary World Tour 1967-1992* (tour book), 1992.

—*Shaun Frentner*

The Jesus Lizard

Rock band

David Yow of The Jesus Lizard. Photo by Ken Settle. Reproduced by permission.

Since the early Nineties the Jesus Lizard have lured a veritable cult following around their sweaty and sometimes shocking live performances. The band emerged out of the much-lauded Austin, Texas outfit Scratch Acid; founders David Yow and David William Sims surfaced in Chicago in the late Eighties to record with legendary indie producer Steve Albini, best known for his work with Nirvana, and regrouped. The Jesus Lizard subsequently recorded several albums filled with nihilistic songs for the Windy City's Touch and Go label, but broke with the notoriously cranky Albini when it came time to record their 1996 major-label debut on Geffen, *Shot.*

The Jesus Lizard, noted Andy Lewis in the *Rough Guide to Rock,* put forth a "primordial, often indigestible stew of blues and punk," and "have consistently managed to reinvigorate a genre often in danger of extinction or self-parody." Most of the band came of age in the thriving Eighties proto-alternative rock scene. Yow grew up in a well-traveled military family that had settled in Texas. He dropped out of college and with Sims formed the art/noise/metal act Scratch Acid. After disbanding in 1987, Yow and Sims found themselves adrift; both wound up separately in Chicago. Sims had joined a band fronted by former Big Black member Steve Albini, while Yow was there to work with guitarist Duane Denison.

Albini's new act never achieved much before falling apart, but the three musicians coalesced as a band and asked Albini to serve as their producer. They recorded the EP *Pure,* and shortly after found a drummer to replace a drum machine they had been using. With Mac McNeilly—a member of whom the band once said was much better than a drum machine, because he could carry gear to and from the road van—the band began touring extensively. From the start, they faced criticism. as simply a knock-off of Big Black, but their odd, seditious lyrics and Yow's vocals set them far away from any other act. "Yow's voice," wrote Lorraine Ali in *Rolling Stone,* "flails between shaky, high-strung whines and a deliriously guttural sing-speak, his words cracking hoarsely in strangles of anger and desperation. His lyrics are disjointed and abstract, evoking nightmarish images and sometimes even nervously funny scenarios."

The band released their first full-length work, *Head,* again on Touch and Go, in April of 1990. Still touring extensively, they cut another record, *Goat,* in Albini's Chicago studio and released it the following year. *Liar* followed in 1992. It was "scarcely easy listening," according to the *Rough Guide*'s Lewis, "but strangely enthralling." By this time, a Jesus Lizard stage show was

Members are **David Yow** (born c. 1961), vocals; **David William Sims** (born c. 1964), bass; **Mac McNeilly** (left band, 1996), drums; **Duane Denison,** guitar; McNeilly replaced by **Jim Kimball**.

The Jesus Lizard formed in Chicago in late 1989. Yow and Sims were founding members of Scratch Acid; Denison and Kimball were in the Denison-Kimball Trio; Kimball was also with Mule and the Laughing Hyenas, and Denison was a veteran of Cargo Cult; McNeilly was a former member of 86 and Phantom 309. They released several LPs on the Touch and Go label, issued a split single with Nirvana, and signed with Capitol Records in 1995.

Addresses: *Record company*—Capitol Records, 1750 North Vine St., Hollywood, CA 90028-5274.

a hot ticket among indie-rock cognoscenti. Yow, like Iggy Pop, was known to mutilate his body onstage, and once even urinated on himself, all while delivering the grisly yet eloquent lyrics that spoke of "violence, bodily corruption and decay," noted Lewis.

Compared to Nirvana

In the early Nineties the Jesus Lizard were often paired with Seattle grunge act Nirvana for tours. They even cut a split single with them, "Puss," (Nirvana's side was "Oh, the Guilt.") in the spring of 1992—after a long negotiation period between executives from both band's labels. SubPop, Nirvana's label, wanted to control the pressing, but the Jesus Lizard insisted that their friends at Touch and Go keep control. Released in 1993, the single made waves in Europe and lured even more fans to Yow's unusual antics. By this point, Nirvana was huge, and some longtime fans may have seen it as a sell-out. But Yow dismissed such charges. "A lot of people may think we're trying to cash in on Nirvana," he told *Rolling Stone* writer Greg Kot at the time. "But this has been in the works for two and a half years, and I still think it's a good idea." Still, the Jesus Lizard remained a pigeonholed indie act at the outermost fringes. Though always a favorite with critics, record sales were often disappointing.

Things began to change with their 1994 release *Down.* In the studio, they managed to boss around Albini for a change, but the contentious atmosphere resulted in

another well-received work, and one slightly more accessible. Tracks on *Down* showcasing Yow's bizarre imagery included "Horse," a tale of southern dysfunction, and "Countless Backs of Sad Losers." The following year, the band played Lollapalooza. On one stop in Cincinnati, Yow took all his clothes off onstage and spent some hours in jail for it. Yet the mainstream alternative tour introduced new fans to the Jesus Lizard experience. Yow was fond of diving into the crowd (and often sported scratches from fans), and reciprocated the hospitality to fans who clambered onstage in a steady stream to do the same. The stage-divers didn't bother Yow: "They're just doing their thing and having fun—plus I'm glad so many people are into what we play," the singer told Keiron Mellotte of *Convulsion.* However, his bandmate Sims has been known to whack stage transgressors in the head with his bass if they venture too close.

Major Label Takes Notice

Their growing fan base attracted the attention of major labels, and late in 1995 the Jesus Lizard signed with Capitol. "We were pretty apprehensive about signing, but we tried desperately to find dirt on [Capitol] and couldn't find any," Yow told *Billboard* writer David Sprague. They were also fortunate to have their former publicist at Touch and Go come to work at Capitol's marketing division. For their 1996 release *Shot,* they kept to their habit of giving four-letter titles to their albums, but broke with Albini as the fifth Lizard. "Steve played a huge role in our past records, but it was getting to be time to move on," Yow told Sprague.

Shot evidenced the typical Jesus Lizard humor in songs like "Skull of a German" and "More Beautiful than Barbie." Other tracks, wrote Rob O'Connor in *Rolling Stone,* "feature Yow's typical lyrical concerns (twisted romance, violent urges and overflowing toilets)." The critic also praised the new slant given by producer GGGarth Richardson, who toned down the emphatic rhythm assault of past works and instead played up Denison's guitar. "With the *Shot* record, we spent more money than we'd ever spent and had more time than we'd ever had," Yow told Jennie Punter of the *Toronto Star.* "And I think the result is [our] most accomplished album, and it sounds the most like us. We're not ones to experiment a lot. We've never really done that."

After their major-label debut, the band underwent some changes. Drummer McNeilly left, a casualty of the band's love of touring and its attendant debauchery; he was replaced by Jim Kimball. Yow tried his hand at directing, working with young punksters the Offspring on a video. He professed to hate the commerciality of such endeavors, however, when it came to his own band: "If it was financially conceivable, I'd love to do a video for every song and then not give them to MTV," Yow told *Billboard*'s Brett Atwood. "There are few things I loathe more than MTV."

Jesus Lizard shows were still a hot ticket, and Punter remarked in the *Toronto Star* that they now enjoy a reputation "as one of the tightest, most dynamic and sonically satisfying live ensembles going." It seemed unlikely that they would tire of the adrenaline rush of performing, though Yow did once assert that most bands, including his, have a definite creative lifespan. "Even though we are getting older, as long as I'm still physically capable of doing it, there's nothing I'd rather do than tour," Yow told *Billboard*'s Sprague. "At least this way, I'm able to plan my personal life so that I'm always in a place like Australia in January. It's a very human way to live."

Selected discography

Pure (EP), Touch and Go, 1989.
Head, Touch and Go, 1990.
Goat, Touch and Go, 1991.
Liar, Touch and Go, 1992.
Down, Touch and Go, 1994.
Show, Collision Arts/Giant, Geffen, 1996.

Also released the split single "Puss" with Nirvana on Touch and Go, 1993.

Sources

Books

The Rough Guide to Rock, Penguin, 1996.

Periodicals

Billboard, March 9, 1996, p. 13; August 3, 1996, p. 102.
Convulsion #4, 1994.
Rolling Stone, April 1, 1993, p. 20; December 15, 1994, p. 97; August 10, 1995, p. 48; May 2, 1996, p. 52.
Toronto Star, January 16, 1997; January 19, 1997.

Additional information for this profile was provided both official and unofficial web pages devoted to the Jesus Lizard.

—*Carol Brennan*

Antonio Carlos Jobim

Jazz guitarist

In the early sixties a new, sophisticated music redolent of 'quiet nights and quiet stars', tropical breezes, beautiful women on white sandy beaches, and clear waters reflecting blue skies came upon the scene. The sound was recognizably Latin, a kind of slowed down samba, quieter, more sensual, and it had a name: Bossa Nova.

Soon, the sound would be known worldwide. Its success in the United States was kicked off with the classic Getz-Gilberto recordings of 1963, featuring the American jazz saxophonist Stan Getz and the Brazilian guitarist João Gilberto. The album featured Gilberto's wife at the time, Astrud, who sang a song which was to become associated in the popular mind, with the music as a whole, "The Girl From Ipanema".And forever the name of Antonio Carlos Jobim, known to his Brazilian fans as Tom Jobim, is linked with Brazil's most successful cultural export.

Antonio Carlos Brasileiro de Almeida Jobim was born in 1927 in the Tijuca section of Rio de Janeiro. His family moved to the Ipanema district, one of the new boroughs in expanding Rio. Jobim grew up surrounded by lush forests which stretched down to the warm waters of the Atlantic. "I believe I learned my songs from the birds of the Brazilian forest," he once said.

Jobim was a beach boy in the 1930s. His father, a diplomat and poet, died when Jobim was eight. His family ran a private school, the Brasiliero de Almeida, and it was that Jobim first encountered the piano. His step-father oversaw Jobim's musical education and he began study with Hans Joachim Koellreutter at the age of fourteen. Soon Jobim added guitar and harmonica to the list of instruments he had mastered.

Jobim grew up listening to samba and other native sounds which he heard in the streets and clubs of Ipanema. Samba was a style of music originating in the Afro-Brazilian *favelas,* or shanty towns, of Rio and other cities. In the thirties, radio play and records made this music became popular among all classes. *Sambistas,* aficionados of the music, would follow their favorite bands from bar to bar, until the sun came up. Later Jobim would come under the influence of the French Impressionists, Debussey and Ravel, as well as the cool jazz of American artists like Miles Davis and Gil Evans. These influences would come together in Jobim's own compositions.

While continuing to play music, Jobim enrolled in an architecture program but quit after one year to work full-time as a musician. First he played piano in little bars called *inferminhos,* little hells. The opportunity arose for Jobim to work as a copyist for radio and recording studios. In 1952 Jobim was hired by the Continental

For the Record . . .

Born Antonio Carlos Brasileiro de Almeida Jobim, January 25, 1927, in the Tijuca section of Rio de Janeiro; died December 8, 1994.

Released first solo record, *The Composer of the Desafinado Plays,* in 1963. Master of numerous instruments, including guitar, harmonica, and piano.

recording company to assist Maestro Radamés Gnatali, the most important arranger of the time. Soon Jobim was arranging and producing for Odeon, one of Brazil's largest record companies.

Jobim might have continued as a well-respect arranger-producer, unknown outside his native country, had he not met Vincius de Moraes, the Oxford educated poet and diplomat, in 1956.
Moraes had adapted the Orpheus legend, transposing the story to the *favelas* of contemporary Brazil. Jobim was asked to write the music. This collaboration resulted in an acclaimed stage production, *Orfeu da Conceição,* performed at the Metropolitan Opera House in Rio. The play was later translated to the screen by the French director Marcel Camus. "Black Orpheus" was the prize winner at the Cannes Film Festival in 1959 and enjoyed worldwide success. The soundtrack, in particular "Felicidade"—Orpheus's theme song, introduced the world to the new samba-inflected music coming out of Brazil.

The Bossa Nova Wave

Bossa Nova, or New Beat, was the new wave in Brazilian music. Derived from samba, it had a cooler, more sophisticated sound, while still relying on the carnivalesque rhythms of its predecessor. It's practitioners were mainly middle-class, educated Euro-Brazilian males with an appreciation of Afro-Brazilian culture. Bossa Nova songs where characterized by their softness. The lyrics were simple, poetic, heartfelt, expressing a love for beautiful women, sun and sea. While Jobim was not the originator of this new sound—he credited João Gilberto with that distinction—he soon distinguished himself as its most sophisticated practitioner. He benefited immensely from his collaborations with singers and fellow songwriters such as de Moraes, Mendonca, and de Oliveira. By the time Bossa Nova hit U.S. shores, Jobim and Bossa Nova were considered one and the same.

Jobim began writing songs with Newton Mendonça, a childhood friend and nightclub pianist. Together they penned the Bossa Nova classics "Samba de Uma Nota Só", "Meditaçao", and "Desafinado". His collaboration with Aloysio de Oliveira, a producer for the Odeon label, produced the classic "Dindi".   In 1958 Jobim met the singer-guitarist João Gilberto. Over the next three years they collaborated on three albums together on which Gilberto recorded 13 Jobim originals. Gilberto's beautiful voice and relaxed guitar playing were perfectly suited for Jobim's compositions. This collaboration yielded the haunting "Chega de Saudade"—*No More Blues,* and consolidated the Bossa Nova style.

In 1962 the American Jazz musicians Stan Getz and Charlie Byrd released an LP called *Jazz Samba.* It was the first introduction of the new Brazilian sound to U.S. audiences. While this record yielded a hit version of "Desafinado," the major breakthrough was to come later. After *Jazz Samba,* Getz went back in the studio, this time with Jobim and Gilberto. Getz version of the Jobim-Moraes penned "The Girl from Ipanema," sung by Gilberto and his then-wife Astrud, was a huge success and kicked off a stateside Bossa Nova craze. Jobim soon found himself one of the most recorded composers as a multitude of performers, from jazz to pop, covered his songs. The culmination of music's popularity is, perhaps, the album "Francis Albert Sinatra and Antonio Carlos Jobim," two sides devoted to the music of Jobim featuring Jobim on piano and accompanying vocals.

As the sixties waned and rock music was ascendant, the cool sounds of Bossa Nova were less frequently heard, with the exception of the Bossa Nova-esque pop covers of Sergio Mendes and Brazil '66.

Jobim Records a Solo Album

Jobim himself an arranger for much of his career, benefited from his collaboration with the arranger Claus Ogerman which began with Jobim's first solo record, in 1963, *The Composer of the Desafinado Plays,* on Verve, and continued off and on into the 1970s. This album was followed by *The Wonderful World of Antonio Carlos Jobim,* arranged by Nelson Riddle. Jobim returned to Ogerman for the Sinatra sessions, and the follow-up, *A Certain Mr. Jobim.*

Part of the success of Jobim in the States has to be attributed to his able translators, Gene Lees foremost among them. Lyrics in English have always been a prerequisite for success in America and Jobim was very particular about the translations. Many of Jobim's songs were translated by himself after he learned English. Still, the majority of Joblm's songs remain untranslated. Ogerman has remarked on the relative dearth of Jobim songs in English. "If somebody brought him a lyric, he usually didn't approve of it. What was missing in his North American career was a steady collaborator, like an Ira Gershwin. That makes life easy."

While Jobim enjoyed wide success in the U.S., Bossa Nova was met with resistance back home. Popularity abroad had generated a backlash, especially by purists who thought the music too American. While there is undoubtedly some jazz influence, Jobim maintained that Bossa Nova was a part of Samba, not jazz. Jobim albums with overt jazz influences did not come until later. The trilogy, *Wave, Tide,* and *Stone Flower*—on A&M— were recorded by Rudy Van Gelder, the preeminent jazz engineer responsible for much of John Coltrane's recordings. But, as Bob Blumenthal has pointed out in his liner notes to *Urubu,* another Ogerman collaboration, "They form a distinct interlude" in Jobim's discography.

Jobim's Orchestral Maneuver

Later albums such as *Jobim,* 1972, and *Urubu,* 1975, show Jobim moving away from the cool, Bossa Nova style and his compositions became more orchestral. These albums reflect his interest not only in native Brazilian music, but jazz as well. Compositions such as "Saudade Do Brasil," "Valse," and "Arquitetura De Morar," show the influence of Debussey as well as Jobim's countryman Heitor Villa-Lobos. These later albums also show Jobim's increased awareness of political issues, in particular environmental concerns.

Jobim and some other leading Brazilian musicians encountered difficulties with the military regime which came into power in the late sixties. Jobim, along with Caetano Veloso, Gilberto Gil, Vincius de Moraes, and Carlos Lyra were detained by the authorities in 1970 and Jobim's songs were scrutinized for subversive lyrics. By the late 1970s, Jobim's contribution to popular music was undisputed. *Terra Brasilis* was released in 1980, a summing up of the composer's more popular work, produced once again by Claus Ogerman. Jobim continued to work with popular Brazilian rhythms as well as classical. A renewed interest in the sophisticated pop of the 1960s brought Jobim to the attention of a new generation in the early 1990s and Jobim was honored by the Mangueira Samba School in the 1992 Carnaval parade in Rio. Jobim died December 8, 1994, leaving a recognizable void in the world of Bossa Nova..

Selected discography

Orfeu da Conceição, EMI-Odeon, 1956.
The Composer of the Desafinado Plays, Verve, 1963.
The Wonderful World of Antonio Carlos Jobim, Warner Bros.,

1964.
A Certain Mr. Jobim, Warner Bros., 1965.
(With Dori Caymmi) *Caymmi Visita Tom,* Elenco 1965.
The Astrud Gilberto Album, Elenco, 1965.
Wave, A&M, 1967.
Stone Flower, CTI, 1970.
Tide, A&M, 1970.
Constução, Philips, 1971.
O Som Do Pasquim, Pasquim, 1972.
Matita Perê, MCA, 1973.
Elis & Tom, Philips, 1974.
Urubu, Warner Bros., 1976.
Miucha e A.C. Jobim, RCA, 1977.
Miucha e Tom Jobim, RCA, 1979.
Chico, Philips, 1980.
Terra Brasilis, Warner Bros., 1980.
A.C. Jobim-Homem Aquarius, Philips, 1981.
Brilhante, Som Livre, 1981.
Edu e Tom, Philips, 1981.
Chico Buarque en Espanol, Philips, 1982.
Gabriela, RCA, 1983.
O Corsario Do Rei, Som Livre, 1983.
Musica em Pessoa, Som Livre, 1985.
O Tempo e O Vento, Som Livre, 1985.
Anos Dourados, Som Livre, 1986.
Estrela da Vida Inteira, Continental, 1986.
A.C. Jobim, Sabía, 1987.
Passarim, Verve, 1987.
Rio Revisited, Verve, 1987.
Cais, Som Livre, 1989.
João de Vale, CBS, 1991.
O Dono do Mundo, Som Livre, 1991.
Gal Costa, RCA, 1992.
Carnegie Hall Salutes the Jazz Masters, Verve, 1993.
Pedra Bonita, Nanã, 1993.
Antonio Brasileiro, Columbia, 1994.
A.C. Jobim Apresenta, Mercury, 1995.

Sources

Periodicals

Village Voice, April 2, 1996, p. 49.

Online

jobim02a.htm

Liner notes

Antonio Carlos Jobim: Composer (Warner Archives), by Bob Blumenthal.
Terra Brasilis (Warner Archives), by Bob Blumenthal.
Urubu (Warner Archives), by Bob Blumenthal
The Antonio Carlos Jobim Songbook (Verve), by Zeca Legiéra.

Eric Johnson

Guitarist, vocalist

Photo by Max Crace. AP/Wide World Photos. Reproduced by permission.

Hailed by many as the best guitarist in the post-Jimi Hendrix era, Eric Johnson has earned high critical praise and a multitude of fans for his blend of classic and contemporary sounds. He established his reputation with his blockbuster *Ah Via Musicom* album released in 1990, which features a wide variety of guitar styles and has been acclaimed as a paragon of guitar mastery.

Johnson has a reputation for perfectionism bordering on obsession, a designation backed up by the fact that it took him nearly six years to record his follow-up album to *Ah Via Musicom*. He has often said that he is more interested in tone than technique, and he has spent much time in the studio fiddling with amps and speakers in search of new sounds that intrigue him. His playing has ranged from soaring rock a la Hendrix to soothing, almost meditative sounds that resemble music produced by the koto, a Japanese zither.

Johnson developed an early passion for music from his parents while growing up in Austin, Texas. "Both my parents loved music, so they tried to get us to take piano lessons and that kind of stuff," Johnson told Raoul Hernandez of the *Austin Chronicle*. Playing the piano at age five, Johnson was already writing songs just three years later. He fell in love with the guitar in 1964 when his brother formed a band and he heard them twanging away in an attempt to sound like the then-popular Ventures. Within a year Johnson had his own guitar and was playing it incessantly. After becoming part of a band called The Id at age thirteen, he played in a series of bands, mostly with older kids who recognized his talent.

When Jimi Hendrix released his *Are You Experienced* album in 1967, Johnson suddenly had to rethink everything he knew about playing guitar. He began experimenting more and looking for ways to get more unique sounds from his instrument. In the late 1960s and early 1970s Johnson immersed himself in the blues, often attending performances of blues legends such as Freddie King and Johnny Winter.

A major influence on Johnson was the work of jazz/rock fusion guitarist John McLaughlin with Chick Corea and Return to Forever on the *Hymn of the Seventh Galaxy* album. Johnson began delving into fusion with his own band, the Electromagnets, while playing in clubs around Austin. Although his group began increasing its base of fans in the mid 1970s, Johnson felt that their songs were becoming too complicated. In 1976 he ventured into the studio solo, and tried singing for the first time. After the Electromagnets disbanded the following year, he taught guitar for a while and then reformed his group with Electromagnets's drummer Bill Maddox and bassist Roscoe Beck.

For the Record . . .

Born August 17, 1954, in Austin, TX.

Began taking piano lessons at age five; wrote first song at age eight; received first guitar, 1965; joined first band at age thirteen; formed own band, the Electromagnets, early 1970s; signed management contract with Lone Wolf Productions, 1977; recorded debut album, *Seven Worlds*, that was never released, late 1970s; began performing on Austin City Limits, 1984; signed recording contract with Warner Brothers; released *Tones*, 1986; signed recording contract with Cinema Records that was later picked up by Capitol Records; released *Ah Via Musicom* , 1990; toured with B.B. King, 1993; released *Venus Isle*, 1996.Awards: Best Overall Guitarist, *Guitar Player* Readers' Poll, 1990–1994; Grammy Award, Best Instrumental ("Cliffs of Dover"), 1992; named one of 100 Greatest Guitarists of the 20th Century, *Musician* magazine.

Addresses: *Record company*—Capitol Records, Hollywood and Vine Streets, Hollywood, CA. *Agent*—Joe Priesnitz Artist Management, P.O. Box 5249, Austin, TX 78763.

Career Stalled by Restrictive Contract

In what turned out to be the greatest roadblock to his career, Johnson singed an exclusive six-year contract with Lone Wolf Productions in 1977. After cutting his debut album, *SevenWorlds*, Johnson had to wait while Lone Wolf rejected offers from some smaller record companies and tried to land a more lucrative deal with a major label. The album was never released and, since Lone Wolf had no long-range plans for Johnson's development as an artist, he was left pretty much in limbo for the duration of his contract. Further hampering his career was Lone Wolf's strategy to keep Johnson out of the public eye in order to increase his "mystique."

When his contract terminated in 1984, Johnson got back into action by becoming part of the lineup on Austin City Limits, a popular venue for musical performers in his hometown. Rumor has it that his playing caught the attention of the rock star formerly known as Prince, who advised Warner Brothers, his label, to sign up Johnson. Before long Johnson was working on an album for Warner's Reprise label, with producer David Tickel. Tickel had produced Split Enz's *Wiatata*, an album that had especially impressed Johnson.

In 1986 the public got its first exposure to Johnson's mastery with his *Tones* LP. In *Guitar Player,* Jas Obrecht called the album "a majestic debut, its collage of guitar sounds ranging from purest-of-pure Strat to Hendrix-heavy psychedelia, from delicate koto chimes to magnificent violin textures." In her review of the album in *The New Age Music Guide,* Patti Jean Birosik wrote, "Johnson plays guitar the way Michelangelo painted ceilings: with a colorful vibrancy that's more real than life." Despite the praise, Warner Brothers did not promote the album heavily and it sold only around 50,000 copies. The figures did not live up to the label's expectations, and Johnson's contract was allowed to lapse. Looking for more creative control over his work, Johnson next signed on with the independent label Cinema Records. When Cinema's distribution arrangement with Capitol Records didn't work out, Capitol was impressed enough with Johnson to transfer his contract to them.

Unlike *Tones,* which was recorded and mixed in only two months, Johnson's next album was a marathon ordeal due to the artist's relentless perfectionism. The effort paid off with the release of *Ah Via Musicom* in 1990. Greeted with rave reviews and benefiting from extensive promotional support from Capitol, the album became a landmark recording in the annals of guitar playing. It featured a number of songs that received major airplay, including Johnson's classic "Cliffs of Dover," "Righteous," "Trademark," and "High Landrons." "Marrying deep emotion with jaw-dropping finesse, portions of *Ah Via Musicom* stand on a par with Jimi Hendrix' "Electric Ladyland," noted Obrecht. The album went gold and has gone on to sell some 800,000 copies. The surge in Johnson's popularity caused by the album also resulted in renewed interest in *Tones,* pushing sales of the release well into the hundreds of thousands.

With *Ah Via Musicom* serving as a testament to his abilities, Johnson was named Best Overall Guitarist along with Steve Vai in *Guitar Player*'s 1990 reader's poll—an award he would also win the next four years in a row. He also won a Grammy Award for "Cliffs of Dover" in 1992 in the Best Instrumental category, and was voted one of the 100 Greatest Guitarists of the Twentieth Century by *Musician* magazine.

With expectations about his next work soaring after *Ah Via Musicom,* Johnson found himself wondering how he could move his music to a new level and avoid repeating himself. He drastically reduced his public appearances over the next three years, surfacing only for a short tour with B.B. King in 1993. Meanwhile, work on a new album creeped along at a snail's pace due to Johnson's continual shifts in direction. "I was looking at my music under a microscope and wanting to get everything perfect," he told *Guitar World.* "It's a phase that I've been going through since I started working on *Musicom*. I'm really aware that I need to become less obsessed." Six years after his last release, the much-awaited *Venus Isle* hit the stores in the fall of 1996. Once again Johnson offered a showcase of his varied talents with songs ranging form the rocking instrumental of "Camel's Night Out," and "Pavilion" to the jazz style of "Manhattan" that is reminiscent of Wes Montgomery. It also featured Johnson on acoustic piano in "Travel One Hope," and in a tribute to the late Stevie Ray Vaughan called "SRV." (Johnson has often stated that he learned a lot from Vaughan.)

Johnson credits extensive meditation for his focus and creativity. In the future he plans to further explore the potential of the guitar in search of a "new" sound. As he told *Guitar World* in 1996, "I really want to find some way to make the guitar into an engine of inspiration that will last for another twenty or thirty years."

Selected discography

Tones, Reprise, 1986.
Ah Via Musicom, Capitol, 1990.
Venus Isle, Capitol, 1996.

Sources

Books

Birosik, Patti Jean, *The New Age Music Guide*, Macmillan, 1989, p. 91.
Erlewine, Michael, Vladimir Bogdanov, and Chris Woodstra, editors, *All Music Guide to Rock*, Miller Freeman, 1995, p. 430.

Periodicals

DownBeat, October 1992, p. 60.
Guitar Player, January 1993, pp. 35–42; January 1995, p. 89, 101

Additional information for this profile was obtained from the Eric Johnson Homepage, Capitol Records website, and *Guitar World* website on the Internet.

—*Ed Decker*

Thad Jones

Jazz trumpeter

Frank Driggs Collection. AP/Wide World Photos. Reproduced by permission.

During the 1950s Thad Jones emerged from the postwar Detroit jazz scene to become an exemplary trumpeter, cornetist, composer, and arranger. A member of a musical family, he shared fame with his older brother Hank, a pianist, and his younger brother, Elvin, who helped to redefine the art of jazz drumming. As Ira Gitler noted in the liner notes to *Elvin!*, "Of all the talented families in jazz, I don't think there any who surpass the three Jones boys." While his brothers earned worldwide recognition, Jones continued on his own creative path as cornetist and arranger with the Count Basie Band and as a co-founder of the Thad Jones-Mel Lewis Orchestra. "Thad is a man of purpose," wrote Raymond Horricks, in *Count Basie and His Orchestra*, "a deep thinker and idealist in his music almost to the point of aestheticism ... He abhors flashy, gallery-fetching tactics in music, believing that if a musician doesn't set out to be creative then there is no point in his playing at all." For nearly half a century, Jones carried forth his creative vision, leaving behind a wealth of compositions, arrangements, and recordings that continued to be studied and performed throughout the world.

Thaddeus Joseph Jones was born one of ten children on March 28, 1923, in Pontiac, Michigan. Jones' father, a Baptist deacon, played guitar. Over the years, the Jones household resonated with the sound of the piano played by Thad's older sister, Olive, who performed at classical recitals, and brothers Hank and Paul. In *The Jazz Scene: An Informal History From New Orleans to 1990*, Jones recalled how the family radio tuned in "a lot of symphony music, especially on Sundays." Thad too listened to radio broadcasts of Louis Armstrong, and after hearing the trumpeter perform in Detroit, became determined to become a trumpeter. Given a second-hand trumpet by his Uncle Williams, Jones soon switched to cornet when he joined the school band (throughout his career Jones performed primarily on cornet). Taught only the rudiments of trumpet in school he pursued the study of his instrument primarily through the use of instruction books. At age sixteen, he and his brother Hank played in a semi-professional ensemble, the Arcadia Club Band, which performed for school functions and weekend events.

In 1941 Jones left the Arcadia Band to perform on a Southern tour with Connie Connell's band. Following his two-year stint with Connell, he played a short engagement with the twelve-piece band of Red Calhoun. Drafted into the military during 1943, he was inducted at Camp Walters, Texas. Though he assigned to checking army cargo, Jones did, a few months before his discharge, join a military band sponsored the 8th Air Force Special Service Division. Following his discharge in Des Moines, Iowa, in 1946, Jones played an engagement at the Silver Slipper Club before joining the band of Charles Young in

Born Thaddeus Joseph Jones, March 28, 1923, in Pontiac, MI; died of cancer on August, 21, 1986, in Copenhagen, Denmark; son of Baptist deacon.

Performed in Arcadia Club Band at age sixteen; 1941 performed in Connie Connell's band; served in U.S. Army 1943-1946; worked with the band of Charles Young (circ. 1946-1948); led own quintet in Detroit; worked in the bands of Candy Johnson and Jimmy Taylor; performed at Blue Bird Inn, Detroit 1952-1954; joined the Count Basie Band in 1954 and performed with Charles Mingus' Jazz Workshop; left the Basie Band and in 1963 worked briefly as a CBS staff arranger; co-led Thad Jones-Mel Lewis Orchestra 1965-1978; led the Danish Radio Orchestra and taught at the Royal Conservatory; 1980 taught Jazz Seminar in Barcelona, Spain; rejoined the Basie Band in 1985;

Awards: *DownBeat* New Star Award 1956.

Oklahoma City. Jones later recalled, as quoted in *Count Basie and His Orchestra,* "Charles Young was the most talented cat I've ever met. He played trumpet, clarinet, baritone, piano, could swing on everything, sing like a bird and write like a demon." With the sudden death of Young at age twenty-six, Jones took over the unit for six months, until the failing health of his father prompted his return to Pontiac.

Detroit's Postwar Jazz Scene

In the Detroit area Jones formed a quintet which included his brother Elvin on drums. Without landing sufficient work, however, Jones went on the road with saxophonist Candy Johnson's band and then worked with the band of Jimmy Taylor. In 1952, he appeared in the house band at Detroit's Blue Bird Inn - an ensemble featuring his brother Elvin, saxophonist Billy Mitchell, bassist James "Beans" Richardson, and pianist Barry Harris. Years later, Mitchell recalled, in *Swing to Bop,* how the band greatly benefitted from "Thad Jones' imagination" as a horn player and arranger. During his two-year stay in the Bluebird house band, Jones too performed with numerous local talents such as guitarist Kenny Burrell and pianist Tommy Flanagan. In the *Detroit News,* Flanagan commented that the early 1950s at the Bluebird proved "a great time. Thad was writing all these original things. The music was played with such high caliber of musicianship." While at the Blue Bird Inn, Jones and his brother Elvin took part in Mitchell's sessions for the Detroit-based Dee Gee label, owned by Dizzy Gillespie and Dave Usher. During a visit to Detroit at this time, Charles Mingus heard Jones, and shortly afterward expressed, as quoted in *Mingus: A Critical Biography,* that "I just heard the greatest trumpet player that I've ever heard in this life. He uses all the classical [compositional] techniques, and is the first man to make them swing."

Member of the Count Basie Band

In May of 1954 Jones joined the Count Basie Band. In his autobiography, Basie related how, after arriving back in America from Europe, he needed "to replace Joe Wilder in the trumpet section, and Frank Wess recommended Thad Jones." As Basie added, "He moved right in and became one of us." After recording on the Clef label with Basie, Jones performed on Basie's 1955 Verve dates which included his celebrated solo on the Basie hit "April in Paris." As a member of the Basie Band, Jones backed vocalist Joe Williams on sides which featured such classic Williams numbers as "Everyday I Have the Blues," "The Comeback," and "Alright, O.K. You Win."

Solo Work

Beginning in August 1954, Jones went into the studio to complete sessions for his album, *Thad Jones,* for Max Roach's and Charles Mingus' Debut label. The critically acclaimed LP utilized two different groups: one featuring Charles Mingus and Max Roach and another guested by Mingus, Hank Jones, and drummer Kenny Clarke. In regard to the Jones-Mingus-Roach ensemble, Nat Hentoff wrote, as quoted in the album's liner notes, "Thad's tone, technique, and his maturely inventive imagination are constantly exciting and sometimes break into startlingly forceful phrases." In 1956 *DownBeat* awarded Jones the "New Star Award." That same year, in his work *Encyclopedia of Jazz,* Leonard Feather listed Jones' Blue Note Lp *Detroit-New York Junction* as one of the finest new jazz albums. In the liner notes to the 1957 Blue Note album, *The Magnificent Thad Jones,* featuring former Detroiters Billy Mitchell, Barry Harris, and Kenny Burrell—Feather described Jones' emerging talent as "magnificent."

In 1957 Jones appeared with the Count Basie Band at a command London performance for Queen Elizabeth, an occasion commemorated in Jones' composition "H.R.H. (Her Royal Highness)." Between November and January of the same year, Jones recorded with saxophonist Sonny Rollins. At this time he continued to earn the praise of leading jazz critics. In 1958 Whitney Balliett wrote, as quoted in his work the *Sound of Surprise*, "Thad Jones is a brassy, sure-footed trumpeter whose solos are now and then so perfectly structured they appear to have been carefully written out before-hand." In the liner notes to Basie's 1959 album, *Chairman of the Board*, Leonard Feather too noted that "Thad Jones has provided some of the pointedly modern sounds emanating from the trumpet team during the last five years." Arranged by Jones, the Lp featured several of the cornetist's original compositions, "The Deacon," "Speaking of Sounds," and "Mutt and Jeff" (previously recorded by Jones as "Sput `n' Jeff").

In 1959 Jones once again assembled several former Detroit jazzmen - Kenny Burrell, Tommy Flanagan, and bassist Paul Chambers - to record his solo effort, *Motor City Scenes* which contained a fine collection of original compositions. In July 1960 and January 1961, he ar-ranged the majority of the material for sessions with singer Sarah Vaughan. Released as the Roulette album *Count Basie & Sarah Vaughan* (minus Basie who sat out the dates in favor of Sarah Vaughan's regular pianist Kirk Stuart), the Lp featured twelve of Jones' arrangements, including Vaughan's outstanding performance of "Perdi-do."

In sessions that took place in the winter and summer of 1961 Jones, along with Basie bandmembers Frank Foster and Frank Wess, provided the horn accompani-ment for his brother's first album *Elvin!* (Riverside 1962). In honor of his brother's debut effort, Jones contributed the original composition "Ray-El" (Elvin's middle name is Ray). Ira Gitler, in the liner notes to *Elvin!*, lauded Thad's cornet work on the Lp: "Whether he is playing open and pugently brassy as on 'Lady Luck,' or insinuatingly and muted as on 'Buzz-at,' he is always vital." In March of 1962, Jones re-entered the studio to record *Count Basie and the Kansas City 7*, the third reincarnation of Basie's smaller seven-piece unit. The recording of the septet - which included Foster and Wess - featured Jones' original compositions "What'cha Talkin'" and "Trey of Hearts," the former of which Stanley Dance described, as quoted in the album's liner notes, as "ingeniously planned blues."

Sideman with Thelonious Monk and Gil Evans

While in Japan in February 1963, Jones worked on the film *Asphalt Girl* with pianist Roland Hanna. In late December of the same year, he played cornet in Thelo-nious Monk's ten piece big band at New York's Philhar-monic Hall (*Monk: Big Band And Quartet in Concert* Columbia). Jones' fluid cornet lines on Monk's title "Four in One" earned him praise from several critics, including Steve Pekar, who in a *DownBeat* review, described the

performance as a "majestic, brilliantly constructed solo." After leaving the Count Basie Band in 1963, he took a job as a CBS staff arranger. In May 1964, Thad joined his brother Elvin in a recording date for pianist and arranger Gil Evans at New York City's Webster Hall. Two of the session's arrangements, the blues traditional "Spoonful" and John Lewis' "Concorde," appeared on Evans' album *The Individualism of Gil Evans*.

The Thad Jones-Mel Lewis Orchestra

In 1965 Jones and Mel Lewis, a former sideman with Stan Kenton and Gerry Mulligan, formed the Thad Jones-Mel Lewis Orchestra—an eighteen piece unit founded for the purpose of offering a creative outlet for New York-based studio jazz musicians. The ensemble performed every Monday night at Max Gordon's Village Vanguard. At this time, Jones, seeking a more appropriate tone for the orchestra's arrangements, performed primarily on flugel-horn. In *Jazz from Its Origins to the Present*, the book's authors—Lewis Porter, Michael Ullman, and Edith Ha-zel—noted Jones' contributions to the orchestra: "From the very beginning Jones' arrangements became more and more challenging, featuring fast, intricate ensem-bles for the winds, or opening odd spaces for duets." In *The Jazz Book*, Joachim E. Brendt, commented that Jones and Lewis "managed to appeal to a large audi-ence and to create an orchestral jazz that, as swinging as it was in the traditional sense, was full of sounds and ideas never heard before." During Jones' co-leadership of the orchestra it included such stellar jazz talents as saxophonists Frank Foster and Pepper Adams, French hornist Peter Gordon, and pianist Roland Hanna. By the 1970s jazz educators had introduced the orchestra's charts to college ensembles, material that often included Jones' "Central Park North" (1969) and his most famous composition "A Child Is Born" (1970).

During the 1970s the Thad Jones and Mel Lewis Big Band made several overseas tours, including a 1972 U.S. State Department sponsored tour of the Soviet Union. While in Yugoslavia in 1978 an unknown assailant caused injury to Jones' lip. Jones then decided to leave the orchestra and moved to Denmark where he briefly took up valve trombone, led the Danish Radio Orchestra, taught at the Royal Conservatory, and eventually re-sumed recording in a small group settings. In 1985, a year following Basie's death, Jones rejoined his former leader's big band. In an effort to bring the band a contemporary sound he commissioned new charts from the band's arrangers Frank Foster, Frank Wess, and Ernie Wilkins. As a result of failing health Jones resigned from the band and returned to Copenhagen, Denmark, where he died of cancer on August, 21, 1986. In *The Jazz Book*, Joachim Brendt lamented that with Jones' passing "contemporary jazz.... Lost one of its important composers and arrangers."

Selected discography

Thad, Debut, 1955.
The Magnificent Thad Jones, Blue Note, 1956.
After Hours, Prestige, 1957.
Motor City Scene, United Artists, 1959
Mad Thad, Period.
Thad Jones and Pepper Adams: Say What You Mean, Original Jazz Classics, 1966.
Thad Jones Quartet, Three & One, Steeplechase.
Basle, TCB, 1969.
Eclipse, Metronome, 1980.
Thad Jones/Danish Radio Big Band, Live at Montmartre, Copenhagen, Storyville.

With Count Basie

April in Paris, Verve.
Count Basie Plays, Joe Williams Sings, Verve, 1957.
Basie in London, Verve.
Count Basie and the Kansas City Seven, (MCA, 1962), Impulse!, 1996.
Everyday I Have the Blues: Joe Williams, Count Basie and His Orchestra, Roulette.
Sing Along with Basie, Roullette.
Chairman of the Board, Roulette.
Basie in Sweden (Recorded Live in Concert), Roulette, 1962.
The Atomic Mr. Basie, Roullette.
The Best of Count Basie: The Roulette Years, Roulette, 1991.
The Essential Count Basie, Verve.
Echoes of an Era: The Best of Count Basie, Roulette, 1972.
Count on the Coast Vol. I, Phonastic.
Eclipse, Metronome, 1980.
Thad Jones/Danish Radio Big Band, Live at Montmartre, Copenhagen, Storyville.

With the Thad Jones-Mel Lewis Orchestra

Presenting Thad Jones and Mel Lewis and the Jazz Orchestra, Solid State, 1966.
Presenting Joe Williams and Thad Jones, Mel Lewis, The Jazz Orchestra, Solid State.
Monday Night at the Village Vanguard, Solid State.
The Big Band Sound of Thad Jones and Mel Lewis, Solid State.
Central Park North, Solid State.
Suite For Pops, Horizon.
The Thad Jones-Mel Lewis Quartet, Artists House, 1977.
Thad Jones-Mel Lewis Orchestra, Blue Note.
New Life, A&M.

With Others

Charles Mingus Jazz Workshop, Impulse.
(With Sonny Rollins) *Lust for Life*, Drive Archive.
(With Frank Wess) *Opus De Blues*, Savoy.
(Curtis Fuller) *Imagination*, Savoy.
(With Charles Mingus) *The Complete Debut Recordings*, Debut.
The Jazz Experiments of Charles Mingus, Bethlehem.
(With Thelonious Monk) *5 by Monk by 5*, Original Jazz Classics.
(With Coleman Hawkins) *The Hawk Swings Vol. I*, Fresh Sound.
Elvin!, Riverside, 1962.
The Individualism of Gil Evans, Verve, 1964.
Thelonious Monk Memorial Album, Classic Performances From His Prestige and Riverside Years, 1952 59, Milestone.
Monk: Big Band and Quartet in Concert, Columbia.
Lionel Hampton/Rare Recordings Vol. I, Telarc.
(With Joe Williams) *Jump for Joy*, Bluebird.
(With Sarah Vaughan) *I'll Be Seeing You*, Vintage Jazz Classics.
(With McCoy Tyner) *Today and Tomorrow*, Impulse! GRP.
(With Jimmy Smith) *The Cat*, Verve.
(With Milt Jackson) *For Someone I Love*, Original Jazz Classics.
(With Ben Webster) *Soulmates*, Original Jazz Classics.
The Jones Boys, Everest.
(With Shirley Scott) *Roll 'Em*, Impulse! GRP.
(With Joe Henderson) *The Blue Note Years*, Blue Note.
(With Horace Parlan) *Glad I Found You*, Steeplechase.
(With Kenny Drew) *Lite Flight*, Steeplechase.

Compilations

The Definitive Jazz Scene, Vol. I, Impulse.

Sources

Books

Balliett, Whitney, *The Sound of Surprise: 46 Pieces in Jazz*, The Jazz Book Club, 1961.
Basie, Count with Albert Murray, *The Autobiography as Told to Albert Murray*, Random House, 1985.
Brendt, Joachim E., revised by Gunther Huesmann, *The Jazz Book from Ragtime to Swing to Fusion and Beyond*, Lawrence Hill Books, 1992.
Feather, Leonard. *Leonard Feather's Encyclopedia of Jazz*, DaCapo, 1956.
Gitler, Ira, *Swing to Bop: An Oral History of the Transition in Jazz in the 1940s*, Oxford University Press, 1985.
Horricks, Raymond. *Count Basie and His Orchestra: Its Music and Musicians*, Negro Universities Press, 1957.

Lee, Gene, *Waiting For Dizzy,* Oxford University, Press, 1991.

Porter, Lewis and Michael Ullman with Edith Hazel, *Jazz from its Origins to the Present,* Prentice Hall, 1993.

Priestly, Brian, *Mingus: A Critical Biography,* Da Capo, 1982.

Stokes, Royal, *The Jazz Scene: An Informal History From New Orleans to 1990,* Oxford University Press, 1991.

Periodicals

Detroit News, September, 26, 1992.

DownBeat, 1964.

Liner notes

Leonard Feather in *Chairman of the Board,* Roulette.

Feather in *The Magnificent Thad Jones,* Blue Note.

Gitler, Ira, *Elvin!*

Stanley Dance in *Count Basie and the Kansas City 7,* Impulse!

Joy Division

Rock band

In a piece cited in a Warner Bros. publicity release *Melody Maker* magazine called Joy Division "the greatest band ever, the group whose music inspired [modern-rock stalwarts] U2, Depeche Mode, Nirvana, Radiohead and countless others." The Northern English band's gloomy post-punk was extremely influential, to be sure, but its mythic importance owes much to the suicide of lead singer Ian Curtis in 1980. The remaining members found greater success as New Order, but Joy Division continued to exert a profound spell on subsequent generations of alternative rock musicians and fans.

The band was born in Manchester, an industrial town in Northern England, in the late 1970s. Punk rock was a burgeoning phenomenon, and the genre's most powerful exemplars, the Sex Pistols, performed at Manchester's Lesser Free Trade Hall in 1976. Attending this performance were three school chums, Bernard Sumner, Peter Hook and Terry Mason. *Sour Times* printed a quote from Sumner regarding the Pistols: "They were terrible," he recalled. "I thought they were great. I wanted to get up and be terrible too." Their musical aspirations kicked into gear by the energy of the punk movement, the three decided to form a band. With Sumner on guitar, Hook on bass and Mason on drums, they lacked only a singer. Curtis, whom they knew from various shows around town, agreed to front the group, which was initially called Stiff Kittens, and then Warsaw. The latter name was inspired by "Warzawa," a moody instrumental on protean British avant-rocker David Bowie's album *Low*.

Mason was replaced by Tony Tabac on drums before Warsaw's first gig, a show at Manchester's Electric Circus in May of 1977 that also featured punk-pop favorites the Buzzcocks. The band continued playing regionally, replacing Tabac with Panik's Steve Brotherdale during the summer, but the latter lasted only a few months—albeit months during which Warsaw made its very first recordings, known collectively in later years as *The Warsaw Demo*. Stephen Morris came on board toward the end of the year. "Steve Morris played cabaret style and we had to teach him the way we wanted him to play, which was difficult," Hook recalled in *Goldmine*, "but when he learned he was brilliant." The new drummer helped the group to forge its sonic identity, and they returned to the studio in December to record four songs for an EP, *An Ideal for Living.* This disc attracted the attention of RCA Records, but the label's attempt to make the group sound "more professional" led to a parting of ways.

"An Important Band"

The success of a London band, Warsaw Pakt, persuaded Warsaw to adopt a new moniker. The name Joy Division came from the term for prostitution units frequented by Nazi officers during World War II; the band learned it from a novel, Karol Cetinsky's *The House of Dolls.* A fight broke out at the first Joy Division show, and riots became a staple of their live appearances. Their name and cryptic, frequently Germanic artwork inspired speculation that the group members were Nazi sympathizers, a charge they passionately denied.

Joy Division eventually signed a deal with Factory Records, which was founded by local music producers Tony Wilson and Rob Gretton. Their initial release on the label was part of a compilation called *A Factory Sampler*, which featured two Joy Division songs; the band also re-released their first EP and recorded some material for influential BBC disc jockey John Peel's program. Their full-length debut came with 1979's *Unknown Pleasures*, which *Goldmine*'s Fernando Lopez De Victoria called "one of the most impressive debut albums ever issued." The group began playing more high-profile shows, even opening for popular alternative-rockers The Cure In London. The music paper *NME* wrote, "Joy Division now sketch withering grey abstractions of industrial malaise," adding "Musically Joy Division is more punishing than any Heavy Metal band.... When Joy Division left the stage I felt emotionally drained. They are, without any exaggeration, an Important Band." Later in the year, the group joined the Buzzcocks on tour, and recorded what would become their signature song, "Love Will Tear Us Apart," for Peel's program. Though not yet commercially available, it became extremely popular.

For the Record . . .

Members include **Ian Curtis** (born July 15, 1956; died May 18, 1980), vocals; **Peter Hook** (born February 13, 1956), bass; **Stephen Morris** (born October 28, 1957; joined group 1977), drums; **Bernard Sumner** (born Bernard Albrecht, January 4, 1956), guitar; **Steve Brotherdale** (bandmember 1977), drums; **Terry Mason** (bandmember 1977), drums; **Tony Tabac** (bandmember 1977), drums.

Band formed c. 1976, Manchester, England; initially called Warsaw. Released EP *An Ideal for Living* on own Enigma label, 1978; signed with Factory Records and contributed songs to *A Factory Sample* compilation EP, 1978; released album debut *Unknown Pleasures*, 1979; dissolved after suicide of Curtis, 1980; singer's widow, Deborah Curtis, published *Touching from a Distance*, a remembrance of Curtis and the band, 1995; band was subject of tribute album *A Means to an End* on Virgin label and compilation *Permanent: The Best of Joy Division* on Qwest, 1995.

Addresses: *Record company*—Qwest/Warner Bros., 3800 Barham Blvd., Ste. 503, Los Angeles, CA 90068. *Website*—Warner Bros: http://www.wbr.com; Factory Records "Fac 2.07" site: http://www.u-net.com/factory/; Joy Division Shadowplay: http://subnet.virtual-pc.com/~wa540709/.

Success and Suicide

The band toured across Europe in early 1980, but the bloom began to come of the rose of success for Curtis. His marriage was compromised by his relationship with a Belgian woman, Annik Honore, and he suffered an epileptic fit after a London concert in April. Never previously diagnosed with the illness, he was devastated by it. "He was only like 22 or something," Sumner told *The New Music* television program, which was transcribed for the *Much Music* web site. "We took him to the hospital and they said, 'Yeah, he's had an epileptic fit.' After that, he just got really bad and he started getting it more and more." The treatment offered at the time, Sumner added, "was just to dose someone up with barbs, so he was on really heavy barbiturates all the time and that just changed his whole personality, really, but there was nothing we could do about it." In a book written by Curtis' widow some years later, Hook maintains that the singer nonetheless concealed the extent of his despair. "He must have been a pretty good actor," asserted the bassist. "We didn't have a bleeding clue what was going on. You tried to help him with your limited experience, and you did what you could, but as soon as you left him, he went back, you know?"

"Love Will Tear Us Apart" appeared on Joy Division's second full-length album, *Closer,* which received excellent reviews. Yet the content of the recording was a tip-off for some of Curtis' deteriorating emotional condition. And Deborah herself later acknowledged—in a radio interview transcribed for a web site–that Curtis had long contemplated ending his life. "He'd always said that he would kill himself and he didn't want to live after the age of 25," she affirmed, but recalled hoping "he'd grow out of it," since the two had a child and the band was doing well. Yet Curtis also pictured himself as a pop-cultural martyr, like singer Jim Morrison of the Doors or movie idol James Dean, both of whom died young and left behind powerful myths. Whatever his motivations, Curtis hanged himself at his home in the town of Macclesfield on May 18, 1980, just before Joy Division was scheduled to leave on a tour. He had apparently just watched a dark German film on television; an album by proto-punk trailblazer Iggy Pop was allegedly on his turntable when his body was found.

Posthumous Influence

In the wake of Curtis' suicide, *Closer* sold briskly; the remaining members of the band went on to form the far more successful band New Order. 1981 saw the release of a posthumous collection, *Still.* Though many fans viewed the latter as an opportunistic release, the legacy of Joy Division exerted a powerful force on the subsequent generation of alternative rock. "It was very important," singer U2 singer Bono of the band in an interview for *The New Music.* Trent Reznor of Nine Inch Nails covered a Joy Division song for a film soundtrack some years later, and a couple of tribute albums during the mid-1990s testified to the staying power of Joy Division's songs, with contributions by techno artist Moby, Billy Corgan of Smashing Pumpkins, Girls Against Boys and many others.

In 1995, Qwest Records released *Permanent,* a collection comprising most of Joy Division's celebrated recordings and a remix of "Love Will Tear Us Apart." That song in particular had come to be recognized as a defining moment in the history of rock, and Bill Wyman listed a portion of the track at the top of his list of "100 Greatest Rock 'N' Roll Moments" for *Addicted to Noise.* "'Love Will Tear Us Apart' may contain one of the most haunting melodies every concocted," claimed Johnny Angel of the *San Francisco Bay Guardian.* "Ian Curtis and Joy Division were one of the turning point of rock music," said Tom Atencio, an executive producer of one tribute anthology and American representative of New Order, in *Billboard.* "The Sex Pistols, Joy Division, and Nirvana are all essential for modern rock." Mark Williams, then an executive at Virgin Records, described Joy Division in the same article as "our generation's [cult-rock phenomenon] Velvet Underground. "More people know about them than actually bought their records when they came out."

Selected discography

An Ideal for Living, Enigma, 1978.
A Factory Sampler, Factory, 1978.
The Peel Sessions, Dutch East India, 1979.
Unknown Pleasures, Factory, 1979.
Closer (includes "Love Will Tear Us Apart"), Factory, 1980.
Still, Factory, 1981.
Substance, 1977-80, Qwest, 1988.
Permanent: The Best of Joy Division, Qwest, 1995.

Sources

Periodicals

Addicted to Noise, January 11, 1996.
Billboard, August 5, 1995.
Chicago Tribune, January 12, 1996; May 13, 1996.
Goldmine, February 7, 1992.
Melody Maker, June 1995.
New Musical Express (*NME*), May 26, 1979.
San Francisco Bay Guardian, July 9, 1996.
Sounds, November 21, 1981.

Additional information was provided by Warner Bros./Qwest publicity materials, and from the Internet sites *HotWired, Joy Division Shadowplay, Much Music, Sour Times* and various unofficial Joy Division sites.

—*Simon Glickman*

R.
Kelly

Singer, songwriter

Singer, songwriter, and record producer R. Kelly arrived on the music scene with a sound reminiscent of traditional R&B music. Kelly's music often explores sexual themes, both openly and through sly innuendo—an aspect to be found in one of the very sources of contemporary R&B, the blues. On the other hand, the spiritual lyrics and powerful vocal delivery of Kelly's performances are clearly marked by the influence of gospel, another cornerstone in African-

American music and culture. Some critics and listeners have found the marriage of sexuality and religion to be troubling, but that barrier has already been broken by once shocking but now revered acts such as Marvin Gaye and Prince. As *Essence* writer Gordon Chambers asserted, "Like many of our great soulmen, Robert Kelly sings about the needs of both the flesh and the spirit." Like Prince, Kelly is a one-man dynamo who, in addition to producing and arranging his own recordings, also plays most of the instruments on them. However, no matter what his precedents may be, and despite any critical backlash, R. Kelly pushes his influences to new extremes.

Raised Out of Poverty

R. Kelly's story is a familiar rags-to-riches ascent. Born on January 8, 1968, in the south side of Chicago, Kelly was surrounded by hardship and poverty from the beginning. One of four children, Kelly was raised by a struggling single mother and schoolteacher, Joanne, in Chicago's housing projects. Even before he had reached adolescence, Kelly was assailed by negative peer pressures and the violent seduction of teen crime. However, the young Kelly eluded the aversive lures of his environment, thanks largely to the spiritual guidance of his mother and the introduction of music into his life. At Joanne's suggestion, Kelly sang backup for a local church choir that performed in storefronts. Not only did Kelly begin to shape the vocal style that launched his career within the church, he also found an uplifting network of support outside of the fraternity of street gangs.

When Kelly was 16 years old, his mother managed to move her family away from the projects and enroll her son into Kenwood Academy, a Chicago public school. It was there that Kelly met his mentor, Lena McLin, who chaired Kenwood's music faculty and of whom Kelly later described as a second mother. McLin immediately spotted the natural yet unpolished musical talent within Kelly, and pushed him to harness it through participation in school and church choir groups, and intense piano training. But McLin's influence went beyond that of a mere tutor. Sympathetic to Kelly's economic position, McLin would often buy her needy student food or clothes. More importantly, she pressed Kelly to have faith in his abilities, assuring him that one day he would record with his idol, singer Michael Jackson. "She made me feel I could do anything," Kelly told *People* in 1994.

Breaks into Performing

Kelly's first burst of success came when McLin placed him in a local talent show to perform a version of "Ribbon in the Sky," a song by Motown legend Stevie Wonder. During the show, he donned a pair of jet black sunglasses, which, along with his cleanly shaven head, were to become his trademark. The performance met with unequivocal approval from a screaming audience, and for the first time Kelly felt that the hopes McLin held for him were within his reach. Armed with a boosted self-confidence and the beginnings of an image, Kelly was ready to break into the record industry.

Before being discovered, Kelly took his act to the streets. Backed up by a clique of partners in song, Kelly became a fixture on the sidewalks of Chicago, crooning to passersby as he accompanied with a modest electronic keyboard. It was not long before the collection hat at Kelly's feet began amassing several hundred dollars per day from appreciative onlookers. Kelly's collection of

For the Record . . .

Born Robert Kelly on January 8, 1968, in Chicago, IL; son of Joanne Kelly (a schoolteacher).

Awards: Named Number One R&B Producer and R&B Artist of the Year, *Billboard* magazine, 1994.

Addresses: *Home*—Chicago, IL. *Record company*—Jive Records, 137-139 West 25th St., New York, NY 10001.

street performers eventually evolved into a bona fide R&B outfit called MGM, which built upon the growing success of the street group. After MGM won a $100,000 grand prize on a syndicated television talent show called *Big Break*, Kelly was tapped by Jive Records agent Wayne Williams. In 1990, Jive Records signed Kelly onto their roster of artists, and ushered him into the recording studio.

Within a year of joining Jive Records, Kelly released his debut album entitled *Born into the 90s*, a polished collection of the kind of slow tempo R&B Kelly had been perfecting on the streets. The record sold over a million copies and featured several single releases including "She's Got That Vibe" and "Honey Love." Even though *Born into the 90s* scored on the R&B and soul charts, it was largely ignored by critics as well as by the mainstream of record buyers.

Becomes a Superstar

After the release of his follow-up album *12 Play* in 1994, Kelly ranked as a true R&B superstar. He took hold of media attention, both positive and negative. On this album, which Kelly wrote, produced, and arranged, smooth harmonies were accompanied by sexual lyrics that pushed the limits of what mainstream radio airplay would allow. Kelly's live stage performance shifted to reflect this as well. Surrounded by an entourage of scantily dressed stage dancers, Kelly would season his singing with suggestive body language and often doff his pants at the concerts' peaks. Besides winning a legion of often screaming female fans, Kelly's unbridled celebration of sex provoked censure from critics and moral watchdogs. Much of the music press regarded Kelly as a mere shock artist, and he was also attacked for being too explicit for young listeners. Nonetheless, Kelly's popularity outweighed any backlash, and he became a mainstay in R&B pop music. As Kelly told

Newsweek, "I wouldn't say my music is raunchy—just sexually aware. Criticizing me is like criticizing the evening news for showing what's really going on."

12 Play sold over five million copies worldwide, offering two gold singles on its lineup, "Sex Me" and "Your Body's Callin'," as well as the platinum-selling "Bump N' Grind." The latter became the longest running number one R&B hit in over 30 years on the singles chart in *Billboard* magazine. The overwhelming popularity of *12 Play* ensued in a largely sold-out world tour with rap act Salt N' Pepa, and at the end of 1994 Kelly was voted number one R&B producer and R&B Artist of the Year by *Billboard.*

Impressed by the production work on *12 Play,* an array of artists, including Aaliyah, Changing Faces, Toni Braxton, Johnny Gill, and Quincy Jones, approached Kelly as a producer and arranger for their own recordings. In addition, Kelly was contacted by singer Janet Jackson to write a ballad especially for her brother, Michael. The result was the number one hit "You Are Not Alone," fulfilling the hopeful prediction made by Lena McLin years earlier. The song is evidence of Kelly's understanding of gospel music, an aspect that had been present in his first two recordings, but one that did not flourish until this time. Feeling the emotional toll of his mother Joanne's death in 1993, Kelly found himself looking in more spiritual directions, which was reflected in his music.

The 1996 album titled simply *R. Kelly* still contained Kelly's trademark sexual ballads, but it also offered a stronger concentration on gospel styled numbers, most notably "Religious Love" and "Trade in My Life," which featured an impressive choral arrangement. The album's biggest hit "(Keep It On The) Down Low," a melodramatic ballad about a secret love tryst, also focused more on emotional rather than sexual content. "With the gospel, I'm not just trying to entertain," Kelly told *Ebony* in 1996. "At my age, I'm going through things within myself; thinking about what I want to do in the future; what I'm doing now in my life and in my career." Clearly this kind of introspection changed Kelly's music, while much of it remains steeped in carnal reference. Nevertheless, the work on *R. Kelly* was generally seen by many critics as a turning point, and Kelly gained kudos for his extension of the gospel tradition. The record was also a smash with the public, and Kelly became one of the industry's more sought after producers.

Kelly has remained in the south side of Chicago but, instead of living in poverty, he resides in an opulent mansion (converted from a church in an exclusive part of the neighborhood). His settlement in Chicago has served to make Kelly feel closer to his late mother, who serves as a spiritual inspiration for the singer's work and life. In addition, Kelly uses the solitude his mansion provides as a place of solitude in which to develop and expand his musical ideas. "I want everyone to recognize me as a true artist, a true writer—a person who is married to his work," Kelly told *Ebony.* "I like to think I'm the weird scientist in the basement."

Selected discography

Born into the 90s (includes "She's Got That Vibe"), Jive Records, 1991.
12 Play (includes "Sex Me," "Bump N' Grind," and "Your Body's Callin'"), Jive Records, 1994.
R. Kelly (includes "[Keep It On The] Down Low"), Jive Records, 1996.

Sources

Periodicals

Ebony, July 1996.
Essence, February 1996.
Newsweek, November 6, 1995.
People, May 30, 1994.

Online

http://members.aol.com/markndark/web/Sept96.htm#R.Kelly
http://www.peeps.com/rkelly

—*Shaun Frentner*

Chaka Khan

Chaka Khan has enjoyed a long and fruitful recording career that spans over two decades, but her soaring voice has failed to put her in the same superstar strata as other African American divas of her generation like Patti LaBelle or Tina Turner. Khan's career came of age as disco dawned in the early 1970s, and with her first hit as a member of Rufus, she became a dynamic presence on the scene. "She was funkier, more contemporary than Aretha Franklin, as she could be just as diverse. Within a mere six years, she would have her own cult of singers who would try to emulate her sound," wrote Curtis Bagley in *Essence.* An even more successful solo career followed, as well as more Grammy Awards, but her presence on the pop/R&B scene by the mid-1990s had become a lightweight one. The London-based singer was remedying that with her contributions to the soundtracks of several successful films.

Khan was born Yvette Stevens, the oldest of four children, on the south side of Chicago. Both parents worked for the University of Chicago, one as a photographer, the other as a research supervisor. Unlike other future R&B stars who cut their musical teeth in church gospel choirs, Khan was raised Roman Catholic—but was exposed to jazz. The singer recalled for *Essence* writer Isabel Wilkerson that she was first exposed to Billie Holiday through her grandmother's record collection. "She's one of my mentors," Khan said of Holiday. "She's one of the first jazz players I ever heard.... The naivete, the suffering, the pain and all the things that come along with the suffering and the pain. She was victimized, and that led to excesses I can relate to and understand. She's a Black woman who went through a lot."

Began Performing at an Early Age

Khan formed her first ensemble with a group of her preteen friends who called themselves the Crystalettes. Their name came from her observation of how the street lights sparkled against the new snow below their Hyde Park high-rise. Big fans of Gladys Knight, Khan and the Crystalettes sang in talent shows where local fans dubbed her "Little Aretha." The official name change to "Chaka" came when she was thirteen and joined an African music group called Shades of Black; it was the onset of the Black Power movement in the mid-1960s and its leader rechristened her Chaka Adunne Aduffe Hodarhi Karifi. Her teen years were spent singing in a number of bands, but Khan also pushed her luck in more potentially self-destructive ways. She told *Essence* that she used to carry a gun, and even practiced with it once a week: "When I did think about killing people with it, I developed

For the Record . . .

Born Yvette Stevens, March 23, 1953, in Chicago, IL; daughter of a photographer and a research supervisor; married Assan Khan, c. 1970 (marriage ended); married again briefly in the mid-1970s; children: Milini, Damien.

Singer. Joined musical group Rufus in 1972; released first two albums *Rufus* and *From Rags to Rufus,* both 1973, for ABC-Dunhill Records; had gold record with single "Tell Me Something Good" from *From Rags to Rufus,* 1974; left group to pursue solo career, 1978; signed with Warner Brothers Records, 1978; released first solo LP, *Chaka,* in 1979; released several solo LPs, but scored hit with the song "I Feel for You," written by Prince, 1984; recorded several other albums and songs for movie soundtracks throughout the 1980s and 1990s.

Awards: Grammy Awards, National Academy of Recording Arts and Sciences, for best group vocal and vocal arrangements, 1983, and for best rhythm and blues female vocal performance, 1983 and 1984.

Addresses: *Home*—London, England. *Office*—Geffen Records, 9130 Sunset Blvd., Los Angeles, CA 90069.

ulcers, and I just threw the gun in the lake."

After dropping out of high school, Chaka moved out of her parents' house when she entered into a common-law marriage with Assan Khan, a bass player from East India. Both wore matching bleached blond coifs, and she was now singing in a group called Lock and Chain. Khan then jumped ship to an act called Lyfe before joining up with another ensemble called Rufus, which had attracted a large Chicago-area following. Working as a file clerk by day, she began hanging around Rufus by night and befriended their frontperson, a woman named Paulette McWilliams. At the time, Rufus was doing dance songs and Sly and the Family Stone covers; when McWilliams quit in 1972, Khan took her place. She was eighteen.

Enters the Majors with Rufus

Rufus won a record deal with ABC-Dunhill, and Khan followed them out to California. Their debut LP, *Rufus,* was released in 1973 to scant notice and little commercial success. During the recording of a second release,

recent Grammy Award-winner Stevie Wonder showed up one day at the Torrance studio, much to the astonishment of the band. The visit would spark Rufus's first hit, the Grammy-winning "Tell Me Something Good." Khan recalled the event in a 1974 interview with Jay Grossman of *Rolling Stone.* "[Wonder] sat down at the clavinet, y'know, and just wrote the song.... The first tune that he laid down, y'know, the first rhythm track, I said, `I don't like that one so much.' And it seemed as though he was a little upset over that, and I thought, `Well, a lot of people must not say that to him!' So he said, `What's your birth sign?' I said `Aries-Pisces,' and he said, `Oh, well here's a song for you.'"

After members of Rufus wrote lyrics for the track, Khan began to sing the "Tell Me Something Good" in her own style, but Wonder, still at the studio, interrupted. "NO NO NO!" In the *Rolling Stone* interview with Grossman, Khan recalled him protesting, "`Sing it like this!' And it turned out for the better." She continued, "I don't know what would have happened if I'd done it myself, but just him being there—I'd been loving this guy for like 10 years." Khan was nine months pregnant when she recorded the LP; they exited the studio on December 17, 1973, and she gave birth to daughter Milini four days later.

"Tell Me Something Good" catapulted Khan and Rufus to instant stardom, complete with gold records on their living-room walls, a Grammy, sold-out tours—and the accompanying heady lifestyle. Khan soon gained a reputation as a wild child of the 1970s. To *Essence*'s Wilkerson, Khan described those drug-fueled days of her life as a "runaway carriage, the reins flying." Much of it she only knows through others' accounts of her behavior. Discussing the possibility of an autobiography, the singer told Wilkerson that "I need to get a hypnotist, okay? I'm trying to write my life story, and it's like we're going to have to call in a professional at some point and put me in a trance because it's deep."

Despite the substance abuse problems, Khan still went on to record several hit albums with Rufus during the 1970s, such as *Rufus Featuring Chaka Khan.* Her career was her saving grace, she told Bagley in *Essence.* "Throughout all my whimsical flights, I have never let anything get completely away from me," Khan said. "Music has always been a grounding factor for me. It has been my one reality check. Even when my head was in the clouds, I always had at least one foot on the ground. That's why I'm alive today."

Solo Efforts Met with Further Acclaim

In 1978 Khan made a successful transition to a solo recording career when she signed with Warner Brothers.

Her solo debut came later that year with *Chaka Khan,* an overwhelming hit buoyed by its first single, "I'm Every Woman." She continued to record several solo efforts, achieving a minor hit in 1981 with *Whatcha Gonna Do for Me?* However, Khan preferred to make scat and jazz-influenced records instead of straightforward, commercial R&B, until Warner Brothers insisted on a more mainstream sound in 1984 when it came time for her to record her sixth solo effort. Khan remembered a song called "I Feel for You" by Prince that appeared on his second album in 1979. Her producer modernized it a bit for her, bringing in Stevie Wonder to blow harp and Grandmaster Melle Mel, then one of the biggest names in the breaking rap scene, to add his own distinctive voice to the mix.

"I Feel for You" was an overwhelming success upon release, charting in the Top Five, and perhaps best remembered for Melle Mel's distinctive triple-fast "Cha-ka Khan" rap. Khan recalled the moment she first heard it in an interview with *Rolling Stone*'s Debby Bull. After laying down her own vocals, Khan went into the studio the next day and listened to the new version. "I thought `Oh, God.' It was great, yes, except for how am I going to live this down? Every time a guy walks up to me on the street, I think he's going to break into that rap. And most of them do." The album, also entitled *I Feel for You,* won Khan her third Grammy and was her biggest success to date.

By this time Khan was living in New York City with Milini and son Damien, born in 1979. She was married a second time briefly in the 1970s but during the mid-1980s was romantically involved with a Harlem schoolteacher who had originally tutored her daughter: "His salary is no-where near mine, but he still brings his money in. He didn't give up his job like my other two husbands did— immediately stop work and groove and say, `My work is now you,'" Khan told Bull in *Rolling Stone.* "No woman wants to hear that. A woman wants to wake up in the morning to the smell of aftershave lotion and not see anybody there."

Khan Found Peace Abroad

Still single, Khan relocated her family to London at the onset of the 1990s after stopping briefly there on a tour and falling in love with the city. She also thought it would be a better environment in which to bring up her teenage son. "Right now in America there's a bounty on young Black boys," Khan told Wilkerson in *Essence.* "And I want him to get some kind of quality education, to speak other languages and live until he's 20 at least." Other members of her family stay for extended periods, including Milini with Khan's granddaughter Raeven, Khan's father from Chicago and sister Yvonne, who followed her older sister into the music business in the 1970s as Taka Boom.

Khan continues to record, and has done a number of works for the soundtracks of popular movies. For the Wesley Snipes/Patrick Swayze film *To Wong Foo: Thanks for Everything, Julie Newmar,* Khan contributed "Free Yourself." She also sang "Love Me Still," the theme song for the 1995 Spike Lee film *Clockers.* The singer also considers making a transition from singer to actress via a television sitcom, perhaps inspired by seeing her contemporary Patti LaBelle excel in the medium. In early 1995 Khan did a stint on the London stage as Sister Carrie in the gospel musical *Mama, I Want to Sing.* She hobnobs in aristocratic circles and enjoys a cult-like following in Europe, where she tours occasionally to great success. Khan seems happy to have grown up, settled down, cleaned up, and found an inner peace. Of that last personal achievement, the singer explained to Wilkerson that "it's a place you evolve to, not a place you go to consciously, you dig? You wake up better and better. Sometimes you slip. Basically, you just live."

Selected discography

(With Rufus) *Rufus,* 1973.
(With Rufus) *From Rags to Rufus,* 1973.
(With Rufus) *Rufus Featuring Chaka Khan,* mid-1970s.
Chaka Khan, 1979.
Whatcha Gonna Do for Me?, 1981.
I Feel for You, mid-1980s.

Sources

Essence, January 1986, p. 69; October 1995, p. 84.
Rolling Stone, October 24, 1974, p. 17; February 14, 1985, p. 11.

—*Carol Brennan*

Dave Koz

Saxophonist

Photo by Henry Diltz/MICHAEL OCHS ARCHIVES/Venice, CA

It is an extremely rare occurrence, within the music industry, that an artist is critically acknowledged at the very beginning of his or her career. However, occasionally one musician's work stands out among thousands of releases presented that year and that artist achieves not only success but personal growth and the respect of his or her peers as well. Dave Koz may very well be one of Adult Contemporary Jazz's greatest success stories and perhaps one of its most inspirational.

Impassioned by music at a young age, Koz recalls being captivated by the soaring horn section of his favorite band, Tower of Power. However it may have been older brother Jeff who was most directly responsible for Dave's progression from fan to performer. When he was just 13, Dave watched his older sibling, a guitarist, lead his own band vigorously around the wedding, bar-mitzvah, and fraternity circuits. Tempted by a need for pocket cash and figuring it was more enterprising than a part-time career in fast food, the younger Koz begged to be a part of the group. Since the ensemble was missing a consistent saxophone player, Jeff insisted if Dave learned the instrument and rehearsed he could join. Practicing fiendishly, Dave eventually obtained the much-coveted spot with the group. "I remember that wedding like it was yesterday," Koz jokingly told *USA Today.* "Everybody got paid $100 and I got paid $10 and I've been getting back at my brother ever since." Koz progressed on his instrument by studying privately, playing with high school bands and—what he considers his most prized way of learning—blowing along to favorite records, such as James Taylor's *Mud Slide Slim and the Blue Horizon.* Koz also cites Pat Metheny, Stevie Wonder, Tom Scott, David Sanborn, Michael Breckner and Tower of Power as cherished influences.

Level-headed and uncertain about the future, while Koz was studying the saxophone and performing a wide range of music with his brother's band, he was simultaneously working towards a degree in Mass Communications at the University of California, Los Angeles. After graduation in 1986, the ambitious musician gave himself an intriguing option. Rather than heading straight for an office and a possible business career, Koz allowed himself six months to see if he could gain any attention as a professional musician or at least earn a living. Fate and perseverance took hold of the situation and within a few weeks he received a welcome call from vocalist Bobby Caldwell to join his band. "That was a great gig," Koz told the *Jazz Times.* "Bobby is like the singer's singer and those gigs were attended by everybody in the music business; singers, musicians, record company people. So it was great way to get exposure."

From Sideman to Solo

The exposure generated from those shows helped garner the attention of Jeff Lorber. Highly impressed by Koz's now obvious abilities, Lorber recruited the burgeoning saxophonist to join his touring band. In a peculiar twist, it was at Lorber's insistence that Koz first considered pursuing a solo career. Lorber and Caldwell both helped Koz to create the demo tapes which caught the attention of Capitol Records

Dave Koz's self-titled debut was released on October 10, 1990. It established Koz as a highly respectable and personable figure in the area of contemporary jazz. Bridging stylistically between the languid flow of adult contemporary and modern jazz, Koz's musical category is debatable. Koz also questions his own categorization. As he explained to the *Jazz Times*, "Because you play the saxophone, people automatically assume you're a jazz musician and they kind of get down on contemporary sax players because they say it's jazz-lite. I agree that it's not as challenging or complex, but you know, it's music that's honestly from me and it's real for me.... The public is not dumb. People can pick up when it's real or not. I think as long as an artist is true to themselves and making music that's vibrant and a true reflection of who they are, then whatever style it is, its okay."

Only twenty-six at the time of his debut, Koz managed to impress and delight a music-loving public. His debut album received gracious critical praise as well as varied prestigious triumphs. Internationally, *Dave Koz* managed to achieve double platinum status in Malaysia and gold status in Singapore. He also landed a number-one single in the Philippines, Malaysia, and Hong Kong with the melodic, breezy, "Emily." In the States there were equally dynamic accomplishments. His first album spent 25 weeks on *Billboard's* contemporary music chart and gave birth to the prolific saxophonist's first number-one single "Nothing But the Radio On." *Dave Koz* reached number eight on *Billboard's* list of top contemporary jazz recordings for the year. With the record's success, the talented Koz was offered a wide array of opportunities that not were not only due to his musical abilities but additionally attributable to his warm and affable personality.

Part of "The Posse"

In 1991 and 1992, Koz regularly sat in with the *Arsenio Hall Show* house band, The Posse. The now-defunct late-night talk show was hosted by vibrant comedian Arsenio Hall and seen throughout the United States. Koz appeared in over eighty episodes. The prolific young musician also appeared on the soap opera *General Hospital*, ABC'S prime time sitcom, *Family Matters* and teen television hit, *Beverly Hills 90210.*

In 1993 the saxophonist released his second album, entitled *Lucky Man.* The record not only achieved more impressive sales figures than his first effort, it also brought Koz under the glow of the music industry's limelight. *Lucky Man* spent an impressive two years on *Billboard's* jazz contemporary charts, achieving RIAA certified gold status. Partly responsible was the single "Faces of the Heart" (co-written by Jeff Koz), as it became the first new theme in twenty years for the soap opera *General Hospital.* Koz launched his first solo tour in 1993, playing 132 dates, where he performed for sold-out crowds and had the opportunity to warm the stages for both Kenny Loggins and Michael Bolton.

Idol Chatter

Koz was granted a unique opportunity to be on the other side of the mike when he became the host of *Personal Notes with Dave Koz.* The two-hour weekly adult alternative radio show debuted on January 21, 1995. As he told Phyllis Stark of *Billboard* magazine, "It's sort of intimidating to get behind a mike when you don't have a saxophone. The concern is, is there enough inside me to make this interesting?" His doubts proved unnecessary, however, since the show, which is syndicated by Sony Worldwide networks, has become extremely popular and is broadcast from over 100 different stations. On the air, Koz's insight as an artist helps to initiate interesting interviews with prestigious musical peers such as Al Jarreau, Stanley Clark, and Anita Baker. Even though quite a successful musician himself, Koz has not lost his ability to be a fan. In many magazine interviews, Koz cites one of the highlights of his career as being able to perform along with such legendary musicians as Grover Washington Jr. and Tom Scott at President Clinton's Inaugural Ball. On *Personal Notes,* when given the opportunity to interview one of his idols, David Sanborn, Koz humbly explained to *Billboard,* "Half the interview was me gushing. He finally told me to stop. It's kind of funny and fun to be able to be put in that position. I've had two successful records, but I still consider myself a new kid on the block." Koz generally records *Personal Notes* from his home; however, when he is away the network outfits him with gear to record the show on the road.

A Different Path

For all that Koz has accomplished at such a young age, the musician does seem to carry some slight regrets. When asked by Cheryl Lavin of the *Chicago Tribune Magazine* what he would do over if he could, Koz replied, "I would have spent my 20s working more on who I am as opposed to what I do." With a hectic tour schedule, a radio show, and the many appearances that he has made in the course of his career, Koz has found he has been left with little personal time. After *Lucky Man,* he felt that both a personal and musical change were in order. He moved from his long-time home of Los Angeles to northern California in an effort to slow down the pace of his frantic schedule. He explained the move to *Smooth Notes* magazine: "I'm thirty-three, and I'm after balance in my life. After ten years or so of going through life with blinders on—worrying about making records. . . . Other than being concerned with the health and happiness of my family, all I thought about was working. I think there's more to life than selling records and touring, and I kinda think I got away from that. I wanted to refocus my life'"

Koz's album *Off the Beaten Path* (Capitol Records 1996) was almost a direct result of his deviation both physically and mentally from his earlier career path. Instead of being under the disguising layer of synthesizers and drum machines, the record displays a more vulnerable folksy quality. Instruments not necessarily associated with jazz, such as mandolins, harmonicas, and various guitars, changed Koz's sound for this recording. "This is a new sound for both me and my

listeners," Koz explained to *Jazziz* magazine, "It's a logical progression from my earlier music. This isn't change for the sake of change, or jumping on any kind of bandwagon. I truly feel this sound found me." The record also boasted Koz's first vocal effort as well as a guest appearance by former Fleetwood Mac diva Stevie Nicks. Dave Koz explains to *Jazz Flyte* magazine about the change in his work, "while I am proud of my last two records—they're very good records, good songwriting and good playing. I think for me a lot of it was hiding behind technology. I tend to come from a school of naturally over production where you put the string pad and the bells and the whistles on. When you put all that stuff on, the saxophone becomes smaller and smaller. I think it was really fear of being vulnerable. Not that I would've attached that label to it in the past. But now, in retrospect, I look at it and say I was afraid to let it all hang out. On this record there was a real conscious effort, from the very first time we started, to make the saxophone really *vulnerable.* To let it out, surround it with instruments that really complement it and not just populate the listening field. I wanted to give it a new complementary sound. That theme goes through this record".

While *Off the Beaten Path* was a change for Koz, it still managed to provoke an audience response. Both "Let Me Count The Ways and "Don't Look Back" have become radio hits. Dave Koz continues to remain a talent and beloved personality in the world of adult contemporary music.

Selected discography

Dave Koz, Capitol Records, 1990.
Lucky Man, Capitol Records, 1993.
Off the Beaten Path, Capitol Records, 1996

Sources

Periodicals

Billboard, April 1, 1995; July 13, 1996, p. 14; September 7, 1996.
Cash Box, August 31, 1996, p. 5.
Chicago Tribune Magazine, September 8, 1996, section 10.
Jazz Flyte, August 1996, p. 5.
Jazz Times, December 1996.
Jazziz, December 1996, p. 24; January 1997.
Smooth Notes, 1996.
USA Today, October 16, 1996.

Online

www.davekoz@aol.com
Press information provided by Capitol Records and the Mitch
Schneider Organization.

—Nicole Elyse

Barbara Lamb

Fiddler

Photo courtesy of Sugar Hill Records. Reproduced by permission.

Barbara Lamb was born in Seattle, Washington, on January 14, 1958. Her father was a music teacher and a musician, and he opened the door to Lamb's view of music. They listened to all types of music, including square dance music. When she was seven years old, Lamb's parents would take her to the local square dance every Friday night. It was there that she first heard old-time fiddling. She loved it so much that at eight years old she picked up her first fiddle and started lessons. Lamb cites her influences as Kenny Baker and Byron Burline, Bill Monroe, Jim and Jessie, and her own fiddling teacher, Vivian Williams.

Though she does sing, Lamb does not profess to be a vocalist. She prefers to be called a fiddler who likes to sing a little bit, as opposed to a singer who fiddles a little bit. She has always sung in every band she has been in, but she is more of a harmony singer, only taking the occasional lead.

Lamb's dream was to move to Nashville. She told herself that if she didn't move before she turned 40, she would never get there. Six months after moving to Nashville, Lamb relocated again, this time to Austin, Texas to do a 12 month tour with Asleep at the Wheel. She was there almost a year and a half, moving back to Nashville in 1996. In addition to performing on the road with Asleep at the Wheel, Lamb also performed with the Seattle band Ranch Romance on Sugar Hill Records. Lamb left Ranch Romance in December 1993, stating that it was just a natural ending, a "time to move on" kind of feeling. It was a good parting and the band members have remained very close, which Lamb feels makes it great because it leaves the door open for reunion gigs. (The members of the band collectively agreed that they should be broken up for about three years before they started hitting the reunion circuit. They feared people would think they never actually broke up if they started playing together sooner than that.)

Lamb was with Ranch Romance for seven years but is now strictly a freelance player. In 1996 she did some shows with two Nashville bands, Riders in the Sky and a blue grass band called Continental Divide. For the most part, Lamb tries not to go out on the road often. She has her own deal with Sugar Hill Records which affords her the luxury to tour and play under her own name. While on tour or in the recording studio, she hires a guitar player and a bass player to accompany her; but she mostly stays at home in Nashville working as a freelance producer, session player, and occasional substitute.

As a solo artist, Lamb feels it's her energy that makes people relate to her music. She states that she is very

For the Record . . .

Born January 14, 1958, in Seattle, WA; married in 1984 but divorced shortly after

Addresses: *Home*—Nashville, TN. *Record company*—Sugar Hill, P.O. Box 55300, Durham, NC 27717-5300; phone (919) 489-4349.

energetic on stage and feels that it comes out on recordings as well. Lamb's music can be generally categorized as country/folk or bluegrass. Lamb believes that if somebody states that they hate country music, they aren't necessarily saying they don't like bluegrass. They are usually referring to what they hear on top-forty radio. Bluegrass is acoustic music that is vocally driven; no drums. It always has bass, banjo, guitar, and either mandolin or a fiddle or both. Lamb states that sometimes people call it the "high lonesome sound", because bluegrass singing tends to be in a high vocal register for both men and women.

Lamb is planning some work with Laura Love, which will be her first venture outside the world of country. Lamb recorded on all three of Love's records but has never performed with her. Lamb feels Love plays really great African rhythms and she is very excited to do more work with her. Lamb has also said she would love to tour with Emmylou Harris. She has always liked Harris and her choice of music. On a grander scale, Lamb would like to tour with Sting and do something in a very large pop vein.

Lamb also hopes to do more producing, including soundtracks for film. She feels that producing is like being a teacher and likes the idea of being able to use different instruments that she does not play—such as all types of percussion—to bring about a musical texture. She particularly likes working with visuals for soundtracks. Though she is steering towards producing, Lamb wants to be able to do it all, creating a nice balance of performing, producing, and working as a freelance session player in Nashville.

Lamb's newest business venture is a Nashville-based song writing camp. It is a camp for adults and happens during the first week of September. Musicians camp out in a rustic cabin in Montgomeryville State Park and study every day with hit song writers from Nashville. The school will also teach mandolin, banjo, guitar and fiddling. Lamb doesn't call it a bluegrass camp, but all the instruments being taught are in the bluegrass vein. Lamb will be one of the teachers for fiddling.

With all these irons in the fire, Barbara Lamb is building a very successful career and enjoying every minute of it.

Selected Discography

Sources

Online

www.tpoint.net/~wallen/country/twangin1.txt-
www.dne.wvnet.edu/augusta/workshops/themes/
workshop/bluegrass.html
www.musicblvd.com

Interview with Barbara Lamb, March 1997

—Robyn Weiss

Lisa Loeb

Pop guitarist, singer, songwriter

Photo by Ken Settle. Reproduced by permission

Lisa Loeb's talent as a folk/pop rock musician was brought into the mainstream with her "discovery" in 1994. Loeb's neighbor and friend, actor Ethan Hawke, admired her songs and brought a tape of her song "Stay" to movie producer Ben Stiller. At the time, Stiller was producing the movie *Reality Bites,* in which Hawke starred. Stiller added the song to the movie soundtrack, and Loeb made history. She became the first unsigned artist to reach number one on the Billboard pop chart with the single "Stay."

Even though her trademark tortoise-shell, horn-rimmed glasses look like a signature fashion statement, Loeb insists they are necessary. Contact lenses cannot correct her vision. She told *Seventeen,* "My glasses are a normal and real part of me. They aren't an act. I'd be selling out if I didn't wear them." She believes the glasses, her college education, and wordy lyrics contribute to her "nerdy" image, but that's fine with her. She thinks nerds are the most interesting people.

Lisa Loeb was born in 1968 and grew up in Dallas. Her father is a doctor; her mother a homemaker. Loeb started playing the piano at a young age, but then took guitar lessons in junior high so she could imitate Andy Summers of The Police. When she switched to guitar, she also began writing her own songs. For 12 years, Loeb attended The Hockaday School in Dallas, a very discipline-oriented prep school. She excelled there, finding the academic challenge rewarding. She was an honor student and student council president while acting in school plays, performing music, and disc jockeying at a local school FM station. She then attended Brown University, studying comparative literature and Spanish literature. At Brown, her roommate Liz was also a singer. They formed a duo, Lisa and Liz, and performed around campus with acoustic guitars and their own folk songs. In 1990, she graduated from Brown and moved to New York.

After college, Loeb briefly took voice lessons and studied for a summer at the Berklee School of Music in Boston. She was eager to perform, though, and began touring with Liz. They eventually formed a band, called Nine Stories, but after a year of lineup changes, Liz ultimately parted with the band. Loeb's first studio recording came in December of 1992. It did not include her band because they were taking a break while their drummer toured with the band They Might Be Giants" During this hiatus she met Juan Patiño, a record engineer and producer, and they recorded *The Purple Acoustic Tape,* available for sale only at her shows. Loeb continued to play the smoky coffeehouse scene in New York solo and with her band.

With the band Nine Stories, "Stay" was released in 1994 on the *Reality Bites* soundtrack, produced and engineered by Juan Patiño, Loeb's boyfriend at the time. "Stay" was inspired by an argument between her and Patiño. She told *Seventeen*, "I think that's what art is all about-taking a little truth and turning it into a good story." Loeb managed to shrewdly own the master tape of "Stay," so RCA paid to lease the song for the soundtrack. When the single hit the top of the charts, the major record companies came calling. Loeb earned a Grammy nomination for best new artist. The single eventually went gold, selling nearly a million copies. Six of the biggest labels wanted to sign her to a contract. After being wined and dined by all six, Loeb finally chose Geffen, an alternative music label (representing Hole among others), and they gave her an advance to record an album.

One of the surprising aspects of Loeb's career is the fact that her album *Tails* was not released until September 1995—an entire year after the success of "Stay." That fact did not surprise or trouble the executives at Geffen, though. The album started from scratch, and the collaborating team of Loeb and Patiño is meticulous, if not perfectionist, in their record-making effort. What Loeb thought would take a month in the studio took much longer because they were so detailed in their approach.

Geffen understood that Loeb also had to fulfill promotional obligations for "Stay."

Music for the Masses

When Geffen released her album in September 1995, they had the task of promoting an artist who was not proven in her ability to sell an entire album, but whose single had sold nearly a million copies. Loeb told *Billboard* magazine that she hoped "success at top 40 won't preclude airplay at college radio." Loeb feels that her music is right for a college audience—her lyrics have often been labeled "dormitory." Her image remained bookish—especially with the acknowledgment that her band was named after a J. D. Salinger collection of short stories.

The critics gave mixed reviews to *Tails*. Andrew Abrams in *People* wrote, "She tries to meld a kind of soft-grunge electric sound and her more comfortable coffeehouse-on-campus folk guitar style with varying effect." Rolf Rykken of *Critics' Choice* remarked, "While she lacks the edge of Alanis Morissette, she is eminently listenable." Gina Arnold of *Metro* wrote that the album "is not a striking effort in any way." She added, "Loeb is the queen of the undamaged psyche, the princess of bedroom poetry." Arnold described Loeb's style, saying she "has a high, pretty soprano voice and a sure way with a melody." Parke Puterbaugh of *Stereo Review* wrote, "Loeb braids folk and pop into a fetching union, singing in a breathy, insistent voice that has a lovely, limpid timbre."

Changes in the Band

Lisa Loeb & Nine Stories toured to promote their album. However, Loeb and Patiño replaced two of the original three bandmembers. The band that appeared on the album included Tim Bright on electric guitars, Jonathan Feinberg on drums/percussion, and Joe Quigley on bass. Only Quigley remained on tour—joined by Mark Spencer on lead guitar, and Ronny Crawford on drums. Juan Patiño told *Entertainment Weekly*, "Nine Stories is a revolving door." Jane Stevenson of the *Toronto Sun* rated one of their concerts a four out of five and commented that Loeb has a number of assets, including: a powerful voice, accomplished guitar playing, and a composed intelligence and sense of humor.

In 1996, Loeb wrote a new song for the *Twister* movie soundtrack and she appeared very briefly—for about ten seconds—in a film starring Donnie Wahlberg titled *Black Circle Boys*. With Loeb's varied background and talent, her future looks bright.

Selected discography

Albums

Purple Acoustic Tape, produced by Juan Patiño, December, 1992.
Naked Rhythm (compilation), Steam Records, August, 1993.
SXSW Live Vol. Two (compilation), March, 1994.
Mud on the Wheel (compilation), Earth Music/Cargo Records, July, 1994.
Reality Bites (soundtrack), RCA, 1994.
Tails, Geffen Records, September, 1995.

Sources

Billboard, August 5, 1995.
Critics' Choice, November 13, 1995.
Entertainment Weekly, October 6, 1995.
Madamoiselle, September, 1995.
New York, September, 1995.
People, October 2, 1995.
Seventeen, April, 1995.
Stereo Review, February, 1996.
Toronto Sun, December 20, 1995.

Additional information provided by the Lisa Loeb website at http://www.geffen.com.

—*Christine Morrison*

Frank Loesser

Composer, lyricist

APWide World Photos. Reproduced by permission.

When Broadway legend Frank Loesser died in 1969, he left behind a remarkable legacy: five musicals, including *Guys and Dolls,* and numerous hit songs sung by some of Hollywood's biggest stars in over 60 motion pictures. Loesser was as talented as he was prolific, many of his songs became standards in the repertoire of singers such as Frank Sinatra. Loesser won multiple Tony awards, an Oscar, and the Pulitzer Prize. The success he enjoyed during his lifetime has endured even after his death. In 1992, a full 23 years after Loesser's death, *Guys and Dolls* was revived on Broadway and won the Tony Award for Best Revival. A glowing review of that revival, in *New York* magazine, stated "The show has radiantly renewed the New York-Broadway love affair that used to be the symbol of the city's vitality."

Loesser grew up in New York surrounded by music. His father was a classical piano teacher and his uncle was both a respected pianist and a music critic. Loesser's burgeoning love of popular music was not well received by his family. By the time Loesser was in his early teens, he played both the harmonica and the piano. He was largely self-taught and was never to study the classical music loved by his father.

After high school, Loesser attended City College of New York. He abandoned his studies when the Depression hit, and for the next several years he held a variety jobs, among them, newspaper ad salesman and city editor for a New Rochelle, New York newspaper. It was during this stint as an editor that Loesser began writing sketches and radio scripts.

First Published Song Lyrics

Loesser's first published song lyrics were "In Love With a Memory of You," which he co-wrote with the future president of Juilliard School of Music, the noted composer William Schuman. Loesser worked in vaudeville and was involved with the *Ziegfield Follies of 1934,*

With Louis Hersher, Loesser wrote the lyrics and music for the film *Poetic Gems* in 1936. Around this time Loesser was doing a nightclub act, singing and playing the piano, in collaboration with the composer Irving Actman. The duo's contribution to *The Illustrators' Show* on Broadway in 1936 got the attention of Hollywood. This earned Loesser a contract with Universal Studios. Loesser made the move west and ultimately landed at Paramount.

In 1937, Loesser and Alfred Newman collaborated on the song "The Moon of Mankoora" for the picture *Hurricane,* That year he also worked on *The Mysterious Crossing,*

For the Record . . .

Born June 29, 1910 in New York, NY; died July 26, 1969 in New York, NY; married twice; second wife's name, Jo Sullivan,

Awards: Tony awards for Best Musical, Best Score, Best Actor, Best Director, Best Supporting Actress, Best Choreographer, Best Book, 1950, for *Guys and Dolls*.

Three Smart Girls and *Turkey Dinner.* In 1938 Loesser worked with Hoagy Carmichael, Burton Lane, and Manning Sherwin on the films *College Swing, Men with Wings,* and *Thanks for the Memory.* In 1939, Loesser did the Lawrence Welk theme song, "Bubbles In The Wine" with Bob Calame and worked on the movies *Beau Geste, Destry Rides Again, Some Like It Hot,* and *St. Louis Blues.*

Begins Composing Music

When war broke out, Loesser found himself for the first time without a partner. Assigned to the Special Services division, Loesser was charged with providing lyrics for military troop shows. During his service, he worked with other composers and now began composing for himself. The result of his first solo effort was a hit, "Praise the Lord and Pass the Ammunition" (1942), and the start of a long and successful career as both composer and writer. Loesser would soon enough be regarded as "more than just another pop tune writer from Hollywood."

Loesser continued to write for motion pictures, including *Let's Dance, Neptune's Daughter, Red, Hot And Blue* (Loesser made his only on-screen appearance here as the piano-playing gangster), *Hans Christian Anderson,* and *My Son John.* Additionally, in the late 1940s, he formed Frank Music Corp. through which he strove to identify and develop up-and-coming composers and lyricists. Jerry Ross, Richard Adler and Meredith Wilson, successful theater songwriters from the 1950s, are just three of the many talents whose careers were given a boost by Frank Music Corp.

Broadway Career

Loesser's enormously successful career on Broadway commenced after the war when he was persuaded to create the music for *Where's Charley?* This musical, produced by Ernest Martin and Cy Feuer, opened on October 11, 1948, and was a smash. Two years later

Loesser wrote the score for *Guys and Dolls,* a musical adaptation of Damon Runyan's fictional world of card-sharks, cheats, molls, and mobsters. *Guys and Dolls* opened on November 24, 1950 to critical acclaim. The musical cleaned up at the Tony Awards, winning the Best Musical, Best Score, Best Actor, Best Director, Best Supporting Actress, Best Choreographer and Best Book categories.

Loesser's next project was even more ambitious. He wrote both the score and the book for *The Most Happy Fella.* During the production, Frank had a sign made reading "Loud is Good" to remind the cast how he wanted the songs done. The play opened May 3, 1956 and ran for the next two years. *Fella* contained the hits "Standing on the Corner" and "Big D" and Columbia Records released a complete recording of the musical from start to finish. A first. It was during the run of *The Most Happy Fella* that Loesser fell in love with his leading lady, Jo Sullivan, who was to become his second wife.

Loesser was never content to repeat himself and his third Broadway endeavor was *Greenwillow,* a kind of "country music fable." Though it was nominated for several Tony Awards, it was not the success Loesser hoped it to be and it closed in 1960 after 95 shows. *Greenwillow* did, however, produce a hit some years later, when the song "Never Will I Marry" was covered by Barbra Streisand.

Undaunted by the disappointing reception to *Greenwillow,* Loesser undertook what was to be his next smash hit. On October 14, 1961, *How to Succeed in Business without Really Trying* opened on Broadway. It was a huge success and ran for the next four years. The Pulitzer Prize-winning production included the hits "I Believe in You" and "Brotherhood of Man." The show also took seven Tonys, including Best Musical.

Singers were especially important to Loesser. He worked with some of the best on Broadway and in Hollywood. He was a perfectionist and had a precise idea of how his songs should be sung. He viewed the singers primarily as an "instrument through which he spoke to an audience". The strength of Loesser's opinions regarding how his music should be performed led to a falling out with Frank Sinatra, resulting in a lifelong grudge. Loesser's temper got the better of him on more than one occasion, leading to physical violence and, in one case, to leaving a show for a period. In the biography of her father, Susan Loesser has written "Singers had a strong effect on my father. He reviled them or he adored them or he married them." Both Loesser's wives were actress/singers.

A constant breakneck pace enabled Loesser to accomplish a phenomenal amount of superior and lasting work in his 59 years. It was a rare occasion that Loesser slept more than four hours at a time. The fruits of this labor are evident in the lasting quality of his work. In addition to the revival of *Guys and Dolls*, the nineties has seen a revival of *How to Succeed in Business without Really Trying*.

Frank Music Corp. is still in business and there have been recent releases of Loesser's music *An Evening with Frank Loesser*, a collection of demos from three of his Broadway shows, and *Loesser by Loesser*, a compilation of pieces sung by Jo Sullivan Loesser and family. Loesser's daughter Susan has published a biography of her father, *A Most Remarkable Fella* and as long as standards are played on the radio, Loesser's music will remain in the public consciousness.

Selected discography

Stage Shows

Zeigfield Follies of 1934, 1934.
The Illustrator's Show, 1950.
Guys and Dolls, 1950.
The Most Happy Fella, 1956.
Greenwillow, 1960.
How to Succeed in Business without Really Trying, 1961.
Pleasures and Palaces, 1965.
Senior Discretion (unproduced), 1969.

Films

Poetic Gems, 1934.
The Man I Marry, 1936.
Postal Inspector, 1936.
Blossoms on Broadway, 1937.
The Duck Hunt, 1937.
Everybody Sings, 1937.
The Golfers, 1937.
The Hurricane, 1937.
The Mysterious Crossing, 1937.
Three Smart Girls, 1937.
Turkey Dinner, 1937.
Vogues of 1938, 1937.
Yellowstone, 1937.
Coconut Grove, 1938.
College Swing, 1938.
Fight for Your Lady, 1938.
Freshman Year, 1938.
Give Me a Sailor, 1938.
Men with Wings, 1938.
Sing You Sinners, 1938.
A Song is Born, 1938.
Spawn of the North, 1938.
Stolen Heaven, 1938.

The Texans, 1938.
Thanks for the Memory, 1938.
$1,000 a Touchdown, 1939.
Beau Geste, 1939.
Cafe Society, 1939.
Dance with the Devil, 1939.
Destry Rides Again,
The Gracie Allen Murder Case, 1939.
Hawaiian Nights, 1939.
Heritage of the Desert, 1939.
Invitation to Happiness, 1939.
Island of Lost Men, 1939.
The Llano Kid, 1939.
Man about Town, 1939.
Some Like it Hot, 1939.
St. Louis Blues, 1939.
The Star Maker, 1939.
Zaza, 1939.
Adventures in Diamonds, 1940.
All Women Have Secrets, 1940.
At Good Old Siwash, 1940.
Buck Benny Rides Again, 1940.
The Farmer's Daughter, 1940.
The Great Victor Herbert, 1940.
Dancing for Nickels and Dimes, 1940.
Moon over Burma, 1940.
A Night at Earl Carroll's, 1940.
Northwest Mounted Police, 1940.
The Quarterback, 1940.
The Road to Singapore, 1940.
Seven Singers, 1940.
Seventeen, 1940.
Typhoon, 1940.
Youth Will be Served, 1940.
Aloma of the South Seas, 1941
Arizona Sketches, 1941.
Birth of the Blues, 1941.
Caught in the Draft, 1941.
Dancing on a Dime, 1941.
Glamour Boy, 1941.
Henry for President, 1941.
Hold Back the Dawn, 1941.
Kiss the Boys Goodbye, 1941.
Las Vegas Nights, 1941.
Manpower, 1941.
Mr. Bug Goes to Town, 1941.
Sailors on Leave, 1941.
Sis Hopkins, 1941.
There's Magic in Music, 1941.
World Premiere, 1941.
Beyond the Blue Horizon, 1942.
The Forest Rangers, 1942.
Priorities on Parade, 1942.
Reap the Wild Wind, 1942.
Seven Days Leave, 1942.
Sweater Girl, 1942.

This Gun for Hire, 1942.
Tortilla Flat, 1942.
True to the Army, 1942.
Army Show, 1943.
Happy-Go-Lucky, 1943.
Riding High, 1943.
Thank Your Lucky Stars, 1943.
About Face, 1944.
And the Angels Sing, 1944.
Christmas Holiday, 1944.
Duffy's Tavern, 1944.
Heavenly Days, 1944.
Hi, Yank, 1944.
See Here, Private Hargrove, 1944.
The Shining Future, 1944.
Skirts, 1944.
Tornado, 1944.
The W.A.C. Musical, 1944.
Behind City Lights, 1945.
The Day Before Spring, 1946.
Lady Called Lou, 1946.
Strange Triangle, 1946.
A Miracle Can Happen, 1947.
The Perils of Pauline, 1947.

Variety Girl, 1947.
Lady from Lariat Loop, 1948.
Let's Dance, 1948.
Neptune's Daughter, 1948.
Where's Charley, 1948.
Red, Hot, and Blue, 1949.
Roseanna McCoy, 1949.
The College Bowl, 1951.
Hans Christian Anderson, 1952.
My Son John, 1952.
Guys and Dolls, 1955.
The Trouble with Harry, 1952.
How to Succeed in Business without Really Trying, 1966.

Sources

Books

The Frank Loesser Songbook, Frank Music Corp., DATE?
Loesser, Susan, *The Most Happy Fella,* Penguin Books, 1994.

—*Kevin O'Sullivan*

Luscious Jackson

Rock band

Jill Cunniff told the *Detroit Free Press* of her band, Luscious Jackson, "People are always telling us, 'I don't know how to describe it and where to put it, ... We're just making this music, y'know—it's just about liking music and being able to dance to it and having a great time." The group, which began when bassist-singer Cunniff and guitarist-singer Gabby Glaser created some homemade recordings, has evolved into a foursome that melds alternative rock, hip hop, soul and virtually every other genre into an unclassifiable stew. "I like the fact that people can't really label us," Glaser confirmed in the online magazine *Intune.*

Glaser, Cunniff and drummer Kate Schellenbach grew up in New York City, absorbing everything from punk rock to rap with equal voraciousness. Glaser and Cunniff were pals from adolescence on. "We wanted to attract attention," Cunniff told Chris Heath of *Details.* "We made a spectacle of ourselves—the way we dressed, the way we danced, the music we liked." Eventually they met Schellenbach, and the three got more and more involved in the developing punk rock scene. "We saw a lot of great bands [together], but we also dug early hip hop," Schellenbach said in a Grand Royal records publicity interview. "It was very connected to growing up in the public school system; party music without a lot of meaning, that played with words and breakbeats. The cool kids in high school were into hip hop, and we'd learn all the rhymes. There was great dancing, and graffiti art. It was very New York."

Beastie Girls and New Ventures

By her teens, Schellenbach was playing drums for a punkish New York rap/rock band called The Beastie Boys. Yet when the group hooked up with rising record maven Rick Rubin, they fired her; Rubin disliked the idea of a female rapper. "I was mad but I really repressed it," she recalled. Glaser and Cunniff knew members of the band, too, from the New York scene, and had played with Beastie Mike D. in a group called the Young Aboriginies; relations with the Beastie Boys would be patched up later on—in grand style.

Cunniff went to school in California, while Glaser went abroad. When they returned to New York, they began playing music together. Their mutual love of sampled instruments, funky grooves and underground rock led to the EP *In Search of Manny,* which was released on the Grand Royal label, run by Beastie Boy Mike D. Schellenbach and Cunniff's keyboardist friend Vivian Trimble joined up just before the disc was completed. *Billboard* compared the EP to "a radio tuned to several stations at once." A substantial buzz was generated by *Manny—*

For the Record . . .

Members include **Jill Cunniff,** bass, vocals; **Gabby Glaser,** guitar, vocals; **Kate Schellenbach,** drums; **Vivian Trimble,** keyboards.

Band formed early 1990s in New York, NY. Released debut EP, *In Search of Manny,* on Grand Royal/Capitol label, 1992; released full-length debut, *Natural Ingredients,* 1994; played Lollapalooza rock festival, 1994; contributed songs to soundtracks of films *Clueless* (1995) and *Girlstown* (1996); contributed tracks to compilations *Ain't Nuthin' but a She Thing* (1995) and *O Come All Ye Faithful: Rock for Choice* (1996); Cunniff and Trimble released album as the Kostars, 1996; Schellenbach performed in duo Ladies Who Lunch.

Addresses: *Record company*—Grand Royal, P.O. Box 26689, Los Angeles, CA 90026. *E-mail*—lusciousjackson@grandroyal.com. *Website*—http://www.grandroyal.com/Bands/LusciousJackson/.

including a good spot on the prestigious Jazz & pop poll of *Village Voice* critics—and the group set to work on their first full-length album, *Natural Ingredients.* Released in 1994, that album made good on the promise of the debut EP and showed an expanded range. Enthused *Spin*'s Terri Sutton, "*Natural Ingredients* is defiantly catchy, the sensual soup of pop and soul, musicianship and sampling, that LJ's debut EP, *In Search of Manny,* struggled to stir up."

High-Profile Tours

One track from the album, "City Song," appeared on the soundtrack of the hit film *Clueless,* and soon Luscious Jackson was on tour with the Beastie Boys and megastars R.E.M. Perhaps more exciting, however, was their spot on the 1994 Lollapalooza tour, alternative rock's high-profile traveling festival. "Oh, it was *great* exposure—and a lot of fun," Cunniff recalled in the *Detroit Free Press.* "We'd play to so many kids every day, huge crowds of people. I don't know if they all knew who we were or not, but it certainly helped us on the tour we're doing now [fall of 1994]; we're selling lots of tickets in the cities we played during Lollapalooza." 1994 also saw the band performing original music to accompany *Easy,* a Dance Theater Workshop production choreographed by Vivian Trimble, the group's keyboard player.

Luscious Jackson returned to the studio in 1996 with producer Daniel Lanois, best known for his work with U2, Peter Gabriel and other rock luminaries. Lanois' gift for finding the emotional core of groove-based music had made him a hot property, and he told *Rolling Stone* what drew him to Luscious Jackson. "What attracted me was that I thought they were smart lyricists," he explained to the magazine's Keith Spera. "And secondly, I thought they had a fresh angle, and selfish me would like to be associated with something new." Cunniff, meanwhile, compared Lanois to "a long-lost brother," and gave her impressions of the producer's New Orleans studio/home: "It's like your rich aunt's house that you never had."

"From a Completely Different Place"

Lanois and the band placed the emphasis this time on a more live feel. "We really wanted to look at arrangements and think about arrangements from a completely different place," Trimble explained in *Gavin.* "Starting with a simple song and then building from there as opposed to the kind of building process that had happened more often in the past, which was in the studio with looping." The result of this collaboration was the album *Fever in, Fever Out,* a more expansive collection of material that showed a newfound maturity and confidence. The single "Naked Eye" enjoyed substantial rotation on radio and MTV.

Fever in, Fever Out didn't bowl over the critics, however. "Unfortunately, the group seems to have lost some of its bounce," ventured *People* reviewer Peter Castro, who bemoaned the presence on *Fever* of "slow, edgeless departures from the funky formula that made [the band] so entertaining in the past." Sara Scribner of the *Los Angeles Times,* meanwhile, found the album little more than "palatable," placing much of the blame on Lanois. "He layers and layers their sounds," she wrote, "until each beat, every loop, feels muffled and twice removed." The *San Francisco Bay Guardian* disagreed, crediting Lanois with "drawing the band out of their creative shell and lending a luxuriant denseness to the barest of dance loops." The members of Luscious Jackson, meanwhile, paid little heed to reviews. Cunniff explained in *Gavin* that *Fever* "is not about abrasive sounds. It's about appealing, inviting sounds. We tried to make an effort to keep it smooth and nice to listen to." She elaborated on the issues informing this decision: "A lot of it is our time," she reflected. "People in the '70s were living fast and dying young, and most of those lyrics came from rockers who were hanging out in the studios doing coke all night. I think times now are really rough, and death is so around us with AIDS and violence. It seems like life is so precious, you know?"

Selected discography

On Grand Royal, except where noted

In Search of Manny, 1992.
Natural Ingredients (includes "City Song"), 1994.
"Here," *Clueless* (soundtrack), Capitol, 1995.
"69 Annee Erotique," *Ain't Nuthin' but a She Thing*, London, 1995.
"Strong Man," *Girlstown* soundtrack, Mercury, 1996.
"Queen of Bliss," *O Come All Ye Faithful: Rock for Choice*, Columbia, 1996.
Fever in Fever Out (includes "Naked Eye"), 1996.

Sources

Billboard, July 16, 1994.
B-Side, August 1994.

Details, October 1994.
Detroit Free Press, October 7, 1994.
Entertainment Weekly, August 26, 1994.
Gavin, November 1, 1996.
Intune, May 1995.
Los Angeles Times, November 9, 1996.
Musician, September 1994; April 1996.
People, November 18, 1996.
Pulse!, June 1994.
Rolling Stone, September 22, 1994; May 30, 1996.
San Francisco Bay Guardian, October 16, 1996.
Spin, September 1993; February 1994; September 1994.
Vibe, June 1994; September 1994.

Additional information was provided by the Grand Royal site on the World Wide Web.

—Simon Glickman

Mahavishnu Orchestra

Jazz-Fusion Band

The Mahavishnu Orchestra was arguably the most influential, and certainly one of the best, jazz fusion groups ever. The band's leader, John McLaughlin, inspired a generation of jazz-rockers with both his guitar wizardry and his flair as a composer. In forming the Mahavishnu Orchestra, McLaughlin brought together an unprecedented combination of elements--a background in jazz and blues, a passionate interest in Eastern (particularly Indian) music, a rock beat, and world class chops--that set the standard for fusion bands for years to come.

When the Mahavishnu Orchestra was created in 1971, it seemed like a logical next step in McLaughlin's already illustrious musical career. Like so many British guitarists, he had been fascinated by American blues as a teenager. He next steeped himself in the jazz of such giants as Charles Mingus, Art Blakey, Miles Davis, and John Coltrane. By the early 1960s, McLaughlin was living in London and playing music professionally. His jazz dabblings led to a role with the Graham Bond Organization, a seminal British fusion group that includ-

John McLaughlin and Mahavishnu Orchestra. MICHAEL OCHS ARCHIVES/Venice, CA. Reproduced by permission.

ed future Cream members Jack Bruce and Ginger Baker.

McLaughlin's Guru Provided Name

In 1969 McLaughlin moved to the U.S. to join Lifetime, a new band led by drummer Tony Williams. In America, he quickly met Miles Davis, and Davis invited him to play on his album *In a Silent Way.* McLaughlin later contributed to several other Davis masterpieces, including *Bitches Brew,* which many consider to be the single album most responsible for making jazz-rock fusion a legitimate musical category. With the encouragement of Davis, McLaughlin left Lifetime in 1971 to form his own band. By this time, he had become a follower of the guru Sri Chinmoy. He decided to name his band after the name he had been given by his spiritual leader: Mahavishnu. In fact, for several years he went by the name Mahavishnu John McLaughlin.

The first incarnation of the Mahavishnu Orchestra included keyboardist Jan Hammer, bassist Rick Laird, violinist Jerry Goodman, drummer Billy Cobham, and McLaughlin on electric guitar. The group was an instant sensation. Its marriage of Eastern and Western sounds captured the attention of both jazz and rock mavens. *Newsweek* described their sound during an early performance as a blending of "instrumental voices swooping like electronic swallows in a summer storm." This version of the Orchestra produced three albums: *The Inner Mounting Flame* (1972), *Birds of Fire* (1973), and

Between Nothingness and Eternity (1973). *Birds of Fire* made it into the top twenty on the album charts for 1973, but by the end of that year internal conflicts led to the dissolution of the band.

Ponty's Violin Distinguished Second Version

McLaughlin quickly put together a new version of the Orchestra, featuring electric violin virtuoso Jean-Luc Ponty. The album *Apocalypse,* released in 1974, also showcased members of the London Symphony Orchestra. That was followed by *Visions of the Emerald Beyond* in 1975 and *Inner Worlds* in 1976. Meanwhile, McLaughlin's interest in Indian music continued to grow. While the second version of Mahavishnu was still active, he began to spend more and more time working with an all-acoustic group of mostly Indian musicians, playing a slightly jazzed-up take on authentic classical music from South India. By 1976, McLaughlin had given up on the Mahavishnu Orchestra--and the guru who had given him the name--and was focusing on Shakti, the new acoustic group, full-time.

Over the next several years, McLaughlin wandered through several different musical formats, always with the thought in the back of his mind of re-emerging with a new Mahavishnu Orchestra. When his interest in Shakti waned after only a couple of years, McLaughlin picked up his electric guitar once again to perform briefly with a group he dubbed the One Truth Band, which also featured L. Shankar, the violinist from Shakti. This band released one album, *Electric Dreams,* in 1979. In 1978 he formed a trio with two other acoustic guitar dynamos, Paco De Lucia and Larry Cornell. Cornell was replaced in 1980 by Al Di Meola, and this group put out albums in 1981 and 1983.

80's Version Featured Evans' Sax

The following year, McLaughlin's background desire to re-form Mahavishnu finally came to fruition. The group did not exactly reunite--the only other returning member was drummer Cobham--but the new version of the band carried on the musical spirit and vision of the original Orchestra. The 1980s edition of the band featured saxophonist Bill Evans, who had previously played with Miles Davis; former Pat Metheny drummer Danny Gottlieb; bassist Jonas Hellborg, and keyboardist Mitch Forman. The presence of Evans' sax and the absence of Ponty's violin distinguished the new Mahavishnu from the earlier version. McLaughlin's composing and guitar fireworks, however, provided continuity.

The third incarnation of the Mahavishnu Orchestra released an album called *Mahavishnu* in 1984. The last album to date recorded under the Mahavishnu name--Jim Beard on keyboards in place of Forman was the only lineup change--was *Adventures in Radioland,* released in 1987. Both albums took full advantage of the amazing advances in the technology of electronic music that had taken place during the previous decade. While he had long since removed Mahavishnu from his personal name, McLaughlin had no qualms about using it for the new band, since the music so clearly descended from that of the earlier versions.

Since 1987, McLaughlin has tended to focus primarily on acoustic music. He has toured as a duo with bassist Hellborg, written and performed orchestral works, and was briefly reunited with Miles Davis before Davis' death in 1992. McLaughlin has always been quick to explain that music is part of a spiritual voyage for him, whether attached to a particular religious sect or not. "My work in music is a work of the spirit; it's a development of my spirit, and the development of myself as a human being," he was quoted as saying in a 1985 *Down Beat* interview. "We don't know if there's a God, but if there is a God, I think music is the face of God." Many listeners would be delighted if McLaughlin's spiritual voyage happens to carry him in the direction of another Mahavishnu Orchestra along the way.

Selected Discography

The Inner Mounting Flame, Columbia, 1972.
Birds of Fire, Columbia, 1973.
Between Nothingness and Eternity, Columbia, 1973.
Apocalypse, Columbia, 1974.
Visions of the Emerald Beyond, Columbia, 1975.
Inner Worlds, Columbia, 1976.
Mahavishnu, Warner Bros., 1984.
Adventures in Radioland, Verve, 1987.

Sources

Books

Berendt, Joachim, *The New Jazz Book,* translated by Margenstern, et al., Lawrence Hill, 1975.
Sallins, James, ed., *Jazz Guitars,* Quill, 1984.

Periodicals

DownBeat, March 1985; May 1991.
High Fidelity, January 1987.
Newsweek, March 27, 1972.
Rolling Stone, July 13, 1978.

—*Robert R. Jacobson*

Liza Minnelli

Singer, actress

For the children of the very famous, perhaps the most daunting task of their lives is to emerge from the larger-than-life shadow cast by their parents and become their own persons. For Liza Minnelli, this process has been doubly difficult because she chose to make a name for herself on the stage, thus following in the footsteps of a mother who was one of the most famous performers of the twentieth century. That Minnelli succeeded is a testament both to her artistic gifts and her independent She remains one of the most versatile, and energetic performers on the American music scene.

Minnelli's life began in the glow of the spotlight and has never really left it. She was born on March 12, 1946 in Hollywood, California to singer/actress Judy Garland and the second of her five husbands, film director, Vincente Minnelli. Liza grew up in the shadow of the studios, visiting her parents on sound stages, absorbing the details of the film-making process. She was particularly interested in dancers such as Gene Kelly and Fred Astaire, whom she watched rehearse for hours, and at an early age she was given dance lessons by MGM choreographer Nico Charisse. By time she was three, Liza had appeared in one of her mother's films, *In the Good Old Summertime,* and at age eight she danced on stage in New York as a backup to her mother singing "Swanee." Although Vincente Minnelli and Garland were divorced in 1951, both would play key roles in Minnelli's artistic development, as she acknowledged in a *New York Times* interview, "I got my drive from my mother and my dreams from my father."

The Legacy of A Voice

If Minnelli's was a glamorous upbringing, it had a dark side as well. Judy Garland's later years were marked by addictions to tranquilizers and alcohol, illnesses, and episodes of emotional instability resulting in a series of failed marriages and strained relationships with everyone close to her. Almost from infancy, Minnelli was pressed into service as her mother's confidante, and by time she was a teenager she was managing her mother's household, paying bills, hiring staff, and supporting Garland through her mental crises. For all that, a strong emotional bond linked the mother and daughter, and to this day Minnelli remembers Garland with fondness for her supportiveness and her efforts to encourage Liza's artistic development.

Perhaps Garland's greatest legacy to Minnelli was her voice. Liza inherited many of Garland's mannerisms and vocal effects. As *New York Times* music writer Michiko Kakutani pointed out in a 1984 article, "Although [Minnelli's] voice possesses a harder... edge, it

For the Record . . .

Born Liza May Minnelli on March 12, 1946 in Hollywood, CA; daughter of Vincente Minnelli (film director) and Judy Garland (singer/actress); married Peter Allen 1967 (divorced 1972); married Jack Haley 1974 (divorced 1979); married Mark Gero (divorced 1992); educated in United States and Europe.

First performed in 1961; made Off-Broadway debut in 1963; made Broadway debut in 1965; has toured extensively in United States, Europe, Australia, and Japan; has appeared or recorded with Judy Garland, Johnny Mathis, Frank Sinatra, Sammy Davis, Jr., Chita Rivera, Goldie Hawn, Vic Damone, Donna Summer, Joel Grey, Charles Aznavour, Marvin Hamlisch; film credits include *Charlie Bubbles*; *The Sterile Cuckoo*; *Tell Me That You Love Me, Junie Moon*; *Cabaret*; *That's Entertainment*; *Lucky Lady*; *A Matter of Time*; *New York, New York*; *Arthur*; *Rent-A-Cop*; *Arthur 2—On the Rocks*; *Stepping Out.*

Awards: Tony Award, 1965; David di Donatello (Italy), 1970; Academy Award, 1972; Golden Globe Award, 1972; British Academy Award, 1972; Entertainer of the Year, American Guild of Variety Artists, 1972; David di Donatello, 1972; Emmy Award, 1972; Tony Award, 1973; Tony Award, 1977; Golden Globe, 1985.

Addresses: *Home*—New York, NY. *Management*— Lee Salter Co., Los Angeles, CA.

---

carries echoes of the throbbing emotion that Judy Garland imparted to all her songs; her stage presence, too—histrionic, nervous, at once vulnerable and brassy—can also conjure up images of her mother." In the early years of her career Minnelli would consciously distant herself from her mother's image, refusing to sing Garland's songs and taking movie roles that portrayed her as worldly and tough as opposed to the wide-eyed innocent Garland often played. But in time she would come to accept and be honored that her audience saw her mother in her.

Minnelli's interest in performing came to the fore in 1960 when she saw the Broadway musical *Bye Bye Birdie.* She recognized in the atmosphere of the stage a world in which she felt completely at home. Successful tours with her school drama club and in local theaters followed, and in 1962 she decided to take the plunge, dropping out of school and moving to New York to pursue a stage career. Although her parents refused to pull strings for the aspiring sixteen-year-old actress, good auditions and curiosity based on her name resulted in her being cast in an Off-Broadway revival of the musical *Best Foot Forward.* The show opened in April 1963, and Minnelli was praised by critics for her confident and accomplished stage presence. After the show ended, Minnelli recorded her first album and went on the road touring with musicals, slowly but surely moving up the ladder to success by dint of what, in a *Washington Post* article, she called "slogging along every day... step by step by step."

Competes With A Legend

The most prominent step in Minnelli's developing career, however, was when she appeared on stage with Judy Garland at the London Palladium on November 8, 1964. Overwhelmed by the thought of having to sing alongside a living legend, who also happened to be her mother, Minnelli was at first terrified, but her talent quickly asserted itself and she proved more than equal to the occasion. So much so, in fact, that Garland became jealous and paid her the supreme compliment of trying to outperform her, as if she were any other competitor. It was an electrifying moment for Minnelli, confirming that she had arrived as a musical talent. She recalled in a *New York Times* interview, "It was like Mama suddenly realized I was good.... One minute she smiled at me, and the next minute she was like the lioness that owned the stage and suddenly found somebody invading her territory."

In 1965, Minnelli's new status as a rising stage star was reaffirmed by her performance in the Broadway musical *Flora the Red Menace*, a lighthearted spoof of the American Communist movement of the 1930s. Although the show received mediocre reviews and closed after only a few weeks, Minnelli was critically applauded and received the Tony Award as best actress in a musical for her work in the title role. At nineteen, she was the youngest actress in Broadway history to be so honored.

More importantly, she established a connection with *Flora's* song-writing team, Fred Ebb and John Kander, who would arrange much of her work from that point on. By characterizing Minnelli as an eccentric but resilient waif with a flashy exterior and inner vulnerability, Kander and Ebb were able to imbue her with a stage personality that, while drawing on her mother's image, was distinctly separate from it. This would be key to Minnelli shedding the critical distinction of being "just like Judy Garland" and emerging into her own as a performer.

Makes Nightclub and Film Debut

With the support of Ebb, Minnelli made her cabaret debut in Washington, D.C. in sold-out performances at the Shoreham Hotel's Blue Room. As was the case with *Flora,* she received accolades from the critical establishment and went on to tour successfully in the United States and abroad. The nightclub milieu was one in which Minnelli felt very much at ease, bringing a relentless energy and stage presence to the smaller venues regarded by most other performers as merely a sidebar between stage shows. As she explained in a 1970 *After Dark* article, "The way I do my club act—it is theater ... I have too much energy to stand still and be cool." Her audiences invariably responded to her enthusiasm and to this day, her nightclub act is the foundation for her continuing appeal.

In 1968, Minnelli ventured into the world of film for the first time, taking the role of the American secretary to Albert Finney in the British comedy *Charlie Bubbles.* Favorable reviews resulted in her being cast in *The Sterile Cuckoo.* Her role of Pookie Adams, a slightly crazy, love-starved college student gave her an opportunity to display her considerable acting talent and would garner her a best actress Oscar nomination. It also served notice that she could do more than just sing and dance, and was in fact a multi-dimensional talent.

In 1969, Minnelli had just begun work on a third film, Otto Preminger's *Tell Me That You Love Me, Junie Moon,* when she received word that Judy Garland had died from an accidental overdose of sleeping pills. Although she must have been devastated, she calmly took charge of the events surrounding her mother's funeral and the settling of her estate, much the same way she had run her mother's household as a child. Plunging back into work afterwards, Minnelli filmed her first television special, entitled *Liza Minnelli,* for NBC in 1970 and went on tour with her cabaret act. In 1971, she was selected to play the female lead in Bob Fosse's *Cabaret,* a film version of writer Christopher Isherwood's short story collection, *Berlin Stories.*

Wins Triple Crown

The role of Sally Bowles, a down-on-her-luck cabaret singer struggling to survive in the amoral atmosphere of 1930s Nazi Germany was tailor-made for Minnelli. On the strength of an excellent score by Kander and Ebb, director Fosse was able to draw a powerful, well rounded performance from Minnelli, showcasing her singing abilities and highlighting the tough/vulnerable dichoto-my that was her hallmark. On its 1972 release, *Cabaret* was hailed by the critics and audiences alike and Minnelli received the Golden Globe, the Academy Award, the British Academy Award and Entertainer of the Year from the American Guild of Variety Artists. As if to crown her laurels, a NBC television special of her singing act, *Liza With a Z,* earned Minnelli an Emmy Award, raising her into the select group of artists who had won a Tony, an Academy Award, and an Emmy, the "Triple Crown" of show business.

Having firmly established herself as a star in her own right, Minnelli continued the relentless schedule that had brought her to the pinnacle of recognition. For the next several years, she toured extensively, playing venues all over the United States. A one-woman show, *Liza,* was the basis for a world tour and garnered her a special Tony Award. In 1974, she was a narrator for *That's Entertainment,* a highly successful film tribute to MGM musicals which prominently featured her mother's work. She also provided voice-overs for the character of Dorothy in *Journey Back To Oz,* an animated feature that allowed Minnelli to reprise Garland's most famous role.

After such a meteoric rise, it seemed inevitable that Liza's career should hit some sour notes. *Lucky Lady,* an adventure film starring Minnelli, Burt Reynolds, and Gene Hackman, was released in 1975 to harsh reviews in spite of the assembled talent. Similarly, when *A Matter of Time,* a Cinderella-type story directed by her father, hit the screens in 1976, her performance was thoroughly panned as mawkish and unconvincing. Perhaps the greatest disappointment for Minnelli, however, was the reception accorded to *New York, New York* which appeared in 1977. She had jumped at the chance to work with Martin Scorcese on the film, a 1940s style musical with Robert de Niro that would afford her the opportunity to star in the same kind of role that had made her mother famous. Once again, however, the critics were less than charitable, charging that she had merely copied her mother's mannerisms, and the film was a box-office disaster.

As if to redeem herself, Minnelli returned to the Broadway stage in late 1977 with *The Act,* the story of a has-been singer trying to reclaim her earlier success. The verve of her live performances, a domain which seemed to suit her more than the screen, pleased the theater-going public and critics alike, and resulted in her third Tony Award. Likewise, her concert appearances continued to attract overflow audiences, with a 1979 Carnegie Hall engagement setting a record for that venerable theater. In 1981, Minnelli returned to film with the hit movie *Arthur,* the story of the unlikely match between a waitress and a drunken millionaire. Capitalizing on that success, Minnelli launched an international tour of her stage show and in 1983 earned a Tony Award for her starring role in *The Rink*, a musical with the close-to-home subject of a daughter coming to terms with her estranged mother.

Overcomes Drug Addiction

In spite of her continued success, or perhaps because of it, Minnelli's personal life began to go out of control. Part of a sophisticated, fast-living crowd in the seventies and early eighties, Minnelli, in a haunting parallel to her mother, developed addictions to alcohol and several different types of drugs, particularly Valium. Gradually she became more and more withdrawn and began to miss concert dates, until in 1984, she entered the Betty Ford Center for detoxification treatment. Several months' intensive therapy cured her of her drug habit and Minnelli emerged from the Center feeling renewed. In 1985, she mounted a hit tour that was a comeback of sorts for her, as well as appearing in a NBC made-for-television movie *A Time to Live* that brought her a second Golden Globe award.

Since the mid-eighties, Minnelli's career has leveled off. She has had little success on the silver screen, starring in *Rent-A-Cop* in 1987, *Arthur 2 - On the Rocks* in 1988, and *Stepping Out* in 1991 with minimal critical or box-office impact. However she has found the medium of television much friendlier, appearing in a series of highly acclaimed specials including *Liza in London*, an HBO pay-per-view event in 1986, *Minnelli on Minnelli: Liza Remembers Vincente*, a 1987 PBS tribute to her father who had died the previous year, and *Liza Minnelli: Sam Found Out*, three one-act plays on ABC in 1988.

Minnelli's greatest success, however, has come in her continually sold-out appearances in theaters and clubs, a forum in which she has the greatest latitude to showcase her high-energy performance style. In 1987, Minnelli appeared in a three-week engagement at Carnegie Hall, recording the concerts as a best-selling live album, her first in almost a decade. A worldwide tour in 1988 with Frank Sinatra and Sammy Davis, Jr. was billed as "The Ultimate Event" and proved to be very lucrative as a pay-per-view special. Minnelli appeared for several weeks in 1991 at New York's Radio City Music Hall, selling out every performance and recording a PBS special that was nominated for six Emmy Awards.

Through the seventies, eighties, and on into the nineties, Minnelli has also kept up a high profile as a recording artist, releasing albums steadily. Although her record-ed output has not achieved the kind of recognition her film, television, and stage work did, all of her albums have sold well, reflecting the extreme devotion of the following she has maintained over the years. A 1996 recording of smoky-sounding romantic standards entitled *Gently* is a distinct change from the show tune-oriented albums she has done in the past and has been generally well received by music critics.

Now in her fifties, Liza Minnelli can look back over a career that has seen many highs and some lows as well. From her teenage years on, she has walked a fine line, striving to establish herself as an artist in the face of inevitable comparisons to her legendary mother. That she has succeeded in making a name for herself is beyond doubt, and in many ways she has become a more well-rounded, if not as compelling, an entertainer as Garland. In the process she has, if anything, extended her mother's renown by giving fresh life to the musical domain Garland had her greatest triumphs, a fact that *New York Times* critic Stephen Holden underlined in extolling Liza Minnelli as "an exuberant, brash entertainer who may be the last great practioner of the brassy and at times proudly vulgar American music-hall tradition."

Selected discography

Albums

Liza! Liza! Capitol, 1964.
It Amazes Me, Capitol, 1965.
Judy Garland & Liza Minnelli Live at the London Palladium, Capitol, 1965.
Flora, The Red Menace, RCA Victor, 1965.
There is a Time, Capitol, 1966.
Liza Minnelli, A&M, 1968.
Cabaret: Original Soundtrack, MCA, 1972.
Liza with a Z, Columbia, 1972.
Liza Minnelli: The Singer, Columbia, 1973.
Live at the Winter Garden, Columbia, 1974.
New York, New York, EMI, 1977.
Tropical Nights, Columbia, 1977.
The Act, DRG, 1978.
Best Foot Forward, Picc-a-dilly, 1980.
Liza Minnelli Live at Carnegie Hall, Caltel, 1981.
The Rink, Polydor, 1984.
I Believe In Music, CBS, 1986.
Liza Minnelli At Carnegie Hall, Telarc, 1987.
Lovely! Lively! Liza! Capitol, 1987.
The Liza Minnelli Four Sider, A&M, 1988.
Results, Epic, 1989.
Love Pains, Epic, 1990.
Stepping Out, Milan America, 1991.
Liza Minnelli: Live from Radio City Music Hall, Columbia, 1992.

Liza, Sony, 1993.
Gently, Angel, 1996.

Films

Charlie Bubbles, 1968.
The Sterile Cuckoo, 1969.
Tell Me That You Love Me, Junie Moon, 1971.
Cabaret, 1972.
Lucky Lady, 1975.
A Matter of Time, 1976.
New York, New York, 1977.
Arthur, 1981.
Rent-A-Cop, 1987.
Arthur 2 - On The Rocks, 1988.
Stepping Out, 1991.

Television

Liza With A Z, 1972.
Goldie and Liza Together, 1980.
Baryshnikov on Broadway, 1980.
A Time to Live, 1985.
Liza In London, 1986.
Liza Minnelli: Sam Found Out, 1988.
The Ultimate Event, 1989.
Liza: Live at Radio City Music Hall, 1992.
Parallel Lives, 1994.
The West Side Waltz, 1995.

Theater

Best Foot Forward, 1963.
Flora, the Red Menace, 1965.
Liza at the Winter Garden, 1973.
Chicago, 1975.
The Act, 1977.
The Rink, 1984.

Sources

Periodicals

After Dark, April 1970.
Boston Globe, April 18, 1996.
Harper's Bazaar, August 1990.
New York Newsday, April 23, 1991.
New York Times, September 6, 1979; March 4, 1984; May 31, 1987; April 25, 1991.
USA Today, April 16, 1996.
Vanity Fair, June 1987.
Washington Post, July 9, 1988.

Additional material for this profile was furnished by Angel/EMI Records, 1996.

—Daniel Hodges

Alanis Morissette

Pop singer

AP/Wide World Photos. Reproduced by permission

Alanis Morissette's 1995 release *Jagged Little Pill* sold over ten million copies and won her four Grammy Awards. Its slew of hit singles, kicked off with the vituperative "You Oughta Know," made Morissette an alternative music star overnight. Yet the singer-songwriter also endured some flak for her success, especially after word leaked out that she had suffered a rather unsuccessful earlier incarnation as a big-haired, drum-machine-backed teen singer in Canada. Nevertheless, the candid songs of *Jagged Little Pill*, penned by Morissette as she matured out of her teens, spoke to a broad cross-section of adolescents and adults alike.

Morissette was born June 1, 1974, in Ottawa, Ontario, one of a set of twins born to Alan and Georgia Morissette. Alanis and he twin Wade joined older brother Chad, and for a time the family lived in Europe when the elder Morissettes—both teachers—took jobs at a military base school. As a young teen in Ottawa again, Morissette attended Catholic schools and was straight-A student. A self-described overachiever, she began piano at age of six and wrote her first song at age nine, and her talents eventually landed her on television. Her biggest success came with a recurring role on *You Can't Do That on Television*, a kids' show on the Nickelodeon cable channel in the mid-1980s.

Debbie Gibson of Canada

With the earnings from the television show, Morissette produced her first single on her own label, Lamor Records. The 1987 release, "Fate Stay with Me," was recorded with the musical expertise from former members of the Stampeders, Canadian rockers who had a 1971 hit with "Sweet City Woman." As a single written by a thirteen-year-old, "Fate Stay with Me" was no monster hit but did attract the attention of MCA Canada, who signed Morissette. Her first full-length record, *Alanis*, debuted in 1991, followed by *Now Is the Time* a year later.

But it was not yet Morissette's time at all. Her career enjoyed some minor successes, but she remained pigeonholed; MCA even had her touring with the always-maligned Vanilla Ice. She did get a chance to hone her songwriting skills over two albums, however, and later, after her major success with *Jagged Little Pill*, refused to be embarrassed by a persona whom unkind journalists compared with Debbie Gibson or Tiffany. "I wasn't writing to communicate anything, and I was definitely not ready on the self-esteem level to indulge myself and all my personal turmoil," she told J. D. Considine of the *Chicago Sun-Times*.

For the Record . . .

Born Alanis Nadine Morissette, June 1, 1974, in Ottawa, Ontario, Canada; daughter of Alan (a high school principal) and Georgia (a teacher) Morissette.

Worked as a child actor, mid-1980s; released first single, "Fate Stay with Me," on Lamor Records, 1987; signed with MCA Canada; released first full-length LP, *Alanis*, in 1991; signed with Maverick Records, 1994; released *Jagged Little Pill*, 1995.

Awards: Juno Award, Most Promising Female Artist, 1992, for *Alanis*; *Jagged Little Pill* earned Grammy Awards in 1996 for Album of the Year, Best Rock Album, Best Rock Song (for "You Oughta Know"), and Best Female Rock Vocal Performance (for "You Oughta Know").

Addresses: Publicist—MSO, 14724 Ventura Blvd., Suite 410, Sherman Oaks, CA 91403.

Jagged Little Pill would bare some of the personal dramas that engulfed Morissette in typical coming-of-age passages, but she has spoken about certain moments in her late teens as definite turning points. In one incident, she had a breakdown in front of her parents—partly as a result of the pressures she felt as a combination teen star/overachiever/perfect daughter. Discovering the 1991 Tori Amos LP *Little Earthquakes* helped inspire Morissette to begin writing from the heart. Coincidentally, Amos had also suffered an off-target launch as an alterna-pop performer under the moniker Y Kant Tori Read, and later succeeded by writing straightforward, deeply personal songs.

Morissette came to see the necessity of leaving Canada for the more inspiring climes of Los Angeles. Like Axl Rose stepping off the bus in the video for "Welcome to the Jungle," she underwent the usual big-city trials during her first weeks. She was held up at gunpoint. She was broke. She tried to find someone to work with, but no one seemed to click. Finally she approached Glen Ballard, an unlikely hero. Ballard was a producer with a home studio who had crafted tunes for Wilson Phillips and Paula Abdul. But he didn't try to mold her into something salable: "I felt that he wasn't judging me, and I felt that he had enough security within himself to give the ball to a 20-year-old and let her go with it," she told J. D. Considine of the *Chicago Sun-Times*. Within a period of two weeks, they recorded most of what would become *Jagged Little Pill*, and shopped their demo tape around. Executives at Maverick Records heard it and signed Morissette in 1994. Their ultimate boss, however, is none other than Madonna, who became CEO of the subsidiary as part of her lavish contract with Warner Brothers. Morissette was just twenty.

Unimaginable Success

Jagged Little Pill, released in the spring of 1995, displayed a drastic change from Morissette's former recording efforts. "The sound is more muscular; her voice is rawer, the guitar work more aggressive," wrote Christopher John Farley in *Time*, "and while the words are rarely as smart as they seem to think they are, this is straight-ahead rock, sweetened somewhat with pop melodiousness." Its initial single, "You Oughta Know," was a catchy diatribe against a former lover. Later, rumors surfaced that Morissette may have been writing about someone specific she had dated, such as television comic Dave Coulier, but the singer has said that it was merely a composite of several doomed relationships.

Success made Morissette an easy target for criticism, however, once her new American fans—who had never heard of her—discovered her previous incarnation via snipey rock critics. There were rumors that Maverick was surreptitiously buying up all unsold copies of the early-'90s releases, and worse, that Ballard had done much of the work for *Jagged Little Pill*. Yet Morissette refused to evade her former teenybopper persona, and debunked the tales of Maverick's attempts to hide it. Instead, she told Jon Beam of the *Minneapolis-St. Paul Star Tribune* that her early brush with fame helped her keep a level head when the real fame came knocking. Her experiences, she asserted, "made me not become a heroin addict and become completely overwhelmed with how crazy this life is that I'm leading right now."

Morissette's newly out-of-control life included extensive touring in support of *Jagged Little Pill* throughout much of 1995 and 1996. In early 1996 the record won four Grammy Awards, including Album of the Year, and *Jagged Little Pill* would eventually sell a staggering ten million copies. Nor surprisingly—given the fervor of her fan base—Morissette has described singing on stage as similar to a religious experience: "When I'm onstage, it's very spiritual. I feel very close to God when I'm up there," she told *Rolling Stone*'s David Wild. Another journalist likened Morissette's stage show to "kind of like waiting for someone to have a breakdown," wrote Jae-Ha Kim in the *Chicago Sun-Times*. "Flailing her arms and moving about in a pigeon-toed stance, she appears most comfortable when her face is covered by her mane of hair."

Still, fame did have its pressures. She began avoiding interviews with members of the Canadian media, granting access only to American journalists. Fans eagerly awaited a follow-up to *Jagged Little Pill,* but, after finishing a heavy year of touring in 1996, Morissette was reportedly staying close to home, and eschewing all interviews and appearances. It seems unlikely, however, that the outspoken Morissette would retire permanently from public life, and a return to acting was one possibility. "I love doing things that scare me," she told Beam in the *Minneapolis-St. Paul Star Tribune* interview. "It makes me feel alive and challenged. It makes me feel like I'm growing. That comfort-zone area, I hate it."

Selected discography

"Fate Stay with Me," Lamor, 1987.
Alanis, MCA Canada, 1991.
Now Is the Time, MCA Canada, 1992.
Jagged Little Pill, Maverick, 1995.

Sources

Billboard, May 13, 1995, p. 7; March 9, 1996, p. 1.
Chicago Sun-Times, March 1, 1996, p. 14; March 4, 1996, p. 29.
Minneapolis-St. Paul Star Tribune, March 11, 1996, p. 10B.
People, December 30, 1996, p. 86.
Rolling Stone, November 2, 1995, p. 40.
San Diego Union-Tribune, March 6, 1996, p. E6.
Time, February 26, 1996, p. 66.

—*Carol Brennan*

Nas

Rap singer

Photo by Ernest Paniccioli. The Bettmann Archive/Newsphotos, Inc.

With just two albums to his credit, rapper Nas has achieved critical and popular acclaim, demonstrated a sensitivity and perception unusual in the aggressive hip-hop world. He has been favorably compared with Rakim, whom many consider the best rapper ever. "Hip-hop is the most controversial music of the '90s," Nas said during an Internet chat session with fans. "I am proud to be a part of it."

The rapper, whose given name is Nasir Jones, was raised by his mother, Fannie Ann Jones, in New York City's tough Queensbridge housing projects. His father is Olu Dara, a jazz and blues trumpeter who has performed and recorded with Art Blakey, Taj Mahal, Bobby Womack and David Murray, among others. Dara chose the name Nasir for his son; it means "helper" and "protector" in Arabic. As a teen-aged break dancer, Nasir used the name Kid Wave.

Growing up in the projects of Queens, "it sometimes seemed to (Nas) his whole world was ill and being eaten away," Christopher John Farley wrote in *Time* magazine. "Drugs were devouring minds, crime was destroying families, poverty was gnawing at souls. Then in May 1992, Jones' brother and best friend were shot on the same night. His brother, Jungle, lived. His friend died." "That was a wake-up call for me," he told Farley. The result of that awakening arrived two years later— in the debut album *Illmatic.* One song on the album, which has been called a classic of the genre, includes the line: "I never sleep, 'cause sleep is the cousin of death."

Nas created *Illmatic* with help from "a who's who of hip-hop producers," wrote *Entertainment Weekly*. The magazine went on to say "his witty lyrics and gruffly gratifying beats draw listeners into (his neighborhood's) lifestyle with poetic efficiency." Farley wrote that the record "captures the ailing community he was raised in—the random gunplay, the whir of police helicopters, the homeboys hanging out on the corner sipping bottles of Hennessey." Nas's songs, however, typically do not glorify the violent, desperate world from which he came the way the music of gangsta rappers does. Instead, he evokes sadness and outrage as he paints that world in rhythm and rhyme. Farley suggested the rapper delivers his songs with "submerged emotion" and dispassionately details the tragedy of urban America "like an anchorman relaying the day's grim news." The *New York Times* concluded that, on *Illmatic*, Nas "imbues his chronicle with humanity and humor, not just hardness. . . . (He) reports violence without celebrating it, dwelling on the way life triumphs over grim circumstances rather than the other way around." Nas, for his part, has taken pains to set himself apart, declaring "I'm not a gangsta rapper."

For the Record . . .

Born Nasir Jones in Queens, NY; son of Fannie Ann Jones and Olu Dara (jazz trumpeter).

Addresses: *Record company*—Columbia Records, 550 Madison Ave., New York, NY 10022-3211. *Website*—http://www.music.sony.co/artistinfo/nas

The young musician's delicate touch amid brutal realities is apparent on the song "One Love," about writing to friends in prison. On the song, Nas raps: "So stay civilized, time flies, though incarcerated your mind dies. I hate it when your mom cries." Or consider "I Gave You Power" from his chart-topping second album, *It Was Written.* The song tells a metaphoric tale from the point of view of a handgun and includes this lyric: "My owner fell to the floor, his wig split so fast. I didn't know he was hit, but it's over with. Heard mad niggas running, cops is comin'. Now I'm happy until I felt somebody else grab me. . . . Damn." The rap also contains the chilling refrain: "I might have took your first child, scarred your life, crippled your style. (But) I gave you power. . . . "

It Was Written, released in 1996, sold more than a million copies and was seen as evidence of Nas's staying power on the music scene. Like *Illmatic,* it was recorded with a variety of hip-hop producers, including the legendary Dr. Dre. The album, however, was criticized for its "utter amorality" as well as "violent episodes and sometimes needlessly rough language"—and for its frustrating contradictions. Take, for example, the hit single "If I Ruled The World (Imagine That)" on which Nas is accompanied by Lauryn Fill of the Fugees. The song depicts paradise as a "better livin' type of place to raise our kids in"—but also as a world in which cocaine comes uncut so more money can be made from it. In a review published in *Rolling Stone* magazine, Mark Coleman noted that Nas "possesses a phenomenal way with words and some savvy musical sense. It's a pity he doesn't put his verbal dexterity and powers of observation to better use." *It Was Written,* Coleman wrote, is "just the latest blatant example of trashy tough-guy talk. When Nas finally aligns his mind with his mouth, he'll truly be dangerous."

In the *New York Times,* music writer Touré suggested there is a strong musical link between Nas and his father, Olu Dara, even though they come from different backgrounds and musical schools: "Nas's music is characterized by a laid-back cool, with a penchant for medium-pace tempos and relatively sparse tracks, all of which are hallmarks of his father's music." "He has different genres of songs," Nas' father, who played a trumpet solo on *Illmatic,* told Touré. " But in each one the chords he has going, the economy, the smoothness, the non-aggressiveness. . . . His aggressive is cool. Not like "I'm angry! I'm mad!" It's cool. And that's the way my music is." Vernon Reid, a gifted rock guitarist who has played with Dara, also sees similarities between father and son. "Both have a finely tuned sense of irony, which I think is evident in Nas's lyrics and Olu's playing," Reid said. "There's a kind of cockeyed way of looking at the world. A raised eyebrow. Sly. They're seeing what's going on underneath the surface."

Touré, meanwhile, describes Nas as "quiet and pensive, an introspective old soul" and strongly suggests the young rapper will be around awhile. "Music is in my blood," Nas told the writer. "I could have chosen to do a lot of other things. I could have been a scientist, a lawyer. But this is where I'm comfortable at, right here."

Selected discography

Illmatic, Columbia, 1994.
It Was Written, Columbia, 1996.

Sources

Periodicals

Entertainment Weekly, April 22, 1994, p. 58; July 26, 1996, p. 56.
New York Times, Oct. 6, 1996, sec. 2.
Rolling Stone, Sept. 16, 1996, pp. 83-84; Dec. 26, 1996, pp. 194-195.
Time, June 20, 1994, p. 62; July 29, 1996, p. 79.

Online

Sony Music home page: (http://www.music.sony.co.artistinfo/nas/)

Peter Nero

Pianist, conductor, arranger, composer

Pianist Peter Nero's virtuoso musical skills and warm stage presence have won him a loyal and enthusiastic following around the world. "There are hundreds of pianists who have extraordinary technical abilities, but Peter has a rare combination: a fantastic technique, a unique touch, and a penetrating musical intelligence. You can hear his knowledge of orchestration when he plays," wrote Swedish conductor Sixteen Ehrling in *Keyboard Classics.* Nero is also a much-in-demand arranger and conductor, holding regular posts with the Philly (Philadelphia) Pops, the Tulsa Philharmonic, and Florida Philharmonic. Since 1961, he has made dozens of recordings and had a Top-40 hit with the theme from the film *The Summer of '42* in 1971.

Peter Nero was born Bernard Nierow in Brooklyn, New York, in 1934. Though his family was non-musical, Nero began piano lessons at age seven and from the start showed a remarkable natural ability. By age eleven, he could play Haydn's *Piano Concerto in D Major* from memory; in his early teens he was performing at small, local engagements. While attending New York's High

AP/Wide World Photos. Reproduced by permission.

For the Record . . .

Born Bernard Nierow on May 22, 1934 in New York, NY; the son of Julius Nierow and Mary Menasche; married Marcia Dunner, 1956 (divorced); married Peggy Altman, 1977; children: (from first marriage), Jedd and Beverly. *Education:* Attended High School of Music and Arts; New York City; Brooklyn College, B.A., 1956; also attended Juilliard School of Music, and studied music privately with Constance Keene, 1951-1957.

Since the early 1950s has made numerous appearances as a pianist in concert halls, theatres, and night clubs and on television throughout North America and Europe; has also appeared as a guest artist with various orchestras, including the Boston Pops. Conductor and music director for the Philly Pops since 1979; pop music director and conductor for the Florida Philharmonic since 1981, and for the Tulsa Philharmonic since 1987; has been guest conductor for dozens of other orchestras. Composer of *Sunday in New York* (film score); *Blue Fantasy and Improvisations; His World; 70 & Suite in Four Movements; The Diary.*

Awards: Grammy Award for Best New Artist, 1961; Grammy Award for Best Performance by an Orchestra or Instrumentalist with Orchestra (not Jazz or Dancing) for *The Colorful Peter Nero,* 1962. Other awards include a Gold Album for *The Summer of '42,* 1972; Best Pop Pianist award, *Contemporary Keyboard* magazine, 1980; International Society of Performing Arts Administrators Presenters Award for "Excellence in the Arts," 1986; induction into the Philadelphia Walk-of-Fame, 1996; World's Number One Instrumentalist, *Cashbox* magazine; Brooklyn College, honorary doctorate.

Addresses: *Office*—Gurtman and Murtha Associates, 450 Seventh Ave., #603, New York, NY, 10123.

School of Music and Art, he won a scholarshp to study part-time at the prestigious Juilliard School of Music in Manhattan. At this point, his extraordinary natural talent began to be something of a liability since it led him to disdain the long hours of practice necessary to hone his skills. "My facility had helped in the beginning, but I hadn't built on it. I was told I was lazy," Nero told *High Fidelity Magazine.*

In 1951, Nero participated in a contest run by the New York radio station WQXR called "Musical Talent in Our Schools." The contest's jury consisted of top names in the classical musical world, including pianist Vladimir Horowitz. The seventeen-year old Nero's piano skills deeply impressed the illustrious jury, especially Horowitz who became a dedicated Nero fan. Abram Chasins, WQXR music director, was in charge of the contest and he listened to Nero warming up just before going on the air. "What I heard was an improvisation that disclosed a strong poetic musical individuality. A remarkable blend of the classical, romantic, impressionistic and popular idioms," Chasins wrote in the liner notes to the album *Nero-ing in on the Hits.* After winning the WQXR contest, Nero asked Chasins for advice on how to become a professional concert pianist. Chasins arranged for him to study with piano Constance Keene, and composition, harmony, and orchestration with Joe Cacciola, a top Broadway musician.

Nero went on to win several other talent contests, including Arthur Godfrey's *Talent Scouts* and Paul Whiteman's *TV Teen Club,* both nationally broadcast programs. For each contest Nero played his own piano transcription of *La Virgen de la Macarena.* He knew the piece only as the theme from *The Brave Bulls,* a then-current movie starring Anthony Quinn. Whiteman asked Nero to appear on his 1952 TV special. Nero played piano with Whiteman leading the orchestra on Gershwin's *Rhapsody in Blue.*

A Growing Interest in Jazz

Nero recognized his problems with jazz and thought that performing in a trio, with a bassist and drummer, would improve his sound. In 1957, Nero moved to Las Vegas, accepting an opportunity to lead a trio at the newly opened Tropicana Hotel. While in Las Vegas he dropped the i from his last name and became known as Bernie Nerow. "Every night was torture. I had a sound in my ear, but I couldn't reproduce the feeling of a phrase on the piano," Nero said of his Las Vegas stint to *High Fidelity.* "I had become hip in the sense that I knew the hip rules--no interpolation of classics, no use of counterpoint--but I was trying to work in groove that was foreign to me."

After two years in Las Vegas, Nero returned to New York and his old job the Hickory House. He also began playing at a musician's hangout called Jilly's. His jazz technique began to improve but he was becoming dissatisfied with the genre, especially with its tendency towards musical repetition and the ultra-hip attitudes of jazz denizens.

In the late 1950s and early 1960s, RCA Victor records was in search of a popular pianist to add to its roster of recording artists. RCA Victor talent scout Stan Greeson heard about young "Bernie Nerow" and went to Jilly's to have a listen. Greeson was pleased with Nero's superb keyboard skills, and with his good looks, but wondered if his jazz-oriented playing was in keeping with the more mainstream performer RCA had in mind. Later, in a private session, Nero showed he had a solid background in classical music. A blend of jazz and classical was exactly what RCA was looking for to create a "popular" sound and the company signed Nero to a contract. RCA changed its new artist's first name from Bernie to the more elegant sounding Peter and dropped the w from his last name.

Nero's first album, *Piano Forte,* debuted in April 1961. "On the first album I did for RCA, there must have been twelve tunes with eight different approaches. One was Mozartean, the next one was in the style of Rachmaninoff, the next was a straight ballad and another was a jazz approach. The idea was to see what came out of this and the response was that everybody liked something different. In other words, the material dictates the approach," Nero told the *Daily Oklahoman* in an article reproduced on the Peter Nero website.

The sales and reviews of *Piano Forte* exceeded expectations and RCA feared that Nero might be a "flash in pan" who could not follow up on his initial success. This proved not to be the case and sales figures went up on subsequent albums, such as *New Piano in Town.* Nero began touring with a trio in night clubs and made frequent concert appearances. In 1961, he won the Grammy Award for best new artist, beating a hodge-podge roster of nominees, including actress/singer Ann-Margaret, comedian Dick Gregory, and the singing quartet The Lettermen. Nero was nominated for another Grammy in his debut year of 1961, for Best Arrangement for *New Piano in Town.* The blow of losing was softened somewhat by the fact that the winner was the great Henry Mancini's *Moon River,* which contained the now-classic theme song from the movie *Breakfast at Tiffany's.*

Composer and Conductor

In 1963, Nero composed the score for the film *Sunday in New York,* a romantic comedy starring Jane Fonda as a naive single girl in the big city. "Peter Nero's score is perky," wrote Leonard Maltin in his *Video and Movie Guide.* Nero made a brief appearance as himself in the film.

Nero stayed with RCA Victor until the late 1960s, recording over twenty albums for the company and picking up a second Grammy Award in 1962 for Best Performance by an Orchestra or Instrumentalist with an Orchestra for

The Colorful Peter Nero. He earned several Grammy nominations, including a nod in 1964 for Best Instrumental Performance, Non-Jazz, for "For As Long As He Needs Me," a ballad from the musical *Oliver!* He lost the 1964 award again to Henry Mancini, who won this time for the theme from the film *The Pink Panther.* Despite their Grammy rivalry, Nero was a fan and friend of Mancini and participated in a tribute to the late composer/conductor at the Hollywood Bowl in 1996.

Leaving RCA, Nero moved to Columbia Records and had a million-selling single record and album with an instrumental version of the theme from the movie *The Summer of '42,* a nostalgic tale of two teenage boys enjoying their last days of adolescence as the United States enters World War II. The wistful, melancholic tune, composed by Michel Legrand, with lyrics by Marilyn and Alan Bergman, won the Oscar for best song. In recent years Nero has recorded for both Intrasound and Concord Records.

Nero's thorough musical knowledge and versatility led him to conducting and serving as musical director for orchestras. Since 1977, he has been conductor and musical director of the Philly Pops. "There's always a problem reviewing a performance of Peter Nero and the Philly Pops. You want to single out the best number, or maybe two or three best, and you can't, because there are so many," wrote Leonard W. Boasberg of the *Philadelphia Inquirer.* Nero is also conductor and director of popular music for the Tulsa Philharmonic and the Florida Philharmonic. A typical Nero concert features a mix of Broadway tunes, popular music, and some classical works. "With pops concerts, you're dealing with people who are exposed to everything in the media. That makes them a tough audience. They don't want just to be entertained, they have to be moved," Nero told the *Daily Oklahoman.*

Throughout his career, Nero has avoided categorization. Finding connections between different types of music is a Nero trademark. An example of Nero's approach is his picking up on a Mozart-like sound in Richard Rodgers' snappy showtune *Mountain Greenery.* "This is strictly an expression of myself, an expression of my impatience with both jazz and classical music," he told *High Fidelity.*

Nero has long been interested in electrical gadgetry and electronics. At age fifteen, he designed and built an electric baseball game using a battery and flashlight bulbs. Although he does not use an electronic synthesizer on stage, considering it an entirely different instrument from the acoustic piano, he is a computer aficionado off-stage. He has written software programs to help him forecast the profitability of performing engagements, and to aid him in putting together imaginative concert selections. He has also designed a program to keep track of airline bonus miles which, since he is on the road half the year, can add up to a significant savings. Nero told *Personal Computing,* "The reason I got into programming, aside from my passion for electronics, is that I was bogged down in paperwork. The amount of time I actually spend with music is about 10 percent of my time. The other 90 percent is business. I have a lot of people who perform services for me ... but somebody has to watch the store. I've found that unless the artist himself is really on top of everything and knows what's going on things don't quite get done the way they should."

In addition to performing over one hundred recital and symphony concerts each season, Nero also tours with a trio. The Peter Nero Trio has appeared in Atlantic City, Lake Tahoe, Las Vegas, and with Frank Sinatra at Radio City Music Hall in New York. Primary among Nero compositions is *The Diary,* based on the writings of Anne Frank. In keeping with Nero's eclectic style, the work includes original songs combining rock and traditional music. Producer Sheldon Saltman is developing *The Diary* for Broadway.

Nero has been married to Peggy Altman since 1977. His previous marriage ended in divorce. He has two children from his first marriage, Jedd, a New York real estate entrepreneur, and Beverly, an aspiring actress in California.

"Ultimately, audiences want you to make them want to come back again," is how Nero summed up his attitude toward performing and conducting to the *Daily Oklahoman.* "So I tell the players they can't just play the notes. They have to approach the music the same way as if they were playing a Beethoven symphony. You've got to have the same attention to detail and dynamics. When that happens, it makes everything worthwhile. You can look out into the hall and see that people smiling. Then you know they're having a good time."

Selected discography

Albums

Piano Forte, RCA, 1961.
New Piano in Town, RCA, 1961.
Young and Warm and Wonderful, RCA, 1962.
For the Nero Minded, RCA, 1962.
The Colorful Peter Nero, RCA, 1962.
Hail the Conquering Nero, RCA, 1963.
Three Great Pianos (with Frankie Carle and Floyd Cramer), RCA, 1963.

Peter Nero in Person, RCA, 1963.
Sunday in New York, RCA, 1964.
Reflections, RCA, 1964.
Peter Nero Plays Songs You Won't Forget, RCA, 1964.
The Best of Peter Nero, RCA, 1965. *Career Girls,* RCA, 1965.
Nero Goes Pops (with the Boston Pops), RCA, 1965.
Peter Nero Up Close, RCA, 1966.
Music to Paint By, RCA, 1996. *Peter Nero on Tour,* RCA, 1966.
The Screen Scene, RCA, 1966.
Nero-ing in on the Hits, RCA, 1967.
Peter Nero Plays a Salute to Herb Alpert and the Tijuana Brass, RCA, 1967.
Tender is the Night, RCA, 1967.
Xochimilco, RCA, 1967.
Peter Nero Plays "Born Free" and Others, RCA, 1967.
Peter Nero Plays "Love is Blue" and Ten Other Great Songs, RCA, 1968.
Fantasy and Improvisations (Blue Fantasy), RCA, 1968.
If Ever I Would Leave You, RCA, 1968.
Gershwin's Concerto in F, RCA, 1968. *I mpressions. The Great Songs of Burt Bacharach and Hal David,* RCA, 1968.
Love Trip, RCA, 1969.
Music Festival of Hits, RCA, 1969.
From "Hair" to Hollywood, Columbia, 1969.
I've Gotta Be Me, Columbia, 1969.
I'll Never Fall in Love Again: Peter Nero Plays the Great Love Songs of Today, Columbia, 1970. *Love Story,* Columbia, 1970.
Peter Nero!, RCA, 1970.
Fiedler and His Friends (with the Boston Pops), RCA, 1971.
This is Broadway, RCA, 1971.
The Summer of '42, Columbia, 1971.
Peter Nero Plays Music from Great Motion Pictures, RCA, 1972.
This is Peter Nero, RCA, 1972.
The World's Favorite Gershwin, RCA, 1972.
The First Time Ever (I Saw Your Face), Columbia, 1972.
'S Wonderful, 'S Marvelous, 'S Gershwin, Daybreak, 1972.
Say, Has Anybody Seen My Sweet Gypsy Rose, Columbia, 1973.
The World of Peter Nero, Columbia, 1973.
A Quadraphonic Concert! (with Andre Kostelanetz), Columbia, 1973.
Peter Nero's Greatest Hits, Columbia, 1974.
The Best of Burt Bacharach, RCA, 1975.
Disco, Dance, and Love Themes of the '70s, Arista, 1975.
Wives and Lovers, Pickwick, 1976.
The Wiz, Crystal Clear Records, 1977.
Peter Nero Now, Concord, 1977.
Peter Goes Pop, Allegiance, 1987.
The Sounds of Love, Bainbridge, 1987.
Peter Nero Plays Great Songs from the Movies, Sony, 1990.
Anything But Lonely, Intersound, 1990.
(With the Rochester Philharmonic) *Classic Connections,* Intersound, 1991.

Peter Nero Plays the Hits, Intersound, 1993.
It Had to Be You, Intersound, 1994.

Sources

Books

Maltin, Leonard. *Leonard Maltin's Movie and Video Guide.*
New York: Signet, 1996.

Periodicals

American Record Guide, May 1969, p.782.
Computers & Electronics, November 1983, p.62-66.

High Fidelity Magazine, February 1963, p.57-59, 122.
Keyboard Classics, September/October 1991, p.8-9.
New York Times, April 11, 1994, p.C16
Personal Computing, December 1984, p.49-50.

Online

www.peternero.com

Information also obtained from Gurtman and Murtha Associates.

—Mary C. Kalfatovic

Northern Lights

Bluegrass band

Although the roots of bluegrass music tap deep into the soil of the Appalachian Mountain region, its branches have stretched over the entire United States and beyond, adapting to the varied climates wherein they eventually find themselves. Of New England-variety bluegrass, none is more popular than the music of the Boston-based band called Northern Lights. With its progressive, up tempo bluegrass salted with elements of western swing, blues, folk, Cajun, and classical music, the band's renown has spread outside of the northeast to reach even some of the more traditional bluegrass strongholds. "This phenomenal quartet of singing, picking, and songwriting talents keeps earning respect and building audiences nationwide," notes Richard D. Smith in his *Bluegrass: An Informal Guide;* "a true achievement for a band that was founded some degrees of latitude away from the Mason-Dixon line."

Since forming during the mid-1970s, Northern Lights has recorded several albums, and has toured extensively throughout the United States on the bluegrass festival circuit. Each of the group's three albums on

Photo by Linda Armerding. Reproduced by permission.

For the Record . . .

Members include **Taylor Armerding**, mandolin, vocals; **Bill Henry**, lead and rhythm guitar, vocals (1982—); **Mike Kropp**, banjo (1984—); **Jeff Horton**, electric bass, vocals (1989-94); **Jake Armerding**, fiddle, vocals (1990—); **Chris Miles**, electric bass, vocals (1994—).

Began as How Banks Fail, Boston, Massachusetts, 1975; changed name to Northern Lights, 1976; signed with Flying Fish Records, 1989; signed with Red House Records, 1996. Have performed at festivals throughout the United States, including the Winterhawk Bluegrass Festival, 1996.

Awards: Third place award, Kentucky Fried Chicken Best New Bluegrass Band Contest, 1986; "Winterhawk" was a song-of-the-year finalist, International Bluegrass Music Association, 1990.

Addresses: *Record company*—Red House Records P.O. Box 4044 St. Paul, MN 55104. *Management*—Linda Bolton 161 Pantry Rd., Sudbury, MA 01776-1112.

Flying Fish Records (a Chicago-based label now owned by Rounder) reached the top 10 spot on countrywide bluegrass radio playlists, according to the *Bluegrass Unlimited* National Bluegrass Survey. Northern Lights signed with Minnesota-based Red House Records in 1996; their first Red House album, *Living in the City*, was released that July. The group's broad-minded approach to what constitutes "bluegrass" music, while possibly not appealing to dyed-in-the-wool bluegrass purists, has gained them a large base of younger fans who will carry an appreciation for this traditional American music into the next century.

Beantown-based Bluegrass

Northern Lights is one of several popular New England-based bluegrass bands—among them the Beacon Hill Billies, Southern Rail, and the Kennebec Valley Boys—to build a strong regional following. Started by mandolinist Taylor Armerding and friends in 1975 as a local bar band called How Banks Fail, the group changed its moniker to Northern Lights the following year. Although the group disbanded a few years later, Armerding met up with a guitar enthusiast named Bill Horton in 1981, and the two decided to give Northern Lights another go.

The band was reformed with new members in 1982.

Joined by such talented young players as Californian banjoist Alison Brown during her stint at Harvard Business School, the rejuvenated band exhibited the kind of "revolving-door" membership so common to local bluegrass groups. When banjoist Mike Kropp signed on in 1984, the band's roster began to stabilize and the group finally had the chance to work on developing a unique "sound." At this point, Northern Lights began to build a strong regional following, bounding into the national spotlight for the first time in 1986 as third-place winners in the annual Kentucky Fried Chicken Best Bluegrass Band playoffs in Louisville, Kentucky. Although they were nudged out of second place by a mere teenager, Northern Lights had no cause not to be proud of their achievement—the teen that bested them was then-fifteen-year-old *wunderkind* Alison Krauss, a bluegrass fiddler and vocalist who has gone on to Grammy Award-winning acclaim with her band Union Station. Krauss would join Northern Lights on their first album, *Take You to the Sky*, in 1990.

Northern Lights Roster

Unlike country groups, where band members stand well to the back of a cowboy-hatted or big-haired singer, a bluegrass band is judged on the strength of each of its pickers as individual musicians. It's a tradition dating back to the early 1940s, when a mandolinist from Kentucky named Bill Monroe first set fire to the ballads and mountain music he had heard as a child and listeners dubbed the new sound "bluegrass." And in the case of Northern Lights, there's definitely fire in the oven. While the band's members have a vast array of musical influences between them—everything from classical to rock—as banjoist Mike Kropp told Fran Larkin in *Acoustic Musician,* "'In Northern Lights, the place where we meet is bluegrass.'" The progressive edge to their sound is honed by their more sophisticated, urban backgrounds in New England, a far cry from the high hills and shady hollers of Bill Monroe country.

Mandolinist, lead vocalist, and songwriter Taylor Armerding builds his love of bluegrass on classical music roots—he played piano and clarinet as a child—and on the vocal harmonizing he learned while singing in his hometown church choir. During high school Armerding got hooked on folk music and taught himself guitar; the bluegrass bug would bite several years later when he attended a Oldtime Fiddlers convention while on leave from the army in 1972. After his discharge three years later, Armerding linked up with the first incarnation of Northern Lights—the Boston-area-based How Banks

Fail. He has been the main force behind the band ever since. Two of Armerding's compositions from 1990's *Take You to the Sky*— "Northern Rail" and "Winterhawk"—charted in *Bluegrass Unlimited* magazine's top ten; "Winterhawk" would go on to be a finalist for 1990's International Bluegrass Music Association Song of the Year honors.

The second half of the band's founding team, Connecticut-born Bill Henry, started flat-picking after hearing guitar genius Doc Watson work his magic on a six-string. To encourage his son's interest in music, Henry's father made his son a guitar, which Henry still uses for practice. Jazz entered Henry's musical mix during his attendance at Boston's famed Berklee School of Music, and he went on to perform with several regional jazz bands, including Boston's Hot off the Frets, and as part of the Big Apple-based Charged Particles. Henry's uniquely complex guitar work has added much to Northern Lights' sound since he joined Armerding in 1982, and his instrumental compositions, which feature strong guitar leads, have been featured on several of the band's albums.

Newer Members, Tradition, and Experience

Like many banjo pickers of his generation, Mike Kropp's life changed when he heard the music of banjoist extraordinaire Earl Scruggs: He picked up a banjo at age fifteen and has yet to put it down. Building on a base of classical and old-timey banjo techniques, including clawhammer and two-finger style, Kropp was quick to master the three-fingered Scruggs-style picking. Before joining Armerding and Henry as part of Northern Lights in mid-1984 Kropp played with Connecticut bluegrass bands Bluegrass Special and Special Delivery, and hosted a Massachusetts bluegrass radio show. A studio veteran of both sides of the mixing board, Kropp has recorded or performed with artists that include bluegrassers Peter Rowan and Vassar Clements and Carole King, David Bromberg, Don MacLean, Jose Feliciano, and Eric Weissberg. He also worked as a staff producer for Columbia Records in New York City.

It wasn't only the strong bluegrass tradition of family-based bands that made it inevitable that Jake Armerding (son of founder Taylor) would join Northern Lights: scarcely out of high school, Jake was already a seasoned veteran. Studying both classical violin and bluegrass fiddle since he was a child, the younger Armerding was winning musical awards even in middle school. And in 1991, at the age of thirteen, he won the Lowell, Massachusetts, Fiddle Contest, where he competed against fiddlers many years his senior. First appearing alongside his father and the rest of Northern

Lights during a concert in Nantucket, Rhode Island, in May of 1990, Jake performed with the band on a part-time basis while finishing high school and learning Northern Lights' progressive bluegrass repertoire. He became a full-time member in November, 1992, and has since contributed several original tunes to the band's playlist.

Bassist and vocalist Jeff Horton linked up with Northern Lights in the fall of 1989. Horton was raised in a musical family, which includes a brother who is a talented and prolific songwriter. He sang throughout his high school years in Mansfield, Massachusetts, while mastering the upright bass, forming a country/bluegrass band the year of his college graduation. From 1979 to 1987 Horton played and recorded with the Rhode Island-based Neon Valley Boys; a stint with Boston's Bluegrass Special would introduce him to Northern Lights banjoist Kropp. Meanwhile, attendees at bluegrass festivals in the area would occasionally spot Horton jamming with Armerding and Henry. Horton played bass and sang lead, baritone, and tenor vocals in a local country band before returning to his bluegrass roots and joining Northern Lights.

After working with Northern Lights for five years, Horton left the band in the summer of 1994, and was replaced by fellow New Englander Chris Miles. Strongly influenced by both jazz and opera—his mother was a student at New York City's Metropolitan Opera—Miles has a background in trumpet and clarinet, in addition to providing the band with a measured bass line and well-schooled vocals. In true bluegrass style, Miles honed up on the band's repertoire quickly enough to join them on stage at the 1996 Winterhawk Bluegrass Festival in New York state, where the group performed before one of the largest crowds of bluegrass aficionados in the nation. His bass playing has been the driving force behind the Northern Lights sound ever since.

Reaching out to Larger Audiences

With a membership that remains committed to furthering their collective bluegrass music accomplishments, Northern Lights has appeared at major festivals and concert venues from New England to California, and has performed on stage alongside such well-known bluegrassers as Peter Rowan, Jonathan Edwards, fiddler Vassar Clements, Dave Mallett, the Seldom Scene, the Tony Rice Unit, Tim O'Brien, the Austin Lounge Lizards, and Ranch Romance. While their success has made the group a stand-out among the many bluegrass bands that perform throughout the nation, they continue to work to perfect their sound. Leader Taylor Armerding is clearly focused on the group's goals: "I'd love to see us make better music, and I'd love to see us get a wider audience," he told Larkin. "If there's a goal, I would love for [the music we make] to get a little more recognition, for people to acknowledge that it's good music." It's a goal that the band is sure to achieve, in characteristic Northern Lights style. "Somehow you have to get five people to agree on [the band's sound]," Henry explained, to Larkin, describing the group's dynamic. "Everyone is always gracious to give something a try. Sometimes you have to scrap a little bit." "It depends on what feels comfortable," Kropp added. "I think there's a nice blend happening."

Selected discography

(With Alison Krauss, Peter Rowan, and Matt Glaser) *Take You to the Sky,* Flying Fish, 1990.
(With Vassar Clements, Glaser, and Stuart Duncan) *Can't Buy Your Way*, Flying Fish, 1992.
(With others) *The Third Winterhawk Scholarship Album,*
Gordo, c. 1993.
Wrong Highway Blues, Red House Records, 1994.
Living In the City, Red House Records, 1996.

Sources

Books

Smith, Richard D., *Bluegrass: An Informal Guide,* A Cappella Press (Chicago), 1995.

Periodicals

Acoustic Musician, January 1996; September 1996, pp. 16-20.
Bluegrass Unlimited, February 1994.

Additional information for this profile was provided by Linda Bolton, Northern Lights Management.

—*Pamela Shelton*

The Offspring

Rock group

Achieving superstar status with their repertoire of punk songs that cross the border into tuneful pop, The Offspring have carved out a unique place for themselves in rock music. "We've approached the punk-rock thing as a legitimate style of music, and we try to play it like a real band and write lyrics that people can identify with," claimed the group's songwriter and lead singer Dexter Holland in *Rolling Stone.* Jon Pareles acknowledged the group's versatility in the *New York Times,* calling their music "a grab-bag of Southern California rock: speedy punk and ska, twangy surf-rock, hefty hard rock, nasal grunge melodies and ardent new wave." Offspring became one of the super groups on the alternative rock circuit after scoring a surprise number-one hit with "Come Out and Play (You Gotta Keep 'Em Separated)" in 1994 from their widely popular *Smash* album.

Unlike typical punk music stars whose anger was ignited by urban blight, the members of The Offspring were more geeks than rebels, and they grew up fairly well-to-do in the suburbs of California's Orange County. Group

Photo by F. Scott Shafer. Columbia Records. Reproduced by permission.

Members include **Bryan "Dexter" Holland,** vocals, guitar; **Greg "Noodles" Wasserman**, guitar and vocals; **Greg "Greg K." Kriesel,** bass; **Ron Welty,** drums.

First began rehearsing as a band (Holland and Kriesel), 1984; began performing at 924 Gilman Street club in Berkeley, CA, 1986; paid to release its first single, 1987; signed recording contract with Nemesis, 1989; released first album, *The Offspring,* on Nemesis, 1989; signed contract with Epitaph Records, 1990s; released *Ignition* on Epitaph, 1992; scored first hit single with "Come Out and Play," 1994; generated biggest sales of all time for an album on an independent label (*Smash*), 1994; performed as opening act for telecast of the *Billboard Music Awards,* 1994; re-released *The Offspring* on their own label, Nitro, 1995; performed in Reading Festival, U.K.; Bizarre Festival, Germany; and Pukklepop Festival, Belgium, 1996; signed recording contract with Columbia, 1996; released *Ixnay on the Hombre* on Columbia, 1997.

Addresses: *Record company*—Columbia Records, 550 Madison Avenue, New York, NY 10022-3211.

leader Bryan "Dexter" Holland was valedictorian of his high school class, became a pre-med student in college and is currently close to earning his Ph.D. in microbiology. He first became enamored with punk music in his senior year at Pacifica High School in California, after hearing music by T.S.O.L., The Adolescents, and Agent Orange. "Something about those bands at the time made me really excited, and got me interested enough to want to start a band," said Holland in *RIP.* Holland and Greg Kriesel, both of whom ran on the school's cross-country team, formed the group Manic Subsidal with two other teammates in 1984 despite not knowing how to play any instruments. "Bryan and I both learned together, and he wasn't even playing chords at the time, so he'd play on one string, and I tried to do the same thing," Kriesel told *Rolling Stone.*

After graduating from high school, Holland and Kriesel went off to college and were limited to rehearsing on weekends. Kevin Wasserman, an older Pacifica graduate who was working as the school janitor, came into the

group when their guitarist left the band. Ron Welty took over drumming duties permanently after frequent stand-ins for the regular drummer, who was attending medical school and was increasingly unavailable. Meanwhile, Holland was venturing into songwriting and the group was eager to get into the studio.

Signed with Small Label

In 1987 the group used their own money to record a seven-inch single, but then couldn't sell it. Two years of rough times followed before they landed a contract with Nemesis, a small punk label distributed by Cargo. With Nemesis they produced another seven-inch single called "Baghdad" and their first album called *The Offspring* in 1989. Producing the album was Thom Wilson, who had also produced songs for T.S.O.L., The Vandals, and The Dead Kennedys.

Offspring's first recordings were standard punk songs. "All punk bands back in '84 wrote about was police, death, religion and war," said Holland in *Rolling Stone.* "So that's what we did." As the group began sending out demo recordings to the full gamut of punk labels, they attracted the attention of Brett Gurewitz, the guitarist with Bad Religion who also owned Epitaph Records. Epitaph signed the group and released its *Ignition* LP in 1992, which sold over 30,000 copies. Word got out on the potential of Offspring, resulting in a bidding war between major record labels, but the group decided to stay with Epitaph.

Had Surprise Hit

"You could tell as the tracks starting going down that there was something kind of neat going on," Holland told the *Los Angeles Times* about the recording of *Smash* in 1994. "And like when we got done we thought, 'Wow, we made a neat little record.'" However, no one in the group anticipated the tremendous impact that the album had on the music world. When Epitaph tried to promote airplay of the album's "Come Out and Play" on the Los Angeles alternative-rock station KROQ, no one in the band felt that the song was that special, according to the *Los Angeles Times.* Before long the song was being played frequently on many commercial stations, as well as on television. After "Come Out and Play," which *Rolling Stone* called "worthy of the best rock-songwriting tradition," soared up the charts, the Offspring soon became superstars whose fame rivaled that of punkdom's Green Day. The singles "Self-Esteem" and "Gotta Get Away" from *Smash* also proved popular, helping boost worldwide sales of the album to over nine million and making it the top-selling LP ever on an independent label.

After the release of *Smash,* the Offspring toured extensively in the U.S., Europe, Japan, and Australia. In 1996 they signed a contract with Columbia Records after disagreements with Epitaph. Their first release on the new label was *Ixnay on the Hombre* in 1997. The release was produced by Dave Jerden, who had worked with Social Distortion and Jane's Addiction. As on *Smash,* the group offered a mix of hardcore music, hard rock, pop, and ska on the new album. *Ixnay on the Hombre* also featured much experimenting with different tempos and rhythms. "Gone Away" starts slowly, luring the listener into thinking it's a ballad before erupting into ferocious rock, and mideastern guitar riffs add an exotic flair to "Me & My Old Lady."

Although known as tireless performers who gladly take to the road, Offspring has not embraced their current fame without reservation. "Sometimes we feel the spotlight," Holland told the *Los Angeles Times.* "It gets kind of uncomfortable, you know, having people watch you all the time."

Selected discography

The Offspring, Nemesis, 1989.
Ignition, Epitaph, 1992.
Smash, Epitaph, 1994.
Ixnay on the Hombre, Columbia, 1997.

Sources

Periodicals

Entertainment Weekly, August 12, 1994, pp. 54–55.
Los Angeles Times, January 29, 1995, p. 8
Musician, August 1994, p. 90.
New York Times, February 22, 1997, p. A17.
RIP, October 1994, pp. 8–10.
Rolling Stone, November 3, 1994, pp. 25–27; February 9, 1995, pp. 43–45.
Spin, November 1994, pp. 47–50; March 1995, pp. 24–25.

Additional information for this profile was obtained from publicity materials from the Mitch Schneider Organization released by Sony Records.

—Ed Decker

Joan Osborne

Singer, songwriter

AP/Wide World Photos. Reproduced by permission.

When Joan Osborne sauntered onto the music scene in 1995 with her major label debut *Relish*, she commanded notice. With her big bluesy voice, unconventional sex appeal, and smart feminist attitude, critics and fans could not help but like her. *Entertainment Weekly* named her double platinum *Relish* the number one album of 1995, and it garnered seven Grammy nominations. It is not where Osborne expected to end up, but now that she has arrived, she has made herself right at home.

Joan Elizabeth Osborne was born the second oldest of six children in the small town of Anchorage, Kentucky, not far from Louisville. She was a feisty and arty kid and not a backwoods hick, as she likes to point out. Called Elizabeth until first grade, she promptly came home one day and told the family her name was Joan and that is what they were to call her. She has always been socially conscious and always a natural performer.

In high school, Osborne got into punk rock music and musical theater. Her mom proudly encouraged Osborne. She was also an excellent student, causing hopes in the family that she might be a doctor. She herself never could imagine a performer's life. "Where I'm from," she told *Rolling Stone's* Ann Powers, "the notion of becoming a professional artist is looked upon as being unrealistic and sort of conceited."

Apparently though, when this lapsed Catholic first "fell from grace"—her mother found out she was having sex at 17—she was asked to leave. She graduated high school in 1980, then went to Louisville and began studying theater arts at the state university, but left school after 18 months. She had been singing in musicals and even worked briefly at the Burt Reynolds Dinner Theater in Jupiter, Florida.

In the mid 1980s, Osborne received a small scholarship to go to film school at New York University. But after three years her money simply ran out. Letters from Anchorage encouraged her to come home and be sensible. Although she felt lost in New York and was quickly losing her sense of self worth, Osborne stuck it out. She happened to wander into a cool club one night in Greenwich Village and found a scene in which she felt welcome. One drunken night at a place called the Abilene Cafe, with all her friends were rooting her on, Osborne climbed up on the stage and belted out the gospel standard "God Bless the Child." They asked her back for their weekly jam session. As Powers wrote, "Sitting in with these [local] bands, Osborne quickly realized that the Janis Joplin-inspired balls-out blues queen was one persona that could accommodate her gifts."

For the Record . . .

Born July 8, 1962, in Anchorage, KY; daughter of Jerry (a general contractor) and Ruth (an interior decorator; maiden name, Yunker) Osborne. Education: attended film school at New York University, mid 1980s.

Singer and songwriter. Began singing at blues clubs around New York City, late 1980s; released *Soul Show* on her own Womanly Hips Music label, 1991; major label debut, *Relish*, 1995.

Addresses: *Record Company*—Mercury Records, Worldwide Plaza, 825 Eighth Ave., New York, NY 10019.

Osborne quickly immersed herself in R&B greats like Otis Redding, as well as the Library of Congress's recordings of singing cotton field hands and Appalachian backwoods types. Osborne was hooked. Pretty soon she had a band and was playing gigs five nights a week. A few things worried her though: Would she be considered a pretender singing the blues? Would mainstream America accept an average-looking woman as opposed to some fashion model? But the singing just felt right, and, as she remarked to *Out's* Tom Donghy regarding some of her R&B and soul influences including Etta James, Aretha Franklin, and Mavis Staples, "Those women were unabashedly sexual, but in that was a sense of humor, strength, and real humanness." And to Chris Willman of *Entertainment Weekly*, "[They] seemed to be almost like this feminist ideal. You could be sexual and strong and funny, but you didn't have to look airbrushed. It seemed a more accurate reflection of the way I feel about sexuality than anything I generally see in the media."

From Womanly Hips to Blue Gorilla

In 1991, Osborne released a live album, *Soul Show,* on her own Womanly Hips Music label. Two years later she released the album *Blue Million Miles.* Although the first record was in strict Janis Joplin mode, the album had a bit more of a rock flavor. Meanwhile, Osborne was waiting for the right deal. In 1993, producer Rick Chertoff needed talent for his new label, Blue Gorilla. A friend, Rob Hyman, with whom Chertoff had worked in the band the Hooters back in the 1980s, proposed Osborne. Chertoff loved her work and suggested she collaborate with him, Hyman, and another former member of the

Hooters, Eric Bazalian. Osborne was hesitant, but "within four or five hours of meeting for the first time we'd written 'Dracula Moon,'" she told *Q's* Phil Sutcliffe. "Ideas flow out of them like water."

The eventual result was 1995's *Relish.* The single "One of Us," about imagining God as just a regular person, worried Osborne. Bazalian had written this one by himself and Osborne was not sure it was true to the rest of the album. It became a huge hit, however, and if people were thrown off by the rest of Osborne's work, few complained.

Reviews of *Relish*

Rolling Stone wrote in their four star review, "Osborne astutely conflates the sacred and profane, and over inventive alterna-cool arrangements ... lets her strong, bluesy vocals rip.... What's especially winning about the woman is her range: Sexy and earnest, her voice, all on its own, conveys whole choirs of feeling." And Jon Pareles wrote of her live show in the *New York Times,* "The songs acknowledge both lust and disillusion without cynicism, and Ms. Osborne's voice teases out every undertone of her smart, subtle lyrics."

Although her work was nominated for seven Grammys, Osborne did not receive any. She did not particularly care, though. Joan Osborne is exactly where she wants to be and she is doing it on her own terms. A long time friend Kirsten Ames told *Rolling Stone's* Powers, "there was always this peace with Joan. She knew everything was going to happen. She's a great example of someone who had to play the game for a while and then reached the moment she'd been waiting for. I think she's going to get what she wants out of this."

Selected discography

Soul Show, Womanly Hips Music, 1991.
Blue Million Miles, Womanly Hips Music, 1993.
Relish (includes "One of Us"), Blue Gorilla/Mercury, 1995.

Sources

Billboard, January 14, 1995.
Entertainment Weekly, December 29, 1995; February 2, 1996.
Gavin, April 14, 1995.
Louisville, December 1995.
New York, June 3, 1996.
New York Times, February 9, 1995; March 5, 1995.
Out, June 1996.

Philadelphia Inquirer, June 27, 1995.

Pollstar, October 30, 1995.

Q, June 1996.

Request, February 1996.

Rockpile, November 1995.

Rolling Stone, May 4, 1995; March 21, 1996.

USA Today, December 4, 1996.

Washington Post, December 19, 1995.

Additional information for this profile was provided by Mercury Records press materials, 1996.

—Joanna Rubiner

Pigface

Alternative industrial act

Pigface defies categorization. Less an actual band than a recording and performing ensemble of well-known musicians in the alternative/industrial genre, it is also, in a way, a political statement. Founding member Martin Atkins had tired of the "rock" star attitudes he witnessed as a member of successful bands like Public Image Limited and Killing Joke; in addition, despite the fact that both acts presented groundbreaking, anti-establishment-themed sonic artistry, both remained under the thumb of record label executives. Sandy Masuo, writing about Pigface in *Option* magazine, equated it with "a savvy, calculating brand of post-punk punk attitude—one that's all about recapturing the means of production that was supposedly seized in the '70s" with the birth of the punk movement.

Pigface was formed in the wake of several musicians—already acquainted with one another's work—who remained in Chicago after the end of a Ministry tour (Ministry founder Al Jourgensen as well as his bandmates are Windy City residents). The founding members coalesced around William Tucker from and William

Photo by John Hughes. MICHAEL OCHS ARCHIVES/Venice, CA. Reproduced by permission.

For the Record . . .

Consistent members include **Martin Atkins** (born in England; married; wife's name, Leila Eminson Atkins), **William Rieflin, William Tucker, En Esch, Nivek Ogre,** and **Chris Connelly.** Occasional members include Trent Reznor, Lesley Rankine, Fuzz, Flour, Andrew Weiss, Paul Raven, Mary Byker, and Genesis P. Orridge, among others.

Band formed c. 1990; Atkins was the original drummer for Public Image Limited (PiL) and later for Killing Joke; after falling upon hard times in the mid-1980s, during which he worked as a landscaper, he founded his own label, Invisible Records, in Chicago with wife Leila Eminson in 1987. Rieflin was a veteran of Ministry, as was Tucker, who also played in My Life with the Thrill Kill Kult; En Esch was a founding member of KMFDM, and Ogre was a founding member of Skinny Puppy; Chris Connelly was part of a Ministry side project, the Revolting Cocks.

Addresses: Record company—Invisible Records, P.O. Box 16008, Chicago, IL 60616.

Rieflin, both from Ministry; Skinny Puppy's Nivek Ogre; Chris Connelly from the Revolting Cocks, a Ministry side project; German musician En Esch of KMFDM, an opening act for Ministry on that tour; and finally, guiding force Martin Atkins. Rieflin and Atkins had met as dual drummers for the Ministry tour. It was Atkins who came up with the name Pigface for the collective; long ago, he had been in a band of the same name that played strip shows. Moving on to better projects, he later served as the original drummer for PiL, the group formed by John Lydon (formerly Johnny Rotten) in the aftermath of the Sex Pistols' demise. After leaving the group in 1984, he became an occasional drummer for the British band Killing Joke, considered the forefathers of today's alternative/industrial genre. In 1987 he founded his own record label, Invisible, in Chicago with wife Leila Eminson.

Debuted with *Gub*

The aforementioned six musicians recorded Pigface's debut, *Gub,* bringing on board legendary Chicago sound engineer Steve Albini, creative mind behind the band Big Black. It was recorded in less than a week. David Yow of the Jesus Lizard as well as Paul Barker,

Connelly's colleague from Ministry and Revolting Cocks, joined them in the studio; an up-and-coming Cleveland musician named Trent Reznor also helped out. Atkins then went on tour with Killing Joke, and nearly a year after the recording of *Gub,* contacted the other members and suggested a tour. (Standard practice holds that bands tour at the time of a record's release, in order to boost sales.) The tour line-up was slightly different, with Atkins, Connelly, Ogre, Tucker, Matt Schultz, and Paul Raven, another Killing Joke alumnus. Sharon O'Connell, writing for *Melody Maker,* caught a London date of the European leg and described the supergroup as "all muscle, mean, chewed sinew tensed to the point of rigidity, but somehow still with room to get funky. Well, as funky as a machine punch can get, I guess."

All shows from the first Pigface tour were recorded on DAT (digital audio tape, a superior but expensive recording technology introduced in the mid-1980s), and Atkins assembled them into the live album *Welcome to Mexico,* released in 1991. The sheer logistics of recruiting members of various bands to assemble for a specific block of time—then winning permission from the various labels involved—was difficult. Joining the party were various other musicians picked up along the way for a show or two, including members of Silverfish, Front Line Assembly, Devo, and GWAR. "Yet a cohesive unit they are turning out to be, and a particularly fine and confrontational one," wrote *Melody Maker*'s Neil Perry in a review. "As a document of chaos in motion, 'Welcome to Mexico' is scorched around the edges but well worthy of your attention."

Added New Members

Bands signed generally had some ties to Pigface, such as Murder, Inc., featuring members of Killing Joke. In 1992 Atkins' Invisible label released *Fook,* Pigface's second full-length studio LP. The line-up consisted of Atkins, Mary Byker (from Gaye Bykers on Acid), Ogre, Connelly, En Esch, Flour, Tucker, Raven, Lesley Rankine from Silverfish, Rollins Band alumni Chris Haskett and Andrew Weiss, Barbara Hunter on cello, Sean Joyce, and David Sims of the Jesus Lizard. Atkins' former Killing Joke mate Geordie Walker also helped out. Christina Zafiris, writing for *College Music Journal,* called *Fook* "more diverse" than the previous effort, and the newer members "[gave] the songs a deeper perspective." The tour roster for live dates was even more unwieldy.

As Pigface grew to achieve cult-like status among the more dedicated fans of the major-label bands, some members of the press began referring to it as a "supergroup." Atkins has voiced mixed opinions about the use of the term. "We are a 'super group,' not a bunch of old has-been dinosaurs wheeled out in oxygen tanks trying to recapture old faded glories," as Atkins told *Alternative Press* writer Jason Pettigrew, but also he dispelled any notion of Pigface as simply a big-name-ridden grasp for money. "Having the glorious position of being the guy who writes the checks on tour, I can tell you that if Pigface was a money-making scam, a picture of Trent Reznor would have been on the front cover of *Gub*..." Atkins told Pettigrew. In another interview, this time with Jon Seltzer of *Melody Maker*, Atkins explained the positive aspects of such a stellar amalgamation of musicians. "It's a reaction and a result of all the things that all of us have done," Atkins said of Pigface. "In some ways, it's like a rejuvenation for everyone who's in it. There are so many levels. We all get together, and we'll talk about who's getting what for tee-shirts, or which promoters are ripping who off. We check out each other's production techniques, each other's way of living, and it's great."

Gristle and Chili Pepper

In 1993 the double LP *Truth Will Out* was released overseas. Cathi Unsworth, reviewing it for *Melody Maker*, asserted *Truth Will Out* called to mind "a bleak, frozen landscape," and declared in conclusion that "numbing repetition and a sterile lack of humanity make an agonising truth drug." The next Pigface effort was *Notes from Thee Underground*, released on Invisible in 1994. Like the other releases, Atkins was responsible for both percussion and production. Guests included Genesis P. Orridge, founder of the seminal bands Throbbing Gristle and Psychic TV; Jello Biafra, formerly of the Dead Kennedys; Flea from the Red Hot Chili Peppers, and even diminutive Japanese girl-popsters Shonen Knife. In their press release for the record attempted to sum up their vision: "Have you ever left a show and thought about the way things could be? So have we. Have you ever felt cheated by the half-baked regurgitations of automatons? So have we. Have you ever wondered what's the point? So have we." *Option* magazine's Masuo called it "eclectic, eccentric, smart and beefy"; Atkins concurred, telling Masuo "it's user-friendly Pigface for sure."

The tour line-up for *Notes from Thee Underground* was even more complex. Permanent road players included Atkins, Byker, Taime Down (of Faster Pussycat), Meg Lee Chin (from Crunch), Charles Levi from My Life with the Thrill Kill Kult, Skinny Puppy alumnus Pat Sprawl, James Teitelbaum of the Evil Clowns, and Joe Trump of Elliot Sharp's Carbon. Coming aboard for certain dates were Orridge, Paul Ferguson (of both Killing Joke and The Orb), Danny Carey from Tool, Caspar Brotzman of German band Massaker, and Ogre. Again, the logistics of coordinating such a roster were nightmarish.

Reverse Attrition

In 1995, Pigface again recruited legendary industrial godfather Genesis P. Orridge, who claimed that when Atkins originally contacted him about participating in the Pigface line-up, "I didn't want to do it," he told Pettigrew in *Alternative Press*. "To be honest, I thought, `That sounds horrible, all those people from all those bands in one place, at one time.' And that's why I did it. Out of spite to myself. I really enjoyed not being in charge of the band." Such sentiments are common to Pigface's dedicated participants. "We have been dubbed the Alternative Traveling Wilburys," founding member Chris Connelly told *Melody Maker*'s Perry— referring to the late 1980s supergroup that included Tom Petty, Johnny Cash, and the late Roy Orbison— "and it's easy to say that, but that definitely isn't the point. One of the greatest things about Pigface is that there is total freedom, and allowances are made.... Pigface never went out to follow a certain path, and a year ago we never would have thought it could sound like this. William and I were thinking it would be great if in two years time none of us were in the band and it was a whole new set of people."

Selected discography

Albums; all on the Invisible label unless otherwise noted

Gub, 1990.
Welcome to Mexico (live), 1991.
Fook, 1992.
Truth Will Out (import), Devotion, 1993.
Notes from Thee Underground, 1994.

Also contributed tracks to the Invisible compilation *Feels Like Heaven*.

Sources

Periodicals

Alternative Press, November 1994.
College Music Journal, November 27, 1992.
Melody Maker, November 9, 1991, p. 26; November 23, 1991; December 12, 1992; November 6, 1993, p. 30.
Option, July/August 1994.

--Carol Brennan

Awadagin Pratt

Pianist

Pianist Awadagin Pratt is an engaging and exciting new presence in the world of classical music, where his passionate playing and unique interpretations have invigorated works by such composers as Brahms, Beethoven, Franck, and Liszt. Pratt, however, has garnered as much attention for superficialities that set him apart on the classical concert stage as he has for his musical prowess. First of all, he is young—in his early 30s—and he is black. He wears his shoulder-length hair in dreadlocks. He lives in Albuquerque, New Mexico, far from the glitter. When he plays, he sits at a low-riding 14-inch bench. And he is likely to perform in T-shirt or a black shirt and pants accented with a colorful tie rather than the more traditional tuxedo. Pratt—whose first name is pronounced ah-wah-DODGE-in—told *Newsweek's* Yah-lin Chang that people who learn he is a musician often assume he is part of a rock band. That is something, however, he finds uninteresting. "I don't have an interest in pop music," he said. "By and large, I find it to be boring. Rhythmically boring, harmonically boring, and melodically possibly interesting but for a very short time."

Pratt burst onto the scene in 1992, when he won the prestigious Naumburg International Piano Competition at Lincoln Center in New York City. He was the first African-American to win an international instrumental competition and first black instrumentalist since Andre Watts to get a recording contract with a major label. He is described as an independent and strong-willed man who has brought a challenging style and a sensual, intellectual virtuosity to classical music. "Pratt plays with a full-bodied intensity that can be at turns intimate and grandly heart-wrenching," Chang wrote. "He has a story to tell, and you can hear him agonizing over every twist. . . . Pratt commands your unfailing attention—without ever getting ostentatious."

Robin P. Robinson , writing in *Emerge* magazine, said Pratt "challenges the establishment and fans alike, forcing them to rethink the way music is perceived and heard." In the *New York Times*, James Barron called Pratt "a hot young pianist with a big sound and a knack for tackling fast, risky passages." And Robert Mann, president of the Naumburg Foundation, said the young pianist "has a rare gift. Very few artists create a sense that the music is theirs."

A Normal Childhood

Pratt was born in Pittsburgh and grew up in Normal, IL, where his father was a physics professor and his mother was a professor of social work at Illinois State University.

He began studying piano at age 6 and the violin when he was 9. As a child, however, tennis was more important to Pratt than music—and he was good enough at the game to turn professional. "I was aware that I showed some reasonable level of proficiency (as a musician), but it was never a prodigy-type thing," he told Robinson. "I was much more involved in tennis. My sister and I were both ranked regionally. It wasn't until I was about 16 that I decided to pursue music seriously." Pratt, in fact, appropriated his dreadlock hairstyle from tennis star Yannick Noah.

A Triple Talent

Pratt enrolled in the University of Illinois to study piano and violin. At age 18, he declared himself financially independent from his parents because they disapproved of his plans to be a performer rather than a music instructor. After three years at Illinois, he prepared to transfer to another institution. The New England Conservatory accepted him as a violinist but not as a pianist, while the Cleveland Institute accepted him as a pianist, but not as a violinist. Pratt elected to attend the Peabody Institute of Music in Baltimore, where he became the first person in the school's 137-year history to graduate with three areas of concentration: piano, violin and conducting. In 1990, he decided to focus on the piano and conducting—and let the violin go. "It's just that the piano has more repertoire," he said. "There's a much greater selection of music I like."

Pratt's victory in the Naumburg Competition in May 1992—and the $5,000 prize, lucrative 40-city concert tour, and recording contract it brought him—came just in time. He had passed up another competition the previous month because he couldn't scrape together the $60 entrance fee. Even so, he never lost sight of his purpose.

After winning Naumburg, Pratt told *People* magazine: "The audience—the people—you want them to be moved by your music. I always figured if I had that going for me, everything else would work out—regardless of whether someone thought I should cut my hair."

Pratt's repertoire puts a new spin on classic compositions. "He leans toward . . . probing, dense pieces by composers such as Brahms, Franck, and Liszt, rather than the more commercially popular Mozart or Vivaldi," Robinson wrote in *Emerge.* "Some critics have found Pratt's style and interpretation of the music a bit disconcerting because it doesn't always sound the way they're accustomed to hearing it. The criticism seems not to faze him. As far as he's concerned, no two musicians should be able to play the same piece of music exactly the same way. 'If one does completely play, internalizes the music, and comes to terms with it, without concern for how it will be perceived, it's bound to sound different,'" Pratt told Robinson. " 'I want to leave an audience with a sense of what these pieces of music are all about, why the composers were so moved they had to write it down on paper.'" In his interview with *Newsweek's* Chang, Pratt said, "I'll listen to five or six recordings (of a composition), and all the musicians are doing the same thing. And the interpretation will make no sense."

Pratt's approach has earned him prestigious awards, critically acclaimed albums, and an invitation to play at the White House in 1994. Following the release of his debut record—called A Long Way from Normal — reviewers raved about his ability to bring fire and freshness to familiar works, including Franck's *Prelude, Chorale* and *Fugue.* "Pratt has plenty of taste, artistry, and insight, all of which are immediately apparent in his comparatively light-textured, deftly colored rendition of Liszt's *Funerailles,*" *Stereo Review* magazine opined. "(He) seems to be a rare bird among competition winners: He's at home in the virtuoso repertory but comes across best in more introspective works that require genuine artistry ... (T)his is a wonderfully satisfying and promising debut album."

Pratt's Community Concerns

An unavoidable subtext to Pratt's story is his race. "The number of African-American pianists can be counted on one hand," Robinson pointed out. "Until recently, the best-known black soloists have been Leon Bates and Andre Watts, both of whom had established their careers by the time Pratt was born." Pratt's agent, Linda Marder, told one interviewer it was important for Pratt to be "taken seriously as a concert pianist—not qualified as an 'African-American concert pianist." On the other hand, Pratt's race carries with it special opportunities and responsibilities. His audiences, for example, are more racially integrated than most that attend classical concerts. And Pratt regularly plays for and talks about music with minority school children. His goal, Barron wrote in *New York Times*, is "to be a role model for black teenagers, to demystify classical music, and to prove that professional sports are not are only paths to fame." Pratt, meanwhile, sees a day when his race and the superficial differences that set him apart will stop garnering notice—and the attention will focus where it belongs, on his music. "I sort of expect that, in time, all the excess stuff won't be news: the bench, the dreadlocks, the blackness," he told Barron. "Not new news. When I wear t-shirts at a performance, that's what makes me comfortable. A tux, that creates barriers."

Selected discography

A Long Way from Normal, 1994, EMI Classics.
Beethoven Piano Sonatas, 1996, EMI Classics.

Sources

American Visions, October/November 1994, pp. 48.
Emerge, February 1995, p. 72.
Newsweek, Nov. 25, 1996, p. 79C.
New York Times, February 1995, pp. 244-245.
People, August 17, 1992.
Stereo Review, September 1994, pp. 111-112.

Lou Rawls

Rhythm and blues singer

AP/Wide World Photos. Reproduced by permission.

L ou Rawls is a rhythm and blues (R & B) singer with extraordinary career longevity and great generosity. His soulful singing career spans over 30 years, and his philanthropy includes helping to raise over 150 million dollars for The College Fund/United Negro College Fund (UNCF). His lengthy singing career began ironically after his life nearly ended in 1958 in a car accident.

Rawls was born on December 1, 1936 in Chicago, home to many great blues musicians. Son of a Baptist minister, he was raised on the South Side of Chicago where he started singing in church at age seven. In the mid-1950s, he toured with his gospel group, The Pilgrim Travelers, until he joined the United States Army in 1956. He served with the 82nd Airborne Division in Fort Bragg, North Carolina for two years. When he returned from military service, he toured again in 1958 with The Pilgrim Travelers. One rainy night the group was on their way to one of their concerts when they were in a car wreck. They collided with an 18-wheeler. Rawls was initially pronounced dead; Eddie Cunningham was killed; Cliff White broke his collarbone; Sam Cooke was hardly injured. Rawls wasn't dead, but lay in a coma for five days before waking and eventually recovering from the severe concussion.

In 1959, The Pilgrim Travelers broke up, and Rawls embarked on a solo career. The Pilgrim Travelers were based in Los Angeles, so Rawls stayed there after the breakup and toured the nightclubs and coffee shops. His location helped him earn a small acting role in the television series *77 Sunset Strip*. Rawls' big break came when he sang in a coffee shop called Pandora's Box. A producer from Capitol Records, Nick Benet, was in the coffee shop. To Rawls' surprise and delight, Benet asked him to record an audition tape. Capitol eventually signed Rawls to a contract in 1962. That same year, Rawls recorded a duet with Sam Cooke called "Bring It on Home to Me," now considered a classic. Sam Cooke moved on to a very successful singing and songwriting career before his untimely death at the age of 33.

Rawls first recordings were fairly successful. His first album was *Stormy Monday*. His 1963 album, *Black and Blue*, made the pop chart, but it wasn't until the 1966 album, *Lou Rawls Live*, that he crossed over to major market success. *Lou Rawls Live* was his first gold album. In 1966 the song "Love Is a Hurtin' Thing" went to number 13 on the pop charts, and hit number one on the R & B charts. Finally, Rawls was reaching white audiences with his smooth baritone. During the mid-1960s, Rawls liked to mix his songs with spoken monologues. In 1967 one of those songs, "Dead End Street," was number 29 on the pop charts and number three on the R & B charts. "Dead End Street" earned him his first

Born Louis Allen Rawls, December 1, 1936, in Chicago, IL; son of Virgil (a Baptist minister) and Evelyn (a homemaker) Rawls; married Lana Jean, 1962 (marriage ended, 1972); children: Louanna, Lou Jr.; *Military service*: United States Army, 1956-1958.

Started singing gospel music in church at age seven; member of the gospel group Pilgrim Travelers, mid-1950s; near fatal car wreck on way to Pilgrim Travelers' concert, 1958; solo career as rhythm and blues singer started 1959; toured Los Angeles nightclubs until signed by Capitol, 1962; first album *Stormy Monday*, 1962; major market success began with first gold album *Lou Rawls Live*, 1966; starred in numerous television variety shows and Las Vegas shows, 1960s and 1970s; national spokesperson for Budweiser, 1976; honorary chairman for The College Fund/United Negro College Fund (UNCF), 1980; began hosting the "Parade of Stars" televised telethon for The College Fund/UNCF, 1980; still tours and records; acted in several films 1969-1995.

Awards: Three Grammy Awards for "Dead End Street," 1967, *A Natural Man*, 1971, and *Unmistakably Lou*, 1977; one Platinum and four Gold albums; American Music Award for "You'll Never Find Another Love Like Mine," 1976; street named after him in Chicago, 1987.

Addresses: *Record company*—Philadelphia International Records care CBS Records, Inc, 51 West 52nd Street, New York, NY 10019.

Grammy Award. In the mid and late 1960s, Rawls guest-starred on many television variety shows and played the Las Vegas nightclub scene. In 1969 he even appeared in a movie, *Angel Angel Down We Go*.

In 1970 Rawls recorded a single called "Your Good Thing Is About to Come to an End," a title that contradicted the success he experienced in the Seventies. The song was nominated for a Grammy Award. Rawls changed record companies in 1971, signing with MGM Records. *A Natural Man* was the first album he recorded with MGM. His first single "A Natural Man" earned Rawls a second Grammy Award in 1972. The song reached number 17 on the pop and R & B charts. Rawls released only one more album with MGM before signing with Philadelphia International records.

The signing with Philadelphia International was memorable because it paired Rawls with legendary producers Kenny Gamble and Leon Huff. His first album with Gamble and Huff was his only platinum album: *All Things in Time*. It reached number 3 on the R & B charts. Rawls' most notable single was the first single recorded with Gamble and Huff in 1976 called "You'll Never Find Another Love Like Mine." It reached number two on the pop charts and number one on the R & B charts, and was played in virtually every disco across the country. The song was Rawls' first gold single and it won him an American Music Award and a Grammy nomination. "Groovy People" was the next single recorded with Gamble and Huff; it also earned a Grammy nomination. Other singles released with Gamble and Huff include: "See You When I Git There," "Lady Love," and "Let Me Be Good to You."

In 1977 Rawls won his third Grammy Award. This time it was for the best male rhythm and blues performance for the album *Unmistakably Lou*. Rawls was seen on television often in the 1970s on variety shows and as an actor. Rawls also represented Budweiser as a national spokesperson in the late 1970s. His voice was heard in the background of many Budweiser commercials. One of Rawls' album titles, *When You've Heard Lou, You've Heard It All*, was based on the famous Budweiser slogan.

Rawls' last notable single was "I Wish You Belonged to Me," which reached number 28 on the R & B chart and was also produced by Gamble & Huff. *At Last*, recorded in 1989, earned a Grammy nomination and included many guest stars. James T. Jones of *Down Beat* suggested the title was appropriate and added, "Rawls returns to singing blues and supper-club jazz within the same acoustic setting of his '62 debut *Stormy Monday*...." On that album, Rawls included some Lyle Lovett tunes. He told *Down Beat*, "I like his songs. They have a light touch; they're not so heavy. He's a country singer. But when I get through with his tunes, they're hardly country." When *Portrait of the Blues* was released in 1993, Phyl Garland of *Stereo Review* commented on Rawls, "Central to his longevity have been the undeniable appeal of his deep baritone voice and his craftsmanship as a singer." Underscoring the accomplishment of his longevity, Garland also remarked, "In a pop world where the duration of fame seems to have been cut back from 15 to 10 minutes, Lou Rawls has maintained his popularity over more than thirty years."

Noteworthy Priorities

Rawls still tours and records, and has appeared in many television shows and films, including the 1995 Mike Figgis film *Leaving Las Vegas*. Throughout the 1980s and 1990s, however, he mainly established himself as a generous humanitarian. He put his money where his mouth is when he was quoted as saying, "Educating the youth of our nation is priority one." Through his efforts as honorary chairman, he has raised over 150 million dollars for The College Fund/UNCF as their honorary chairman. He has accomplished this by hosting a televised telethon every January called the "Parade of Stars." Since 1980 Rawls has invited fellow performers to appear live on the show to raise money for this important fund. Guests have included: Marilyn McGoo, Gladys Knight, Ray Charles, Patti LaBelle, Luther Vandross, Peabo Bryson, Sheryl Lee Ralph, Take 6, Jody Watley, Tevin Campbell, Anita Baker, Boyz II Men, Me'Shell NdegeOcello, Eddie Murphy, and Whoopi Goldberg. Anheuser-Busch Companies Inc. is the founding sponsor of the telethon. Rawls is adamant in his opinion about the role of education in guiding today's youth. He told *Jet*, "If you look around you, you see the adults constantly pointing the finger at the kids, saying, 'You're doing wrong.' But do you give them an option? I think the option should be education. Our future depends on it, man."

In 1989 Rawls' hometown of Chicago named a street after him. South Wentworth Avenue was renamed Lou Rawls Drive. In 1993 Rawls attended ceremonies for the groundbreaking of the Lou Rawls Theater and Cultural Center. His cultural center includes a library, two cinemas, a restaurant, a 1500-seat theater, and a roller skating rink. The center is built on the original site of the Regal Theater on the south side of Chicago. The gospel and blues music played at the Regal Theater in the 1950s inspired a young Lou Rawls. Now his name is immortalized at the site of where it all began.

Selected discography

Stormy Monday, Blue Note, 1962.
Black and Blue, Capitol, 1963.
Tobacco Road, Capitol, 1963.
For You My Love, Capitol, 1964.
Lou Rawls and Strings, Capitol, 1965.
Merry Christmas Ho! Ho! Ho!, Capitol, 1965.
Nobody but Lou, Capitol, 1965.
Lou Rawls Live, Capitol, 1966.
Lou Rawls Soulin', Capitol, 1966.
Lou Rawls Carryin' On, Capitol, 1966.
Soul Stirring Gospel Sounds of the Sixties, Capitol, 1966.
That's Lou, Capitol, 1967.
Too Much, Capitol, 1967.

You're Good for Me, Capitol, 1968.
Feelin' Good, Capitol, 1968.
Best from Lou Rawls, Capitol, 1968.
The Way It Was/The Way It Is, Capitol, 1969.
Your Good Thing, Capitol, 1969.
A Natural Man, MGM, 1971.
Silk and Soul, MGM, 1972.
All Things in Time (includes "You'll Never Find Another Love Like Mine" and "Groovy People"), Philadelphia International, 1976.
Philly Years, Philadelphia International, 1976.
Unmistakably Lou (includes "See You When I Git There" and "Lady Love"), Philadelphia International, 1977.
When You Hear Lou, You've Heard It All, Philadelphia International, 1977.
Lou Rawls Live, Philadelphia International, 1978.
Let Me Be Good to You, Philadelphia International, 1979.
Sit Down and Talk to Me, Philadelphia International, 1980.
Shades of Blue, Philadelphia International, 1981.
When the Night Comes, Epic, 1983.
At Last, Blue Note, 1989.
Greatest Hits, Curb, 1990.
It's Supposed to Be Fun, Blue Note, 1990.
Portrait of the Blues, Manhattan, 1993.
Christmas is the Time, Manhattan, 1993.

Sources

Books

Hawkins, Walter L., editor, *African American Biographies- Profiles of 558 Current Men and Women*, McFarland and Company, Inc., 1992.
Patricia Romanowski, editor, *The New Rolling Stone Encyclopedia of Rock & Roll*, Fireside, 1995.

Periodicals

DownBeat, January, 1990.
Jet, June 26, 1989; August 30, 1993; January 9, 1995; January 13, 1997.
Stereo Review, July, 1993.

Additional information provided by the website *All-Music Guide: A Complete Online Database of Recorded Music* by Matrix Software, copyright 1991-97.

—*Christine Morrison*

Leon Redbone

Singer, guitarist

When Leon Redbone burst on the scene in the early 1970s, he did so under a shroud of mystery. No one, not even those considered his friends, knew where he was from, how old he was, or his real name. A walking caricature, Redbone shuffled through folk festivals in his rumpled three-piece suits from the Twenties, a wide-brim hat, sunglasses, and thick mustache. The only thing widely known about him was that he was a gifted singer and guitarist with a thorough knowledge of blues, urban folk, jazz, and ragtime. "Mr. Redbone doesn't just dig up the past, he embodies it," wrote *New York Times* reviewer Stephen Holden in 1981, "by dressing himself in the clothes of an old-time traveling minstrel and singing in a voice that is a stylistic composite of early Southern blues and vaudeville performers." Although today his voice is familiar to many, due to countless television jingles hawking everything from beer to laundry detergent, he remains an enigmatic figure whose musical tastes and presentations have gone unchanged for more than twenty years.

"Sixteen seventy was the year as I recall. July the tenth," Redbone responded when asked by *Rolling Stone*'s Steve Weitzman when he was born. As Weitzman put forth the question in 1974, it seemed obvious he was interviewing a man approaching his 304th birthday. "Of course I don't know," Redbone added. "It's just something I vaguely recall. I can't say for sure." In the same interview, Redbone went on to mention that his father was the Italian violinist/composer Paganini, who died in 1840, and his mother was Swedish soprano Jenny Lind, who died in 1887. Two years earlier when asked to submit biographical information for the 1972 Mariposa Folk Festival magazine, Redbone sent in a crumpled up, old photo of Bob Dylan and a sheet of paper saying, "My name is Blind James Hocum. I come from New Orleans and the reason I wear dark glasses all the time is because I use to lead Blind Blake around the South." Blind Blake, in addition to being a profound influence on Redbone, was a blues and ragtime guitarist who died in the early 30s.

Mysterious Entrance

With all the sidestepping about his past, one thing about Redbone is certain; very few people know anything about his life before 1970, and those who do don't talk about it. When asked about Redbone's real name and age, his manager Beryl Handler, told Weitzman, "You'd have to ask Leon Redbone. To him it's irrelevant." What is known about Redbone is that he suddenly appeared as part of the Toronto folk scene in 1970. Even then he was determined to be a mystery. Tam Kearny, manager of a Toronto club Redbone used to play at, reminisced to Weitzman about Redbone's efforts to retain his enigmatic stature. "We used to give him lifts home after the gigs and he'd have us drop him off in a different part of the city every night," Kearny said. "After we'd drive away we could see him come back out of the apartment building he'd just entered and start walking down the street. And if he took the subway home and people would follow him to try and find out where he lived, he would have to lose them in the subway. But he always did."

While performing at the 1971 Mariposa Folk Festival outside of Toronto, Redbone so impressed musicians David Bromberg and Ramblin' Jack Elliot, that when they returned to New York they began to tell everyone they knew about Redbone's musical breadth and mysterious eccentricities. The next year Bonnie Raitt, John Prine, Maria Muldaur, and Bob Dylan went to the festival to hear Redbone. "He's just amazing," Raitt told Weitzman of *Rolling Stone.* "He's probably the best combination singer guitarist I've heard in years." Raitt went on to tell her tale of being unable to get past the Redbone persona. "I spent an afternoon with him in a hotel room," Raitt said, "and I was wondering when he was going to become normal. He never did."

Gets *On the Track*

Dylan was so taken with Redbone's musical prowess and archival sensibilities he declared that if he had a record label, Redbone would be the first musician he'd

sign. True to his word, when Dylan was about to start his own label, Ashes & Sand, in the mid-70s, Redbone was going to be the initial artist to sign on. Neither event occurred, however. Instead, with the support and championing of so many influential musicians, Redbone eventually signed with Warner Bros. and released his first album, *On the Track,* in 1975.

On the Track, however, did not make much of an impact on the charts. Amidst the era of Led Zeppelin arena-rock and the infancies of punk and disco, not many people were likely to tune into a gruff voiced crooner slur his way through "Polly Wolly Doodle" and Fats Waller's "Ain't Misbehavin'." After almost a year the album only sold 15,000 copies. Then, in February of 1976, Redbone performed on *Saturday Night Live*—back in the days when it was called *NBC's Saturday Night*—and appeared again the following May. After performing before an estimated 18-22 million viewers, Redbone's album began to sell at the rate of 8,000 copies a week. By the end of that year, he sold almost 200,000 albums without any publicity from Warner Bros.

Just A Novelty Act?

More concerts and albums followed, all consisting of old standards and period pieces. Although the albums sold enough to make the charts—1977's *Double Time* went gold—and concerts were well attended, critics began to wonder if Redbone was little more than a novelty act. "By treating everything as a joke," wrote the *Village Voice*'s Geoffrey Stokes in 1978, "he avoids the risks involved in making a 'sophisticated' audience feel the awkward pain which originally lay behind some of his songs." Stokes went as far as to compare Redbone to a magician who performs the same trick over and over. His faithful interpretations, however, of long forgotten music eased the sting of some critical barbs. Robert Palmer, reviewing a 1977 show for the *New York Times* accused Redbone of placing the mannerisms of his droll character over the content of the songs. "But ultimately," Palmer conceded, "one forgave him because the music was so much fun."

In 1978 Redbone was asked by Dan Forte of *Guitar Player* if the image of being a nostalgic novelty bothered him. "Everything bothers me," Redbone responded. "At the same time, nothing bothers me....If something isn't right it's annoying to me—I don't care what it is.... If someone's going to write about something and make a comment on it, it should be right." He added, "I'm basically a very serious fellow, but at the same time I'm very indifferent to a lot of things, and I think a little humor is necessary. Consequently, people tend to pick up and focus on that humor."

In a 1990 interview with Pete Feenstra of England's *Folk Roots* magazine, Redbone claimed it was the media, not him, who perpetuated his mythic persona. "Well the media painted me as something of a recluse," he said, "somebody who was mysterious. Back in the 70s I was regarded as someone who wouldn't talk much about myself. But the problem was the media always ended up asking me the obvious non-musical questions...about what I wear, and what I like to eat, etc. When it came down to the music itself they weren't particularly interested in music from the 1920s. And so when I wouldn't talk much about things non-musical they put together their own image of me."

From Budweiser to Ballet

Ultimately, Leon said, it's this style of music that should be in the foreground. "I don't regard them as old standard tunes or a nostalgia-type thing," he told *Rolling Stone*'s Weitzman in 1976. "I just happen to do whatever I do simply because that's what I hear." And what Redbone hears, as someone who's musical interests lies between the period of 1830 to 1930, is the common thread of romance. "To me, Blind Lemon Jefferson was the same as Chopin," he explained to Forte. "They were both romantics. A romantic, to me, is someone with a depressed, tormented soul. I would say almost everything I do is romantic." Romantic or not, critics continued to assail Redbone's excessive use of his persona at the expense of the music, although the music itself was held in high regard.

In the early 80s Madison Avenue tapped Redbone's style and the singer found himself crooning about ALL laundry detergent and Budweiser beer, to name a few. As long as the jingle was something he could work with, Redbone said, he had no qualms with doing the commercials. "Most of what I've done so far seems to have worked without too much difficulty," he told Feenstra. "Basically as long as I get to play my music, and as long as it's got the necessary feel then there's not really a problem." The commercials may have, in fact, helped in bringing Redbone back to the public's attention after years of a break in recording. As the nineties began, Redbone was touring and recording only slightly less than during his rise to prominence almost twenty years earlier.

In 1996 ballet choreographer Elliot Feld created "Paper Tiger," a suite of dances set to 11 Leon Redbone songs for his company, Feld Ballets/NY. It was no less than Mikhail Baryshnikov who suggested to Feld that he considered Redbone's music for a dance score, although Feld had long been a fan. "I adore Leon Redbone," he told Elizabeth Zimmer of the *Los Angeles Times.* "The interpretation of music is very important to me. How Leon sings these songs gives them a world, a universe. He's a tragic clown." For his part, Redbone was delighted by the dance. "I was quite fascinated by the whole thing," he told Zimmer. "I have a visual sense for the music, it has to stay true to a certain sense of period. I rely on a sense of colors and mood in my approach to the arrangement.... I was surprised to see all those things I think of when I put the music together actually represented."

Whether described as a novelty act, cult hero, or, as Stokes dubbed him, "Johnny One-Trick," no description of Redbone doesn't include the fact that he has been a singular force in bringing a style and period of music to many people who may not have heard it otherwise. While critics may argue about the emphasis placed on his persona, his reverence for the music has never been questioned. With a desire to remain true to himself—whoever he is—and Blind Blake, Jelly Roll Morton, Blind Lemon Jefferson, and the rest of his idols, Redbone is more an educator than performer, a professor of one of the richest periods in American music. And although he told *Rolling Stone*'s Weitzman, that regarding himself, "I don't want them to know anything that they don't know already," he'd like more people to know about this music.

Selected discography

On the Track, Warner Bros., 1976.
Double Time, Warner Bros., 1977.
Champagne Charlie, Warner Bros., 1978.
From Branch to Branch, Atco/Emerald, 1981.
Red to Blue, August, 1986.
No Regrets, Sugar Hill, 1988.
Christmas Island, Private Music, 1990.
Sugar, Private Music, 1990.
Up a Lazy River, Private Music, 1992.
Whistling in the Wind, Private Music, 1994.

Sources

Books

Nite, Norm N., *Rock On: The Illustrated Encyclopedia of Rock n' Roll, Vol. 3,* Harper & Row, 1985.
Penguin Encyclopedia of Popular Music, edited by Donald Clarke, Viking, 1987.

Periodicals

DownBeat, November 16, 1978, p. 28.
Folk Roots, June 1990, p. 27.
Guitar Player, April 1978, p. 34.

Los Angeles Times, June 18, 1994, p. F1; April 7, 1996, p.7.

Melody Maker, February 7, 1976, p. 14.

New York Times, April 1, 1977; May 27, 1981, p. C26

Newsday (New York), March 5, 1996, p.B7.

Rolling Stone, May 9, 1974, p. 14; December 18, 1975, p. 64; February 26, 1976, p. 94; November 18, 1976, p. 24; March 10, 1977, p. 64; June 25, 1981, p. 39.

Village Voice, September 18, 1978, p. 100.

—*Brian Escamilla*

Reverend Horton Heat

Rockabilly band

Photo by Marina Chavez. Courtesy of Atomic Music Group/Highwest Mgmt. Reproduced by permission.

The trio Reverend Horton Heat mixes a brand of maniacal, Texas-based rockabilly—or "psychobilly" and "trashbilly"—with edgy, high-octane punk and old-fashioned Jerry Lee Lewis-style rock 'n' roll to create a uniquely potent style of wild, Texas punk-metal-rockabilly fusion. James Heath, known as The Reverend Horton Heat, plays with bassist Jimbo and drummer Scott Churilla, known as Taz; the purposely demented three-some began as a rockabilly band and then, after evolving into a punkbilly band, would present a show of mock religious preaching, complete with tongue-in-cheek warnings of hellfire-and-brimstone and a clearly inebriated "preacher" in the form of Heath. Although The Reverend Horton Heat has dropped the religious humor from their live shows and lyrics, they retained the original name of their band.

A Wild Teen Who Loved Fast Music

The Reverend Horton Heat appeals most widely to the independent record crowd, offering songs that entail precision-like guitar work and enthusiastically crazed drumming. Tony Ferguson, an Interscope A & R man, brought the Reverend Horton Heat to the label because he felt psychobilly/punkbilly bands have the potential for a broad appeal in the current market. He told *Billboard*'s Chris Morris, "I think people are getting a little fed up with the dark grunge metal stuff, and it's a pleasant thing to hear these cross-musical ideas with a rockabilly base."

Heath was raised in Corpus Christi, TX, and picked up his first guitar at the age of 6. He spent his adolescent years in various Texas juvenile correctional facilities after having committed a string of petty crimes. He told *RIP* magazine's Steffan Chirazi, "I started hangin' out with the kids who smoked cigarettes at the bowling alley, playing foosball, tryin' to get older kids to buy us bottles of booze, hangin' at the local record store." Heath became a noted pool hustler, a talent he retained throughout the decades. One of Heath's formative experiences was listening to Johnny Cash's "Folsum Prison Blues" with his cousin, a former point-man for the Marines in the Vietnam War. He told Chirazi, "That song was the coolest song I ever heard in my life, so I had to learn to play like it. "

Tirelessly Tours Between Albums

Heath formed his first band, Chantilly Lace, in junior high school and played standards from the 1950s. Heath loved the music of Jerry Lee Lewis in particular. He told Chirazi, "I always lived fast music ... I always have liked the 'edge' performers, Jerry Lee Lewis, Little Richard,

For the Record . . .

The Reverend Horton Heat trio consists of **James Heath**, known as the Reverend, vocals; **Jimbo,** bassist ; **Scott Churilla,** known as Taz, drums.

Band formed in 1987. They released *Smoke 'Em If You Got 'Em* on Sub-Pop in 1987 and *The Full-Custom Gospel Sounds of Reverend Horton Heat* in 1993, produced by Gibby Haynes of the Butthole Surfers. *Liquor in the Front*, released in 1994, was their first joint Sub Pop/Interscope album, produced by Ministry's Al Jourgensen. *It's Martini Time*, released in 1996, was produced by Thom Panunzio, who worked with U2, John Lennon, and Rocket From The Crypt.

Addresses: *Record company*—Interscope Records, 10900 Wilshire Boulevard, Suite 1230, Los Angeles, CA 90024, (310) 208-6547.

Chuck Berry...I love a lotta Buddy Holly's music but some of it's too sweet and cutsie, and once you start getting cutsie you start to lose me."

In 1987 Heath formed a band with old friend Taz and newer friend Jimbo; they released *Smoke 'Em If You Got 'Em* on the Sub-Pop label that year, followed by *The Full-Custom Gospel Sounds of Reverend Horton Heat,* which was produced by Gibby Haynes of the Butthole Surfers. Between album releases, the trio tours seemingly without a break, usually playing more than 200 live shows a year. *Liquor in the Front*, released in 1994, was the band's first album as part of a joint agreement between Sub Pop and Interscope Records; it was produced by Ministry's Al Jourgensen in a style consistent with Heath's band: fast, loud, and raucous. Heath was introduced to Jourgensen by Haynes, and knew a working partnership was born when Jourgensen got down on his knees and licked the band's shoes after a performance in Chicago. *It's Martini Time* was released in 1996.

Improving One Step at a Time

Heath used to feign "preaching" on stage, which was in keeping with the band's name, but he grew tired of it after deciding that the band was considerably more than a novelty act. Due to his moniker, friends often ask him to officiate at weddings and he turns their requests down without a second thought. The band started out in 1987 as a rockabilly band playing mostly originals and made

a conscious effort to create a "harder and faster" sound. Heath told *Guitar Player's* Chris Gill, "We're not really looking for that big break that's going to vault us into rock stardom ...We just want to make sure that things get a little better, one step at a time."

Liquor in the Front differed from the bands earlier material in that it reveals the Latin-music influence of Heath's youth in Texas. While growing up in Corpus Christi, Heath played in bands with Mexican-Americans and was influenced by Tex-Mex music, authentic Mexican music, and Chicano music. The album is about "good ole times" and sex, liquor, cars, love, and brawls. Songs range from surf to country, from the pointedly humorous to gentle ballads to deep-country inspired songs and twangy covers. The band's drunken rendition of "The Entertainer" includes belches as memorable sound effects.

Heath told Gill, "My latest guy to rip off is Carlos Santana. I love the way he plays guitar. That's what it's all about, man." The band experimented with a more psychedelic sound, coupled with a faster beat than was found on previous albums. Their music is upright bass music, with many of the songs relying on the rhythmic aspect. Heath told Gill, "Taz is really good at double kick. It doesn't fit with most rockabilly bands, but he plays it so good that it's got to be heard."

Puts Heart into Music

It's Martini Time featured breezy jazz tunes, howling guitar psychobilly songs, rollicking dance tunes, and country swing lilts. The band's fourth album was produced by Thom Panunzio instead of Jourgensen; Panunzio worked with U2, John Lennon, and Rocket From The Crypt. *It's Martini Time* differs from the band's previous albums by being calmer and infused with more humor, and the album utilizes horns, piano, accordion steel guitar and sound loops for the first time.

The band writes partially about their true experiences and wants listeners to appreciate the straightforward lyrics. Heath told Gill, "It doesn't matter what kind of guitar you play. It's how you play it ... it's what comes out of your heart." The band has opened for a remarkable variety of artists:Smashing Pumpkins, White Zombie, Willie Nelson, Toadies, Butthole Surfers, and Nine Inch Nails.

The Reverend Horton Heat earned more money when touring around town on the blues circuit because of the vastly lower overhead, but they found the blues audiences to be too polite and restrained; they took a cut in pay to tour punk clubs across the country, savoring the beer-sloshing, mosh-pit diving enthusiasm of rock fans.

Heath enthused to Dama Darzin of *Cash Box,* "We're really lucky. We've managed to drive ourselves through the cracks."

Selected discography

Smoke 'Em If You Got 'Em, Sub Pop, 1987.
The Full-Custom Gospel Sounds of Reverend Horton Heat, Sub Pop, 1993.
Liquor in the Front, Sub Pop/Interscope, 1994.
It's Martini Time, Sub Pop/Interscope, 1996.

Sources

Periodicals

Cash Box, July 13, 1996.
Entertainment Weekly, July 29, 1994.
Guitar Player, July 1994; September 1996.
RIP, September, 1996.
Rolling Stone, October 6, 1994; June 13, 1996.
Los Angeles Times, September 11, 1996.
Tribe (New Orleans), June/July 1996.
Vanity Fair, August 1993.

—*B. Kim Taylor*

LeAnn Rimes

Country singer

AP/Wide World Photos. Reproduced by permission.

Assessing the career of adolescent country singer LeAnn Rimes is much like squinting to count tree-rings in a sapling oak—one might say she has only stepped on the precipice of what could be called a career. Yet Rimes has demonstrated a mastery of performance as well as huge mass appeal, evidenced by her 1997 Grammy Award for Best Female Vocalist in Country Music. While some critics have written off Rimes's style as derivative of earlier country music heroes like as Patsy Cline, and have chalked up her popularity to novelty appeal, few have discounted her powerful voice itself.

Born on August 28, 1982 to parents Belinda and Wilbur in Jackson, Mississippi, Rimes was initiated into the performing arts at a surprisingly early age. Having no siblings, she received the lavish affection parents of only children often afford, and was enrolled in vocal and dance training by the age of two. Whether she was motivated by avid stage parents or by an indelible performing urge, Rimes was singing in pitch when she was 18 months, assuring Belinda and Wilbur to continue nurturing their precocious child's talents. Following the advice of LeAnn's vocal coach, Rimes's parents decided to plunge their daughter into the often hectic world of child talent competitions, and successfully ushered her on the stage by age five. Within a year, Rimes won her first song and dance contest, with her version of "Getting to Know You," and professed to her parents that she wanted performing to be a permanent part of her life.

Lone Star Stardom

Eager to realize his daughter's dreams, Wilbur Rimes "sold his truck and his dogs and everything," as LeAnn told USA Today, and left Jackson in 1988 to relocate to Garland, Texas. It was in the Lone Star State that the youthful star-to-be began making rapid inroads to success. Rimes nearly landed the lead role in a sequel to the blockbuster Broadway musical Annie. Persistent, she continued auditioning for stage roles until she was chosen to play Tiny Tim in a Dallas production of A Christmas Carol. After a triumph on the television showcase for aspiring amateurs, Star Search, and a string of appearances on Johnny High's Country Music Revue in Fort Worth, Texas, Rimes began to attract the attention of national talent scouts.

Not even a decade old, Rimes was already a virtual veteran of live performances. She regularly performed an a capella rendition of "The Star Spangled Banner" during the opening ceremonies of Dallas Cowboys football games, adding to her local legion of fans. In addition, Rimes and her father embarked on trips around

For the Record . . .

Born August 28, 1982, in Jackson, MS; daughter of Belinda (a homemaker) and Wilbur (a salesman), moved to Garland, TX, in 1988.

Began singing when 18 months old, won first talent contest at age six for performing "Getting To Know You;" competed on the television talent showcase *Star Search*, 1988; performed "The Star Spangled Banner" at Dallas Cowboys football games in early 1990s.

Awards: Grammy Award for best female vocalist in Country and Western, 1997.

Addresses: *Record company*--Curb, 3300 Warner Blvd., Burbank, CA 91510.

the country to perform over a hundred stage dates per year. Nonetheless, touring and word of mouth could only generate so much attention, and the next logical step in Rimes's career path was to enter the recording studio.

The creation of Rimes's debut album, *After All,* was a relatively quiet affair. Recorded at an old studio in Clovis, New Mexico for the independent label Nor Va Jak, *After All* did not receive the promotional fanfare that accompanies major label debuts. Rimes's father, a salesman by profession, served as the record's producer, and the result was neither slick nor seamless. While the album saw an impressive sales run within Texas, Nor Va Jak could not give *After All* the push it needed to sweep a national audience. Yet, Rimes and her father were quickly hit by an onslaught of contract offers from major labels to record a second album.

Shocks Country Music Community

The primary source of record industry hype over Rimes's debut, *After All,* was largely provoked by that album's cut "Blue," a bittersweet composition that perfectly displayed the range of Rimes's vocal stylings. The song was penned over 30 years prior to its recording, and was originally intended for country legend Patsy Cline, who died tragically before she could perform it. Cline's distinctive, haunting voice had served to influence several generations of singers, many of them outside the realm of country music. For them, Cline stood as a model not only of artistic precision and clarity, but also of resonant emotional expression. In order for the song's

author Bill Mack to have given to a newcomer a piece tailored expressly for Cline's style and mastery, Rimes must have evidenced some of the elder singer's attributes. Indeed, some critics have argued that Rimes's talent is only in reproducing Cline's unique sound without offering any innovation, while others have claimed that although technically almost flawless, Rimes's singing is devoid of emotional depth that only a life of experience can provide. In fact, Rimes's father initially turned down "Blue" on the grounds that a sensual lament of love was not appropriate for a young girl's repertoire. "My dad said the song was too old for me," Rimes remembered. "I loved it, though, and I kept bugging him about it. Then I got the idea to put the yodel thing to it." Whether though her yodeled twists or through her youthful freshness, Rimes managed to make "Blue" her own, and whatever the critical verdict, she was on the eve of becoming a national sensation.

In the meantime, Rimes's personal life underwent some changes. With so much public attention imbued upon her as well as the beginnings of a plane-hopping lifestyle, Rimes quickly found herself at odds with the normal routine of a young student. By the time she entered junior high school, Rimes was occasionally harassed by classmates in response to her rising fame. For sake of convenience, she withdrew from school and continued her education with a tutor. While a private education only helped Rimes excel, it also effectively withdrew her from her peers at a critical age. However, Rimes sees the experience as a positive one. "I don't think I'm giving up a lot, because I'm achieving a lot right now," she told the *Los Angeles Times.* "I do have a different life and I've grown up in an adult world ... I don't mind giving up the prom kind of thing and all that. I really don't think I'm missing out on anything 'cause this is what I want to do."

With this kind of devotion, Rimes began work on her sophomore release, after signing with the Curb label, an outfit known for its roster of country artists. The result was the album *Blue,* whose title cut was a reworked version from *After All,* now made available to audiences around the world. The album included "Cattle Call," a duet between Rimes and country great Eddy Arnold; "I'll Get Even With You," another refurbishing from *After All;* and "Talk To Me," which the then 13 year old Rimes co-wrote. However, it was still "Blue" itself that turned heads and invaded radio playlists. With no video promotion, the single "Blue" debuted at number 49 on *Billboard* magazine's country music charts, making Rimes the youngest singer to do so, and the single rapidly peaked in the Top 10. The album *Blue* fared equally well in sales, and Rimes was instantly country music's hottest property.

Whatever speculations some critics may have made, Rimes was showered with kudos from the music industry. She was nominated for both Single of the Year and the Horizon Award by the Country Music Association (CMA), making her the youngest nominee in CMA's history. More impressively, Rimes earned the Grammy Award for best female vocalist in Country and Western, beating out four other seasoned nominees as the youngest recipient ever to win that award. Slowly, the voices accusing Rimes of being a mere novelty began to subside, if not disappear.

Rimes greater role in the history of country music remains to be written, but a spirit of devotion and expansion cannot said to be lacking. "I want to continue singing and writing songs," Rimes told the Great American Country website. "I'd like to act. College is also an option for me. I've always wanted to help children and I've thought about studying speech pathology."

Selected discography

After All, Nor Va Jak, 1994.
Blue, Curb, 1996.

Sources

Periodicals

Los Angeles Times, July 27, 1996; November 6, 1996.
USA Today, June 11, 1996.

Online

http://www.countrystars.com/artists/lrimes.html

—*Shaun Frentner*

Ryuichi Sakamoto

Keyboardist, composer

Though Ryuichi Sakamoto has cited nineteenth-century French composer Claude Debussy and 1970s-era German synthesizer act Kraftwerk as his biggest influences, his style is far beyond a mere hybrid of classical impressionism and technopop. Sakamoto is known for coupling a melodic touch with technological mastery, but the depth evident in his work derives from a deep interest in multicultural forces. His compositions have combined elements from the musical traditions of Asia and other cultures with the European formalism and American hip-hop. This cultural integration was an influential precursor to the world music of the Nineties, just as Sakamoto's electronic lyricism broke ground for contemporary ambient and new-age movements.

Sakamoto was born in Japan in 1952. He began piano training at the age of three, and by his tenth year had begun composing. By the time he was eleven, his musical interests ranged from the Beatles to Beethoven and he began to study under a professor at the Tokyo University of the Arts. He enrolled formally as a student there in 1971, and came into contact with synthesizers for the first time. The university owned several, which were then fairly expensive and rare. Sakamoto eventually earned a B.A. in composition and later a master's degree with a concentration in electronic and ethnic music; his university years also introduced him to radical politics, and he was associated with a leftist student group, Zen Ga Kren. In 1977, he began work as a composer, arranger, and studio musician with some of Japan's most popular rock, jazz, and classical artists.

Within a few years, he became a noted producer, arranger, and keyboardist.

Formed Yellow Magic Orchestra

In 1978, Sakamoto released his first solo album, *The Thousand Knives of Ryuichi Sakamoto.* That same year, he and two fellow young, avant-garde Tokyo rockers, Haruomi Hosano and Yukihiro Takahashi, formed Yellow Magic Orchestra (YMO). With a sound that drew heavily from progressive European music of the 1970s—especially the German band Kraftwerk—but also presented a distinctly Japanese sonic touch, Sakamoto and the others became celebrities. "They were the Great Yellow Hope, the group that would crack the Anglo curtain and do for Japanese musicians what the Beatles did for the British," wrote Bob Doerschuk in Keyboard magazine.

YMO became wildly popular in Japan, but also found an audience abroad. "Computer Game," a track from their debut, became a staple in both discotheques and new wave clubs in America and Europe. Their second album, *Solid State Survivor,* released in 1979, sold well over a million copies, which led to the first of many world tours. In his travels, Sakamoto became acquainted firsthand with the cultures of much of the international music that had long fascinated him. Between 1978 and 1984, YMO released 13 albums, plus another 13 albums of other material and remixes over the next dozen years. Though they disbanded in 1983, with members wishing to move on to other projects, YMO remained popular even in the late 1990s, with several Internet Web sites devoted to the group. Sakamoto's contributions to the group's prolific output demonstrated his interest in such diverse sources as jazz, classical, Jamaican dub, Latin bossa nova, and Indonesian gamelan as well as his interest in pioneering electronic equipment.

Menaced David Bowie on Film

Sakamoto segued from pop stardom to a career in film. He scored the 1983 film *Merry Christmas, Mr. Lawrence,* and starred opposite David Bowie in the World War II-set drama. He became involved in other media as well. In 1984, he formed his own publishing company, Hon Hon Doh, and published Long Calls, a dialogue with Yuji Takahashi. Subsequent issuances have included dialogues with composers and philosophers. In 1987, Sakamoto's score for the Bernardo Bertolucci epic *The Last Emperor,* written with Talking Heads founder David Byrne and Cong Su, won an Oscar, a Grammy, a Golden Globe, and the New York, Los Angeles, and British Film Critics Association awards for best original score. Sakamoto also acted in a minor but pivotal role in the film. "The

Born in Japan in 1952; once married to keyboardist Akiko Yano. Education: Received degree in music composition, and advanced degree in electronic and ethnic music, both mid-1970s, from Tokyo's National University of Fine Arts and Music.

Began composing music at the age of eleven; formed Yellow Magic Orchestra with two other Japanese musicians, 1977; released several albums with group, 1978-83; group disbanded, 1983 (reformed briefly, 1993); began solo career with *The Thousand Knives of Ryuichi Sakamoto* on Nippon Columbia, 1978; released several other solo albums from throughout career; began composing film scores with *Merry Christmas, Mr. Lawrence,* 1983; has collaborated with numerous musicians and producers from around the globe.

Sakamoto's soundtrack for the 1987 Bernardo Bertolucci film *The Last Emperor,* composed with Cong Su and David Byrne, earned a Grammy Award, a Golden Globe, and several other awards for best film score.

Addresses: *Home*—New York City. *Record company*—Island Records, 400 Lafayette St., fifth floor, New York, NY 10003.

director asked me to act first then I asked to compose the music so it was a good trade," he said on an America Online chat.

Since then he has worked with Volker Schlondorff (*The Handmaid's Tale*), Oliver Stone (the television series *Wild Palms*), Pedro Almodovar (*High Heels*), Bertolucci again (*The Sheltering Sky, Little Buddha*), and others. Of his working relationship with Bertolucci, he said in the America Online interview: "We're friends, but when we work, we, of course, fight. I'm always the loser, because it's his film. That's what he says, `It's my film.'" Sakamoto's film roles have led to an appearance in Madonna's "Rain" music video, and he has even worked as a menswear model for top designers. In Japan, his famous face appears frequently on billboards pitching a variety of products. Since 1990 he has lived in New York City's Greenwich Village, but he described living there as "a disaster," to Mark Prendergast in *New Statesman & Society.* "It's quite violent.... When I'm driving in Manhattan and you stop at the lights people come at you from all sides banging on your windows for money."

Composed 1992 Olympic Theme

The list of contributors Sakamoto has worked with musically is a long one: the aforementioned Byrne and Bowie, as well as Public Image Limited (PiL), Iggy Pop, Jamaican reggae artist Sly Dunbar, Thomas Dolby, Beach Boy Brian Wilson, David Sylvain, and Caetano Veloso as well as the writers William Burroughs, celebrated video-installation artist Nam June Paik, and cyberpunk trailblazer William Gibson. One of Sakamoto's more noted accomplishments was the invitation to compose a musical work in honor of the 1992 Summer Olympics, held in Barcelona, Spain. He conducted the piece, "El Mar Mediterano," for the opening ceremony.

In addition to his work with YMO—they reunited for one album in 1993—the film scores, and the extensive collaborative efforts, Sakamoto has enjoyed an impressive solo career. Between 1978 and 1996, he released several solo albums, including as 1984's *Illustrated Musical Encyclopedia, Neo Geo,* released in 1987, and 1990's acclaimed *Beauty.* On this latter effort, Sakamoto's vision brought together the diverse talents of the Beach Boy, the rasta Dunbar, and Senegalese vocalist Youssou N'Dour all on one track, "Calling from Tokyo." The Band's Robbie Robertson and Ravi Shankar also guested in the studio, and Sakamoto even undertook a rare concert tour for the work. Doerschuk called it "an album that fully lives up to its name," he wrote in a 1990 issue of Keyboard. "It's a complex beauty, at times even unsettling."

For Sakamoto's 1992 solo album, *Heartbeat,* the composer branched out from the Middle Eastern and African rhythms that had peppered Beauty and found inspiration in house music. He invited Dee-Lite's DJ Dmitri to appear on it, as well as Lounge Lizard John Lurie, who played alto sax. *Smoochy,* released in 1995, was influenced by Sakamoto's trip to Rio de Janeiro and that city's diverse culture. The following year he made a return to more classical form with 1996, in which Sakamoto abandoned the tablas and synthesizers in favor of an actual piano and string instruments. He writes and records music via a Macintosh computer, however, and his years of experience and resulting proficiency in electronic music and cutting-edge technology allow him to arrange and conduct his compositions not in a studio, with other musicians present, but on computer disk.

A Futurist at Heart

In Sakamoto's 1985 interview with *Keyboard,* he predicted the demise of record and CD sales. "Soon music will primarily be sold as data over telephone lines and cable," he told Doerschuk. "To prepare for this, I've started gearing toward audio-visual projects, like videos and cable television." Several years later, Sakamoto was lauding the technology had brought new immediacy to connecting with others across the globe. He noted in a 1996 interview with *Billboard*'s Steve McClure that "some record companies are very nervous" about the Internet. "It's a new medium through which you can transmit any information, without a third party, directly to the world.... You don't need [label executives], you don't need a CD factory, you don't need trucks to bring the CDS to the stores."

Sakamoto's musical interests, always geographically expansive, have broadened in a conceptual sense as well. Three of his live performances—a June 1996 show at the Knitting Factory in New York, a July concert at London's Royal Festival Hall, and another at Orchard Hall in Tokyo the following month—were broadcast on the Internet. He also has a radio program in Japan, and his guest lecture at Keio University is available on the Internet as well. Sakamoto continues to explore new musical concepts and technologies—in 1996 he was releasing work on laser disc as well—and anticipates the music of the next century. He theorized that the earth's inhabitants "will have to move to a big space station in the next hundred years. We will have to bring Earth culture with us—not space station culture, but culture of this world," he mused in the 1990 interview with Doerschuk. His online diary for September, 1996 reflected his vision for even more dramatic possibilities: "I ask myself what the sound of music originating from something as immense as the Internet would sound like. The music would be without a center. Perhaps a key in understanding of what this kind of music would sound like lies in the music of the Pygmy tribes in Africa or in sounds made by whales."

Selected discography

Solo LPs

The Thousand Knives of Ryuichi Sakamoto, Nippon Columbia, 1978.
B-2 Unit, Alfa, 1980.
Left Handed Dream, Alfa, 1981.
Coda, London, 1983.
Illustrated Musical Encyclopedia, Midi, 1984.
Esperanto, Midi, 1985.
Media Bahn Live, Midi, 1986.
Future Boy, Midi, 1986.
Neo Geo, CBS Sony/Epic, 1987.
Beauty, Virgin, 1988.
Playing the Orchestra, Virgin, 1988.

Gruppo Musicale, Midi, 1989.
Ryuichi Sakamoto in the 90's, Mark Plati remix, Alfa, 1991.
Heartbeat, Virgin, 1992.
Ryuichi Sakamoto Virgin Tracks, Toshiba EMI, 1993.
Ryuichi Sakamoto Soundtracks, Toshiba EMI, 1993.
Gruppo Musicale II, Midi, 1993.
Sweet Revenge Tour 1994, For Life/Gut, 1994.
Hard Revenge, For Life/Gut, 1994.
Sweet Revenge, For Life/Gut-Elektra, 1994.
Smoochy, For Life/Gut, 1995.
1996, For Life/Gut, 1996.
Snooty, For Life/Gut, 1996.

Albums with Yellow Magic Orchestra; on Alfa unless otherwise noted

Yellow Magic Orchestra, 1978.
Solid State Survivor, 1979.
Yellow Magic Orchestra--U.S. Remix, 1979.
Multiples (album version), 1980.
Multiples (with Snakeman Show; 10-inch vinyl), 1980.
Public Pressure (live), 1980.
Technodelic, 1981.
BGM, 1981.
Service, 1983.
Naughty Boys (instrumental), 1983.
Naughty Boys, 1983.
After Service (live), 1984.
Sealed limited edition compilation, 1984.
YMO Mega Mix, 1990.
Faker Holic, YMO World Tour Live, 1991.
YMO in the 90's—Peter Lorimar remix, 1991.
Techno Bible, YMO, 1992.
Live at Budhokkan 1980, 1993.
Technodon Live, Toshiba EMI, 1993.
Technodon Remixes remix by the Orb, Toshiba EMI, 1993.
Technodon Remixes remix by Tei Towa and Go Hotoda, Toshiba EMI, 1993.
Technodon, Toshiba EMI, 1993.
YMO vs. The Human League, 1993.
YMO/Over Seas Collection, 1995.
YMO—Winter—Live—1981, 1995.
YMO World Tour 1980, 1996.

Other

Summer Nerves, with The Kakutogi Session, CBS Sony, 1979.
The Arrangement, with Robin Scott, Alfa, 1982.
The End of Asia, with Danceries, Nippon Columbia, 1982.
(Producer/arranger) *Virginia Astley, Hope in a Darkened Heart*, WEA, 1986
Let It Be, with Aki Takahashi, Toshiba EMI, 1992.
(Producer/arranger) *Aztec Camera, Dreamland*, Sire/WEA, 1993.
Asian Games, with Yosuke Yamashita and Bill Laswell, Mercury, 1993.

A Chance Operation—A Tribute to John Cage, Koch Classics, 1993.

The Geisha Girls, The Geisha Girls—Remix, For Life/Gut, 1994.

(Producer) *The Geisha Girls, The Geisha Girls Show,* For Life/Gut, 1995.

The Geisha Girls, The Geisha "Remix" Girls Show, For Life/Gut, For Life/Gut, 1995.

E Preciso Perdoar—Red Hot + Rio, with Caetano Veloso and Cesaria Evora, Antilles/Verve, 1996.

(Producer) *Syokumotsu-rensa, Miki Nakatani,* For Life/Gut, 1996.

Film soundtracks

Merry Christmas, Mr. Lawrence, London/Milan, 1983.

Kitten Story (Koneko Monogatari), Midi, 1986.

Aile De Honneamise, Midi, 1987.

The Last Emperor, Virgin, 1988.

The Sheltering Sky, Virgin, 1990.

The Handmaid's Tale, Japan Record, 1990.

Wild Palms, Capitol, 1992.

Wuthering Heights, Capitol, 1992.

Peach Boy (Momotaro), Rabbit Ear Productions, 1992.

High Heels, Island/Virgin, 1992.

Little Buddha, Milan, 1993.

Sources

Books

(Ryuichi Sakamoto and Ryu Murakami) *A Writer's Sonata: A Musician's Story,* Shinchosha, 1996.

Periodicals

Billboard, April 14, 1990, p. 32; June 29, 1996; August 31, 1996.

Keyboard, August 1985, p. 32; July 1990, p. 49.

Musician, October 1994, p. 48.

New Statesman, June 24, 1992, p. 32; July 19, 1996, p. 17.

Online

http://www.kab.com./m/siteskmt

Other sources used in compilation of this profile included Tokyo Melody, a documentary by produced by a French television network, 1985; a transcript from America Online chat with Ryuichi Sakamoto, June 13, 1996; an on-line diary, September, 1996; publicity material from RZO Advisory Group, 1996.

—Link Yaco

Adam Sandler

Comedian, singer

Photo by Chris Pizzello. AP/Wide World Photos. Reproduced by permission.

Former NBC *Saturday Night Live* cast member and comedy writer Adam Sandler successfully fused his own brand of goofy, offbeat humor with rock music in his 1993 platinum debut album, they're *all gonna laugh at you!,* which was nominated for a Grammy Award. When he released What *the Hell Happened to Me?* in 1995, he cemented his popularity and proved that his foray into music was more than just a temporary comedic fluke.

Although Sandler's material is created for comedic effect, his band has proven to be genuinely accomplished and impressive. Sandler's band is led by guitarist Waddy Wachtel, who toured with Keith Richards and the X-Pensive Winos and played with Fleetwood Mac. Bassist Bob Glaub, a longtime L.A. session pro, worked with Bob Seger, Rod Stewart, Ringo Starr, John Lennon, and Bruce Springsteen. Guitarist Teddy Castilucci arranged and worked with Michael Jackson, Smokey Robinson, and Michael Bolton. Drummer Don Heffington worked with Bob Dylan, and keyboardist Mike Thompson played on Alanis Morissette's *Jagged Little Pill* album.

Sandler's musical tours and albums are best described as an accomplished musical rock comedy show with scatological undertones. He plays original, humorous songs like "Lunchlady Land" and "Red Hooded Sweatshirt," and covers rock classics by musicians such as Led Zeppelin, Barry White, and Bob Marley—musicians and groups he listened to as a teenager in Manchester, NH. He told the *Hartford Courant*'s Roger Catlin, "I had a garage band in high school called Final Warning. That was the best name we came up with. And we did Led Zeppelin." Sandler was also influenced in high school by Aerosmith and Black Sabbath.

Although he was born in Brooklyn, NY, Sandler spent most of his childhood in Manchester, NH, where he lived from the age of 5 through 17, and where most of his immediate family still resides. Sandler's father, a retired electrical engineer, served as one of Sandler's earliest test audiences, as did Sandler's mother, a retired nursery school teacher, and his brother and two sisters. "Most of what I think came from my years in New Hampshire," he told the *Boston Herald*'s Dean Johnson, "You learn to respect the beauty of the place." He told Johnson that he went into comedy because he "didn't have anything else to do."

Started with Stand-Up Comedy

In 1984 Sandler and his brother went to the Boston comedy club Stitches where, at his brother's urging, the 17 year-old Sandler took the stage and first tried his hand

For the Record . . .

Born in 1967, in Brooklyn, NY; moved to Manchester, NH at age 5; father a retired electrical engineer, mother a retired nursery school teacher. Education: Earned a Fine Arts degree from New York University.

Began career in comedy at age 17 when he tried stand-up for the first time at Boston's Stitches club; discovered by Dennis Miller of NBC's *Saturday Night Live* and signed on as a writer for the show by Lorne Michaels in 1990. Stayed at *Saturday Night Live* for five years.

Released *they're gonna laugh at you!* in 1993; album went platinum; released *What the Hell Happened to Me?* in 1996; album went gold. Appeared in films *Airheads, Mixed Nuts,* and *Coneheads.* Cowrote and starred in *Billy Madison* and *Happy Gilmore.* Costarred in *Bulletproof* and *The Wedding Band.*

Awards: Best Film Fight Award from MTV for fight scene with Bob Barker in *Happy Gilmore* in 1996.

Addresses: *Record company*—Warner Brothers/Reprise Records, 75 Rockefeller Plaza, New York, NY 10019 (212) 275-4600, fax: (212) 275-4600.

at stand-up comedy. He was going to attend New York University, and hadn't planned on becoming a comedian until that fateful night—even though he bombed on stage.

While earning a fine arts degree from New York University, Sandler managed to balance schoolwork with appearances at Manhattan comedy clubs. Comedian Dennis Miller, then a cast member on Saturday *Night Live,* saw one of Sandler's shows and told his boss, Lorne Michaels, about Sandler's comedy prowess. Michaels then saw the show himself and hired Sandler for a writing slot on "Saturday Night Live" in 1990. Sandler told the *Pittsburgh Press's* Ed Masley, "I would write myself into the skits. I snaked my way onto the air. The old dipsy-doodle, I pulled."

Sandler performed musical comedy for five years on *Saturday Night* Live, appearing as Axl Rose, Eddie Vedder, Opera Man, Canteen Boy, Cajun Man, or a banjo-strumming singing poet, but he enjoyed a wider berth on his own albums, with R-rated lyrics far racier than the material allowed on television. Sandler told

Catlin, "I do curse a lot, I must tell you. But it's not mean-spirited". Sandler's home page on the Internet includes a warning not to read it if you're under the age of 17 or if your parents are home.

Humorous Spin On Classics

Since leaving "Saturday Night Live," Sandler sold over 1.5 million copies of his two musical comedy albums. "The Chanukah Song" on What *the Hell Happened to Me?* was immensely popular in 1995, and the album surpassed gold status halfway through 1996. Sandler took a summer tour in 1996 to promote What *the Hell Happened to Me?,* and described the tour Scott Cronick of the Atlantic *City Daily* as, "a backyard rock 'n' roll party for you and 5,000 of your friends." Sandler incorporated video into his live performances and created a stage set that looked like his parents' back porch, complete with lawn chairs and an amplifier propped up in a garbage can. He told Johnson, "It (the live show) has a party feel, and I'm going to try to make people laugh, dance, and have fun."

Sandler's first album underscored his comedy-writing talent with hilariously original songs like "Toll Booth Willie," but his second album showcased the songs more than the lyrics, and demonstrated that he and his band can play genuine music. The reggae melody to Bob Marley's "Buffalo Soldier" was used for "Ode To My Car," a song in which Sandler's details the woes of owning an old junker, and the live, acoustic "The Chanukah Song" lists to music all of the noted people who celebrate Chanukah. Director Stephen Spielberg called Sandler after the release of "The Chanukah Song" to request a copy of the lyrics, and rabbis called Sandler to say it was a positive song; the single was one of 1996's most requested songs at major radio stations during the winter holiday season. Sandler also covers Springsteen's "Out On The Streets" and Marvin Gaye's "Let's Get It On," and he performed Led Zeppelin's "Communication Breakdown" on The Tonight Show in June of 1996.

they're *all gonna laugh at you!* spent over 100 weeks on the *Billboard* Heatseeker's Chart, garnered a Grammy nomination, and went platinum. What *the Hell Happened to Me?* achieved gold status, and prompted Sandler to take a 21-city U.S. tour.

Balances Film and Music Career

Sandler's first comedy/song album, they're *all gonna laugh at you!,* was released in 1993 just as his film career was taking off. By then Sandler had appeared in *Coneheads, Mixed Nuts,* and *Airheads* In 1995 Sandler left

Saturday Night Live and cowrote, along with friend Tim Herlihy, and starred in *Billy Madison.* He then cowrote and starred in *Happy Gilmore* in 1996, garnering MTV's Best Fight Award for his character's sparring scene with 72-year old actor and former television game show host Bob Barker. After releasing *What the Hell Happened to Me?* in 1996, Sandler costarred in 1997 with James Caan and Damon Wayans in the action comedy *Bulletproof* and the went to work on *The Wedding Band,* a movie about a wedding DJ who wants to be married.

When asked if he planned to release a third album, Sandler told *Scene's* Steven Battan, "I have some other ideas for songs, some duet-kind of things that I want to do, but we'll see." Sandler told Gary Graff of *Detroit Jewish News,* "I never had the discipline for anything but comedy and acting ... But I do have the discipline to stay up all night and make sure I write something that, to me, feels good. That I'll do."

Selected discography

they're all gonna laugh at you!, Warner Brothers, 1993.
What the Hell Happened to Me?, Warner Brothers, 1996.

Sources

Periodicals

Atlantic City Press, June 8, 1996.
Boston Herald, June 14, 1996.
Bucks County Courier Times (Levittown, PA), June 12, 1996.
Columbus Dispatch, June 24, 1996.
Dallas Morning News, July 5, 1996; July 8, 1996.
Detroit Jewish News, June 21, 1996.
Everybody's News (Cincinnati, OH), June 21, 1996.
Fort Worth Star-Telegram, July 5, 1996.
Grand Rapids Press, June 27, 1996.
Hartford Courant, April 25, 1996; June 6, 1996; June 10, 1996.
Oakland Press (Pontiac, MI), June 28, 1996.
Philadelphia Weekly, June 12, 1996.
Pitch Weekly (Kansas City, MO), June 20, 1996.
Pittsburgh Press, June 23, 1996.
Scene (Cleveland, OH), June 1996.
Sunday Republican (Waterbury, CT), June 9, 1996.
Valley Advocate (Hatfield, MA), May 16, 1996.
Willoughby News-Herald (Ohio), May 24, 1996.

—*B. Kim Taylor*

Carlos Santana

Jazz, rock guitarist

Photo by Jack Dempsey. AP/Wide World Photos. Reproduced by permission.

Carlos Santana's music, an eclectic blend of international rhythms, has proved more durable than the Rhythm-and-Blues sound that dominated the sixties, and indeed than later trends such as the disco movement of the 1970s. Santana's concerts, with their trademark searing guitar solos over a background of powerful Afro-Cuban style percussion, continue to attract a worldwide audience.

Santana's origins are about as far from the mainstream as could be imagined. He was born July 20, 1947 in Autlan de Navarro, a remote village in the state of Jalisco, Mexico. His father, Jose Santana, was a violinist of some local renown and through him Carlos had his earliest exposure to music in the form of the traditional Mexican violin. Although he never found the violin to his liking, Santana acquired a definite appreciation for music and the determination to make performing his career. When the Santana family moved to the border city of Tijuana in 1955, Carlos discovered American music. Rock-and-roll and blues artists such as Freddy King, B.B. King, Ray Charles, and Little Richard were given heavy air play on the radio and by local cover bands, and the teenaged Carlos found something soul-stirring in the powerful electric rhythms. His father gave him a guitar and by the early sixties, he became a professional musician, playing long hours in the thriving Tijuana strip club scene.

Discovers a Musical Cornucopia

In 1961, Santana's father moved to San Francisco to seek work and, soon after, the rest of the family followed him. Carlos disliked the United States at first and returned to Tijuana to live on his own and support himself as a club musician. Although this brief spell of freedom was stimulating, the harsh lifestyle of the club circuit took its toll and in late 1963, Santana returned to San Francisco for good. Here he found a new variety of music, discovering jazz, international folk music, classic salsa from the likes of Tito Puente and Eddie Palmieri, and seeing artists like B.B. King, whose records he had memorized note-by-note, perform live. To his young, fertile mind, the Bay Area was, as Carlos remembered in a *Billboard* interview, "a cornucopia...."

It was also the area where the hippie movement was coming to life in a ferment of confusion and creativity. Santana observed the scene from its margins, absorbing its eclectic ideals and cultivating his own musical abilities. Employed full-time as a dishwasher at a downtown diner, he jammed on weekends with anyone he could find, playing for spare change in the street while sizing up musicians for his band. When, one day in 1966, the band members of Grateful Dead happened to pull up to the diner in limousines, Santana came to the sudden realization that he was just as good a musician as they were and capable of being just as successful. Deciding to take the plunge and become a full-time musician, he quit on the spot and joined forces with fellow street musicians bassist David Brown and keyboard player Gregg Rolie to form the Santana Blues band.

Amid the noise of the many San Francisco rock groups that came into being at the same time, the Santana Blues Band—quickly shortened to "Santana"—had to struggle to be heard. Fortunately for them, their sound, a fast-tempo, improvisational take on Latin music that fused elements of jazz, blues, salsa, and African music, proved immediately appealing to club audiences. One person who was particularly taken with them was rock promoter Bill Graham, a moving force behind the Bay Area music scene, who was looking for an alternative to the countless sound-alike blues bands. Impressed by the distinct Afro-Cuban resonance of the band, Graham booked them in 1968 at his Fillmore West and Winterland clubs and promoted them vigorously. Their fortunes underwent a steady rise, culminating in a legendary performance at the Woodstock Music and Arts Festival in 1969.

Revelation at Woodstock

Face-to-face with some half million revelers, the band—consisting of Santana, Rolie, Brown, Mike Shrieve on drums, and Jose Areas and Mike Carrabello on percussion—was nervous, but elated. As Santana recalled in a *Rolling Stone* article commemorating the festival's twentieth anniversary, "It was a bit scary to go out there and plug into this ocean of hair, teeth, eyes, and arms. It was incredible." Their set was a revelation to an audience which had little or no previous experience with Latin or jazz music and definitely liked what it heard. Music executives were just as appreciative and the band's first album, *Santana*, was released by Columbia in 1969. It would remain on the *Billboard* charts for over two years and become a triple platinum album, selling nearly four million copies.

Santana had arrived and the success of their first album, exemplified by the top 10 single "Evil Ways," was just the beginning. In 1970, the band released a second album, *Abraxas*, that yielded two hit singles, "Oye Como Va" and "Black Magic Woman," and went platinum. *Santana III*, a gold album in 1971, and *Caravanserai*, a platinum album in 1972 followed. During the same period, a deepening interest in jazz led Carlos to his first collaborative effort outside the group in the form of *Live!*, recorded with jazz drummer Buddy Miles in the crater of Hawaii's Diamond Head volcano.

The band underwent a number of personnel changes during this period as Carlos experimented with a shifting mix of musicians. Guitarist Neal Schon joined the group in 1971 and then left in 1973 after the release of *Caravanserai* with Gregg Rolie, one of the Santana Blues Band's original founders, to form the group Journey. In time, Carlos was the only member from the original group left, and Santana, the band, came to be almost exclusively associated with him and his Latin rock/jazz fusion guitar playing. Although many groups might have foundered under the pressure of so much tinkering with internal chemistry, Carlos seemed to have a gift for choosing musicians who would meld together effortlessly, as he explained in a *Down Beat* interview, "[I had] to learn how to be wise getting a person who has his identity but is like water ... because I don't play just one idiom of music."

Undergoes Spiritual Conversion

Santana's personal life also continued to change and evolve in ways that would effect the group's music. Disheartened by the alienation he saw in the music world at the beginning of the 1970s, reflected in the drug-induced deaths of many prominent musicians, he became a follower of Sri Chimnoy, a guru and proponent of meditation, who gave Santana the name Devadip, meaning "the light of the lamp of the supreme." His identification with Chimnoy's teachings, as well as a deep fascination with the eastern-influenced music of jazz master John Coltrane, brought him together with fellow Chimnoy devotee and guitar wizard, Mahavishnu John McLaughlin. They released the spiritually-oriented jazz-fusion album *Love, Devotion, Surrender* in 1973 and it went gold, testifying to the popular draw of value-based religious music. Over the next decade, Santana released four more similar-themed solo albums, recording with the likes of Turiya Alice Coltrane, Herbie Hancock, Wayne Shorter, and Ron Carter.

Although Santana's religiosity would be very important to him throughout the seventies and early eighties, he managed to keep it separate from the more pop-oriented work he was doing with his band. Over the course of the decade, the group released a string of albums, including the highly successful *Amigos* in 1976, and *Zebop* in 1981, both of which marked a return to the latin-based rock with which the group was so strongly identified. With the exception of the live album *Lotus*, all of the records released by the group between 1969 and 1981 went gold or platinum, a track record which few other bands at the time could match.

In 1982, Santana ended his association with Sri Chimnoy, feeling that he had outgrown a need for a spiritual advisor and preferring to let music alone guide him. As he commented in a *Billboard* interview, "...the tone of Miles [Davis] or the moan of John Lee Hooker, that stuff ... touches me way deeper than a hundred gurus, a thousand yogis, fifteen hundred popes." However, he continued to explore jazz, touring with Wayne Shorter in 1988, and recording solo albums such as *Blues for Salvador*, released in 1987, which garnered Santana his first Grammy award.

With the decline of commercial interest in jazz/rock fusion during the 1980s, Santana's group recorded less frequently, releasing only five albums over the course of the decade as opposed to the twelve they had recorded during the seventies. Nonetheless the band maintained a high public profile, touring extensively to sold-out auditoriums and appearing at the US Festival, LiveAid, and on the first Amnesty International concert tour. Like many artists from the sixties, Carlos felt that the most important thing about his group was what took place on stage, the spontaneity and communication with the audience, rather than the number of albums they sold. Discussing his musical goals in a 1988 *Down Beat* article, he asserted, "I don't measure my life according to *Rolling Stone* or the Pope or *Billboard*.... If I can give myself chills or make my hair stand up, it doesn't matter whether I'm [playing] in front of Macy's or in Madison Square Garden...."

In 1991, Carlos ended his twenty-two year relationship with Columbia/CBS and signed with Polydor, releasing the albums *Milagro in 1992*, and *Sacred Fire: Live in South America* in 1993. In 1994, Carlos founded his own label, called Guts and Grace, and released a solo album, *Brothers*, a collaboration between Carlos, his brother Jorge Santana, and nephew Carlos Hernandez that was nominated for a best rock instrumental Grammy Award. Twenty-five years after his arrival at Woodstock, he exposed a whole new generation of music fans to his fiery guitar work at the commemorative Woodstock '94 festival. In 1995, he played with blues legend John Lee Hooker on the album *Chill Out* and in 1996 received the Century Award from *Billboard* magazine in recognition of his impact over thirty years on the American music scene.

Santana's music continues to hold audiences around the world spellbound. Although it might be tempting to dismiss him as a musical relic whose durability is based on nostalgia for the sixties, one would be greatly mistaken in doing so. Santana appeals to contemporary listeners for the same reason that his group originally interested Bill Graham: an ability to reach beyond artistic boundaries and find something new. Two decades before "world music" was recognized by the public and record executives, Santana made it an art form. From the departure point of his Latin roots, Santana and a host of accompanying musicians blended Eastern music, Rhythm-and-Blues, Afro-Cuban jazz, African drumming, and innumerable other influences into a searing, multicultural mix that transcends musical and spiritual borders. In doing so, he created, and continues to create, a uniquely American hybrid.

Selected discography

Santana, Columbia, 1969.
Abraxas, Columbia, 1970.
Santana III, Columbia, 1971.
Caravanserai, Columbia, 1972.
(With Buddy Miles) *Carlos Santana & Buddy Miles! Live!* Columbia, 1972
Welcome, Columbia, 1973.
(With Mahavishnu John McLaughlin) *Love, Devotion, Surrender,* Columbia, 1973
Greatest Hits, Columbia, 1974.
Borboletta, Columbia, 1974.
Illuminations, Columbia, 1974.
Lotus, Columbia, 1975.
Amigos, Columbia, 1976.
Festival, Columbia, 1976.
Moonflower, CBS, 1977.
Inner Secrets, Columbia, 1978.
Marathon, Columbia, 1979.
Oneness, Silver Dreams-Golden Reality, Columbia, 1979.
The Swing of Delight, Columbia, 1980.
Zebop, Columbia, 1981.
Shango, Columbia, 1982.
Havana Moon, Columbia, 1983.
Beyond Appearances, Columbia, 1985.
Freedom, Columbia, 1987.
Blues for Salvador, Columbia, 1987.
Viva Santana!, Columbia, 1988.
The Sound of Carlos Santana, Pair, 1989.
Spirits Dancing in the Flesh, CBS Records, 1990.
Milagro, Polygram Records, 1992.
Sacred Fire, Polydor, 1993.
Brothers, Polygram Records, 1994.

Sources

Periodicals

Billboard, April 6, 1996; December 7, 1996.
Down Beat, February 1988; August 1991.
Guitar Player, January 1993.
Rolling Stone, August 24, 1989.
Stereo Review, February 1989.

Additional information for this profile was provided by Island Records, New York, NY and Jensen Communications, Pasadena, CA, 1997.

—Daniel Hodges

Screaming Trees

Rock band

Gary Lee Conner of Screaming Trees. Photo by Ken Settle. Reproduced by permission.

Despite the tempestuous relationships between its members and repeated commercial and other frustrations, the Washington-based band Screaming Trees has remained a vital creative institution for well over a decade. While many of their peers in the world of Northwest "grunge" rock have seen big-time success—and a few have not survived it—the Trees have been perpetual underdogs. "Screaming Trees have made a career of turning unlikely situations into transcendent rock & roll," according to *Rolling Stone's* Jason Fine. Yet their powerful, psychedelia-tinged rock has continued to mature, and their 1996 album, *Dust,* made many critics' and fans' best-of lists for that year.

Though usually listed alongside their friends in Nirvana, Soundgarden and other "grunge" acts as a Seattle band, the Trees originated in 1985 in the town of Ellensburg, which is located over 100 miles from the Seattle. Brothers Gary Lee (a.k.a. Lee) and Van Conner, whose parents owned the town's one video store, grew up loving both heavy metal and punk rock. An affinity for the latter usually aroused the suspicions of local toughs, and Van, five years younger than Lee, faced threats of violence from his schoolmates for his musical tastes. He did, however, make friends with singer Mark Lanegan, a fan of punk and new wave rock. Later, after Lanegan met Lee, the three decided to form a band, taking their name from a guitar effects pedal by Electro-Harmonix. They added drummer Mark Pickerel and began playing locally, selling a six-song tape at their shows. "We were all nerds," Van told *Rolling Stone,* "but Lee was the king. He was kind of a mama's-boy nerd who was really shy. Then we played our first gig. We count, 'One, two, three, four,' and suddenly Lee's diving all over the stage." The Screaming Trees released their debut album, *Clairvoyance,* on the Velvetone label the following year.

From Indie to Major Label

After attending a show in Olympia by Black Flag—one of L.A.'s best-known punk bands—they gave a tape to Black Flag guitarist/leader Greg Ginn. Shortly thereafter, they were offered a deal with Ginn's label, SST. The band soldiered on for several years, weathering tours and fights, putting out a string of releases on SST between 1987 and 1989. Lanegan also released a solo album on the Sub Pop label that featured members of Nirvana. College radio success landed the Trees a deal with the major label Epic Records in 1990; Soundgarden frontman Chris Cornell co-produced their Epic debut, *Uncle Anesthesia.* Jim Greer of *Spin* would later write that the album's "relative incoherence reflected the less than easy relations among the band itself." Pickerel departed soon thereafter, and was replaced by Barrett Martin,

For the Record . . .

Members include **Gary Lee Conner** (born c. 1963, Ellensburg, WA), guitar; **Van Conner** (born c. 1968, Ellensburg, WA), bass; **Josh Homme** (joined 1996), guitar; **Mark Lanegan** (born c. 1965, Ellensburg, WA), vocals; **Barrett Martin** (born Tumwater, WA; joined band 1991), drums; **Mark Pickerel** (left band 1991), drums.

Formed c. 1985, Ellensburg, WA; released cassette-only EP *Other Worlds*, 1985; released debut album, *Clairvoyance*, on Velvetone label, 1986; signed with SST records and released *Even If and Especially When*, 1987; released Sub Pop EP *Change Has Come*, 1989; Lanegan released solo debut, *The Winding Sheet*, on Sub Pop, 1989; signed with Epic Records, 1990, and released album *Uncle Anesthesia*, 1991; song "Nearly Lost You" appeared on soundtrack of film *Singles*, 1992; Lanegan and Martin appeared on Mad Season album *Above*, Columbia, 1995; appeared on Lollapalooza tour, 1996.

Addresses: *Record company*—Epic Records, 550 Madison Ave., New York, NY 10022; 2100 Colorado Ave., Santa Monica, CA 90404.

formerly of the band Skin Yard.

In the space between the Trees' Epic bow and their subsequent release, Seattle became hot. This was due in large part to the success of Nirvana's *Nevermind*, the massive sales of which turned the music industry on its ear and ushered in the new "alternative" era. Numerous other Seattle bands and practitioners of so-called "grunge," such as Soundgarden, Pearl Jam, and Alice inChains, benefited from Nirvana's breakthrough. The Trees, meanwhile, were stunned; they'd been Nirvana fans since the latter group's earliest club shows. "All of a sudden there was a market for our kind of music," Lee told *Rolling Stone*. "It was weird—like everything sort of slipped into this alternative universe."

Praised for *Oblivion*

1992 saw the release of the Trees' *Sweet Oblivion*, which boasted the hit single "Nearly Lost You." The song, which also appeared on the soundtrack to the Seattle-themed movie *Singles*, brought the band greater recognition than it had ever had. But *Sweet Oblivion* also showed a more unified and mature group, perhaps because the

intermittent feuding between members—especially the Conner brothers, who would hurl their substantial bulk at each other during gigs and would, like their bandmates, erupt into shouting matches when interviewed together—led them to believe it would be their last record. "So we actually worked together on the songs for the first time in years," Van explained in *Spin*. "In the course of which we also became friends again." Critics were effusive about the album; a *Village Voice* reviewer proclaimed, "these Northwest veterans have started roiling and hooking and knocking 'em dead at the very moment they seemed ready to expire of corporate torpor."

After touring to promote *Oblivion*, the Trees returned to the studio and commenced work on a follow-up. Unfortunately, it didn't come out to their satisfaction. "It was too soon, and none of us were ready to interact," Lanegan told *Rolling Stone*. They decided instead to scrap the record and begin working on another one virtually from scratch. They also changed producers, moving from Don Fleming, who'd helmed *Oblivion*, to George Drakoulias, best known for his work with the Black Crowes and the Jayhawks. Keyboardist Benmont Tench, of Tom Petty's band, was brought in to provide some flourishes on mellotron and other instruments, and a variety of exotic percussion was employed on what would become *Dust*, released in 1996. In the interim, Lanegan released a second solo album, and he and Martin worked with the Seattle supergroup Mad Season.

"Childhood Dream Come True"

The deaths of Nirvana leader Kurt Cobain, Hole bassist Kristen Pfaff and Gits leader Mia Zapata, among others, led Lanegan into detox; they also inspired much of the material on *Dust*, notably the song "Dying Days," which features a solo by Pearl Jam guitarist Mike McCready. Yet despite such dark subject matter, the album rose above the angst-rock that had become the staple of "alternative" music in the preceding several years. "Unlike their gloomy Washington state peers," noted *USA Today*, "The Trees create a kaleidoscopic sound that never descends into dark 'n' stark grunge. Ferocious and fanciful, the music reflects a restless energy." *BAM*, meanwhile, declared, "*Dust* is a welcome rarity—a contemporary album that rewards repeated listens from beginning to end." Pronounced *Newsday*, "Screaming Trees has developed, even above Soundgarden, into grunge rock's most accomplished band."

Screaming Trees appeared on the 1996 Lollapalooza tour, alongside longtime rock heroes the Ramones and metal superstars Metallica; they added a second guitarist, Josh Homme of Kyuss, to their touring lineup.

"Playing with the Ramones is like a childhood dream come true," Van noted in the band's record company biography. "I told my dad we were playing with them on Lollapalooza. He said, 'Y'know, that's all you cared about when you were 16 years old: Playing on the same bill as the Ramones.' Now we're doing that ... and a whole lot more." Though the Trees still haven't become superstars, they've survived more than a decade of adversity, and managed to improve steadily. "This is not an easy band to be in," Martin averred in *Rolling Stone.* "It's like there's this fine line between healthy creative tension and total misery and self-destruction. We've definitely seen both, but I think we've gotten a lot better at staying on this side of the line."

Selected discography

Other Worlds (EP), 1985 (cassette only); SST, 1988.
Clairvoyance, Velvetone, 1986.
Even If and Especially When, SST, 1987.
Invisible Lantern, SST, 1988.
Buzz Factory, SST, 1989.
Change Has Come (EP), Sub Pop, 1989.
Anthology, SST, 1991.
Uncle Anesthesia, Epic, 1991.
(Contributor) *Singles* (soundtrack), Epic, 1992.
Sweet Oblivion (includes "Nearly Lost You"), Epic, 1992.
Dust (includes "Dying Days"), Epic, 1996.

Mark Lanegan solo

The Winding Sheet, Sub Pop, 1989.
Whiskey for the Holy Ghost, Sub Pop, 1994.

With Mad Season

Above, Columbia, 1995.

Sources

Periodicals

Addicted to Noise, June 3, 1996.
BAM, July 12, 1996.
Guitar Player, February 1993.
I-Magazine, October 1996.
Musician, December 1992; March 1994; October 1996.
Newsday, August 18, 1996.
Rocket, July 24, 1996.
Rolling Stone, February 18, 1993; May 16, 1996; August 22, 1996.
Spin, March 1993; February 1994.
USA Today, July 19, 1996.
Village Voice, March 9, 1993.

Additional information was provided by Epic Records publicity materials, 1996.

—*Simon Glickman*

DJ
Shadow

Hip-Hop Artist

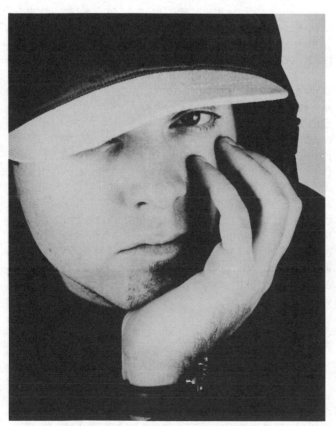

London Records/Mo' Wax. Reproduced by permission.

D J Shadow's debut album, *Endtroducing,* cemented his standing as one of the foremost instrumental hip-hop, trip-hop, and "techno" artists of the 1990s. Spin magazine included Endtroducing in its 20 Best Albums of 1996 list, and the release is serving as an example of what the future of pop music may sound like within the realm of mainstream music. Shadow is considered an innovator, along with DJ Krush, the Aphex Twin, Dr. Octagon, Tranquility Bass, and DJ Spooky, for creating personal compositions that use the entire history of music as material.

Since DJ Shadow's music is instrumental and comprised solely of hundreds of obscure, unrecognizable musical samples, it poses a dilemma for those who want to label it. Shadow is adamant about the fact that his music is hip-hop music. He told *Vibe*'s Andrea Duncan, "Hip-hop is about eliminating genre barriers in music," and told *Details* magazine, "Hip-hop used to represent everything from Kraftwerk to the Rolling Stones to James Brown. It was about innovation at any cost. It's ironic that people now think ... we don't need any more innovation. Of course we do."

DJ Shadow, born Josh Davis in 1972, was raised in a middle-class family in the rural suburb of Davis, CA, where he took piano lessons and wanted to study drums. He heard his first hip-hop album, Grandmaster Flash's *The Message,* at the age of ten when it played over his little clock-radio cube. He immediately rolled over and pressed "record" on his tape recorder just as his parents were entering his room to say goodnight. He told Spin's Stephen Stickler, "You can hear me on the tape going, 'Shh, Shh' (to his parents). That song was the most direct form of communication I'd ever heard and it may sound corny, but it changed my life." He began mixing by the age of 12.

Although Shadow was living in the proximity of the college town where independent guitar bands like True West and Thin White Rope had created a legacy, he remained devoted to hip-hop through a steady stream of new record releases. His earliest influences were Afrika Bambaata, Flash, Steinski, Latin Rascals, Mantronik, and Prince Paul. In addition to the beat and sound of hip-hop, Shadow liked the social and philosophical tenants of the music. He told Mills, "Hip-hop used to represent unity through music. When Bambaata played, he was called 'the peacemaker'."

Shadow was already scratching and mixing by the time he enrolled at University of California-Davis, and in 1989—following the success of the Beastie boys and Public Enemy—at the age of 17, Shadow chose his moniker and began pursuing his own vision of hip-hop. His first record, "Lesson 4," appeared in 1991 on the

Hollywood Basic label, which was a subsidiary of Disney. Shadow's work for Hollywood Basic entailed "promo only" records or "vinyl only" and"compilation only," which rendered it obscure.

Shadow was part of a generation of people who fell in love with hip-hop's "let's change the world" philosophy, and when it spiralled down into boastful gangsta rap, he and others began to forge new inroads by founding their own small labels, playing underground hip-hop on college stations and pirate radio, starting 'zines and internet connections, creating websites, and releasing 12" singles. Shadow produced mixes for the San Francisco radio station KMEL between 1987 and 1991, and in 1992 he scratched on Oakland-based rapper Paris's "Sleeping with the Enemy" track.

Founded Solesides

In 1991 the English DJ James Lavelle, known as U.N.K.L.E., discovered Shadow's vinyl EP "Zimbabwe Legit." Lavelle founded the Mo' Wax label with the intention of specializing in acid jazz, hip-hop avant garde, and abstract techno music. Lavelle and Shadow met and agreed that modern music needed more breathing room to grow and expand. In 1993 when Mo' Wax released Shadow's "In/Flux," both Shadow and Mo'

Wax were given rave reviews.

Shadow then founded his own rap-oriented label, Solesides, with Jeff "Zen" Chang, which issued his "Entropy" release. In 1995 Mo' Wax released several more Shadow EPs, most notably "What Does Your Soul Look Like," as Shadow was remixing and producing for DJ Krush, Lateef the Truth Seeker, Blackalicious, and the Roots. Other Soleside artists include The Invisible Scratch Pickles, Mixmaster Mike, Apollo, ShortKut, Q-Bert, Peanut Butter Wolf, Dan "The Automator" Nakamura, and Dr. Octagon.

In spite of his early foray into scratching and mixing, the low-key Shadow didn't perform before a live audience until 1993. James Lavelle taught him how to "read a crowd," and Shadow discovered that he enjoyed surprising his audience. He told Mills, "My favorite thing is doing the opposite of what I think the crowd is expecting....If I look out and see a bunch of hip-hop headz ... I'll play, oh, Black Sabbath's "Wall of Sleep".

Mystery and Originality

Shadow spent six months in preproduction for *Endtroducing,* which represents the culmination of his knowledge of records, hip-hop culture, and technical artistic ability. The songs reflect his mood at the time they were conceived and created, and no one song was completed before he started the next, a process akin to a writer working on many chapters of a book at once instead of following a progression.

Unlike most hard-core rappers or hip-hop artists, Shadow is white, from the suburbs, and he's popular in England. The term "trip-hop" was first applied to Shadow's "In/Flux" single by English fans. *Endtroducing* includes choruses of angels, cello solos, pipe organs, haunted, moaning voices, pipe organs, and live drummers. With the exception of rap-inspired "TheNumber Song," Shadow once again surprised his audience by delivering organic, urban classical music culled from thousands of dime-store and used record store finds. He told *Rolling Stone*'s Josh Kun, "You're not contributing anything to the genre by putting out a record that sounds just like somebody else. All you're doing is weighing it down."

Shadow keeps his musical sources a mystery and never lifts samples from bootlegs, compilations, or reissues. He sculpts songs out of layers and layers of sampled instruments as well as other interesting sound fragments, most of which he processes, loops, and rearranges beyond recognition. He is content to remain in his hometown and isn't hungry for fame. As he said to

Cheo Hodari Coker of the *Los Angeles Times,* "I just want to be remembered as someone who make a difference, even if my name isn't on everybody's lips."

Selected discography

Albums

Endtroducing, Mo'Wax/ffrr, 1996.

Singles/EPs

"Lesson 4," Hollywood Basic, 1991.
"Zimbabwe Legit: Legitimate Mix," Hollywood Basic, 1991.
"Entropy," Solesides, 1993.
"In/Flux & Hindsight," Mo' Wax/Solesides, 1993.
"What Does Your Soul Look Like," Mo' Wax, 1995.
"Hardcore Instrumental Hip-Hop" (as the Grooverobbers), Mo' Wax Excursions/Solesides, 1995.
"Midnight In A Perfect world," Mo' Wax, 1996.
"Stem," Mo' Wax, 1996.

Compilations

Royalties Overdue, Mo' Wax, 1994.
Headz, Mo' Wax, 1994.
The Groove Action Collection, OM, 1995.
Headz 2-B, Mo' Wax, 1996.
Excursions, Mo' Wax, 1997.

DJ Shadow has also appeared on records by Blackalicious, Dr. Octagon, Lateef the Truth Seeker, the Roots, and DJ Krush.

Sources

Periodicals

Billboard, November 23, 1996.
Chicago Tribune, February 2, 1997.
Details, December 1996; January 1997.
Entertainment Weekly, November 1996.
High Times, March 1997.
Los Angeles Times, December 15, 1996; December 29, 1996; February 2, 1997.
Magnet, February/March 1997.
Musician, February 1997.
New York Post, November 20, 1996.
Option, January 1997.
Paper, December 1996.
Philadelphia Weekly, December 18, 1996.
Playboy, February 1997.
Rap Pages, October 1996.
Raygun, November 1996.
Request, December 1996.
Rolling Stone, January 21, 1997; March 6, 1997.
San Francisco Bay Guardian, December 4, 1996.
Spin, December 1996; January 1997; March 1997; April 1997.
Stranger, November 7, 1996.
Time Out, November 21-28, 1996.
Urb, November 1996.
Vibe, February 1997.
Village Voice, November 19, 1996; February 25, 1997.
Wired, March 1997.

—*B. Kim Taylor*

Shaggy

Reggae Artist

Orville Burrell was born in Kingston, Jamaica on October 22, 1968 and earned his nick-name, "Shaggy" from the animated Saturday morning show, *Scooby Doo.* Scooby's side-kick, "Shaggy" was the ever-hungry hippie on the show, and his friends thought it fitting for Burrell. He left his native Jamaica at age 18, to join his mother in the Flatbush section of Brooklyn, New York where he soon found himself a place in the local New York reggae scene. While in high school, Shaggy would use his lunch break to recite lyrics and perform on the benches outside.

Shaggy's recording career started in his 20th year, debuting with "Man A Mi Yard," "Bullet Proof Buddy," followed by "Big Hood" and "Duppy Or Uglyman" for producer Lloyd "Spiderman" Campbell but his musical career took a higher leap after he hooked up with New York's premier reggae radio D.J. and producer, Sting—not to be confused with pop rock recording artist and former Police member, Sting. Shaggy cut "Mampie," with Sting and the song rose to number one in the New York reggae charts along with his next single, "Big Up."

Shaggy's musical career was temporarily halted in 1988. After a difficult year trying to find work with a steady paycheck, and wanting to escape the gun-to-your-head mentality of the streets of Brooklyn where the only work that could be found was illegal, Shaggy joined the United States Marines. Thinking this was a way out of possible poverty and a vacation from the harsh streets of Brooklyn, he was sadly mistaken and found himself in the middle of the Gulf War. What he thought was going to be something like summer camp turned out to be war on the front-line. He also found himself driving an armored HumVee tank through an Iraqi minefield. Shaggy joked many times about that experience, "Some people go in the military for 20 years and never see fighting. I go for four years and get straight into a war."

When Shaggy returned from the Gulf War, he was stationed in Camp LeJeune, in North Carolina. While he had been in the Gulf, the New York street tunes he had first recorded made him a local star. Every weekend while he was on active duty, Shaggy made a pilgrimage, driving 18 hours to New York City to record his music. There, he would live the life of a star, but during the week, he was back on base with a mop and bucket.

Success was right around the corner for Shaggy when in 1993, he released, "Oh Carolina," a remake of an old Prince Buster classic. "Oh Carolina" became a surprise smash hit topping charts around the world. He became a world traveler, performing in an endless number of countries. He was also the first dance hall artist to perform in South Africa following the abolishment of

Photo by Eric Draper. AP/Wide World Photos. Reproduced by permission.

apartheid. His debut album, *Pure Pleasure* established Shaggy as one the most exciting new voices in the reggae movement. With the release of *Boombastic*, Shaggy's audience expanded across all formats.

The Grammy-winning album, *Boombastic,* derived its name from a Jamaican word meaning anything sensational. Since it's release in July 1995, it has shattered barriers worldwide—taking reggae music to new heights on Pop, Rap, and R&B charts throughout the world and reaching gold record sales in the United States. *Boombastic* took the 1996 Grammy Award for "Best Reggae Album" and dominated the top spot on *Billboard's* Reggae Album Chart, where it held the number one slot for 30 consecutive weeks; making *Boombastic* the longest number one reign in the chart's history.

Boombastic Tops *Billboard*

The title track of the album went platinum and emerged as one of 1995's biggest hits. Boombastic ripped through format boundaries and topped the following *Billboard* charts: Hot R&B singles, Hot R&B singles Sales, Hot Rap Singles, and Rap Airplay Monitor and rose to number three on *Billboard's* Hot 100 Singles chart on the strength of it's number one showing on the Hot 100 Singles Sales chart. Worldwide, *Boombastic* hit number one on the national singles charts in Italy, Sweden, New Zealand Ireland. It went to the top five in Germany, Holland, Span, Denmark, Greece, Finland, Switzerland Austria, Norway, and Belgium.

"Why You Treat Me So Bad," one of the singles from *Boombastic*, features a guest performance from ex-Brand Nubian rapper Grand Puba; following such gems as "Summertime," a high spirited update of the Mungo Jerry classic, and "The Train Is Coming," which was featured in the movie, *Money Train*. Another of Shaggy's songs, not from the *Boombastic* album, was used in the remake of the movie, *Flipper*.

Most of *Boombastic*'s 14 tracks were produced by the New York team of Sting and Robert Livingston, who have done a great job at capturing Shaggy's raucous, fun-loving approach to Reggae. No one in the 1990s has done more for Reggae in earning the world wide attention than Shaggy. He has admitted his desire to advance a culture—specifically, the musical culture of reggae—and to be an ambassador and a positive representative of this music. With this purpose in mind, Shaggy is campaigning to get a star placed on the Hollywood Walk of Fame for the late reggae legend, Bob Marley. He feels Marley deserves that star achieving the highest point in reggae, making music from his heart—with no compromises. Shaggy won't relent until that star shines with Marley's name.

Thanks to the help of Sting, Robert Livingston and long time partner Rayvon, Shaggy's monetary concerns are in the past. Above all, Shaggy's success mirrors his personal motto "No matter where you go or what you do, make an impression."

Selected discography
Albums

Pure Pleasure, Cema/Virgin, 1993
Boombastic, Cema/Virgin, 1995.
Original Doberman, Greensleeves, 1996.

Sources
Periodicals

Ebony Man, May 1996.
People, August 14, 1996

Online

http://www.jamweb.com/shaggy.html
http://www.pegasus.rutgers.edu/~albe/shaggy.html
http://www.musicblvd.com

—*Robyn Weiss*

Horace Silver

Jazz pianist and composer

Frank Driggs Collection. Archive Photos, Inc. Reproduced by permission.

In 1996 Horace Silver released a recording called *The Hardbop Grandpop.* That could just as well be the title of his biography. Silver helped define the jazz style known as hard-bop back in the 1950s. Nearly half a century later, he remains among the jazz elite. Silver's status as a giant of jazz is reflected by the list of artists with whom he has been associated. He got his first big break from Stan Getz, learned his basics from Coleman Hawkins and Lester Young, honed his style with Miles Davis, broke ground with Art Blakey, and taught the ropes to Tom Harrell and the Brecker brothers, Michael and Randy. Along the way, by making the rhythm funky and keeping the melody simple, Silver has produced a huge body of jazz classics that continues to grow.

Horace Silver was born on September 2, 1928 in Norwalk, Connecticut. His father, John, was an immigrant from Cape Verde, a group of islands off the western coast of Africa, and the Latin-flavored folk music of that country would later find its way into Horace's compositions. Silver began taking piano lessons when he was about ten years old. A couple of years later, he was bitten by the jazz bug when he heard the legendary Jimmy Lunceford's band perform at a nearby amusement park. From that point on, Silver knew that he wanted to be a musician.

Discovered by Stan Getz

By his teens, Silver was copying note-for-note the solos of early jazz pianists such as Earl Hines and Art Tatum. For a while he took up tenor sax, with the great Lester Young serving as his role model. Silver's self-education then led him to listen to bebop pioneers Charlie Parker and Dizzy Gillespie. Eventually, he settled on Bud Powell and Thelonius Monk as his main jazz heroes. By the time he finished high school, Silver was a regular on the local club scene and even led his own trio. Silver's big break came in 1950, when his trio was serving as the backup band for the visiting Stan Getz at Hartford, Connecticut's Sundown Club. Getz was so impressed that he quickly hired Silver on as a member of his quartet for the next two years.

After his stint with Getz, Silver decided he was ready to move to New York. He quickly found work playing with some of the very musicians he had been idolizing for years, including Hawkins and Young. In 1953 Silver cut the first of his many albums on the Blue Note label, as part of a trio. By the following year, he was leading a group that included tenor saxophonist Hank Mobley and bassist Doug Watkins. This ensemble had a steady gig at a Harlem club called Minton's. Silver was named top "new star" for 1954 in *DownBeat* magazine's annual poll.

Born Horace Ward Martin Tavares Silver, September 2, 1928, in Norwalk, CT; son of John and Gertrude (Edmounds) Silver.

Toured with Stan Getz, 1950-52; Blue Note recording artist, 1953-1980; led quartet at Minton's in Harlem, 1954; co-founded Jazz Messengers with drummer Art Blakey, 1954; leader, Horace Silver Quintet, 1955—; recorded hit "Song for My Father," 1964; founded Silveto record label, 1980; Impulse! recording artist, 1996—.

Awards: DownBeat "New Star," 1954; Budweiser Musical Excellence Award, 1958; Citizen Call Entertainment Award, 1960; Down Beat Hall of Fame, 1996.

Addresses: Agent—Joanne Jimenez, The Bridge Agency, 110 Salem Rd., Pound Ridge, NY 10516; Record company—GRP/Impulse Records, 555 West 57th Street, New York, NY 10019.

The Minton's band soon evolved into the Jazz Messengers, with the addition of drummer and co-leader Art Blakey and trumpet player Kenny Dorham. They recorded a 1954 album under the name Horace Silver and the Jazz Messengers.

Left Messengers to Front Own Group

The Jazz Messengers—without Silver's name in front—recorded a live album in 1955. Silver then left the band, taking Mobley and Dorham with him, while Blakey carried on as leader of a group by that name for decades to come. With his new quintet, Silver began to further develop a distinct identity as a composer. By taking bebop and eliminating some of the complexity, while injecting elements of gospel, blues, and soul, and funkifying the beat a tad, Silver and his imitators were inventing "hard-bop."

Silver's 1956 album Six Pieces of Silver produced his first hit, "Señor Blues." From that point on, he was in more or less constant demand. For the next few years, his band was a revolving-door unit, with a shifting cast that included at different times Mobley, Dorham, Art Farmer, Doug Watkins, Art Taylor, and Clifford Jordan. From 1958 to 1964, Silver's band had a fairly stable lineup that featured the front line of Blue Mitchell on trumpet and Junior Cook on tenor sax. This group recorded some of Silver's best-known compositions, including "Sister Sadie" from Blowin' The Blues Away (1959) and "Nica's Dream" from Horace-Scope (1960).

In 1964, Silver recorded "Song For My Father" on an album of the same title. The song became a huge hit, and the album made Billboard's top 200 pop chart. Audiences since then have almost never allowed Silver to leave the stage without playing the song. In 1965 he released the album Cape Verdean Blues, a tribute to the folk music he had learned from his father. In the late 1960s, Silver experienced a sort of spiritual awakening, which was reflected in his music. In 1970 he released an album called The United States of Mind, which included Silver's own quasi-philosophical lyrics.

Provided "University" for Younger Players

In the 1970s Silver collaborated with arranger Wade Marcus on a series of albums with similar titles: Silver 'n Brass, Silver 'n Wood, and Silver 'n Voices. During this period, his bands included a number of young musicians who have gone on to become stars in their own right, including Michael Brecker and trumpeter Tom Harrell. Brecker, according to Down Beat, said his stint with Silver "was like a university of jazz." While Silver felt that his more spiritually oriented work of the 1970s was important, he believed that the people at Blue Note wanted him to go back to the more straight ahead brand of jazz that had sold so well in the 1960s. Unwilling to haggle over the direction of his music, Silver left Blue Note, the only company he had ever recorded for, in 1980 and formed his own label, Silveto.

Silver continued to record and tour steadily throughout the 1980s. Among his albums of that period were Spiritualizing the Senses and Music to Ease Your Disease. He also put out an album of previously unreleased live material from 1964. Silver showed no signs of slowing down in the 1990s. He released three new albums between 1990 and 1996—It's Got to Be Funky, Pencil Packin' Papa, and The Hardbop Grandpop—in spite of serious health problems that put him out of action for a period in 1993 and 1994.

In 1996 Silver became the Down Beat Hall of Fame's 86th member, joining Getz, Blakey, and a host of others whose music he had enhanced over the years with his own magic. As he approached the age of 70, Silver insisted that he still had musical goals. Above all, he expressed a hope to continue spreading jazz, which he sees as a unique and spiritually uplifting art form, to new audiences. To Silver, the music itself is the healing force that keeps him going.

Selected discography

Horace Silver and the Jazz Messengers, Blue Note, 1954.
Six Pieces of Silver, Blue Note, 1956.
The Stylings of Silver, Blue Note, 1957.
Finger Poppin', Blue Note, 1959.
Blowin' the Blues Away, Blue Note, 1959.
Horace-Scope, Blue Note, 1960.
Doin' the Thing, Blue Note, 1961.
Silver's Serenade, Blue Note, 1963.
Song for My Father, Blue Note, 1964.
The Cape Verdean Blues, Blue Note, 1965.
That Healin' Feelin' (The United States of Mind, Phase I), Blue Note, 1970.
Total Response (Phase II), Blue Note, 1971.
In Pursuit of the 27th Man, Blue Note, 1972.
All (Phase III), Blue Note, 1973.
Silver 'n Brass, Blue Note, 1975.
Silver 'n Wood, Blue Note, 1976.
Silver 'n Voices, Blue Note, 1977.
Silver 'n Percussion, Blue Note, 1977.
Silver 'n Strings Play the Music of the Spheres, Blue Note, 1978.
It's Got to Be Funky, Columbia, 1993.
Pencil Packin' Papa, Columbia, 1994.
The Hardbop Grandpop, Impulse, 1996.

Sources

Books

Lyons, Len, and Don Perlo, *Jazz Portraits,* Morrow, 1989.
Reisner, Robert, *The Jazz Titans,* DeCapo, 1977.
Ullman, Michael, *Jazz Lives,* New Republic Books, 1980.

Periodicals

DownBeat, November 1980; September 1994; December 1996.
New Republic, July 8, 1978.

Additional material was provided by GRP/Impulse Records.

—*Robert R. Jacobson*

Social Distortion

Punk Rock Band

In 1996 Social Distortion, Orange County, California punk stalwarts, released their third major label album, *White Light, White Heat, White Trash,* to critical acclaim. It was the band's first album in four years, the belated follow up to their first major success, *Somewhere Between Heaven and Hell.* In those interim years the band lost its longtime drummer and would lose a second drummer before the album was released. Mike Ness, the pumped-up, tattooed singer and songwriter, struggled with new material. The band spent a year in the recording studio, the final results sounding much like previous Social D albums, with its signature blend of roots rock and punk, angry, angst-ridden lyrics and Ness's gravelly baritone. Upon the album's release, the band netted legendary punk drummer Chuck Biscuits, of Black Flag, Circle Jerks, and D.O.A. fame.

Formed in 1979 by childhood friends Mike Ness and Dennis Danell, Social Distortion came at the tail end of the initial punk movement. From the beginning, Ness's songs were marked with anger and frustration. As it was in the beginning, so it is with *White Light, White Heat, White Trash.* As Lorraine Ali, wrote in *Rolling Stone,* "One reason for Social D's longevity is that they never have bought into any one trend but instead have written songs with a timeless, outlaw attitude." The band has stayed close to the essentials; loud guitars, angry vocals, hard-beaten drums. Social Distortion's voice, which grew out of angry adolescence, has not changed.

The early Social D played hard-driving Ramones-style songs typifying teenage attitudes like distrust of parents and of authority. Suburban punks from Orange County, they entered a scene dominated by Los Angeles groups like X, the Weirdos, and proto-hardcore bands like Black Flag and the Circle Jerks. The band's early years were tumultuous. Fast driving hard core was replacing the punk rock of the seventies. Sid Vicious of the Sex Pistols was dead of an overdose and a hero to some. Hard drugs were rampant. "I started drinking and doing drugs when I was eleven," said Ness. "I did them until I was twenty-three. I got thrown out of my house when I was fifteen. Then I just survived. My houses were mostly just a bunch of dope fiends shooting up," he told Chris Mundy of *Rolling Stone.*

Ness and the band itself were on shaky ground when they toured cross-country in an old, unreliable tour bus. The film Another State of Mind documents that troubled tour. There was a defection of two original members and Ness fell deeper into addiction. John Maurer, a childhood friend of Ness and a former roadie for the band, took over as bass player in 1984.

Later that same year, Chris Reece, from the San Francisco punk band, The Lewd, became their drummer. The band tried to get it together to record while Ness battled his drug addiction. Social D reformed itself, releasing *Prison Bound* in 1988, their first recording since Ness got clean. Their early punk, Ramones-style sound took on a rockabilly/country flavor which was to become, over the next several albums, their signature style. The band was blues-based, set at punk pace. "We were never hardcore," says Ness. "And by 1984 punk had lost it. Like anything, when it gets big, it gets diluted. " he told Mundy. The album included a cover of the Johnny Cash classic, "Ring of Fire." The band continued to tour, much as they had in the early days, and in 1990 they released *Social Distortion,* their major label debut. They toured that year as the supporting act to Neil Young.

Persistence and Success

Their follow-up album, *Somewhere Between Heaven and Hell* was released in February of 1992. It marked the band's first real commercial success. The video for "I Was Wrong" was in heavy rotation on MTV's "Buzz Bin" for 12 weeks. The album sold over 400,000 copies. With songs titled "Born To Lose," "King of Fools," and "Bad Luck," the album continued Ness's interest in the dark side of country while remaining true to the band's punk origins. Various critics decried the record as sounding like a shotgun wedding between two disparate types of music, a wedding that was surprisingly successful. A review in the *Los Angeles Reader* described *Somewhere*

For the Record . . .

Original members include **Mike Ness**, guitar and vocals; **Dennis Danell**, guitar; **Brent Liles** (left band in 1988) bass; **Derek O'Brien** (left band in 1988), vocals, drums. Later members include **John Maurer** (joined band in 1984), bass; **Chris Reece** (member 1988-1994), drums; **Chuck Biscuits** (joined band in 1996), drums.

Addresses: *Record company*—Sony Music, Attn: Dave Gottlieb, 550 Madison Ave., New York, NY 10022-3211; phone: 212 8330-8491; fax: 212 833-4060.

Between Heaven and Hell as "somewhere between the Ramones and Johnny Cash."

Persistence had finally paid off. The band's longevity, it's origins in the tail end of the initial punk wave, and Ness's personal history had earned the band the recognition it deserved. While the outlaw pose adopted by Ness and the songs about drifters, losers and hard luck were rock and roll clichés, Ness had lived what he sang about, and this authenticity shined through. The band toured for nearly sixteen months, co-billed with the Ramones, and later headlining with the Rev. Horton Heat.

Four years passed before the release of their next album, *White Light, White Heat, White Trash.* During this time Social Distortion was engaged in a lengthy legal battle to reclaim ownership of its back catalogue. They were eventually victorious and the early singles were released on a compilation on Mainliner records, as well as their first EP and "Mommy's Little Monster." The band also assumed ownership of "The Casbah," the Orange County studio where they recorded their first two albums, after its owner died in an accident. Chris Reece, who had been with the band for over ten years, left at the end of 1994, as Ness struggled to write new songs. A replacement drummer lasted little more than a year and it was only upon completion of *White Light, White Heat, White Trash* that Chuck Biscuits, legendary drummer for Black Flag, Circle Jerks, D.O.A. and recently Danzig, joined the band.

White Light, White Heat, White Trash marked both a return to the roots of the band and a culmination of all that the band had worked through over the years. Ness sings "in a compassionate growl that fuses pain, anger, shame, and courage, he's chased by memories he can't outrun," wrote Ira Robbins, in *Rolling Stone.* Ness did not veer from the familiar terrain of frustration, anger, and contrition. However, while the subjects seem familiar, they are viewed with a more mature and wizened outlook. The first single and video "I Was Wrong" reflects upon the singer's self-destructive past; it is the song of a survivor.

The album was produced by Michael Beinhorn who has recorded Soundgarden, and the Red Hot Chili Peppers. Basic tracks were recorded in New York; overdub and mixing were done in Los Angeles. Ness, a Southern California native, immersed himself in the local scene while continuing to write songs. The sound is more raw, less country than the roots-punk of *Social Distortion* and *Somewhere Between Heaven and Hell.* As Ness explained, "Every record I write is an example of what I'm listening to. The last two albums, I was listening to a lot of Hank Williams and dark rockabilly and blues as well, so that came out. What I've been listening to the last couple of years is back to Johnny Thunders and the Clash and Ramones and Dead Boys, as well as early LA bands: X, the Dickies, stuff like that. That stuff has so much more soul and substance than what's called alternative now."

Selected discography

Albums

Mommy's Little Monster, Time Bomb Records, 1982.
Prison Bound, Sticky Fingers Records, 1988.
Social Distortion, Epic, 1990.
Somewhere Between Heaven and Hell, Epic, 1992.
Mainliner: Wreckage From the Past, Time Bomb Recordings, 1995.
White Light, White Heat, White Trash, Sony 550 Music, 1996.

With others

Future Looks Bright Ahead, Posh Boy, 1981.
Rodney on the ROQ Vol. II, Posh Boy, 1981.
Someone Got Their Head Kicked In, B.Y.O. Records, 1981.
Hell Comes to Your House Vol. I, Bemisbrain, 1982.
More Than A State of Mind, Restless, 1990.

Sources

Los Angeles Reader, March 6, 1992.
New York Times, November 29, 1996.
Rolling Stone, July 9-23, 1992; October 3, 1996.

Online

http://www.socialdistortion.com

Additional information gathered from publicity materials
provided by 550 Music.

—Kevin O'Sullivan

Spearhead

Rap, soul group

The genre-defying music of Spearhead draws upon such influential R&B, soul, reggae and hip-hop artists as Stevie Wonder, Curtis Mayfield, Bob Marley, Marvin Gaye and Public Enemy, but the band refuses to engage in mere revivalism. Singer-rapper-songwriter Michael Franti's vision is at once political and personal; Spearhead represents a warmer, more approachable take on the issues of color and community he once tackled with his former bands, the Beatnigs and Disposable Heroes of Hiphoprisy. The band's debut album saw some small-scale success, and the advent of viable "alternative soul" acts in the following years opened the possibility of mainstream popularity by the time Spearhead's sophomore set hit the streets in 1997.

Franti told Ian Rogers of the online magazine *Crash,* "a lot of R&B and early soul music is what was in my house when I was a kid." Yet inspiring as these records would later prove to be, they didn't move the young Franti directly into music. Indeed, well into his days at the University of San Francisco, his mind was on hoops. "I was just a jock," he recalled to Rogers, "that's all I

Photo by Chapman Baehler. Capitol Records. Reproduced by permission.

For the Record . . .

Members include **Michael Franti**, vocals; **Mary Harris** (bandmember 1994-95), vocals, drums; **James Gray**, drums; **David James**, guitar; **Oneida James** (joined c. 1995), bass, vocals; **Le Le Jamison** (bandmember c. 1994-95), keyboards; **Keith McArthur** (bandmember c. 1994-95), bass; **Trinna Simmons** (joined c. 1995), vocals; **Sub Commander Ras I Zulu**, vocals.

Band formed c. 1994, Philadelphia, PA and San Francisco, CA; signed with Capitol Records and released debut album *Home*, 1994; song "Positive" appeared on GRP compilation *Stolen Moments: Red Hot & Cool*, 1994 and used in Red Cross AIDS outreach program, 1996; appeared on House of Blues Smokin' Grooves Tour with Fugees, Ziggy Marley, Cypress Hill, A Tribe Called Quest, Busta Rhymes, 1996.

Awards: CLIO award for "Hole in the Bucket" video, 1994; *Stolen Moments* voted Record of the Year by *Time* magazine, 1994.

Addresses: *Record company*—Capitol Records, 1750 North Vine St., Los Angeles, CA 90028. *Website*—http://www.hollywoodandvine.com/Spearhead/. *Fan Mail*—Spearhead Intelligence Agency, PO Box 423480, San Francisco, CA 94142-3480. *E-mail*—MFSPEAR1@aol.com. (online address for Michael Franti).

wanted to do: eat, sleep and think basketball. Then I started to get really disillusioned with sports and the whole business of it, so I decided to get into the music business—which is even more corrupt!"

His first foray into music was with the San Francisco troupe The Beatnigs, which *Billboard* would later describe as a "noisy, post-industrial junkyard band." Franti's attempts to move beyond the stubbornly underground ethic of the band led to hard feelings; by the time he'd formed the more directly political industrial rap project The Disposable Heroes of Hiphoprisy, his former bandmates were already accusing him of selling out. "What Michael's doing," said ex-Beatnig Troy Dixon in *Option*, "is a calculated attempt to avoid disturbing his white listeners." The Heroes—which consisted of Franti and DJ Rono Tse, with various guests, including guitarist Charlie Hunter—released one album, *Hiphoprisy Is the Greatest Luxury*, an imposing set of political treatis-

es recited over edgy beats, noise and scratching. *Option* quoted hip-hop writer Michael Gonzalez, who opined that the Heroes "borrowed the worst from Public Enemy and [jazz-funk poet and composer] Gil Scott-Heron. [Public Enemy MC} Chuck D can't flow and Gil Scott-Heron can't sing." *Entertainment Today*, in an article praising Spearhead, decried the Heroes' "dour political sermonizing."

"About Seduction"

After a handful of collaborations with cutting-edge artists like punk provocateur Jello Biafra and writer William S. Burroughs, Franti dissolved the Heroes and began to rethink his musical approach. "The Heroes came to a point when there was a clash musically, you know?" He recalled to the electronic 'zine *The Buzz*. "We were both doing our own thin and, when we came to record the album, we discovered that we were just too far apart to come together on it." In forming Spearhead, he returned to the warm, progressive soul of his youth. The new group's name came from the innovation of the Zulu king Shaka, who modified the traditional Africanspear for modern use. Likewise, Spearhead would use the penetrating power of old-school black music to reach contemporary audiences. "Hiphoprisy was about gettin' in people's faces," he told Merrell Noden of the Internet magazine *Grooves*. "Spearhead is more about seduction." Collaborating in Philadelphia with producer Joe "The Butcha" Nicolo, Franti enlisted singer-drummer Mary Harris, guitarist David James, keyboardist Le Le Jamison and dancer/rapper Ras I Zulu, among others.

The result was Spearhead's Capitol Records debut, *Home*. With tracks like the evocative "Hole in the Bucket" and the celebratory "People in the Middle," the album managed to fuse Franti's political concerns with more small-scale, vulnerable lyrics. The result, according to *Entertainment Today*, was a recording that "verges on a miraculous"; the magazine added, "Spearhead has studied its music history and come up with spellbinding grooves, perfectly apt arrangements, and insinuating melodies, all of which perfectly complement rhymes that manage to be intimate and global, angry and loving, meditative and playful all at once. In short, they write good songs, regardless of the genre."

Home was hamstrung by its own ambitions, to some degree. R&B radio was too conservative to embrace Spearhead's sound, and only alternative rock radio, among pop formats, gave any rotation to "Hole in the Bucket." Yet the band earned numerous honors for "Hole" and its video, and the song "Positive"—a somber, personalized meditation on HIV—was included on the benefit album *Stolen Moments: Red Hot & Cool* and was central to a teen outreach program sponsored by the Red Cross. Spearhead also managed to gain fans worldwide with their loose, energetic live shows, and in 1996 participated in the House of Blues Smokin' Grooves tour with the Fugees, Ziggy Marley, Cypress Hill, A Tribe Called Quest and Busta Rhymes.

Chocolate: Hip-Hop as Internet

Spearhead emerged again in 1997 with a follow-up album, *Chocolate Supa Highway.* Contrasting the media's preoccupation with the Internet with the oral traditions of black culture, Franti proposed a funkier concept than the information superhighway. The album's title comes, he elaborated in the *Telluride Daily Planet,* "from the other side of the information superhighway, the Black realm. The way we as a people communicate ... that comes from a shared history of battling to retain our way of living in the face of colonialism ... hip-hop is our world-wide Internet." He also presented a retooled Spearhead, with Harris replaced by singer Trinna Simmons, Carl Young taking over on keyboards, and new bassist Oneida James sharing vocals. The infiltration of black radio by such progressive soul artists as the Fugees, D'Angelo and Me'Shell Ndegeocello in the mid-1990s, meanwhile, made Capitol more optimistic about Spearhead's chances for mainstream success. *Playboy* called the album "an impressive improvement on the band's debut," while *Gavin* declared Franti "at the forefront of hip-hop's renaissance." Even so, not everyone was thrilled with the group's new direction. *CMJ* lamented that *Chocolate* "lacks the immediacy and punch of the earlier effort; it's just as dense, and more subtle, but less catchy and less fun."

Franti – never one to be hindered by doubters—shared his thoughts about his own mission with the *San Francisco Bay Guardian:* "I feel like the information is already gone," he asserted. "Right now, we're in the inspiration era. People are looking to find something in their lives that is gonna bring them peace and inspire them to be creative and help them get through the bullshit." To *Metro Active,* he elaborated on his approach: "I'm not so much into education as I am into inspiration," he said. "I'm not much into politics; I'm more into having fun, but being in the space where I'm free to have fun."

Selected discography

Home (includes "Hole in the Bucket," "People in the Middle" and "Positive"), Capitol, 1994.
Chocolate Supa Highway, Capitol, 1997.

Sources

Billboard, February 8, 1997.
CMJ (*College Music Journal*), April 1997.
Entertainment Today, October 26, 1995.
Gavin, February 21, 1997.
Metro Active, August 29, 1996; December 5, 1996.
Option, January 1993.
Playboy, April 1997.
San Francisco Bay Guardian, March 5, 1997.
Telluride Daily Planet, December 6, 1996.

Additional information was provided by Capitol Records' Internet site, the unofficial Spearhead home page and the online publications The Buzz, Crash and *Grooves.*

—*Simon Glickman*

Spencer Davis Group

Rock band

The Spencer Davis Group, originally formed in 1963 in Birmingham, England, had a major impact on the music of other British rock stars of the sixties. Considered the band to see by other musicians, including such luminaries as the Beatles and the Rolling Stones, the members of the group seemed destined for success. Recalling the impact of the group, Ian Whitcomb stated in *Rock Odyssey: A Musician's Chronicle of Rock,* "only The Who, The Kinks and the Spencer Davis Group were keeping the rock pulse running." Davis, lead vocalist and guitar player, the Winwood brothers—Muff on bass and Steve on vocals, guitar, and keyboard—and drummer Pete York were the original members. They spent four years touring England and the world and producing chart-topping hits. Songs such as "Gimme Some Lovin'" and "I'm a Man," driven by Steve's blues-tinged vocals and infectious keyboard riffs, became almost instant classics. By 1967, however, Steve and Muff decided to leave the band. Though Davis soon enlisted replacements, the band never again enjoyed the acclaim that had defined their early years. In 1970 the

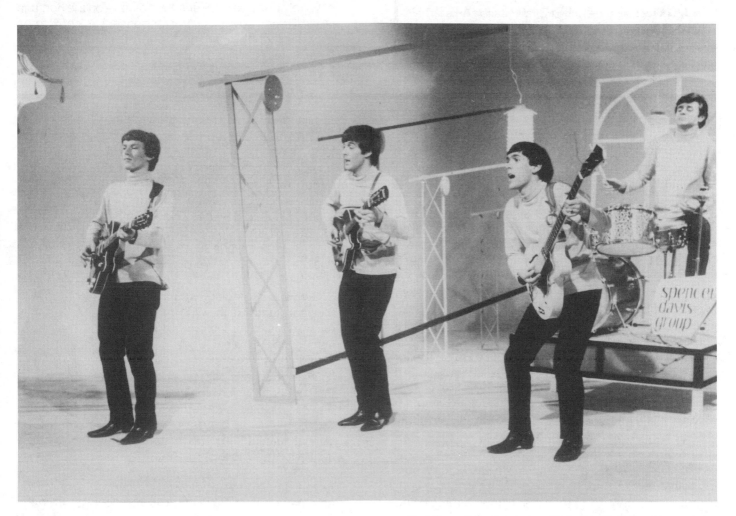

Frank Driggs Collection. Archive Photos, Inc. Reproduced by permission.

Founding members include **Spencer Davis** (born July 17, 1942, Swansea, Wales), guitar, vocals, and harmonica; **Steve Winwood** (born May 12, 1948, Birmingham, England), vocals, keyboards, and guitar; **Muff Winwood** (born Mervyn Winwood on June 14, 1943, Birmingham, England), bass; **Pete York** (born August 15, 1942, Middlesborough, England) drums. Steve and Muff Winwood left group, 1967. Pete York left original group 1969. Subsequent members include: **Phil Sawyer,** guitar; **Eddie Hardin,** keyboards and vocals; **Ray Fenwick,** guitar; **Dee Murray,** bass; **Nigel Olsson,** drums.

Group formed in Birmingham, England, 1963; released first British number one hit, "Keep On Running," 1965; named Best New Group in Britain, 1966; first American top ten hit, "Gimme Some Lovin'," 1967.

Addresses: *Agent*—Robert Birk, Paradise Artists, 108 East Matilija St., Ojai, CA 92023. *E-mail*—spencer@gsmmedia.com.

notice for his musical abilities. A child pianist, he turned to guitar in his early teens and later spent a year in music college where he learned to compose songs. Muff, five years older than Steve, also began his music training early and, by the time he formed Muff Woody, he was an accomplished jazz musician. When Davis saw the brothers' musical versatility, he knew he had found his band. He soon persuaded them to join him and drummer Pete York as the Rhythm and Blues Quartet. Playing mainly R & B covers, they landed a regular gig at a club in London within a year.

Topping the Charts

By 1964 they had adopted the name Spencer Davis Group and began to get some very famous attention. "Rock celebrities flocked to see them," Dave McAleer wrote in *The Fab British Rock `N' Roll Invasion of 1964.* He also referred to them as a "group's group," a title that would be applied to them often during those early years. The music industry buzz quickly reached the record labels and the band soon released it's first single—a cover of John Lee Hooker's "Dimples"—on the Fontana label. It received a lukewarm response. Their next three releases,though reaching the top fifty on the U. K.'s record charts, still did not garner the attention that the band did during a live show. That would soon change.

Chris Blackwell, visionary music promoter and founder of Island Records, heard the Spencer Davis Group perform at a London bar and was blown away. On Island's Web site, he recalled how Steve "could sing like Ray Charles whilst still sounding like himself." He introduced the group to another one of his artists, Jamaican singer-songwriter Jackie Edwards, and in 1965 the group released Edwards' "Keep On Running." It was a runaway hit, knocking the Beatles' "We Can Work It Out" out of the number one spot on the U. K. charts. Their next release, another Edwards composition, "Somebody Help Me" also hit number one. Their success in Great Britain was immediate. Touring on their own and with musical giants like the Who and the Rolling Stones, they amassed a loyal following. Early in 1966 they were named the Best New Group in Britain. In addition to the singles they also released three albums during this time. Though less popular than the single releases, all three albums, which highlighted the band's rhythm and blues style, still managed to make the U. K.'s top ten. Like so many pop bands of that era, they also made an obligatory film debut in a campy adventure movie entitled "The Ghost Goes Gear."

group disbanded. Davis and York occasionally revived the group, playing to audiences worldwide.

Their story begins in the early 1960s. Davis, a language scholar at University of Birmingham, England, decided he wanted to start a rock band. As a child he had learned to play harmonica and piano accordion. By sixteen he was hooked on the guitar and the American rhythm and blues music that was slowly making it's way across the Atlantic. With few opportunities to hear R & B in England, Davis avidly sought out any performance that came to town. When he heard a Dixieland band perform a skiffle version of the R & B song "John Henry," he was blown away. Skiffle—music played using standard instruments as well as improvisational objects such as washboards, jugs, and kazoos—was to Great Britain's R & B sound, what the Blues was to America's R&B. It influenced bands like the Animals, the Rolling Stones, and Manfred Mann, and provided Davis with the perfect outlet for his distinctive sound to take root. After a stint playing skiffle as a solo artist, Davis was ready to apply his skill to his own R & B band.

In 1963 Davis went to a local tavern to see Muff Woody, a traditional jazz band featuring Muff and Steve Winwood. Steve, only 15 at the time, was already gaining

As their fame grew, so did Steve Winwood's reputation as a natural musical talent. His vocal range, from the high of a pre-pubescent boy to the deep soul-scratching wail of a bluesman, was a mesmerizing draw. He slowly began to eclipse the band. On their second album, *Autumn 66,* songs like "When A Man Loves A Woman" and "Dust My Blues" highlighted his songwriting abilities as well as his vocals.

Despite their popularity in Great Britain, they weren't able to make an impact on the American music charts. Then in 1966 they released the original composition "Gimme Some Lovin'." Written quickly, under the exacting guidance of Blackwell, the song was an easy collaboration among the members. Driven by an infectious dance beat and a chorus that demands to be sung along with, it was destined to become a classic. American audiences went wild for it. Already a number three hit in the U. K., it climbed to number seven on the American charts by early 1967. Within two months, "I'm A Man," another original song, also hit the top ten in both Great Britain and America. The Spencer Davis Group was an international sensation. Steve, however, had already decided to leave the group to start his own band, Traffic. Muff also gave notice, choosing to pursue the business side of the music industry.

Though the loss of the Winwood brothers was a dramatic blow to the group, Davis was not about to let his namesake band fold easily. He soon enlisted Phil Sawyer for guitar and Eddie Hardin for vocals and keyboards. Their first release together was for a 1967 movie soundtrack *Here We Go 'Round The Mulberry Bush,* that also featured the music of Steve Winwood's new venture, Traffic. In 1968, after replacing Sawyer with veteran guitarist Ray Fenwick, the Spencer Davis Group released the aptly named album *With Their New Face On.* Though it clearly lacked the distinctive sound that made the original group so successful, it did send two songs—"Time Seller" and "Mr. Second Class"—to the charts. Despite this minor success, the band continued to suffer. York, who had experienced both the highs and the lows, decided to pursue a duo career with Hardin. Still committed to the group, Davis recruited bassist Dee Murray and drummer Nigel Olsson to join him and Fenwick, and in 1969 they released two albums, *Heavies* and *Funky.* Neither album produced a hit and by 1970 Olsson and Murray left to join Elton John's band. No more replacements were sought and within the year Davis packed his guitar and moved to California.

Though the original Spencer Davis Group was gone, their reputation lived on. Considered to be one of the most influential of the "British Invasion" bands, Davis and the rest of the original band members discovered that many of their songs were considered classics. Referring to "Gimme Some Lovin'," Davis told a Penn-sylvania newspaper reporter, "We had no idea when we wrote it that it would turn out to be an evergreen, a classic." Perhaps, hoping to recapture some of that classic spirit, Davis briefly reformed the Spencer Davis Group in 1973. Featuring Davis, York, Hardin, Fenwick, and newcomer Charlie McCracken on bass, the group put out two albums, *Gluggo* and *Living in a Back Street.* The former featured "Catch You On The Rebop," an infectious tune that enjoyed some success.

After the Breakup

Throughout the seventies and eighties the original band members pursued various avenues of the music business. Steve Winwood, following the disbanding of Traffic, spent time in the groups Blind Faith and Airforce. He later struck out on his own and developed an international following for his solo work. His brother Muff eventually became head of Artist Development at CBS Records in England. Pete York pursued a successful career as a jazz drummer, playing in various groups as well as completing studio work. Davis has worked in the music industry as a promoter for artists such as Robert Palmer and Bob Marley and as a consultant for music video producers. In addition he has appeared in television commercials and sitcoms, including a co-starring role on *Married with Children.* He is also in demand as a lecturer on the history of rock and roll. Despite his busy schedule, he has always taken time out for his first love—making music. He produced solo albums in 1972 and 1984, collaborated on a couple of folk music albums, and toured the world with a group of classic rock stars. Since the early nineties, he and York reunite each year and tour Europe as the Spencer Davis Group. Performing their classic hits for new audiences, as well as those old enough to remember when, it seems that, thirty years after their first hit, the Spencer Davis Group are determined to 'keep the rock pulse running' a little longer.

Selected discography

First Album (includes "Dimples"), Fontana, 1965.
Second Album (includes "Keep On Runnin'"), Fontana 1966.
Autumn '66 (includes "Dust My Blues" and "When A Man Loves A Woman"), Fontana, 1966.
Gimme Some Lovin' (includes "Gimme Some Lovin'"), United Artists, 1967
I'm A Man (includes "I'm A Man"), United Artists, 1967.
With Their New Face On (includes "Time Seller" and "Mr. Second Class"), United Artists, 1968.
Heavies, United Artists, 1969.

Funky, 1969.

Gluggo (includes "Catch You On The Rebop"), Vertigo, 1973.

Sources

Books

McAleer, Dave, *The Fab British Rock 'N' Roll Invasion of 1964,* St. Martin's Press, 1994.

Whitcomb, Ian, *Rock Odyssey: A Musician's Chronicle of Rock,* Dolphin Books, 1983.

Periodicals

The Daily News (McKeesport, PA), December 24, 1991.

Online

http://www.webcom.com/spencer/welcome.html.

Additional information was provided by Paradise Artists publicity materials, 1997.

Steeleye Span

Folk rock group

Playing electrified, rock-and-roll versions of traditional folk songs, Steeleye Span became one of the most long-lasting of the British folk-rock bands that sprung up in the late 1960s. As Robin Denselow wrote of the group in the liner notes of *The Steeleye Span Story: Original Masters*, "Of all the excellent, varied bands in recent British rock history, they are the only one who have stuck with their original aim and ideal—to promote British traditional songs to mass audiences, while branching out as far as they could."

The genesis of Steeleye Span began with Tim Hart and Maddy Prior in 1967, who established their reputation as top performers of old folk songs and recorded three albums of traditional music. "Maddy's exquisite clean voice, Tim's harmonies and acoustic guitar playing quickly put the duo at the top of the folk club scene," noted Denselow. The group began to take shape when Tiger Hutchings, a bass player for the popular folk-group Fairport Convention, started scouting around to create a new band . He formed the core of Steeleye Span in 1969 with Hart, Prior, and the folk-singing

For the Record . . .

Original members included **Maddy Prior** (born August 14, 1947, in Blackpool, UK), vocals; **Ashley Hutchings** (born January 1945, in London, UK), bass; **Tim Hart** (born January 9, 1948, in Lincoln, UK), guitar, vocals, dulcimer; **Gay Woods**, vocals, concertina; **Terry Woods**, guitar. Later members included **Martin Carthy,** guitar; **Peter Knight,** fiddle, mandolin, vocals; **Rick Kemp** (born November 15, 1941, Little Handford, UK), bass, vocals; **Bob Johnson,** lead guitar, vocals; **Nigel Pegrum,** drums.

Tyger Hutchings recruited Hart, Prior, and Gay and Terry Woods to form group, 1969; released first album, *Hark! the Village Wait,* 1970; guitarist Martin Carthy and fiddle player Peter Knight replaced the Woodses; group performed in *Corunna,* a play written for them; Hutchings and Carthy were replaced by Rick Kemp on bass and Bob Johnson on guitar; Kemp and Prior were married, 1979; released *Below the Salt*, an album with a stronger rock orientation, 1972; released first charting single, "Gaudete," 1972; Nigel Pegrum became first drummer with group, 1973; manager/prouder Sandy Robertson was replaced by Joe Lustig; signed major recording deal with Chrysalis Records; became major international group, mid 1970s; began experimenting with reggae and heavier rock rhythms, late 1970s; disbanded, 1978; reformed to release *Sails of Silver,* 1980; played occasionally for reunion concerts and festivals, 1980s–90s; released *Time,* 1996.

Addresses: *Record company*—Shanachie Entertainment, P.O. Box 284, Newton, New Jersey 07860.

Guinness Encyclopedia of Popular Music, the album was "expertly arranged and performed to encompass the rock-based perspective Hutchings helped create on the Fairport's Liege and Lief, while retaining the purity of the songs." On the *All-Music Guide* website, reviewer Bruce Eder added that "Prior's voice was never better than on this album" and that "This was probably the best singing edition of Steeleye Span...."

Soon after the album was released, the Woodses left to join the group Doctor Strangely Strange and were replaced by guitarist Martin Carthy and fiddle player Peter Knight. Terry Woods eventually ended up with the Pogues in the 1980s. Group solidarity began developing cracks while the group was performing in a play entitled *Corunna* that had been written for Steeleye Span by Keith Dewhurst. When the play was about to move to a larger London theater, Hutchings decided he didn't want to stay with it or tour America with the group. At this time the band was progressing to a louder, more rock-and-roll sound that strayed from Hutchings' plans, and he left the group to play with the more traditional-sounding Albion Country Band.

Disputes over Hutchings' replacement led to the defection of Carthy, resulting in a major change in the structure of the group. Hutchings and Carthy were replaced by Rick Kemp on bass and Bob Johnson on guitar, two musicians with extensive rock experience but who were largely unknown at the time. Kemp and Prior were married in 1979. Johnson had previously played in a folk due with Knight. "The blend of Bob and Rick's rock approach, with Tim, Maddy and Pete's folk style gave Steeleye its firm identify and sense of direction—and they sounded like a fully-fledged band, not just a collection of individuals playing together," claimed Denselow. This collection of personnel released two of the group's most highly regarded albums, *Below the Salt* in 1972 and *Parcel of Rogues* in 1973. Both albums featured a strong rock orientation and showed a wide range of musical styles.

"There's not a weak note here, and all of it has a harder, more muscular sound courtesy of Kemp and Johnson, matched to impeccable vocals and uniformly excellent material," said Eder about Below the Salt. This album's lineup featured Nigel Pegrum, the group's first drummer who had played with Gnidgrolog. It also contained "Gaudete," Steeleye Span's first song to make it onto the British charts. They had more hit singles with "Thomas the Rhymer" from 1974's *Now We Are Six*, which was produced by Ian Anderson of Jethro Tull, and the title track from *All Around My Hat* in 1975. Discussing "Thomas the Rhymer," Denselow wrote that the song "showed Steeleye mixing harmony and rock with even more energy and attack...." By this time the group was

couple of Gay and Terry Woods, who had previously performed with the Irish folk-rock group Sweeney's Men. Hart purportedly came up with the name of the group from a character in an old ballad called "Horkstow Grange."

Acclaimed Debut Album

Hutchings' goal with the new group was to perform traditional music with electric instruments. His aim was realized in 1970 with the release of the group's first album, *Hark! the Village Wait.* Electric instruments were used subtly on this debut LP, without excessive amplification, and no drummer was used. According to the writing many of their own songs and settings to match traditional lyrics.

Became Major International Group

With the enlistment of new manager/producer Joe Lustig, the group secured a new recording arrangement with Chrysalis Records and became a major group on the international scene in the mid-1970s. "Between 1972 and 1976 they were the group that most extensively and logically explored the folk-rock formula...," claimed Dafydd Rees and Luke Crampton in the *Encyclopedia of Rock Stars.* Public acceptance of the group began to wane in the late 1970s when it began experimenting with reggae and heavier rock rhythms, according to Guinness.

After breaking up in 1978, the group reformed in 1980 and released *Sails of Silver.* Throughout the 1980s the group got together from time to time for reunion concerts and appearances at festivals, while Prior and Hart also pursued successful solo careers. Steeleye Span proved it was still a very viable group with its release of *Time* on the Shanachie label in 1996. On the Dirty Linen website, reviewer Steve Winick said that the album "shows them to be much like the Steeleye Span of the mid-1970s, committed to combining traditional music with rock and roll in powerful and interesting ways."

Selected discography

Albums

Hark! the Village Wait, Shanachie, 1970.

Please to See the King, Shanachie, 1971.
Ten Man Top, Shanachie, 1971.
Below the Salt, Shanachie, 1972.
Parcel of Rogues, Shanachie, 1973.
Now We Are Six, BGO, 1974.
All Around My Hat, Shanachie, 1975.
Live at Last, Chrysalis, 1978.
Sails of Silver, Chrysalis, 1980.
Tempted and Tried, Shanachie, 1989.
Time, Shanachie, 1996.

Sources

Books

Clarke, Donald, editor, *The Penguin Encyclopedia of Popular Music,* Viking, 1989, p. 1116.
Larkin, Colin, editor, *The Guinness Encyclopedia of Popular Music,* Volume 5, Guinness Publishing, 1995, p. 3953.
Rees, Dafydd, and Luke Crampton, *Encyclopedia of Rock Stars,* Dorling Kindersley, 1996, p. 420.
Romanowski, Patricia, and Holly George-Warren, editors, *The New Rolling Stone Encyclopedia of Rock & Roll,* Rolling Stone Press, 1995, pp. 948–949.

Additional information for this profile was obtained from the liner notes of *The Steeleye Span Story: Original Masters,* a Chrysalis release, as well as the *All-Music Guide, CD Universe,* and Dirty Linen websites on the Internet.

—Ed Decker

Sting

Singer, songwriter, actor

Sting is one of the few musicians to experience huge success both as a member of a band and as a solo artist. His band, the Police, reached the highest possible peak in pop rock after the release of *Synchronicity*. *Synchronicity* was number one on the charts for 17 consecutive weeks, and the band was selling out major venues on their world tour. However, one night before a concert at Shea Stadium, where they sold out 70,000 seats, the band members all looked at one another and realized that it would not get any better. The Police went out with a bang; *Synchronicity* inadvertently turned out to be their last album. Sting then embarked on a very successful solo career. He enjoyed the freedom of songwriting without having to achieve consensus, and the freedom to become an actor without having to adjust schedules.

Sting continues to produce quality music that resists classification. Sting is a star with substance, "the pop idol adults can admire," according to *Rolling Stone* writer Anthony DeCurtis. His songwriting within the confinement of his former band proved insightful and adventurous even while vaulting them to megastar status in the pop world. His risk-taking as a solo artist keeps Police fans interested while appealing to a new set of fans of jazz-inflected rock. Sting's appeal goes well beyond his music, or the effective dramatic performances he has given on stage and screen. His dedicated work to preserve the Amazon's vanishing rain forest makes him an inspirational figure for anyone concerned about the pressing environmental problems facing the world today.

Growing up in the bleak English industrial town of Newcastle-upon-Tyne, Sting—then known as Gordon Sumner—was primarily concerned with breaking free from the dead-end life that most of the people in town seemed resigned to living. Sting often made offensive comments about his family and his reasons for wanting to leave Newcastle. Making music was Sting's uncertain ambition. He never had formal lessons, but by the age of 17 he was working semi-professionally in local jazz clubs, where he had learned from older players to play bass guitar and read music. Members of one of the jazz bands he joined back then gave him his nickname "Sting" one day when he wore a yellow and black striped sweater to one of their gigs. After he briefly attended Warwick University, he worked at odd jobs, like construction, until 1971 when he trained to be a schoolteacher. By day he was a mild mannered English teacher. By night, he played punk rock with a band he formed with three friends, called Last Exit. When he referred to this period of time, Sting once said that he had settled into a life that he could project thirty years down the road, and that terrified him. Even though he married Frances

Born Gordon Matthew Sumner, October 2, 1951, in Newcastle-upon-Tyne, England; son of Ernest Matthew (a milkman and small dairy owner) and Audrey (a homemaker; maiden name, Cowell) Sumner; married Frances Eleanor Tomelty (an actress), May 1, 1976 (divorced March 1984); two children with Tomelty: Joseph and Katherine; married Trudie Styler (actress and producer), August 22, 1992; four children with Styler.

School teacher in Newcastle-upon-Tyne, 1975-76; member of several jazz ensembles and band Last Exit, 1971-76; acquired nickname "Sting" from fellow musicians commenting on striped sweater, 1975; met Stewart Copeland and performed with the Police, 1976-83; "Roxanne" recorded, 1978; the Police recorded six albums before disbanding in 1983; *Synchronicity*, most successful of the six albums, stayed number one for 17 consecutive weeks, 1983; Sting teamed with Branford Marsalis, Kenny Kirkland in first solo effort *The Dream of the Blue Turtles*, 1985; *Bring on the Night* documentary traces the making of *The Dream of the Blue Turtles*, 1985; Recorded seven solo albums, 1985-1996; acted on stage in *The Threepenny Opera*, 1989; appeared in numerous films including: *Brimstone and Treacle, Dune, The Bride, Plenty, Julia and Julia, Stormy Monday, The Adventures of Baron Munchausen, Gentlemen Don't Eat Poets*, 1982-1997;

Awards: Winner of five Grammy Awards with the Police and four Grammy Awards as a solo artist; (with the Police) named best new artist in *Rolling Stone* Critics' Poll, 1979; received numerous awards, as a member of the Police and as a solo artist from *DownBeat* magazine's readers' and critics' polls.

Addresses: *Office*—Firstars, Bugle House 21A Noel St, London W1V 3PD, England; Firstars, 3520 Hayden Ave, Culver City, CA 90232-2413.

Tomelty in May of 1976 and their first child was born in October, Sting ran for the school exit by the end of the year.

Goodbye Dead End Job

Sting and his band, Last Exit, headed for London where he met with Stewart Copeland, a drummer who was combing the club scene for members of a new band. Doubting themselves, the members of Last Exit ran back to Newcastle. In 1976 Copeland, Sting, and Andy Summers performed as the Police. It was the heyday of the punk/new wave movement. The Police were frequently called a new wave group, but their music was more complex than that of most in that genre. Sting contributed highly literate lyrics, and their music used polyrhythmic structures and lush chordal work to create a truly unique sound. Stewart Copeland's brother owned a record label, Illegal Records. The Police recorded a single for him, called "Fall Out," that sold about 10,000 copies and led to a contract with A & M Records.

Elated over signing with a major label, the band members decided that they had to conquer America immediately. Despite strenuous protests from A & M, they began planning a club tour of the States, where no one had heard of them and they had not released any music. "It was right in the middle of corporate rock and roll, where to tour in America you had to support Foreigner," Sting recalled in *Rolling Stone*. "You'd go on as the doors opened, people would be eating popcorn or whatever and would hate you. Instead, we headlined every night— but sometimes to three people. We played to three people in Poughkeepsie, New York ... It was a great show.... We did four or five encores for those three people." That sort of energy and dedication saw them through the many rough moments of their first American tour.

Proof of their success came with the release of the haunting single "Roxanne." Suddenly, the Police was a bigger hit than any of the already-established new wave groups. Sting wrote nearly every song the band performed and eventually recorded. In 1979, A & M rushed to release their debut LP, *Outlandos d'Amour*, which they recorded for a mere $6000. *Reggatta De Blanc* was released that same year, and *Zenyatta Mondatta* followed early in 1980. The three albums made them superstars. In 1980 they embarked on a tour that included many Third World venues. Sting credits that tour as really opening his world view. Shortly after the tour, he told *Guitar Player*, "I've developed my songwriting away from the subjects of love, alienation, and devotion to a more political, socially aware viewpoint." The evolution was evident in the songs on the group's fourth and fifth albums: *Ghost in the Machine* and *Synchronicity*.

Sting often speaks of how the band's greatest success came at a time of failure in his personal life. In 1982 his marriage with Frances Tomelty ended in divorce. The turmoil of that break-up was, in Sting's words, "the worst thing that ever happened to me." *Synchronicity* reflected the upheaval he incurred that year. The lyrics of songs like "King of Pain," "Wrapped Around Your Finger," and "Every Breath You Take" resonate with the anguish felt when love and intimacy result in legal bickering and jealousy. The songs "Synchronicity" and "Synchronicity II" were inspired by the psychotherapy Sting received during the divorce, which was based on the philosophies of Carl Jung. Sting and Frances remain friends; she lives down the road from Sting and his second wife, actress and producer Trudie Styler.

Going Solo

Copeland, Summers, and Sting stayed together through the rigors of their rise to the top, but by 1983, three large egos in one group created too much tension. "In our final year, it was very clear to me that for the sake of sanity, for the sake of dignity, we should end it," Sting told DeCurtis."We had the big song of the year, the big album of the year, the big tour of the year. We were it. We'd made it—everything we attempted, we'd achieved to the power of ten." The group disbanded at the height of its popularity. For Sting, there are no regrets. "I'm very proud of the legend of the Police—I think it's intact. And I want to keep it intact. I'm very proud of the work we did, and I'm proud of my association with Andy and Stewart.... But it's in the past. I don't want to return to the Police for nostalgic reasons or for money. That would spoil it."

Sting's first priority after the breakup of the Police was to devote time to one of his longtime interests: acting. His first role had been that of the hypocritical rebel Ace Face in the Who's 1980 rock film *Quadrophenia.* He appeared in *The Secret Policeman's Other Ball* and *Brimstone and Treacle* in 1982. As time went on, Sting acquired bigger parts in more movies, including science fiction epic *Dune;* the Frankenstein remake *The Bride;* and the war drama *Plenty,* which starred Meryl Streep. He appeared on Broadway to mixed reviews in the role of *Macheath* in Bertolt Brecht's *Threepenny Opera.* His best acting to date was in the 1989 Mike Figgis film *Stormy Monday,* and the 1997 film *Gentlemen Don't Eat Poets,* produced by his wife, Trudie Styler. *Stormy Monday* was set in Sting's hometown of Newcastle, and Figgis created a character for Sting well suited to his dark, moody side. *Gentlemen Don't Eat Poets,* based on the Patrick McGrath novel, *The Grotesque,* inspired Owen Gleiberman of *Entertainment Weekly* to write that Sting is "one of the few rock stars who actually knows how to act." His performances, according to DeCurtis of *Rolling Stone,* "attest to a range of talents that is increasingly rare in what often seems the increasingly one-dimensional world of pop culture."

Sting released his first solo album in 1985. *The Dream of the Blue Turtles* combined Sting's intelligent lyrics and the Police's rhythmic sophistication with a fresh jazz sound. Backing Sting were jazz musicians Branford Marsalis, Darryl Jones, Kenny Kirkland, and Omar Hakim. A documentary was released in theaters in 1985 called *Bring on the Night.* The film traced the making of *The Dream of the Blue Turtles* and Sting's first solo concert in Paris with his new band. One memorable scene included Miles Copeland, Sting's manager, explaining why he would not pay the other musicians what Sting was paid for the concert tour. When the musicians asked him what money was on the table, Miles replied, "It's not your table." He explained to them that if one of them didn't show up for the concert, the audience would not react; but if Sting didn't show up, there was no concert. Sting was pleased with the album, but when it was nominated for a Grammy in the jazz category, he was "horrified and dismayed," and relieved not to win.

Nothing Like the Sun, released in 1987, had a sound much like *The Dream of the Blue Turtles* and was equally popular. Sting dedicated the album to his mother, who died suddenly while he was recording it. Six months later, Sting's father died. "I was told about it just before I went onstage in front of about 250,000 people in Rio for the first gig of the world tour," Sting told Phil Sutcliffe of *Us* magazine. "I had to do the show. I wanted to. In a way, it was a wake for my father. It was great—seething with energy. But I never cried for him." He told DeCurtis, "I figured the modern way to cope with death is to ignore it, just work through it. It's the modern thing to do—you go to work. Really, I think, it's fear. You're scared to actually deal with the enormity of what's happened and you try to pretend it hasn't happened. So I did that. I worked my butt off .... I just didn't stop. I didn't want to think about it."

Sting paid a high price for his emotional denial. The once prolific writer found himself unable to write a word for three years. When at last he confronted this frightening block, he realized he was "going to have to write a record about death," he told DeCurtis. "I didn't really want to." Once he sat down to do it, *The Soul Cages* poured forth in about two weeks. "It was quite painful, a bit overwhelming," he told Sutcliffe. "But I'm glad I did it." Sting dedicated *The Soul Cages* to his father, and he has said that the album has reconciled him with the family and background he once rejected so vehemently. "It's the old ping-pong of wanting to escape and then having to go back and face it," he commented. "Wanting to escape the idea of death, yet having to go back and face it. Wanting to escape where I came from, yet having to come back and face it.... My relationship with my father was complex, and it wasn't resolved.... I think now, through some psychic working, it seems to be resolved."

Ten Summoner's Tales, Sting's follow-up album to *The Soul Cages*, was more upbeat. He recorded it on his farm in Wiltshire, England, where he lives with his wife Trudie Styler and their four children. "But less and less do I know what a hit record will be," he told *Rolling Stone*. "I used to have a very clear idea. Now I'm not so sure. I like to think I'm less about rock and roll and more about songs. I think songwriting is a tradition that's older than rock and roll. I could live without rock and roll. I haven't got this sort of religious reverie for rock and roll. I think it's incredibly reactionary and boring."

Mercury Falling was released in 1996, and Sting toured again to promote it. He actually "commuted" to his concerts with a private jet and two pilots on standby. His family would stay in one of three houses that were home-bases. He would fly out at night to a gig and come back to wake up in the morning with "my babies." Christopher John Farley of *Time* magazine wrote, "*Mercury Falling* stands out as his most consistently entertaining effort. The lyrics are smart but not ostentatiously cerebral. The instrumental work of [Kenny] Kirkland, who performs on all the new tracks, and [Branford] Marsalis, who plays on two, adds shading and sophistication."

Shadows in the Rain

Sting devotes a great deal of time and money to human rights and ecological causes. He explained to DeCurtis: "I'm still, in a sense, a believer in transcendent cures for various problems .... But it's getting a bit late, unfortunately. I feel that with certain issues, like the environment, for example, you have to be active. You can't just sit there with your legs crossed and hope that the air is going to be fit to breathe tomorrow. I think we don't have very long left, frankly."

In trying to do his part for the environment, Sting focuses on the preservation of the Amazon rain forest, which is vital to the health of the earth's atmosphere. To that end, he founded the Rain Forest Foundation. It originated in 1987, after he went deep into the jungle to meet with the natives there. He developed a close friendship with one of the chiefs, Raoni. The two traveled to Rio de Janiero to appeal to the government to stop the forest destruction. Then-president Jose Sarney promised that if Sting raised $1,000,000 to cover expenses, an area the size of England—including Raoni's homeland—would be demarcated as Xingo Park. Sting agreed to do so, generating much favorable publicity for Sarney. However, when Sting produced the money, Sarney refused to hold up his end of the deal. It was a painful lesson in politics for both Sting and the natives, and led to some criticism of the

Rain Forest Foundation. Sting now directs part of the Rain Forest Foundation's money into programs to educate and empower the natives in their rights and the workings of politics. He is also involved with Amnesty International, and has organized and performed in concerts to raise funds for that cause.

Sting learned another painful lesson in 1995. His long-time accountant, Keith Moore, was sentenced in London to six years in prison for embezzling $9.4 million from Sting's account. He siphoned the money between 1988 and 1992. Sting's bank reimbursed him $7.5 million that they transferred to Moore's account without permission. "The person who did it shocked me," Sting told *Rolling Stone*. "It made me look very seriously at the idea of wealth, and I came up with the conclusion that wealth isn't about what you have in the bank. Your wealth is your friendships, family, health and happiness."

Selected discography

With the Police; released by A & M

Outlandos d'Amour (includes "Roxanne"), 1979.
Reggatta de Blanc, 1979.
Zenyatta Mondatta, 1980.
Ghost in the Machine, 1981.
Synchronicity (includes "King of Pain," "Wrapped Around Your Finger," "Every Breath You Take," "Synchronicity," and "Synchronicity II"), 1983.
Every Breath You Take-The Singles, 1986.
Message in a Box-The Complete Recordings of the Police (box compilation), 1993.

Solo releases

The Dream of the Blue Turtles, A & M, 1985.
Bring on the Night (live recording), A & M, 1986.
Nothing Like the Sun, A & M, 1987.
Nada Como el Sol..., A & M, 1988.
The Soul Cages, A & M, 1991.
Ten Summoner's Tales, A & M, 1993.
The Best of Sting-Fields of Gold, A & M, 1994.
Sting: All This Time (CD-ROM for Windows 95 or higher), Starwave, 1996.
Mercury Falling, A & M, 1996.

Other album appearances

Brimstone & Treacle (soundtrack), A & M, 1982.
Party, Party (soundtrack), 1982.
The Secret Policeman's Other Ball (soundtrack), 1982.
Money for Nothing (Dire Straits), 1988.
Peter and the Wolf, Deutsche Gramm, 1991.
Pavarotti & Friends, 1993.

The Three Musketeers (soundtrack), 1993.
Demolition Man (soundtrack), 1993.
Leaving Las Vegas (soundtrack), 1995.
Sabrina (soundtrack), 1995.

Sources

Periodicals

DownBeat, December 1983; May 1984; August 1984; December 1984; May 1985; November 1986; December 1987; December 1988.
Entertainment Weekly, August, 1996; March 21, 1997.
Guitar Player, September 1982.
Guitar World, April 1988; October 1988.
Musician, September 1987.
Rolling Stone, June 14, 1979; December 13, 1979; November 16, 1980; December 25, 1980; February 19, 1981; September 1, 1983; September 25, 1986; November 5, 1987; February 7, 1991; May 27, 1993.
Spin, May 1991.
Time, April 1, 1996.
Us, May 16, 1991.

Additional information provided by *The Message in a Box* liner notes and additional material.

—*Christine Morrison*

Sublime

Alternative rock band

Sublime came together when the future band members were children. "Bud" Floyd Gaugh and Eric Wilson grew up across the alley from each other and met when they had a head on collision on their Big Wheels. Wilson's father was a former big band drummer and taught his son how to play drums. Wilson met Nowell in the sixth grade; Nowell was a gifted student without many friends and was bussed to a magnet school. Quite a few years later, while Nowell was on break from the University of California, Santa Cruz, where he was studying finance, Wilson introduced him to Gaugh and a short time later the three began to jam. It was Nowell who first introduced his bandmates to ska and reggae. They formed Sublime in 1988 and went out to the club circuit but were refused bookings due to their strange-sounding hybrid act. Being the innovative personalities they were, Sublime founded their own label, Skunk Records, just so they could tell clubs they were "Skunk Records recording artists.".

The 1992 debut of *40 oz. to Freedom* was almost forgotten until two years later when Los Angeles's world famous KROQ radio station put the song, "Date Rape," into heavy rotation. The song was attacked for turning a sensitive subject into a farce. Little did the band know that "Date Rape" would become an independent rock hit and catapult *40 oz. to Freedom* on the Soundscan alternative chart for 70 consecutive weeks. This shot the band from punk-garage-playing wanna-be's to overnight stardom in the music kingdom of their genre. Their follow-up, *Robbin' the Hood*, was recorded in 1994 in an earthquake-damaged house with pirated electricity.

In 1995, Sublime played on the first Warped tour (an annual skateboarding/ska/punk traveling music festival) and was the first to be thrown off the tour for one week because of their unruly behavior. Their daily regimen was waking up, drinking, drinking more as the day went on, playing, and then drinking all night long. Nowell's dog, a Dalmatian named Lou, traveled with them, and when they brought the dog out on stage one night, Lou bit some skaters. That was basically the last straw for the promoters and people trying to keep the peace during their shows.

Unexpected Death

The drinking, unpredictability, and the out-of-control Dalmatian were all part of Sublime's explosive appeal. Gaugh's stock answer to their appeal is that the band is looking for extremes—the raw experience that could help them write and perform compelling music—but for Nowell, his wild ride to artistic inspiration was fueled by harder drugs than alcohol.

On May 25, 1996, Nowell woke up in a San Francisco hotel room early in the morning. His life had taken quite a few fortunate twists. He was trying to turn his life around and had begun to shake his reputation for wildness and womanizing. He had just gotten married to his girlfriend Troy in a Hawaiian-theme ceremony in Las Vegas, he was doing what he loved; playing his music and touring and the band had just finished recording an album which received rave reviews from anyone who heard it; stating that it was going to be a smash. Life was good. He decided to take Lou, the Dalmatian for a walk along the beach and tried to convince Wilson to get out of bed and join him on the beach. Being that it was around 6:30 a.m., Wilson ignored him. It would be the last time that anyone would see Nowell alive.

There were a few different reports and accounts of what happened that morning. One of them was that Gaugh had raided Nowell's stash in San Francisco and shot up while Nowell was out walking the dog. When he woke up hours later, he found that he'd been joined by Nowell, who was lying stiffly on the bed. Gaugh told a reporter in July that he felt the Grim Reaper had been actually looking for him but confused the two and took Nowell by mistake. Another report said that Gaugh found him lying on his hotel-room bed, dead of an overdose.

Nowell's bandmates profess that they tried to help him but, if drug abuse was mentioned in Nowell's presence, he would get angry and talk about other artists who died as a result of an accidental overdose. He would say how stupid these other artists were and that they shot too much because they didn't know what they were doing. Two months after Nowell's death, Sublime instantly had a hit song on their hands. While this should have been their moment in the sun, Sublime had effectively ceased to exist.

The untimely death of Nowell pushed Sublime into the limelight. Their record sales increased substantially and, while MCA wanted to sell records, they were wary of appearing like opportunists. With that in mind, MCA included a press release stating their wish that Sublime's recordings stand as Nowell's last gift to his family and fans.

Selected discography

40 oz. to Freedom, UNI/MCA, 1996.
Robbin' the Hood, UNI/MCA, 1996.
Sublime, UNI/MCA, 1996.
Living in a Boring Nation, Liberation/Mushroom, 1997.

With others

Misfits of Ska, Dill Records, 1994.
Hempilation, Capricorn Records, 1995.
Mallrats (soundtrack), MCA , 1995.
Punk Rock Jukebox, Revelation, 1995.
Punk Sucks, Liberation, 1995.
Saturday Morning: Cartoon's Greatest Hits, MCA, 1995.
Fox Hunt, Rhino Records, 1996.
MOM: Music for Our Mother Earth, Surf Dog/Interscope Records, 1996.

Sources

Periodicals

Billboard, May 6, 1995; August 10, 1996.
People, September 30, 1996.

Online

http://www.hallucinet.com/sublime/history.html
http://www.musicblvd.com
http://www.ubl.com
http://www.iuma.com/IUMA-2.0/ads/html/usrics/mix-17.html
http://www.takeme.com/lint/vol-1/sublime.html

--Robyn Weiss

Talk Talk

Pop Band

The English act Talk Talk is best remembered as low-key but successful players in the 1980s Britpop scene. Label executives signed the unassuming musicians in an early Eighties effort to locate and profit from what they thought could be the next Duran Duran. At this time, punk and disco had given way to a return to catchy pop melodies played by photogenic musicians, and a synthesizer-based sound came to predominate. Grouped around the "New Romantic" tag, bands such as Duran Duran and Reflex were topping the charts with the combination of drum-machine rhythms and a definite sense of fashion. Talk Talk, while initially going along with this program, moved farther and farther away from such single-fueled pop success with every one of their releases during the 1980s. After being dropped by EMI, the band attracted notoriety and set legal precedent for suing the label over the re-issue and remixing of its previous work.

Talk Talk was formed in the early 1980s when Paul Webb and Lee Harris did some studio work with a producer named Ed Hollis, who suggested the two should meet his younger brother. Mark Hollis had already tried his hand at songwriting, and the trio immediately clicked and began arranging Hollis's tunes and even writing their own together. Recruiting a keyboardist, Simon Brenner, the group coalesced as Talk Talk after mining their growing roster of new song titles for a name. They had no guitarist, a purposeful omission, and EMI expressed i the band's wry humor. Released in 1982, the work contained the aforementioned "Talk Talk" single as well

as the debut single, "Mirror Man" and "It's So Serious." Reviewing the release for *Melody Maker,* Ian Pye faulted the production of what could have been a more dynamic album, he opined. "Hollis' plaintive and sometimes richly melodic songs deserve much more than the sterile setting they've been coldly placed in."

Enthusiastic Critical and Commercial Reception

Talk Talk's second album came two years later—a very long stretch by pop standards of the day— after Hollis spent several months writing new songs and recruiting a roster of studio musicians to add more complexity to the band's sound. *It's My Life* would be their most successful record. Paul Strange, reviewing the 1984 release for *Melody Maker,* declared that he originally loathed the group—"but this second Talk Talk album is a surprise—a delight that has made me change my opinions." Strange lauded such tracks as "Dum Dum Girl," which he termed "dashing and dangerous," and the trumpet employed on "Rennee." Talk Talk had also taken a hiatus from performing in public, after one particularly disastrous 1982 outdoor concert during which the audience threw plastic bottles at them, but returned to the stage in 1984 to support their record. They also crafted a well-received video for the song "It's My Life."

After another two-year hiatus, Talk Talk returned in early 1986 with the acclaimed *Colour of Spring.* Accompanying the band in the studio at various points were Steve Winwood and David Rhodes, a guitarist with Peter Gabriel. Barry McIlheney of *Melody Maker* termed it "ambient, timeless music." Fellow *Melody Maker* writer Strange noticed and lauded the "more provocative, more accessible, and above all more direct material" than contained in their two previous works. Strange termed the album's debut single, "Life's What You Make It," "haunting and utterly infuriating," and also heaped praise upon the video for it. Directed by Tim Pope, best known for his work with nearly all of the videos for The Cure, the film montage included sequences of foxes and beavers.

Released Abstruse Spirit of Eden

Melody Maker's Steve Sutherland explained that at this point EMI held high hopes for Talk Talk, envisioning them "filling stadia around the world." But when confronted in a 1988 interview by Sutherland's question as to whether Hollis felt comfortable as a pop star, the lead singer replied "No, absolutely not. This is the perfect situation for me—I just go in and make the albums I want to make and that's it. There's nothing more I want. I have no ambition to do anything else." In other interviews, Hollis seemed reluctant to talk about the creative process and unwilling to share any details of a life lived outside the studio. He did, however, cite such jazz greats as Ornette Coleman, Miles Davis, and John Lee Hooker as inspiration, and confessed to enjoying artists as diverse as Frank Sinatra and 1970s German art-rock ensemble Can.

With their fourth album, *Spirit of Eden,* Talk Talk ventured as far from Duran-like sensibility as possible. The six cuts on the 1988 release segue into one another, inciting *Melody Maker*'s Sutherland to pin it "nearer the free jazz ethic of vintage Miles Davis than the soaring inanities of Simple Minds." At the time of its release, Harris tried to explain his vision to Sutherland, and decried the overcommercialization of popular music via technology at the same time. "If I have any impression it's that, where technology has entered, it's actually divorced people from music," Hollis said in *Melody Maker.* "It's funny because, when the synthesizer first became popular, it looked to me as if it could be something that made music more accessible for people but I think it's actually done the opposite and got people over-concerned with the technicality of what a good sound it."

Severed Association with EMI

Spirit of Eden was disastrously unsuccessful, and EMI released them from their contract. However, to make up for some of the financial losses it had suffered, the label released a compilation album in 1990 without the band's consent. Members of Talk Talk were less than thrilled about *Natural History: The Very Best of Talk Talk,* especially when the record, full of their Eighties hits from *It's My Life* and *Colour of Spring,* did well on the charts. When EMI released a second album of their previous work, *History Revisited—The Remixes,* Talk Talk became doubly incensed. The work was the result of label executives at EMI allowing producers then currently in vogue to remix and rework the original singles. As Hollis told *Melody Maker*'s Sutherland, "To me, it's unbeliev-

able they could do that. To have people overdubbing stuff you've done and putting it out." Hollis had learned of the project prior to its release, and sent letters threatening legal action, which EMI ignored. The bastardized record even earned the unwilling Hollis a nomination for a Brits Award, the English equivalent of a Grammy. For the ceremony, "they showed film of us from 1984," Hollis told *Melody Maker*'s Sutherland. "It was just insulting.... I wasn't happy with it."

Hollis forged ahead with a lawsuit against his former label, but also sunk his energies into recording a new work for a new label. Talk Talk had signed with Verve, a subsidiary of Polydor and known home to avant-garde styles and jazz artists. But *Laughing Stock,* the band's Verve debut, seemed to be an exercise in showing their new label just how expensive the recording process could be. The band swelled to 18 musicians, who were instructed by Hollis to improvise around a basic theme rather than learn a specific song; thus the sessions went on for over a year. Recording in a converted church in Wessex, Hollis recruited a gospel choir and recorded them, then purposely erased the tapes the following day. A string quartet was brought in and recorded over a two-day period, but only one brief section of the tape was used—when the cellist made an error.

Jim Arundel reviewed *Laughing Stock* for *Melody Maker* and noted how the arduous recording process is still evident in the final product. "Talk Talk records breathe," Arundel wrote. "The detail is everything. Often, the tracks sound as if all the superstructure has been removed, like paint separated from its canvas, just a tissue of colour." Arundel also went on to note the evident change in the band's sonic mood. "Where previous albums have been CD clean and icy pure, *Laughing Stock* is bruised and grimy," Arundel declared. "Guitars buzz on the edge of screaming feedback, the strings flirt with discord, the brass is cracked and broken."

Suit against EMI a Triumph

In 1992 Talk Talk won legal victory in their suit against EMI. The label was ordered by the court to reimburse the band for the production costs of the original work, costs which under most contracts between artists and labels are normally deducted from revenues of album sales. The second part of Talk Talk's suit charged "false attribution of authorship," or in other words, releasing an album of Talk Talk's music that the band members did not consider their creation, and they were also successful in a precedent-setting legal victory. Yet instead of freeing the group's creative abilities, the lawsuits seem to have exhausted them. Hollis was still signed to Verve according to a 1995 report, but was mired in another arduous songwriting/recording process. Meanwhile, Harris and Webb formed a band called Orang, and released *Herd of Instinct* on the Echo label in 1994. Hollis explained that such lulls have occurred before. "When I finished *Spirit of Eden,* there was a long period where I never thought I would make another record because I just didn't know where to go or anything," he told *Melody Maker* in 1991. "It's never anything I can predict. It's like, I say I'm in a four album deal [with Verve] but there's no way of knowing that I can ever do four albums. I do not know. The only thing I can ever hope is that I would never make an album for the wrong reasons and just stay with that ethic. I can't see the point of making an album for the sake of it. There's nothing that I would get from it."

Selected discography

The Party's Over, EMI, 1982.
It's My Life, LP, EMI, 1984.

It's My Mix, EMI, 1984.
The Colour of Spring, EMI, 1986.
Spirit of Eden, EMI, 1988.
Natural History: The Very Best of Talk Talk, EMI, 1990.
History Revisited—The Remixes, EMI, 1991.
Laughing Stock, Verve, 1991.

Sources

Books

The Guinness Encyclopedia of Popular Music, edited by Colin Larkin, Guinness Publishing, 1995.

Periodicals

Melody Maker, February 27, 1982, p. 16; July 31, 1982, p. 17; March 3, 1984, p. 26; May 5, 1984, p. 28; February 22, 1986; May 10, 1986, p. 18; September 24, 1988, p. 8; September 7, 1991, p. 33, p. 40; April 11, 1992, p. 5; November 18, 1995, p. 52.

—*Carol Brennan*

Leon Theremin

Inventor

Russian scientist Leon Theremin is considered the founder of electronic music. In 1918, using newly discovered vacuum-tube technology, he designed and built the first musical instrument that relied on electronic oscillation to produce its sound; furthermore, his invention remains the only instrument that is played without actual human contact. The Russian and the instrument that bore his name became renowned in classical music circles, and Theremin lived as somewhat of a celebrity in New York City during the 1930s before he was kidnapped by Soviet agents and returned home. Later, Soviet authorities reported him dead, but he was actually incarcerated in a Siberian prison camp. Theremin went on to use his expertise in electronics to create bugging devices for the Soviet secret police. In the early 1990s, an American filmmaker discovered Theremin in Moscow, then well into his nineties, and brought him to New York City for a visit in conjunction with a documentary film that celebrated the man and the invention: *Theremin: An Electronic Odyssey.*

Theremin was born Lev Termen in 1896 in St. Petersburg, Russia, during the tsarist era. According to one report, his family had emigrated to Russia in the sixteenth century as a result of religious repression in France. Theremin exhibited a keen interest in science from his childhood on, and eventually studied physics and astronomy at the University of St. Petersburg; he also completed training in electrical engineering. His entry into adulthood roughly coincided with the era of World War I and the fall of the Russian monarchy. The Bolsheviks seized power in 1917 and ushered in the world's first communist state, which brought with it radical new thinking in science and the arts. By 1920, Theremin was head of the experimental electronic oscillation laboratory at Petrograd's Institute of Physical Engineering. Through his attempts to devise a new kind of radio, one particular configuration of vacuum tubes and antennae evolved into the Theremin. At first, he called his invention the "aetherphon."

Lenin Owned One

The instrument caused a sensation at the time. "The musician moves his or her hands above the device to disrupt an electromagnetic field and thus coax eerie, piercing notes out of the ether," explained a modern-day article by J. Hoberman in *Premiere.* Its very invention reflected new thinking and progressive ideals of the time--Theremin told a New York audience in 1991 that with his invention he strove to "force modern industrial technologies into the idealized realm of the arts," according to Timothy White in *Billboard.* The perfected theremin evolved into a podium-like device with two antennae. The horizontal antenna controls volume, while the vertical antenna modulates the pitch. Steven M. Martin, the documentary filmmaker who honored Theremin's achievements, told White: "The theremin has produced some of the most haunting and penetrating sounds ever recorded. Imagine what it's like to act as a human capicitator, interrupting an electromagnetic field to create music!"

In 1922 Theremin himself demonstrated his invention for Soviet leader Vladimir I. Lenin, and supposedly Lenin was given a theremin built by its inventor's hand. That same year the first public performance of the theremin was given in the Soviet Union. The device caused a sensation in the world of classical music; the Leningrad Philharmonic performed an original work entitled "A Symphonic Mystery" in 1924 using the instrument. Theremin gained fame and was called the "Soviet Edison." He also conducted experiments that played a role in the development of television technology. In 1926 he gave a demonstration at the Leningrad Polytechnic Institute that heralded the first transmission of non-static images onto a screen. "Although all parts of the device were known long before Theremin, he was the first to assemble them in a sequence that allowed the transmission of moving objects," declared *Soviet Life.*

Toast of Gotham

Meanwhile, Theremin's musical invention was inciting interest among classical musicians elsewhere. He made a tour of Europe in the 1920s with it; on subsequent travels he found himself the toast of New York City in 1927 and decided to stay. The instrument's first public performance in the United States came in February 1928 at New York's Metropolitan Opera House. Manhattan's progressive crowd feted Theremin, and the emigre soon became romantically involved with a violinist--also of Russian heritage--named Clara Rockmore. Through their collaboration Rockmore became the best-known virtuoso of the instrument. (She also played an integral role in Steven Martin's decision to make a film about Theremin and his life.) For several years Theremin ran an informal school in New York City to train enthusiasts on his instrument, which was notoriously difficult to master. Through the Soviet trade commission, Theremin obtained a patent for it, then in 1929 licensed it to RCA for mass production. The company made a thousand of them, but only a quarter of them were sold after the American economy nosedived as a result of the stock market crash in October of that same year.

During his years in New York, Theremin also made the acquaintance of luminaries such as Albert Einstein and Dwight D. Eisenhower; Einstein even played the violin at recitals at Theremin's apartment on West 54th Street. He also created the world's first electronic security system, based partly on technical knowledge gained through perfecting the theremin; he installed the first system of its kind at New York's Sing Sing Prison. Unfortunately such prominence and regard did little but earn him enmity back home, and one day in 1938 Theremin mysteriously disappeared. It was later learned that he had been kidnapped by KGB agents and spirited back to the Soviet Union. He was reported dead, but was actually in a Siberian gulag, where many prominent intellectuals and Russians with contacts in the West were "rehabilitated" in an era of totalitarianist repression in the 1930s.

Instrument Rediscovered, Inventor Disappeared

Theremin was released when the exploitation of his talents became vital to Soviet military authorities. He invented numerous listening devices for the KGB, and was even awarded the Stalin Prize for this efforts. It was during this era that some American musicians working in the film industry began using the theremin to create a spooky, ethereal sound. The instrument had first been used on the soundtrack to the 1935 film *The Bride of Frankenstein,* but made its appearance in two acclaimed films a decade later: *The Lost Weekend,* the story of a man's bleak descent into alcoholism, and Alfred Hitchcock's *Spellbound,* which won an Academy Award for its music. In the latter film, the theremin's sounds were used to foreshadow a coming psychotic attack in the lead,

Gregory Peck. Over the next decade, its unique tones became familiar to younger audiences in such science-fiction thrillers as *The Day the Earth Stood Still* and *It Came from Outer Space,* both dating from the early 1950s. A few odd recordings were made, such as RCA Victor's *Perfume Set to Music,* and the late 1940s albums *Music Out of the Moon* and *Music for Peace of Mind.*

The theremin's use in horror films awakened a new generation to the possibilities of the instrument. Musical pioneer Robert Moog, the inventor of the first synthesizer, or electronic keyboard, constructed a theremin from a magazine diagram when he was still in high school. For years, Moog sold do-it-yourself theremin kits by mail. Brian Wilson, songwriter of the Beach Boys, was moved by his initial experience hearing the theremin, and incorporated its sounds most famously in the 1966 hit "Good Vibrations." Led Zeppelin's Jimmy Page mastered it for "Whole Lotta Love." Another rock act of the era, Lothar and the Hand People, made the theremin sound the centerpiece of entire albums. The Delos record label released a title called *The Art of the Theremin* in the late 1980s that featured Clara Rockmore's earlier performances. It was the aging Rockmore who told filmmaker Steven Martin that Theremin was still alive and well in Moscow. According to a 1988 article on him in *Soviet Life,* at the age of 92 he was still conducting experiments at Moscow University and walked to work each morning. Martin sought him out and brought him to New York City, where he was again feted.

Theremin's experiences in New York, a neon-lit urban landscape and a far different world than the one he left in 1938, were recorded on film for *Theremin: An Electronic Odyssey.* He was also able to spend time with Rockmore once again. The film was the work of Martin, Moog, and producer Hal Willner and was released in 1995, two years after Theremin's death in Moscow at the age of 97. "Since my childhood, the theremin has seemed like a window to another, less pessimistic era when people still believed progress meant a better, more visionary life," Martin told White in *Billboard.* "Leon Theremin pioneered the concept of the artist as scientist. I just want to see the creative journey of a great man come full circle." *Village Voice* writer Amy Taubin called Martin's film tribute "a graceful, evocative documentary about how historical events of great moment disrupt individual lives." By the mid-1990s several alternative bands had discovered the theremin's sound and were using it both onstage and in recordings; the Jon Spencer Blues Explosion is perhaps the best-known example of this resurgence. There is even a Theremin Enthusiasts' Club International.

Sources

Billboard, June 6, 1992, p. 5; November 20, 1993, p. 13.
New Yorker, September 17, 1990, pp. 34-36.
Premiere, February 1995, pp. 44-45.
Soviet Life, May 1988, p. 34.
Village Voice, September 12, 1995, p. 59.

—*Carol Brennan*

Traffic

Rock band

A hybrid of rock, R&B, jazz, and English folk, Traffic was a band with so many starts and stops their name seemed more than appropriate. The group was originally formed in 1967 by keyboardist, guitarist, and singer Steve Winwood; guitarist and singer Dave Mason; saxophone and flute player Chris Wood; and drummer and singer Jim Capaldi. Mason left the group in 1968 only to rejoin a few months later. Then they disbanded in 1969, when Winwood left to form Blind Faith with Eric Clapton, Ginger Baker, and Rick Grech. Following one album and one American tour, Blind Faith ended, with Winwood going on to serve time in Ginger Baker's Airforce. Then, for four years beginning in 1970, Winwood, Capaldi, and Wood formed the nucleus of Traffic while other members, including Mason, would come and go. Twenty years later, in 1994, Winwood and Capaldi joined forces again under the Traffic moniker for an album and tour.

In early 1967, not long after The Spencer Davis Group had two big hits in a row, "Gimme Some Lovin" and "I'm A Man," the band's keyboard player and vocalist, Steve

MICHAEL OCHS ARCHIVES/Venice, CA. Reproduced by permission.

For the Record . . .

Members include **Steve Winwood** (born May 12, 1948, Birmingham, England), vocals, keyboards, guitar; **Jim Capaldi** (born August 24, 1944, Evesham, Worcestershire, England), drums, vocals; **Chris Wood,** (died July 12, 1983), reeds, woodwinds; **Dave Mason** (born May 10, 1945, Worcestershire, England), vocals, guitar, 1967-68, 1971; **Rick Grech,** bass, 1971; **Jim Gordon,** drums, 1971; **Reebop Kwaku Baah,** percussion, 1971-73; **David Hood,** bass, 1972-73; **Roger Hawkins,** drums, 1972-73; **Rosco Gee,** bass, 1973-74, 1994.

Formed in 1967 in Birmingham, England; released first single, "Paper Sun," May 1967; released first album, *Mr. Fantasy,* December 1967; disbanded January 1969; Winwood went on to play with Eric Clapton in Blind Faith, 1969; Winwood, Capaldi, and Wood reformed as a trio for *John Barleycorn Must Die,* 1970; released *The Low Spark of High Heeled Boys,* 1971; various personnel changes, 1971-74; disbanded, 1974; Winwood and Capaldi recorded *Far from Home* and toured under the Traffic name, 1994.

Winwood, decided he'd had enough. The formulaic R&B/pop band had become too restricting for the 18 year-old musician and he'd recently met and began jamming with a band called Deep Feeling at The Elbow Room in Birmingham, England. Led by drummer Jim Capaldi, Deep Feeling would play its normal set and then other musicians, including Winwood, Chris Wood, and Spencer Davis Group roadie/guitarist Dave Mason, would gather for a freeform jam. "It was the end of my Spencer Davis Group days," Winwood told *Rolling Stone*'s Jonathon Cott in 1969, "and we all used to go to this drinking-gambling club where Jim used to play, and like we used to get up and play with him and jam. And we just got together."

Berkshire Poppies

The quartet dubbed themselves Traffic and hid away in a cottage amidst the fields of wheat, barley, and poppies of the Berkshire section of England to write their first album. "When Jim, Dave, Chris Wood, and I went up to the Berkshire cottage in 1967 to start Traffic," Winwood told Timothy White in his anthology *Rock Lives,* "it was

the result of a lot of enthusiastic planning and time spent playing together informally. What came out of those talks and things was a desire on the part of the four of us to make a uniquely British form of rock and roll ... while breaking new ground artistically." For his part, Capaldi recalled that not everything they came up with was that great, in fact, some of it was way off the mark. "But," he told White, "I sometimes look back and feel that we were an experimental group that went out into the natural wilds just to hammer it all out. Back then, all the rock music was anchored to the city life. The fact that the four of us...went back to the country to abandon the urban distractions and get into the music set a definite trend." Soon the band emerged from their secluded rehearsal space with a funky mixture of jazz, folk, and psychedelic R&B to begin recording their first album, *Mr. Fantasy,* at London's Olympic Studios.

Months before the album was out, Island Records, their record company in England, released two singles in the UK. The first single, "Paper Sun," released in May of 1967, reached number five on the UK charts and the song, "Hole In My Shoe" was scheduled for release the following September. Written by Dave Mason, "Hole In My Shoe," was a catchy pop song the rest of the band hated. The record company, however, smelling commercial success, wanted to release it as a single against the strong and vocal desires of Winwood, Capaldi, and Wood. "It was a so silly and poppy and commercial, Capaldi told Chris Welch, author of Winwood's biography, *Roll with It.* "It had nothing to do with Traffic at all.... Me, Chris, and Steve stuck together as a nucleus and the song caused a big rift within the band. We never played it live, ever." Winwood echoed Capaldi's sentiments about the song telling Welch, "It didn't really represent us at all, although in England it's what we're known for. Not so in America! The Americans have never heard "Hole In My Shoe." The song was released in September and reached number two on the UK charts.

"Dear Mr. Fantasy"

In December of 1967 the debut album, *Mr. Fantasy,* was finally released and with the emergence of FM radio in America and their willingness to play long album cuts like the classic "Dear Mr. Fantasy," the album provided an ideal soundtrack to the free wheelin', often drug-induced spirit of the late sixties. "It became one of the strongest things Traffic ever played," Capaldi told Welch. "It broke new ground, influenced people. It had R&B and yet it was different. I remember hearing it on the radio and I knew it was a classic ... that whole first album." In a 1970 interview with *Rolling Stone*'s Jim

Carroll, Chris Wood remembered the *Mr. Fantasy* album fondly. "You don't really know whether something is good until six months or a year later, but on *Fantasy*, well...'Mr. Fantasy' of course, and 'Coloured Rain,''Paper Sun,' and 'Heaven is in Your Mind.' It was kind of our first expression, that album."

One month after the album's release, in January of 1968, Mason left the band, still reeling over the episode involving "Hole In My Shoe." In the end it seemed that Mason was too individualistic and protective about his songs while the others felt it was important to work together in order to get the "Traffic sound." Winwood reminisced about the conflicting work ethic to Welch: "[Mason] would come up and say, 'Right here's my song. Now you do this and you do that. And this is the way it's gonna be, because it's my song.' Well, the rest of us, we never worked that way.... But it became Dave writing songs his way, and the rest of us writing songs another way. It was inevitable that Dave wouldn't agree with the way we wrote songs."

So Winwood, Capaldi, and Wood carried on as a trio and began to tour America. While in New York in May of 1968—where Winwood and Wood guested on Jimi Hendrix's "Voodoo Chile" from his *Electric Ladyland* LP—the group met up with Mason and he joined them for the rest of the tour. "During the first tour of the States we were going through a bad state," Winwood confessed to Cott in 1969, "mainly because we only had about a couple of weeks before we went to the States as a trio and a lot of the numbers we were doing weren't actually written for a trio. We needed somebody else in the group and then Dave appears in New York."

Traffic Stop

Following the tour, the group returned to England to record their second album. Titled simply Traffic, it was released in October 1968 and featured now classic Traffic tunes such as "Feelin' Alright," "40,000 Headmen," and "Pearly Queen." "Traffic is a group that excels at everything except getting it together," Jann Wenner wrote in his review of the album for *Rolling Stone*. "This has been evident not only from the drawn out personnel and touring problems they have had, but also from their records—excruciatingly good in terms of real music—but frustratingly plagued with a severe case of what could only be called 'loose-endism.'" Wenner went on to bemoan the fact that listeners might not ever really hear or see what the band is capable of. "They'll break up first," he predicted. He was right. Following the release of the album, Mason left again,

pretty much for the same reasons as the first time, and in January of 1969, the rest of the group disbanded as well. The following May, their record company released *Last Exit*, a hodgepodge of unreleased songs and live performances and then a *Best of Traffic* LP in October.

Any hopes of Traffic immediately reforming were dashed when Winwood started Blind Faith with Eric Clapton and Ginger Baker, who'd just broken up Cream, and bassist Rick Grech. The first "supergroup" of the era, the band recorded a self-titled LP that was well received and embarked on a U.S. tour that wasn't. While the crowds were somewhat interested in what Blind Faith had to say, they were much more responsive to old Cream and Traffic songs and that's what Blind Faith ended up playing, thus losing their identity and enthusiasm. The group disbanded after the tour and Winwood went on to play with Ginger Baker's Airforce but didn't find that fulfilling either. For their part, Capaldi, Mason, and Wood had a short lived group with friend (Wynder K.) Frog, and Mason began recording a solo album, 1970's *Alone Together*, for the Blue Thumb label.

In 1970 Winwood began work on a own solo album that was to be called *Mad Shadows*. During recording he summoned Capaldi and Wood to the studio and it turned into the Traffic album, *John Barleycorn Must Die*. Released in April of that year, it's considered one of Traffic's classic recordings but, at the time, Rolling Stone's Jon Carroll couldn't shroud his disappointment. "Perhaps part of the problem," Carroll admitted, "is my high expectations of any Traffic album." Still, Carroll confessed, "This is a good album of rock and roll music featuring the best rock and roll woodwind player anywhere and one of the best singers, and maybe the trio is still just getting together again, feeling each other out." A month earlier, in a *Rolling Stone* profile of the band, Carroll proclaimed Traffic as "arguably one of the two or three best rock and roll bands in existence."

"You Just Can't Escape from the Sound"

Following the release of the album, the trio embarked on a tour only to realize they needed more musicians to recreate the effect of their albums on stage. To that end, they recruited bassist Rick Grech, who had played with Winwood in Blind Faith; drummer Jim Gordon, who had worked with Clapton in his Derek And The Dominoes project, and whose presence freed up Capaldi to sing without being tied to the drum kit; percussionist Reebop Kwaku Baah; and for six shows in 1971, Dave Mason. This version of the band is documented in the luke-warm live album, *Welcome To The Canteen*, released in September of 1971. Between performances the band, minus Dave Mason, were in the studio recording what would be their most critically and commercially successful album, *The Low Spark of High Heeled Boys*, released just two months after *Canteen*.

David Lubin of *Rolling Stone* credits Winwood for his meticulous job as *Low Spark*'s producer. "His work with the tracks in every case produced an integration of sounds which left nothing either crowded or isolated," Lubin wrote. "Although he is not up to his highest form as a composer, as musicians he and Traffic have never played better." Of particular interest to Lubin, as well as listeners, was the album's title track, a jazz-influenced rock epic that clocked in at over 12 minutes. "It's a sensuous black jazz piece except for the rock counter-theme, (characteristically Traffic-sounding)," Lubin described, "which comes in with the refrain of every chorus. Each member of the group lays down a track or tracks which could in parts stand alone." Following the American tour to support the album, however, the then twenty-five year old Winwood developed peritonitis, the result of undiagnosed appendicitis. The potentially fatal disease sent Winwood a message that it was time to slow down, so Traffic was sidelined once again until he recovered.

The band then set off for Jamaica to record their next album, this time with the famed Muscle Shoals rhythm section of bassist David Hood and drummer Roger Hawkins in place of Grech and Gordon. The result, 1973's *Shootout at the Fantasy Factory*, received mixed reviews, not surprising following such a landmark recording as *The Low Spark of High Heeled Boys*. This version of the band is also featured on another luke-warm live album, *On the Road*, released the same year. Traffic's concerts had in fact become luke-warm experiences themselves, some rising to the occasion brilliantly, others just phoned-in performances of Traffic favorites. Capaldi and Wood had taken to drinking too much before performances and Winwood would often appear joyless throughout the entire show. By the end of 1973 Hood, Hawkins, and Reebop were gone and with Jamaican bassist Rosco Gee, the band recorded *When the Eagle Flies*, released in September of 1974.

Generally regarded as a bleak and somber album, *When the Eagle Flies*, was nonetheless recommended by *Rolling Stone*'s Ken Emerson who asserted that Traffic was moving away from "the loose, interminable nodding-out riffing with which it has dawdled for the past couple of years" and heading towards "sharply defined and relatively concise songs." Winwood, in reflecting on the album to *White in Rock Lives*, said, "It doesn't seem like a Traffic record very much, does it? The whole record is very doomy, and I suppose it's the way we saw both Traffic and the music of the era going."

Less than a month before the album's release, Traffic played what was to be its last concert for twenty years at the Reading Festival in England. Though there was never any formal announcement, Traffic just came to a halt. "I'd had enough of this album, tour, album, tour," Winwood confessed to Rolling Stone in 1988. "It was like I was on a treadmill and there was no way of getting off. I just had to say, `That's it with Traffic; no way can I do that anymore.'"

End of the Road?

So the nucleus of Winwood, Capaldi, and Wood split and went their own ways in 1974. Capaldi recorded a few solo albums, though none came close to matching those of the Traffic era; Wood died of a liver ailment in 1983 following years of drinking and drug abuse; and Winwood went on to meteoric solo success in the 1980s with hugely successful pop albums such as 1980's *Arc of a Diver*, the Grammy-award winning *Back in the Highlife* in 1986, and 1988's *Roll with It*. Winwood, however, fell back into the trap of playing the kind of saccharine-laced pop he accused the Spencer Davis Group of playing when he left that band. His antidote in 1967 was to form Traffic; the answer in 1994, he felt, was to reform Traffic. "My own solo work had gotten a little pasteurized," he confessed to Jeff Gordinier of *Entertainment Weekly*. "Traffic put a little bacteria back into it. By bacteria, I mean a certain looseness, nonconformity, freedom."

With Wood gone, however, and Dave Mason recording and touring with the umpteenth version of Fleetwood Mac, that left just Winwood and Capaldi to get Traffic moving again. They began with the album, *Far from Home*, and carried through with a world tour that included Woodstock '94. Reviews of both the album and tour were decidedly mixed. J.D. Considine of *Rolling Stone* suggested the album "easily suited the soulful spirit and jazzy groove of *Mr. Fantasy* or *The Low Spark of High Heeled Boys*," but conceded, "what passes for melody on most of the songs is generic and forgettable." Parke Puterbaugh of *Stereo Review* concurred, stating that while pleasant, Winwood and Capaldi "coast along on autopilot, providing comfortable background music that packs little of the emotional shiver of which the duo is capable." Deborah Frost of *Entertainment Weekly*, however, took out both guns and blasted the twosome for the "fairly crass attempt to jump-start two stalled solo careers and exploit a legendary brand name in the process."

Whether or not the 1994 version of Traffic is truly the last one is unknown, but it seems without the presence of Wood, the band misses a vital ingredient. Winwood himself said as much in Welch's biography: "Jim and I could play and sing, but Chris gave the band it's character. Traffic must belong...to Chris Wood. He was more responsible for the sound than anyone else." And it was the sound of Traffic, after all, which gave the band such a distinct voice during the late 60s and early 70s. "We'd listen to different kinds of music," Winwood recalled to *Rolling Stone* in 1988. "Classical, folk, jazz, all kinds of ethnic music, country music, early rock, blues, and the only thing we calculated was to try in some way to incorporate all of them. We were trying to get ourselves a sound which was purely Traffic and couldn't be mistaken for anybody else."

Selected discography

Mr. Fantasy, United Artist, 1967.
Traffic, United Artists, 1968.
Last Exit, United Artists, 1969.
The Best of Traffic, United Artists, 1969.
John Barleycorn Must Die, United Artists, 1970.
Welcome to the Canteen, United Artists, 1971.
The Low Spark of High-Heeled Boys, Island, 1971.
Shoot Out at the Fantasy Factory, Island, 1973.

On the Road, Island, 1973.
Where the Eagle Flies, Island, 1974.
Smiling Phases, Island, 1991.
Far from Home, Virgin, 1994.

Sources

Books

Welch, Chris, and Steve Winwood, *Roll with It,* Perigree Books, 1990.
White, Timothy, *Rock Lives,* Henry Holt & Co., 1990.

Periodicals

Entertainment Weekly, May 6, 1994, p. 65.
Rolling Stone, January 4, 1969, p. 28; May 3, 1969, p.17; August 6, 1970, p. 26; September 3, 1970, p. 42; June 20, 1972, p. 48; November 7, 1974, p.62; December 1, 1988, p. 46; June 16, 1994, p. 108; October 25, 1994, p. 46.
Stereo Review, July 1994, p. 86.

—Brian Escamilla

Uriah Heep

Rock band

U riah Heep was one of a handful of important progressive rock bands to emerge from Britain during the 1970s. They combined the hard, guitar-focused sound of traditional heavy metal bands like Deep Purple and Led Zeppelin with extended jazz-like orchestrations and multi-part vocal harmonies which had great impact on later harmonic bands, such as Queen. During the 1970s, the band's heyday, Uriah Heep sold some 30 million records and toured all over the world. The band's line-up changed regularly, but the core group that produced much of the important work from the 1970s consisted of Mick Box, David Byron, Ken Hensley, Gary Thain and Lee Kerslake. Much of the music was composed by Hensley, Box, and Byron, in various combinations, and they are considered the core members of the group.

Uriah Heep took their name from a character in Charles Dickens' novel *David Copperfield* (using Dickens' character names for bands would become something of a trend with Mott the Hoople and Jethro Tull). Their first album, released in 1970, *Very 'eavy, Very 'umble* was,

AP/Wide World Photos. Reproduced by permission

For the Record . . .

Founding members include **David Byron** (born January 29, 1947, in Epping, England; died February 28, 1985), vocals; **Mick Box** (born June 8, 1947, in London, England), guitar, vocals; **Ken Hensley** (born August 24, 1945, in London, England), guitar, keyboards, vocals;
Paul Newton (born 1946, in Andover, England), bass; **Gary Thain** (born May 15, 1948, in Wellington, New Zealand; died March 19, 1976), bass.

Addresses: *Fan Club*—Official Uriah Heep Appreciation Society, P.O. Box 268, Telford, Shropshire, England TF2 6XA.

as dictated by the times, psychedelic and progressive. Most of the music coming out of Britian at the time was psychedelic and the heavy metal bands that dominated the popular music scene at the time—including Deep Purple, Pink Floyd and Vanilla Fudge—had been crossing psychedelia and heavy metal for a few years, creating a really quite unique sound. This type of music featured a wall of sound combination of keyboards and guitars highlighted by highly structured vocal harmonies. Lyrics often featured medieval and Renaissance themes—lost princesses, black magic, mythical creatures—which were highly romanticized by the disaffected youth culture of Britian.

Releasing a Future Classic

In 1971, Uriah Heep released *Salisbury*, considered by many to a classic album of this genre. The title track, in fact, is a fifteen-minute, highly orchestrated piece featuring multi-part harmonies and the overdubbing of orchestral music. Also released that year was *Look at Yourself*, a less orchestrated work but still brimming with psychedelic romanticism and heavy guitar-keyboard work. Manfred Mann, who would later establish himself as an important figure in electronic-synthesized music, played keyboards on a couple of tracks and the band also used members of an Africa percussion band on the album's title track.

1972 saw the release of the definitive Uriah Heep album, *Demons and Wizards*. The title itself indicates that the band was still romantically working medieval myth into their songs, but they were now doing so in a more straight-forward, hard-rocking way. The feel of the earlier albums of highly produced, orchestrated works was abandoned with this album and instead the band began playing a much more traditional heavy metal sound. They did, however, maintain their trademark vocal harmonies, they just did so with less emphasis and without the use of too much studio wizardry. Aficionados of the band consider *Demons and Wizards* to be the their crowning achievement and indeed, as far as popular and critical success, this era marks the band's apex, reaching number 20 on the British charts and number 23 on the U.S. This was about as high as any album of theirs would ever go (1973's *Sweet Freedom* would make 18 on the British charts but only 33 on the U.S.). The first single from the album, "Easy Livin'" became a popular song, although it did not exactly scream up the charts, and is one of two or three songs by the group that can still be heard on commercial radio in the United States—generally on stations dedicated to what is called "classic rock."

In 1973, the band released *Sweet Freedom* which included one of the band's most recognizable songs, "Stealin'." The song, in fact, became something of a trademark in later years and can still be heard on classic rock stations. Also released in 1973 was *Uriah Heep Live* which featured a medley of early rock songs which was a staple of FM radio play at the time. In 1974, the band released *Wonderworld*, which, although it sold pretty well, was panned by the critics. One of the reasons the album was considered so lackluster was that some of the members of the group at this time started having troubles with drugs. It was also during this period that the band's personnel began to change. In 1975, Gary Thain, the band's bassist since 1969, was replaced with John Wetton (formerly of King Crimson) for the recording of *Return to Fantasy*, the band's best-selling album in Britain. Also in 1975, the band released a greatest hits album titled, *The Best of Uriah Heep*.

A Changed Uriah Heep

The next year saw the beginning of the end for the band as David Byron, one of the core members and the lead vocalist, left to pursue a solo career. The band hired John Lawton to take his place and found their third bass player in Trevor Bolder, who had worked with David Bowie in his back-up band The Spiders from Mars. This newly reworked lineup released *High & Mighty* in 1976, a largely forgettable album by most accounts. By 1980, the band had essentially disappeared from public view, except for a group of hardcore fans who dubbed themselves Heepsters. They continued to release albums and tour, although they were reduced to very small venues. They have always been much more popular in Europe and Britain than in the United States and especially so in pop-culture-starved Eastern Europe, where they were cult heroes. In 1988, the band, or what was left of it, played a series of sellout concerts in Lenningrad (now St. Petersburg) and Moscow, just as the Soviet Union was beginning its thaw with the west.

Uriah Heep released *Sea of Light* in 1995 and *Spellbinder* in 1996. The band toured Europe after releasing *Sea of Light*, with the Mick Box as the last original band member. As children of the late 1970s and early 1980s matured, there came a renewed interest in many bands from that period. Though numerous bands regrouped and toured in the 1990s, the original members of Uriah Heep had no plans on attempting any kind of a reunion.

Selected discography

Very 'eavy Very 'umble, Bronze 1970.
Salisbury, Bronze 1971.
Look at Yourself, Bronze 1971.
Demons and Wizards, Bronze 1972.
The Magician's Birthday, Bronze 1972.
Uriah Heep Live, Bronze 1973.
Sweet Freedom, Bronze 1973.

Wonderworld, Bronze 1974.
Return to Fantasy, Bronze 1975.
The Best of Uriah Heep, Bronze 1975.
High and Mighty, Bronze 1976.
Firefly, Bronze 1977.
Innocent Victim, Bronze 1977.
Fallen Angel, Bronze 1978.
Conquest, Bronze 1980.
Abominog, Bronze 1982.
Head First, Bronze 1983.
Equator, Bronze 1985.
Live in Europe 1979, Raw Power 1987.
Live in Moscow, Bronze 1988.
Raging Silence, Legacy 1989.
Still 'eavy, Still Proud, Legacy 1990.
Different World, Legacy 1991.
Rarities from the Bronze Age, Sequel 1992.
Sea of Light, Castle 1995.
Spellbinder, Castle 1996

Sources

Guinness Encyclopedia of Popular Music, Guinness Publishing, Ltd. Middlesex, England, 1994.

The Ventures

Rock instrumental group

Called "one of the first, best, more lasting and influential of instrumental guitar-based rock combos" by *The New Rolling Stone Encyclopedia of Rock & Roll*, the Ventures had remarkable staying power since the burst on to the rock scene with their hit single "Walk Don't Run" in 1960. Between 1960 and the mid 1970s, thirty-seven of the group's more than fifty albums placed on the U.S. pop charts.

The Ventures were known for their crisp rocking sound with driving percussion and light, twanging electric guitars. They had a significant influence on the surf music of the Beach Boys, and traces of their style can be heard in songs by groups such as Blondie, the B-52's, the Go-Go's, and others. The group survived through the decades by continually updating their sound to match the musical style of the era, copying many other bands and experimenting with everything from disco and reggae to psychedelic rock. Their albums have featured recordings of songs written by everyone from Richard Rodgers, Irving Berlin, and Henry Mancini, to Duke Ellington, Paul McCartney, and Booker T.

Archive Photos, Inc. Reproduced by permission.

Bob Bogle was the key force behind the birth of the Ventures. An avid guitar player since his teens, Bogle met fellow guitarist Don Wilson in Seattle in the late 1950s when both of them were working as mortar removers on construction sites. By 1959 the twosome was performing as the Impacts with a pick-up rhythm section in local clubs. In 1960, after expanding into a quartet with Nokie Edwards on bass guitar and Skip Moore on drums, the group renamed themselves the Versatones. Moore was later replaced by Howie Johnston. Eager to record, the Versatones formed their own label called Blue Horizon with the help of Don Wilson's mother, who became the group's manager. In

early 1960 they broke into vinyl with "Cookies and Coke," which was recorded in a Seattle studio. Soon afterwards the group dubbed themselves the Ventures.

After hearing the song "Walk Don't Run" on a Chet Atkins's album, the group began performing the song and it became a favorite with audiences. "We were asked to play it half a dozen times a night and decided this is the song to record," said Bogle, according to Bob Shannon and John Javna in Behind the Hits. After sending demos of the song to various record labels without success, Wilson's mother decided to release it on their Blue Horizon label. They played a copy of it for Bob Reisdorff, the manager of the Fleetwoods and owner of the local Dolton recording label, but Reisdorff rejected it. After shopping the song around to radio stations, the group lucked when out when Pat O'Day, a friend who was a local deejay, made the song a local favorite by playing it after each news bulletin on station KJR in Seattle. Reisdorff changed his own tune on the song after hearing it on radio and agreed to release it on his label. The contract negotiated by Wilson's mother gave the group artistic control over their releases via their Blue Horizon Productions.

Second Single A Runaway Hit

"Walk Don't Run" became a major hit, selling over a million copies and rising to number two on the U.S. pop charts. "Initially a jazz instrumental, it ["Walk Don't Run"] nonetheless lent itself to simplified chord structure and by emphasizing its beat, the Ventures constructed a powerful, compulsive sound which not only became their trademark, but was echoed in the concurrent surfing style," commented The Guinness Encyclopedia of Popular Music.

The success of "Walk Don't Run" allowed Wilson and Bogle to give up their construction jobs for a full-time music career. Dolton's distribution by Liberty Records resulted in the Ventures relocating their recording activities to the Los Angeles base of Liberty. According to Shannon and Javna, Liberty Records owner Bob Bennett offered the group some prophetic advice. "Don't change the image," Bennett supposedly told the group. "You can add to it but don't change it. Don't ever try a vocal."

Chart success greeted the group again with their 1960 release of "Perfidia." This Latin tune first released by Alberto Dominquez in 1939, became a number-fifteen hit for the Ventures. At this point, the band focused on albums, releasing their first in a long string of LPS in

1961. This first release, *The Ventures,* featured a collection of mostly covers of other group's instrumental hits. Confirming the popularity of the group, the album rose up the U.S. pop charts to the number eleven slot and the Ventures were invited to perform in the "Alan Freed Spectacular" at the Hollywood Bowl with stars such as Brenda Lee, Bobby Vee, B.B. King, the Shirelles, and others. That same year, Mel Taylor replaced Howie Johnson on drums after Johnson quit following a car accident.

In 1962, the Ventures revealed their willingness to embrace new elements in their music with their release of "2000 Pound Bee," which featured the first-time recording of fuzz-guitar in a song. They had their most successful LP release in 1963 with *The Ventures Play Telstar,* and *The Lonely Bull,* an album that achieved gold-record status and topped out at number eight on the charts. At this time Edwards took over lead guitar duties, while Bogle switched to bass guitar. In 1964 the group proved that lightning can strike twice, when they made the top ten with a new version of "Walk Don't Run" that incorporated various influences from popular surf music of the time.

Immensely Popular in Japan

Coinciding with the first availability of electric guitars on a mass scale in Japan, the Ventures's initial tour of that country in the mid 1960s made them overnight superstars there. Their instrumentals bypassed any language barrier, and before long, the group had established a popularity in Japan that rivaled the Beatles. The Ventures remained a major draw in Japan after their fame waned in the U.S., and they performed a series of concerts there each year for over a quarter century. The Japanese demand for their music was so high that the Ventures often wrote songs designed for Japanese lyricists to add words to in their own language.

Dance music also proved a gold mine for the Ventures, and they had big sellers with their *Twist with the Ventures* and other albums designed for dancing. In 1965 they released one of the first instructional records, *Play Guitar with the Ventures.* Tie-ins to current pop culture were common for the group, as shown by their covers of theme songs for television shows such as *Batman, The Man from U.N.C.L.E., Secret Agent Man,* and *Hawaii Five-O.* Their *Hawaii Five-O* recording in 1969 brought the group their last hit single, topping out at number eleven. That same year the group released their last charting single, a cover of Percy Faith's "Theme for A Summer Place." That song peaked at eighty-three on the hit parade.

Throughout the 1960s and 1970s, the Ventures toured and recorded extensively. They also worked as guest and session players for artists such as Harvey Mandel, Leon Russell, and David Gates. Edwards left the band in 1968 to pursue a solo career and was replaced by Jerry McGee, who had played with the Everly Brothers, Elvis Presley, the Monkees, and Kris Kristofferson. The addition of keyboardist Johnny Durrill, who had formerly played with the Five Americans, made the group a quintet in 1969. When McGee left to record with Delaney and Bonnie Bramlett, Edwards returned to the group in 1972. Taylor and Durrill later left the group, and drummer Jo Barile came on board. The group took more artistic control over their music when they founded their Tridex label, and in 1979 Taylor returned to the group.

After fading from the popular scene in the 1970s, the Ventures enjoyed a resurgence in 1981 with their recording of "Surfin' and Spyin'," a song written by the Go-Go's Charlotte Caffey. The song was particularly popular in California thanks to a revival of surf music there, and the group played numerous gigs on the west coast to wide acclaim. Since that time the Ventures have maintained an active presence on the nostalgia circuit and continue to be a major draw in Japan, where their album sales have topped the forty-million mark.

Selected discography

Singles

"Walk Don't Run," 1960.
"Perfidia," 1960
"Ram-Bunk Shush, 1961.
"The 2,000-Pound Bee," 1962.
"Telstar," 1963.
"Diamondhead," 1965.
"Hawaii Five-O," 1969.

Albums

The Ventures, Dolton, 1961.
Surfing, Dolton, 1963.
Play Guitar with the Ventures (instructional), Dolton, 1965.
Ventures A-Go-Go, Dolton, 1965.
Super Psychedelics, Liberty, 1967.
Walk Don't Run: The Best of the Ventures, EMI America, 1990.

Sources

Books

Clarke, Donald, editor, *The Penguin Encyclopedia of Popular Music,* Viking, 1989, p. 200.

Hitchcock, H. Wiley, and Stanley Sadie, editors, *The New Grove Dictionary of American Music,* Volume 4, Macmillan, 1986, p. 456.

Larkin, Colin, editor, *The Guinness Encyclopedia of Popular Music,* Volume 5, Guinness Publishing, 1995, pp. 4321-22.

Rees, Dafydd, and Luke Crampton, *Encyclopedia of Rock Stars,* Dorling Kindersley, 1996, pp. 898–99.

Romanowski, Patricia, and Holly George-Warren, editors, *The New Rolling Stone Encyclopedia of Rock & Roll,* Rolling Stone Press, 1995, p. 1046.

Shannon, Bob, and John Javna, *Behind the Hits,* Warner Books, 1986, p. 102.

Additional information for this profile was obtained from the All-Music Guide and CD Universe websites on the Internet.

—Ed Decker

Gene Vincent

Singer

In Timothy White's anthology, *Rock Lives*, White recalled a 1983 interview with singer/songwriter, Paul Simon. When Simon was asked the smartest thing he had ever heard anybody say in rock-and-roll, his response was simple: "Be-Bop-A-Lula, she's my baby." With that quote, Simon gave a nod to Gene Vincent and his 1956 hit, "Be-Bop-A-Lula." Whether Simon was sincere about Gene Vincent's first and biggest hit reaching the height of profundity, in 1956, the song did reach the height of popularity. Driven by a rockabilly beat and featuring Vincent's raw, Presley-esque vocals, "Be-Bop-A-Lula" took Gene Vincent and his Blue Caps to the top of the rock world. Vincent's stay at the top, however, was shortened both by his excessive drinking and his addiction to pain pills. The pills were the result of a 1955 motorcycle accident which necessitated the use of a heavy metal leg brace for the rest of his life. Vincent would achieve fame in England during the early 1960s, but to Americans, he was another aging rock-and-roller who sang recycled versions of his old hits with pick-up bands. A final American comeback attempt in the late 60s was stunted by his ill health and the changing music climate. Vincent died in 1971 at the age of 36.

Born Vincent Eugene Craddock February 17, 1935, in Norfolk, Virginia, his birthdate is usually quoted as February 11th, a result of his mother's handwriting being misread on his birth certificate application. In 1942, the Craddock family moved to the rural Munden Point, Virginia, where parents Kie and Louise Craddock opened a general store. At this point in young Gene's life—everyone always called him Gene—he had only heard country music. The racially mixed area of Munden Point, however, initiated him to the sounds of blues and gospel. The mix of Grand Ole Opry music emanating from the family radio with the spiritual sounds of the neighborhood gospel singers proved irresistible to Vincent, and he begged his parents for a guitar and music lessons. Soon, people began to notice the skinny kid with the big guitar on the porch of the Craddock's store. "There was lots of colored folks around there and they'd sit on the porch and sing and sometimes Gene would play his guitar for them," Vincent's younger sister Evelyn told Britt Hagarty, author of Vincent's biography, *The Day the World Turned Blue*. "That's where his sound came from."

An Early Passion

When Vincent was 13, the Craddocks sold their store and moved back to Norfolk. Small and thin, Vincent would often be the subject of taunts and teasing at school and would always end up in fights. Frustrated by his size and the fact he wasn't doing well in his classes, Vincent quit school during the ninth grade and decided to join the

Born Vincent Eugene Craddock February 17, 1935 in Norfolk, VA; died October 12, 1971 in Newhall, CA of a seizure attributed to a bleeding ulcer. Married four times: Ruth Ann, Darlene, Margie, Jackie; children: Melody, Gene Jr., Sherri Ann. Served in the U.S. Naval Service 1953-55; served in Korea and was awarded two Distinguished Service Medals.

Began professional career after singing on *Country Showtime*, in Norfolk, VA, 1956; recorded "Be-Bop-A-Lula" with the Blue Caps, 1956; appeared in film *The Girl Can't Help It* with Jayne Mansfield and Little Richard, 1957; had a hit with "Lotta Lovin'," 1957; appeared in film *Hot Rod Gang*, 1958; moved to England, early 60s; toured Europe throughout the 1960s; returned to America, 1969; released comeback album, *I'm Back and I'm Proud*, 1970; died 1971.

Navy. His father, who'd been in the coast guard during World War II, signed the permission papers to let the seventeen-year-old enlist during the height of the Korean War. Vincent would often sing and play guitar with the other sailors and soon found another interest that would rival his passion for music—motorcycles.

In March of 1955, with a year of service left, Vincent re-enlisted for another six years in order to receive a reenlistment bonus. With this $612.39 bonus, Vincent bought a big Triumph motorcycle. In July of that year, while on leave in Norfolk, Vincent was hit by a car while riding his Triumph, leaving his left leg crushed. After being rushed to the hospital, doctors decided to amputate the leg, but Vincent begged his mother not to sign the forms permitting them to do so. Although she granted her son's request, years later Louise Craddock would admit to Hagarty, "I tell you, when I looked into his eyes, I knew I couldn't do it.... But now I wish I had." Vincent would spend the next six months in and out of the Portsmouth Naval Hospital and the rest of his life in a heavy metal leg brace.

While in the hospital, Vincent tried his hand at songwriting and penned "Race with the Devil" and "Be-Bop-A-Lula," a song inspired by a popular comic strip, "Little Lulu." Following his release, Vincent met and married his first wife, Ruth Ann, and with the encouragement of his new wife and his mother, he auditioned for a local talent show put on by Norfolk's WCMS radio called *Country Showtime*. For his audition, Vincent sang Elvis Presley's current hit, "Heartbreak Hotel" and brought the house down. "I never heard such sweet sounds," "Sheriff Tex" Davis, a WCMS-DJ, talent show judge, and soon-to-be Vincent manager, told Hagarty. "He was great!"

"Be-Bop-A-Lula"

Davis, WCMS station manager Roy Lamear, and booking agent Sy Blumenthal knew record companies were looking for the "new Elvis." They thought Vincent had a chance and formed a band for Gene to play with. Soon, Vincent was rehearsing with rhythm guitarist Willie Williams, bassist Jack Neal, drummer Dickie Harrell, and lead guitarist Cliff Gallup. After the group made a demo recording of "Be-Bop-A-Lula" at the WCMS studios, Davis sent it to producer Ken Nelson of Capitol Records. Less than a month later, in May of 1956, Vincent and the band were signed to the label and found themselves in a real Nashville recording studio. Producer Nelson was unsure of the young musicians from Norfolk and brought in some of Nashville's finest session musicians to back up Vincent, but that plan was scrapped as soon as they heard Cliff Gallup on lead guitar. Considered one of the greatest guitarists of 50s rock-and-roll, Gallup influenced guitarists such as Jerry Garcia, Jeff Beck, Dave Edmunds, and Bryan Setzer.

The band played so loudly in the recording studio that Vincent had to record his vocals in a stairway so he could hear himself over the band. After the recording, Nelson suggested using Vincent instead of Craddock as a surname, and to also find a name for the band. Drummer Harrell, who'd taken to wearing small hats when he played, suggested "The Blue Caps." One month later, "Be-Bop-A-Lula" was released as the B-side to the single "Woman Love," on Capitol Records by Gene Vincent and the Blue Caps.

For a short while, no one paid much attention to the record until a DJ in Baltimore started playing its B-side. By the end of June, "Be-Bop-A-Lula" had sold 200,000 copies, and Capitol rushed the band into the studio to record four more songs. Vincent and the Blue Caps were also touring steadily as "Lula" raced up the charts. By September, the song was in the top ten and Capitol released the group's first album, *Blue Jean Bop*. Although the album sold well, a second single, "Race with the Devil," faded quickly.

The Beginning of the Descent

By the end of 1956, *Blue Jean Bop* was still selling well, but Vincent's marriage was ending, his management team had broken up, and two Blue Caps left the band. Ruth Ann, tired of her husband's constant traveling and rumors of infidelity, left Vincent during what would be the height of his career. On the business side, Vincent sided with Davis in a management dispute that left Lamear and Blumenthal out of the picture, although Davis himself was out of the picture a short time later. Guitarist Willie Williams and lead guitarist Cliff Gallup left the band because of the strain of touring on their family lives. Vincent, however, loved to travel, perform, and the money, but he admitted that it all came too fast. "Listen, I never wanted to make money," he's quoted as saying in Hagarty's book. "I never wanted it. I'm a singer, man. My only thought was just to make a living singing. But all of a sudden I was getting $1500 a night.... It shouldn't have happened on that first record. I just didn't know how to handle it."

On stage, however, if there was anything wrong with Vincent and the Blue Caps, no one knew it. Even with his near-crippled leg, Vincent was an exciting, enthusiastic performer who never let an audience down, unless he was drunk. To handle the pain Vincent found refuge in pain pills, which he often washed down with a bottle of whiskey. The changing musical landscape of the late 50s was also a source of pain for Vincent. Although he scored another hit with 1957's "Lotta Lovin," the rockabilly sound of rock-and-roll had all but disappeared, replaced with new hitmakers like Frankie Avalon, Fabian, and Bobby Rydell. Even Elvis, with songs like "Are You Lonesome Tonight?" began to record songs in a pop vein. Soon, the Blue Caps were gone and Vincent began to tour England where there was still an audience for American rock-and-roll.

By 1960, Vincent and his second wife, Darlene, had a home in Portland, Oregon with Darlene's daughter from a previous marriage, Debbie, and their own daughter, Melody. But Vincent would often be touring in Europe, once again straining the relationship with his wife. On one tour with fellow American rocker and his best friend, Eddie Cochran, in April of that year, Vincent and company were in a car crash. Vincent suffered a broken collar bone and broken ribs, and Cochran was killed. "Gene was really shook up," Darlene told Hagarty. "He and Eddie were very close. He talked a lot about Eddie and sent flowers to the funeral. But he didn't go because he didn't think he'd be able to handle it." Six months later Darlene gave birth to their son, Gene Jr., but by the next year, she and the kids were gone. Vincent's drinking, mood swings, and his erratic life on the road resulted in another divorce.

With no one to go home to in America, Vincent moved to England and toured Europe almost constantly with a variety of backup bands. At one show in Hamburg, Germany in 1962, he was backed up by the then-unknown Beatles when his regular touring band failed to arrive on time. Vincent's drinking was at an all time high, as was his reliance on pain pills. For the remainder of the decade, he still, he managed to perform to enthusiastic audiences in Europe, while in America he was all but forgotten. Married and divorced two more times during the 1960s, the only relationship Vincent seemed able to sustain was with the audience. By the end of the decade, his health left him in awful shape.

Simon Frith, in a 1970 Rolling Stone article heralding the release of two greatest hits packages and an American comeback album, *I'm Back and I'm Proud*, recalled a then recent performance by Vincent. "He was in pain throughout and sang kneeling, his bad leg stretched out straight behind him.... He was fat, ugly, and greasier than Joe Cocker. There were no girls in the audience but for the assembled rockers he was the ultimate in rock and roll—offering nothing but music and sacrificing everything to that music, their music. I've never seen another rock star so worshipped and held in such awe by an audience." In talking about the albums, Frith held the most enthusiasm for the vintage recordings of the 1950s. "Nobody makes records like that anymore," Frith declared, "not even Gene Vincent."

The next year, Vincent died in his parents' home after a fall caused a seizure brought on by a bleeding ulcer. He was 36 years old. Though to some he's just the guy who sang "Be-Bop-A-Lula, she's my baby," his imprint on the early days of rock-and-roll goes far beyond that, even though that particular tune had sold nearly nine million copies by the time of his death. A number of later musicians named him as a primary influence, and British rock guitarist Jeff Beck recorded an entire album of Vincent and the Blue Caps songs on his 1993 album, *Crazy Legs*. Additionally, the resurgence of rockabilly in the 1980s with bands like the Blasters and the Stray Cats introduced new fans to the style of Vincent and his contemporaries. Members of the Blue Caps still get together to celebrate the music they made forty years earlier with the skinny kid from Norfolk. Though not every detail of his legacy remains impressive, Vincent's awareness of the impact of the music secures him a prominent place in the history of rock-and-roll.

Selected discography

Blue Jean Bop, Capitol, 1957.
Gene Vincent and the Blue Caps, Capitol, 1957.
Gene Vincent Rocks and the Blue Caps Roll, Capitol, 1958.
A Gene Vincent Record Date, Capitol, 1958.
The Best of Gene Vincent, Capitol, 1970.
I'm Back and I'm Proud, Dandelion/Elektra, 1970.
If Only You Could See Me Today, Kama Sutra, 1970.

The Day the World Turned Blue, 1971.
Capitol Collectors Series, Capitol, 1990.
Gene Vincent and His Blue Caps, Curb, 1993.
Screaming End: The Best of Gene Vincent and His Blue Caps,
    Razor and Tie Music, 1997.

Sources

Books

Encyclopedia of Rock, edited by Tony Russell, Crescent
    Books, 1983.
Encyclopedia of Rock, edited by Phil Hardy and Dave Laing,
    Schirmer Books, 1988.
Hagarty, Britt, *The Day the World Turned Blue: A Biography
    of Gene Vincent,* Talonbooks, 1983.
The New Rolling Stone Encyclopedia of Rock and Roll, edited
    by Patricia Romanowski and Holly George-Warren, Roll-
    ing Stone Press, 1995.
Perkins, Carl and David McGee, *The Life and Times of Carl
    Perkins,* Hyperion, 1996.

Periodicals

Rolling Stone, March 7, 1970, p. 52; November 11, 1971.
Los Angeles Times, August 17, 1996, p. F2.

—Brian Escamilla

Weather Report

Jazz band

With its mixture of electronic instrumentation and jazz sensibilities, Weather Report became the jazz-rock, or fusion, band against which all others were measured. For 15 years after the band's inception in 1971, Weather Report was steered through personnel changes and compositional experiments under the auspices of co-leaders keyboardist Joe Zawinul and saxophonist Wayne Shorter. Both musicians had been accomplished performers and composers, veterans of the hard-bop era of the late 1950s and early 1960s. Ten years later when the styles of rock began to merge with jazz, both men had front row seats playing with Miles Davis on his groundbreaking fusion albums, *In a Silent Way*—for which Zawinul composed the theme song—and *Bitches Brew.* During the band's heyday of the mid-to-late 1970s, when the group included bass virtuoso Jaco Pastorius, Weather Report was fundamental in taking jazz out of the clubs and into arenas. Zawinul and Shorter laid the band to rest in 1986 and ten years later announced that Weather Report would record and tour once again. Months later, however, another announcement signaled the end to those plans.

AP/Wide World Photos. Reproduced by permission.

For the Record . . .

Members include **Josef Zawinul** (born July 7, 1932, Vienna, Austria), keyboards, 1971-86; **Wayne Shorter** (born August 25, 1933, Newark, N J), saxophone, 1971-86; **Mirslav Vitous** (born December 6, 1947, Prague, Czechoslovakia), bass, 1971-73; **Alphonse Mouzon** (born November 21, 1948, Charleston, SC), drums, 1971; **Airto Moreira** (born August 5, 1941, Itaiopolis, Brazil), percussion, 1971; **Eric Gravatt**, drums, 1971-72; **Dom Um Romao**, percussion, 1971-73; **Ishmael Wilburn**, drums, 1972; **Alphonso Johnson**, bass, 1973-75; **Ndugu** (born Leon Chancler, 1952); **Chester Thompson**, drums, 1975-76; **Jaco Pastorius** (born John Francis Pastorius, December 1, 1951, Norristown, PA; died September 21, 1987, Fort Lauderdale, FL, bass, 1976-82; **Alejandro Acuna** (born December 12, 1944, Pativika, Peru), percussion, 1976-77; **Manola Badrena**, percussion, 1977; **Peter Erskine** (born June 5, 1954, Somers Pt., NJ), drums, 1978-82, 1986; **Victor Bailey**, bass, 1982-86; **Jose Rossy**, percussion, 1982-85; **Omar Hakim**, drums, 1982-85; **Mino Cinelu**, percussion, 1986.

Formed 1971 in New York by Zawinul, Shorter, and Vitous; signed to Columbia Records and released debut, *Weather Report,* 1971; Vitous left in 1973, replaced by Alphonso Johnson; a series of drummers and percussionists have recorded and toured, 1971-86; bassist Johnson left 1975, replaced by virtuoso bassist Jaco Pastorius; recorded album *Heavy Weather* in 1977, featuring the popular "Birdland"; Pastorius left 1979; group disbanded 1986.

Awards: Voted *DownBeat* Band of the Year by readers, 1971-78.

Addresses: *Record company*—Columbia Records, 550 Madison Ave., New York, NY 10022-3211.

The path to Weather Report begins with the singular careers of Joe Zawinul, born in Vienna, Austria, and Wayne Shorter, a native of Newark, New Jersey. Zawinul arrived in America in 1959, the result of a scholarship to Boston's Berklee School of Music. With the decision that a better classroom would be on the bandstand, Zawinul left Berklee after a few weeks to play piano for Maynard Ferguson's band, where he first worked with Shorter, then Ferguson's saxophonist. Shorter left the band after a month to play with Art Blakey's Jazz Messengers while Zawinul was fired after eight months following conflicts with Ferguson.

Before the Weather Changed

Beginning in 1960, Zawinul embarked on a 19-month stint as singer Dinah Washington's accompanist, and it was during this period that he first played an electric piano. "Dinah Washington and I toured with Ray Charles in 1960," he recalled to *DownBeat*'s Conrad Silvert, "and we did a couple of tunes when both Ray and Dinah would sing and I'd accompany on Ray's Wurlitzer electric piano." Zawinul then went on to join alto saxophonist Cannonball Adderly's group for nine years beginning in 1961. During his time with the group, he played the electric piano, and in 1966, one of his compositions was the band's first hit, "Mercy, Mercy, Mercy."

Shorter, meanwhile, was having considerable success with Blakey's Jazz Messengers contributing such compositions as "Lester Left Town" and "Free for All" and acquiring the coveted role of the band's musical director. In 1963 he left Blakey's band and after recording a few albums as leader, Shorter joined Miles Davis's band in 1964, filling the chair vacated by John Coltrane. Along with bassist Ron Carter, drummer Tony Williams, and pianist Herbie Hancock, Shorter was part of Davis's seminal mid-1960s quintet that's credited with bringing Davis back to the musical vanguard in jazz. "Those were all young guys," Davis wrote in his autobiography, *Miles: The Autobiography*, "and although they were learning from me, I was learning from them, too, about the new thing, the free thing." He added about Shorter, "When he came into the band it started to grow a whole lot faster, because Wayne is a real composer..... Wayne also brought in a kind of curiosity about working with musical rules. If they didn't work, then he broke them, but with a musical sense; he understood that freedom in music was the ability to know the rules in order to bend them to your satisfaction and taste."

The Birth of Fusion

In the late 1960s one of the ways to break the rules in jazz was in integrating electronic instruments. Zawinul was at the forefront of electronic instrumentation and Davis so admired the sound of his electric piano work in Adderly's band and his compositions, that in 1969 he invited Zawinul to bring both to a recording session for Davis's next album. One song Zawinul brought, "In A Silent Way," became the album's title tune and marked the first time Zawinul and Shorter played together since

Ferguson's band a decade earlier. Zawinul also contributed songs and playing on Davis's second album that fused the elements of jazz and rock, *Bitches Brew*. It became the biggest selling jazz album ever.

Two years later, Shorter, who had left Davis's group in the fall of 1969, was talking with Zawinul, who had just left Adderly's band, and bassist Miroslav Vitous, who had just been freed up from duties in Herbie Mann's group. The three decided to form a group that would take the music that came out of Davis's fusion recording sessions and move it a few steps further. "We kind of always talked about doing something together," Zawinul explained to *Rolling Stone*'s Bob Blumenthal, referring to himself and Shorter. "If we met in a club we used to talk about music ... for a while we didn't see each other at all; I was going one way with Cannon's group, Wayne would be somewhere else with Miles. Then I heard *Nefertiti* [a 1967 Davis album featuring three Shorter compositions] and that's when I felt Wayne was the guy I should do something with. He had the new thinking."

Weather Report

The trio made a demo tape with stand-in drummer Billy Cobham, although Columbia Records signed them without even listening to it. Drummer Alphonse Mouzon and guest percussionist Airto Morirera were recruited and the band went into rehearsals. "Rehearsing was quite something," Zawinul told *DownBeat*'s Dan Morgenstern. "Every day when we got home we'd be exhausted, there was so much music going on." Their debut album, *Weather Report*, was released in May of 1971 to much anticipation and fanfare. Here was a supergroup of jazz virtuosos, each superb soloists, who placed solos aside to emphasize the ensemble feel of playing, each instrument blending to support the theme of the composition. According to Zawinul, it was the compositions, after all, which were the essence of the band. "One thing made me certain we could be the greatest band in the world: the compositions," he declared to Blumenthal. "Composing is always the thing that lasts, and I knew that both Wayne and I can write our asses off. And the playing is right behind."

Mouzon left the band after the first tour and was replaced by Eric Gravatt with Dom Um Romao handling percussion duties for the band's next album, *I Sing the Body Electric*. With one side consisting of studio recordings and the other a live recording from Tokyo, *Rolling Stone*'s Robert Palmer called it a "beautiful, near perfect LP," and went on to describe the band's live side as "a group that has reorganized the role of the traditional rhythm section in an unusual way. Joe Zawinul uses his electronic keyboard like a hornplayer ... to engage in a

dialogue of equals with saxophonist Shorter. Vitous uses his bass as a third voice in this ongoing conversation, which often leaves drummer Gravatt to handle the rhythmic chores, a job he performs with style and grace." *DownBeat*'s Gary Giddins declared, "there is no question that Weather Report is into something new and stimulating."

The next album, 1973's *Sweetnighter,* sold well but wasn't as successful with the critics as the previous two efforts, and Gravatt was absent on three tracks, having left the group during recording. On that album, however, the group began to make the transition to synthesizers and electric bass, a move completed by the band's next release, 1974's *Mysterious Traveller* with drummer Ishmael Wilburn. Bassist and founding member Vitous was only heard on one tune, having left the band, to be replaced, for this album, by the layered textures of Zawinul's synthesizers. "Synthesizers don't complicate anything," Zawinul insisted to *Melody Maker*'s Steve Lake. "Our music is so simple, man, and it's getting more simple the more familiar we are getting with electronics. When the music is right synthesizers don't sound like synthesizers. They just sound like some beautiful instrument which you can't put your finger on." Indeed, instead of being a cold, programmed sound, *Rolling Stone*'s Robert Palmer called it "the triumph of feeling over technology," and proclaimed the album "reintroduces human proportion into the mix and is far and away Weather Report's most complete and perfect statement."

Jaco Joins the Group

Bassist Alphonso Johnson was in the group by 1975 with drummer Ngudu appearing on that year's *Tale Spinnin'*, an album that brought solos back into the mix. This was followed by 1976's Black Market, the first album to include a volatile young bass player from Florida, Jaco Pastorius. "I met Jaco in Miami after one of our concerts," Zawinul told *DownBeat*'s Silvert. "He was talking with a certain confidence and with such a knowledge of what's going on, I figured there was a good chance he was really into something. Either he was an incredible musician or a fool." Pastorius sent Zawinul some tapes and he was sufficiently impressed to invite him to play on the *Black Market* album on the song "Cannonball," an ode to Zawinul's old boss Julian "Cannonball" Adderly, also a Florida native. Zawinul thought Pastorius's bass would give the tune "that Florida sound."

Shortly after they recorded "Cannonball," Pastorius was invited to join the group and added one of his own tunes, "Barbary Coast," to the *Black Market* album. Now the band had three capable composers and Weather Report seemed unstoppable. The addition of Pastorius with his virtuosic sensibilities and flamboyant stage antics were well in tune with the direction the band was going. The first full album with Pastorius, 1977's *Heavy Weather,* ranks among their best. Featuring their most well known tune, "Birdland,"—later a vocal hit for the Manhattan Transfer—*HeavyWeather* also incorporated Latin American sounds with an increasing blend of R&B. Reviewer Dan Oppenheimer of *Rolling Stone* credited Pastorius with anchoring the band. "He's vital to them now," Oppenheimer wrote, "because he fills up the music where it used to diffuse, which suits their apparent aims just fine."

Weather Report followed up with 1978's *Mr. Gone,* an album that brought drummer Peter Erskine into the mix and featured Zawinul's new Prophet synthesizer, an ingredient he thought would help make *Mr. Gone* their best record yet. "This Prophet keyboard is an incredible machine," Zawinul exclaimed to *Rolling Stone*'s Blumenthal. "It has what I've always needed to make the music come off. I have forty-four different programs, including a string sound that you will not know isn't a symphony orchestra." Unfortunately, *Mr. Gone* and the Prophet keyboard received a disappointing one star review from *DownBeat.* "Zawinul's insistent multi-tracking distorts the sound," the reviewer said. "... Zawinul's use of his electronic keyboards is too rigid and confining, and it is as if in his attempt to free the band from the restriction of conventional acoustic instrumentation, he has established a whole new set of equally restrictive guidelines."

Beginning of the End

A 1979 live album, *8:30,* brought back some of the luster to Weather Report and showcased their impressive improvisational abilities. The group continued as a quartet for the next three years releasing two like-minded albums that failed to match their earlier work both critically and commercially. About 1982's *Weather Report,* the last album to include Pastorius and Erskine, *Rolling Stone*'s J.D. Considine wrote, "More often than not ... the members of Weather Report engage in a kind of push-and-pull performing that ends up blunting the music's intensity." Pastorius went on to form the 20-piece Word of Mouth band while Erskine left to do some solo recording and extensive session work.

In 1983 bassist Victor Bailey, drummer Omar Hakim, and percussionist Jose Rossy, formed the rhythm section of the band and the band in this quintet format would record three albums: *Procession, Domino Theory, and Sportin' Life.* The last Weather Report album, 1986's *This is This* featured the return of Peter Erskine, percussionist Mino Cinelu in the place of Rossy, and guest guitarist Carlos Santana. When the time came to tour in support of the album, however, Shorter toured with his own quartet leaving Zawinul to go out with a band he dubbed "Weather Update," featuring Erskine, Bailey, percussionist Bobby Thomas, Jr., and guitarist Steve Kahn.

Weather Report Update?

In the years that followed the 1986 breakup, Shorter recorded and toured with various musicians as a leader and Zawinul formed the Weather Report-influenced Zawinul Syndicate. In 1987 Pastorius died from injuries he received in a fight outside a bar in Fort Lauderdale, Florida. To the dismay of their fans, nothing in the post-breakup years indicated that Weather Report would ever reform. Then in April 1996, *DownBeat* reported that the band would record the following Fall and tour in the Spring and Summer of 1997. "We want to make a new record with newmusic," Zawinul told *DownBeat*'s Zan Stewart. "And on the tour, we'll probably play the new music, as well as recalling some of the old tunes." For his part, Shorter affirmed that the time was right to reform the band. "When we were working on Weather Report, we always said that ours was the folk music of the future.... Now we're in the future as opposed to being back then.... By doing what [Joe and I] did, going on our separate paths, we gathered experiences, maybe stories that will, whether we want them to or not, manifest themselves on the new record."

In July of 1996, Shorter lost his niece and Ana Maria, his wife of some thirty years, in the TWA Flight 800 crash off the coast of New York. A few months later it was announced that Weather Report would not be reforming, although no explanations were given or necessary. Shorter went on to win a Grammy for his 1996 album, *High Life,* while Zawinul was nominated for a Grammy as well, in a separate category, for the Zawinul Syndicate's *My People.* While both musicians continue to make music that's appreciated by fans and critics alike, it's unknown whether Shorter or Zawinul will ever perform together again under the Weather Report banner. When asked by *DownBeat*'s Larry Birnbaum in 1979 why Weather Report was still going strong while other fusion groups slipped away, Zawinul responded, "It's because we're saying what we're saying and it goes on strong because it's real and it's genuine and there's nothing false about it. It was always real, good or bad, but it's real." If Weather Report has anything left to say then, good or bad, at least it'll be real. "

Selected discography

Weather Report, Columbia, 1971.
I Sing the Body Electric, Columbia, 1972.
Sweetnighter, Columbia, 1973.
Mysterious Traveller, Columbia, 1974.
Tale Spinnin', Columbia, 1975.
Black Market, Columbia, 1976.
Heavy Weather, Columbia, 1977.
Mr. Gone, Columbia, 1978.
8:30, Columbia, 1979.
Night Passages, Columbia, 1980.
Weather Report, Columbia, 1982.
Procession, Columbia, 1983.
Domino Theory, Columbia, 1984.
Sportin' Life, Columbia, 1985.
This is This, Columbia, 1986.

Sources

Books

Carr, Ian, et al., *Jazz: The Rough Guide*, Rough Guides Ltd., 1995.

Case, Brian and Stan Britt, *The Harmony Illustrated Encyclopedia of Jazz*, Harmony Books, 1986.
Davis, Miles with Quincy Troupe, *Miles: The Autobiography*, Touchstone, 1989.
Lyons, Len and Don Perlo, *Jazz Portraits: The Lives and Music of the Jazz Masters*, Quill, 1989.

Periodicals

DownBeat, May 27, 1971, p. 14; October 26, 1972, p. 30; June 1, 1978, p. 13; June 15, 1978, p. 21; July 1994, p. 60, 94; April 1996, p. 14; November 1996, p. 6.
Melody Maker, December 20, 1975, p. 33; October 15, 1977.
Rolling Stone, July 6, 1972, p. 55; September 27, 1973, p. 24; August 1, 1974, p. 50; May 5, 1977, p. 24; June 10, 1977, p. 105; December 28, 1978, p. 64; April 15, 1982, p.88.

—Brian Escamilla

Slim Whitman

Folk singer

Once dubbed "America's Favorite Folk singer," Slim Whitman was brought to the attention of a new generation of listeners with the 1997 release of *Mars Attacks!,* director Tim Burton's spoof of the 1950's alien invasion films. In Burton's film, it is Whitman's version of "Indian Love Call" which repels the invading Martians and saves the world from imminent defeat. With more than 103 albums to his credit, a majority now available on CD, Whitman enjoys international popularity in countries such as England, Australia, and Holland. Among his famous fans are Michael Jackson, and George Harrison and Paul McCartney of the *Beatles.* In the U.S., World War II hero Audie Murphy was a fan, as was Elvis Presley who toured with Whitman at the beginning of his own career. It is therefore surprising that Whitman has not yet been inducted into the Country Music Hall of Fame, which is not to say he has gone unrecognized. Whitman has a star on the Hollywood Walk of Fame and in Holland both a rose and tulip have been named after him. Whitman has sold more than 70 million records worldwide and he continues to play to packed houses and audiences which span nearly three generations.

Ottis Dewey Whitman, Jr. was born January 20, 1929 in Tampa, Florida, where he grew up playing baseball, fishing, and listening to Montana Slim and Jimmie Rodgers, the father of country music. Whitman had a close-knit family, with two brothers and two sisters. At age fifteen Whitman met Geraldine "Jerry" Christ, the preacher's daughter. They fell in love and Whitman married her two years later. After graduating from high school, Whitman took a job in a meat packing plant. He later found work as a shipfitter and boilermaker at a Tampa shipyard.

In 1943, Whitman joined the Navy. He was stationed on the *USS Chilton* in the South Pacific. It was onboard the *Chilton* that Whitman found a guitar and began to play. The left-handed Whitman restrung the guitar upside-down. Each week, during happy hour, he entertained the sailors by either boxing or singing. Fifty years after his service, Navy buddies still approached him with recollections of their time onboard the Chilton.

Honorably discharged in 1946, Whitman returned home to Tampa and his job at the shipyard. He also played baseball with the Plant City Berries, a class C team in the Orange Belt League. With his skillful left-handed pitch and a batting average of .360, Whitman helped his team take the pennant in 1947. Friends, however, urged him to pursue his singing career, so in 1948, he gave up baseball and began to sing professionally.

He started out on Florida radio station WDAE, then moved on to WHBO and WFLA until September 1949, when he teamed up with The Lightcrust Doughboys to do a series of programs through the Mutual Network. The programs were then picked up by a Shreveport Louisiana station, KWKH, and incorporated as part of the "Louisiana Hayride." Up to this point, Whitman had a stutter and was very shy; it was Hank Williams who helped him overcome this obstacle.

A happy accident during one of these radio broadcasts would change electric steel guitar playing forever. Hoot Rains, guitarist in Slim's band, overshot a note. The sound was so unique it was incorporated by the band. It became the definitive "shooting arrow" sound heard on all of Slim's subsequent recordings. The pay for these radio shows was minimal—$18 per week—and Slim had to take a second job as a postal worker to make ends meet. Colonel Tom Parker, who would later become famous as Elvis Presley's manager, heard Whitman on WFLA and, in 1948, helped him get signed to RCA. At the beginning of Presley's career, he toured as the opening act for Slim Whitman. Whitman received $500 per show while Elvis Presley received $50.

There are two stories about how Whitman got the nickname "Slim." One has it that the 6'2" Whitman received it in the Navy. The other has it that management changed his name while he was off fishing, totally unbeknownst to Whitman. However he came by the name it stuck, and in 1952 Slim Whitman was signed to Imperial Records, where he recorded "Lovesong of the Waterfall". He remained with Imperial until 1970.

Whitman's Success Abroad

Slim Whitman released his biggest stateside hit, "Indian Love Call" in July of 1952. The song had been his favorite when he was a boy, and his cover version brought him his highest mark ever on the American Country charts—

three weeks at number two, and 21 weeks at number three. It also made the Top 10 on the pop charts. In November 1953 Whitman's "North Wind" was number eight for five weeks and paved the way for his January 1954 cover of "Secret Song," first sung by Doris Day.

His success in the U.S. has been marginal compared to his international reception, especially in Great Britian. In May of 1954, Whitman released "Rose Marie". It went straight to number one on the U.K. pop chart where it remained for 11 weeks. The release of "Indian Love Call" and it's B-side single, "China Doll" were also eagerly received and, in 1956, Whitman became the first Country artist ever to play the London Palladium. He is still a big draw in the U.K.; in 1974, 1975, 1978, 1979, and 1980, Slim was named "International Male Vocalist" at The Wembley Festival and, in 1991, Slim and his son Byron headlined at the final Wembley Festival.

Perhaps Whitman's avoidance of drinking and cheating songs confused American audiences and prevented him from achieving the kind of success at home that he had long enjoyed overseas. Or perhaps it was bad timing. Whitman's unusual three octave singing ability and his knack for yodeling may have seen out of place at a time when rock and roll was first making an impact. Whatever the case, it wasn't until 1965, with the release of "More Than Yesterday" that Whitman returned to the limelight. Whitman placed eleven songs on the charts between 1966 and 1969, and in 1970 he was invited back to the U.K. where he played three packed shows. Whitman's longtime label, Imperial, was absorbed by United Artists (UA) in 1970 and Whitman remained on UA until 1974. During his United years, Whitman had hits with "Guess Who", "Something Beautiful (to Remember)", "It's a Sin to Tell a Lie" and "Happy Anniversary," which made it to number 14 on the British pop chart in 1974.

In 1977, Whitman toured Great Britian again, this time with his son, Byron, who had an album out at the time under the moniker Byron Keltgh. Speaking of touring with his son, Whitman has said "He does have his own style, especially on record. On stage we also team up into the two Whitmans, 'The Powerhouse' we call it, with the two high yodels, the two high voices."

In 1979 Whitman released a 20 track television album, *All My Best*, through Suffolk Marketing. This album went on to sell a record four million copies. Following up on this success, Suffolk released another compilation in 1989, entitled *Just For You*. Whitman then signed with Cleveland International Records and returned to the top 15 with "When." He recorded two more records with Cleveland: *That Silver-haired Daddy of Mine*, and *Can't Help Falling in Love.* Two years later, he recorded *Angeline*, produced by Bob Montgomery, which contains a duet with Byron Whitman titled "Four Walls." Heartland released *Slim Whitman-Best Loved Favorites* in 1989 and Progressive Music released *20 Precious Memories,* a religious record, in 1991. Both were television records and both were successes. When asked how he'd like to be remembered, Slim said, "As a nice guy with a white hat, you might say. I'd like my son to remember me as a good dad. I'd like the people to remember me as having a good voice and a clean suit."

Selected discography

America's Favorite Folk Artist, Imperial, 1954.
Favorites, Imperial, 1956.
Unchain My Heart, Sunset, 1968.
The Best of Slim Whitman, United Artists, 1972.
All My Best, Suffolk, 1979.
Ghost Riders in the Sky, Liberty, 1981.
Angeline, Epic/Cleveland International, 1984.
One of a Kind, Pair, 1984.
The Very Best of Slim Whitman, Country Store, 1985.

Just for You, Suffolk, 1989.
Greatest Hits, Curb, 1990.
20 Precious Memories, Progressive Music, 1991.
How Great Thou Art, Arrival, 1993.
Vintage Collections, Capitol, 1997.

Sources

Books

Whitburn, Joel, *Joel Whitburn's Top Country Singles; 1944-1993,* Billboard Publications, 1994.

Periodicals

Associated Press AAA Wire, January 28, 1991
Country Music People, March 1987.

Additional information provided by publicity materials from "The Louisiana Hayride" and Epic Records.

—*Kevin O'Sullivan*

Gerald Wilson

Jazz Arranger

Photo by Lyn Sherwood. AP/Wide World Photos. Reproduced by permission.

Dense, assertive brass; cool, dry reeds; strong doses of Mexican, Latin American and rock feeling; arrangements that showcase soloists; solos that complement arrangements. These are some of the elements that identify the various bands of Gerald Wilson. "You can always tell a Gerald Wilson arrangement. He has his own style," said vibraphonist/leader Terry Gibbs. "There's nothing more pretty than eight brass playing a whole chorus, with all eight notes moving, moving." So said Wilson, the maestro, in an interview with Zan Stewart for the January, 1997, *DownBeat.* "Moving" has been a hallmark of the Wilson style. From his early days with the Jimmy Lunceford Band to his current musical activities, Gerald Wilson has usually moved well ahead of the pack.

Wilson's family moved to Detroit from Memphis when he was about 14. Wilson had already grounded himself in a jazz tradition, through early piano lessons with his mother and sessions listening and talking with his brother Shelby. A Tuskegee Institute classmate of jazz legend Teddy Wilson, Shelby brought a jazz perspective to his younger brother. Detroit's Cass Technical High School, then a Mecca for talented students of many disciplines, provided the basis for Wilson's formal training. There, he was taught by Clarence Byrne, the father of trombonist/ band leader Bobby Byrne.

With this background, and still in his teens, Wilson launched his career, first as a trumpeter at Detroit's Plantation Club in 1936-37, then touring with Chic Carter. In 1939, he joined the famous Jimmy Lunceford Band, replacing trumpeter/arranger Sy Oliver, whose charts, trumpet solos and vocals had helped propel this band to the forefront of swing groups. Oliver had shifted to the Tommy Dorsey Orchestra, where his arrangements were responsible for helping Dorsey record some of his greatest hits. Initially, Wilson was limited to playing trumpet, but soon he began to contribute arrangements to the Lunceford band, whose position was being challenged by many other groups of the day. Two of his best-known recorded arrangements for Lunceford were "Hi Spook" and "Yard Dog Mazurka," "the opening of which Stan Kenton appropriated, lock, stock, and barrel a few years later for 'Intermission Riff,'" Gunther Schuller noted in his *The Swing Era.* Composer credit for this hit Kenton recording is assigned to Kenton trumpeter Ray Wetzel. Schuller also pointed out that several Wilson arrangements helped sustain the fading Lunceford group.

By the time Wilson left Lunceford in 1942 and moved to California, he had established himself as a distinguished arranger. Once on the West Coast, he played with the bands of Les Hite and Benny Carter, picking up writing and arranging tips along the way. Next came a stint in the U.S. Navy at the Great Lakes Naval Training Center, where Wilson performed and probably arranged in a band led by reedman Willie Smith, an old Lunceford compatriot. Trumpet section-mates there included the inimitable Clark Terry and Ernie Royal. Upon his discharge in December, 1944, Wilson formed his first band in the midst of the fermenting California music scene.

Wilson's Ascent to Fame

Wilson's band commanded immediate attention, and embarked on a successful performing tour throughout the country. Singer Joe Williams was with the band briefly in 1946, and they played Los Angeles, St. Louis and Chicago with stars such as Ella Fitzgerald and Sammy Davis, Jr. Despite an enthusiastic welcome at New York's demanding Apollo Theater that capped-off this tour, Wilson decided to quit the business for a while. He felt he was not yet ready to sustain the responsibilities of leader, arranger, composer, trumpeter. Returning to California, Wilson spent some time playing and writing for the Count Basie and Dizzy Gillespie bands through 1947 and 1949. During that time, he also began a long period of writing intermittently for Duke Ellington's band

in 1947.

Throughout this period and well into the 1950s, Wilson managed to maintain bands of his own, mostly to play music which he had written and arranged. In addition, these writing and arranging skills lead to assignments for television and film work for NBC and MGM. He also conducted albums for a variety of artists, including Ray Charles, Nancy Wilson, Nat Cole, Billie Holiday and Harry Belafonte, as well as pianist Les McCann and guitarist B. B. King. Of his preparation for these responsibilities, Wilson told writer John William Hardy, "Nobody can say they have taught me how to write or orchestrate—I haven't studied with or under anyone—but that is not to say I haven't studied long and hard on my own. I don't feel that my lack of formal training means that I am in any way limited in my approach to the job."

In the 1960s, with the dedicated push of producer Albert Marx for Pacific Jazz records, Wilson recorded a string of albums that showcased his own writing and arranging. Partly because this was studio work, and because of the exciting material, Wilson was able to attract some of the better musicians. Among these were: trumpeters Al Porcino, Conte Candoli and Carmell Jones; trombonists Bob Edmondson and Les Robertson; reedmen Teddy Edwards, Harold Land, Jack Nimitz, and Bud Shank; guitarists Joe Pass and Laurindo Almeida; vibist Bobby Hutcherson; drummer Mel Lewis.

Embracing a Culture

It was also during this period that Wilson developed a fascination for Mexico. His Mexican wife, Josephina, became the subject of one of his compositions, as has Mexican culture in general: bullfighters, pyramids, folklore. These themes are represented principally on 1966's *Torero Impressions in Jazz: The Golden Sword*, which includes such titles as "Carlos" (dedicated to bullfighter Carlos Arruza), "Mi Corazon," and three selections from a from a larger work, for the 2,000-year-old pyramid, the "Teotihuacan Suite." Wilson affected a Mexican persona; his on-stage and rehearsal demeanor with his orchestra is both commanding and exciting—not unlike that of a great toreador. It is not surprising that he did some acting, including a televised appearance in 1959's *The Lineup*.

Wilson studied the writing of modern classicists such as Aram Khatchaturian, Manuel de Falla and Joaquin Rodrigo. In addition, he incorporated many characteristics of rock music into his writing and arrangements, leading to the jazz/rock phenomenon that remains. Any residual doubts Wilson had about his ability to write with sustaining interest, such as inhibited him with his 1946 band, were dispelled when Zubin Mehta, conductor of the Los Angeles Philharmonic, commissioned him to write an extended work for that orchestra's 1972 season. Because of the scope and success of this work, he told writer Zan Stewart, "That was the day I realized I could compose anything I wanted." When Wilson came to New York in 1988 to conduct the American Jazz Orchestra playing his music, it marked his first appearance there in 25 years. That orchestra's manager, Loren Schoenberg, told *New York Times* writer Peter Watrous: "Gerald's concept is completely modern. The music he's writing here doesn't have much to do with the Lunceford style. . . . Gerald's pieces are all extended. . . . They're almost hypnotic. . . . Only a master can keep the interest going that long, and he does."

Wilson's approach is often compared to that of Duke Ellington. Each served as leader, composer, arranger and player. (Because of dental problems, Wilson laid aside his trumpet in the mid-1970s.) Like Ellington, Wilson considered his orchestra to be his main instrument, and though Wilson was never afforded the luxury of having the same instrument, with only evolutionary changes over a period of decades, his sporadic bands of the 1940s and the 1960s and beyond did attract a stable of some of the best players of the West Coast galaxy. It was for this changing cast that he wrote, and, like Ellington, he often altered arrangements to enhance a solo or the length of a solo to enrich the arrangement.

An example of Wilson's arranging skill for Ellington is pointed out in the five CD 1995 Smithsonian collection, *Big Band Renaissance.* In his collection notes Bill Kirchner wrote, "Though some listeners may be surprised to find a non Ellington/Strayhorn arrangement in an Ellington sampling, there are several reasons for inlcuing this recording of "Perdido": it is an ingenious reworking of a tune introduced by the Ellington band in 1942, it enables us to hear a number of the band's soloists, and it is an electrifying performance—one of the best recordings ever—of one of the most frequently performed themes in jazz." Wilson's own band is also represented in this magnum collection.

Wilson and Stan Kenton are also often compared, and not only because they plowed the same California soil. Many musicians worked in both bands at one time or another; each band was heavy on the brass; each used Latin rhythms extensively; each played its share of jazz/rock numbers; each experimented with extended works. Whereas Wilson rarely traveled, Kenton was on the road for most of his career.

Wilson stays young by mentoring young musicians. He began teaching at California State University—Northridge in 1970 and also taught at Cal State—Los Angeles, then joined the faculty of the University of California in Los Angeles in 1991. These contacts with interested students and his continuing writing provide the challenges Wilson craves. As he told *DownBeat's* Stewart: "I have a big class, about 550 students, and I have fun with them. . . . I cover ragtime through swing in one section, bebop up through today in the other. It's really a kick."

Selected discography

Albums

Moment of Truth, Pacific Jazz, 1962.
Portraits, Pacific Jazz, 1963.
Gerald Wilson: On Stage, Pacific Jazz, 1965.
The Golden Sword, Pacific Jazz, 1966.
The Best of the Gerald Wilson Orchestra, Pacific Jazz, c. 1968.
Eternal Equinox, Pacific Jazz, 1969.
State Street Sweet, MAMA, 1994.
Suite Memories, MAMA, 1996.

Sources

Books

Erlewine, Michael, et al, Eds., *All Music Guide to Jazz,* Miller Freeman Books, 1996.
Feather, Leonard, *The New Edition of the Encyclopedia of Jazz,* Bonanza Books, 1965.
Gioia, Ted, West Coast Jazz: Modern Jazz in California, 1945-1960,; Oxford University Press, 1992.
Schuller, Gunther, *The Swing Era: The Development of Jazz, 1930-1945,* Oxford University Press, 1989.

Periodicals

DownBeat, January, 1997.
New York Times, October 20, 1988.

Monograph

Kirchner, Bill, *Notes for Big Band Renaissance,* Smithsonian Institution, 1995.

Album Liner Notes

Moment of Truth, notes by John William Hardy, Pacific Jazz, 1962.
Portraits, notes by Eliot Tiegel, Pacific Jazz, 1963.
Torero Impressions In Jazz: The Golden Sword, notes by Leonard Feather, Pacific Jazz, 1966.

—*Robert Dupuis*

Mac Wiseman

Singer, guitarist, songwriter, producer

Photo by Jon Sievert. *MICHAEL OCHS ARCHIVES/Venice, CA. Reproduced by permission.*

Known to fans as the "Voice with a Heart" because of his distinctive, mellow, tenor vocals, singer and guitarist Mac Wiseman is renowned as a bluegrass music artist, although his music also encompasses old-time, modern, and even pop styles. Despite bluegrass's reputation as a "feudin'" music, with stylistic hardliners holding to various opposing camps, Wiseman has graciously moved in and out of both the more rigid, tradition-laced Bill Monroe-inspired school and the more progressive brand of bluegrass, making him one of the few performers of the genre to transcend such time-honored factionalism. Introducing the twin-fiddle sound to the bluegrass mix through his own innovations during the 1950s, Wiseman has otherwise specialized in more traditional, sentimental material, such as the A. P. Carter-penned "Jimmy Brown the Newsboy" and the old-time classic "Letter Edged in Black."

Malcolm B. "Mac" Wiseman was born in the town of Crimora, near Waynesboro, Virginia, on May 23, 1925. Performing country and mountain music in the area of the Shenandoah Valley where Wiseman was raised was a common pastime that sometimes even bordered on folk art; young Mac learned a great deal from the talented friends, neighbors, and family members that he watched interpret traditional Appalachian melodies. The Wiseman home was a popular gathering spot for the musically inclined, as Mac's father had one of the only phonograph players in the area, and even owned a battery-powered radio. "I recall that people came from several miles distance on Saturday night to listen to the *[Grand Ole] Opry* and the *WLS Barn Dance*," Wiseman recalled in *Music City News*, "often staying until the wee hours of the morning or sometimes all night, and then having breakfast and going home." Wiseman taught himself to play the guitar when he was twelve years old, and soon built a large repertoire of traditional songs.

From Disc Jockey to Performer

During high school, Wiseman grew more and more interested in music, and decided to find a way to make it his livelihood. After high school, he attended Dayton, Virginia's Shenandoah Conservatory of Music. Graduating from their music program in about 1945, Mac went on to join the announcing staff of radio station WSVA in Harrisburg, Virginia, as newscaster and disc jockey. As his on-air schedule permitted, Wiseman made extra money by writing advertising copy for WSVA sponsors. He also indulged in his favorite pastime—music—by performing with local country bands on the weekends. These stints onstage made Wiseman realize how much he enjoyed performing in front of a live audience, and in 1947 he began to orchestrate a shift in his career. While hosting WCYB radio's *Farm and Fun Time* show in Bristol, Virginia, Wiseman began playing bass guitar with mountain singer Molly O'Day, whom he would later describe to Don Rhodes in *Bluegrass Unlimited* as, "without a doubt, the female Hank Williams." Already a talented guitarist and in possession of a warm, fluid tenor voice, Wiseman was soon sought out by other bands, including a popular country group called the Blue Grass Boys, led by a fearsome mandolin picker by the name of Bill Monroe. Wiseman liked the group's fast, loud sound, and recorded several sessions with them, singing harmony to Monroe's lead vocals. It would be a few years before their sound, with its high, wailing tenor vocals and intricate acoustic instrumentals, would bear the name "bluegrass."

Joins Flatt & Scruggs

Wiseman spent most of 1947 playing guitar with Bill Monroe and the Blue Grass Boys, which then featured what came to be known as the group's classic lineup: fiddle player Chubby Wise, guitarist Lester Flatt, bass player Cedrick Rainwater (Howard Watts), banjoist Earl Scruggs, and Monroe on mandolin and lead vocals. As fate would have it, Wiseman also found himself taking part in one of the most historic "splits" in bluegrass

music. In January of 1948, guitarist Flatt and banjo-picker extraordinaire Scruggs--inventor of the much imitated three-fingered banjo picking style that now bears his name--left Monroe to form their own band, the Foggy Mountain Boys. Their departure from Monroe's band was not solo: Wise and Rainwater would also leave during the same period. Rainwater had linked up with Flatt & Scruggs and the Blue Grass-turned-Foggy Mountain Boys were now performing on WCYB. The group, which would record for Mercury from 1948 through 1950, featured Flatt, Scruggs, Rainwater on bass, and Jim Shumate on fiddle. As Neil Rosenberg notes of the high strung Father of Bluegrass in his classic *Bluegrass: A History;* "Monroe had previously had the experience of band members leaving him to strike out on their own. But he had never had most of the band leave and go into direct competition with him.... he did not like it." Wiseman would join the Foggy Mountain Boys during their first year—even playing second rhythm guitar and performing tenor vocals on the group's first recording for Mercury in 1948—then left to play guitar for Monroe's band for a season before launching his own band in 1950. While Wiseman successfully transcended the historic split, it would be several decades before the rift between Flatt & Scruggs and Monroe would heal.

Begins Career as Solo Recording Artist

After one year fronting his own band, Wiseman signed with Dot Records as a solo artist. His association with Dot--a new, independent record company based out of Gallatin, Tennessee—would be a long and fruitful one, producing a number of best-selling singles, including the recordings that have earned Wiseman his enduring reputation. Hits with Dot included "'Tis Sweet to Be Remembered," "Jimmy Brown the Newsboy" (also a standard for the Foggy Mountain Boys), "Shackles and Chains," "The Ballad of Davy Crockett," and "Love Letters in the Sand."

While working on his recording career, Wiseman established himself as a solo performer beginning in 1951, when he starred on Shreveport's popular *Louisiana Hayride.* Stints on Atlanta's WSB *Barn Dance,* and Knoxville, Tennessee's *Barn Dance* would follow, as well as a guest-starring spot on Nashville's *Grand Ole Opry.* He joined the cast of Richmond, Virginia's WRVA *Old Dominion Barn Dance* in 1953, moving to a regular spot on *Louisiana Hayride* in 1956, which pushed his recordings with Dot to national hit status; Wiseman's poignant rendition of "Jimmy Brown the Newsboy" hung on to a spot on the *Billboard* charts for thirty-three weeks.

The late 1950s would find Wiseman moving to the business side of country. Mac wanted to hold onto his identity as a solo artist and, although his band had a distinctive sound, unlike a true bluegrass act his sidemen were always subordinate to his own lead vocals. "You could see the decline or lack of interest in country music," Wiseman recalled to *Muleskinnner News* interviewer Doug Green, describing the musical climate of the mid-1950s, "and rock music was coming on the scene. It was difficult to get exposure for a straight country product because the volume of the teen market was so big." So, in 1957 Wiseman became the now-California-based Dot Records' country music A&R (artists & repertoire) executive, a job he continued until 1961. During that period he also ran the company's country music division. He recorded and produced for Capitol Records during the early 1960s, returning to Dot in 1966 to record three albums' worth of experimental music featuring string orchestra-backed traditional tunes and folk music.

Folk Music Boom Signals Bluegrass Revivalism

The phenomenal renewal of interest in traditional musical forms during the late 1950s was epitomized by the success of the historic Newport, Rhode Island, Folk Festivals. In addition to performing at Newport in 1959, Wiseman would become a frequent, and popular performer at many of the major festivals spawned by the Newport festival throughout the following decades. Among his many appearances was one at the groundbreaking Roanoke Bluegrass Festival organized by promoter Carleton Haney in Finecastle, Virginia, in 1965, and now considered to be the first large-scale all-bluegrass festival. During the 1970s, as interest in acoustic and folk music rose once again, Mac gained a large following among college students who were captivated by his pleasing vocals and his skillful renditions of traditional songs. In 1973 Wiseman was honored as the only U.S. bluegrass artist invited to perform at England's Wembley Music Festival.

Wiseman has remained a prolific recording artist throughout his career, cutting records for labels that have included Vetco, MGM, CMH, and RCA Victor, which he signed to in 1969. He experienced a resurgence of popularity among veteran bluegrass audiences when he teamed up with Flatt for some earthy bluegrass albums for RCA during the early 1970s, and also built a large following in Great Britain with regular tours and record releases following his appearance at Wembley.

One of the few bluegrass singers who hasn't maintained a regular band, Wiseman frequently teamed up with the popular Osborne Brothers in live performances during the 1980s and 1990s--his *Essential Bluegrass Album,*

recorded with Sonny and Donny Osborne in 1979, is considered a gold mine of traditional bluegrass, much of which the trio would later perform in concert. Wiseman's rich, clear tenor can also be heard in several collaboration albums, such as banjoist Larry Perkins' *A Touch of the Past* (1993), which features Wiseman alongside such bluegrass notables as Scruggs, Alison Krauss, John Hartford, and award-winning bandleader Del McCoury.

In addition to the continued loyalty of his countless fans, Wiseman's pioneering contributions to bluegrass music have been officially acknowledged. In 1994 he was inducted into the International Bluegrass Music Association's Bluegrass Hall of Honor in Owensboro, Kentucky. Apart from the bluegrass festivals where he continues to perform, Wiseman has remained active behind the scenes in the bluegrass music industry. He has most recently recorded for independent labels Churchill Records and the Los Angeles-based CMH, all the while maintaining his traditional bluegrass style.

Selected discography

Mac Wiseman, Dot, 1958.
Twelve Great Hits, 1960.
Keep on the Sunny Side, Dot, 1960.
Fireball Mail, Dot, 1962.
Bluegrass Favorites, Capitol, 1962.
This is Mac Wiseman, Dot, 1966.
Master at Work, Dot, 1966.
Songs of the Dear Old Days, Hamilton, 1966.
Johnny's Cash and Charlie's Pride, RCA, 1970.
Concert Favorites, RCA, c. 1971.
(With Lester Flatt) *Lester 'n' Mac*, RCA, 1971.
The Mac Wiseman Story, CMH, 1976 (1991).
(With the Osborne Brothers) *The Essential Bluegrass Album*, CMH, 1979.
Twenty-four Greatest Hits, Deluxe, 1987.
Classic Bluegrass, Rebel, 1989.
Grassroots to Bluegrass: A Very Special Collection, CMH, 1990.
Early Dot Recordings (three volumes), County, 1990-92.
Teenage Hangout, Bear Family, 1993.
(With others) *A Touch of the Past*, Pinecastle, 1993.
(With Shenandoah Cut-ups) *New Traditions* (two volumes), Vetco, reissued as *Bluegrass Classics*, Rebel.
Golden Classics, Gusto.
Shenandoah Valley Memories, Canaan.
Country Music Memories, CMH.
Songs that Made the Jukebox Play, CMH.
Greatest Bluegrass Hits, CMH.
Sings Gordon Lightfoot, CMH.

Sources

Books

Smith, Richard, D., *Bluegrass: An Informal Guide,* A Cappella Books (Chicago), 1995.

Comprehensive Country Music Encyclopedia, Times Books (New York), 1994.

Encyclopedia of Folk and Country & Western Music, edited by Irwin Stamblen and GrelunLandon, St. Martin's Press, 1983.

Rosenberg, Neil V., *Bluegrass: A History,* University of Illinois Press (Chicago), 1985.

Periodicals

Bluegrass Unlimited, July 1975.

Muleskinner News, July 1972, pp. 2-8.

Music City News, October 1973, p. 30.

—Pamela Shelton

Jimmy Witherspoon

Singer

One of the last of the great post-war blues shouters, Jimmy Witherspoon, or 'Spoon, as he's known throughout the jazz and blues world, performs with no signs of slowing down. Sidelined at times by illness and tough times, the soulful singer who helped introduce gospel inflections to jazz and blues rhythms has persevered. His 1996 album, *Live at the Mint,* was nominated for a Grammy and he continues to perform for old fans as well as legions of newer fans curious to hear one of the original voices of blues influenced jazz. More than any other male singer, Witherspoon straddled the line between blues and jazz, becoming an integral participant in the history of both of these classic genres of American music.

Born August 8, 1923, in Gurdon, Arkansas, the young James Witherspoon sang in church choirs much like his railroad worker father. Confidence came early as he won first prize in a singing competition at the age of five. While in his midteens, Witherspoon decided to try his luck pursuing a singing career and ran away to Los Angeles. It was there that he decided to become a blues singer after seeing a performance by Big Joe Turner. "I like Jimmy Rushing, but Joe Turner was my idol," he told Arnold Shaw, author of *Honkers and Shouters,* "I knew him from `Wee Baby Blues'.... He's a blues singer. Before that, I didn't dig the blues because I'd been told it was a dirty word. You couldn't sing in church and sing the blues."

Discovered by Jay McShann

Bouncing around from job to job and not having much success as a singer, Witherspoon joined the merchant marines in 1941. As a cook and a steward, Witherspoon didn't pursue singing until one night while on leave in Calcutta, India. There he found Chicago pianist Teddy Weatherford performing with a big band and decided to sit in. "They were playing Benny Goodman's `Why Don't You Do Right?,'" he told Shaw, "so I walked up and sang with them." Witherspoon's performance was so well received, his confidence was instantly boosted; he knew he could make it as a singer.

By the time his stint in the merchant marines ended, Witherspoon's mother had moved to San Francisco where he joined her in 1944. With a day job as a boiler in a steel mill, Witherspoon would sing on weekends at a club called The Waterfront in nearby Vallejo, California. While singing at the club one night, Witherspoon got his big break when he was heard by bandleader Jay McShann. McShann led one of the finest blues bands of the era, rivaling that of the great Count Basie, and had been a starting point for the young Charlie Parker before

AP/Wide World Photos. Reproduced by permission.

For the Record . . .

Born August 8, 1923, in Gurdon, AR; served in the merchant marines, 1941-44.

Began singing in Vallejo, CA nightclub, 1944; joined bandleader Jay McShann's band, 1944; left McShann's band and started solo career, 1948—; recorded hit song, "Ain't Nobody's Business," 1949; performed at 1959 Monterey Jazz Festival; appeared in film, *The Black Godfather*, 1974; returned to charts with "Love is a Five Letter Word," 1974; diagnosed with and treated for throat cancer, late 1970s; recorded and toured with Van Morrison, 1994; album *Live at the Mint*, on Private Music label.

Addresses: *Record company*—Private Music, 9014 Melrose Ave., Los Angeles, CA 90069.

the alto saxophonist went to New York to help usher in the language of bebop. McShann and his original singer, Walter Brown, who together wrote their hits "Confessin' the Blues" and "Hootie's Blues," had a falling out leading McShann to recruit Witherspoon. At least on one tune, Witherspoon was persuaded to imitate Brown's style. "Jay McShann told me," Witherspoon recalled to Shaw, "'Spoon, they know me by 'Confessin the Blues,' so sing it with Brown's sound, but the rest, you go your own way.'"

Ain't Nobody's Business

Witherspoon eventually did go his own way with, leaving McShann's band after a few years to record as a soloist for the Supreme label. In 1949, after a few recordings that went nowhere, 'Spoon recorded a version of "Ain't Nobody's Business," a song originally recorded by blues singer Bessie Smith in 1922. 'Spoon's version, which would become his signature song and featured McShann and others from the old band, went to number one on the R&B charts and stayed on the charts for 34 months, longer than any previous R&B tune. Witherspoon's next release, "In the Evening When the Sun Goes Down," reached the number five spot. Following this, 'Spoon released a number of albums on a variety of labels including Modern, Federal, and the legendary Chess label. Unlike his idol, the blues shouter Big Joe Turner, Witherspoon had difficulty making the transition to rock n' roll, which by then was sweeping the country. Turner, whose hits included "Shake, Rattle, and Roll," "Honey Hush," and "Flip, Flop and Fly," was considered

a sort of father figure in the burgeoning rock n' roll scene, where Witherspoon's rich, smooth vocals were more suited to jazz.

Virtually ignored by jazz and rock audiences and with financial hardships stalling large, swinging blues bands like McShann's, the rest of the 1950s found Witherspoon playing the chitlin circuit, a network of small black-owned clubs that played to mostly black audiences. For a while he played bass and sang at a club in Newport, Kentucky in a small band that also featured famed blues pianist Charles Brown. In 1959, however, 'Spoon was invited to appear at the Monterey Jazz Festival with an all-star group that included tenor saxophonist Ben Webster, trumpeter Roy Eldridge, alto saxophonist Coleman Hawkins, clarinetist Woody Herman, trombonist Urbie Green, and pianist Earl "Fatha" Hines. The electrifying performance, recorded and released as Jimmy Witherspoon at Monterey, propelled Witherspoon into the limelight as one of the leading singers of blues-laced jazz and put his career back on track. 'Spoon landed a recording contract with Atlantic, began to sing for larger crowds, and was featured in Jon Hendricks's historic program, "Evolution of the Blues," at the 1960 Monterey Jazz Festival.

Like most jazz and blues performers, Witherspoon was especially successful in Europe and toured and recorded there many times since the early 1960s. Although he continued to record and tour, success on the record charts proved elusive for Witherspoon. In the 1970s, while hosting a late night radio blues program in Los Angeles and appearing in the film *The Black Godfather*, Witherspoon had his first chart success since 1960 with the song, "Love is a Five Letter Word" on Capitol Records. The song hit number 31 on the R&B charts but did little in raising the status of Witherspoon's career. He continued, however, to record and perform for enthusiastic, albeit smaller, audiences.

Cancer Scare

In the late 1970s, Witherspoon was diagnosed with throat cancer and faced the possibility of never being able to sing again. For a while he couldn't even swallow. A throat operation and radiation treatment in England kept Witherspoon out of recording studios and clubs for a few years and took its toll on the veteran singer's dynamic style. "I had to learn to sing all over again," he confessed to Joel Silver in a Private Music promotional biography. After getting his singing back to where it was, Witherspoon noticed he could now reach a lower vocal register that before his operation was unattainable.

The mid-1990s found Witherspoon at his most active, including touring with singer Van Morrison, in support of

Morrison's *A Night in San Francisco* album, on which Witherspoon appeared, as well as his own headlining gigs to promote reissues of earlier Witherspoon albums and recent releases. One such album, a live album with guitarist Robben Ford, entitled *Live at the Mint,* was the most welcome. A return to his roots but with a more upbeat feel, courtesy of Ford and his band, Witherspoon shouts through lively renditions of songs, some of which he'd been singing for more than 40 years. "'Spoon's swinging Jazz sensibilities are front and center on songs like Basie's 'Goin' to Chicago" and his signature tune, 'Ain't Nobody's Business,'" wrote *DownBeat* reviewer Michael Point, "but he's lost none of his ability to drop down into a convincing blues mood, as amply demonstrated by his powerful renditions of 'Goin' Down Slow' and an assortment of Big Bill Broonzy classics."

Live at the Mint went on to be nominated for a Grammy Award for Best Traditional Blues recording only to lose out to harmonica player Junior Wells. Still, the warm reception to the album and Grammy nomination did much to introduce—or reintroduce—Witherspoon to a group of fans.

Selected discography

(With Jay McShann) Goin *to Kansas City Blues,* RCA, 1958.
'Spoon Concerts, Fantasy, 1959.
Evening*' Blues,* Original Blues Classics, 1963.
Baby, Baby, Baby, Original Blues Classics, 1963.
Spoon's Life, Evidence, 1980.
(Wth Big Joe Turner) *Patcha, Patcha All Night Long,* Original Jazz Classics, 1985.
(Wth Panama Francis) *Savoy Sultans,* Black and Blue, 1980.
Rockin' L.A., Fantasy, 1989.
Blowin' in from Kansas City, Flair, 1991.
Blues, the Whole Blues, and Nothin' but the Blues, Indigo, 1992.

(With Jay McShann) *Jimmy Witherspoon/Jay McShann,* Black Lion, 1992.
Spoonful, Avenue Jazz, 1994.
(With Van Morrison) *A Night in San Francisco,* Polydor, 1994.
Spoon's Blues, Stony Plain, 1995.
(With Howard Scott) *American Blues,* Avenue Jazz, 1995.
(With Groove Holmes) *Spoon and Groove,* Tradition/Rykodisc, 1996.
Live at the Mint, Private Music, 1996.
Spoon So Easy: The Chess Recordings, Chess.

Sources

Books

Carr, Ian, et al., *Jazz: The Rough Guide,* Rough Guides Ltd., 1995.
Crowther, Bruce and Mike Pinfold, *The Jazz Singers: From Ragtime to the New Wave,* Blandford Press, 1986.
Herzhaft, Gerard, *Encyclopedia of the Blues,* University of Arkansas Press, 1992.
Santelli, Robert, *The Big Book of Blues,* Penguin Books, 1993.
Shaw, Arnold, *Honkers and Shouters: The Golden Years of Rhythm & Blues,* Collier Books, 1978.
Sonnier, Austin, Jr., *A Guide to the Blues,* Greenwood Press, 1994.

Periodicals

DownBeat, May 1996, p. 57.
Living Blues, July/August 1994, p. 102; July/August 1995, p. 97; May/June 1996, p.91.

Additional information for this profile was obtained from the liner notes of *The Mercury Blues 'N' Rhythm Story, 1945-1955,* Mercury, 1996, by Dick Shurman; and the Jimmy Witherspoon page of the Private Music label's website.

—*Brian Escamilla*

Wu-Tang Clan

Hip-hop artists

Photo by Ruth Fremson. AP/Wide World Photos. Reproduced by permission.

The Wu-Tang Clan are a large group of lyricists who have assembled an intriguing microcosm of their own culture, both in music and in business. Their aliases are a menacing bunch of terms such as Ghost Face Killer and Inspectah Deck, and their lyrics aren't pretty. However, like a great deal of hip-hop artists, the Clan demonstrates an authentic portrayal of urban grist. The band also has very unusual and progressive business arrangements which have been the focus of much attention and commentary within the record industry.

In *Melody Maker,* writer Simon Grice said "when he hears the Wu-Tang Clan he hears New York"—not the pretty tourist friendly version of NY but the gritty, subway screech sort of variety. He described "crack pipes, garbage blown alleys, and cockroaches." Appropriately, the members responded, "It's our sound." The bands symbiotic relationship with its hometown began many years ago in the streets of the notoriously tough city.

All Wu-Tang members were born in either the outer boroughs of Staten Island or Brooklyn, and have known each other in various incarnations since childhood. "The crew goes back to when we were nine, ten years old. That's when we started experimenting with rapping," RZA explained to *Billboard* Magazine, "Back then, we called what we were doing MCing though." The Clan's roots run deep. RZA and Raekwon were elementary school companions. 'Ol Dirty Bastard, The Genius and Raekwon are cousins.

Committing petty crimes and rehearsing in the basement, the boys developed the Clan hypothetically when they were barely teenagers. Instead of buying clothes and more youthfully cherished items, RZA brought DJ equipment and is said to have stolen his clothes. In 1991, RZA, Genius, and The 'Ol Dirty Bastard finally put their talents together to form the Wu-Tang Clan.

Both the group's concept and name were derived from basic martial arts principles. Wu-Tang means "sword family" and is considered one of the deadliest styles of the martial arts. RZA who besides being a lyricist is the group's producer, claimed he chose the name after reading in the Bible that Jesus said, "the tongue is like a double edged sword." RZA thought the group had the best lyrical techniques around, that they were unchallenged in that area; therefore he applied the concept to the band's name.

The band's particular musical style interjects snippets of mafia movie dialogue over lyrics detailing the brutal reality of ghetto life. Their realistic urban rhythms have brought much attention to their music and have in turn generated a large fan base.

When the band first began making demos, they were unable to obtain what they deemed an acceptable record contract. Record labels had offered them extremely small advances—as low as $200,000 for all eight members. Instead, the Clan members pooled their money together. Each member contributed $100 apiece in order to release "Protect Your Neck," their first single in 1991, on the Wu-Tang label. Following the single's release, the group set out on its own promotional tour selling copies of "Protect Your Neck" out of the trunk of their car all the way from Virginia to Ohio. It quickly hit a spot with college radio stations, clubs, and in the ever burgeoning hip-hop scene of New York. Many labels initially uninterested in the Clan were now attempting to coerce the band to sign with their respective companies. Instead, the Clan chose to go with Loud Records—a then-small, unproven rap label. Loud picked up on the buzz generated by these rhyming beat-masters and subsequently inked a contract with the group in 1993.

The Thirty-Six Chambers

The Wu-Tang Clan released their first album *Enter the Wu-tang Clan (Thirty Six Chambers)* in November 1993. The title refers to two special martial arts concepts. One explanation: there are 36 points on the body and 10 degrees between each point—an equation adding up to a perfectly balanced 360 degrees. RZA explained the second meaning of thirty-six chambers to *Billboard* Magazine. "During ancient times, for one, young monks went to Shao Lin to study the Wu-Tang Style. It was all done in secret and students became masters only by advancing through all 35 chambers in the process. One day one of the Monks decided to take the technique to the whole world. The world became the thirty sixth chamber, which would complete a circle. That's what happened with Wu-Tang Clan. We were doing what we were doing on Staten Island for years and years. Nobody outside of here knew there was rap talent we took it to a whole new level. We christened Staten Island Shao-lin."

The band's next full-length single maintained a spot on *Billboard*'s rap singles chart for over 25 weeks. Subsequently "Cash Rules Everything Around Me," otherwise known as "C.R.E.A.M," managed to touch a raw nerve with its provocative lyrics. The song questions that drug money may be the only way out for young urban blacks. It also illustrates the reality of crack addicts and the sort of urban reality which most people want to avoid. The single placed number three on the rap singles chart, number one on the maxi singles sales charts and a top 60 on the pop singles chart. "`C.R.E.A.M.' really says what we went through to get this money. And cash really does rule everything around me but it doesn't rule me. That's how come we got it," explained Wu-Tang Master mind RZA to the *New York Times.* "It's good because we came from the bottom of the bottomless pit."

The Wu-Tang Clan's most surprising feature may very well be their savvy business tactics which have proven quite unique and successful within the music industry. Instead of shopping around for a large record label to sign them after the success of single "Protect Your Neck," the Clan opted to sign with a smaller label. RZA said he learned one of his most crucial business lessons selling marijuana on the streets of New York: "You can sell weed and make a little money but most of it gets made for the guy your selling it for . It's the same thing in the music business except it's legal." The group settled with Loud Records because it offered them a unique record deal. The group agreed to receive a minimal advance while retaining full creative control. It also stipulated that each group member would be able to individually sign separate recording deals. RZA strangely encouraged each of the members to seek solo deals with labels not normally known for their hip-hop prowess.

The band felt strongly that producing solo albums with various labels wouldn't initiate competitiveness among the group but would actually strengthen its position in the marketplace. He was right. Genius signed with Geffen who no longer even had a black music department. Raekwon signed with the Wu-Tang's RCA label also not known for hip-hop savvy, and 'Ol Dirty Bastard secured a contract with Elektra Records. Producer RZA shocked the industry as his prediction proved correct. Each of the member's solo albums went on to sell at least 500,000 copies apiece.

Wu-Wearables

The Wu-Tang Clan has made an impact on the fashion world. In 1995, the ever-enterprising Clan decided to start their own clothing label, Wu-Wear. In describing the clothes to the *Miami Herald*, one teenaged fan said, "I like their style, it's unusual. It's sort of like ruggish, smooth, hard-core." The line boasts oversized hockey jerseys with large symbolic W's, jackets, and t-shirts. All the merchandise can be ordered directly from Wu-Wear's main store in the Clan's homebase of Staten Island. Some of the Clan's stylish marketing gimmicks include gold Vampire fangs as worn by Ol' Dirty Bastard and Method Man and a glass eye also worn by Method Man. The Group has opened other stores in Atlanta and hopes to expand to Virginia and Los Angeles. *Rolling Stone* has criticized the Clan's merchandising through song lyrics to impressionable young kids. Writer S. H. Fernando explained that, "over a gargantuan drum beat and simple melody, the hero becomes highly civilized going through a garment renaissance where he swears off Benetton, Tommy Hilfiger, Liz Claiborne and RZA goes on to describe how the protagonist only buys from black owned companies such as Karl Kani, Cross Colours and Shabazz Naturally." In response to the criticism of the lyrics in the song "Wu-Wear, The Garment Renaissance" (available on the *High School High* soundtrack), RZA responded, "I wanted to do a song that was directed toward the youth. We know what we want to wear".

Even though the Wu-Tang Clan hasn't conjointly recorded an album since their debut in 1993, the band has not splintered and instead has thrived on their family-like existence. As RZA explained to the *New York Times*: "The point is when Wu-tang came together, we vowed brotherhood to each other. When you stick together you can't lose."

Selected discography

Albums

Enter the Wu-Tang Clan (36 Chambers), Loud Records, 1993.
(With others) Batman Forever (soundtrack), Atlantic, 1995.

Sources

Periodicals

Billboard, November 25, 1995, p. 38.
Forty Ounces and a Blunt Magazine, vol. 1, no.3, p. 6.
Four-Thousand Eighty Magazine, November 1995, p. 58.
Melody Maker, August 12, 1995, p.10.
Miami Herald (International Edition) October 8, 1995.
New York Times, December 8, 1996, p. 34.
Spin, January 1995, p. 6.
Source, October 1995, p. 57.

Additional information obtained from publicity materials provided by Loud Records.

—*Nicole Elyse*

Cumulative Indexes

Cumulative Subject Index

Volume numbers appear in **bold**.

A cappella
Bulgarian State Female Vocal Choir, The **10**
Nylons, The **6**
Take 6 **6**
Zap Mama **14**

Accordion
Buckwheat Zydeco **6**
Chenier, C. J. **15**
Chenier, Clifton **6**
Queen Ida **9**
Richard, Zachary **9**
Rockin' Dopsie **10**
Simien, Terrance **12**
Sonnier, Jo-El **10**
Yankovic, "Weird Al" **7**

Ambient/Rave/Techno
Aphex Twin **14**
Deep Forest **18**
KMFDM **18**
Kraftwerk **9**
Orb, The **18**
2 Unlimited **18**
Shadow, DJ **19**

Bandoneon
Piazzolla, Astor **18**

Banjo
Bromberg, David **18**
Clark, Roy **1**
Crowe, J.D. **5**
Eldridge, Ben
  See Seldom Scene, The
Fleck, Bela **8**
  Also see New Grass Revival, The
Hartford, John **1**
Johnson, Courtney
  See New Grass Revival, The
McCoury, Del **15**
Piazzolla, Astor **18**
Scruggs, Earl **3**
Seeger, Pete **4**
  Also see Weavers, The
Skaggs, Ricky **5**
Stanley, Ralph **5**
Watson, Doc **2**

Bass
Bruce, Jack
  See Cream
Carter, Ron **14**

Chambers, Paul **18**
Clarke, Stanley **3**
Collins, Bootsy **8**
Dixon, Willie **10**
Entwistle, John
  See Who, The
Fender, Leo **10**
Haden, Charlie **12**
Hill, Dusty
  See ZZ Top
Hillman, Chris
  See Byrds, The
  Also see Desert Rose Band, The
Johnston, Bruce
  See Beach Boys, The
Jones, John Paul
  See Led Zeppelin
Lake, Greg
  See Emerson, Lake & Palmer/Powell
Laswell, Bill **14**
McCartney, Paul **4**
  Also see Beatles, The
McBride, Christian **17**
McVie, John
  See Fleetwood Mac
Meisner, Randy
  See Eagles, The
Mingus, Charles **9**
Ndegéocello, Me'Shell **18**
Porter, Tiran
  See Doobie Brothers, The
Rutherford, Mike
  See Genesis
Schmit, Timothy B.
  See Eagles, The
Shakespeare, Robbie
  See Sly and Robbie
Simmons, Gene
  See Kiss
Sting **2**
Sweet, Matthew **9**
Vicious, Sid
  See Sex Pistols, The
  Also see Siouxsie and the Banshees
Waters, Roger
  See Pink Floyd
Weymouth, Tina
  See Talking Heads
Wyman, Bill
  See Rolling Stones, The

Big Band/Swing
Andrews Sisters, The **9**
Arnaz, Desi **8**
Bailey, Pearl **5**

Basie, Count **2**
Beiderbecke, Bix **16**
Bennett, Tony **16**
  Earlier sketch in CM **2**
Berrigan, Bunny **2**
Blakey, Art **11**
Calloway, Cab **6**
Carter, Benny **3**
Chenille Sisters, The **16**
Clooney, Rosemary **9**
Como, Perry **14**
Dorsey, Jimmy
  See Dorsey Brothers, The
Dorsey, Tommy
  See Dorsey Brothers, The
Dorsey Brothers, The **8**
Eckstine, Billy **1**
Eldridge, Roy **9**
Ellington, Duke **2**
Ferguson, Maynard **7**
Fitzgerald, Ella **1**
Fountain, Pete **7**
Getz, Stan **12**
Gillespie, Dizzy **6**
Goodman, Benny **4**
Henderson, Fletcher **16**
Herman, Woody **12**
Hines, Earl "Fatha" **12**
Jacquet, Illinois **17**
James, Harry **11**
Jones, Spike **5**
Jordan, Louis **11**
Krupa, Gene **13**
Lee, Peggy **8**
McKinney's Cotton Pickers **16**
Miller, Glenn **6**
Norvo, Red **12**
Parker, Charlie **5**
Prima, Louis **18**
Puente, Tito **14**
Rich, Buddy **13**
Rodney, Red **14**
Roomful of Blues **7**
Scott, Jimmy **14**
Severinsen, Doc **1**
Shaw, Artie **8**
Sinatra, Frank **1**
Strayhorn, Billy **13**
Teagarden, Jack **10**
Torme, Mel **4**
Vaughan, Sarah **2**
Welk, Lawrence **13**
Whiteman, Paul **17**

Bluegrass
Auldridge, Mike **4**

Clements, Vassar **18**
Country Gentlemen, The **7**
Crowe, J.D. **5**
Flatt, Lester **3**
Fleck, Bela **8**
    Also see New Grass Revival, The
Gill, Vince **7**
Grisman, David **17**
Hartford, John **1**
Krauss, Alison **10**
Louvin Brothers, The **12**
Martin, Jimmy **5**
    Also see Osborne Brothers, The
McCoury, Del **15**
McReynolds, Jim and Jesse **12**
Monroe, Bill **1**
Nashville Bluegrass Band **14**
New Grass Revival, The **4**
Northern Lights **19**
O'Connor, Mark **1**
Osborne Brothers, The **8**
Parsons, Gram **7**
    Also see Byrds, The
Reverend Horton Heat **19**
Scruggs, Earl **3**
Seldom Scene, The **4**
Skaggs, Ricky **5**
Stanley Brothers, The **17**
Stanley, Ralph **5**
Stuart, Marty **9**
Watson, Doc **2**
Wiseman, Mac **19**

Blues
Ayler , Albert **19**
Bailey, Pearl **5**
Baker, Ginger **16**
    Also see Cream
Ball, Marcia **15**
Berry, Chuck **1**
Bland, Bobby "Blue" **12**
Block, Rory **18**
Blood, Sweat and Tears **7**
Blues Brothers, The **3**
Broonzy, Big Bill **13**
Brown, Clarence "Gatemouth" **11**
Brown, Ruth **13**
Burdon, Eric **14**
    Also see War
Cale, J. J. **16**
Charles, Ray **1**
Clapton, Eric **11**
  Earlier sketch in CM **1**
    Also see Cream
    Also see Yardbirds, The
Collins, Albert **4**
Cray, Robert **8**
Davis, Reverend Gary **18**
Diddley, Bo **3**
Dixon, Willie **10**
Dr. John **7**
Dupree, Champion Jack **12**
Earl, Ronnie **5**
    Also see Roomful of Blues
Fabulous Thunderbirds, The **1**

Gatton, Danny **16**
Guy, Buddy **4**
Handy, W. C. **7**
Hawkins, Screamin' Jay **8**
Healey, Jeff **4**
Holiday, Billie **6**
Hooker, John Lee **1**
Hopkins, Lightnin' **13**
House, Son **11**
Howlin' Wolf **6**
James, Elmore **8**
James, Etta **6**
Jefferson, Blind Lemon **18**
Johnson, Lonnie **17**
Johnson, Robert **6**
Jon Spencer Blues Explosion **18**
Joplin, Janis **3**
King, Albert **2**
King, B. B. **1**
King, Freddy **17**
Leadbelly **6**
Led Zeppelin **1**
Little Feat **4**
Little Walter **14**
Lockwood, Robert, Jr. **10**
Mayall, John **7**
McClinton, Delbert **14**
McDowell, Mississippi Fred **16**
McTell, Blind Willie **17**
Muldaur, Maria **18**
Patton, Charley **11**
Plant, Robert **2**
    Also see Led Zeppelin
Professor Longhair **6**
Raitt, Bonnie **3**
Redding, Otis **5**
Reed, Jimmy **15**
Rich, Charlie **3**
Robertson, Robbie **2**
Robillard, Duke **2**
Roomful of Blues **7**
Rush, Otis **12**
Shaffer, Paul **13**
Shines, Johnny **14**
Smith, Bessie **3**
Snow, Phoebe **4**
Spann, Otis **18**
Sunnyland Slim **16**
Taj Mahal **6**
Taylor, Koko **10**
Thornton, Big Mama **18**
Toure, Ali Farka **18**
Turner, Big Joe **13**
Ulmer, James Blood **13**
Van Zandt, Townes **13**
Vaughan, Stevie Ray **1**
Waits, Tom **1**
Walker, T-Bone **5**
Wallace, Sippie **6**
Washington, Dinah **5**
Waters, Ethel **11**
Waters, Muddy **4**
Wells, Junior **17**
Weston, Randy **15**
Whitfield, Mark **18**

Whitley, Chris **16**
Williams, Joe **11**
Williamson, Sonny Boy **9**
Wilson, Gerald **19**
Winter, Johnny **5**
Witherspoon, Jimmy **19**
ZZ Top **2**

Cajun/Zydeco
Ball, Marcia **15**
Brown, Clarence "Gatemouth" **11**
Buckwheat Zydeco **6**
Chenier, C. J. **15**
Chenier, Clifton **6**
Doucet, Michael **8**
Landreth, Sonny **16**
Queen Ida **9**
Richard, Zachary **9**
Rockin' Dopsie **10**
Simien, Terrance **12**
Sonnier, Jo-El **10**

Cello
Casals, Pablo **9**
Gray, Walter
    See Kronos Quartet
Harrell, Lynn **3**
Jeanrenaud, Joan Dutcher
    See Kronos Quartet
Ma, Yo-Yo **2**
Rostropovich, Mstislav **17**

Children's Music
Bartels, Joanie **13**
Cappelli, Frank **14**
Chapin, Tom **11**
Chenille Sisters, The **16**
Harley, Bill **7**
Lehrer, Tom **7**
Nagler, Eric **8**
Penner, Fred **10**
Raffi **8**
Rosenshontz **9**
Sharon, Lois & Bram **6**

Christian Music
Ashton, Susan **17**
Chapman, Steven Curtis **15**
dc Talk **18**
Grant, Amy **7**
Duncan, Bryan **19**
Eskelin, Ian **19**
King's X **7**
Paris, Twila **16**
Patti, Sandi **7**
Petra **3**
Smith, Michael W. **11**
Stryper **2**
Waters, Ethel **11**

Clarinet
Adams, John **8**
Bechet, Sidney **17**
Braxton, Anthony **12**
Dorsey, Jimmy
    See Dorsey Brothers, The

Fountain, Pete **7**
Goodman, Benny **4**
Herman, Woody **12**
Shaw, Artie **8**

Classical
Anderson, Marian **8**
Arrau, Claudio **1**
Baker, Janet **14**
Bernstein, Leonard **2**
Boyd, Liona **7**
Bream, Julian **9**
Britten, Benjamin **15**
Bronfman, Yefim **6**
Canadian Brass, The **4**
Carter, Ron **14**
Casals, Pablo **9**
Chang, Sarah **7**
Clayderman, Richard **1**
Cliburn, Van **13**
Copland, Aaron **2**
Davis, Anthony **17**
Davis, Chip **4**
Fiedler, Arthur **6**
Galway, James **3**
Gingold, Josef **6**
Gould, Glenn **9**
Gould, Morton **16**
Hampson, Thomas **12**
Harrell, Lynn **3**
Hayes, Roland **13**
Hendricks, Barbara **10**
Herrmann, Bernard **14**
Hinderas, Natalie **12**
Horne, Marilyn **9**
Horowitz, Vladimir **1**
Jarrett, Keith **1**
Kennedy, Nigel **8**
Kissin, Evgeny **6**
Kronos Quartet **5**
Kunzel, Erich **17**
Lemper, Ute **14**
Levine, James **8**
Liberace **9**
Ma, Yo-Yo **2**
Marsalis, Wynton **6**
Masur, Kurt **11**
McNair, Sylvia **15**
McPartland, Marian **15**
Mehta, Zubin **11**
Menuhin, Yehudi **11**
Midori **7**
Nyman, Michael **15**
Ott, David **2**
Parkening, Christopher **7**
Perahia, Murray **10**
Perlman, Itzhak **2**
Phillips, Harvey **3**
Rampal, Jean-Pierre **6**
Rostropovich, Mstislav **17**
Rota, Nino **13**
Rubinstein, Arthur **11**
Salerno-Sonnenberg, Nadja **3**
Salonen, Esa-Pekka **16**
Schickele, Peter **5**

Schuman, William **10**
Segovia, Andres **6**
Shankar, Ravi **9**
Solti, Georg **13**
Stern, Isaac **7**
Sutherland, Joan **13**
Takemitsu, Toru **6**
Toscanini, Arturo **14**
Upshaw, Dawn **9**
von Karajan, Herbert **1**
Weill, Kurt **12**
Wilson, Ransom **5**
Yamashita, Kazuhito **4**
York, Andrew **15**
Zukerman, Pinchas **4**

Composers
Adams, John **8**
Allen, Geri **10**
Alpert, Herb **11**
Anka, Paul **2**
Atkins, Chet **5**
Bacharach, Burt **1**
Badalamenti, Angelo **17**
Beiderbecke, Bix **16**
Benson, George **9**
Berlin, Irving **8**
Bernstein, Leonard **2**
Blackman, Cindy **15**
Bley, Carla **8**
Bley, Paul **14**
Braxton, Anthony **12**
Britten, Benjamin **15**
Brubeck, Dave **8**
Burrell, Kenny **11**
Byrne, David **8**
    Also see Talking Heads
Cage, John **8**
Cale, John **9**
Casals, Pablo **9**
Clarke, Stanley **3**
Coleman, Ornette **5**
Cooder, Ry **2**
Cooney, Rory **6**
Copeland, Stewart **14**
Copland, Aaron **2**
Crouch, Andraé **9**
Curtis, King **17**
Davis, Anthony **17**
Davis, Chip **4**
Davis, Miles **1**
de Grassi, Alex **6**
Dorsey, Thomas A. **11**
Elfman, Danny **9**
Ellington, Duke **2**
Eno, Brian **8**
Enya **6**
Esquivel, Juan **17**
Evans, Bill **17**
Evans, Gil **17**
Fahey, John **17**
Foster, David **13**
Frisell, Bill **15**
Frith, Fred **19**
Galás, Diamanda **16**

Gillespie, Dizzy **6**
Glass, Philip **1**
Gould, Glenn **9**
Gould, Morton **16**
Green, Benny **17**
Grusin, Dave **7**
Guaraldi, Vince **3**
Hamlisch, Marvin **1**
Hancock, Herbie **8**
Handy, W. C. **7**
Hargrove, Roy **15**
Harris, Eddie **15**
Hartke, Stephen **5**
Henderson, Fletcher **16**
Herrmann, Bernard **14**
Hunter, Alberta **7**
Isham, Mark **14**
Jacquet, Illinois **17**
Jarre, Jean-Michel **2**
Jarrett, Keith **1**
Johnson, James P. **16**
Jones, Hank **15**
Jones, Quincy **2**
Joplin, Scott **10**
Jordan, Stanley **1**
Kenny G **14**
Kern, Jerome **13**
Kitaro **1**
Kottke, Leo **13**
Lateef, Yusef **16**
Lee, Peggy **8**
Legg, Adrian **17**
Lewis, Ramsey **14**
Lincoln, Abbey **9**
Lloyd Webber, Andrew **6**
Loesser, Frank **19**
Loewe, Frederick
    See Lerner and Loewe
Mancini, Henry **1**
Marsalis, Branford **10**
Marsalis, Ellis **13**
Martino, Pat **17**
Masekela, Hugh **7**
McBride, Christian **17**
McPartland, Marian **15**
Menken, Alan **10**
Metheny, Pat **2**
Mingus, Charles **9**
Moby **17**
Monk, Meredith **1**
Monk, Thelonious **6**
Montenegro, Hugo **18**
Morricone, Ennio **15**
Morton, Jelly Roll **7**
Mulligan, Gerry **16**
Nascimento, Milton **6**
Newman, Randy **4**
Nyman, Michael **15**
Oldfield, Mike **18**
Ott, David **2**
Palmieri, Eddie **15**
Parker, Charlie **5**
Parks, Van Dyke **17**
Peterson, Oscar **11**
Piazzolla, Astor **18**

Ponty, Jean-Luc **8**
Porter, Cole **10**
Previn, André **15**
Puente, Tito **14**
Pullen, Don **16**
Reich, Steve **8**
Reinhardt, Django **7**
Ritenour, Lee **7**
Roach, Max **12**
Rollins, Sonny **7**
Rota, Nino **13**
Sakamoto, Ryuichi **19**
Sakamoto, Ryuichi **18**
Salonen, Esa-Pekka **16**
Sanders, Pharoah **16**
Satriani, Joe **4**
Schickele, Peter **5**
Schuman, William **10**
Shankar, Ravi **9**
Shaw, Artie **8**
Shorter, Wayne **5**
Silver, Horace **19**
Solal, Martial **4**
Sondheim, Stephen **8**
Sousa, John Philip **10**
Story, Liz **2**
Strayhorn, Billy **13**
Summers, Andy **3**
Sun Ra **5**
Takemitsu, Toru **6**
Talbot, John Michael **6**
Tatum, Art **17**
Taylor, Billy **13**
Taylor, Cecil **9**
Thielemans, Toots **13**
Threadgill, Henry **9**
Tyner, McCoy **7**
Washington, Grover, Jr. **5**
Weill, Kurt **12**
Weston, Randy **15**
Whiteman, Paul **17**
Williams, John **9**
Wilson, Cassandra **12**
Winston, George
Winter, Paul **10**
Worrell, Bernie **11**
Yanni **11**
York, Andrew **15**
Young, La Monte **16**
Zimmerman, Udo **5**
Zorn, John **15**
Zappa, Frank **17**
 Earlier sketch in CM **1**

Conductors
Bacharach, Burt **1**
Bernstein, Leonard **2**
Britten, Benjamin **15**
Casals, Pablo **9**
Copland, Aaron **2**
Domingo, Placido **1**
Evans, Gil **17**
Fiedler, Arthur **6**
Gould, Morton **16**
Herrmann, Bernard **14**

Jarrett, Keith **1**
Jones, Hank **15**
Kunzel, Erich **17**
Levine, James **8**
Mancini, Henry **1**
Marriner, Neville **7**
Masur, Kurt **11**
Mehta, Zubin **11**
Menuhin, Yehudi **11**
Nero, Peter **19**
Previn, André **15**
Rampal, Jean-Pierre **6**
Rostropovich, Mstislav **17**
Salonen, Esa-Pekka **16**
Schickele, Peter **5**
Solti, Georg **13**
Toscanini, Arturo **14**
von Karajan, Herbert **1**
Welk, Lawrence **13**
Williams, John **9**
Zukerman, Pinchas **4**

Contemporary Dance Music
Abdul, Paula **3**
Aphex Twin **14**
Bee Gees, The **3**
B-52's, The **4**
Brown, Bobby **4**
Brown, James **2**
C + C Music Factory **16**
Cherry, Neneh **4**
Clinton, George **7**
Craig, Carl **19**
Deee-lite **9**
De La Soul **7**
Depeche Mode **5**
Earth, Wind and Fire **12**
English Beat, The **9**
En Vogue **10**
Erasure **11**
Eurythmics **6**
Exposé **4**
Fox, Samantha **3**
Gang of Four **8**
Hammer, M.C. **5**
Harry, Deborah **4**
 Also see Blondie
Ice-T **7**
Idol, Billy **3**
Jackson, Janet **16**
 Earlier sketch in CM **3**
Jackson, Michael **17**
 Earlier sketch in CM **1**
 Also see Jacksons, The
James, Rick **2**
Jones, Grace **9**
Madonna **16**
 Earlier sketch in CM **4**
Massive Attack **17**
Moby **17**
M People **15**
New Order **11**
Peniston, CeCe **15**
Pet Shop Boys **5**
Pizzicato Five **18**

Prince **14**
 Earlier sketch in CM **1**
Queen Latifah **6**
Rodgers, Nile **8**
Salt-N-Pepa **6**
Shadow, DJ **19**
Simmons, Russell **7**
Soul II Soul **17**
Summer, Donna **12**
Technotronic **5**
TLC **15**
Tricky **18**
2 Unlimited **18**
Vasquez, Junior **16**
Village People, The **7**
Was (Not Was) **6**
Waters, Crystal **15**
Young M.C. **4**

Contemporary Instrumental/New Age
Ackerman, Will **3**
Clinton, George **7**
Collins, Bootsy **8**
Davis, Chip **4**
de Grassi, Alex **6**
Enigma **14**
Enya **6**
Esquivel, Juan **17**
Hedges, Michael **3**
Isham, Mark **14**
Jarre, Jean-Michel **2**
Kitaro **1**
Kronos Quartet **5**
Legg, Adrian **17**
Story, Liz **2**
Summers, Andy **3**
Tangerine Dream **12**
Winston, George **9**
Winter, Paul **10**
Yanni **11**

Cornet
Armstrong, Louis **4**
Beiderbecke, Bix **16**
Cherry, Don **10**
Handy, W. C. **7**
Oliver, King **15**

Country
Acuff, Roy **2**
Alabama **1**
Anderson, John **5**
Arnold, Eddy **10**
Asleep at the Wheel **5**
Atkins, Chet **5**
Auldridge, Mike **4**
Autry, Gene **12**
Bellamy Brothers, The **13**
Berg, Matraca **16**
Berry, John **17**
Black, Clint **5**
Blue Rodeo **18**
Bogguss, Suzy **11**
Boone, Pat **13**
Brooks & Dunn **12**

Brooks, Garth **8**
Brown, Junior **15**
Brown, Marty **14**
Brown, Tony **14**
Buffett, Jimmy **4**
Byrds, The **8**
Cale, J. J. **16**
Campbell, Glen **2**
Carpenter, Mary-Chapin **6**
Carter, Carlene **8**
Carter Family, The **3**
Cash, Johnny **17**
  Earlier sketch in CM **1**
Cash, June Carter **6**
Cash, Rosanne **2**
Chesnutt, Mark **13**
Clark, Guy **17**
Clark, Roy **1**
Clark, Terri **19**
Clements, Vassar **18**
Cline, Patsy **5**
Coe, David Allan **4**
Collie, Mark **15**
Cooder, Ry **2**
Cowboy Junkies, The **4**
Crowe, J. D. **5**
Crowell, Rodney **8**
Cyrus, Billy Ray **11**
Daniels, Charlie **6**
Davis, Skeeter **15**
DeMent, Iris **13**
Dean, Billy **19**
Denver, John **1**
Desert Rose Band, The **4**
Diamond Rio **11**
Dickens, Little Jimmy **7**
Diffie, Joe **10**
Dylan, Bob **3**
Earle, Steve **16**
Flatt, Lester **3**
Flores, Rosie **16**
Ford, Tennessee Ernie **3**
Foster, Radney **16**
Frizzell, Lefty **10**
Gayle, Crystal **1**
Germano, Lisa **18**
Gill, Vince **7**
Gilley, Mickey **7**
Gilmore, Jimmie Dale **11**
Gordy, Jr., Emory **17**
Greenwood, Lee **12**
Griffith, Nanci **3**
Haggard, Merle **2**
Hall, Tom T. **4**
Harris, Emmylou **4**
Hartford, John **1**
Hay, George D. **3**
Hiatt, John **8**
Highway 101 **4**
Hill, Faith **18**
Hinojosa, Tish **13**
Howard, Harlan **15**
Jackson, Alan **7**
Jennings, Waylon **4**
Jones, George **4**

Judd, Wynonna
  See Wynonna
Judds, The **2**
Keith, Toby **17**
Kentucky Headhunters, The **5**
Kershaw, Sammy **15**
Ketchum, Hal **14**
Kristofferson, Kris **4**
Lamb, Barbara **19**
Lang, K. D. **4**
Lawrence, Tracy **11**
LeDoux, Chris **12**
Lee, Brenda **5**
Little Feat **4**
Little Texas **14**
Louvin Brothers, The **12**
Loveless, Patty **5**
Lovett, Lyle **5**
Lynn, Loretta **2**
Lynne, Shelby **5**
Mandrell, Barbara **4**
Mattea, Kathy **5**
Mavericks, The **15**
McBride, Martina **14**
McClinton, Delbert **14**
McCoy, Neal **15**
McEntire, Reba **11**
McGraw, Tim **17**
Miller, Roger **4**
Milsap, Ronnie **2**
Moffatt, Katy **18**
Monroe, Bill **1**
Montgomery, John Michael **14**
Morgan, Lorrie **10**
Murphey, Michael Martin **9**
Murray, Anne **4**
Nelson, Willie **11**
  Earlier sketch in CM **1**
Newton-John, Olivia **8**
Nitty Gritty Dirt Band, The **6**
Oak Ridge Boys, The **7**
O'Connor, Mark **1**
Oslin, K. T. **3**
Owens, Buck **2**
Parnell, Lee Roy **15**
Parsons, Gram **7**
  Also see Byrds, The
Parton, Dolly **2**
Pearl, Minnie **3**
Pierce, Webb **15**
Price, Ray **11**
Pride, Charley **4**
Rabbitt, Eddie **5**
Raitt, Bonnie **3**
Raye, Collin **16**
Reeves, Jim **10**
Restless Heart **12**
Rich, Charlie **3**
Rimes, LeAnn **19**
Robbins, Marty **9**
Rodgers, Jimmie **3**
Rogers, Kenny **1**
Rogers, Roy **9**
Sawyer Brown **13**
Scruggs, Earl **3**

Seals, Dan **9**
Shenandoah **17**
Skaggs, Ricky **5**
Sonnier, Jo-El **10**
Statler Brothers, The **8**
Stevens, Ray **7**
Stone, Doug **10**
Strait, George **5**
Stuart, Marty **9**
Sweethearts of the Rodeo **12**
Texas Tornados, The **8**
Tillis, Mel **7**
Tillis, Pam **8**
Tippin, Aaron **12**
Travis, Merle **14**
Travis, Randy **9**
Tritt, Travis **7**
Tubb, Ernest **4**
Tucker, Tanya **3**
Twain, Shania **17**
Twitty, Conway **6**
Van Shelton, Ricky **5**
Van Zandt, Townes **13**
Wagoner, Porter **13**
Walker, Jerry Jeff **13**
Wariner, Steve **18**
Watson, Doc **2**
Wells, Kitty **6**
West, Dottie **8**
White, Lari **15**
Whitley, Keith **7**
Williams, Don **4**
Williams, Hank, Jr. **1**
Williams, Hank, Sr. **4**
Willis, Kelly **12**
Wills, Bob **6**
Wynette, Tammy **2**
Wynonna **11**
  Also see Judds, The
Yearwood, Trisha **10**
Yoakam, Dwight **1**
Young, Faron **7**

Dobro
  Auldridge, Mike **4**
    Also see Country Gentlemen, The
    Also see Seldom Scene, The
  Burch, Curtis
    See New Grass Revival, The
  Knopfler, Mark **3**
  Whitley, Chris **16**

Drums
  See **Percussion**

Dulcimer
  Ritchie, Jean **4**

Fiddle
  Lamb, Barbara **19**
  See **Violin**

Film Scores
  Anka, Paul **2**
  Bacharach, Burt **1**

Badalamenti, Angelo **17**
Berlin, Irving **8**
Bernstein, Leonard **2**
Blanchard, Terence **13**
Britten, Benjamin **15**
Byrne, David **8**
    Also see Talking Heads
Cafferty, John
    See Beaver Brown Band, The
Cahn, Sammy **11**
Cliff, Jimmy **8**
Copeland, Stewart **14**
Copland, Aaron **2**
Crouch, Andraé **9**
Dibango, Manu **14**
Dolby, Thomas **10**
Donovan **9**
Eddy, Duane **9**
Elfman, Danny **9**
Ellington, Duke **2**
Ferguson, Maynard **7**
Froom, Mitchell **15**
Gabriel, Peter **16**
    Earlier sketch in CM **2**
    Also see Genesis
Galás, Diamanda **16**
Gershwin, George and Ira **11**
Gould, Glenn **9**
Grusin, Dave **7**
Guaraldi, Vince **3**
Hamlisch, Marvin **1**
Hancock, Herbie **8**
Harrison, George **2**
Hayes, Isaac **10**
Hedges, Michael **3**
Herrmann, Bernard **14**
Isham, Mark **14**
Jones, Quincy **2**
Knopfler, Mark **3**
Lennon, John **9**
    Also see Beatles, The
Lerner and Loewe **13**
Loesser, Frank **19**
Mancini, Henry **1**
Marsalis, Branford **10**
Mayfield, Curtis **8**
McCartney, Paul **4**
    Also see Beatles, The
Menken, Alan **10**
Mercer, Johnny **13**
Metheny, Pat **2**
Montenegro, Hugo **18**
Morricone, Ennio **15**
Nascimento, Milton **6**
Nilsson **10**
Nyman, Michael **15**
Parks, Van Dyke **17**
Peterson, Oscar **11**
Porter, Cole **10**
Previn, André **15**
Reznor, Trent **13**
Richie, Lionel **2**
Robertson, Robbie **2**
Rollins, Sonny **7**
Rota, Nino **13**

Sager, Carole Bayer **5**
Sakamoto, Ryuichi **18**
Schickele, Peter **5**
Shankar, Ravi **9**
Taj Mahal **6**
Waits, Tom **12**
    Earlier sketch in CM **1**
Weill, Kurt **12**
Williams, John **9**
Williams, Paul **5**
Willner, Hal **10**
Young, Neil **15**
    Earlier sketch in CM **2**

Flugelhorn
Sandoval, Arturo **15**

Flute
Anderson, Ian
    See Jethro Tull
Galway, James **3**
Lateef, Yusef **16**
Mann, Herbie **16**
Rampal, Jean-Pierre **6**
Ulmer, James Blood **13**
Wilson, Ransom **5**

Folk/Traditional
Altan **18**
America **16**
Arnaz, Desi **8**
Baez, Joan **1**
Belafonte, Harry **8**
Black, Mary **15**
Blades, Ruben **2**
Bloom, Luka **14**
Blue Rodeo **18**
Brady, Paul **8**
Bragg, Billy **7**
Bromberg, David **18**
Buckley, Tim **14**
Bulgarian State Female Vocal Choir, The
    10
Byrds, The **8**
Carter Family, The **3**
Chandra, Sheila **16**
Chapin, Harry **6**
Chapman, Tracy **4**
Chenille Sisters, The **16**
Cherry, Don **10**
Chieftains, The **7**
Childs, Toni **2**
Clegg, Johnny **8**
Cockburn, Bruce **8**
Cohen, Leonard **3**
Collins, Judy **4**
Colvin, Shawn **11**
Cotten, Elizabeth **16**
Crosby, David **3**
    Also see Byrds, The
Cruz, Celia **10**
de Lucia, Paco **1**
DeMent, Iris **13**
Donovan **9**
Dr. John **7**

Drake, Nick **17**
Dylan, Bob **3**
Elliot, Cass **5**
Enya **6**
Estefan, Gloria **15**
    Earlier sketch in CM **2**
Fahey, John **17**
Feliciano, José **10**
Galway, James **3**
Germano, Lisa **18**
Gilmore, Jimmie Dale **11**
Gipsy Kings, The **8**
Gorka, John **18**
Griffith, Nanci **3**
Grisman, David **17**
Guthrie, Arlo **6**
Guthrie, Woody **2**
Hakmoun, Hassan **15**
Hardin, Tim **18**
Harding, John Wesley **6**
Hartford, John **1**
Havens, Richie **11**
Henry, Joe **18**
Hinojosa, Tish **13**
Ian and Sylvia **18**
Iglesias, Julio **2**
Indigo Girls **3**
Ives, Burl **12**
Khan, Nusrat Fateh Ali **13**
Kingston Trio, The **9**
Klezmatics, The **18**
Kottke, Leo **13**
Kuti, Fela **7**
Ladysmith Black Mambazo **1**
Larkin, Patty **9**
Lavin, Christine **6**
Leadbelly **6**
Lightfoot, Gordon **3**
Los Lobos **2**
Makeba, Miriam **8**
Masekela, Hugh **7**
McLean, Don **7**
Melanie **12**
Mitchell, Joni **17**
    Earlier sketch in CM **2**
Moffatt, Katy **18**
Morrison, Van **3**
Morrissey, Bill **12**
Nascimento, Milton **6**
N'Dour, Youssou **6**
Near, Holly **1**
Ochs, Phil **7**
O'Connor, Sinead **3**
Odetta **7**
Parsons, Gram **7**
    Also see Byrds, The
Paxton, Tom **5**
Pentangle **18**
Peter, Paul & Mary **4**
Pogues, The **6**
Prine, John **7**
Proclaimers, The **13**
Redpath, Jean **1**
Ritchie, Jean, **4**
Roches, The **18**

Rodgers, Jimmie **3**
Sainte-Marie, Buffy **11**
Santana, Carlos **1**
Seeger, Pete **4**
  Also see Weavers, The
Selena **16**
Shankar, Ravi **9**
Simon, Paul **16**
  Earlier sketch in CM **1**
Snow, Pheobe **4**
Steeleye Span **19**
Story, The **13**
Sweet Honey in the Rock **1**
Taj Mahal **6**
Thompson, Richard **7**
Tikaram, Tanita **9**
Toure, Ali Farka **18**
Van Ronk, Dave **12**
Van Zandt, Townes **13**
Vega, Suzanne **3**
Wainwright III, Loudon **11**
Walker, Jerry Jeff **13**
Watson, Doc **2**
Weavers, The **8**
Whitman, Slim **19**

French Horn
Ohanian, David
  See Canadian Brass, The

Funk
Bambaataa, Afrika **13**
Brand New Heavies, The **14**
Brown, James **2**
Burdon, Eric **14**
  Also see War
Clinton, George **7**
Collins, Bootsy **8**
Fishbone **7**
Gang of Four **8**
Jackson, Janet **3**
Khan, Chaka **9**
Mayfield, Curtis **8**
Meters, The **14**
Ohio Players **16**
Parker, Maceo **7**
Prince **14**
  Earlier sketch in CM **1**
Red Hot Chili Peppers, The **7**
Stone, Sly **8**
Toussaint, Allen **11**
Worrell, Bernie **11**

Funky
Front 242 **19**
Wu-Tang Clan **19**

Fusion
Anderson, Ray **7**
Beck, Jeff **4**
  Also see Yardbirds, The
Clarke, Stanley **3**
Coleman, Ornette **5**
Corea, Chick **6**
Davis, Miles **1**

Fishbone **7**
Hancock, Herbie **8**
Harris, Eddie **15**
Johnson, Eric **19**
Lewis, Ramsey **14**
Mahavishnu Orchestra **19**
McLaughlin, John **12**
Metheny, Pat **2**
O'Connor, Mark **1**
Ponty, Jean-Luc **8**
Reid, Vernon **2**
Ritenour, Lee **7**
Shorter, Wayne **5**
Summers, Andy **3**
Washington, Grover, Jr. **5**

Gospel
Anderson, Marian **8**
Boone, Pat **13**
Brown, James **2**
Caesar, Shirley **17**
Carter Family, The **3**
Charles, Ray **1**
Cleveland, James **1**
Cooke, Sam **1**
  Also see Soul Stirrers, The
Crouch, Andraé **9**
Dorsey, Thomas A. **11**
Five Blind Boys of Alabama **12**
Ford, Tennessee Ernie **3**
Franklin, Aretha **17**
  Earlier sketch in CM **2**
Green, Al **9**
Hawkins, Tramaine **17**
Houston, Cissy **6**
Jackson, Mahalia **8**
Kee, John P. **15**
Knight, Gladys **1**
Little Richard **1**
Louvin Brothers, The **12**
Mighty Clouds of Joy, The **17**
Oak Ridge Boys, The **7**
Paris, Twila **16**
Pickett, Wilson **10**
Presley, Elvis **1**
Redding, Otis **5**
Reese, Della **13**
Robbins, Marty **9**
Smith, Michael W. **11**
Soul Stirrers, The **11**
Sounds of Blackness **13**
Staples, Mavis **13**
Staples, Pops **11**
Take 6 **6**
Waters, Ethel **11**
Watson, Doc **2**
Williams, Deniece **1**
Williams, Marion **15**
Winans, The **12**
Womack, Bobby **5**

Guitar
Ackerman, Will **3**
Adé, King Sunny **18**
Allman, Duane

  See Allman Brothers, The
Alvin, Dave **17**
Atkins, Chet **5**
Autry, Gene **12**
Baxter, Jeff
  See Doobie Brothers, The
Beck **18**
Beck, Jeff **4**
  Also see Yardbirds, The
Belew, Adrian **5**
Benson, George **9**
Berry, Chuck **1**
Berry, John **17**
Bettencourt, Nuno
  See Extreme
Betts, Dicky
  See Allman Brothers, The
Block, Rory **18**
Bloom, Luka **14**
Boyd, Liona **7**
Bream, Julian **9**
Bromberg, David **18**
Brown, Junior **15**
Buck, Peter
  See R.E.M.
Buckingham, Lindsey **8**
  Also see Fleetwood Mac
Burrell, Kenny **11**
Campbell, Glen **2**
Chesnutt, Mark **13**
Christian, Charlie **11**
Clapton, Eric **11**
  Earlier sketch in CM **1**
  Also see Cream
  Also see Yardbirds, The
Clark, Roy **1**
Cockburn, Bruce **8**
Collie, Mark **15**
Collins, Albert **19**
Collins, Albert **4**
Cooder, Ry **2**
Cotten, Elizabeth **16**
Cray, Robert **8**
Cropper, Steve **12**
Dale, Dick **13**
Daniels, Charlie **6**
Davis, Reverend Gary **18**
de Grassi, Alex **6**
de Lucia, Paco **1**
Dickens, Little Jimmy **7**
Diddley, Bo **3**
DiFranco, Ani **17**
Di Meola, Al **12**
Drake, Nick **17**
Earl, Ronnie **5**
  Also see Roomful of Blues
Eddy, Duane **9**
Edge, The
  See U2
Ellis, Herb **18**
Etheridge, Melissa **16**
  Earlier sketch in CM **4**
Fahey, John **17**
Feliciano, José **10**
Fender, Leo **10**

Flatt, Lester **3**
Flores, Rosie **16**
Ford, Lita **9**
Frampton, Peter **3**
Frehley, Ace
  See Kiss
Fripp, Robert **9**
Frisell, Bill **15**
Frith, Fred **19**
Garcia, Jerry **4**
  Also see Grateful Dead, The
Gatton, Danny **16**
George, Lowell
  See Little Feat
Gibbons, Billy
  See ZZ Top
Gill, Vince **7**
Gilmour, David
  See Pink Floyd
Gorka, John **18**
Green, Grant **14**
Green, Peter
  See Fleetwood Mac
Guy, Buddy **4**
Haley, Bill **6**
Hardin, Tim **18**
Harper, Ben **17**
Harrison, George **2**
Hatfield, Juliana **12**
  Also see Lemonheads, The
Havens, Richie **11**
Healey, Jeff **4**
Hedges, Michael **3**
Hendrix, Jimi **2**
Hillman, Chris
  See Byrds, The
  Also see Desert Rose Band, The
Hitchcock, Robyn **9**
Holly, Buddy **1**
Hooker, John Lee **1**
Hopkins, Lightnin' **13**
Howlin' Wolf **6**
Iommi, Tony
  See Black Sabbath
Ives, Burl **12**
James, Elmore **8**
Jardine, Al
  See Beach Boys, The
Jefferson, Blind Lemon **18**
Jobim, Antonio Carlos **19**
Johnson, Eric **19**
Johnson, Lonnie **17**
Johnson, Robert **6**
Jones, Brian
  See Rolling Stones, The
Jordan, Stanley **1**
Kantner, Paul
  See Jefferson Airplane
Keith, Toby **17**
King, Albert **2**
King, B. B. **1**
King, Freddy **17**
Klugh, Earl **10**
Knopfler, Mark **3**
Kottke, Leo **13**

Landreth, Sonny **16**
Larkin, Patty **9**
Leadbelly **6**
Legg, Adrian **17**
Lennon, John **9**
  Also see Beatles, The
Lindley, David **2**
Lockwood, Robert, Jr. **10**
Loeb, Lisa **19**
Marr, Johnny
  See Smiths, The
  See The The
Martino, Pat **17**
May, Brian
  See Queen
Mayfield, Curtis **8**
McClinton, Delbert **14**
McCoury, Del **15**
McDowell, Mississippi Fred **16**
McGuinn, Roger
  See Byrds, The
McLachlan, Sarah **12**
McLaughlin, John **12**
McReynolds, Jim
  See McReynolds, Jim and Jesse
McTell, Blind Willie **17**
Metheny, Pat **2**
Mitchell, Joni **17**
  Earlier sketch in CM **2**
Montgomery, Wes **3**
Morrissey, Bill **12**
Muldaur, Maria **18**
Nugent, Ted **2**
Oldfield, Mike **18**
Owens, Buck **2**
Page, Jimmy **4**
  Also see Led Zeppelin
  Also see Yardbirds, The
Parkening, Christopher **7**
Parnell, Lee Roy **15**
Pass, Joe **15**
Patton, Charley **11**
Perkins, Carl **9**
Perry, Joe
  See Aerosmith
Petty, Tom **9**
Phair, Liz **14**
Phillips, Sam **12**
Prince **14**
  Earlier sketch in CM **1**
Raitt, Bonnie **3**
Ray, Amy
  See Indigo Girls
Redbone, Leon **19**
Reed, Jimmy **15**
Reid, Vernon **2**
  Also see Living Colour
Reinhardt, Django **7**
Richards, Keith **11**
  Also see Rolling Stones, The
Richman, Jonathan **12**
Ritenour, Lee **7**
Robbins, Marty **9**
Robertson, Robbie **2**
Robillard, Duke **2**

Rodgers, Nile **8**
Rush, Otis **12**
Saliers, Emily
  See Indigo Girls
Santana, Carlos **19**
Santana, Carlos **1**
Satriani, Joe **4**
Scofield, John **7**
Segovia, Andres **6**
Sharrock, Sonny **15**
Shines, Johnny **14**
Simon, Paul **16**
  Earlier sketch in CM **1**
Skaggs, Ricky **5**
Slash
  See Guns n' Roses
Springsteen, Bruce **6**
Stewart, Dave
  See Eurythmics
Stills, Stephen **5**
Stuart, Marty **9**
Summers, Andy **3**
Taylor, Mick
  See Rolling Stones, The
Thielemans, Toots **13**
Thompson, Richard **7**
Tippin, Aaron **12**
Toure, Ali Farka **18**
Townshend, Pete **1**
Travis, Merle **14**
Tubb, Ernest **4**
Ulmer, James Blood **13**
Vai, Steve **5**
Van Halen, Edward
  See Van Halen
Van Ronk, Dave **12**
Vaughan, Jimmie
  See Fabulous Thunderbirds, The
Vaughan, Stevie Ray **1**
Wagoner, Porter **13**
Waits, Tom **12**
  Earlier sketch in CM **1**
Walker, Jerry Jeff **13**
Walker, T-Bone **5**
Walsh, Joe **5**
  Also see Eagles, The
Wariner, Steve **18**
Watson, Doc **2**
Weir, Bob
  See Grateful Dead, The
Weller, Paul **14**
White, Lari **15**
Whitfield, Mark **18**
Whitley, Chris **16**
Wilson, Nancy
  See Heart
Winston, George **9**
Winter, Johnny **5**
Wiseman, Mac **19**
Wray, Link **17**
Yamashita, Kazuhito **4**
Yarrow, Peter
  See Peter, Paul & Mary
Young, Angus
  See AC/DC

Young, Malcolm
  See AC/DC
York, Andrew **15**
Young, Neil **15**
  Earlier sketch in CM **2**
Zappa, Frank **17**
  Earlier sketch in CM **1**

Harmonica
Dylan, Bob **3**
Guthrie, Woody **2**
Horton, Walter **19**
Lewis, Huey **9**
Little Walter **14**
McClinton, Delbert **14**
Musselwhite, Charlie **13**
Reed, Jimmy **15**
Thielemans, Toots **13**
Waters, Muddy **4**
Wells, Junior **17**
Williamson, Sonny Boy **9**
Wilson, Kim
  See Fabulous Thunderbirds, The
Wonder, Stevie **17**
  Earlier sketch in CM **2**
Young, Neil **15**
  Earlier sketch in CM **2**

Heavy Metal
AC/DC **4**
Aerosmith **3**
Alice in Chains **10**
Anthrax **11**
Black Sabbath **9**
Blue Oyster Cult **16**
Cinderella **16**
Circle Jerks **17**
Danzig **7**
Deep Purple **11**
Def Leppard **3**
Dokken **16**
Faith No More **7**
Fishbone **7**
Ford, Lita **9**
Guns n' Roses **2**
Iron Maiden **10**
Judas Priest **10**
King's X **7**
Led Zeppelin **1**
L7 **12**
Megadeth **9**
Metallica **7**
Mötley Crüe **1**
Motörhead **10**
Nugent, Ted **2**
Osbourne, Ozzy **3**
Pantera **13**
Petra **3**
Queensryche **8**
Reid, Vernon **2**
  Also see Living Colour
Reznor, Trent **13**
Roth, David Lee **1**
  Also see Van Halen
Sepultura **12**

Skinny Puppy **17**
Slayer **10**
Soundgarden **6**
Spinal Tap **8**
Stryper **2**
Suicidal Tendencies **15**
Warrant **17**
Whitesnake **5**
White Zombie **17**

Humor
Borge, Victor **19**
Coasters, The **5**
Jones, Spike **5**
Lehrer, Tom **7**
Pearl, Minnie **3**
Russell, Mark **6**
Sandler, Adam **19**
Schickele, Peter **5**
Shaffer, Paul **13**
Spinal Tap **8**
Stevens, Ray **7**
Yankovic, "Weird Al" **7**

Inventors
Fender, Leo **10**
Harris, Eddie **15**
Paul, Les **2**
Scholz, Tom
  See Boston
Teagarden, Jack **10**
Theremin, Leon **19**

Jazz
Adderly, Cannonball **15**
Allen, Geri **10**
Allison, Mose **17**
Anderson, Ray **7**
Armstrong, Louis **4**
Bailey, Mildred **13**
Bailey, Pearl **5**
Baker, Anita **9**
Baker, Chet **13**
Baker, Ginger **16**
  Also see Cream
Basie, Count **2**
Bechet, Sidney **17**
Beiderbecke, Bix **16**
Belle, Regina **6**
Bennett, Tony **16**
  Earlier sketch in CM **2**
Benson, George **9**
Berigan, Bunny **2**
Blackman, Cindy **15**
Blakey, Art **11**
Blanchard, Terence **13**
Bley, Carla **8**
Bley, Paul **14**
Blood, Sweat and Tears **7**
Brand New Heavies, The **14**
Braxton, Anthony **12**
Bridgewater, Dee Dee **18**
Brown, Ruth **13**
Brubeck, Dave **8**
Burrell, Kenny **11**

Burton, Gary **10**
Calloway, Cab **6**
Canadian Brass, The **4**
Carter, Benny **3**
  Also see McKinney's Cotton Pickers
Carter, Betty **6**
Carter, James **18**
Carter, Ron **14**
Chambers, Paul **18**
Charles, Ray **1**
Cherry, Don **10**
Christian, Charlie **11**
Clarke, Stanley **3**
Clements, Vassar **18**
Clooney, Rosemary **9**
Cole, Holly **18**
Cole, Nat King **3**
Coleman, Ornette **5**
Coltrane, John **4**
Connick, Harry, Jr. **4**
Corea, Chick **6**
Davis, Anthony **17**
Davis, Miles **1**
DeJohnette, Jack **7**
Di Meola, Al **12**
Eckstine, Billy **1**
Eldridge, Roy **9**
  Also see McKinney's Cotton Pickers
Ellington, Duke **2**
Ellis, Herb **18**
Evans, Bill **17**
Evans, Gil **17**
Ferguson, Maynard **7**
Ferrell, Rachelle **17**
Fitzgerald, Ella **1**
Flanagan, Tommy **16**
Fleck, Bela **8**
  Also see New Grass Revival, The
Fountain, Pete **7**
Frisell, Bill **15**
Galway, James **3**
Getz, Stan **12**
Gillespie, Dizzy **6**
Goodman, Benny **4**
Gordon, Dexter **10**
Grappelli, Stephane **10**
Green, Benny **17**
Green, Grant **14**
Guaraldi, Vince **3**
Haden, Charlie **12**
Hampton, Lionel **6**
Hancock, Herbie **8**
Hargrove, Roy **15**
Harris, Eddie **15**
Hawkins, Coleman **11**
Hawkins, Erskine **19**
Hedges, Michael **3**
Henderson, Fletcher **16**
Henderson, Joe **14**
Herman, Woody **12**
Hines, Earl "Fatha" **12**
Hirt, Al **5**
Holiday, Billie **6**
Horn, Shirley **7**
Horne, Lena **11**

Humes, Helen **19**
Hunter, Alberta **7**
Incognito **16**
Isham, Mark **14**
Jackson, Milt **15**
Jacquet, Illinois **17**
James, Harry **11**
Jarreau, Al **1**
Jarrett, Keith **1**
Jobim, Antonio Carlos **19**
Johnson, James P. **16**
Johnson, Lonnie **17**
Jones, Elvin **9**
Jones, Hank **15**
Jones, Philly Joe **16**
Jones, Quincy **2**
Jones, Thad **19**
Jordan, Stanley **1**
Kennedy, Nigel **8**
Kenny G **14**
Kirk, Rahsaan Roland **6**
Kitt, Eartha **9**
Klugh, Earl **10**
Kronos Quartet **5**
Krupa, Gene **13**
Laine, Cleo **10**
Lateef, Yusef **16**
Lee, Peggy **8**
Lewis, Ramsey **14**
Lincoln, Abbey **9**
Israel "Cachao" Lopez **14**
Lovano, Joe **13**
Mahavishnu Orchestra **19**
Mancini, Henry **1**
Manhattan Transfer, The **8**
Mann, Herbie **16**
Marsalis, Branford **10**
Marsalis, Ellis **13**
Marsalis, Wynton **6**
Martino, Pat **17**
Masekela, Hugh **7**
McBride, Christian **17**
McFerrin, Bobby **3**
McKinney's Cotton Pickers **16**
McLaughlin, John **12**
McPartland, Marian **15**
McRae, Carmen **9**
Metheny, Pat **2**
Mingus, Charles **9**
Monk, Thelonious **6**
Montgomery, Wes **3**
Morgan, Frank **9**
Morton, Jelly Roll **7**
Mulligan, Gerry **4**
Nascimento, Milton **6**
Norvo, Red **12**
Oliver, King **15**
Palmieri, Eddie **15**
Parker, Charlie **5**
Parker, Maceo **7**
Pass, Joe **15**
Paul, Les **2**
Pepper, Art **18**
Peterson, Oscar **11**
Ponty, Jean-Luc **8**

Powell, Bud **15**
Previn, André **15**
Professor Longhair **6**
Puente, Tito **14**
Pullen, Don **16**
Rampal, Jean-Pierre **6**
Redman, Joshua **12**
Reeves, Dianne **16**
Reid, Vernon **2**
   Also see Living Colour
Reinhardt, Django **7**
Rich, Buddy **13**
Roach, Max **12**
Roberts, Marcus **6**
Robillard, Duke **2**
Rodney, Red **14**
Rollins, Sonny **7**
Sanborn, David **1**
Sanders, Pharoah **16**
Sandoval, Arturo **15**
Santana, Carlos **19**
Santana, Carlos **1**
Schuur, Diane **6**
Scofield, John **7**
Scott, Jimmy **14**
Scott-Heron, Gil **13**
Severinsen, Doc **1**
Sharrock, Sonny **15**
Shaw, Artie **8**
Shorter, Wayne **5**
Silver, Horace **19**
Simone, Nina **11**
Solal, Martial **4**
Strayhorn, Billy **13**
Summers, Andy **3**
Sun Ra **5**
Take 6 **6**
Tatum, Art **17**
Taylor, Billy **13**
Taylor, Cecil **9**
Teagarden, Jack **10**
Thielemans, Toots **13**
Threadgill, Henry **9**
Torme, Mel **4**
Tucker, Sophie **12**
Turner, Big Joe **13**
Turtle Island String Quartet **9**
Tyner, McCoy **7**
Ulmer, James Blood **13**
US3 **18**
Vaughan, Sarah **2**
Walker, T-Bone **5**
Washington, Dinah **5**
Washington, Grover, Jr. **5**
Weather Report **19**
Webb, Chick **14**
Weston, Randy **15**
Whiteman, Paul **17**
Whitfield, Mark **18**
Whittaker, Rodney **19**
Williams, Joe **11**
Wilson, Cassandra **12**
Wilson, Nancy **14**
Winter, Paul **10**
Witherspoon, Jimmy **19**

Young, La Monte **16**
Young, Lester **14**
Zorn, John **15**

Juju
Adé, King Sunny **18**

Keyboards, Electric
Aphex Twin **14**
Bley, Paul **14**
Brown, Tony **14**
Corea, Chick **6**
Davis, Chip **4**
Dolby, Thomas **10**
Emerson, Keith
   See Emerson, Lake & Palmer/Powell
Eno, Brian **8**
Foster, David **13**
Froom, Mitchell **15**
Hancock, Herbie **8**
Jackson, Joe **4**
Jarre, Jean-Michel **2**
Jones, Booker T. **8**
Kitaro **1**
Manzarek, Ray
   See Doors, The
McDonald, Michael
   See Doobie Brothers, The
McVie, Christine
   See Fleetwood Mac
Pierson, Kate
   See B-52's, The
Sakamoto, Ryuichi **19**
Sakamoto, Ryuichi **18**
Shaffer, Paul **13**
Sun Ra **5**
Waller, Fats **7**
Wilson, Brian
   See Beach Boys, The
Winwood, Steve **2**
Wonder, Stevie **17**
   Earlier sketch in CM **2**
Worrell, Bernie **11**
Yanni **11**

Liturgical Music
Cooney, Rory **6**
Talbot, John Michael **6**

Mandolin
Bromberg, David **18**
Bush, Sam
   See New Grass Revival, The
Duffey, John
   See Seldom Scene, The
Grisman, David **17**
Hartford, John **1**
Lindley, David **2**
McReynolds, Jesse
   See McReynolds, Jim and Jesse
Monroe, Bill **1**
Rosas, Cesar
   See Los Lobos
Skaggs, Ricky **5**
Stuart, Marty **9**

Musicals

Allen, Debbie **8**
Allen, Peter **11**
Andrews, Julie **4**
Andrews Sisters, The **9**
Bacharach, Burt **1**
Bailey, Pearl **5**
Baker, Josephine **10**
Berlin, Irving **8**
Brown, Ruth **13**
Buckley, Betty **16**
  Earlier sketch in CM **1**
Burnett, Carol **6**
Carter, Nell **7**
Channing, Carol **6**
Chevalier, Maurice **6**
Crawford, Michael **4**
Crosby, Bing **6**
Curry, Tim **3**
Davis, Sammy, Jr. **4**
Garland, Judy **6**
Gershwin, George and Ira **11**
Hamlisch, Marvin **1**
Horne, Lena **11**
Johnson, James P. **16**
Jolson, Al **10**
Kern, Jerome **13**
Laine, Cleo **10**
Lerner and Loewe **13**
Lloyd Webber, Andrew **6**
LuPone, Patti **8**
Masekela, Hugh **7**
Menken, Alan **10**
Mercer, Johnny **13**
Moore, Melba **7**
Patinkin, Mandy **3**
Peters, Bernadette **7**
Porter, Cole **10**
Robeson, Paul **8**
Rodgers, Richard **9**
Sager, Carole Bayer **5**
Shaffer, Paul **13**
Sondheim, Stephen **8**
Waters, Ethel **11**
Weill, Kurt **12**

Oboe

Lateef, Yusef **16**

Opera

Adams, John **8**
Anderson, Marian **8**
Baker, Janet **14**
Bartoli, Cecilia **12**
Battle, Kathleen **6**
Bumbry, Grace **13**
Callas, Maria **11**
Carreras, José **8**
Caruso, Enrico **10**
Copeland, Stewart **14**
Cotrubas, Ileana **1**
Davis, Anthony **17**
Domingo, Placido **1**
Freni, Mirella **14**
Gershwin, George and Ira **11**

Graves, Denyce **16**
Hampson, Thomas **12**
Hendricks, Barbara **10**
Herrmann, Bernard **14**
Horne, Marilyn **9**
McNair, Sylvia **15**
Norman, Jessye **7**
Pavarotti, Luciano **1**
Price, Leontyne **6**
Sills, Beverly **5**
Solti, Georg **13**
Sutherland, Joan **13**
Te Kanawa, Kiri **2**
Toscanini, Arturo **14**
Upshaw, Dawn **9**
von Karajan, Herbert **1**
Weill, Kurt **12**
Zimmerman, Udo **5**

Percussion

Baker, Ginger **16**
  Also see Cream
Blackman, Cindy **15**
Blakey, Art **11**
Bonham, John
  See Led Zeppelin
Burton, Gary **10**
Collins, Phil **2**
  Also see Genesis
Copeland, Stewart **14**
DeJohnette, Jack **7**
Densmore, John
  See Doors, The
Dunbar, Aynsley
  See Jefferson Starship
  Also See Whitesnake
Dunbar, Sly
  See Sly and Robbie
Fleetwood, Mick
  See Fleetwood Mac
Hampton, Lionel **6**
Hart, Mickey
  See Grateful Dead, The
Henley, Don **3**
Jones, Elvin **9**
Jones, Kenny
  See Who, The
Jones, Philly Joe **16**
Jones, Spike **5**
Kreutzman, Bill
  See Grateful Dead, The
Krupa, Gene **13**
Mason, Nick
  See Pink Floyd
Moon, Keith
  See Who, The
N'Dour, Youssou **6**
Otis, Johnny **16**
Palmer, Carl
  See Emerson, Lake & Palmer/Powell
Palmieri, Eddie **15**
Peart, Neil
  See Rush
Powell, Cozy
  See Emerson, Lake & Palmer/Powell

Puente, Tito **14**
Rich, Buddy **13**
Roach, Max **12**
Sheila E. **3**
Starr, Ringo **10**
  Also see Beatles, The
Walden, Narada Michael **14**
Watts, Charlie
  See Rolling Stones, The
Webb, Chick **14**

Piano

Allen, Geri **10**
Allison, Mose **17**
Amos, Tori **12**
Arrau, Claudio **1**
Bacharach, Burt **1**
Ball, Marcia **15**
Basie, Count **2**
Berlin, Irving **8**
Blake, Eubie **19**
Bley, Carla **8**
Bley, Paul **14**
Borge, Victor **19**
Britten, Benjamin **15**
Bronfman, Yefim **6**
Brubeck, Dave **8**
Bush, Kate **4**
Charles, Ray **1**
Clayderman, Richard **1**
Cleveland, James **1**
Cliburn, Van **13**
Cole, Nat King **3**
Collins, Judy **4**
Collins, Phil **2**
  Also see Genesis
Connick, Harry, Jr. **4**
Crouch, Andraé **9**
DeJohnette, Jack **7**
Domino, Fats **2**
Dr. John **7**
Dupree, Champion Jack **12**
Esquivel, Juan **17**
Ellington, Duke **2**
Evans, Bill **17**
Evans, Gil **17**
Feinstein, Michael **6**
Ferrell, Rachelle **17**
Flack, Roberta **5**
Flanagan, Tommy **16**
Frey, Glenn **3**
Galás, Diamanda **16**
Glass, Philip **1**
Gould, Glenn **9**
Green, Benny **17**
Grusin, Dave **7**
Guaraldi, Vince **3**
Hamlisch, Marvin **1**
Hancock, Herbie **8**
Helfgott, David **19**
Henderson, Fletcher **16**
Hinderas, Natalie **12**
Hines, Earl "Fatha" **12**
Horn, Shirley **7**
Hornsby, Bruce **3**

Horowitz, Vladimir **1**
Jackson, Joe **4**
Jarrett, Keith **1**
Joel, Billy **12**
  Earlier sketch in CM **2**
John, Elton **3**
Johnson, James P. **16**
Jones, Hank **15**
Joplin, Scott **10**
Kissin, Evgeny **6**
Levine, James **8**
Lewis, Jerry Lee **2**
Lewis, Ramsey **14**
Liberace **9**
Little Richard **1**
Manilow, Barry **2**
Marsalis, Ellis **13**
McDonald, Michael
  See Doobie Brothers, The
McPartland, Marian **15**
McRae, Carmen **9**
McVie, Christine
  See Fleetwood Mac
Milsap, Ronnie **2**
Mingus, Charles **9**
Monk, Thelonious **6**
Morton, Jelly Roll **7**
Newman, Randy **4**
Nero, Peter **19**
Palmieri, Eddie **15**
Perahia, Murray **10**
Peterson, Oscar **11**
Powell, Bud **15**
Pratt, Awadagin **19**
Previn, André **15**
Professor Longhair **6**
Puente, Tito **14**
Pullen, Don **16**
Rich, Charlie **3**
Roberts, Marcus **6**
Rubinstein, Arthur **11**
Russell, Mark **6**
Schickele, Peter **5**
Sedaka, Neil **4**
Shaffer, Paul **13**
Solal, Martial **4**
Solti, Georg **13**
Spann, Otis **18**
Story, Liz **2**
Strayhorn, Billy **13**
Sunnyland Slim **16**
Tatum, Art **17**
Taylor, Billy **13**
Taylor, Cecil **9**
Tyner, McCoy **7**
Waits, Tom **12**
  Earlier sketch in **1**
Waller, Fats **7**
Weston, Randy **15**
Wilson, Cassandra **12**
Winston, George **9**
Winwood, Steve **2**
Wonder, Stevie **17**
  Earlier sketch in CM **2**
Wright, Rick

  See Pink Floyd
Young, La Monte **16**

Piccolo
  Galway, James **3**

Pop
Abba **12**
Abdul, Paula **3**
Adam Ant **13**
Adams, Bryan **2**
Adams, Oleta **17**
All-4-One **17**
Alpert, Herb **11**
America **16**
Amos, Tori **12**
Andrews Sisters, The **9**
Armatrading, Joan **4**
Arnold, Eddy **10**
Astley, Rick **5**
Atkins, Chet **5**
Avalon, Frankie **5**
Bacharach, Burt **1**
Bailey, Pearl **5**
Basia **5**
Beach Boys, The **1**
Beatles, The **2**
Beaver Brown Band, The **3**
Bee Gees, The **3**
Belly **16**
Bennett, Tony **16**
  Earlier sketch in CM **2**
Benson, George **9**
Benton, Brook **7**
B-52's, The **4**
Better Than Ezra **19**
Blige, Mary J. **15**
Blondie **14**
Blood, Sweat and Tears **7**
Blue Rodeo **18**
BoDeans, The **3**
Bolton, Michael **4**
Boone, Pat **13**
Boston **11**
Bowie, David **1**
Boyz II Men **15**
Bragg, Billy **7**
Branigan, Laura **2**
Braxton, Toni **17**
Brickell, Edie **3**
Brooks, Garth **8**
Brown, Bobby **4**
Browne, Jackson **3**
Bryson, Peabo **11**
Buckingham, Lindsey **8**
  Also see Fleetwood Mac
Buckley, Tim **14**
Buffett, Jimmy **4**
Burdon, Eric **14**
  Also see War
Cabaret Voltaire **18**
Campbell, Glen **2**
Campbell, Tevin **13**
Cardigans **19**
Carey, Mariah **6**

Carlisle, Belinda **8**
Carnes, Kim **4**
Carpenters, The **13**
Case, Peter **13**
Chandra, Sheila **16**
Chapin, Harry **6**
Chapman, Tracy **4**
Charlatans, The **13**
Charles, Ray **1**
Checker, Chubby **7**
Cher **1**
Cherry, Neneh **4**
Chicago **3**
Chilton, Alex **10**
Clapton, Eric **11**
  Earlier sketch in CM **1**
  Also see Cream
  Also see Yardbirds, The
Clayderman, Richard **1**
Clooney, Rosemary **9**
Coasters, The **5**
Cocker, Joe **4**
Cocteau Twins, The **12**
Cole, Lloyd **9**
Cole, Natalie **1**
Cole, Nat King **3**
Collins, Judy **4**
Collins, Phil **2**
  Also see Genesis
Colvin, Shawn **11**
Como, Perry **14**
Connick, Harry, Jr. **4**
Cooke, Sam **1**
  Also see Soul Stirrers, The
Cope, Julian **16**
Costello, Elvis **12**
  Earlier sketch in CM **2**
Cranberries, The **14**
Crash Test Dummies **14**
Crenshaw, Marshall **5**
Croce, Jim **3**
Crosby, David **3**
  Also see Byrds, The
Crow, Sheryl **18**
Crowded House **12**
Daltrey, Roger **3**
  Also see Who, The
D'Arby, Terence Trent **3**
Darin, Bobby **4**
Dave Clark Five, The **12**
Davies, Ray **5**
Davis, Sammy, Jr. **4**
Davis, Skeeter **15**
Dayne, Taylor **4**
DeBarge, El **14**
Del Amitri **18**
Denver, John **1**
Depeche Mode **5**
Des'ree **15**
Devo **13**
Diamond, Neil **1**
Dion **4**
Dion, Céline **12**
Doc Pomus **14**
Donovan **9**

Doobie Brothers, The **3**
Doors, The **4**
Duran Duran **4**
Dylan, Bob **3**
Eagles, The **3**
Earth, Wind and Fire **12**
Easton, Sheena **2**
Edmonds, Kenneth "Babyface" **12**
Electric Light Orchestra **7**
Elfman, Danny **9**
Elliot, Cass **5**
Enigma **14**
En Vogue **10**
Estefan, Gloria **15**
  Earlier sketch in CM **2**
Eurythmics **6**
Everly Brothers, The **2**
Everything But The Girl **15**
Exposé **4**
Fabian **5**
Feliciano, José **10**
Ferguson, Maynard **7**
Ferry, Bryan **1**
Fiedler, Arthur **6**
Fisher, Eddie **12**
Fitzgerald, Ella **1**
Flack, Roberta **5**
Fleetwood Mac **5**
Fogelberg, Dan **4**
Fordham, Julia **15**
Foster, David **13**
Four Tops, The **11**
Fox, Samantha **3**
Frampton, Peter **3**
Francis, Connie **10**
Franklin, Aretha **17**
  Earlier sketch in CM **2**
Frey, Glenn **3**
  Also see Eagles, The
Garfunkel, Art **4**
Gaye, Marvin **4**
Gayle, Crystal **1**
Geldof, Bob **9**
Genesis **4**
Gershwin, George and Ira **11**
Gibson, Debbie **1**
Gift, Roland **3**
Gin Blossoms **18**
Goodman, Benny **4**
Gordy, Berry, Jr. **6**
Grant, Amy **7**
Grebenshikov, Boris **3**
Green, Al **9**
Guthrie, Arlo **6**
Hall & Oates **6**
Hammer, M.C. **5**
Hancock, Herbie **8**
Harding, John Wesley **6**
Harrison, George **2**
  Also see Beatles, The
Harry, Deborah **4**
  Also see Blondie
Healey, Jeff **4**
Henley, Don **3**
  Also see Eagles, The

Herman's Hermits **5**
Hitchcock, Robyn **9**
Holland-Dozier-Holland **5**
Hootie and the Blowfish **18**
Horne, Lena **11**
Hornsby, Bruce **3**
Houston, Whitney **8**
Human League, The **17**
Humperdinck, Engelbert **19**
Ian, Janis **5**
Idol, Billy **3**
Iglesias, Julio **2**
Indigo Girls **3**
Ingram, James **11**
Isaak, Chris **6**
Isley Brothers, The **8**
Jackson, Janet **16**
  Earlier sketch in CM **3**
Jackson, Joe **4**
Jackson, Michael **17**
  Earlier sketch in CM **1**
  Also see Jacksons, The
Jacksons, The **7**
Jam, Jimmy, and Terry Lewis **11**
James **12**
James, Harry **11**
James, Rick **2**
Jarreau, Al **1**
Jayhawks, The **15**
Jefferson Airplane **5**
Jodeci **13**
Joel, Billy **12**
  Earlier sketch in CM **2**
Johansen, David **7**
John, Elton **3**
Jolson, Al **10**
Jones, Quincy **2**
Jones, Rickie Lee **4**
Jones, Tom **11**
Joplin, Janis **3**
Khan, Chaka **9**
King, Ben E. **7**
King, Carole **6**
Kiss **5**
Kitt, Eartha **9**
Knight, Gladys **1**
Knopfler, Mark **3**
Kool & the Gang **13**
Kraftwerk **9**
Kristofferson, Kris **4**
LaBelle, Patti **8**
Lauper, Cyndi **11**
Lee, Brenda **5**
Leiber and Stoller **14**
Lemper, Ute **14**
Lennon, John **9**
  Also see Beatles, The
Lennon, Julian **2**
Lennox, Annie **18**
    Also see Eurythmics, The
Lewis, Huey **9**
Liberace **9**
Lightfoot, Gordon **3**
Loeb, Lisa **19**
Loggins, Kenny **3**

Lovett, Lyle **5**
Lowe, Nick **6**
Lush **13**
Lynne, Jeff **5**
MacColl, Kirsty **12**
Madonna **16**
  Earlier sketch in CM **4**
Mancini, Henry **1**
Manhattan Transfer, The **8**
Manilow, Barry **2**
Marley, Bob **3**
Marley, Ziggy **3**
Marsalis, Branford **10**
Martin, Dean **1**
Martin, George **6**
Marx, Richard **3**
Mathis, Johnny **2**
Mazzy Star **17**
McCartney, Paul **4**
  Also see Beatles, The
McFerrin, Bobby **3**
McLachlan, Sarah **12**
McLean, Don **7**
Medley, Bill **3**
Melanie **12**
Michael, George **9**
Midler, Bette **8**
Mike & the Mechanics **17**
Miller, Mitch **11**
Miller, Roger **4**
Milli Vanilli **4**
Mills Brothers, The **14**
Minnelli, Liza **19**
Mitchell, Joni **17**
  Earlier sketch in CM **2**
Money, Eddie **16**
Monkees, The **7**
Montand, Yves **12**
Morrison, Jim **3**
Morrison, Van **3**
Morissette, Alanis **19**
Morrissey **10**
Mouskouri, Nana **12**
Moyet, Alison **12**
Murray, Anne **4**
Myles, Alannah **4**
Neville, Aaron **5**
    Also see Neville Brothers, The
Neville Brothers, The **4**
New Kids on the Block **3**
Newman, Randy **4**
Newton, Wayne **2**
Newton-John, Olivia **8**
Nicks, Stevie **2**
Nilsson **10**
Nitty Gritty Dirt Band **6**
Nyro, Laura **12**
Oak Ridge Boys, The **7**
Ocasek, Ric **5**
Ocean, Billy **4**
O'Connor, Sinead **3**
Oldfield, Mike **18**
Orlando, Tony **15**
Osborne, Joan **19**
Osmond, Donny **3**

Page, Jimmy **4**
    Also see Led Zeppelin
    Also see Yardbirds, The
Page, Patti **11**
Parks, Van Dyke **17**
Parsons, Alan **12**
Parton, Dolly **2**
Pendergrass, Teddy **3**
Peniston, CeCe **15**
Penn, Michael **4**
Pet Shop Boys **5**
Peter, Paul & Mary **4**
Phillips, Sam **12**
Piaf, Edith **8**
Pizzicato Five **18**
Plant, Robert **2**
    Also see Led Zeppelin
Pointer Sisters, The **9**
Porter, Cole **10**
Prefab Sprout **15**
Presley, Elvis **1**
Prince **14**
    Earlier sketch in CM **1**
Proclaimers, The **13**
Pulp **18**
Queen **6**
Rabbitt, Eddie **5**
Raitt, Bonnie **3**
Rea, Chris **12**
Redding, Otis **5**
Reddy, Helen **9**
Reeves, Martha **4**
R.E.M. **5**
Richard, Cliff **14**
Richie, Lionel **2**
Riley, Teddy **14**
Robbins, Marty **9**
Robinson, Smokey **1**
Rogers, Kenny **1**
Rolling Stones **3**
Ronstadt, Linda **2**
Ross, Diana **1**
Roth, David Lee **1**
    Also see Van Halen
Ruffin, David **6**
Sade **2**
Sager, Carole Bayer **5**
Sainte-Marie, Buffy **11**
Sanborn, David **1**
Seal **14**
Seals, Dan **9**
Seals & Crofts **3**
Secada, Jon **13**
Sedaka, Neil **4**
Selena **16**
Shaffer, Paul **13**
Sheila E. **3**
Shirelles, The **11**
Shonen Knife **13**
Siberry, Jane **6**
Simon, Carly **4**
Simon, Paul **16**
    Earlier sketch in CM **1**
Sinatra, Frank **1**
Smiths, The **3**

Snow, Pheobe **4**
Sparks **18**
Spector, Phil **4**
Springfield, Rick **9**
Springsteen, Bruce **6**
Squeeze **5**
Stansfield, Lisa **9**
Starr, Ringo **10**
Steely Dan **5**
Stereolab **18**
Stevens, Cat **3**
Stewart, Rod **2**
Stills, Stephen **5**
Sting **19**
    Earlier sketch in CM **2**
Story, The **13**
Straw, Syd **18**
Streisand, Barbra **2**
Summer, Donna **12**
Supremes, The **6**
Sweat, Keith **13**
Sweet, Matthew **9**
SWV **14**
Talking Heads **1**
Talk Talk **19**
Taylor, James **2**
Tears for Fears **6**
Teenage Fanclub **13**
Temptations, The **3**
10,000 Maniacs **3**
The The **15**
They Might Be Giants **7**
Thomas, Irma **16**
Three Dog Night **5**
Tiffany **4**
Tikaram, Tanita **9**
Timbuk 3 **3**
TLC **15**
Toad the Wet Sprocket **13**
Tony! Toni! Toné! **12**
Torme, Mel **4**
Townshend, Pete **1**
    Also see Who, The
Turner, Tina **1**
Valli, Frankie **10**
Vandross, Luther **2**
Vega, Suzanne **3**
Vinton, Bobby **12**
Walsh, Joe **5**
Warnes, Jennifer **3**
Warwick, Dionne **2**
Was (Not Was) **6**
Washington, Dinah **5**
Waters, Crystal **15**
Watley, Jody **9**
Webb, Jimmy **12**
"Weird Al" Yankovic **7**
Weller, Paul **14**
Who, The **3**
Williams, Andy **2**
Williams, Deniece **1**
Williams, Joe **11**
Williams, Lucinda **10**
Williams, Paul **5**
Williams, Vanessa **10**

Williams, Victoria **17**
Wilson, Jackie **3**
Wilson Phillips **5**
Winwood, Steve **2**
Womack, Bobby **5**
Wonder, Stevie **17**
    Earlier sketch in CM **2**
XTC **10**
Young, Neil **15**
    Earlier sketch in CM **2**
Young M.C. **4**

Producers
Ackerman, Will **3**
Albini, Steve **15**
Alpert, Herb **11**
Austin, Dallas **16**
Baker, Anita **9**
Benitez, Jellybean **15**
Bogaert, Jo
    See Technotronic
Brown, Junior **15**
Brown, Tony **14**
Browne, Jackson **3**
Burnett, T Bone **13**
Cale, John **9**
Clarke, Stanley **3**
Clinton, George **7**
Collins, Phil **2**
    Also see Genesis
Combs, Sean "Puffy" **16**
Costello, Elvis **2**
Cropper, Steve **12**
Crowell, Rodney **8**
Dixon, Willie **10**
DJ Premier
    See Gang Starr
Dr. Dre **15**
    Also see N.W.A.
Dolby, Thomas **10**
Dozier, Lamont
    See Holland-Dozier-Holland
Edmonds, Kenneth "Babyface" **12**
Enigma **14**
Eno, Brian **8**
Ertegun, Ahmet **10**
Foster, David **13**
Fripp, Robert **9**
Froom, Mitchell **15**
Gordy, Jr., Emory **17**
Gray, F. Gary **19**
Grusin, Dave **7**
Holland, Brian
    See Holland-Dozier-Holland
Holland, Eddie
    See Holland-Dozier-Holland
Jackson, Millie **14**
Jam, Jimmy, and Terry Lewis **11**
Jones, Booker T. **8**
Jones, Quincy **2**
Jourgensen, Al
    See Ministry
Krasnow, Bob **15**
Lanois, Daniel **8**
Laswell, Bill **14**

Leiber and Stoller **14**
Lillywhite, Steve **13**
Lynne, Jeff **5**
Marley, Rita **10**
Martin, George **6**
Mayfield, Curtis **8**
Miller, Mitch **11**
Parks, Van Dyke **17**
Parsons, Alan **12**
Prince **14**
  Earlier sketch in CM **1**
Riley, Teddy **14**
Robertson, Robbie **2**
Rodgers, Nile **8**
Rubin, Rick **9**
Rundgren, Todd **11**
Shocklee, Hank **15**
Simmons, Russell **7**
Skaggs, Ricky **5**
Spector, Phil **4**
Sure!, Al B. **13**
Sweat, Keith **13**
Swing, DeVante
  See Jodeci
Too $hort **16**
Toussaint, Allen **11**
Tricky **18**
Vandross, Luther **2**
Vasquez, Junior **16**
Vig, Butch **17**
Walden, Narada Michael **14**
Wexler, Jerry **15**
Willner, Hal **10**
Wilson, Brian
  See Beach Boys, The
Winbush, Angela **15**

Promoters
Clark, Dick **2**
Geldof, Bob **9**
Graham, Bill **10**
Hay, George D. **3**
Simmons, Russell **7**

Ragtime
Johnson, James P. **16**
Joplin, Scott **10**

Rap
Anthony, Marc **19**
Arrested Development **14**
Austin, Dallas **16**
Bambaataa, Afrika **13**
Basehead **11**
Beastie Boys, The **8**
Biz Markie **10**
Black Sheep **15**
Bone Thugs-N-Harmony **18**
Busta Rhymes **18**
Campbell, Luther **10**
Cherry, Neneh **4**
Combs, Sean "Puffy" **16**
Coolio **19**
Cypress Hill **11**
Das EFX **14**

De La Soul **7**
Digable Planets **15**
Digital Underground **9**
DJ Jazzy Jeff and the Fresh Prince **5**
Dr. Dre **15**
  Also see N.W.A.
Eazy-E **13**
  Also see N.W.A.
EPMD **10**
Eric B. and Rakim **9**
Franti, Michael **16**
Fugees, The **17**
Gang Starr **13**
Geto Boys, The **11**
Grandmaster Flash **14**
Hammer, M.C. **5**
Heavy D **10**
House of Pain **14**
Ice Cube **10**
Ice-T **7**
Jackson, Millie **14**
Kane, Big Daddy **7**
Kid 'n Play **5**
Knight, Suge **15**
Kool Moe Dee **9**
Kris Kross **11**
KRS-One **8**
L.L. Cool J. **5**
MC Breed **17**
MC Lyte **8**
MC 900 Ft. Jesus **16**
MC Serch **10**
Nas **19**
Naughty by Nature **11**
N.W.A. **6**
Pharcyde, The **17**
P.M. Dawn **11**
Public Enemy **4**
Queen Latifah **6**
Rage Against the Machine **18**
Riley, Teddy **14**
Rubin, Rick **9**
Run-D.M.C. **4**
Salt-N-Pepa **6**
Scott-Heron, Gil **13**
Shaggy **19**
Shanté **10**
Shocklee, Hank **15**
Simmons, Russell **7**
Sir Mix-A-Lot **14**
Snoop Doggy Dogg **17**
Spearhead **19**
Special Ed **16**
Sure!, Al B. **13**
TLC **15**
Tone-L c **3**
Too $hort **16**
Tribe Called Quest, A **8**
2Pac **17**
Tricky **18**
US3 **18**
Vanilla Ice **6**
Wu-Tang Clan **19**
Young M.C. **4**
Yo Yo **9**

Record Company Executives
Ackerman, Will **3**
Alpert, Herb **11**
Brown, Tony **14**
Busby, Jheryl **9**
Combs, Sean "Puffy" **16**
Davis, Chip **4**
Davis, Clive **14**
Ertegun, Ahmet **10**
Foster, David **13**
Gabriel, Peter **16**
  Earlier sketch in CM **2**
  Also see Genesis
Geffen, David **8**
Gordy, Berry, Jr. **6**
Hammond, John **6**
Harley, Bill **7**
Harrell, Andre **16**
Jam, Jimmy, and Terry Lewis **11**
Knight, Suge **15**
Koppelman, Charles **14**
Krasnow, Bob **15**
LiPuma, Tommy **18**
Madonna **16**
  Earlier sketch in CM **4**
Marley, Rita **10**
Martin, George **6**
Mayfield, Curtis **8**
Mercer, Johnny **13**
Miller, Mitch **11**
Mingus, Charles **9**
Near, Holly **1**
Ostin, Mo **17**
Penner, Fred **10**
Phillips, Sam **5**
Reznor, Trent **13**
Rhone, Sylvia **13**
Robinson, Smokey **1**
Rubin, Rick **9**
Simmons, Russell **7**
Spector, Phil **4**
Teller, Al **15**
Too $hort **16**
Wexler, Jerry **15**

Reggae
Bad Brains **16**
Black Uhuru **12**
Burning Spear **15**
Cliff, Jimmy **8**
Dube, Lucky **17**
Inner Circle **15**
Marley, Bob **3**
Marley, Rita **10**
Marley, Ziggy **3**
Mystic Revealers **16**
Skatalites, The **18**
Sly and Robbie **13**
Steel Pulse **14**
Third World **13**
Tosh, Peter **3**
UB40 **4**
Wailer, Bunny **11**

Rhythm and Blues/Soul
Abdul, Paula **3**

Adams, Oleta **17**
Alexander, Arthur **14**
All-4-One **17**
Austin, Dallas **16**
Ballard, Hank **17**
Baker, Anita **9**
Ball, Marcia **15**
Basehead **11**
Belle, Regina **6**
Berry, Chuck **1**
Bland, Bobby "Blue" **12**
Blige, Mary J. **15**
Blues Brothers, The **3**
Bolton, Michael **4**
Boyz II Men **15**
Brandy **19**
Braxton, Toni **17**
Brown, James **16**
  Earlier sketch in CM **2**
Brown, Ruth **13**
Bryson, Peabo **11**
Burdon, Eric **14**
  Also see War
Busby, Jheryl **9**
C + C Music Factory **16**
Campbell, Tevin **13**
Carey, Mariah **6**
Charles, Ray **1**
Cole, Natalie **1**
Cooke, Sam **1**
  Also see Soul Stirrers, The
Cropper, Steve **12**
Curtis, King **17**
D'Arby, Terence Trent **3**
DeBarge, El **14**
Des'ree **15**
Dibango, Manu **14**
Diddley, Bo **3**
Domino, Fats **2**
Dr. John **7**
Earth, Wind and Fire **12**
Edmonds, Kenneth "Babyface" **12**
En Vogue **10**
Evora, Cesaria **19**
Fabulous Thunderbirds, The **1**
Four Tops, The **11**
Fox, Samantha **3**
Franklin, Aretha **17**
  Earlier sketch in CM **2**
Gaye, Marvin **4**
Gordy, Berry, Jr. **6**
Green, Al **9**
Hall & Oates **6**
Hayes, Isaac **10**
Holland-Dozier-Holland **5**
Incognito **16**
Ingram, James **11**
Isley Brothers, The **8**
Jackson, Freddie **3**
Jackson, Janet **3**
Jackson, Michael **17**
  Earlier sketch in CM **1**
  Also see Jackson, The
Jackson, Millie **14**
Jacksons, The **7**

Jam, Jimmy, and Terry Lewis **11**
James, Etta **6**
Jodeci **13**
Jones, Booker T. **8**
Jones, Grace **9**
Jones, Quincy **2**
Jordan, Louis **11**
Kelly, R. **19**
Khan, Chaka **19**
Khan, Chaka **9**
King, Ben E. **7**
Knight, Gladys **1**
Kool & the Gang **13**
LaBelle, Patti **8**
Los Lobos **2**
Mayfield, Curtis **8**
Medley, Bill **3**
Meters, The **14**
Milli Vanilli **4**
Moore, Melba **7**
Morrison, Van **3**
Ndegéocello, Me'Shell **18**
Neville, Aaron **5**
  Also see Neville Brothers, The
Neville Brothers, The **4**
Ocean, Billy **4**
Ohio Players **16**
O'Jays, The **13**
Otis, Johnny **16**
Pendergrass, Teddy **3**
Peniston, CeCe **15**
Pickett, Wilson **10**
Pointer Sisters, The **9**
Prince **14**
  Earlier sketch in CM **1**
Rawls, Lou **19**
Redding, Otis **5**
Reese, Della **13**
Reeves, Martha **4**
Richie, Lionel **2**
Riley, Teddy **14**
Robinson, Smokey **1**
Ross, Diana **6**
  Also see Supremes, The
Ruffin, David **6**
  Also see Temptations, The
Sam and Dave **8**
Scaggs, Boz **12**
Secada, Jon **13**
Shanice **14**
Shirelles, The **11**
Shocklee, Hank **15**
Sledge, Percy **15**
Soul II Soul **17**
Stansfield, Lisa **9**
Staples, Mavis **13**
Staples, Pops **11**
Stewart, Rod **2**
Stone, Sly **8**
Subdudes, The **18**
Supremes, The **6**
  Also see Ross, Diana
Sure!, Al B. **13**
Sweat, Keith **13**
SWV **14**

Temptations, The **3**
Third World **13**
Thomas, Irma **16**
TLC **15**
Thornton, Big Mama **18**
Tony! Toni! Toné! **12**
Toussaint, Allen **11**
Turner, Tina **1**
Vandross, Luther **2**
Was (Not Was) **6**
Waters, Crystal **15**
Watley, Jody **9**
Wexler, Jerry **15**
Williams, Deniece **1**
Williams, Vanessa **10**
Wilson, Jackie **3**
Winans, The **12**
Winbush, Angela **15**
Womack, Bobby **5**
Wonder, Stevie **17**
  Earlier sketch in CM **2**

Rock
AC/DC **4**
Adam Ant **13**
Adams, Bryan **2**
Aerosmith **3**
Afghan Whigs **17**
Albini, Steve **15**
Alexander, Arthur **14**
Alice in Chains **10**
Allman Brothers, The **6**
Alvin, Dave **17**
America **16**
American Music Club **15**
Anthrax **11**
Babes in Toyland **16**
Bad Brains **16**
Baker, Ginger **16**
  Also see Cream
Ballard, Hank **17**
Band, The **9**
Barenaked Ladies **18**
Basehead **11**
Beach Boys, The **1**
Beastie Boys, The **8**
Beatles, The **2**
Beaver Brown Band, The **3**
Beck, Jeff **4**
  Also see Yardbirds, The
Beck **18**
Belew, Adrian **5**
Belly **16**
Benatar, Pat **8**
Berry, Chuck **1**
Bettie Serveert **17**
Biafra, Jello **18**
Big Audio Dynamite **18**
Bjork **16**
Black Crowes, The **7**
Black, Frank **14**
Black Sabbath **9**
Blackman, Cindy **15**
Blondie **14**
Blood, Sweat and Tears **7**

Blue Oyster Cult **16**
Blue Rodeo **18**
Blues Traveler **15**
Blur **17**
BoDeans, The **3**
Bon Jovi **10**
Boston **11**
Bowie, David **1**
Bragg, Billy **7**
Breeders **19**
Brickell, Edie **3**
Browne, Jackson **3**
Buckingham, Lindsey **8**
   Also see Fleetwood Mac
Buckley, Tim **14**
Buffalo Tom **18**
Burdon, Eric **14**
   Also see War
Burnett, T Bone **13**
Bush **18**
Butthole Surfers **16**
Buzzcocks, The **9**
Byrds, The **8**
Byrne, David **8**
   Also see Talking Heads
Cale, J. J. **16**
Cale, John **9**
Captain Beefheart **10**
Cardigans **19**
Catherine Wheel **18**
Cave, Nick **10**
Charlatans, The **13**
Cheap Trick **12**
Cher **1**
Chicago **3**
Church, The **14**
Cinderella **16**
Circle Jerks, The **17**
Clapton, Eric **11**
   Earlier sketch in CM **1**
      Also see Cream
      Also see Yardbirds, The
Clash, The **4**
Clemons, Clarence **7**
Clinton, George **7**
Coasters, The **5**
Cocker, Joe **4**
Collective Soul **16**
Collins, Phil **2**
   Also see Genesis
Cooder, Ry **2**
Cooke, Sam **1**
   Also see Soul Stirrers, The
Cooper, Alice **8**
Cope, Julian **16**
Costello, Elvis **12**
   Earlier sketch in CM **2**
Cougar, John(ny)
   See Mellencamp, John "Cougar"
Counting Crows **18**
Cracker **12**
Cramps, The **16**
Cranberries, The **14**
Crash Test Dummies **14**
Cream **9**

Creedence Clearwater Revival **16**
Crenshaw, Marshall **5**
Crosby, David **3**
   Also see Byrds, The
Crow, Sheryl **18**
Crowded House **12**
Cult, The **16**
Cure, The **3**
Curry, Tim **3**
Curve **13**
Dale, Dick **13**
Daltrey, Roger **3**
   Also see Who, The
Daniels, Charlie **6**
Danzig **7**
D'Arby, Terence Trent **3**
Dave Clark Five, The **12**
Dave Matthews Band **18**
Davies, Ray **5**
dc Talk **18**
Dead Can Dance **16**
Deep Purple **11**
Def Leppard **3**
Del Amitri **18**
Depeche Mode **5**
Devo **13**
Diddley, Bo **3**
DiFranco, Ani **17**
Dinosaur Jr. **10**
Doc Pomus **14**
Dokken **16**
Doobie Brothers, The **3**
Doors, The **4**
Duran Duran **4**
Dylan, Bob **3**
Eagles, The **3**
Eddy, Duane **9**
Einstürzende Neubauten **13**
Electric Light Orchestra **7**
Elliot, Cass **5**
Emerson, Lake & Palmer/Powell **5**
English Beat, The **9**
Eno, Brian **8**
Erickson, Roky **16**
Escovedo, Alejandro **18**
Etheridge, Melissa **16**
   Earlier sketch in CM **4**
Eurythmics **6**
Everclear **18**
Extreme **10**
Faithfull, Marianne **14**
Faith No More **7**
Fall, The **12**
Ferry, Bryan **1**
fIREHOSE **11**
Fishbone **7**
Fleetwood Mac **5**
Flores, Rosie **16**
Fogelberg, Dan **4**
Fogerty, John **2**
   Also see Creedence Clearwater Revival
Ford, Lita **9**
Fox, Samantha **3**
Frampton, Peter **3**
Franti, Michael **16**

Frey, Glenn **3**
   Also see Eagles, The
Front 242 **19**
Froom, Mitchell **15**
Fugazi **13**
Gabriel, Peter **16**
   Earlier sketch in CM **2**
      Also see Genesis
Gang of Four **8**
Garcia, Jerry **4**
   Also see Grateful Dead, The
Gatton, Danny **16**
Genesis **4**
Gift, Roland **3**
Gin Blossoms **18**
Glitter, Gary **19**
Goo Goo Dolls, The **16**
Graham, Bill **10**
Grant Lee Buffalo **16**
Grateful Dead **5**
Grebenshikov, Boris **3**
Green Day **16**
Guided By Voices **18**
Guns n' Roses **2**
Gwar **13**
Hall & Oates **6**
Harper, Ben **17**
Harrison, George **2**
   Also see Beatles, The
Harry, Deborah **4**
   Also see Blondie
Harvey, Polly Jean **11**
Hatfield, Juliana **12**
   Also see Lemonheads, The
Healey, Jeff **4**
Helmet **15**
Hendrix, Jimi **2**
Henley, Don **3**
   Also see Eagles, The
Henry, Joe **18**
Hiatt, John **8**
Hole **14**
Holland-Dozier-Holland **5**
Hootie and the Blowfish **18**
Idol, Billy **3**
INXS **2**
Iron Maiden **10**
Isaak, Chris **6**
Jackson, Joe **4**
Jagger, Mick **7**
   Also see Rolling Stones, The
Jane's Addiction **6**
Jayhawks, The **15**
Jefferson Airplane **5**
Jesus Lizard **19**
Jesus and Mary Chain, The **10**
Jethro Tull **8**
Jett, Joan **3**
Joel, Billy **2**
Johansen, David **7**
John, Elton **3**
Jon Spencer Blues Explosion **18**
Joplin, Janis **3**
Joy Division **19**
Judas Priest **10**

KMFDM **18**
Kennedy, Nigel **8**
Kidjo, Anjelique **17**
King Crimson **17**
Kinks, The **15**
Kiss **5**
Knopfler, Mark **3**
Kravitz, Lenny **5**
Landreth, Sonny **16**
Led Zeppelin **1**
Leiber and Stoller **14**
Lemonheads, The **12**
Lennon, John **9**
  Also see Beatles, The
Lennon, Julian **2**
Lindley, David **2**
Little Feat **4**
Little Texas **14**
Live **14**
Living Colour **7**
Loggins, Kenny **3**
Los Lobos **2**
Love and Rockets **15**
L7 **12**
Luna **18**
Luscious Jackson **19**
Lush **13**
Lydon, John **9**
  Also see Sex Pistols, The
Lynne, Jeff **5**
Lynyrd Skynyrd **9**
Madder Rose **17**
Marilyn Manson **18**
Martin, George **6**
Marx, Richard **3**
McCartney, Paul **4**
  Also see Beatles, The
McClinton, Delbert **14**
MC5, The **9**
McKee, Maria **11**
McMurtry, James **10**
Meat Loaf **12**
Meat Puppets, The **13**
Megadeth **9**
Mekons, The **15**
Mellencamp, John "Cougar" **2**
Metallica **7**
Midnight Oil **11**
Mike & the Mechanics **17**
Miller, Steve **2**
Ministry **10**
Moby Grape **12**
Money, Eddie **16**
Moody Blues, The **18**
Morphine **16**
Morrison, Jim **3**
  Also see Doors, The
Morrison, Van **3**
Mötley Crüe **1**
Motörhead **10**
Mould, Bob **10**
Mudhoney **16**
Muldaur, Maria **18**
Myles, Alannah **4**
Nelson, Rick **2**

New York Dolls **19**
Newman, Randy **4**
Nicks, Stevie **2**
Nirvana **8**
NRBQ **12**
Nugent, Ted **2**
Oasis **16**
Ocasek, Ric **5**
O'Connor, Sinead **3**
Offspring **19**
Ono, Yoko **11**
Orbison, Roy **2**
Osbourne, Ozzy **3**
Page, Jimmy **4**
  Also see Led Zeppelin
  Also see Yardbirds, The
Palmer, Robert **2**
Pantera **13**
Parker, Graham **10**
Parker, Maceo **7**
Parsons, Alan **12**
Parsons, Gram **7**
  Also see Byrds, The
Pavement **14**
Pearl Jam **12**
Pere Ubu **17**
Perkins, Carl **9**
Petty, Tom **9**
Phillips, Sam **5**
Phish **13**
Pigface **19**
Pink Floyd **2**
Plant, Robert **2**
  Also see Led Zeppelin
Pogues, The **6**
Poi Dog Pondering **17**
Poison **11**
Pop, Iggy **1**
Presley, Elvis **1**
Pretenders, The **8**
Primal Scream **14**
Primus **11**
Prince **14**
  Earlier sketch in CM **1**
Prine, John **7**
Proclaimers, The **13**
Pulp **18**
Queen **6**
Queensryche **8**
Rage Against the Machine **18**
Raitt, Bonnie **3**
Ramones, The **9**
Red Hot Chili Peppers, The **7**
Reed, Lou **16**
  Earlier sketch in CM **1**
  Also see Velvet Underground, The
Reid, Vernon **2**
  Also see Living Colour
R.E.M. **5**
Replacements, The **7**
Residents, The **14**
Reverend Horton Heat **19**
Reznor, Trent **13**
Richards, Keith **11**
  Also see Rolling Stones, The

Richman, Jonathan **12**
Robertson, Robbie **2**
Rolling Stones, The **3**
Rollins, Henry **11**
Roth, David Lee **1**
  Also see Van Halen
Rubin, Rick **9**
Rundgren, Todd **11**
Rush **8**
Ryder, Mitch **11**
Santana, Carlos **19**
Satriani, Joe **4**
Scaggs, Boz **12**
Scorpions, The **12**
Screaming Trees **19**
Seal **14**
Seger, Bob **15**
Sepultura **12**
Sex Pistols, The **5**
Shaffer, Paul **13**
Shannon, Del **10**
Shocked, Michelle **4**
Shonen Knife **13**
Simon, Carly **4**
Simon, Paul **16**
  Earlier sketch in CM **1**
Siouxsie and the Banshees **8**
Skinny Puppy **17**
Slayer **10**
Smashing Pumpkins **13**
Smith, Patti **17**
  Earlier sketch in CM **1**
Smithereens, The **14**
Smiths, The **3**
Social Distortion **19**
Sonic Youth **9**
Soul Asylum **10**
Soundgarden **6**
Sparks **18**
Spector, Phil **4**
Spencer Davis Group **19**
Spin Doctors **14**
Spinal Tap **8**
Sponge **18**
Springsteen, Bruce **6**
Squeeze **5**
Starr, Ringo **10**
Steeleye Span **19**
Steely Dan **5**
Stevens, Cat **3**
Stewart, Rod **2**
Stills, Stephen **5**
Sting **2**
Stone Roses, The **16**
Stone, Sly **8**
Stone Temple Pilots **14**
Straw, Syd **18**
Stray Cats, The **11**
Stryper **2**
Sublime **19**
Sugarcubes, The **10**
Suicidal Tendencies **15**
Summers, Andy **3**
Tears for Fears **6**
Teenage Fanclub **13**

Television **17**
10,000 Maniacs **3**
Tesla **15**
Texas Tornados, The **8**
The The **15**
They Might Be Giants **7**
Thin Lizzy **13**
Thompson, Richard **7**
Three Dog Night **5**
Throwing Muses **15**
Timbuk 3 **3**
Toad the Wet Sprocket **13**
Townshend, Pete **1**
  Also see Who, The
Traffic **19**
Tragically Hip, The **18**
T. Rex **11**
Turner, Tina **1**
U2 **12**
  Earlier sketch in CM **2**
Ulmer, James Blood **13**
Urge Overkill **17**
Uriah Heep **19**
Vai, Steve **5**
Valli, Frankie **10**
Van Halen **8**
Vaughan, Stevie Ray **1**
Velvet Underground, The **7**
Ventures **19**
Verve, The **18**
Vincent, Gene **19**
Violent Femmes **12**
Waits, Tom **12**
  Earlier sketch in CM **1**
Walsh, Joe **5**
  Also see Eagles, The
War **14**
Warrant **17**
Weller, Paul **14**
Whitesnake **5**
White Zombie **17**
Whitley, Chris **16**
Who, The **3**
Winter, Johnny **5**
Winwood, Steve **2**
Wray, Link **17**
X **11**
Yardbirds, The **10**
Yes **8**
Young, Neil **15**
  Earlier sketch in CM **2**
Zappa, Frank **17**
  Earlier sketch in CM **1**
Zevon, Warren **9**
ZZ Top **2**

Rock and Roll Pioneers
Ballard, Hank **17**
Berry, Chuck **1**
Clark, Dick **2**
Darin, Bobby **4**
Diddley, Bo **3**
Dion **4**
Domino, Fats **2**
Eddy, Duane **9**

Everly Brothers, The **2**
Francis, Connie **10**
Glitter, Gary **19**
Haley, Bill **6**
Hawkins, Screamin' Jay **8**
Holly, Buddy **1**
James, Etta **6**
Jordan, Louis **11**
Lewis, Jerry Lee **2**
Little Richard **1**
Nelson, Rick **2**
Orbison, Roy **2**
Otis, Johnny **16**
Paul, Les **2**
Perkins, Carl **9**
Phillips, Sam **5**
Presley, Elvis **1**
Professor Longhair **6**
Sedaka, Neil **4**
Shannon, Del **10**
Shirelles, The **11**
Spector, Phil **4**
Twitty, Conway **6**
Valli, Frankie **10**
Wilson, Jackie **3**
Wray, Link **17**

Saxophone
Adderly, Cannonball **15**
Ayler , Albert **19**
Bechet, Sidney **17**
Braxton, Anthony **12**
Carter, Benny **3**
  Also see McKinney's Cotton Pickers
Carter, James **18**
Chenier, C. J. **15**
Clemons, Clarence **7**
Coleman, Ornette **5**
Coltrane, John **4**
Curtis, King **17**
Dibango, Manu **14**
Dorsey, Jimmy
  See Dorsey Brothers, The
Getz, Stan **12**
Gordon, Dexter **10**
Harris, Eddie **15**
Hawkins, Coleman **11**
Henderson, Joe **14**
Herman, Woody **12**
Jacquet, Illinois **17**
Kenny G **14**
Kirk, Rahsaan Roland **6**
Koz, Dave **19**
Lateef, Yusef **16**
Lopez, Israel "Cachao" **14**
Lovano, Joe **13**
Marsalis, Branford **10**
Morgan, Frank **9**
Mulligan, Gerry **16**
Parker, Charlie **5**
Parker, Maceo **7**
Pepper, Art **18**
Redman, Joshua **12**
Rollins, Sonny **7**
Sanborn, David **1**

Sanders, Pharoah **16**
Shorter, Wayne **5**
Threadgill, Henry **9**
Washington, Grover, Jr. **5**
Winter, Paul **10**
Young, La Monte **16**
Young, Lester **14**
Zorn, John **15**

Sintir
Hakmoun, Hassan **15**

Songwriters
Acuff, Roy **2**
Adams, Bryan **2**
Albini, Steve **15**
Alexander, Arthur **14**
Allen, Peter **11**
Allison, Mose **17**
Alpert, Herb **11**
Alvin, Dave **17**
Amos, Tori **12**
Anderson, Ian
  See Jethro Tull
Anderson, John **5**
Anka, Paul **2**
Armatrading, Joan **4**
Astbury, Ian
  See Cult, The
Atkins, Chet **5**
Autry, Gene **12**
Bacharach, Burt **1**
Baez, Joan **1**
Baker, Anita **9**
Balin, Marty
  See Jefferson Airplane
Barrett, (Roger) Syd
  See Pink Floyd
Basie, Count **2**
Becker, Walter
  See Steely Dan
Beckley, Gerry
  See America
Belew, Adrian **5**
Benton, Brook **7**
Berg, Matraca **16**
Berlin, Irving **8**
Berry, Chuck **1**
Bjork **16**
  Also see Sugarcubes, The
Black, Clint **5**
Black, Frank **14**
Blades, Ruben **2**
Blige, Mary J. **15**
Bloom, Luka **14**
Bono
  See U2
Brady, Paul **8**
Bragg, Billy **7**
Brickell, Edie **3**
Brooke, Jonatha
  See Story, The
Brooks, Garth **8**
Brown, Bobby **4**
Brown, James **16**
  Earlier sketch in CM **2**

Brown, Junior **15**
Brown, Marty **14**
Browne, Jackson **3**
Buck, Peter
  See R.E.M.
Buck, Robert
  See 10,000 Maniacs
Buckingham, Lindsey **8**
  Also see Fleetwood Mac
Buckley, Tim **14**
Buffett, Jimmy **4**
Bunnell, Dewey
  See America
Burdon, Eric **14**
  Also see War
Burnett, T Bone **13**
Burning Spear **15**
Bush, Kate **4**
Byrne, David **8**
  Also see Talking Heads
Cahn, Sammy **11**
Cale, J. J. **16**
Cale, John **9**
Calloway, Cab **6**
Captain Beefheart **10**
Carpenter, Mary-Chapin **6**
Carter, Carlene **8**
Cash, Johnny **17**
  Earlier sketch in CM **1**
Cash, Rosanne **2**
Cetera, Peter
  See Chicago
Chandra, Sheila **16**
Chapin, Harry **6**
Chapman, Steven Curtis **15**
Chapman, Tracy **4**
Charles, Ray **1**
Chenier, C. J. **15**
Childs, Toni **2**
Chilton, Alex **10**
Clapton, Eric **11**
  Earlier sketch in CM **1**
  Also see Cream
  Also see Yardbirds, The
Clark, Guy **17**
Clements, Vassar **18**
Cleveland, James **1**
Clinton, George **7**
Cockburn, Bruce **8**
Cohen, Leonard **3**
Cole, Lloyd **9**
Cole, Nat King **3**
Collins, Albert **4**
Collins, Judy **4**
Collins, Phil **2**
  Also see Genesis
Cooder, Ry **2**
Cooke, Sam **1**
  Also see Soul Stirrers, The
Collie, Mark **15**
Cooper, Alice **8**
Cope, Julian **16**
Corgan, Billy
  See Smashing Pumpkins
Costello, Elvis **12**

Earlier sketch in CM **2**
Cotten, Elizabeth **16**
Crenshaw, Marshall **5**
Croce, Jim **3**
Crofts, Dash
  See Seals & Crofts
Cropper, Steve **12**
Crosby, David **3**
  Also see Byrds, The
Crow, Sheryl **18**
Crowe, J. D. **5**
Crowell, Rodney **8**
Daniels, Charlie **6**
Davies, Ray **5**
  Also see Kinks, the
DeBarge, El **14**
DeMent, Iris **13**
Denver, John **1**
Des'ree **15**
Diamond, Neil **1**
Diddley, Bo **3**
Difford, Chris
  See Squeeze
DiFranco, Ani **17**
Dion **4**
Dixon, Willie **10**
Doc Pomus **14**
Domino, Fats **2**
Donelly, Tanya
  See Belly
  Also see Throwing Muses
Donovan **9**
Dorsey, Thomas A. **11**
Doucet, Michael **8**
Dozier, Lamont
  See Holland-Dozier-Holland
Drake, Nick **17**
Dube, Lucky **17**
Duffy, Billy
  See Cult, The
Dulli, Greg **17**
  See Afghan Whigs, The
Dylan, Bob **3**
Earle, Steve **16**
Edge, The
  See U2
Edmonds, Kenneth "Babyface" **12**
Eitzel, Mark
  See American Music Club
Elfman, Danny **9**
Ellington, Duke **2**
Emerson, Keith
  See Emerson, Lake & Palmer/Powell
Enigma **14**
Erickson, Roky **16**
Ertegun, Ahmet **10**
Escovedo, Alejandro **18**
Estefan, Gloria **15**
  Earlier sketch in CM **2**
Etheridge, Melissa **16**
  Earlier entry in CM **4**
Everly, Don
  See Everly Brothers, The
Everly, Phil
  See Everly Brothers, The

Fagen, Don
  See Steely Dan
Faithfull, Marianne **14**
Ferry, Bryan **1**
Flack, Roberta **5**
Flatt, Lester **3**
Fogelberg, Dan **4**
Fogerty, John **2**
  Also see Creedence Clearwater Revival
Fordham, Julia **15**
Foster, David **13**
Frampton, Peter **3**
Franti, Michael **16**
Frey, Glenn **3**
  Also see Eagles, The
Fripp, Robert **9**
Frizzell, Lefty **10**
Gabriel, Peter **16**
  Earlier sketch in CM **2**
  Also see Genesis
Garcia, Jerry **4**
  Also see Grateful Dead, The
Gaye, Marvin **4**
Geldof, Bob **9**
George, Lowell
  See Little Feat
Gershwin, George and Ira **11**
Gibb, Barry
  See Bee Gees, The
Gibb, Maurice
  See Bee Gees, The
Gibb, Robin
  See Bee Gees, The
Gibbons, Billy
  See ZZ Top
Gibson, Debbie **1**
Gift, Roland **3**
Gill, Vince **7**
Gilley, Mickey **7**
Gilmour, David
  See Pink Floyd
Goodman, Benny **4**
Gordy, Berry, Jr. **6**
Gorka, John **18**
Grant, Amy **7**
Green, Al **9**
Greenwood, Lee **12**
Griffith, Nanci **3**
Guthrie, Arlo **6**
Guthrie, Woodie **2**
Guy, Buddy **4**
Haggard, Merle **2**
Hall, Daryl
  See Hall & Oates
Hall, Tom T. **4**
Hamlisch, Marvin **1**
Hammer, M.C. **5**
Hammerstein, Oscar
  See Rodgers, Richard
Harrison, George **2**
  Also see Beatles, The
Harry, Deborah **4**
  Also see Blondie
Hart, Lorenz
  See Rodgers, Richard
Hartford, John **1**

Hatfield, Juliana **12**
    Also see Lemonheads, The
Hawkins, Screamin' Jay **8**
Hayes, Isaac **10**
Healey, Jeff **4**
Hedges, Michael **3**
Hendrix, Jimi **2**
Henley, Don **3**
    Also see Eagles, The
Henry, Joe **18**
Hersh, Kristin
    See Throwing Muses
Hiatt, John **8**
Hidalgo, David
    See Los Lobos
Hillman, Chris
    See Byrds, The
    Also see Desert Rose Band, The
Hinojosa, Tish **13**
Hitchcock, Robyn **9**
Holland, Brian
    See Holland-Dozier-Holland
Holland, Eddie
    See Holland-Dozier-Holland
Holly, Buddy **1**
Hornsby, Bruce **3**
Howard, Harlan **15**
Hutchence, Michael
    See INXS
Hynde, Chrissie
    See Pretenders, The
Ian, Janis **5**
Ice Cube **10**
Ice-T **7**
Idol, Billy **3**
Isaak, Chris **6**
Jackson, Alan **7**
Jackson, Janet **16**
    Earlier sketch in CM **3**
Jackson, Joe **4**
Jackson, Michael **17**
    Earlier sketch in CM **1**
    Also see Jacksons, The
Jackson, Millie **14**
Jagger, Mick **7**
    Also see Rolling Stones, The
Jam, Jimmy, and Terry Lewis **11**
James, Rick **2**
Jarreau, Al **1**
Jennings, Waylon **4**
Jett, Joan **3**
Joel, Billy **12**
    Earlier sketch in CM **2**
Johansen, David **7**
John, Elton **3**
Johnson, Lonnie **17**
Johnson, Matt
    See The The
Jones, Brian
    See Rolling Stones, The
Jones, George **4**
Jones, Mick
    See Clash, The
Jones, Quincy **2**
Jones, Rickie Lee **4**

Joplin, Janis **3**
Judd, Naomi
    See Judds, The
Kane, Big Daddy **7**
Kantner, Paul
    See Jefferson Airplane
Kee, John P. **15**
Keith, Toby **17**
Kelly, R. **19**
Ketchum, Hal **14**
Khan, Chaka **9**
King, Albert **2**
King, B. B. **1**
King, Ben E. **7**
King, Carole **6**
King, Freddy **17**
Kirkwood, Curt
    See Meat Puppets, The
Knopfler, Mark **3**
Kottke, Leo **13**
Kravitz, Lenny **5**
Kristofferson, Kris **4**
Lake, Greg
    See Emerson, Lake & Palmer/Powell
Landreth, Sonny **16**
Lang, K. D. **4**
Larkin, Patty **9**
Lavin, Christine **6**
LeDoux, Chris **12**
Lee, Peggy **8**
Lehrer, Tom **7**
Leiber and Stoller **14**
Lennon, John **9**
    Also see Beatles, The
Lennon, Julian **2**
Lewis, Huey **9**
Lightfoot, Gordon **3**
Little Richard **1**
Llanas, Sammy
    See BoDeans, The
L.L. Cool J **5**
Loggins, Kenny **3**
Love, Courtney
    See Hole
Loveless, Patty **5**
Lovett, Lyle **5**
Lowe, Nick **6**
Lydon, John **9**
    Also see Sex Pistols, The
Lynn, Loretta **2**
Lynne, Jeff **5**
Lynne, Shelby **5**
Lynott, Phil
    See Thin Lizzy
MacColl, Kirsty **12**
MacDonald, Barbara
    See Timbuk 3
MacDonald, Pat
    See Timbuk 3
Madonna **16**
    Earlier sketch in CM **4**
Manilow, Barry **2**
Manzarek, Ray
    See Doors, The
Marley, Bob **3**

Marley, Ziggy **3**
Marx, Richard **3**
Mattea, Kathy **5**
May, Brian
    See Queen
Mayfield, Curtis **8**
MC Breed **17**
McCartney, Paul **4**
    Also see Beatles, The
McClinton, Delbert **14**
McCoury, Del **15**
McDonald, Michael
    See Doobie Brothers, The
McGuinn, Roger
    See Byrds, The
McLachlan, Sarah **12**
McLean, Don **7**
McMurtry, James **10**
MC 900 Ft. Jesus **16**
McTell, Blind Willie **17**
McVie, Christine
    See Fleetwood Mac
Medley, Bill **3**
Melanie **12**
Mellencamp, John "Cougar" **2**
Mercer, Johnny **13**
Merchant, Natalie
    See 10,000 Maniacs
Mercury, Freddie
    See Queen
Michael, George **9**
Miller, Roger **4**
Miller, Steve **2**
Milsap, Ronnie **2**
Mitchell, Joni **17**
    Earlier sketch in CM **2**
Moffatt, Katy **18**
Morrison, Jim **3**
Morrison, Van **3**
Morrissey **10**
Morrissey, Bill **12**
Morton, Jelly Roll **7**
Mould, Bob **10**
Moyet, Alison **12**
Nascimento, Milton **6**
Ndegéocello, Me'Shell **18**
Near, Holly **1**
Nelson, Rick **2**
Nelson, Willie **11**
    Earlier sketch in CM **1**
Nesmith, Mike
    See Monkees, The
Neville, Art
    See Neville Brothers, The
Newman, Randy **4**
Newmann, Kurt
    See BoDeans, The
Nicks, Stevie **2**
Nilsson **10**
Nugent, Ted **2**
Nyro, Laura **12**
Oates, John
    See Hall & Oates
Ocasek, Ric **5**
Ocean, Billy **4**

Ochs, Phil **7**
O'Connor, Sinead **3**
Odetta **7**
Orbison, Roy **2**
Osbourne, Ozzy **3**
Oslin, K. T. **3**
Owens, Buck **2**
Page, Jimmy **4**
  See Led Zeppelin
    Also see Yardbirds, The
Palmer, Robert **2**
Paris, Twila **16**
Parks, Van Dyke **17**
Parnell, Lee Roy **15**
Parker, Graham **10**
Parsons, Gram **7**
  Also see Byrds, The
Parton, Dolly **2**
Paul, Les **2**
Paxton, Tom **5**
Peniston, CeCe **15**
Penn, Michael **4**
Perez, Louie
  See Los Lobos
Perkins, Carl **9**
Perry, Joe
  See Aerosmith
Petty, Tom **9**
Phair, Liz **14**
Phillips, Sam **12**
Pickett, Wilson **10**
Pierson, Kate
  See B-52's, The
Plant, Robert **2**
  Also see Led Zeppelin
Pop, Iggy **1**
Porter, Cole **10**
Prince **14**
  Earlier sketch in CM **1**
Prine, John **7**
Professor Longhair **6**
Rabbitt, Eddie **5**
Raitt, Bonnie **3**
Ray, Amy
  See Indigo Girls
Rea, Chris **12**
Redding, Otis **5**
Reddy, Helen **9**
Reed, Lou **16**
  Earlier sketch in CM **1**
    Also see Velvet Underground, The
Reid, Charlie
  See Proclaimers, The
Reid, Craig
  See Proclaimers, The
Reid, Vernon **2**
  Also see Living Colour
Rich, Charlie **3**
Richards, Keith **11**
  Also see Rolling Stones, The
Richie, Lionel **2**
Richman, Jonathan **12**
Riley, Teddy **14**
Ritchie, Jean **4**
Robbins, Marty **9**

Roberts, Brad
  See Crash Test Dummies
Robertson, Robbie **2**
Robillard, Duke **2**
Robinson, Smokey **1**
Rodgers, Jimmie **3**
Rodgers, Richard **9**
Roland, Ed
  See Collective Soul
Roth, David Lee **1**
  Also see Van Halen
Russell, Mark **6**
Rutherford, Mike
  See Genesis
Sade **2**
Sager, Carole Bayer **5**
Saliers, Emily
  See Indigo Girls
Sandman, Mark
  See Morphine
Satriani, Joe **4**
Scaggs, Boz **12**
Schneider, Fred III
  See B-52's, The
Scott-Heron, Gil **13**
Scruggs, Earl **3**
Seal **14**
Seals, Dan **9**
Seals, Jim
  See Seals & Crofts
Secada, Jon **13**
Sedaka, Neil **4**
Seeger, Pete **4**
  Also see Weavers, The
Seger, Bob **15**
Shannon, Del **10**
Sheila E. **3**
Shocked, Michelle **4**
Siberry, Jane **6**
Simmons, Gene
  See Kiss
Simmons, Patrick
  See Doobie Brothers, The
Simon, Carly **4**
Simon, Paul **16**
  Earlier sketch in CM **1**
Skaggs, Ricky **5**
Sledge, Percy **15**
Slick, Grace
  See Jefferson Airplane
Smith, Patti **17**
  Earlier sketch in CM **1**
Smith, Robert
  See Cure, The
    Also see Siouxsie and the Banshees
Snoop Doggy Dogg **17**
Sondheim, Stephen **8**
Spector, Phil **4**
Springsteen, Bruce **6**
Stanley, Paul
  See Kiss
Stanley, Ralph **5**
Starr, Ringo **10**
  Also see Beatles, The
Stevens, Cat **3**

Stevens, Ray **7**
Stewart, Dave
  See Eurythmics, The
Stewart, Rod **2**
Stills, Stephen **5**
Sting **2**
Stipe, Michael
  See R.E.M.
Strait, George **5**
Straw, Syd **18**
Streisand, Barbra **2**
Strickland, Keith
  See B-52's, The
Strummer, Joe
  See Clash, The
Stuart, Marty **9**
Summer, Donna **12**
Summers, Andy **3**
Sure!, Al B. **13**
Sweat, Keith **13**
Sweet, Matthew **9**
Swing, DeVante
  See Jodeci
Taj Mahal **6**
Taylor, James **2**
Taylor, Koko **10**
Thompson, Richard **7**
Thornton, Big Mama **18**
Tikaram, Tanita **9**
Tilbrook, Glenn
  See Squeeze
Tillis, Mel **7**
Tillis, Pam **8**
Timmins, Margo
  See Cowboy Junkies, The
Timmins, Michael
  See Cowboy Junkies, The
Tippin, Aaron **12**
Tone-L c **3**
Torme, Mel **4**
Tosh, Peter **3**
Toussaint, Allen **11**
Townshend, Pete **1**
  Also see Who, The
Travis, Merle **14**
Travis, Randy **9**
Tricky **18**
Tritt, Travis **7**
Tubb, Ernest **4**
Twain, Shania **17**
Twitty, Conway **6**
2Pac **17**
Tyler, Steve
  See Aerosmith
Vai, Steve **5**
  Also see Whitesnake
Vandross, Luther **2**
Van Halen, Edward
  See Van Halen
Van Ronk, Dave **12**
Van Shelton, Ricky **5**
Van Zandt, Townes **13**
Vedder, Eddie
  See Pearl Jam
Vega, Suzanne **3**

Wagoner, Porter **13**
Waits, Tom **12**
  Earlier sketch in CM **1**
Walden, Narada Michael **14**
Walker, Jerry Jeff **13**
Walker, T-Bone **5**
Waller, Fats **7**
Walsh, Joe **5**
  Also see Eagles, The
Wariner, Steve **18**
Waters, Crystal **15**
Waters, Muddy **4**
Waters, Roger
  See Pink Floyd
Webb, Jimmy **12**
Weill, Kurt **12**
Weir, Bob
  See Grateful Dead, The
Welch, Bob
  See Fleetwood Mac
Weller, Paul **14**
West, Dottie **8**
White, Lari **15**
Whitley, Chris **16**
Whitley, Keith **7**
Williams, Deniece **1**
Williams, Don **4**
Williams, Hank, Jr. **1**
Williams, Hank, Sr. **4**
Williams, Lucinda **10**
Williams, Paul **5**
Williams, Victoria **17**
Wills, Bob **6**
Wilson, Brian
  See Beach Boys, The
Wilson, Cindy
  See B-52's, The
Wilson, Ricky
  See B-52's, The
Winbush, Angela **15**
Winter, Johnny **5**
Winwood, Steve **2**
Womack, Bobby **5**
Wonder, Stevie **17**
  Earlier sketch in CM **2**
Wray, Link **17**
Wynette, Tammy **2**
Yoakam, Dwight **1**
Young, Angus
  See AC/DC
Young, Neil **15**
  Earlier sketch in CM **2**
Zappa, Frank **17**

Earlier sketch in CM **1**
Zevon, Warren **9**

Trombone
Anderson, Ray **7**
Dorsey, Tommy
  See Dorsey Brothers, The
Miller, Glenn **6**
Teagarden, Jack **10**
Watts, Eugene
  See Canadian Brass, The

Trumpet
Alpert, Herb **11**
Armstrong, Louis **4**
Baker, Chet **13**
Berigan, Bunny **2**
Blanchard, Terence **13**
Cherry, Don **10**
Coleman, Ornette **5**
Davis, Miles **1**
Eldridge, Roy **9**
    Also see McKinney's Cotton Pickers
Ferguson, Maynard **7**
Gillespie, Dizzy **6**
Hargrove, Roy **15**
Hawkins, Erskine **19**
Hirt, Al **5**
Isham, Mark **14**
James, Harry **11**
Jones, Quincy **2**
Jones, Thad **19**
Loughnane, Lee **3**
Marsalis, Wynton **6**
Masekela, Hugh **7**
Mills, Fred
  See Canadian Brass, The
Oliver, King **15**
Rodney, Red **14**
Romm, Ronald
  See Canadian Brass, The
Sandoval, Arturo **15**
Severinsen, Doc **1**

Tuba
Daellenbach, Charles
  See Canadian Brass, The
Phillips, Harvey **3**

Vibraphone
Burton, Gary **10**
Hampton, Lionel **6**
Jackson, Milt **15**

Norvo, Red **12**

Viola
Dutt, Hank
  See Kronos Quartet
Jones, Michael
  See Kronos Quartet
Killian, Tim
  See Kronos Quartet
Menuhin, Yehudi **11**
Zukerman, Pinchas **4**

Violin
Acuff, Roy **2**
Anderson, Laurie **1**
Bromberg, David **18**
Bush, Sam
  See New Grass Revival, The
Chang, Sarah **7**
Clements, Vassar **18**
Coleman, Ornette **5**
Daniels, Charlie **6**
Doucet, Michael **8**
Germano, Lisa **18**
Gingold, Josef **6**
Grappelli, Stephane **10**
Gray, Ella
  See Kronos Quartet
Harrington, David
  See Kronos Quartet
Hartford, John **1**
Hidalgo, David
  See Los Lobos
Kennedy, Nigel **8**
Krauss, Alison **10**
Lewis, Roy
  See Kronos Quartet
Marriner, Neville **7**
Menuhin, Yehudi **11**
Midori **7**
O'Connor, Mark **1**
Perlman, Itzhak **2**
Ponty, Jean-Luc **8**
Salerno-Sonnenberg, Nadja **3**
Shallenberger, James
  See Kronos Quartet
Sherba, John
  See Kronos Quartet
Skaggs, Ricky **5**
Stern, Isaac **7**
Whiteman, Paul **17**
Wills, Bob **6**
Zukerman, Pinchas **4**

Cumulative Musicians Index

Volume numbers appear in **bold**.

Abba **12**
Abbott, Jacqueline
  See Beautiful South
Abbruzzese, Dave
Anthony, Marc **19**
Ayler , Albert **19**
Abdul, Paula **3**
Abong, Fred
  See Belly
Abrahams, Mick
  See Jethro Tull
Abrantes, Fernando
  See Kraftwerk
AC/DC **4**
Ackerman, Will **3**
Acland, Christopher
  See Lush
Acuff, Roy **2**
Adam Ant **13**
Adamendes, Elaine
  See Throwing Muses
Adams, Bryan **2**
Adams, Clifford
  See Kool & the Gang
Adams, Craig
  See Cult, The
Adams, Donn
  See NRBQ
Adams, John **8**
Adams, Oleta **17**
Adams, Terry
  See NRBQ
Adcock, Eddie
  See Country Gentleman, The
Adderly, Cannonball **15**
Adderly, Julian
  See Adderly, Cannonball
Adé, King Sunny **18**
Adler, Steven
  See Guns n' Roses
Aerosmith **3**
Afghan Whigs **17**
Afonso, Marie
  See Zap Mama
AFX
  See Aphex Twin
Ajile
  See Arrested Development
Alabama **1**
Albarn, Damon
  See Blur
Alberti, Dorona
  See KMFDM
Albini, Steve **15**
Albuquerque, Michael de

See Electric Light Orchestra
Alexakis, Art
  See Everclear
Alexander, Arthur **14**
Alexander, Tim
  See Asleep at the Wheel
Alexander, Tim "Herb"
  See Primus
Ali
  See Tribe Called Quest, A
Alice in Chains **10**
Allcock, Martin
  See Jethro Tull
Allen, April
  See C + C Music Factory
Allen, Dave
  See Gang of Four
Allen, Debbie **8**
Allen, Duane
  See Oak Ridge Boys, The
Allen, Geri **10**
Allen, Johnny Ray
  See Subdudes, The
Allen, Papa Dee
  See War
Allen, Peter **11**
Allen, Red
  See Osborne Brothers, The
Allen, Rick
  See Def Leppard
Allen, Ross
  See Mekons, The
All-4-One **17**
Allison, Mose **17**
Allman, Duane
  See Allman Brothers, The
Allman, Gregg
  See Allman Brothers, The
Allman Brothers, The **6**
Allsup, Michael Rand
  See Three Dog Night
Alpert, Herb **11**
Alphonso, Roland
  See Skatalites, The
Alston, Andy
  See Del Amitri
Alston, Shirley
  See Shirelles, The
Altan **18**
Alvin, Dave **17**
  Also see X
Am, Svet
  See KMFDM
Amedee, Steve
  See Subdudes, The

Ament, Jeff
  See Pearl Jam
America **16**
American Music Club **15**
Amos, Tori **12**
Anastasio, Trey
  See Phish
Anderson, Al
  See NRBQ
Anderson, Cleave
  See Blue Rodeo
Anderson, Emma
  See Lush
Anderson, Gladstone
  See Skatalites, The
Anderson, Ian
  See Jethro Tull
Anderson, John **5**
Anderson, Jon
  See Yes
Anderson, Laurie **1**
Anderson, Marian **8**
Anderson, Pamela
  See Incognito
Anderson, Ray **7**
Anderson, Signe
  See Jefferson Airplane
Andersson, Benny
  See Abba
Andrews, Barry
  See XTC
Andrews, Julie **4**
Andrews, Laverne
  See Andrews Sisters, The
Andrews, Maxene
  See Andrews Sisters, The
Andrews, Patty
  See Andrews Sisters, The
Andrews Sisters, The **9**
Andy, Horace
  See Massive Attack
Anger, Darol
  See Turtle Island String Quartet
Anka, Paul **2**
Anselmo, Philip
  See Pantera
Ant, Adam
  See Adam Ant
Anthony, Marc **19**
Anthony, Michael
  See Massive Attack
Anthony, Michael
  See Van Halen
Anthrax **11**
Anton, Alan
  See Cowboy Junkies, The

Antunes, Michael
    See Beaver Brown Band, The
Aphex Twin 14
Appice, Vinnie
    See Black Sabbath
Araya, Tom
    See Slayer
Ardolino, Tom
    See NRBQ
Arm, Mark
    See Mudhoney
Armatrading, Joan 4
Armstrong, Billie Joe
    See Green Day
Armstrong, Louis 4
Arnaz, Desi 8
Arnold, Eddy 10
Arnold, Kristine
    See Sweethearts of the Rodeo
Arrau, Claudio 1
Arrested Development 14
Arthurs, Paul
    See Oasis
Ash, Daniel
    See Love and Rockets
Ashcroft, Richard
    See Verve, The
Ashton, Susan 17
Asleep at the Wheel 5
Astbury, Ian
    See Cult, The
Astley, Rick 5
Astro
    See UB40
Asuo, Kwesi
    See Arrested Development
Atkins, Chet 5
Atkinson, Sweet Pea
    See Was (Not Was)
Auf Der Maur, Melissa
    See Hole
Augustyniak, Jerry
    See 10,000 Maniacs
Auldridge, Mike 4
    Also see Country Gentlemen, The
    Also see Seldom Scene, The
Austin, Cuba
    See McKinney's Cotton Pickers
Austin, Dallas 16
Autry, Gene 12
Avalon, Frankie 5
Avery, Eric
    See Jane's Addiction
Avory, Mick
    See Kinks, The
Aykroyd, Dan
    See Blues Brothers, The
Ayler, Albert 19
B, Daniel
    See Front 242
Babes in Toyland 16
Babjak, James
    See Smithereens, The
Babyface
    See Edmonds, Kenneth "Babyface"

Bacharach, Burt 1
Badalamenti, Angelo 17
Bad Brains 16
Bad Livers 19
Badger, Pat
    See Extreme
Baez, Joan 1
Bailey, Mildred 13
Bailey, Pearl 5
Bailey, Phil
    See Earth, Wind and Fire
Baker, Anita 9
Baker, Bobby
    See Tragically Hip , The
Baker, Chet 13
Baker, Ginger 16
    Also see Cream
Baker, Janet 14
Baker, Jon
    See Charlatans, The
Baker, Josephine 10
Balakrishnan, David
    See Turtle Island String Quartet
Baldursson, Sigtryggur
    See Sugarcubes, The
Baldwin, Donny
    See Starship
Baliardo, Diego
    See Gipsy Kings, The
Baliardo, Paco
    See Gipsy Kings, The
Baliardo, Tonino
    See Gipsy Kings, The
Balin, Marty
    See Jefferson Airplane
Ball, Marcia 15
Ballard, Florence
    See Supremes, The
Ballard, Hank 17
Balsley, Phil
    See Statler Brothers, The
Baltes, Peter
    See Dokken
Bambaataa, Afrika 13
Band, The 9
Banks, Nick
    See Pulp
Banks, Peter
    See Yes
Banks, Tony
    See Genesis
Baptiste, David Russell
    See Meters, The
Barbata, John
    See Jefferson Starship
Barber, Keith
    See Soul Stirrers, The
Barbero, Lori
    See Babes in Toyland
Barenaked Ladies 18
Bargeld, Blixa
    See Einstürzende Neubauten
Bargeron, Dave
    See Blood, Sweat and Tears
Barham, Meriel

    See Lush
Barker, Paul
    See Ministry
Barlow, Barriemore
    See Jethro Tull
Barlow, Lou
    See Dinosaur Jr.
Barnes, Danny
    See The Bad Livers
Barnes, Micah
    See Nylons, The
Barnwell, Ysaye Maria
    See Sweet Honey in the Rock
Barr, Ralph
    See Nitty Gritty Dirt Band, The
Barre, Martin
    See Jethro Tull
Barrere, Paul
    See Little Feat
Barrett, (Roger) Syd
    See Pink Floyd
Barron, Christopher
    See Spin Doctors
Bartels, Joanie 13
Bartholomew, Simon
    See Brand New Heavies, The
Bartoli, Cecilia 12
Barton, Lou Ann
    See Fabulous Thunderbirds, The
Bartos, Karl
    See Kraftwerk
Basehead 11
Basher, Mick
    See X
Basia 5
Basie, Count 2
Batchelor, Kevin
    See Steel Pulse
Batel, Beate
    See Einstürzende Neubauten
Battin, Skip
    See Byrds, The
Battle, Kathleen 6
Bauer, Judah
    See Jon Spencer Blues Explosion
Baumann, Peter
    See Tangerine Dream
Bautista, Roland
    See Earth, Wind and Fire
Baxter, Jeff
    See Doobie Brothers, The
Bayer Sager, Carole
    See Sager, Carole Bayer
Baynton-Power, David
    See James
Beach Boys, The 1
Beale, Michael
    See Earth, Wind and Fire
Beard, Frank
    See ZZ Top
Beasley, Paul
    See Mighty Clouds of Joy, The
Beastie Boys, The 8
Beatles, The 2
Beauford, Carter
    See Dave Matthews Band

Beautiful South **19**
Beaver Brown Band, The **3**
Bechet, Sidney **17**
Beck, Jeff **4**
  Also see Yardbirds, The
Beck, William
  See Ohio Players
Beck **18**
Becker, Walter
  See Steely Dan
Beckford, Theophilus
  See Skatalites, The
Beckley, Gerry
  See America
Bee Gees, The **3**
Beers, Garry Gary
  See INXS
Behler, Chuck
  See Megadeth
Beiderbecke, Bix **16**
Belafonte, Harry **8**
Belew, Adrian **5**
  Also see King Crimson
Belfield, Dennis
  See Three Dog Night
Bell, Andy
  See Erasure
Bell, Derek
  See Chieftains, The
Bell, Eric
  See Thin Lizzy
Bell, Jayn
  See Sounds of Blackness
Bell, Melissa
  See Soul II Soul
Bell, Ronald
  See Kool & the Gang
Belladonna, Joey
  See Anthrax
Bellamy, David
  See Bellamy Brothers, The
Bellamy, Howard
  See Bellamy Brothers, The
Bellamy Brothers, The **13**
Belle, Regina **6**
Bello, Frank
  See Anthrax
Belly **16**
Belushi, John
  See Blues Brothers, The
Benante, Charlie
  See Anthrax
Benatar, Pat **8**
Benedict, Scott
  See Pere Ubu
Benitez, Jellybean **15**
Bennett, Tony **16**
Earlier sketch in CM **2**
Bennett-Nesby, Ann
Eskelin, Ian **19**
Evora, Cesaria **19**
  See Sounds of Blackness
Benson, George **9**
Benson, Ray
  See Asleep at the Wheel

Benson, Renaldo "Obie"
  See Four Tops, The
Bentley, John
  See Squeeze
Benton, Brook **7**
Bentyne, Cheryl
  See Manhattan Transfer, The
Berenyi, Miki
  See Lush
Berg, Matraca **16**
Berigan, Bunny **2**
Berlin, Irving **8**
Berlin, Steve
  See Los Lobos
Bernstein, Leonard **2**
Berry, Bill
  See R.E.M.
Berry, Chuck **1**
Berry, John **17**
Berry, Robert
  See Emerson, Lake & Palmer/Powell
Best, Nathaniel
  See O'Jays, The
Best, Pete
  See Beatles, The
Bettencourt, Nuno
  See Extreme
Better Than Ezra **19**
Bettie Serveert **17**
Betts, Dicky
  See Allman Brothers, The
Bevan, Bev
  See Black Sabbath
  Also see Electric Light Orchestra
B-52's, The **4**
Biafra, Jello **18**
Big Audio Dynamite **18**
Big Mike
  See Geto Boys, The
Big Money Odis
  See Digital Underground
Bingham, John
  See Fishbone
Binks, Les
  See Judas Priest
Birchfield, Benny
  See Osborne Brothers, The
Bird
  See Parker, Charlie
Birdsong, Cindy
  See Supremes, The
Biscuits, Chuck
  See Danzig
Bishop, Michael
  See Gwar
Biz Markie **10**
Bizzy Bone
  See Bone Thugs-N-Harmony
Bjelland, Kat
  See Babes in Toyland
Björk **16**
  Also see Sugarcubes, The
Black, Clint **5**
Black Crowes, The **7**
Black Francis

  See Black, Frank
Black, Frank **14**
Black, Mary **15**
Black Sabbath **9**
Black Sheep **15**
Black Uhuru **12**
Black, Vic
  See C + C Music Factory
Blackman, Cindy **15**
Blackmore, Ritchie
  See Deep Purple
Blades, Ruben **2**
Blake, Eubie **19**
Blake, Norman
  See Teenage Fanclub
Blakey, Art **11**
Blanchard, Terence **13**
Bland, Bobby "Blue" **12**
Bley, Carla **8**
Bley, Paul **14**
Blige, Mary J. **15**
Block, Rory **18**
Blondie **14**
Blood, Sweat and Tears **7**
Bloom, Eric
  See Blue Oyster Cult
Bloom, Luka **14**
Blue Oyster Cult **16**
Blue Rodeo **18**
Blues, Elwood
  See Blues Brothers, The
Blues, "Joliet" Jake
  See Blues Brothers, The
Blues Brothers, The **3**
Blues Traveler **15**
Blunt, Martin
  See Charlatans, The
Blur **17**
BoDeans, The **3**
Bob, Tim
  See Rage Against the Machine
Bogaert, Jo
  See Technotronic
Bogdan, Henry
  See Helmet
Bogguss, Suzy **11**
Bolade, Nitanju
  See Sweet Honey in the Rock
Bolan, Marc
  See T. Rex
Bolton, Michael **4**
Bon Jovi **10**
Bon Jovi, Jon
  See Bon Jovi
Bonebrake, D. J.
  See X
Bone Thugs-N-Harmony **18**
Bonham, John
  See Led Zeppelin
Bonnecaze, Cary
  See Better Than Ezra
Borge, Victor **19**
Bonner, Leroy "Sugarfoot"
  See Ohio Players
Bono
  See U2

Bonsall, Joe
  See Oak Ridge Boys, The
Books
  See Das EFX
Boone, Pat 13
Booth, Tim
  See James
Bordin, Mike
  See Faith No More
Borg, Bobby
  See Warrant
Borge, Victor 19
Borowiak, Tony
  See All-4-One
Bostaph, Paul
  See Slayer
Boston 11
Bostrom, Derrick
  See Meat Puppets, The
Bottum, Roddy
  See Faith No More
Bouchard, Albert
  See Blue Oyster Cult
Bouchard, Joe
  See Blue Oyster Cult
Bouchikhi, Chico
  See Gipsy Kings, The
Bowen, Jimmy
  See Country Gentlemen, The
Bowens, Sir Harry
  See Was (Not Was)
Bowie, David 1
Bowman, Steve
  See Counting Crows
Boyd, Liona 7
Boyz II Men 15
Brady, Paul 8
Bragg, Billy 7
Bramah, Martin
  See Fall, The
Brand New Heavies, The 14
Brandy 19
Branigan, Laura 2
Brantley, Junior
  See Roomful of Blues
Braxton, Anthony 12
Braxton, Toni 17
B-Real
  See Cypress Hill
Bream, Julian 9
Breeders 19
Brevette, Lloyd
  See Skatalites, The
Brickell, Edie 3
Bridgewater, Dee Dee 18
Bright, Ronnie
  See Coasters, The
Briley, Alex
  See Village People, The
Britten, Benjamin 15
Brittingham, Eric
  See Cinderella
Brix
  See Fall, The
Brockie, Dave

See Gwar
Bromberg, David 18
Bronfman, Yefim 6
Brooke, Jonatha
  See Story, The
Brookes, Jon
  See Charlatans, The
Brooks, Baba
  See Skatalites, The
Brooks, Garth 8
Brooks, Leon Eric "Kix"
  See Brooks & Dunn
Brooks & Dunn 12
Broonzy, Big Bill 13
Brotherdale , Steve
  See Joy Division
Brown, Bobby 4
Brown, Clarence "Gatemouth" 11
Brown, Duncan
  See Stereolab
Brown, George
  See Kool & the Gang
Brown, Harold
  See War
Brown, Ian
  See Stone Roses, The
Brown, James 16
Earlier sketch in CM 2
Brown, Jimmy
  See UB40
Brown, Junior 15
Brown, Marty 14
Brown, Mick
  See Dokken
Brown, Norman
  See Mills Brothers, The
Brown, Ruth 13
Brown, Selwyn "Bumbo"
  See Steel Pulse
Brown, Tony 14
Browne, Jackson 3
  Also see Nitty Gritty Dirt Band, The
Brubeck, Dave 8
Bruce, Jack
  See Cream
Bruford, Bill
Bruford, Bill
  See King Crimson
  Also see Yes
Bruster, Thomas
  See Soul Stirrers, The
Bryan, David
  See Bon Jovi
Bryan, Karl
  See Skatalites, The
Bryan, Mark
  See Hootie and the Blowfish
Bryant, Elbridge
  See Temptations, The
Bryson, Bill
  See Desert Rose Band, The
Bryson, David
  See Counting Crows
Bryson, Peabo 11
Buchholz, Francis

See Scorpions, The
Buchignani, Paul
  See Afghan Whigs
Buck, Mike
  See Fabulous Thunderbirds, The
Buck, Peter
  See R.E.M.
Buck, Robert
  See 10,000 Maniacs
Buckingham, Lindsey 8
  Also see Fleetwood Mac
Buckley, Betty 16
Earlier sketch in CM 1
Buckley, Tim 14
Buckwheat Zydeco 6
Budgie
  See Siouxsie and the Banshees
Buerstatte, Phil
  See White Zombie
Buffalo Tom 18
Buffett, Jimmy 4
Bulgarian State Female Vocal Choir, The
  10
Bulgarian State Radio and Television
  Female Vocal Choir, The
  See Bulgarian State Female Vocal Choir,
  The
Bumbry, Grace 13
Bumpus, Cornelius
  See Doobie Brothers, The
Bunker, Clive
  See Jethro Tull
Bunnell, Dewey
  See America
Bunskoeke, Herman
  See Bettie Serveert
Burch, Curtis
  See New Grass Revival, The
Burden, Ian
  See Human League, The
Burdon, Eric 14
  Also see War
Burgess, Tim
  See Charlatans, The
Burke, Clem
  See Blondie
Burnett, Carol 6
Burnett, T Bone 13
Burnette, Billy
  See Fleetwood Mac
Burnham, Hugo
  See Gang of Four
Burning Spear 15
Burns, Bob
  See Lynyrd Skynyrd
Burns, Karl
  See Fall, The
Burr, Clive
  See Iron Maiden
Burrell, Kenny 11
Burrell
  See King Crimson
Burton, Cliff
  See Metallica
Burton, Gary 10

Busby, Jheryl **9**
Bush **18**
Bush, Dave
　See Fall, The
Bush, John
　See Anthrax
Bush, Kate **4**
Bush, Sam
　See New Grass Revival, The
Bushwick Bill
　See Geto Boys, The
Busta Rhymes **18**
Butler, Terry "Geezer"
　See Black Sabbath
Butterfly
　See Digable Planets
Butthole Surfers **16**
Buzzcocks, The **9**
Byrds, The **8**
Byrne, David **8**
　Also see Talking Heads
Byrne, Dermot
　See Altan
C + C Music Factory **16**
Cabaret Voltaire **18**
Cachao
　See Lopez, Israel "Cachao"
Caesar, Shirley **17**
Cafferty, John
　See Beaver Brown Band, The
Cage, John **8**
Cahn, Sammy **11**
Cale, J. J. **16**
Cale, John **9**
　Also see Velvet Underground, The
Calhoun, Will
　See Living Colour
Callahan, Ken
　See Jayhawks, The
Callas, Maria **11**
Callis, Jo
　See Human League, The
Calloway, Cab **6**
Cameron, Duncan
　See Sawyer Brown
Cameron, Matt
　See Soundgarden
Campbell, Ali
　See UB40
Campbell, Glen **2**
Campbell, Kerry
　See War
Campbell, Luther **10**
Campbell, Phil
　See Motörhead
Campbell, Robin
　See UB40
Campbell, Tevin **13**
Canadian Brass, The **4**
Cantrell, Jerry
　See Alice in Chains
Canty, Brendan
　See Fugazi
Cappelli, Frank **14**
Captain Beefheart **10**

Cardigans **19**
Carey, Mariah **6**
Carlisle, Belinda **8**
Carlos, Bun E.
　See Cheap Trick
Carlos, Don
　See Black Uhuru
Carlson, Paulette
　See Highway 101
Carnes, Kim **4**
Carpenter, Bob
　See Nitty Gritty Dirt Band, The
Carpenter, Karen
　See Carpenters, The
Carpenter, Mary-Chapin **6**
Carpenter, Richard
　See Carpenters, The
Carpenters, The **13**
Carr, Eric
　See Kiss
Carrack, Paul
　See Mike & the Mechanics
　Also see Squeeze
Carreras, José **8**
Carrigan, Andy
　See Mekons, The
Carroll, Earl "Speedo"
　See Coasters, The
Carruthers, John
　See Siouxsie and the Banshees
Carter, Anita
　See Carter Family, The
Carter, A. P.
　See Carter Family, The
Carter, Benny **3**
　Also see McKinney's Cotton Pickers
Carter, Betty **6**
Carter, Carlene **8**
Carter, Helen
　See Carter Family, The
Carter, James **18**
Carter, Janette
　See Carter Family, The
Carter, Jimmy
　See Five Blind Boys of Alabama
Carter, Joe
　See Carter Family, The
Carter, June **6**
　Also see Carter Family, The
Carter, Maybell
　See Carter Family, The
Carter, Nell **7**
Carter, Ron **14**
Carter, Sara
　See Carter Family, The
Carter Family, The **3**
Caruso, Enrico **10**
Casady, Jack
　See Jefferson Airplane
Casale, Bob
　See Devo
Casale, Gerald V.
　See Devo
Casals, Pablo **9**
Case, Peter **13**

Cash, Johnny **17**
　Earlier sketch in CM **1**
Cash, Rosanne **2**
Cates, Ronny
　See Petra
Catherall, Joanne
　See Human League, The
Catherine Wheel **18**
Caustic Window
　See Aphex Twin
Cauty, Jimmy
　See Orb, The
Cavalera, Igor
　See Sepultura
Cavalera, Max
　See Sepultura
Cave, Nick **10**
Cavoukian, Raffi
　See Raffi
Cease, Jeff
　See Black Crowes, The
Cervenka, Exene
　See X
Cetera, Peter
　See Chicago
Chamberlin, Jimmy
　See Smashing Pumpkins
Chambers, Martin
　See Pretenders, The
Chambers, Paul **18**
Chambers, Terry
　See XTC
Chance, Slim
　See Cramps, The
Chandra, Sheila **16**
Chang, Sarah **7**
Channing, Carol **6**
Chapin, Harry **6**
Chapin, Tom **11**
Chapman, Steven Curtis **15**
Chapman, Tony
　See Rolling Stones, The
Chapman, Tracy **4**
Chaquico, Craig
　See Jefferson Starship
Charlatans, The **13**
Charles, Ray **1**
Chea, Alvin "Vinnie"
　See Take 6
Cheap Trick **12**
Checker, Chubby **7**
Cheeks, Julius
　See Soul Stirrers, The
Chenier, C. J. **15**
Chenier, Clifton **6**
Chenille Sisters, The **16**
Cher **1**
Cherone, Gary
　See Extreme
Cherry, Don **10**
Cherry, Neneh **4**
Chesnutt, Mark **13**
Chevalier, Maurice **6**
Chevron, Phillip
　See Pogues, The

Chicago **3**
Chieftains, The **7**
Childress, Ross
   See Collective Soul
Childs, Toni **2**
Chilton, Alex **10**
Chimes, Terry
   See Clash, The
Chopmaster J
   See Digital Underground
Christ, John
   See Danzig
Christian, Charlie **11**
Christina, Fran
   See Fabulous Thunderbirds, The
   Also see Roomful of Blues
Chuck D
   See Public Enemy
Chung, Mark
   See Einstürzende Neubauten
Church, Kevin
   See Country Gentlemen, The
Church, The **14**
Cinderella **16**
Circle Jerks, The **17**
Clapton, Eric **11**
Earlier sketch in CM **1**
   Also see Cream
   Also see Yardbirds, The
Clark, Dave
   See Dave Clark Five, The
Clark, Dick **2**
Clark, Gene
   See Byrds, The
Clark, Guy **17**
Clark, Keith
   See Circle Jerks, The
Clark, Mike
   See Suicidal Tendencies
Clark, Roy **1**
Clark, Steve
   See Def Leppard
Clark, Terri **19**
Clarke, "Fast" Eddie
   See Motörhead
Clarke, Michael
   See Byrds, The
Clarke, Stanley **3**
Clarke, Vince
   See Depeche Mode
   Also see Erasure
Clarke, William
   See Third World
Clash, The **4**
Clayderman, Richard **1**
Claypool, Les
   See Primus
Clayton, Adam
   See U2
Clayton, Sam
   See Little Feat
Clayton-Thomas, David
   See Blood, Sweat and Tears
Cleaves, Jessica
   See Earth, Wind and Fire

Clegg, Johnny **8**
Clements, Vassar **18**
Clemons, Clarence **7**
Cleveland, James **1**
Cliburn, Van **13**
Cliff, Jimmy **8**
Clifford, Douglas Ray
   See Creedence Clearwater Revival
Cline, Patsy **5**
Clinton, George **7**
Clivilles, Robert
   See C + C Music Factory
Clooney, Rosemary **9**
Coasters, The **5**
Cobain, Kurt
   See Nirvana
Cockburn, Bruce **8**
Cocker, Jarvis
   See Pulp
Cocker, Joe **4**
Cocking, William "Willigan"
   See Mystic Revealers
Cocteau Twins, The **12**
Codenys, Patrick
   See Front 242
Coe, David Allan **4**
Coffey, Jeff
   See Butthole Surfers
Coffie, Calton
   See Inner Circle
Cohen, Jeremy
   See Turtle Island String Quartet
Cohen, Leonard **3**
Cohen, Porky
   See Roomful of Blues
Colbourn, Chris
   See Buffalo Tom
Cole, David
   See C + C Music Factory
Cole, Holly **18**
Cole, Lloyd **9**
Cole, Natalie **1**
Cole, Nat King **3**
Cole, Ralph
   See Nylons, The
Coleman, Ornette **5**
Collective Soul **16**
Colley, Dana
   See Morphine
Collie, Mark **15**
Collin, Phil
   See Def Leppard
Collins, Albert **19**
 Earlier sketch in CM **4**
Collins, Allen
   See Lynyrd Skynyrd
Collins, Bootsy **8**
Collins, Judy **4**
Collins, Mark
   See Charlatans, The
Collins, Mel
   See King Crimson
Collins, Phil **2**
   Also see Genesis
Collins, Rob

   See Charlatans, The
Collins, William
   See Collins, Bootsy
Colomby, Bobby
   See Blood, Sweat and Tears
Colt, Johnny
   See Black Crowes, The
Coltrane, John **4**
Colvin, Shawn **11**
Combs, Sean "Puffy" **16**
Comess, Aaron
   See Spin Doctors
Como, Perry **14**
Conneff, Kevin
   See Chieftains, The
Connelly, Chris
   See KMFDM
Connick, Harry, Jr. **4**
Connors, Marc
   See Nylons, The
Conti, Neil
   See Prefab Sprout
Conway, Billy
   See Morphine
Conway, Gerry
   See Pentangle
Cooder, Ry **2**
Cook, Jeff
   See Alabama
Cook, Paul
   See Sex Pistols, The
Cook, Stuart
   See Creedence Clearwater Revival
Cooke, Sam **1**
   Also see Soul Stirrers, The
Cool, Tre
   See Green Day
Coolio **19**
Cooney, Rory **6**
Cooper, Alice **8**
Cooper, Michael
   See Third World
Cooper, Paul
   See Nylons, The
Coore, Stephen
   See Third World
Cope, Julian **16**
Copeland, Stewart **14**
Copland, Aaron **2**
Copley, Al
   See Roomful of Blues
Corea, Chick **6**
Corgan, Billy
   See Smashing Pumpkins
Corina, Sarah
   See Mekons, The
Cornelius, Robert
   See Poi Dog Pondering
Cornell, Chris
   See Soundgarden
Cornick, Glenn
   See Jethro Tull
Corrigan, Brianna
   See Beautiful South
Costello, Elvis **12**
Earlier sketch in CM **2**

Coté, Billy
  See Madder Rose
Cotoia, Robert
  See Beaver Brown Band, The
Cotrubas, Ileana **1**
Cotten, Elizabeth **16**
Cotton, Caré
  See Sounds of Blackness
Cougar, John(ny)
  See Mellencamp, John "Cougar"
Counting Crows **18**
Country Gentlemen, The **7**
Coury, Fred
  See Cinderella
Coverdale, David
  See Whitesnake **5**
Cowan, John
  See New Grass Revival, The
Cowboy Junkies, The **4**
Cox, Andy
  See English Beat, The
Cox, Terry
  See Pentangle
Coxon, Graham
  See Blur
Cracker **12**
Craig, Carl **19**
Crain, S. R.
  See Soul Stirrers, The
Cramps, The **16**
Cranberries, The **14**
Crash Test Dummies **14**
Crawford, Dave Max
  See Poi Dog Pondering
Crawford, Ed
  See fIREHOSE
Crawford, Michael **4**
Cray, Robert **8**
Creach, Papa John
  See Jefferson Starship
Cream **9**
Creedence Clearwater Revival **16**
Creegan, Andrew
  See Barenaked Ladies
Creegan, Jim
  See Barenaked Ladies
Crenshaw, Marshall **5**
Cretu, Michael
  See Enigma
Criss, Peter
  See Kiss
Croce, Jim **3**
Crofts, Dash
  See Seals & Crofts
Cropper, Steve **12**
Crosby, Bing **6**
Crosby, David **3**
  Also see Byrds, The
Cross, David
  See King Crimson
Cross, Mike
  See Sponge
Cross, Tim
  See Sponge
Crouch, Andraé **9**

Crow, Sheryl **18**
Crowded House **12**
Crowe, J. D. **5**
Crowell, Rodney **8**
Cruz, Celia **10**
Cuddy, Jim
  See Blue Rodeo
Cult, The **16**
Cummings, David
  See Del Amitri
Cure, The **3**
Curless, Ann
  See Exposé
Curley, John
  See Afghan Whigs
Curran, Ciaran
  See Altan
Currie, Justin
  See Del Amitri
Currie, Steve
  See T. Rex
Curry, Tim **3**
Curtis, Ian
  See Joy Division
Curtis, King **17**
Curve **13**
Custance, Mickey
  See Big Audio Dynamite
Cuthbert, Scott
  See Everclear
Cutler, Chris
  See Pere Ubu
Cypress Hill **11**
Cyrus, Billy Ray **11**
Dacus, Donnie
  See Chicago
Dacus, Johnny
  See Osborne Brothers, The
Daddy G
  See Massive Attack
Daddy Mack
  See Kris Kross
Daellenbach, Charles
  See Canadian Brass, The
Dahlheimer, Patrick
  See Live
Daisley, Bob
  See Black Sabbath
Dale, Dick **13**
Daley, Richard
  See Third World
Dall, Bobby
  See Poison
Dalton, John
  See Kinks, The
Dalton, Nic
  See Lemonheads, The
Daltrey, Roger **3**
  Also see Who, The
Dando, Evan
  See Lemonheads, The
D'Angelo, Greg
  See Anthrax
Daniels, Charlie **6**
Daniels, Jack

  See Highway 101
Danko, Rick
  See Band, The
Danny Boy
  See House of Pain
Danzig **7**
Danzig, Glenn
  See Danzig
D'Arby, Terence Trent **3**
Darin, Bobby **4**
Darling, Eric
  See Weavers, The
Darriau, Matt
  See Klezmatics, The
Darvill, Benjamin
  See Crash Test Dummies
Das EFX **14**
Daugherty, Jay Dee
  See Church, The
Daulne, Marie
  See Zap Mama
Dave Clark Five, The **12**
Dave Matthews Band **18**
Davenport, N'Dea
  See Brand New Heavies, The
Davidson, Lenny
  See Dave Clark Five, The
Davies, Dave
  See Kinks, The
Davies, Ray **5**
  Also see Kinks, The
Davies, Saul
  See James
Davis, Anthony **17**
Davis, Chip **4**
Davis, Clive **14**
Davis, Michael
  See MC5, The
Davis, Miles **1**
Davis, Reverend Gary **18**
Davis, Sammy, Jr. **4**
Davis, Skeeter **15**
Davis, Steve
  See Mystic Revealers
Davis, Zelma
  See C + C Music Factory
Dawdy, Cheryl
  See Chenille Sisters, The
Dayne, Taylor **4**
dc Talk **18**
de la Rocha, Zack
  See Rage Against the Machine
de Coster, Jean Paul
  See 2 UnlimitedDeBarge, El **14**
DeLeo, Dean
  See Stone Temple Pilots
DeLeo, Robert
  See Stone Temple Pilots
dePrume, Ivan
  See White Zombie
de Albuquerque, Michael
  See Electric Light Orchestra
Deacon, John
  See Queen
Dead Can Dance **16**

Deakin, Paul
    See Mavericks, The
Deal, Kelley
    See Breeders
Deal, Kim
    See Breeders
Dean, Billy **19**
Dee, Mikkey
    See Dokken
    Also see Motörhead
Deee-lite **9**
Deep Forest **18**
Deep Purple **11**
Def Leppard **3**
DeGarmo, Chris
    See Queensryche
de Grassi, Alex **6**
Deily, Ben
    See Lemonheads, The
DeJohnette, Jack **7**
De La Soul **7**
DeLorenzo, Victor
    See Violent Femmes
Del Amitri **18**
Del Mar, Candy
    See Cramps, The
Delp, Brad
    See Boston
de Lucia, Paco **1**
De Meyer, Jean-Luc
    See Front 242
DeMent, Iris **13**
Demeski, Stanley
    See Luna
Demos, Greg
    See Guided By Voices
Dempsey, Michael
    See Cure, The
Denison, Duane
    See Jesus Lizard
Dennis, Garth
    See Black Uhuru
Densmore, John
    See Doors, The
Dent, Cedric
    See Take 6
Denton, Sandy
    See Salt-N-Pepa
Denver, John **1**
De Oliveria, Laudir
    See Chicago
Depeche Mode **5**
Derosier, Michael
    See Heart
Desert Rose Band, The **4**
Des'ree **15**
DeVille, C. C.
    See Poison
Deschamps, Kim
    See Blue Rodeo
Destri, Jimmy
    See Blondie
Deupree, Jerome
    See Morphine
Devo **13**

Devoto, Howard
    See Buzzcocks, The
DeWitt, Lew C.
    See Statler Brothers, The
de Young, Joyce
    See Andrews Sisters, The
Diagram, Andy
    See James
Diamond "Dimebag" Darrell
    See Pantera
Diamond, Mike
    See Beastie Boys, The
Diamond, Neil **1**
Diamond Rio **11**
Di'anno, Paul
    See Iron Maiden
Dibango, Manu **14**
Dickens, Little Jimmy **7**
Dickerson, B. B.
    See War
Dickinson, Paul Bruce
    See Iron Maiden
Dickinson, Rob
    See Catherine Wheel
Diddley, Bo **3**
Diffie, Joe **10**
Difford, Chris
    See Squeeze
DiFranco, Ani **17**
Digable Planets **15**
Diggle, Steve
    See Buzzcocks, The
Digital Underground **9**
DiMant, Leor
    See House of Pain
Di Meola, Al **12**
DiMucci, Dion
    See Dion
DiNizo, Pat
    See Smithereens, The
Dilworth, Joe
    See Stereolab
Dinning, Dean
    See Toad the Wet Sprocket
Dinosaur Jr. **10**
Dio, Ronnie James
    See Black Sabbath
Dion **4**
Dion, Céline **12**
Dirks, Michael
    See Gwar
Dirnt, Mike
    See Green Day
Dittrich, John
    See Restless Heart
Dixon, Jerry
    See Warrant
Dixon, Willie **10**
DJ Domination
    See Geto Boys, The
DJ Fuse
    See Digital Underground
DJ Jazzy Jeff and the Fresh Prince **5**
D.J. Lethal
    See House of Pain

D.J. Minutemix
    See P.M. Dawn
DJ Muggs
    See Cypress Hill
DJ Premier
    See Gang Starr
DJ Ready Red
    See Geto Boys, The
DJ Terminator X
    See Public Enemy
Doc Pomus **14**
Dombroski, Vinnie
    See Sponge
Donovan, Bazil
    See Blue Rodeo
Doth, Anita
    See 2 Unlimited
Downie, Gordon
    See Tragically Hip , The
Doyle, Candida
    See Pulp
Dr. Dre **15**
    Also see N.W.A.
Dr. John **7**
Doe, John
    See X
Dokken **16**
Dokken, Don
    See Dokken
Dolby, Thomas **10**
Dolenz, Micky
    See Monkees, The
Domingo, Placido **1**
Domino, Fats **2**
Don, Rasa
    See Arrested Development
Donelly, Tanya
    See Belly
    Also see Throwing Muses
    Also see Breeders
Donovan **9**
Doobie Brothers, The **3**
Doodlebug
    See Digable Planets
Doors, The **4**
Dorge, Michel (Mitch)
    See Crash Test Dummies
Dorsey, Jimmy
    See Dorsey Brothers, The
Dorsey, Thomas A. **11**
Dorsey, Tommy
    See Dorsey Brothers, The
Dorsey Brothers, The **8**
Doucet, Michael **8**
Douglas, Jerry
    See Country Gentlemen, The
Dowd, Christopher
    See Fishbone
Downes, Geoff
    See Yes
Downey, Brian
    See Thin Lizzy
Downing, K. K.
    See Judas Priest
Dozier, Lamont
    See Holland-Dozier-Holland

Drake, Nick **17**
Drayton, Leslie
　See Earth, Wind and Fire
Dreja, Chris
　See Yardbirds, The
Drew, Dennis
　See 10,000 Maniacs
Drumbago,
　See Skatalites, The
Drumdini, Harry
　See Cramps, The
Drummond, Don
　See Skatalites, The
Drummond, Tom
　See Better Than Ezra
Dryden, Spencer
　See Jefferson Airplane
Dubbe, Berend
　See Bettie Serveert
Dube, Lucky **17**
Duffey, John
　See Country Gentlemen, The
　Also see Seldom Scene, The
Duffy, Billy
　See Cult, The
Duffy, Martin
　See Primal Scream
Dulli, Greg
　See Afghan Whigs
Dunbar, Aynsley
　See Jefferson Starship
　Also see Whitesnake
Dunbar, Sly
　See Sly and Robbie
Duncan, Steve
　See Desert Rose Band, The
Duncan, Bryan **19**
Duncan, Stuart
　See Nashville Bluegrass Band
Dunlap, Slim
　See Replacements, The
Dunn, Holly **7**
Dunn, Larry
　See Earth, Wind and Fire
Dunn, Ronnie
　See Brooks & Dunn
Dupree, Champion Jack **12**
Duran Duran **4**
Durante, Mark
　See KMFDM
Duritz, Adam
　See Counting Crows
Dutt, Hank
　See Kronos Quartet
Dylan, Bob **3**
E., Sheila
　See Sheila E.
Eagles, The **3**
Earl, Ronnie **5**
　Also see Roomful of Blues
Earle, Steve
　See Afghan Whigs
Earle, Steve **16**
Earth, Wind and Fire **12**
Easton, Sheena **2**

Eazy-E **13**
　Also see N.W.A.
Echeverria, Rob
　See Helmet
Eckstine, Billy **1**
Eddy, Duane **9**
Eden, Sean
　See Luna
Edge, Graeme
　See Moody Blues, The
Edge, The
　See U2
Edmonds, Kenneth "Babyface" **12**
Edwards, Dennis
　See Temptations, The
Edwards, Gordon
　See Kinks, The
Edwards, Leroy "Lion"
　See Mystic Revealers
Edwards, Mike
　See Electric Light Orchestra
Einheit
Einheit, F.M.
　See KMFDM
　See Einstürzende Neubauten
Einstürzende Neubauten **13**
Eitzel, Mark
　See American Music Club
Eklund, Greg
　See Everclear
Eldon, Thór
　See Sugarcubes, The
Eldridge, Ben
　See Seldom Scene, The
Eldridge, Roy **9**
　Also see McKinney's Cotton Pickers
Electric Light Orchestra **7**
Elfman, Danny **9**
Elias, Manny
　See Tears for Fears
Ellefson, Dave
　See Megadeth
Ellington, Duke **2**
Elliot, Cass **5**
Elliot, Joe
　See Def Leppard
Ellis, Bobby
　See Skatalites, The
Ellis, Herb **18**
Ellis, Terry
　See En Vogue
ELO
　See Electric Light Orchestra
Ely, John
　See Asleep at the Wheel
Emerson, Bill
　See Country Gentlemen, The
Emerson, Keith
　See Emerson, Lake & Palmer/Powell
Emerson, Lake & Palmer/Powell **5**
Emery, Jill
　See Hole
English Beat, The **9**
Enigma **14**
Eno, Brian **8**

Enos, Bob
　See Roomful of Blues
Enright, Pat
　See Nashville Bluegrass Band
Entwistle, John
　See Who, The
En Vogue **10**
Enya **6**
EPMD **10**
Erasure **11**
Eric B.
　See Eric B. and Rakim
Eric B. and Rakim **9**
Erickson, Roky **16**
Erlandson, Eric
　See Hole
Ertegun, Ahmet **10**
Esch, En
　See KMFDM
Escovedo, Alejandro **18**
Eshe, Montsho
　See Arrested Development
Eskelin, Ian **19**
Esquivel, Juan **17**
Estefan, Gloria **15**
　Earlier sketch in CM **2**
Estrada, Roy
　See Little Feat
Etheridge, Melissa **16**
　Earlier sketch in CM **4**
Eurythmics **6**
Evan, John
　See Jethro Tull
Evans, Bill **17**
Evans, Dick
　See U2
Evans, Gil **17**
Evans, Mark
　See AC/DC
Evans, Shane
　See Collective Soul
Everclear **18**
Everlast
　See House of Pain
Everly, Don
　See Everly Brothers, The
Everly, Phil
　See Everly Brothers, The
Everly Brothers, The **2**
Everman, Jason
　See Soundgarden
Evora, Cesaria **19**
Extreme **10**
Ezell, Ralph
　See Shenandoah
Fabian **5**
Fabulous Thunderbirds, The **1**
Fadden, Jimmie
　See Nitty Gritty Dirt Band, The
Fagan, Don
　See Steely Dan
Fahey, John **17**
Faithfull, Marianne **14**
Faith No More **7**
Fakir, Abdul "Duke"

See Four Tops, The
Falconer, Earl
  See UB40
Fall, The **12**
Fallon, David
  See Chieftains, The
Fältskog, Agnetha
  See Abba
Farley, J. J.
  See Soul Stirrers, The
Farndon, Pete
  See Pretenders, The
Farrell, Perry
  See Jane's Addiction
Farris, Dionne
  See Arrested Development
Farriss, Andrew
  See INXS
Farriss, Jon
  See INXS
Farriss, Tim
  See INXS
Fay, Johnny
  See Tragically Hip, The
Fay, Martin
  See Chieftains, The
Fearnley, James
  See Pogues, The
Fehlmann, Thomas
  See Orb, The
Feinstein, Michael **6**
Fela
  See Kuti, Fela
Felber, Dean
  See Hootie and the Blowfish
Felder, Don
  See Eagles, Theh
Feldman, Eric Drew
  See Pere Ubu
Fennell, Kevin
  See Guided By Voices
Ferrell, Rachelle **17**
Ficca, Billy
  See Television
Fier, Anton
  See Pere Ubu
Flesh-N-Bone
  See Bone Thugs-N-Harmony
Ford, Penny
  See Soul II Soul
Franklin, Aretha **17**
Franklin, Elmo
  See Mighty Clouds of Joy, The
French, Mark
  See Blue Rodeo
Fricker, Sylvia
  See Ian and Sylvia
Futter, Brian
  See Catherine Wheel
Feliciano, José **10**
Fender, Freddy
  See Texas Tornados, The
Fender, Leo **10**
Ferguson, Keith
  See Fabulous Thunderbirds, The

Ferguson, Maynard **7**
Ferguson, Steve
  See NRBQ
Ferry, Bryan **1**
Fiedler, Arthur **6**
Fielder, Jim
  See Blood, Sweat and Tears
Fields, Johnny
  See Five Blind Boys of Alabama
Finch, Jennifer
  See L7
Finer, Jem
  See Pogues, The
Finn, Micky
  See T. Rex
Finn, Neil
  See Crowded House
Finn, Tim
  See Crowded House
fIREHOSE **11**
Fishbone **7**
Fisher, Eddie **12**
Fisher, Jerry
  See Blood, Sweat and Tears
Fisher, John "Norwood"
  See Fishbone
Fisher, Phillip "Fish"
  See Fishbone
Fisher, Roger
  See Heart
Fishman, Jon
  See Phish
Fitzgerald, Ella **1**
Five Blind Boys of Alabama **12**
Flack, Roberta **5**
Flanagan, Tommy **16**
Flansburgh, John
  See They Might Be Giants
Flatt, Lester **3**
Flavor Flav
  See Public Enemy
Flea
  See Red Hot Chili Peppers, The
Fleck, Bela **8**
  Also see New Grass Revival, The
Fleetwood, Mick
  See Fleetwood Mac
Fleetwood Mac **5**
Flemons, Wade
  See Earth, Wind and Fire
Fletcher, Andy
  See Depeche Mode
Flores, Rosie **16**
Flür, Wolfgang
  See Kraftwerk
Flynn, Pat
  See New Grass Revival, The
Fogelberg, Dan **4**
Fogerty, John **2**
  Also see Creedence Clearwater Revival
Fogerty, Thomas
  See Creedence Clearwater Revival
Foley
  See Arrested Development
Ford, Lita **9**

Ford, Mark
  See Black Crowes, The
Ford, Tennessee Ernie **3**
Fordham, Julia **15**
Fortune, Jimmy
  See Statler Brothers, The
Fossen, Steve
  See Heart
Foster, David **13**
Foster, Malcolm
  See Pretenders, The
Foster, Paul
  See Soul Stirrers, The
Foster, Radney **16**
Fountain, Clarence
  See Five Blind Boys of Alabama
Fountain, Pete **7**
Four Tops, The **11**
Fox, Lucas
  See Motörhead
Fox, Oz
  See Stryper
Fox, Samantha **3**
Frampton, Peter **3**
Francis, Connie **10**
Francis, Mike
  See Asleep at the Wheel
Franke, Chris
  See Tangerine Dream
Franklin, Aretha **17**
  Earlier sketch in CM **2**
Franklin, Larry
  See Asleep at the Wheel
Franklin, Melvin
  See Temptations, The
Franti, Michael **16**
Frantz, Chris
  See Talking Heads
Fraser, Elizabeth
  See Cocteau Twins, The
Freese, Josh
  See Suicidal Tendencies
Frehley, Ace
  See Kiss
Freiberg, David
  See Jefferson Starship
Freni, Mirella **14**
Frey, Glenn **3**
  Also see Eagles, The
Friedman, Marty
  See Megadeth
Friel, Tony
  See Fall, The
Fripp, Robert **9**
  Also see King Crimson
Frisell, Bill **15**
Frith, Fred **19**
Frizzell, Lefty **10**
Froese, Edgar
  See Tangerine Dream
Froom, Mitchell **15**
Front 242 **19**
Frusciante, John
  See Red Hot Chili Peppers, The
Fugazi **13**

Fugees, The **17**
Gabriel, Peter **16**
Earlier sketch in CM **2**
  Also see Genesis
Gadler, Frank
  See NRBQ
Gahan, Dave
  See Depeche Mode
Gaines, Steve
  See Lynyrd Skynyrd
Gaines, Timothy
  See Stryper
Galás, Diamanda **16**
Gale, Melvyn
  See Electric Light Orchestra
Gallagher, Liam
  See Oasis
Gallagher, Noel
  See Oasis
Gallup, Simon
  See Cure, The
Galway, James **3**
Gambill, Roger
  See Kingston Trio, The
Gamble, Cheryl "Coko"
  See SWV
Gane, Tim
  See Stereolab
Gang of Four **8**
Gang Starr **13**
Gano, Gordon
  See Violent Femmes
Garcia, Dean
  See Curve
Garcia, Jerry **4**
  Also see Grateful Dead, The
Garcia, Leddie
  See Poi Dog Pondering
Gardner, Carl
  See Coasters, The
Gardner, Suzi
  See L7
Garfunkel, Art **4**
Garland, Judy **6**
Garrett, Peter
  See Midnight Oil
Garrett, Scott
  See Cult, The
Garvey, Steve
  See Buzzcocks, The
Gaskill, Jerry
  See King's X
Gatton, Danny **16**
Gaudreau, Jimmy
  See Country Gentlemen, The
Gaye, Marvin **4**
Gayle, Crystal **1**
Geary, Paul
  See Extreme
Geffen, David **8**
Geldof, Bob **9**
Genesis **4**
Gentry, Teddy
  See Alabama
George, Lowell

  See Little Feat
George, Rocky
  See Suicidal Tendencies
Georges, Bernard
  See Throwing Muses
Germano, Lisa **18**
Gerrard, Lisa
  See Dead Can Dance
Gershwin, George and Ira **11**
Geto Boys, The **11**
Getz, Stan **12**
Giammalvo, Chris
  See Madder Rose
Gibb, Barry
  See Bee Gees, The
Gibb, Maurice
  See Bee Gees, The
Gibb, Robin
  See Bee Gees, The
Gibbons, Billy
  See ZZ Top
Gibbons, Ian
  See Kinks, The
Gibson, Debbie **1**
Gibson, Wilf
  See Electric Light Orchestra
Gifford, Katharine
  See Stereolab
Gifford, Peter
  See Midnight Oil
Gift, Roland **3**
Gilbert, Gillian
  See New Order
Gilbert, Ronnie
  See Weavers, The
Giles, Michael
  See King Crimson
Gilkyson, Tony
  See X
Gill, Andy
  See Gang of Four
Gill, Janis
  See Sweethearts of the Rodeo
Gill, Pete
  See Motörhead
Gill, Vince **7**
Gillan, Ian
  See Deep Purple
Gillespie, Bobby
  See Primal Scream
Gillespie, Dizzy **6**
Gilley, Mickey **7**
Gillian, Ian
  See Black Sabbath
Gillingham, Charles
  See Counting Crows
Gilmore, Jimmie Dale **11**
Gilmour, David
  See Pink Floyd
Gin Blossoms **18**
Gingold, Josef **6**
Gioia
  See Exposé
Gipsy Kings, The **8**
Glass, Philip **1**

Glasscock, John
  See Jethro Tull
Glennie, Jim
  See James
Glitter, Gary **19**
Glover, Corey
  See Living Colour
Glover, Roger
  See Deep Purple
Gobel, Robert
  See Kool & the Gang
Godchaux, Donna
  See Grateful Dead, The
Godchaux, Keith
  See Grateful Dead, The
Goettel, Dwayne Rudolf
  See Skinny Puppy
Golden, William Lee
  See Oak Ridge Boys, The
Goldstein, Jerry
  See War
Goo Goo Dolls, The **16**
Gooden, Ramone PeeWee
  See Digital Underground
Goodman, Benny **4**
Goodridge, Robin
  See Bush
Gordon, Dexter **10**
Gordon, Dwight
  See Mighty Clouds of Joy, The
Gordon, Kim
  See Sonic Youth
Gordon, Mike
  See Phish
Gordy, Berry, Jr. **6**
Gordy, Emory, Jr. **17**
Gore, Martin
  See Depeche Mode
Gorham, Scott
  See Thin Lizzy
Gorka, John **18**
Gorman, Christopher
  See Belly
Gorman, Steve
  See Black Crowes, The
Gorman, Thomas
  See Belly
Gosling, John
  See Kinks, The
Gossard, Stone
  See Pearl Jam
Gott, Larry
  See James
Goudreau, Barry
  See Boston
Gould, Billy
  See Faith No More
Gould, Glenn **9**
Gould, Morton **16**
Goulding, Steve
  See Poi Dog Pondering
Gracey, Chad
  See Live
Gradney, Ken
  See Little Feat

Graham, Bill **10**
Graham, Johnny
  See Earth, Wind and Fire
Gramolini, Gary
  See Beaver Brown Band, The
Grandmaster Flash **14**
Grant, Amy **7**
Grant, Bob
  See The Bad Livers
Grant Lee Buffalo **16**
Grant, Lloyd
  See Metallica
Grappelli, Stephane **10**
Grateful Dead, The **5**
Graves, Denyce **16**
Gray, Del
  See Little Texas
Gray, Ella
  See Kronos Quartet
Gray, F. Gary **19**
Gray, James
  See Blue Rodeo
Gray, Tom
  See Country Gentlemen, The
  Also see Seldom Scene, The
Gray, Walter
  See Kronos Quartet
Gray, Wardell
  See McKinney's Cotton Pickers
Grebenshikov, Boris **3**
Green, Al **9**
Green, Benny **17**
Green, Charles
  See War
Green Day **16**
Green, Grant **14**
Green, Karl Anthony
  See Herman's Hermits
Green, Peter
  See Fleetwood Mac
Green, Susaye
  See Supremes, The
Green, Willie
  See Neville Brothers, The
Greenhalgh, Tom
  See Mekons, The
Greenspoon, Jimmy
  See Three Dog Night
Greenwood, Gail
  See Belly
Greenwood, Lee **12**
Greer, Jim
  See Guided By Voices
Gregg, Paul
  See Restless Heart
Gregory, Bryan
  See Cramps, The
Gregory, Dave
  See XTC
Griffin, Bob
  See BoDeans, The
Griffin, Kevin
  See Better Than Ezra
Griffin, Mark
  See MC 900 Ft. Jesus

Griffith, Nanci **3**
Grisman, David **17**
Grohl, Dave
  See Nirvana
Grotberg, Karen
  See Jayhawks, The
Groucutt, Kelly
  See Electric Light Orchestra
Grove, George
  See Kingston Trio, The
Grover, Charlie
  See Sponge
Grusin, Dave **7**
Guaraldi, Vince **3**
Guard, Dave
  See Kingston Trio, The
Gudmundsdottir, Björk
  See Björk
  Also see Sugarcubes, The
Guerin, John
  See Byrds, The
Guest, Christopher
  See Spinal Tap
Guided By Voices **18**
Gunn, Trey
  See King Crimson
Guns n' Roses **2**
Gunther, Cornell
  See Coasters, The
Guru
  See Gang Starr
Guss, Randy
  See Toad the Wet Sprocket
Gustafson, Steve
  See 10,000 Maniacs
Gut, Grudrun
  See Einstürzende Neubauten
Guthrie, Arlo **6**
Guthrie, Robin
  See Cocteau Twins, The
Guthrie, Woody **2**
Guy, Billy
  See Coasters, The
Guy, Buddy **4**
Gwar **13**
Hacke, Alexander
  See Einstürzende Neubauten
Hackett, Steve
  See Genesis
Haden, Charlie **12**
Hagar, Sammy
  See Van Halen
Haggard, Merle **2**
Hakmoun, Hassan **15**
Hale, Simon
  See Incognito
Haley, Bill **6**
Haley, Mark
  See Kinks, The
Halford, Rob
  See Judas Priest
Hall, Daryl
  See Hall & Oates
Hall, Lance
  See Inner Circle

Hall, Randall
  See Lynyrd Skynyrd
Hall, Tom T. **4**
Hall, Tony
  See Neville Brothers, The
Hall & Oates **6**
Halliday, Toni
  See Curve
Hamilton, Frank
  See Weavers, The
Hamilton, Milton
  See Third World
Hamilton, Page
  See Helmet
Hamilton, Tom
  See Aerosmith
Hamlisch, Marvin **1**
Hammer, M.C. **5**
Hammerstein, Oscar
  See Rodgers, Richard
Hammett, Kirk
  See Metallica
Hammon, Ron
  See War
Hammond, John **6**
Hammond-Hammond, Jeffrey
  See Jethro Tull
Hampson, Sharon
  See Sharon, Lois & Bram
Hampson, Thomas **12**
Hampton, Lionel **6**
Hancock, Herbie **8**
Handy, W. C. **7**
Hanley, Steve
  See Fall, The
Hanna, Jeff
  See Nitty Gritty Dirt Band, The
Hanneman, Jeff
  See Slayer
Hannon, Frank
  See Tesla
Hansen, Mary
  See Stereolab
Hardin, Tim **18**
Harding, John Wesley **6**
Hardson, Tre "Slimkid"
  See Pharcyde, The
Hargrove, Kornell
  See Poi Dog Pondering
Hargrove, Roy **15**
Harley, Bill **7**
Harper, Ben **17**
Harper, Raymond
  See Skatalites, The
Harrell, Andre **16**
Harrell, Lynn **3**
Harrington, Carrie
  See Sounds of Blackness
Harrington, David
  See Kronos Quartet
Harris, Addie "Micki"
  See Shirelles, The
Harris, Damon Otis
  See Temptations, The
Harris, Eddie **15**

Harris, Emmylou **4**
Harris, Evelyn
  See Sweet Honey in the Rock
Harris, Gerard
  See Kool & the Gang
Harris, R. H.
  See Soul Stirrers, The
Harris, Steve
  See Iron Maiden
Harrison, George **2**
  Also see Beatles, The
Harrison, Jerry
  See Talking Heads
Harrison, Nigel
  See Blondie
Harrison, Richard
  See Stereolab
Harry, Deborah **4**
  Also see Blondie
Hart, Lorenz
  See Rodgers, Richard
Hart, Mark
  See Crowded House
Hart, Mickey
  See Grateful Dead, The
Hartford, John **1**
Hartke, Stephen **5**
Hartman, Bob
  See Petra
Hartman, John
  See Doobie Brothers, The
Harvey, Bernard "Touter"
  See Inner Circle
Harvey, Philip "Daddae"
  See Soul II Soul
Harvey, Polly Jean **11**
Harvie, Iain
  See Del Amitri
Harwood, Justin
  See Luna
Hashian
  See Boston
Haskell, Gordon
  See King Crimson
Haskins, Kevin
  See Love and Rockets
Haslinger, Paul
  See Tangerine Dream
Hassan, Norman
  See UB40
Hatfield, Juliana **12**
  Also see Lemonheads, The
Hauser, Tim
  See Manhattan Transfer, The
Havens, Richie **11**
Hawes, Dave
  See Catherine Wheel
Hawkins, Coleman **11**
Hawkins, Erskine **19**
Hawkins, Nick
  See Big Audio Dynamite
Hawkins, Screamin' Jay **8**
Hawkins, Tramaine **17**
Hay, George D. **3**
Hayes, Isaac **10**

Hayes, Roland **13**
Haynes, Gibby
  See Butthole Surfers
Haynes, Warren
  See Allman Brothers, The
Hays, Lee
  See Weavers, The
Hayward, David Justin
  See Moody Blues, The
Hayward, Richard
  See Little Feat
Headliner
  See Arrested Development
Headon, Topper
  See Clash, The
Healey, Jeff **4**
Heard, Paul
  See M People
Hearn, Kevin
  See Barenaked Ladies
Heart **1**
Heaton,, Paul
  See Beautiful South
Heavy D **10**
Hedges, Michael **3**
Heggie, Will
  See Cocteau Twins, The
Helfgott, David **19**
Hell, Richard
  See Television
Hellerman, Fred
  See Weavers, The
Helm, Levon
  See Band, The
  Also see Nitty Gritty Dirt Band, The
Helmet **15**
Hemingway, Dave
  See Beautiful South
Henderson, Fletcher **16**
Henderson, Joe **14**
Hendricks, Barbara **10**
Hendrix, Jimi **2**
Henley, Don **3**
  Also see Eagles, The
Henrit, Bob
  See Kinks, The
Henry, Joe **18**
Henry, Nicholas "Drummie"
  See Mystic Revealers
Herman, Maureen
  See Babes in Toyland
Herman, Tom
  See Pere Ubu
Herman, Woody **12**
Herman's Hermits **5**
Herndon, Mark
  See Alabama
Herrera, R. J.
  See Suicidal Tendencies
Herrmann, Bernard **14**
Herron, Cindy
  See En Vogue
Hersh, Kristin
  See Throwing Muses
Hester, Paul

  See Crowded House
Hetfield, James
  See Metallica
Hetson, Greg
  See Circle Jerks, The
Hewson, Paul
  See U2
Hiatt, John **8**
Hickman, Johnny
  See Cracker
Hicks, Chris
  See Restless Heart
Hicks, Sheree
  See C + C Music Factory
Hidalgo, David
  See Los Lobos
Higgins, Jimmy
  See Altan
Highway 101 **4**
Hijbert, Fritz
  See Kraftwerk
Hill, Brendan
  See Blues Traveler
Hill, Dusty
  See ZZ Top
Hill, Faith **18**
Hill, Ian
  See Judas Priest
Hill, Lauryn "L"
  See Fugees, The
Hillage, Steve
  See Orb, The
Hillman, Bones
  See Midnight Oil
Hillman, Chris
  See Byrds, The
  Also see Desert Rose Band, The
Hinderas, Natalie **12**
Hinds, David
  See Steel Pulse
Hines, Earl "Fatha" **12**
Hines, Gary
  See Sounds of Blackness
Hinojosa, Tish **13**
Hirst, Rob
  See Midnight Oil
Hirt, Al **5**
Hitchcock, Robyn **9**
Hodo, David
  See Village People, The
Hoenig, Michael
  See Tangerine Dream
Hoffman, Guy
  See BoDeans, The
  Also see Violent Femmes
Hogan, Mike
  See Cranberries, The
Hogan, Noel
  See Cranberries, The
Hoke, Jim
  See NRBQ
Hole **14**
Holiday, Billie **6**
Holland, Brian
  See Holland-Dozier-Holland
Holland, Dave

See Judas Priest
Holland, Eddie
   See Holland-Dozier-Holland
Holland, Julian "Jools"
   See Squeeze
Holland-Dozier-Holland **5**
Holly, Buddy **1**
Holt, David Lee
   See Mavericks, The
Honeyman, Susie
   See Mekons, The
Honeyman-Scott, James
   See Pretenders, The
Hook, Peter
   See Joy Division
   See New Order
Hooker, John Lee **1**
Hooper, Nellee
   See Soul II Soul
   Also see Massive Attack
Hootie and the Blowfish **18**
Hope, Gavin
   See Nylons, The
Hopkins, Doug
   See Gin Blossoms
Hopkins, Lightnin' **13**
Hopwood, Keith
   See Herman's Hermits
Horn, Shirley **7**
Horn, Trevor
   See Yes
Horne, Lena **11**
Horne, Marilyn **9**
Hornsby, Bruce **3**
Horovitz, Adam
   See Beastie Boys, The
Horowitz, Vladimir **1**
Horton, Walter **19**
Hossack, Michael
   See Doobie Brothers, The
House, Son **11**
House of Pain **14**
Houston, Cissy **6**
Houston, Whitney **8**
Howard, Harlan **15**
Howe, Steve
   See Yes
Howell, Porter
   See Little Texas
Howlin' Wolf **6**
H.R.
   See Bad Brains
Hubbard, Greg "Hobie"
   See Sawyer Brown
Hubbard, Preston
   See Fabulous Thunderbirds, The
   Also see Roomful of Blues
Huber, Connie
   See Chenille Sisters, The
Hudson, Earl
   See Bad Brains
Hudson, Garth
   See Band, The
Huffman, Doug
   See Boston

Hughes, Bruce
   See Cracker
Hughes, Glenn
   See Black Sabbath
Hughes, Glenn
   See Village People, The
Hughes, Leon
   See Coasters, The
Human League, The **17**
Humes, Helen **19**
Humperdinck, Engelbert **19**
Hunt, Darryl
   See Pogues, The
Hunter, Alberta **7**
Hunter, Mark
   See James
Hunter, Shepherd "Ben"
   See Soundgarden
Hurley, George
   See fIREHOSE
Hutchence, Michael
   See INXS
Huth, Todd
   See Primus
Hütter, Ralf
   See Kraftwerk
Hutton, Danny
   See Three Dog Night
Huxley, Rick
   See Dave Clark Five, The
Hyman, Jerry
   See Blood, Sweat and Tears
Hynde, Chrissie
   See Pretenders, The
Ian, Janis **5**
Ian, Scott
   See Anthrax
Ian and Sylvia **18**
Ibbotson, Jimmy
   See Nitty Gritty Dirt Band, The
Ibold, Mark
   See Pavement
Ice Cube **10**
   Also see N.W.A
Ice-T **7**
Idol, Billy **3**
Iglesias, Julio **2**
Iha, James
   See Smashing Pumpkins
Incognito **16**
Indigo Girls **3**
Inez, Mike
   See Alice in Chains
Infante, Frank
   See Blondie
Ingram, James **11**
Inner Circle **15**
Innes, Andrew
   See Primal Scream
Innis, Dave
   See Restless Heart
Interior, Lux
   See Cramps, The
INXS **2**
Iommi, Tony

   See Black Sabbath
Iron Maiden **10**
Irons, Jack
   See Red Hot Chili Peppers, The
Isaak, Chris **6**
Isham, Mark **14**
Isles, Bill
   See O'Jays, The
Isley, Ernie
   See Isley Brothers, The
Isley, Marvin
   See Isley Brothers, The
Isley, O'Kelly, Jr.
   See Isley Brothers, The
Isley, Ronald
   See Isley Brothers, The
Isley, Rudolph
   See Isley Brothers, The
Isley Brothers, The **8**
Ives, Burl **12**
Ivey, Michael
   See Basehead
J.
   See White Zombie
J, David
   See Love and Rockets
Jabs, Matthias
   See Scorpions, The
Jackson, Alan **7**
Jackson, Eddie
   See Queensryche
Jackson, Freddie **3**
Jackson, Jackie
   See Jacksons, The
Jackson, Janet **16**
   Earlier sketch in CM **3**
Jackson, Jermaine
   See Jacksons, The
Jackson, Joe **4**
Jackson, Karen
   See Supremes, The
Jackson, Mahalia **8**
Jackson, Marlon
   See Jacksons, The
Jackson, Michael **17**
   Earlier sketch in CM **1**
   Also see Jacksons, The
Jackson, Millie **14**
Jackson, Milt **15**
Jackson, Randy
   See Jacksons, The
Jackson, Tito
   See Jacksons, The
Jackson 5, The
   See Jacksons, The
Jacksons, The **7**
Jacobs, Walter
   See Little Walter
Jacox, Martin
   See Soul Stirrers, The
Jacquet, Illinois **17**
Jagger, Mick **7**
   Also see Rolling Stones, The
Jairo T.
   See Sepultura

Jam, Jimmy
   See Jam, Jimmy, and Terry Lewis
Jam, Jimmy, and Terry Lewis **11**
Jam Master Jay
   See Run-D.M.C.
James **12**
James, Alex
   See Blur
James, Andrew "Bear"
   See Midnight Oil
James, Cheryl
   See Salt-N-Pepa
James, Doug
   See Roomful of Blues
James, Elmore **8**
James, Etta **6**
James, Harry **11**
James, Richard
   See Aphex Twin
James, Rick **2**
Jane's Addiction **6**
Janovitz, Bill
   See Buffalo Tom
Jansch, Bert
   See Pentangle
Jardine, Al
   See Beach Boys, The
Jarobi
   See Tribe Called Quest, A
Jarre, Jean-Michel **2**
Jarreau, Al **1**
Jarrett, Irwin
   See Third World
Jarrett, Keith **1**
Jasper, Chris
   See Isley Brothers, The
Jay, Miles
   See Village People, The
Jayhawks, The **15**
Jayson, Mackie
   See Bad Brains
Jazzie B
   See Soul II Soul
Jean, Wyclef "Clef"
   See Fugees, The
Jeanrenaud, Joan Dutcher
   See Kronos Quartet
Jefferson, Blind Lemon **18**
Jefferson Airplane **5**
Jefferson Starship
   See Jefferson Airplane
Jenifer, Darryl
   See Bad Brains
Jennings, Greg
   See Restless Heart
Jennings, Waylon **4**
Jerry, Jah
   See Skatalites, The
Jessie, Young
   See Coasters, The
Jesus and Mary Chain, The **10**
Jesus Lizard **19**
Jethro Tull **8**
Jett, Joan **3**
Jimenez, Flaco

   See Texas Tornados, The
Jobim, Antonio Carlos **19**
Jobson, Edwin
   See Jethro Tull
Jodeci **13**
Joel, Billy **12**
   Earlier sketch in CM **2**
Johansen, David **7**
Johanson, Jai Johanny
   See Allman Brothers, The
Johansson, Lars-Olof
   See Cardigans
John, Elton **3**
Johnson, Brian
   See AC/DC
Johnson, Courtney
   See New Grass Revival, The
Johnson, Daryl
   See Neville Brothers, The
Johnson, Eric **19**
Johnson, Gene
   See Diamond Rio
Johnson, Gerry
   See Steel Pulse
Johnson, James P. **16**
Johnson, Lonnie **17**
Johnson, Matt
   See The The
Johnson, Mike
   See Dinosaur Jr.
Johnson, Ralph
   See Earth, Wind and Fire
Johnson, Robert **6**
Johnson, Scott
   See Gin Blossoms
Johnson, Shirley Childres
   See Sweet Honey in the Rock
Johnson, Tamara "Taj"
   See SWV
Johnston, Bruce
   See Beach Boys, The
Johnston, Tom
   See Doobie Brothers, The
JoJo
   See Jodeci
Jolly, Bill
   See Butthole Surfers
Jolson, Al **10**
Jon Spencer Blues Explosion **18**
Jones, Booker T. **8**
Jones, Brian
   See Rolling Stones, The
Jones, Busta
   See Gang of Four
Jones, Claude
   See McKinney's Cotton Pickers
Jones, Davy
   See Monkees, The
Jones, Elvin **9**
Jones, Geoffrey
   See Sounds of Blackness
Jones, George **4**
Jones, Grace **9**
Jones, Hank **15**
Jones, Jamie

   See All-4-One
Jones, Jim
   See Pere Ubu
Jones, John Paul
   See Led Zeppelin
Jones, Kendall
   See Fishbone
Jones, Kenny
   See Who, The
Jones, Marshall
   See Ohio Players
Jones, Maxine
   See En Vogue
Jones, Michael
   See Kronos Quartet
Jones, Mic
   See Big Audio Dynamite
   Also see Clash, The
Jones, Philly Joe **16**
Jones, Quincy **2**
Jones, Rickie Lee **4**
Jones, Robert "Kuumba"
   See Ohio Players
Jones, Sandra "Puma"
   See Black Uhuru
Jones, Simon
   See Verve, The
Jones, Spike **5**
Jones, Steve
   See Sex Pistols, The
Jones, Thad **19**
Jones, Tom **11**
Jones, Will "Dub"
   See Coasters, The
Joplin, Janis **3**
Joplin, Scott **10**
Jordan, Lonnie
   See War
Jordan, Louis **11**
Jordan, Stanley **1**
Jorgensor, John
   See Desert Rose Band, The
Joseph-I, Israel
   See Bad Brains
Jourgensen, Al
   See Ministry
Joyce, Mike
   See Buzzcocks, The
   Also see Smiths, The
Joy Division **19**
Judas Priest **10**
Judd, Naomi
   See Judds, The
Judd, Wynonna
   See Judds, The
   Also see Wynonna
Judds, The **2**
Juhlin, Dag
   See Poi Dog Pondering
Jukebox
   See Geto Boys, The
Jungle DJ "Towa" Towa
   See Deee-lite
Jurado, Jeanette
   See Exposé
Kabongo, Sabine

See Zap Mama
Kahlil, Aisha
  See Sweet Honey in the Rock
Kakoulli, Harry
  See Squeeze
Kalligan, Dick
  See Blood, Sweat and Tears
Kaminski, Mik
  See Electric Light Orchestra
Kamomiya, Ryo
  See Pizzicato Five
Kanawa, Kiri Te
  See Te Kanawa, Kiri
Kane, Big Daddy 7
Kane, Nick
  See Mavericks, The
Kannberg, Scott
  See Pavement
Kanter, Paul
  See Jefferson Airplane
Karajan, Herbert von
  See von Karajan, Herbert
Kath, Terry
  See Chicago
Kato, Nash
  See Urge Overkill
Katz, Steve
  See Blood, Sweat and Tears
Kaukonen, Jorma
  See Jefferson Airplane
Kavanagh, Chris
  See Big Audio Dynamite
Kaye, Tony
  See Yes
Kay Gee
  See Naughty by Nature
K-Ci
  See Jodeci
Kean, Martin
  See Stereolab
Keane, Sean
  See Chieftains, The
Kee, John P. 15
Keelor, Greg
  See Blue Rodeo
Keifer, Tom
  See Cinderella
Keitaro
  See Pizzicato Five
Keith, Jeff
  See Tesla
Keith, Toby 17
Kelly, Charlotte
  See Soul II Soul
Kelly, Kevin
  See Byrds, The
Kelly, R. 19
Kelly, Rashaan
  See US3
Kendrick, David
  See Devo
Kendricks, Eddie
  See Temptations, The
Kennedy, Delious
  See All-4-One

Kennedy, Frankie
  See Altan
Kennedy, Nigel 8
Kenner, Doris
  See Shirelles, The
Kenny G 14
Kentucky Headhunters, The 5
Kern, Jerome 13
Kershaw, Sammy 15
Ketchum, Hal 14
Key, Cevin
  See Skinny Puppy
Khan, Chaka 9
Khan, Nusrat Fateh Ali 13
Kibble, Mark
  See Take 6
Kibby, Walter
  See Fishbone
Kick, Johnny
  See Madder Rose
Kid 'n Play 5
Kidjo, Anjelique 17
Kiedis, Anthony
  See Red Hot Chili Peppers, The
Kilbey, Steve
  See Church, The
Killian, Tim
  See Kronos Quartet
Kimball, Jennifer
  See Story, The
Kimball, Jim
  See Jesus Lizard
Kimble, Paul
  See Grant Lee Buffalo
Kincaid, Jan
  See Brand New Heavies, The
Kinchla, Chan
  See Blues Traveler
King, Albert 2
King, B. B. 1
King, Ben E. 7
King, Bob
  See Soul Stirrers, The
King, Carole 6
King, Ed
  See Lynyrd Skynyrd
King, Freddy 17
King, Jon
  See Gang of Four
King, Kerry
  See Slayer
King, Philip
  See Lush
King Ad-Rock
  See Beastie Boys, The
King Crimson 17
Kingston Trio, The 9
King's X 7
Kinks, The 15
Kinney, Sean
  See Alice in Chains
Kirk, Rahsaan Roland 6
Kirk, Richard H.
  See Cabaret Voltaire
Kirkwood, Cris

See Meat Puppets, The
Kirkwood, Curt
  See Meat Puppets, The
Kirtley, Peter
  See Pentangle
Kirwan, Danny
  See Fleetwood Mac
Kiss 5
Kisser, Andreas
  See Sepultura
Kissin, Evgeny 6
Kitaro 1
Kitt, Eartha 9
Klein, Jon
  See Siouxsie and the Banshees
Klezmatics, The 18
Klugh, Earl 10
Kmatsu, Bravo
  See Pizzicato Five
KMFDM 18
Knight, Gladys 1
Knight, Jon
  See New Kids on the Block
Knight, Jordan
  See New Kids on the Block
Knight, Suge 15
Knopfler, Mark 3
Know, Dr.
  See Bad Brains
Knowledge
  See Digable Planets
Knox, Nick
  See Cramps, The
Knudsen, Keith
  See Doobie Brothers, The
Konietzko, Sascha
  See KMFDM
Konishi, Yasuharu
  See Pizzicato Five
Konto, Skip
  See Three Dog Night
Kool & the Gang 13
Kool Moe Dee 9
Kooper, Al
  See Blood, Sweat and Tears
Koppelman, Charles 14
Koppes, Peter
  See Church, The
Kottke, Leo 13
Kotzen, Richie
  See Poison
Kowalczyk, Ed
  See Live
Koz, Dave 19
Kraftwerk 9
Krakauer, David
  See Klezmatics, The
Kramer, Joey
  See Aerosmith
Kramer, Wayne
  See MC5, The
Krasnow, Bob 15
Krause, Bernie
  See Weavers, The
Krauss, Alison 10

Krauss, Scott
    See Pere Ubu
Kravitz, Lenny 5
Krayzie Bone
    See Bone Thugs-N-Harmony
Krazy Drayz
    See Das EFX
Kretz, Eric
    See Stone Temple Pilots
Kreutzman, Bill
    See Grateful Dead, The
Krieger, Robert
    See Doors, The
Kris Kross 11
Kristofferson, Kris 4
Krizan, Anthony
    See Spin Doctors
Kronos Quartet 5
KRS-One 8
Krupa, Gene 13
Krusen, Dave
    See Pearl Jam
Kulick, Bruce
    See Kiss
Kunkel, Bruce
    See Nitty Gritty Dirt Band, The
Kunzel, Erich 17
Kuti, Fela 7
LaBar, Jeff
    See Cinderella
LaBelle, Patti 8
Lady Miss Kier
    See Deee-lite
Ladybug
    See Digable Planets
Ladysmith Black Mambazo 1
Lafalce, Mark
    See Mekons, The
Laine, Cleo 10
Laine, Denny
    See Moody Blues, The
Lake, Greg
    See Emerson, Lake & Palmer/Powell
    Also see King Crimson
LaLonde, Larry "Ler"
    See Primus
Lally, Joe
    See Fugazi
Lamb, Barbara 19
Lamm, Robert
    See Chicago
Landreth, Sonny 16
Lane, Jani
    See Warrant
Lane, Jay
    See Primus
lang, k. d. 4
Langford, Jon
    See Mekons, The
Langley, John
    See Mekons, The
Langlois, Paul
    See Tragically Hip, The
Langston, Leslie
    See Throwing Muses

Lanier, Allen
    See Blue Oyster Cult
Lanois, Daniel 8
Larkin, Patty 9
Laswell, Bill 14
Lataille, Rich
    See Roomful of Blues
Lateef, Yusef 16
Laughner, Peter
    See Pere Ubu
Lauper, Cyndi 11
Laurence, Lynda
    See Supremes, The
Lavin, Christine 6
Lavis, Gilson
    See Squeeze
Lawlor, Feargal
    See Cranberries, The
Lawrence, Tracy 11
Lawry, John
    See Petra
Laws, Roland
    See Earth, Wind and Fire
Lawson, Doyle
    See Country Gentlemen, The
Layzie Bone
    See Bone Thugs-N-Harmony
Leadbelly 6
Leadon, Bernie
    See Eagles, The
    Also see Nitty Gritty Dirt Band, The
Leary, Paul
    See Butthole Surfers
Leavell, Chuck
    See Allman Brothers, The
LeBon, Simon
    See Duran Duran
Leckenby, Derek "Lek"
    See Herman's Hermits
Ledbetter, Huddie
    See Leadbelly
LeDoux, Chris 12
Led Zeppelin 1
Lee, Beverly
    See Shirelles, The
Lee, Brenda 5
Lee, Geddy
    See Rush
Lee, Peggy 8
Lee, Pete
    See Gwar
Lee, Sara
    See Gang of Four
Lee, Tommy
    See Mötley Crüe
Leen, Bill
    See Gin Blossoms
Leese, Howard
    See Heart
Legg, Adrian 17
Lehrer, Tom 7
Leiber, Jerry
    See Leiber and Stoller
Leiber and Stoller 14
Lemmy

    See Motörhead
Lemonheads, The 12
Le Mystère des Voix Bulgares
    See Bulgarian State Female Vocal Choir,
    The
Lemper, Ute 14
Lenners, Rudy
    See Scorpions, The
Lennon, John 9
    Also see Beatles, The
Lennon, Julian 2
Lennox, Annie 18
    Also see Eurythmics
Leonard, Glenn
    See Temptations, The
Lerner, Alan Jay
    See Lerner and Loewe
Lerner and Loewe 13
Lesh, Phil
    See Grateful Dead, The
Lessard, Stefan
    See Dave Matthews Band
Levene, Keith
    See Clash, The
Levert, Eddie
    See O'Jays, The
Levin, Tony
    See King Crimson
Levine, James 8
Levy, Andrew
    See Brand New Heavies, The
Levy, Ron
    See Roomful of Blues
Lewis, Huey 9
Lewis, Ian
    See Inner Circle
Lewis, Jerry Lee 2
Lewis, Marcia
    See Soul II Soul
Lewis, Otis
    See Fabulous Thunderbirds, The
Lewis, Peter
    See Moby Grape
Lewis, Ramsey 14
Lewis, Roger
    See Inner Circle
Lewis, Roy
    See Kronos Quartet
Lewis, Samuel K.
    See Five Blind Boys of Alabama
Lewis, Terry
    See Jam, Jimmy, and Terry Lewis
Lhote, Morgan
    See Stereolab
LiPuma, Tommy 18
Libbea, Gene
    See Nashville Bluegrass Band
Liberace 9
Licht, David
    See Klezmatics, The
Lifeson, Alex
    See Rush
Lightfoot, Gordon 3
Ligon, Willie Joe
    See Mighty Clouds of Joy, The

Lilienstein, Lois
　See Sharon, Lois & Bram
Lilker, Dan
　See Anthrax
Lillywhite, Steve **13**
Lincoln, Abbey **9**
Lindley, David **2**
Linna, Miriam
　See Cramps, The
Linnell, John
　See They Might Be Giants
Lipsius, Fred
　See Blood, Sweat and Tears
Little, Keith
　See Country Gentlemen, The
Little Feat **4**
Little Richard **1**
Little Texas **14**
Little Walter **14**
Live **14**
Living Colour **7**
Llanas, Sammy
　See BoDeans, The
L.L. Cool J. **5**
Lloyd, Richard
　See Television
Lloyd Webber, Andrew **6**
Lockwood, Robert, Jr. **10**
Lodge, John
　See Moody Blues, The
Loeb, Lisa **19**
Loesser, Frank **19**
Loewe, Frederick
　See Lerner and Loewe
Loggins, Kenny **3**
Lombardo, Dave
　See Slayer
London, Frank
　See Klezmatics, The
Lopes, Lisa "Left Eye"
　See TLC
Lopez, Israel "Cachao" **14**
Lord, Jon
　See Deep Purple
Lorson, Mary
　See Madder Rose
Los Lobos **2**
Los Reyes
　See Gipsy Kings, The
Loughnane, Lee
　See Chicago
Louison, Steve
　See Massive Attack
Louris, Gary
　See Jayhawks, The
Louvin, Charlie
　See Louvin Brothers, The
Louvin, Ira
　See Louvin Brothers, The
Louvin Brothers, The **12**
Lovano, Joe **13**
Love, Courtney
　See Hole
Love, Gerry
　See Teenage Fanclub

Love, Mike
　See Beach Boys, The
Love and Rockets **15**
Loveless, Patty **5**
Lovering, David
　See Cracker
Lovett, Lyle **5**
Lowe, Chris
　See Pet Shop Boys
Lowe, Nick **6**
Lowery, David
　See Cracker
Lozano, Conrad
　See Los Lobos
L7 **12**
Luccketta, Troy
　See Tesla
Lucia, Paco de
　See de Lucia, Paco
Luke
　See Campbell, Luther
Lukin, Matt
　See Mudhoney
Luna **18**
Lupo, Pat
　See Beaver Brown Band, The
LuPone, Patti **8**
Luscious Jackson, **19**
Lush **13**
Lydon, John **9**
　Also see Sex Pistols, The
Lynch, George
　See Dokken
Lyngstad, Anni-Frid
　See Abba
Lynn, Loretta **2**
Lynne, Jeff **5**
　Also see Electric Light Orchestra
Lynne, Shelby **5**
Lynott, Phil
　See Thin Lizzy
Lynyrd Skynyrd **9**
Lyons, Leanne "Lelee"
　See SWV
Ma, Yo-Yo **2**
MacColl, Kirsty **12**
MacGowan, Shane
　See Pogues, The
MacKaye, Ian
　See Fugazi
Mack Daddy
　See Kris Kross
Mackey, Steve
　See Pulp
MacPherson, Jim
　See Breeders
Madder Rose **17**
Madonna **16**
　Earlier sketch in CM **4**
Mael, Ron
　See Sparks
Mael, Russell
　See Sparks
Maginnis, Tom
　See Buffalo Tom

Magnie, John
　See Subdudes, The
Magoogan, Wesley
　See English Beat, The
Maher, John
　See Buzzcocks, The
Mahavishnu Orchestra **19**
Maimone, Tony
　See Pere Ubu
Makeba, Miriam **8**
Malcolm, Hugh
　See Skatalites, The
Malcolm, Joy
　See Incognito
Malins, Mike
　See Goo Goo Dolls, The
Malkmus, Stephen
　See Pavement
Malley, Matt
　See Counting Crows
Mallinder, Stephen
　See Cabaret Voltaire
Malo, Raul
　See Mavericks, The
Malone, Tom
　See Blood, Sweat and Tears
Malone, Tommy
　See Subdudes, The
Mancini, Henry **1**
Mandrell, Barbara **4**
Maness, J. D.
　See Desert Rose Band, The
Manhattan Transfer, The **8**
Manilow, Barry **2**
Mann, Herbie **16**
Manuel, Richard
　See Band, The
Manzarek, Ray
　See Doors, The
Marie, Buffy Sainte
　See Sainte-Marie, Buffy
Marilyn Manson **18**
Marini, Lou, Jr.
　See Blood, Sweat and Tears
Marley, Bob **3**
Marley, Rita **10**
Marley, Ziggy **3**
Marr, Johnny
　See Smiths, The
　Also see The The
Marriner, Neville
Mars, Chris
　See Replacements, The
Mars, Mick
　See Mötley Crüe
Marsalis, Branford **10**
Marsalis, Ellis **13**
Marsalis, Wynton **6**
Marsh, Ian Craig
　See Human League, The
Marshal, Cornel
　See Third World
Martin, Barbara
　See Supremes, The
Martin, Christopher
　See Kid 'n Play

Martin, Dean **1**
Martin, George **6**
Martin, Greg
  See Kentucky Headhunters, The
Martin, Jim
  See Faith No More
Martin, Jimmy **5**
  Also see Osborne Brothers, The
Martin, Johnney
  See Mighty Clouds of Joy, The
Martin, Phonso
  See Steel Pulse
Martin, Sennie
  See Kool & the Gang
Martin, Tony
  See Black Sabbath
Martino, Pat **17**
Marx, Richard **3**
Mascis, J
  See Dinosaur Jr.
Masdea, Jim
  See Boston
Masekela, Hugh **7**
Maseo, Baby Huey
  See De La Soul
Mason, Nick
  See Pink Floyd
Masse, Laurel
  See Manhattan Transfer, The
Massey, Bobby
  See O'Jays, The
Massive Attack **17**
Mastelotto, Pat
  See King Crimson
Masur, Kurt **11**
Material
  See Laswell, Bill
Mathis, Johnny **2**
Matlock, Glen
  See Sex Pistols, The
Mattea, Kathy **5**
Matthews, Dave
  See Dave Matthews Band
Matthews Band, Dave
  See Dave Matthews Band
Matthews, Quinn
  See Butthole Surfers
Matthews, Scott
  See Butthole Surfers
Maunick, Bluey
  See Incognito
Mavericks, The **15**
May, Brian
  See Queen
Mayall, John **7**
Mayfield, Curtis **8**
Mays, Odeen, Jr.
  See Kool & the Gang
Mazelle, Kym
  See Soul II Soul
Mazibuko, Abednigo
  See Ladysmith Black Mambazo
Mazibuko, Albert
  See Ladysmith Black Mambazo
Mazzola, Joey

  See Sponge
Mazzy Star **17**
MCA
  See Yauch, Adam
McAloon, Martin
  See Prefab Sprout
McAloon, Paddy
  See Prefab Sprout
McBrain, Nicko
  See Iron Maiden
MC Breed **17**
McBride, Christian **17**
McBride, Martina **14**
McCabe, Nick
  See Verve, The
McCall, Renee
  See Sounds of Blackness
McCarrick, Martin
  See Siouxsie and the Banshees
McCarroll, Tony
  See Oasis
McCartney, Paul **4**
  Also see Beatles, The
McCarty, Jim
  See Yardbirds, The
MC Clever
  See Digital Underground
McCary, Michael S.
  See Boyz II Men
McClinton, Delbert **14**
McCollum, Rick
  See Afghan Whigs
McConnell, Page
  See Phish
McCook, Tommy
  See Skatalites, The
McCoury, Del **15**
McCowin, Michael
  See Mighty Clouds of Joy, The
McCoy, Neal **15**
McCracken, Chet
  See Doobie Brothers, The
McCready, Mike
  See Pearl Jam
McCulloch, Andrew
  See King Crimson
McDaniels, Darryl "D"
  See Run-D.M.C.
McDermott, Brian
  See Del Amitri
McDonald, Barbara Kooyman
  See Timbuk 3
McDonald, Ian
  See King Crimson
McDonald, Michael
  See Doobie Brothers, The
McDonald, Pat
  See Timbuk 3
McDorman, Joe
  See Statler Brothers, The
McDowell, Hugh
  See Electric Light Orchestra
McDowell, Mississippi Fred **16**
McEntire, Reba **11**
MC Eric

  See Technotronic
McEuen, John
  See Nitty Gritty Dirt Band, The
McFee, John
  See Doobie Brothers, The
McFerrin, Bobby **3**
MC5, The **9**
McGeoch, John
  See Siouxsie and the Banshees
McGinley, Raymond
  See Teenage Fanclub
McGraw, Tim **17**
McGuigan, Paul
  See Oasis
McGuinn, Jim
  See McGuinn, Roger
McGuinn, Roger
  See Byrds, The
M.C. Hammer
  See Hammer, M.C.
McGuire, Mike
  See Shenandoah
McIntosh, Robbie
  See Pretenders, The
McIntyre, Joe
  See New Kids on the Block
McKagan, Duff
  See Guns n' Roses
McKay, Al
  See Earth, Wind and Fire
McKay, John
  See Siouxsie and the Banshees
McKean, Michael
  See Spinal Tap
McKee, Maria **11**
McKeehan, Toby
  See dc Talk
McKernarn, Ron "Pigpen"
  See Grateful Dead, The
McKinney, William
  See McKinney's Cotton Pickers
McKinney's Cotton Pickers **16**
McKnight, Claude V. III
  See Take 6
McLachlan, Sarah **12**
McLaughlin, John **12**
McLean, Don **7**
McLeod, Rory
  See Roomful of Blues
MC Lyte **8**
McLoughlin, Jon
  See Del Amitri
McMeel, Mickey
  See Three Dog Night
McMurtry, James **10**
McNabb , Travis
  See Better Than Ezra
McNair, Sylvia **15**
McNeilly, Mac
  See Jesus Lizard
MC 900 Ft. Jesus **16**
McPartland, Marian **15**
McQuillar, Shawn
  See Kool & the Gang
McRae, Carmen **9**
M.C. Ren

See N.W.A.
McReynolds, Jesse
    See McReynolds, Jim and Jesse
McReynolds, Jim
    See McReynolds, Jim and Jesse
McReynolds, Jim and Jesse **12**
MC Serch **10**
McShane, Ronnie
    See Chieftains, The
McShee, Jacqui
    See Pentangle
McTell, Blind Willie **17**
McVie, Christine
    See Fleetwood Mac
McVie, John
    See Fleetwood Mac
Mdletshe, Geophrey
    See Ladysmith Black Mambazo
Meat Loaf **12**
Meat Puppets, The **13**
Medley, Bill **3**
Medlock, James
    See Soul Stirrers, The
Megadeth **9**
Mehta, Zubin **11**
Meine, Klaus
    See Scorpions, The
Meisner, Randy
    See Eagles, The
Mekons, The **15**
Melanie **12**
Melax, Einar
    See Sugarcubes, The
Mellencamp, John "Cougar" **2**
Mengede, Peter
    See Helmet
Menken, Alan **10**
Menuhin, Yehudi **11**
Menza, Nick
    See Megadeth
Mercer, Johnny **13**
Merchant, Natalie
    See 10,000 Maniacs
Mercier, Peadar
    See Chieftains, The
Mercury, Freddie
    See Queen
Mertens, Paul
    See Poi Dog Pondering
Mesaros, Michael
    See Smithereens, The
Metallica **7**
Meters, The **14**
Methembu, Russel
    See Ladysmith Black Mambazo
Metheny, Pat **2**
Meyers, Augie
    See Texas Tornados, The
Mhaonaigh, Mairead Ni
    See Altan
Michael, George **9**
Michaels, Bret
    See Poison
Michel, Prakazrel "Pras"
    See Fugees, The

Middlebrook, Ralph "Pee Wee"
    See Ohio Players
Midler, Bette **8**
Midnight Oil **11**
Midori **7**
Mighty Clouds of Joy, The **17**
Mike & the Mechanics **17**
Mike D
    See Beastie Boys, The
Mikens, Dennis
    See Smithereens, The
Mikens, Robert
    See Kool & the Gang
Milchem, Glenn
    See Blue Rodeo
Miles, Richard
    See Soul Stirrers, The
Millar, Deborah
    See Massive Attack
Miller, Charles
    See War
Miller, Glenn **6**
Miller, Jacob "Killer" Miller
    See Inner Circle
Miller, Jerry
    See Moby Grape
Miller, Mark
    See Sawyer Brown
Miller, Mitch **11**
Miller, Rice
    See Williamson, Sonny Boy
Miller, Roger **4**
Miller, Steve **2**
Milli Vanilli **4**
Mills, Donald
    See Mills Brothers, The
Mills, Fred
    See Canadian Brass, The
Mills, Harry
    See Mills Brothers, The
Mills, Herbert
    See Mills Brothers, The
Mills, John, Jr.
    See Mills Brothers, The
Mills, John, Sr.
    See Mills Brothers, The
Mills, Sidney
    See Steel Pulse
Mills Brothers, The **14**
Milsap, Ronnie **2**
Mingus, Charles **9**
Ministry **10**
Minnelli, Liza **19**
Miss Kier Kirby
    See Lady Miss Kier
Mitchell, Alex
    See Curve
Mitchell, John
    See Asleep at the Wheel
Mitchell, Joni **17**
Earlier sketch in CM **2**
Mitchell, Keith
    See Mazzy Star
Mitchell, Mitch
    See Guided By Voices

Mittoo, Jackie
    See Skatalites, The
Mize, Ben
    See Counting Crows
Mizell, Jay
    See Run-D.M.C.
Moby **17**
Moby Grape **12**
Modeliste, Joseph "Zigaboo"
    See Meters, The
Moffatt, Katy **18**
Moginie, Jim
    See Midnight Oil
Molloy, Matt
    See Chieftains, The
Moloney, Paddy
    See Chieftains, The
Money B
    See Digital Underground
Money, Eddie **16**
Monk, Meredith **1**
Monk, Thelonious **6**
Monkees, The **7**
Monroe, Bill **1**
Montand, Yves **12**
Montenegro, Hugo **18**
Montgomery, John Michael **14**
Montgomery, Wes **3**
Monti, Steve
    See Curve
Montoya, Craig
    See Everclear
Moody Blues, The **18**
Moon, Keith
    See Who, The
Mooney, Tim
    See American Music Club
Moore, Alan
    See Judas Priest
Moore, Angelo
    See Fishbone
Moore, Johnny "Dizzy"
    See Skatalites, The
Moore, LeRoi
    See Dave Matthews Band
Moore, Melba **7**
Moore, Sam
    See Sam and Dave
Moore, Thurston
    See Sonic Youth
Morand, Grace
    See Chenille Sisters, The
Moraz, Patrick
    See Moody Blues, The
    Also see Yes
Morello, Tom
    See Rage Against the Machine
Morgan, Frank **9**
Morgan, Lorrie **10**
Morissette, Alanis **19**
Morley, Pat
    See Soul Asylum
Morphine **16**
Morricone, Ennio **15**
Morris, Keith
    See Circle Jerks, The

Morris, Kenny
    See Siouxsie and the Banshees
Morris, Nate
    See Boyz II Men
Morris, Stephen
    See New Order
    See Joy Division
Morris, Wanya
    See Boyz II Men
Morrison, Bram
    See Sharon, Lois & Bram
Morrison, Claude
    See Nylons, The
Morrison, Jim 3
    Also see Doors, The
Morrison, Sterling
    See Velvet Underground, The
Morrison, Van 3
Morrissett, Paul
    See Klezmatics, The
Morrissey 10
    Also see Smiths, The
Morrissey, Bill 12
Morrissey, Steven Patrick
    See Morrissey
Morton, Everett
    See English Beat, The
Morton, Jelly Roll 7
Morvan, Fab
    See Milli Vanilli
Mosbaugh, Garth
    See Nylons, The
Mosely, Chuck
    See Faith No More
Moser, Scott "Cactus"
    See Highway 101
Mosley, Bob
    See Moby Grape
Mothersbaugh, Bob
    See Devo
Mothersbaugh, Mark
    See Devo
Mötley Crüe 1
Motörhead 10
Motta, Danny
    See Roomful of Blues
Mould, Bob 10
Moulding, Colin
    See XTC
Mounfield, Gary
    See Stone Roses, The
Mouquet, Eric
    See Deep Forest
Mouskouri, Nana 12
Moyet, Alison 12
M People 15
Mr. Dalvin
    See Jodeci
Mudhoney 16
Mueller, Karl
    See Soul Asylum
Muir, Jamie
    See King Crimson
Muir, Mike
    See Suicidal Tendencies

Muldaur, Maria 18
Mullen, Larry, Jr.
    See U2
Mulligan, Gerry 16
Murph
    See Dinosaur Jr.
Murphy, Brigid
    See Poi Dog Pondering
Murphey, Michael Martin 9
Murphy, Dan
    See Soul Asylum
Murray, Anne 4
Murray, Dave
    See Iron Maiden
Mushroom
    See Massive Attack
Musselwhite, Charlie 13
Mustaine, Dave
    See Megadeth
    Also see Metallica
Mwelase, Jabulane
    See Ladysmith Black Mambazo
Mydland, Brent
    See Grateful Dead, The
Myers, Alan
    See Devo
Myles, Alannah 4
Mystic Revealers 16
Nadirah
    See Arrested Development
Nagler, Eric 8
Nakamura, Tetsuya "Tex"
    See War
Nakatami, Michie
    See Shonen Knife
Narcizo, David
    See Throwing Muses
Nas 19
Nascimento, Milton 6
Nashville Bluegrass Band 14
Nastanovich, Bob
    See Pavement
Naughty by Nature 11
Navarro, David
    See Jane's Addiction
Nawasadio, Sylvie
    See Zap Mama
N'Dour, Youssou 6
Ndegéocello, Me'Shell 18
Near, Holly 1
Neel, Johnny
    See Allman Brothers, The
Negron, Chuck
    See Three Dog Night
Neil, Vince
    See Mötley Crüe
Nelson, Errol
    See Black Uhuru
Nelson, Rick 2
Nelson, Shara
    See Massive Attack
Nelson, Willie 11
    Earlier sketch in CM 1
Nero, Peter 19
Nesbitt, John

    See McKinney's Cotton Pickers
Nesmith, Mike
    See Monkees, The
Nevarez, Alfred
    See All-4-One
Neville, Aaron 5
    Also see Neville Brothers, The
Neville, Art
    See Meters, The
    Also see Neville Brothers, The
Neville, Charles
    See Neville Brothers, The
Neville, Cyril
    See Meters, The
    Also see Neville Brothers, The
Neville Brothers, The 4
New Grass Revival, The 4
New Kids on the Block 3
Newman, Randy 4
Newmann, Kurt
    See BoDeans, The
New Order 11
New Rhythm and Blues Quartet
    See NRBQ
Newson, Arlene
    See Poi Dog Pondering
Newton, Wayne 2
Newton-Davis, Billy
    See Nylons, The
Newton-John, Olivia 8

Nibbs, Lloyd
    See Skatalites, The
Nicholls, Geoff
    See Black Sabbath
Nichols, Todd
    See Toad the Wet Sprocket
Nicks, Stevie 2
    Also see Fleetwood Mac
Nico
    See Velvet Underground, The
Nicolette
    See Massive Attack
Nielsen, Rick
    See Cheap Trick
Nilsson 10
Nilsson, Harry
    See Nilsson
Nirvana 8
Nisbett, Steve "Grizzly"
    See Steel Pulse
Nitty Gritty Dirt Band, The 6
Nocentelli, Leo
    See Meters, The
Nomiya, Maki
    See Pizzicato Five
Noone, Peter
    See Herman's Hermits
Norica, Sugar Ray
    See Roomful of Blues
Norman, Jessye 7
Norman, Jimmy
    See Coasters, The
Northern Lights 19
Norum, John
    See Dokken

Norvo, Red **12**
Novoselic, Chris
  See Nirvana
NRBQ **12**
Nugent, Ted **2**
Nunn, Bobby
  See Coasters, The
N.W.A. **6**
Nylons, The **18**
Nyman, Michael **15**
Nyolo, Sally
  See Zap Mama
Nyro, Laura **12**
O'Hagan, Sean
  See Stereolab
O'Reagan, Tim
  See Jayhawks, The
Oakey, Philip
  See Human League, The
Oakley, Berry
  See Allman Brothers, The
Oak Ridge Boys, The **7**
Oasis **16**
Oates, John
  See Hall & Oates
O'Brien, Dwayne
  See Little Texas
O'Bryant, Alan
  See Nashville Bluegrass Band
Ocasek, Ric **5**
Ocean, Billy **4**
Oceans, Lucky
  See Asleep at the Wheel
Ochs, Phil **7**
O'Connell, Chris
  See Asleep at the Wheel
O'Connor, Billy
  See Blondie
O'Connor, Daniel
  See House of Pain
O'Connor, Mark **1**
O'Connor, Sinead **3**
Odetta **7**
O'Donnell, Roger
  See Cure, The
Offspring **19**
Ogre, Nivek
  See Skinny Puppy
Ohanian, David
  See Canadian Brass, The
O'Hare, Brendan
  See Teenage Fanclub
Ohio Players **16**
O'Jays, The **13**
Oje, Baba
  See Arrested Development
Olafsson, Bragi
  See Sugarcubes, The
Olander, Jimmy
  See Diamond Rio
Oldfield, Mike **18**
Olds, Brent
  See Poi Dog Pondering
Oliver, Joe
  See Oliver, King

Oliver, King **15**
Olson, Jeff
  See Village People, The
Olson, Mark
  See Jayhawks, The
Onassis, Blackie
  See Urge Overkill
Ono, Yoko **11**
Orb, The **18**
Orbison, Roy **2**
O'Riordan, Cait
  See Pogues, The
O'Riordan, Dolores
  See Cranberries, The
Orlando, Tony **15**
Örn, Einar
  See Sugarcubes, The
Örnolfsdottir, Margret
  See Sugarcubes, The
Orr, Casey
  See Gwar
Orrall, Frank
  See Poi Dog Pondering
Orzabal, Roland
  See Tears for Fears
Osborne, Bob
  See Osborne Brothers, The
Osborne, Joan **19**
Osborne, Sonny
  See Osborne Brothers, The
Osborne Brothers, The **8**
Osbourne, Ozzy **3**
  Also see Black Sabbath
Oskar, Lee
  See War
Oslin, K. T. **3**
Osmond, Donny **3**
Ostin, Mo **17**
Otis, Johnny **16**
Ott, David **2**
Outler, Jimmy
  See Soul Stirrers, The
Owen, Randy
  See Alabama
Owens, Buck **2**
Owens, Ricky
  See Temptations, The
Page, Jimmy **4**
  Also see Led Zeppelin
  Also see Yardbirds, The
Page, Patti **11**
Page, Steven
  See Barenaked Ladies
Paice, Ian
  See Deep Purple
Palmer, Carl
  See Emerson, Lake & Palmer/Powell
Palmer, David
  See Jethro Tull
Palmer, Robert **2**
Palmer-Jones, Robert
  See King Crimson
Palmieri, Eddie **15**
Paluzzi, Jimmy
  See Sponge

Pankow, James
  See Chicago
Pantera **13**
Parazaider, Walter
  See Chicago
Paris, Twila **16**
Parkening, Christopher **7**
Parker, Charlie **5**
Parker, Graham **10**
Parker, Kris
  See KRS-One
Parker, Maceo **7**
Parks, Van Dyke **17**
Parnell, Lee Roy **15**
Parsons, Alan **12**
Parsons, Dave
  See Bush
Parsons, Gene
  See Byrds, The
Parsons, Gram **7**
  Also see Byrds, The
Parsons, Tony
  See Iron Maiden
Parton, Dolly **2**
Partridge, Andy
  See XTC
Pasemaster, Mase
  See De La Soul
Pass, Joe **15**
Paterson, Alex
  See Orb, The
Patinkin, Mandy **3**
Patti, Sandi **7**
Patton, Charley **11**
Patton, Mike
  See Faith No More
Paul, Alan
  See Manhattan Transfer, The
Paul, Les **2**
Paul, Vinnie
  See Pantera
Paulo, Jr.
  See Sepultura
Pavarotti, Luciano **1**
Pavement **14**
Paxton, Tom **5**
Payne, Bill
  See Little Feat
Payne, Scherrie
  See Supremes, The
Payton, Denis
  See Dave Clark Five, The
Payton, Lawrence
  See Four Tops, The
Pearl, Minnie **3**
Pearl Jam **12**
Pearson, Dan
  See American Music Club
Peart, Neil
  See Rush
Pedersen, Herb
  See Desert Rose Band, The
Peduzzi, Larry
  See Roomful of Blues
Peek, Dan
  See America

Peeler, Ben
  See Mavericks, The
Pegg, Dave
  See Jethro Tull
Pendergrass, Teddy **3**
Pengilly, Kirk
  See INXS
Peniston, CeCe **15**
Penn, Michael **4**
Penner, Fred **10**
Pentangle **18**
Pepper, Art **18**
Perahia, Murray **10**
Pere Ubu **17**
Peretz, Jesse
  See Lemonheads, The
Perez, Louie
  See Los Lobos
Perkins, Carl **9**
Perkins, John
  See XTC
Perkins, Percell
  See Five Blind Boys of Alabama
Perkins, Steve
  See Jane's Addiction
Perlman, Itzhak **2**
Perlman, Marc
  See Jayhawks, The
Perry, Brendan
  See Dead Can Dance
Perry, Doane
  See Jethro Tull
Perry, Joe
  See Aerosmith
Persson, Nina
  See Cardigans
Peter, Paul & Mary **4**
Peters, Bernadette **7**
Peters, Dan
  See Mudhoney
Peters, Joey
  See Grant Lee Buffalo
Peterson, Oscar **11**
Petersson, Tom
  See Cheap Trick
Petra **3**
Pet Shop Boys **5**
Petty, Tom **9**
Pfaff, Kristen
  See Hole
Phair, Liz **14**
Phantom, Slim Jim
  See Stray Cats, The
Pharcyde, The **17**
Phelps, Doug
  See Kentucky Headhunters, The
Phelps, Ricky Lee
  See Kentucky Headhunters, The
Phife
  See Tribe Called Quest, A
Phil, Gary
  See Boston
Philips, Anthony
  See Genesis
Phillips, Chynna

See Wilson Phillips
Phillips, Glenn
  See Toad the Wet Sprocket
Phillips, Grant Lee
  See Grant Lee Buffalo
Phillips, Harvey **3**
Phillips, Sam **5**
Phillips, Sam **12**
Phillips, Simon
  See Judas Priest
Phish **13**
Phungula, Inos
  See Ladysmith Black Mambazo
Piaf, Edith **8**
Piazzolla, Astor **18**
Picciotto, Joe
  See Fugazi
Piccolo, Greg
  See Roomful of Blues
Pickering, Michael
  See M People
Pickett, Wilson **10**
Pierce, Marvin "Merv"
  See Ohio Players
Pierce, Webb **15**
Pierson, Kate
  See B-52's, The
Pigface **19**
Pilatus, Rob
  See Milli Vanilli
Pilson, Jeff
  See Dokken
Pinder, Michael
  See Moody Blues, The
Pine, Courtney
  See Soul II Soul
Pink Floyd **2**
Pinkus, Jeff
  See Butthole Surfers
Pinnick, Doug
  See King's X
Pirner, Dave
  See Soul Asylum
Pirroni, Marco
  See Siouxsie and the Banshees
Pizzicato Five **18**
Plakas, Dee
  See L7
Plant, Robert **2**
  Also see Led Zeppelin
Ploog, Richard
  See Church, The
P.M. Dawn **11**
Pogues, The **6**
Poi Dog Pondering **17**
Poindexter, Buster
  See Johansen, David
Pointer, Anita
  See Pointer Sisters, The
Pointer, Bonnie
  See Pointer Sisters, The
Pointer, June
  See Pointer Sisters, The
Pointer, Ruth
  See Pointer Sisters, The

Pointer Sisters, The **9**
Poison **11**
Poison Ivy
  See Rorschach, Poison Ivy
Poland, Chris
  See Megadeth
Pollard, Jim
  See Guided By Voices
Pollard, Robert, Jr.
  See Guided By Voices
Polygon Window
  See Aphex Twin
Pomus, Doc
  See Doc Pomus
Ponty, Jean-Luc **8**
Pop, Iggy **1**
Popper, John
  See Blues Traveler
Porter, Cole **10**
Porter, George, Jr.
  See Meters, The
Porter, Tiran
  See Doobie Brothers, The
Portman-Smith, Nigel
  See Pentangle
Posdnuos
  See De La Soul
Potts, Sean
  See Chieftains, The
Powell, Billy
  See Lynyrd Skynyrd
Powell, Bud **15**
Powell, Cozy
  See Emerson, Lake & Palmer/Powell
Powell, Kobie
  See US3
Powell, William
  See O'Jays, The
Powers, Congo
  See Cramps, The
Prater, Dave
  See Sam and Dave
Pratt, Awadagin **19**
Prefab Sprout **15**
Presley, Elvis **1**
Pretenders, The **8**
Previn, André **15**
Price, Leontyne **6**
Price, Louis
  See Temptations, The
Price, Ray **11**
Price, Rick
  See Electric Light Orchestra
Pride, Charley **4**
Prima, Louis **18**
Primal Scream **14**
Primettes, The
  See Supremes, The
Primus **11**
Prince **14**
  Earlier sketch in CM **1**
Prince Be
  See P.M. Dawn
Prine, John **7**
Proclaimers, The **13**
Professor Longhair **6**

Propes, Duane
  See Little Texas
Prout, Brian
  See Diamond Rio
Public Enemy **4**
Puente, Tito **14**
Pullen, Don **16**
Pulp **18**
Pulsford, Nigel
  See Bush
Pusey, Clifford "Moonie"
  See Steel Pulse
Pyle, Andy
  See Kinks, The
Pyle, Artemis
  See Lynyrd Skynyrd
Q-Tip
  See Tribe Called Quest, A
Quaife, Peter
  See Kinks, The
Queen **6**
Queen Ida **9**
Queen Latifah **6**
Queensryche **8**
Querfurth, Carl
  See Roomful of Blues
Rabbitt, Eddie **5**
Rabin, Trevor
Rotheray, Dave
  See Beautiful South
Rubin, Mark
  See The Bad Livers
  See Yes
Raffi **8**
Rage Against the Machine **18**
Raheem
  See Geto Boys, The
Raitt, Bonnie **3**
Rakim
  See Eric B. and Rakim
Ramone, C. J.
  See Ramones, The
Ramone, Dee Dee
  See Ramones, The
Ramone, Joey
  See Ramones, The
Ramone, Johnny
  See Ramones, The
Ramone, Marky
  See Ramones, The
Ramone, Ritchie
  See Ramones, The
Ramone, Tommy
  See Ramones, The
Ramones, The **9**
Rampal, Jean-Pierre **6**
Ramsay, Andy
  See Stereolab
Ranaldo, Lee
  See Sonic Youth
Randall, Bobby
  See Sawyer Brown
Ranglin, Ernest
  See Skatalites, The
Ranken, Andrew

  See Pogues, The
Ranking Roger
  See English Beat, The
Rarebell, Herman
  See Scorpions, The
Rawls, Lou **19**
Ray, Amy
  See Indigo Girls
Raybon, Marty
  See Shenandoah
Raye, Collin **16**
Raymonde, Simon
  See Cocteau Twins, The
Rea, Chris **12**
Reagon, Bernice Johnson
  See Sweet Honey in the Rock
Redbone, Leon **19**
Redding, Otis **5**
Reddy, Helen **9**
Red Hot Chili Peppers, The **7**
Redman, Don
  See McKinney's Cotton Pickers
Redman, Joshua **12**
Redpath, Jean **1**
Reed, Jimmy **15**
Reed, Lou **16**
  Earlier sketch in CM **1**
  Also see Velvet Underground, The
Reese, Della **13**
Reeves, Dianne **16**
Reeves, Jim **10**
Reeves, Martha **4**
Reich, Steve **8**
Reid, Charlie
  See Proclaimers, The
Reid, Christopher
  See Kid 'n Play
Reid, Craig
  See Proclaimers, The
Reid, Delroy "Junior"
  See Black Uhuru
Reid, Don
  See Statler Brothers, The
Reid, Ellen Lorraine
  See Crash Test Dummies
Reid, Harold
  See Statler Brothers, The
Reid, Janet
  See Black Uhuru
Reid, Jim
  See Jesus and Mary Chain, The
Reid, Vernon **2**
  Also see Living Colour
Reid, William
  See Jesus and Mary Chain, The
Reifman, William
  See KMFDM
Reinhardt, Django **7**
Relf, Keith
  See Yardbirds, The
R.E.M. **5**
Renbourn, John
  See Pentangle
Reno, Ronnie
  See Osborne Brothers, The

Replacements, The **7**
Residents, The **14**
Restless Heart **12**
Reverend Horton Heat **19**
Rex
  See Pantera
Reyes, Andre
  See Gipsy Kings, The
Reyes, Canut
  See Gipsy Kings, The
Reyes, Nicolas
  See Gipsy Kings, The
Reynolds, Nick
  See Kingston Trio, The
Reynolds, Robert
  See Mavericks, The
Reynolds, Sheldon
  See Earth, Wind and Fire
Reznor, Trent **13**
Rhodes, Nick
  See Duran Duran
Rhodes, Philip
  See Gin Blossoms
Rhodes, Todd
  See McKinney's Cotton Pickers
Rhone, Sylvia **13**
Rich, Buddy **13**
Rich, Charlie **3**
Richard, Cliff **14**
Richard, Zachary **9**
Richards, Keith **11**
  Also see Rolling Stones, The
Richie, Lionel **2**
Richman, Jonathan **12**
Rieckermann, Ralph
  See Scorpions, The
Rieflin, William
  See Ministry
Riley, Teddy **14**
Riley, Timothy Christian
  See Tony! Toni! Toné!
Rimes, LeAnn **19**
Rippon, Steve
  See Lush
Ritchie, Brian
  See Violent Femmes
Ritchie, Jean **4**
Ritenour, Lee **7**
Roach, Max **12**
Roback, David
  See Mazzy Star
Robbins, Marty **9**
Roberts, Brad
  See Crash Test Dummies
Roberts, Brad
  See Gwar
Roberts, Dan
  See Crash Test Dummies
Roberts, Marcus **6**
Robertson, Brian
  See Motörhead
  Also see Thin Lizzy
Robertson, Ed
  See Barenaked Ladies
Robertson, Robbie **2**
  Also see Band, The

Robeson, Paul **8**
Robillard, Duke **2**
  Also see Roomful of Blues
Robinson, Arnold
  See Nylons, The
Robinson, Chris
  See Black Crowes, The
Robinson, Dawn
  See En Vogue
Robinson, R. B.
  See Soul Stirrers, The
Robinson, Rich
  See Black Crowes, The
Robinson, Romye "Booty Brown"
  See Pharcyde, The
Robinson, Smokey **1**
Roche, Maggie
  See Roches, The
Roche, Suzzy
  See Roches, The
Roche, Terre
  See Roches, The
Roches, The **18**
Rockenfield, Scott
  See Queensryche
Rocker, Lee
  See Stray Cats, The
Rockett, Rikki
  See Poison
Rockin' Dopsie **10**
Rodford, Jim
  See Kinks, The
Rodgers, Jimmie **3**
Rodgers, Nile **8**
Rodgers, Richard **9**
Rodney, Red **14**
Rodriguez, Rico
  See Skatalites, The
Rodriguez, Sal
  See War
Roe, Marty
  See Diamond Rio
Roeder, Klaus
  See Kraftwerk
Roeser, Donald
  See Blue Oyster Cult
Roeser, Eddie "King"
  See Urge Overkill
Rogers, Kenny **1**
Rogers, Norm
  See Jayhawks, The
Rogers, Roy **9**
Rogers, Willie
  See Soul Stirrers, The
Roland, Dean
  See Collective Soul
Roland, Ed
  See Collective Soul
Rolling Stones, The **3**
Rollins, Henry **11**
Rollins, Sonny **7**
Romm, Ronald
  See Canadian Brass, The
Ronstadt, Linda **2**
Roomful of Blues **7**

Roper, De De
  See Salt-N-Pepa
Rorschach, Poison Ivy
  See Cramps, The
Rosas, Cesar
  See Los Lobos
Rose, Axl
  See Guns n' Roses
Rose, Michael
  See Black Uhuru
Rosen, Gary
  See Rosenshontz
Rosen, Peter
  See War
Rosenshontz **9**
Rosenthal, Jurgen
  See Scorpions, The
Rosenthal, Phil
  See Seldom Scene, The
Ross, Diana **1**
  Also see Supremes, The
Rossdale, Gavin
  See Bush
Rossi, John
  See Roomful of Blues
Rossington, Gary
  See Lynyrd Skynyrd
Rostropovich, Mstislav **17**
Rota, Nino **13**
Roth, David Lee **1**
  Also see Van Halen
Roth, Ulrich
  See Scorpions, The
Rotsey, Martin
  See Midnight Oil
Rotten, Johnny
  See Lydon, John
  Also see Sex Pistols, The
Rourke, Andy
  See Smiths, The
Rowe, Dwain
  See Restless Heart
Rowntree, Dave
  See Blur
Rubin, Rick **9**
Rubinstein, Arthur **11**
Rucker, Darius
  See Hootie and the Blowfish
Rudd, Phillip
  See AC/DC
Rue, Caroline
  See Hole
Ruffin, David **6**
  Also see Temptations, The
Rundgren, Todd **11**
Run-D.M.C. **4**
Rush **8**
Rush, Otis **12**
Rushlow, Tim
  See Little Texas
Russell, Alecia
  See Sounds of Blackness
Russell, Mark **6**
Rutherford, Mike
  See Genesis

  Also see Mike & the Mechanics
Rutsey, John
  See Rush
Ryan, David
  See Lemonheads, The
Ryan, Mick
  See Dave Clark Five, The
Ryder, Mitch **11**
Ryland, Jack
  See Three Dog Night
Rzeznik, Johnny
  See Goo Goo Dolls, The
Sabo, Dave
  See Bon Jovi
Sade **2**
Sadier, Laetitia
  See Stereolab
Sager, Carole Bayer **5**
Sahm, Doug
  See Texas Tornados, The
St. Hubbins, David
  See Spinal Tap
St. John, Mark
  See Kiss
St. Marie, Buffy
  See Sainte-Marie, Buffy
Sainte-Marie, Buffy **11**
Sakamoto, Ryuichi **18**
Salerno-Sonnenberg, Nadja **3**
Saliers, Emily
  See Indigo Girls
Salisbury, Peter
  See Verve, The
  Also see Pizzicato Five
Salmon, Michael
  See Prefab Sprout
Salonen, Esa-Pekka **16**
Salt-N-Pepa **6**
Sam and Dave **8**
Sambora, Richie
  See Bon Jovi
Sampson, Doug
  See Iron Maiden
Samuelson, Gar
  See Megadeth
Samwell-Smith, Paul
  See Yardbirds, The
Sanborn, David **1**
Sanchez, Michel
  See Deep Forest
Sanders, Steve
  See Oak Ridge Boys, The
Sandler, Adam **19**
Sandman, Mark
  See Morphine
Sandoval, Arturo **15**
Sandoval, Hope
  See Mazzy Star
Sanger, David
  See Asleep at the Wheel
Santana, Carlos **19**
  Earlier sketch in CM **1**
Saraceno, Blues
  See Poison
Sasaki, Mamiko

See PulpSanders, Pharoah **16**
Satchell, Clarence "Satch"
 See Ohio Players
Satriani, Joe **4**
Savage, Rick
 See Def Leppard
Sawyer Brown **13**
Saxa
 See English Beat, The
Saxon, Stan
 See Dave Clark Five, The
Scaccia, Mike
 See Ministry
Scaggs, Boz **12**
Scanlon, Craig
 See Fall, The
Scarface
 See Geto Boys, The
Schemel, Patty
 See Hole
Schenker, Michael
 See Scorpions, The
Schenker, Rudolf
 See Scorpions, The
Schenkman, Eric
 See Spin Doctors
Schermie, Joe
 See Three Dog Night
Schickele, Peter **5**
Schlitt, John
 See Petra
Schloss, Zander
 See Circle Jerks, The
Schmelling, Johannes
 See Tangerine Dream
Schmit, Timothy B.
 See Eagles, The
Schmoovy Schmoove
 See Digital Underground
Schneider, Florian
 See Kraftwerk
Schneider, Fred III
 See B-52's, The
Schnitzler, Conrad
 See Tangerine Dream
Scholten, Jim
 See Sawyer Brown
Scholz, Tom
 See Boston
Schrody, Erik
 See House of Pain
Schroyder, Steve
 See Tangerine Dream
Schulze, Klaus
 See Tangerine Dream
Schuman, William **10**
Schuur, Diane **6**
Scofield, John **7**
Scorpions, The **12**
Scott, Ronald Belford "Bon"
 See AC/DC
Scott, George
 See Five Blind Boys of Alabama
Scott, Howard
 See War

Scott, Jimmy **14**
Scott, Sherry
 See Earth, Wind and Fire
Scott-Heron, Gil **13**
Screaming Trees **19**
Scruggs, Earl **3**Schulz, Guenter
 See KMFDM
Seal **14**
Seales, Jim
 See Shenandoah
Seals, Brady
 See Little Texas
Seals, Dan **9**
Seals, Jim
 See Seals & Crofts
Seals & Crofts **3**
Sears, Pete
 See Jefferson Starship
Secada, Jon **13**
Sedaka, Neil **4**
 Seeger, Pete **4**
 Also see Weavers, The
Seger, Bob **15**
Segovia, Andres **6**
Seldom Scene, The **4**
Selena **16**
Sen Dog
 See Cypress Hill
Senior, Milton
 See McKinney's Cotton Pickers
Senior, Russell
 See Pulp
Sensi
 See Soul II Soul
Sepultura **12**
Seraphine, Daniel
 See Chicago
Sermon, Erick
 See EPMD
Setzer, Brian
 See Stray Cats, The
Severin, Steven
 See Siouxsie and the Banshees
Severinsen, Doc **1**
Sex Pistols, The **5**
Seymour, Neil
 See Crowded House
Shabalala, Ben
 See Ladysmith Black Mambazo
Shabalala, Headman
 See Ladysmith Black Mambazo
Shabalala, Jockey
 See Ladysmith Black Mambazo
Shabalala, Joseph
 See Ladysmith Black Mambazo
Shadow, DJ **19**
Shaffer, Paul **13**
Shaggy **19**
Shakespeare, Robbie
 See Sly and Robbie
Shakur, Tupac
 See 2Pac
Shallenberger, James
 See Kronos Quartet
Shane, Bob

 See Kingston Trio, The
Shanice **14**
Shankar, Ravi **9**
Shannon, Del **10**
Shanté **10**
Shapps, Andre
 See Big Audio Dynamite
Sharon, Lois & Bram **6**
Sharrock, Sonny **15**
Shaw, Artie **8**
Shearer, Harry
 See Spinal Tap
Sheehan, Bobby
 See Blues Traveler
Sheehan, Fran
 See Boston
Sheila E. **3**
Shelley, Peter
 See Buzzcocks, The
Shelley, Steve
 See Sonic Youth
Shenandoah **17**
Sherba, John
 See Kronos Quartet
Sherman, Jack
 See Red Hot Chili Peppers, The
Shines, Johnny **14**
Shirelles, The **11**
Shocked, Michelle **4**
Shock G
 See Digital Underground
Shocklee, Hank **15**
Shogren, Dave
 See Doobie Brothers, The
Shonen Knife **13**
Shontz, Bill
 See Rosenshontz
Shorter, Wayne **5**
Shovell
 See M People
Siberry, Jane **6**
Siegal, Janis
 See Manhattan Transfer, The
Sikes, C. David
 See Boston
Sills, Beverly **5**
Silva, Kenny Jo
 See Beaver Brown Band, The
Silver, Horace **19**
Simien, Terrance **12**
Simmons, Gene
 See Kiss
Simmons, Joe "Run"
 See Run-D.M.C.
Simmons, Patrick
 See Doobie Brothers, The
Simmons, Russell **7**
Simon, Carly **4**
Simon, Paul **16**
Earlier sketch in CM **1**
Simone, Nina **11**
Simonon, Paul
 See Clash, The
Simpson, Denis
 See Nylons, The

Simpson, Derrick "Duckie"
  See Black Uhuru
Simpson, Mel
  See US3
Simpson, Ray
  See Village People, The
Sims , David William
  See Jesus Lizard
Sims, Neil
  See Catherine Wheel
Sinatra, Frank **1**
Sinclair, Gord
  See Tragically Hip, The
Sinfield, Peter
  See King Crimson
Singer, Eric
  See Black Sabbath
Singh, Talvin
  See Massive Attack
Sioux, Siouxsie
  See Siouxsie and the Banshees
Siouxsie and the Banshees **8**
Sir Mix-A-Lot
Sir Rap-A-Lot
  See Geto Boys, The
Sixx, Nikki
  See Mötley Crüe
Skaggs, Ricky **5**
  Also see Country Gentlemen, The
Skatalites, The **18**
Skeoch, Tommy
  See Tesla
Skillings, Muzz
  See Living Colour
Skinny Puppy **17**
Sklamberg, Lorin
  See Klezmatics, The
Skoob
  See Das EFX
Slash
  See Guns n' Roses
Slayer **10**
Sledd, Dale
  See Osborne Brothers, The
Sledge, Percy **15**
Slick, Grace
  See Jefferson Airplane
Slijngaard, Ray
  See 2 Unlimited
Slovak, Hillel
  See Red Hot Chili Peppers, The
Sly and Robbie **13**
Smith, Kevin
  See dc Talk
Small, Heather
  See M People
Smalls, Derek
  See Spinal Tap
Smart, Terence
  See Butthole Surfers
Smashing Pumpkins **13**
Smith, Adrian
  See Iron Maiden
Smith, Bessie **3**
Smith, Chad

See Red Hot Chili Peppers, The
Smith, Charles
  See Kool & the Gang
Smith, Curt
  See Tears for Fears
Smith, Debbie
  See Curve
Smith, Fred
  See Blondie
Smith, Fred
  See MC5, The
Smith, Fred
  See Television
Smith, Garth
  See Buzzcocks, The
Smith, Joe
  See McKinney's Cotton Pickers
Smith, Mark E.
  See Fall, The
Smith, Michael W. **11**
Smith, Mike
  See Dave Clark Five, The
Smith, Parrish
  See EPMD
Smith, Patti **17**
Earlier sketch in CM **1**
Smith, Robert
  See Cure, The
  Also see Siouxsie and the Banshees
Smith, Smitty
  See Three Dog Night
Smith, Tweed
  See War
Smith, Wendy
  See Prefab Sprout
Smith, Willard
  See DJ Jazzy Jeff and the Fresh Prince
Smithereens, The **14**
Smiths, The **3**
Smyth, Joe
  See Sawyer Brown
Sneed, Floyd Chester
  See Three Dog Night
Snoop Doggy Dogg **17**
Snow, Don
  See Squeeze
Snow, Phoebe **4**
Soan, Ashley
  See Del Amitri
Social Distortion **19**
Solal, Martial **4**
Soloff, Lew
  See Blood, Sweat and Tears
Solti, Georg **13**
Sondheim, Stephen **8**
Sonefeld, Jim
  See Hootie and the Blowfish
Sonic Youth **9**
Sonnenberg, Nadja Salerno
  See Salerno-Sonnenberg, Nadja
Sonnier, Jo-El **10**
Sorum, Matt
  See Cult, The
Sosa, Mercedes **3**
Soul Asylum **10**

Soul Stirrers, The **11**
Soul II Soul **17**
Soundgarden **6**
Sounds of Blackness **13**
Sousa, John Philip **10**Simins, Russell
  See Jon Spencer Blues Explosion
Spampinato, Joey
  See NRBQ
Spampinato, Johnny
  See NRBQ
Spann, Otis **18**
Sparks **18**
Sparks, Donita
  See L7
Spearhead **19**
Special Ed **16**
Spector, Phil **4**
Speech
  See Arrested Development
Spence, Alexander "Skip"
  See Jefferson Airplane
  Also see Moby Grape
Spence, Skip
  See Spence, Alexander "Skip"
Spencer Davis Group **19**
Spencer, Jeremy
  See Fleetwood Mac
Spencer, Jim
  See Dave Clark Five, The
Spencer, Jon
  See Jon Spencer Blues Explosion
Spencer, Thad
  See Jayhawks, The
Spencer Blues Explosion, Jon
  See Jon Spencer Blues Explosion
Spinal Tap **8**
Spin Doctors **14**
Spitz, Dan
  See Anthrax
Spitz, Dave
  See Black Sabbath
Sponge **18**
Spring, Keith
  See NRBQ
Springfield, Rick **9**
Springsteen, Bruce **6**
Sproule, Daithi
  See Altan
Sprout, Tobin
  See Guided By Voices
Squeeze **5**
Squire, Chris
  See Yes
Squire, John
  See Stone Roses, The
Stacey, Peter "Spider"
  See Pogues, The
Staley, Layne
  See Alice in Chains
Staley, Tom
  See NRBQ
Stanier, John
  See Helmet
Stanley, Ian
  See Tears for Fears

Stanley, Paul
  See Kiss
Stanley, Ralph **5**
Stansfield, Lisa **9**
Staples, Mavis **13**
Staples, Pops **11**
Starling, John
  See Seldom Scene, The
Starr, Mike
  See Alice in Chains
Starr, Ringo **10**
  Also see Beatles, The
Starship
  See Jefferson Airplane
Statler Brothers, The **8**
Stead, David
  See Beautiful South
Steele, Billy
  See Sounds of Blackness
Steele, David
  See English Beat, The
Steeleye Span **19**
Steel Pulse **14**
Steely Dan **5**
Steier, Rick
  See Warrant
Stein, Chris
  See Blondie
Sterban, Richard
  See Oak Ridge Boys, The
Stereolab **18**
Sterling, Lester
  See Skatalites, The
Stern, Isaac **7**
Stevens, Cat **3**
Stevens, Ray **7**
Stevenson, Don
  See Moby Grape
Stewart, Dave
  See Eurythmics
Stewart, Derrick "Fatlip"
  See Pharcyde, The
Stewart, Ian
  See Rolling Stones, The
Stewart, Jamie
  See Cult, The
Stewart, John
  See Kingston Trio, The
Stewart, Larry
  See Restless Heart
Stewart, Rod **2**
Stewart, Tyler
  See Barenaked Ladies
Stewart, William
  See Third World
Stewart, Winston "Metal"
  See Mystic Revealers
Stills, Stephen **5**
Sting **19**
  Earlier sketch in C M **2**
Stinson, Bob
  See Replacements, The
Stinson, Tommy
  See Replacements, The
Stipe, Michael

  See R.E.M.
Stockman, Shawn
  See Boyz II Men
Stoller, Mike
  See Leiber and Stoller
Stoltz, Brian
  See Neville Brothers, The
Stonadge, Gary
  See Big Audio Dynamite
Stone, Curtis
  See Highway 101
Stone, Doug **10**
Stone Roses, The **16**
Stone, Sly **8**
Stone Temple Pilots **14**
Stookey, Paul
  See Peter, Paul & Mary
Story, Liz **2**
Story, The **13**
Stradlin, Izzy
  See Guns n' Roses
Strain, Sammy
  See O'Jays, The
Strait, George **5**
Stratton, Dennis
  See Iron Maiden
Straw, Syd **18**
Stray Cats, The **11**
Strayhorn, Billy **13**
Street, Richard
  See Temptations, The
Streisand, Barbra **2**
Strickland, Keith
  See B-52's, The
Strummer, Joe
  See Clash, The
Stryper **2**
Stuart, Marty **9**
Stubbs, Levi
  See Four Tops, The
Subdudes, The **18**
Sublime **19**
Such, Alec Jon
  See Bon Jovi
Sugarcubes, The **10**
Suicidal Tendencies **15**
Sulley, Suzanne
  See Human League, The
Summer, Donna **12**
Summer, Mark
  See Turtle Island String Quartet
Summers, Andy **3**
Sumner, Bernard
  See New Order
  See Joy Division
Sun Ra **5**
Sunnyland Slim **16**
Super DJ Dmitry
  See Deee-lite
Supremes, The **6**
Sure!, Al B. **13**
Sutcliffe, Stu
  See Beatles, The
Sutherland, Joan **13**
Svenigsson, Magnus

  See Cardigans
Svensson, Peter
  See Cardigans
Svigals, Alicia
  See Klezmatics, The
Sweat, Keith **13**
Sweet, Matthew **9**
Sweet, Michael
  See Stryper
Sweet, Robert
  See Stryper
Sweethearts of the Rodeo **12**
Sweet Honey in the Rock **1**
Swing, DeVante
  See Jodeci
SWV **14**
Sykes, John
  See Whitesnake
Tabor, Ty
  See King's X
TAFKAP (The Artist Formerly Known as
  Prince)
  See Prince
Tait, Michael
  See dc Talk
Taj Mahal **6**
Tajima, Takao
  See Pizzicato Five
Takac, Robby
  See Goo Goo Dolls, The
Takanami
  See Pizzicato Five
Takemitsu, Toru **6**
Take 6 **6**
Talbot, John Michael **6**
Talk Talk **19**
Talking Heads **1**
Tandy, Richard
  See Electric Light Orchestra
Tangerine Dream **12**
Taree, Aerle
  See Arrested Development
Tate, Geoff
  See Queensryche
Tatum, Art **17**
Taylor, Andy
  See Duran Duran
Taylor, Billy **13**
Taylor, Cecil **9**
Taylor, Chad
  See Live
Taylor, Dave
  See Pere Ubu
Taylor, Dick
  See Rolling Stones, The
Taylor, Earl
  See Country Gentlemen, The
Taylor, James **2**
Taylor, James "J.T."
  See Kool & the Gang
Taylor, John
  See Duran Duran
Taylor, Johnnie
  See Soul Stirrers, The
Taylor, Koko **10**

Taylor, Leroy
    See Soul Stirrers, The
Taylor, Mick
    See Rolling Stones, The
Taylor, Philip "Philthy Animal"
    See Motörhead
Taylor, Roger
    See Duran Duran
Taylor, Roger Meadows
    See Queen
Taylor, Teresa
    See Butthole Surfers
Teagarden, Jack **10**
Tears for Fears **6**
Technotronic **5**
Teenage Fanclub **13**
Te Kanawa, Kiri **2**
Television **17**
Teller, Al **15**
Tempesta, John
    See White Zombie
Temple, Michelle
    See Pere Ubu
Temptations, The **3**
Tennant, Neil
    See Pet Shop Boys
10,000 Maniacs **3**
Terminator X
    See Public Enemy
Terrell, Jean
    See Supremes, The
Tesla **15**
Texas Tornados, The **8**
Thacker, Rocky
    See Shenandoah
Thayil, Kim
    See Soundgarden
Theremin, Leon **19**
The The **15**
They Might Be Giants **7**
Thielemans, Toots **13**
Thin Lizzy **13**
Third World **13**
Thomas, Alex
    See Earth, Wind and Fire
Thomas, David
    See Pere Ubu
Thomas, David
    See Take 6
Thomas, David Clayton
    See Clayton-Thomas, David
Thomas, Dennis "D.T."
    See Kool & the Gang
Thomas, George "Fathead"
    See McKinney's Cotton Pickers
Thomas, Irma **16**
Thomas, Mickey
    See Jefferson Starship
Thomas, Olice
    See Five Blind Boys of Alabama
Thomas, Ray
    See Moody Blues, The
Thomas, Rozonda "Chilli"
    See TLC
Thompson, Danny

    See Pentangle
Thompson, Dennis
    See MC5, The
Thompson, Les
    See Nitty Gritty Dirt Band, The
Thompson, Mayo
    See Pere Ubu
Thompson, Porl
    See Cure, The
Thompson, Richard **7**
Thorn, Stan
    See Shenandoah
Thorn, Tracey
    See Everything But The Girl
    Also see Massive Attack
Thornton, Big Mama **18**
Thornton, Willie Mae
    See Thornton, Big Mama
Threadgill, Henry **9**
3-D
    See Massive Attack
Three Dog Night **5**
Throwing Muses **15**
Tiffany **4**
Tikaram, Tanita **9**
Tilbrook, Glenn
    See Squeeze
Tillis, Mel **7**
Tillis, Pam **8**
Timbuk 3 **3**
Timmins, Margo
    See Cowboy Junkies, The
Timmins, Michael
    See Cowboy Junkies, The
Timmins, Peter
    See Cowboy Junkies, The
Timms, Sally
    See Mekons, The
Tinsley, Boyd
    See Dave Matthews Band
Tippin, Aaron **12**
Tipton, Glenn
    See Judas Priest
TLC **15**
Toad the Wet Sprocket **13**
Tolhurst, Laurence
    See Cure, The
Tolland, Bryan
    See Del Amitri
Toller, Dan
    See Allman Brothers, The
Tone-Loc **3**
Tony K
    See Roomful of Blues
Tony! Toni! Toné! **12**
Too $hort **16**
Toohey, Dan
    See Guided By Voices
Took, Steve Peregrine
    See T. Rex
Topham, Anthony "Top"
    See Yardbirds, The
Tork, Peter
    See Monkees, The
Torme, Mel **4**

Torres, Hector "Tico"
    See Bon Jovi
Toscanini, Arturo **14**
Tosh, Peter **3**
Toure, Ali Farka **18**
Tourish, Ciaran
    See Altan
Toussaint, Allen **11**
Townes, Jeffery
    See DJ Jazzy Jeff and the Fresh Prince
Townshend, Pete **1**
    Also see Who, The
Traffic **19**
Tragically Hip, The **18**
Travers, Brian
    See UB40
Travers, Mary
    See Peter, Paul & Mary
Travis, Merle **14**
Travis, Randy **9**
Treach
    See Naughty by Nature
T. Rex **11**
Tribe Called Quest, A **8**
Tricky
    See Massive Attack
Tricky **18**
Tritt, Travis **7**
Trotter, Kera
    See C + C Music Factory
Trucks, Butch
    See Allman Brothers, The
Trugoy the Dove
    See De La Soul
Trujillo, Robert
    See Suicidal Tendencies
Truman, Dan
    See Diamond Rio
Tubb, Ernest **4**
Tubridy, Michael
    See Chieftans, The
Tucker, Moe
    See Velvet Underground, The
Tucker, Sophie **12**
Tucker, Tanya **3**
Tufnel, Nigel
    See Spinal Tap
Turbin, Neil
    See Anthrax
Turner, Big Joe **13**
Turner, Erik
    See Warrant
Turner, Joe Lynn
    See Deep Purple
Turner, Steve
    See Mudhoney
Turner, Tina **1**
Turpin, Will
    See Collective Soul
Turtle Island String Quartet **9**
Tutuska, George
    See Goo Goo Dolls, The
Twain, Shania **17**
Twitty, Conway **6**
2 Unlimited **18**

23, Richard
  See Front 242
2Pac **17**
  Also see Digital Underground
Tyagi, Paul
  See Del Amitri
Tyler, Steve
  See Aerosmith
Tyner, McCoy **7**
Tyner, Rob
  See MC5, The
Tyson, Ian
  See Ian and Sylvia
Tyson, Ron
  See Temptations, The
UB40 **4**
US3 **18**
Ulmer, James Blood **13**
Ulrich, Lars
  See Metallica
Ulvaeus, Björn
  See Abba
Unruh, N. U.
  See Einstürzende Neubauten
Upshaw, Dawn **9**
Urge Overkill **17**
Uriah Heep **19**
U2 **12**
Earlier sketch in CM **2**
Vachon, Chris
  See Roomful of Blues
Vai, Steve **5**
  Also see Whitesnake
Valentine, Gary
  See Blondie
Valentine, Rae
  See War
Valenzuela, Jesse
  See Gin Blossoms
Valli, Frankie **10**
van Dijk, Carol
  See Bettie Serveert
Van Hook, Peter
  See Mike & the Mechanics
Vandenburg, Adrian
  See Whitesnake
Vandross, Luther **2**
Van Halen **8**
Van Halen, Alex
  See Van Halen
Van Halen, Edward
  See Van Halen
Vanilla Ice **6**
Van Ronk, Dave **12**
Van Shelton, Ricky **5**
Van Vliet, Don
  See Captain Beefheart
Van Zandt, Townes **13**
Van Zant, Johnny
  See Lynyrd Skynyrd
Van Zant, Ronnie
  See Lynyrd Skynyrd
Vasquez, Junior **16**
Vaughan, Jimmie
  See Fabulous Thunderbirds, The

Vaughan, Sarah **2**
Vaughan, Stevie Ray **1**
Vedder, Eddie
  See Pearl Jam
Vega, Suzanne **3**
Velvet Underground, The **7**
Ventures **19**
Verlaine, Tom
  See Television
Verta-Ray, Matt
  See Madder Rose
Verve, The **18**
Vettese, Peter-John
  See Jethro Tull
Vicious, Sid
  See Sex Pistols, The
  Also see Siouxsie and the Banshees
Vickrey, Dan
  See Counting Crows
Vig, Butch **17**
Village People, The **7**
Vincent, Gene **19**
Vincent, Vinnie
  See Kiss
Vinnie
  See Naughty by Nature
Vinton, Bobby **12**
Violent Femmes **12**
Virtue, Michael
  See UB40
Visser, Peter
  See Bettie Serveert
Vito, Rick
  See Fleetwood Mac
Voelz, Susan
  See Poi Dog Pondering
Volz, Greg
  See Petra
Von, Eerie
  See Danzig
von Karajan, Herbert **1**
Vox, Bono
  See U2
Vudi
  See American Music Club
Wadenius, George
  See Blood, Sweat and Tears
Wadephal, Ralf
  See Tangerine Dream
Wagoner, Faidest
  See Soul Stirrers, The
Wagoner, Porter **13**
Wahlberg, Donnie
  See New Kids on the Block
Wailer, Bunny **11**
Wainwright III, Loudon **11**
Waits, Tom **12**
Earlier sketch in CM **1**
Wakeling, David
  See English Beat, The
Wakeman, Rick
  See Yes
Walden, Narada Michael **14**
Walford, Britt
  See Breeders

Walker, Colin
  See Electric Light Orchestra
Walker, Ebo
  See New Grass Revival, The
Walker, Jerry Jeff **13**
Walker, T-Bone **5**
Wallace, Ian
  See King Crimson
Wallace, Richard
  See Mighty Clouds of Joy, The
Wallace, Sippie **6**
Waller, Charlie
  See Country Gentlemen, The
Waller, Fats **7**
Wallinger, Karl **11**
Wallis, Larry
  See Motörhead
Walls, Chris
  See Dave Clark Five, The
Walls, Greg
  See Anthrax
Walsh, Joe **5**
  Also see Eagles, The
Walters, Robert "Patch"
  See Mystic Revealers
War **14**
Ward, Bill
  See Black Sabbath
Ware, Martyn
  See Human League, The
Wareham, Dean
  See Luna
Wariner, Steve **18**
Warner, Les
  See Cult, The
Warnes, Jennifer **3**
Warrant **17**
Warren, George W.
  See Five Blind Boys of Alabama
Warren, Mervyn
  See Take 6
Warwick, Clint
  See Moody Blues, The
Warwick, Dionne **2**
Was, David
  See Was (Not Was)
Was, Don
  See Was (Not Was)
Wash, Martha
  See C + C Music Factory
Washington, Chester
  See Earth, Wind and Fire
Washington, Dinah **5**
Washington, Grover, Jr. **5**
Was (Not Was) **6**
Waters, Crystal **15**
Waters, Ethel **11**
Waters, Muddy **4**
Waters, Roger
  See Pink Floyd
Watkins, Christopher
  See Cabaret Voltaire
Watkins, Tionne "T-Boz"
  See TLC
Watley, Jody **9**

Watson, Doc **2**
Watt, Ben
   See Everything But The Girl
Watt, Mike
   See fIREHOSE
Watts, Charlie
   See Rolling Stones, The
Watts, Eugene
   See Canadian Brass, The
Watts, Raymond
   See KMFDM
Weather Report **19**
Weaver, Louie
   See Petra
Weavers, The **8**
Webb, Chick **14**
Webb, Jimmy **12**
Webber, Andrew Lloyd
   See Lloyd Webber, Andrew
Webber, Mark
   See Pulp
Weiland, Scott "Weiland"
   See Stone Temple Pilots
Weill, Kurt **12**
Weir, Bob
   See Grateful Dead, The
Welch, Bob
   See Fleetwood Mac
Welch, Sean
   See Beautiful South
Welk, Lawrence **13**
Weller, Paul **14**
Wells, Cory
   See Three Dog Night
Wells, Junior **17**
Wells, Kitty **6**
Welnick, Vince
   See Grateful Dead, The
West, Dottie **8**
West, Steve
   See Pavement
Westerberg, Paul
   See Replacements, The
Weston
   See Orb, The
Weston, Randy **15**
Wetton, John
   See King Crimson
Wexler, Jerry **15**
Weymouth, Tina
   See Talking Heads
Wheat, Brian
   See Tesla
Wheeler, Audrey
   See C + C Music Factory
Wheeler, Caron
   See Soul II Soul
Wheeler, Robert
   See Pere Ubu
Whelan, Gavan
   See James
White, Alan
   See Oasis
White, Alan
   See Yes

White, Barry **6**
White, Billy
   See Dokken
White, Clarence
   See Byrds, The
White, Dave
   See Warrant
White, Freddie
   See Earth, Wind and Fire
White, Lari **15**
White, Mark
   See Mekons, The
White, Mark
   See Spin Doctors
White, Maurice
   See Earth, Wind and Fire
White, Ralph
   See The Bad Livers
White, Roland
   See Nashville Bluegrass Band
White, Verdine
   See Earth, Wind and Fire
White Zombie **17**
Whitehead, Donald
   See Earth, Wind and Fire
Whiteman, Paul **17**
Whitesnake **5**
Whitfield, Mark **18**
Whitford, Brad
   See Aerosmith
Whitley, Chris **16**
Whitley, Keith **7**
Whitman, Slim **19**
Whitwam, Barry
   See Herman's Hermits
Who, The **3**
Wiggins, Dwayne
   See Tony! Toni! Toné!
Wiggins, Raphael
   See Tony! Toni! Toné!
Wiggs, Josephine
   See Breeders
Wilborn, Dave
   See McKinney's Cotton Pickers
Wilcox, Imani
   See Pharcyde, The
Wilde, Phil
   See 2 Unlimited
Wilder, Alan
   See Depeche Mode
Wilk, Brad
   See Rage Against the Machine
Wilkeson, Leon
   See Lynyrd Skynyrd
Wilkinson, Geoff
   See US3
Wilkinson, Keith
   See Squeeze
Williams, Andy **2**
Williams, Boris
   See Cure, The
Williams, Cliff
   See AC/DC
Williams, Dana
   See Diamond Rio

Williams, Deniece **1**
Williams, Don **4**
Williams, Fred
   See C + C Music Factory
Williams, Hank, Jr. **1**
Williams, Hank, Sr. **4**
Williams, James "Diamond"
   See Ohio Players
Williams, Joe **11**
Williams, John **9**
Williams, Lamar
   See Allman Brothers, The
Williams, Lucinda **10**
Williams, Marion **15**
Williams, Otis
   See Temptations, The
Williams, Paul **5**
   See Temptations, The
Williams, Phillard
   See Earth, Wind and Fire
Williams, Vanessa **10**
Williams, Victoria **17**
Williams, Walter
   See O'Jays, The
Williams, Wilbert
   See Mighty Clouds of Joy, The
Williamson, Sonny Boy **9**
Willie D.
   See Geto Boys, The
Willis, Clarence "Chet"
   See Ohio Players
Willis, Kelly **12**
Willis, Larry
   See Blood, Sweat and Tears
Willis, Pete
   See Def Leppard
Willis, Victor
   See Village People, The
Willner, Hal **10**
Wills, Bob **6**
Willson-Piper, Marty
   See Church, The
Wilmot, Billy "Mystic"
   See Mystic Revealers
Wilson, Anne
   See Heart
Wilson, Brian
   See Beach Boys, The
Wilson, Carl
   See Beach Boys, The
Wilson, Carnie
   See Wilson Phillips
Wilson, Cassandra **12**
Wilson, Cindy
   See B-52's, The
Wilson, Dennis
   See Beach Boys, The
Wilson, Gerald **19**
Wilson, Jackie **3**
Wilson, Kim
   See Fabulous Thunderbirds, The
Wilson, Mary
   See Supremes, The
Wilson, Nancy **14**
   See Heart

Wilson, Ransom **5**
Wilson, Ricky
  See B-52's, The
Wilson, Robin
  See Gin Blossoms
Wilson, Shanice
  See Shanice
Wilson, Wendy
  See Wilson Phillips
Wilson Phillips **5**
Wilton, Michael
  See Queensryche
Wimpfheimer, Jimmy
  See Roomful of Blues
Winans, Carvin
  See Winans, The
Winans, Marvin
  See Winans, The
Winans, Michael
  See Winans, The
Winans, Ronald
  See Winans, The
Winans, The **12**
Winbush, Angela **15**
Winfield, Chuck
  See Blood, Sweat and Tears
Winston, George **9**
Winter, Johnny **5**
Winter, Paul **10**
Winwood, Steve **2**
Wiseman, Bobby
  See Blue Rodeo
Wiseman, Mac **19**
Wish Bone
  See Bone Thugs-N-Harmony
Witherspoon, Jimmy **19**
Wolstencraft, Simon
  See Fall, The
Womack, Bobby **5**
Wonder, Stevie **17**
Earlier sketch in CM **2**
Wood, Danny
  See New Kids on the Block
Wood, Ron
  See Rolling Stones, The
Wood, Roy
  See Electric Light Orchestra
Woods, Terry
  See Pogues, The
Woodson, Ollie
  See Temptations, The
Woody, Allen
  See Allman Brothers, The
Woolfolk, Andrew

  See Earth, Wind and Fire
Worrell, Bernie **11**
Wray, Link **17**
Wreede, Katrina
  See Turtle Island String Quartet
Wren, Alan
  See Stone Roses, The
Wretzky, D'Arcy
  See Smashing Pumpkins
Wright, Adrian
  See Human League, The
Wright, David "Blockhead"
  See English Beat, The
Wright, Jimmy
  See Sounds of Blackness
Wright, Norman
  See Country Gentlemen, The
Wright, Rick
  See Pink Floyd
Wright, Simon
  See AC/DC
Wright, Tim
  See Pere Ubu
Wu-Tang Clan **19**
Wurzel
  See Motörhead
Wu-Tang Clan **19**
Wyman, Bill
  See Rolling Stones, The
Wynette, Tammy **2**
Wynonna **11**
 Also see Judds, The
X **11**
XTC **10**
Ya Kid K
  See Technotronic
Yamamoto, Hiro
  See Soundgarden
Yamano, Atsuko
  See Shonen Knife
Yamano, Naoko
  See Shonen Knife
Yamashita, Kazuhito **4**
Yankovic, "Weird Al" **7**
Yanni **11**
Yardbirds, The **10**
Yarrow, Peter
  See Peter, Paul & Mary
Yates, Bill
  See Country Gentlemen, The
Yauch, Adam
  See Beastie Boys, The
Yearwood, Trisha **10**
Yella

  See N.W.A.
Yes **8**
Yoakam, Dwight **1**
Yoot, Tukka
  See US3
York, Andrew **15**
York, John
  See Byrds, The
Young, Angus
  See AC/DC
Young, Faron **7**
Young, Fred
  See Kentucky Headhunters, The
Young, Gary
  See Pavement
Young, Grant
  See Soul Asylum
Young, Jeff
  See Megadeth
Young, La Monte **16**
Young, Lester **14**
Young, Malcolm
  See AC/DC
Young, Neil **15**
Earlier sketch in CM **2**
Young, Paul
  See Mike & the Mechanics
Young, Richard
  See Kentucky Headhunters, The
Young, Robert "Throbert"
  See Primal Scream
Young M.C. **4**
Yo Yo **9**
Yow, David
  See Jesus Lizard
Yseult, Sean
  See White Zombie
Yule, Doug
  See Velvet Underground, The
Zander, Robin
  See Cheap Trick
Zap Mama **14**
Zappa, Frank **17**
·Earlier sketch in CM **1**
Zevon, Warren **9**
Zimmerman, Udo **5**
Zombie, Rob
  See White Zombie
Zoom, Billy
  See X
Zorn, John **15**
Zukerman, Pinchas **4**
ZZ Top **2**